LIVING DANGEROUSLY

LIVING DANGEROUSLY

The Autobiography of
RANULPH FIENNES

To Janet

with best wishes

Ranulph Fiennes

2002

MACMILLAN

PICTURE ACKNOWLEDGEMENTS

In addition to Ranulph Fiennes' own photographs, the author and publishers wish to thank the following for permission to reproduce their photographs in this book: Bassano and Vandyke Studios, London; Erik Berglund, Bukhang and Omdahl; Michael Boys; Bryn Campbell; Richard Einzig; Mike Hoover; Jackie McConnell; David Mason; Geoffrey Newman; Gerry Nicholson; Lieutenant Colin Sheridan; Jimmy Young.

First published 1987 by Macmillan London Limited
This edition with three new chapters published 1994 by Macmillan London Limited
a division of Pan Macmillan Publishers Limited
Cavaye Place London SW10 9PG
and Basingstoke

Associated companies throughout the world

ISBN 0-333-61701-0

3 5 7 9 8 6 4

A CIP catalogue record for this book is available from
the British Library

Typeset by Parker Typesetting Service, Leicester
Printed and bound in Great Britain by
The Bath Press, Bath

Contents

List of Maps

For Charlie Burton and Ollie Shepard for their strength and their friendship over the years.

Acknowledgements

My thanks to Frances Pajovic for typing the manuscript, Macmillan's editors for ruthlessly cutting things down to size, Bryn Campbell and the others for letting me use their photos and Ginnie for her continued patience.

1

A Timid Disposition

I have been a stranger in a strange land.

EXODUS 18:iii

In 1943 my mother and her three little daughters were living in Sunningdale, Berkshire, with her mother-in-law, Florrie, whose elder son had been killed in the First World War and whose husband Eustace Fiennes had died nine months before. Now only Florrie's younger son, my father Ranulph, was left to her, and he lay wounded in a Naples hospital. On a grey morning late in November the postman delivered a red-edged cablegram and my mother and grandmother learned that their beloved Ranulph would never come back to them. My mother was expecting a child, conceived the last time she saw my father, five months earlier. She consoled herself in her misery with the hope that she would bear the boy they both had wanted.

This was the time of the V2 rockets, when hospitals and nursing homes were over-worked. Eventually, my mother was able to arrange a week's stay at the Princess Christian Nursing Home in nearby Windsor, though it was already full to bursting with babies. When the time arrived she rushed to the Home with a friendly nurse, Miss Lumley. Because the doctor decided to finish his lunch, Nurse Lumley handled the delivery herself, muttering darkly to the doctor when he turned up that I was another BBA baby – born before arrival. _The Guinness Book of Records_ later described me as 'the youngest posthumous baronet'. Then, my curly hair was fair and my eyes hazel; now, sadly, they are mud-brown and mottled green.

When we lived at Granny Florrie's place in Sunningdale, doodle-bugs and bombs were as busy as ever. One especially accurate bomb killed a cow in the local bog. Whenever the parish alarm sounded, my personal guardian, Nanny Wells, would rush me into the dining room and we would crouch together beneath the stout oak table. By the time I was two the war was over. Rationing (as I have subsequently gathered from pieces in _Woman's Own_) had made me a Healthy War Baby.

In her eightieth year, when I was two and a half, Granny Florrie decided to return home to South Africa. There was nothing left for her in England after my father and grandfather had gone, and perhaps she wanted to die in her homeland. But she did not mention this. All the talk was positive – a new house, a new life. The idea rejuvenated Florrie and my mother was carried along in her wake, as were all the furnishings from Sunningdale and we four children.

We crossed the Line on board the good ship _Capetown Castle_, passing the voyage in deck quoits, gin rummy and bingo sessions. An extremely smart widow of Granny Florrie's acquaintance, Mrs Hambro, happened to sail with us. One day, when I was left unattended in her cabin, I located her resurrection-box, removed a porcelain pot of scented rouge and liberally rouged everything within three feet of the ground – clothes, shoes, bed, carpet and toiletry. My mother had a deal of explaining to do and must have regretted leaving old Nurse Wells behind in Surrey.

We arrived in Table Bay at dawn on 23 January 1947. Apart from Granny Florrie (who always wore voluminous apparel) we looked like refugees direct from Belsen, or so my mother was told later: obviously rationing had been very much a reality back in post-war England. A tall, handsome man wearing a small suit and bow tie welcomed us to our new country. This was Richard Butters, the first of a great many cousins we were to meet. Turning to me, he asked Granny: 'And what is her name?' Granny exploded, for she was very proud of her only grandson. 'But,' protested the cousin, 'how can you blame anyone for mistaking his sex when you doll his curly hair up with these long blue ribbons?' The ribbons, the height of Sunningdale kiddies' fashion, were removed that very evening, never to be worn again.

Richard Butters, who became a friend for life, drove us from Cape Town to Wynberg through avenues of oak and creeping plumbago, past wide suburban gardens bright with mimosa, hibiscus and oleander. Every bungalow seemed to have a pool, with children who splashed, shouting, in the rainbows of garden sprinklers. Beyond Wynberg the gardens gave way to vineyards and to pine woods with a strong whiff of resin. The soil was rich and the horizons bounded by wild mountains.

The Brommersvlei Road led us deep into rolling vine country, through narrow friendly lanes, some of tarmac, some of dirt. Richard turned round and smiled at our wondering faces. 'This is Constantia, the Valley of the Vines, where our family lives – the most beautiful place in the world.' And it was. He took us to a white homestead on high ground at the head of an oak-lined drive. Les Marais was 100 years old or more. Rockdoves murmured from a cote in the cobbled stableyard and sun birds whistled in mulberry trees around the parched lawn. The walls were thick, busy with columns of ants that followed long cracks in the mortar and with darting predator lizards. Inside, behind the red-tiled stoeps covered in grapevine and the heavy lace curtains, it was drowsy-cool.

There were thirty-three cousins, most of whom lived, in happy harmony, in or near Constantia. All were descended from the marriage between Johannes Rathfelder, of Prussian descent, and a Scottish lady, 'Miss MacFarlane'. His butcher's shop in Wynberg had earned a handsome income from the British Army during the Boer War. With the proceeds they bought the valley of Constantia, which Johannes first put to the vine and later divided between his brother and his children. Brother Danny owned a magnificent pub in nearby Diep River and had never married. Then came Aunt Ethel, who had married a Mr Marais, after whom she named the white homestead where we were lodged on our arrival. Between Ethel and Florrie there was Stenie, once known in the Cape as a beauty, who had married an English millionaire named Taylor. Finally there was Otto Rathfelder, whose wife, Aunt Evie, lived at the crown of our combe with one unmarried daughter. In the yard of her dark homestead, Belle Ombre, stood a slave-bell that still rang on special occasions, though no longer to call slaves in from the vines.

Aunt Evie was still feuding with Aunt Ethel over an ancient water rights quarrel, and, although they were neighbours, the two women would not speak to each other. Now that Florrie had returned to the valley with her daughter-in-law and grandchildren the clan decided to hold a Great Tea Party at Les Marais to welcome the prodigal home. Aunt Evie and Aunt Ethel were both invited, and at last resolved their differences over sucking pig and trifle. A Great Business Meeting followed the Great Tea Party, and Granny Florrie was given three acres of

Aunt Ethel's vineyard not a mile from Les Marais and close to the Vlei, the marshy land around the valley's stream where the coloured folk lived in small shacks under a clump of pine trees. Granny took us to her new plot and, with a great deal of gesturing, described her plans for the house, which was to be called Broughton, the name of the Fiennes family castle back in England. Until it was built we had no home and we soon moved to St James, a quiet resort on the Cape coast, where we rented a house belonging to one of our cousins.

My sisters were sent to school so I was the sole charge of our English nanny, Nurse Ella Ritson. At just three years old, I was known as the naughtiest boy at St James. We went for afternoon walks on a sandy beach where there were pretty shells and bewitching rock pools, and I would scream when the time came to go home. When Nurse Ritson took my hand, I would go limp, forcing her to drag a dead weight. When she lifted me up, I would scratch at her face, even bite her hands. At other times I loved her dearly and told her so.

Sometimes Granny drove us to watch our Constantia home taking shape on the hill above the vineyards. Broughton cost £17,000 to build – a great deal of money in 1948 – and Granny Florrie was immensely proud of it. When we finally moved in, she entertained almost daily, serving tea and fine-cut brown sandwiches to every relative or past acquaintance she could summon. Granny Florrie advertised in the Vlei for a staff of three full-time servants: cook, housemaid and gardener. Mary the maid and Christine the cook, both local Cape coloureds whose families had at some stage settled in the Constantia Vlei, stayed with us from the beginning. The gardeners, who lived in a small summerhouse-cum-toolshed in the garden, either died or disappeared.

The first was John, who wore a tweed cap day and night. As a four-year-old I would listen for hours to stories of his travels around the Cape. In the pine woods beside Broughton he stashed an old cooking-oil container in which he fermented grapes. This he called *dagga* and said I should tell no one of its presence. John never washed, and he smoked homemade tobacco in an old briar. The sweet, pungent smell lingered in the summerhouse long after he had left us, suddenly and without collecting his pay, never to return.

Abner appeared the very next day, a tall Xhosa from Transkei, not a coloured at all, which was rare in those parts. For a year he stayed with us, but one hot day when the dry Berg wind withered lawns and flowers he failed to appear as usual. I found him curled up on the summerhouse floor under empty potato sacks, his black face shining with sweat. He seemed frightened of me, his lips curled back in snarling rictus, and he ignored me when I poured water into his mug from his clay pitcher. I fetched Mary the maid, who first spoke to him, then shouted. He muttered a reply, not looking at her. His voice was quite changed from its usual deep, proud Xhosa tones, more like a febrile old man. Mary took me away abruptly, one firm hand around my wrist. 'You *not* go back in there.' Later my mother called a doctor and, on his advice, the local priest. 'There is nothing I can do,' he said after visiting Abner. 'The witch doctor has said he will die, and *he* believes it. I have seen this many times before.' Abner's mysterious illness cleared up as suddenly as it had arrived and he remained at Broughton until two years after we left the house, though the new owners later told my mother that he had once again received a witch doctor's curse and died in hospital of an indeterminate sickness.

When children from the Vlei came up to Broughton with messages for Mary or Christine, I waited at the end of our red dirt drive to intercept them. There were no white children of my age in the valley except cousin Bella Rathfelder, who cried all the time. Soon the coloured boys took

3

me to their homes and showed me how to play Pooh-sticks under the plank-bridge by their stream. Over the next four years our gang often roamed the valley together, avoiding the Tokai Forest, with its baboons and packs of wild dogs. Bamboo spears and short leather straps to whip the dirt were *de rigueur* and I became co-leader of the gang along with a one-armed lad named Archie. For some reason, Granny Florrie called me 'Bay', not Ranulph, and whenever I appeared at the Vlei my friends danced out of their homes shouting rhythmically, 'Bay, Bay, Stick fer may' – 'Bee, Bee, sting me'. At Christmas-time Granny Florrie gave everyone from the Vlei a present and the children sang carols in the shade of the stoep with its halo of coral-blue agapanthus and red-hot pokers in place of snow and stars.

From Broughton we could see west across the vineyards to Les Marais and Belle Ombre, and north to the ramparts of Table Mountain, Devil's Peak and Lion's Drift. A sandy lane wound through the vineyards behind the Vlei and I loved to walk along it with my mother – preferably without my sisters, because then I had all her attention. Sometimes these walks took us to Les Marais where Cookie, as old as Aunt Ethel, would bring us lemonade in a jar beneath a beaded lace square, and delectable cinnamon crumble.

I began to go daily to the Little People's School in Wynberg, which was mainly attended by Boer children. The dreadful Alan Read and his cronies chased and beat me with bamboo canes no matter how much I tried to maintain a low profile. Eventually, I was removed to a school called Forres, run by two dear old ladies who did 'not *tolerate* bullying of any sort'. In fact, there was just as much bullying as there had been at the Little People's School, but the Forres monster, Lionel Gertz, warned his victims that, should they tell, their lives would become one long nightmare. Unable to tell my mother or the headmistresses – I was as mesmerised by fear as the next boy – I began to give Gertz my prize marbles, catapult, biltong sticks, anything to placate him. Eventually Gertz left and I have only happy memories of Forres after that. Apart from standard academic lessons, the school emphasised handicrafts. I have long been thankful for the lessons in raffia-work, egg- and teapot-cosy making and, above all, darning and sewing.

Mark Charnock, a Forres friend and fellow six-year-old, often came home with me at weekends and joined in the patrols of the Vlei gang. The coloured children were skilled at hitting moving targets with their bamboo spears and, although not up to their standards, Mark and I would practise on the lawn, away from the others. Taking turns, one of us would throw six spears at the other as he ran across a fifty-yard patch. The 'target' would hold a dustbin lid for protection as he ran. One Sunday after church I hit Mark in the eye with a sharpened bamboo. I was horrified. So was my mother. I was locked in my bedroom and my mother beat me with a cane, as my father would have done – but, I suspect, rather less effectively. Two weeks later we breathed again. Mark's sight had been saved, and in time his scars improved.

Gillian, my third sister, was five years my senior, and at twelve was already showing great talent on a horse. Cousin Richard and his wife Joyce across the valley owned a popular riding school, where their daughter Gonda was the star attraction. For the next twenty-five years cousin Gonda was to shine as South Africa's top eventer and show-jumper, outperforming even Britain's Pat Smythe in the days before South Africa was banned from competing in international events. But Gill, on her Anglo-Arab named Quita, was Gonda's equal at local gymkhanas, and I idolised her. I was given a Zulu pony named Zimba, but I preferred to run barefoot in the sand, so the neglected pony was re-sold.

Celia, my middle sister, was eight years older than me, and Susan an impossible ten years older, so we could hardly play together. Aunt Evie often asked us down to Belle Ombre to swim in the homestead pool. Although the pool was cleaned every few years, the water was ink green and the sides of the pool slippery with slime. My sisters happily swam in this fetid tank, but I went along to catch giant toads in my butterfly net. All around the pool were gazanea, wild nerine and white moonflowers. Clusters of weaver-bird nests hung from bamboo groves. Birds chattered, frogs croaked and sisters splashed, so nobody heard when I took a swipe at a crouching toad and missed. Unable to swim, I struggled and sank into the wet murk. By chance Susan saw my hair surface and shouted to the others. She then plunged in and rescued me.

Through the early Broughton years Granny Florrie went from strength to strength. One of her chief pleasures was family feuding. When Aunts Ethel and Evie both died, Florrie became quite senior in the valley. There had long been talk of relatives who by night moved boundary markers between the vineyards, and one cousin, Joy Packer, had written a colourful novel, *The Valley of the Vines*, encapsulating the various intrigues. The apparent equivalents of Aunts Ethel and Evie were given disguises as thin as cling-wrap, and well-publicised controversy amused the family for many months, doubtless boosting the book's sales locally.

At midnight one New Year's Eve an especially spirited cousin, Googie Marais, whose land lay to our northeast, conducted the traditional 'Beating the Bounds' ceremony by firing his rifle at our roof. The impact was intended to arouse Florrie's wrath, but Googie hit the wrong end of the house and panicked a temporary nanny, who packed her bags and left us the very next day.

In October 1950 Florrie suffered a stroke, and a nurse watched by her bedside for eight weeks. She died quietly in the house she loved and was mourned by everyone in the valley. The funeral was held in the Anglican church in Constantia, although our normal place of worship was St Saviour's in Claremont, where the priest, Canon Wade, had two skinny little daughters. The younger, Virginia, later became an English tennis star.

With the wonderfully strong spirit of Florrie Fiennes at rest, there was nothing to keep my mother in South Africa. The call of England was strong, but the family's funds were partially tied up in Broughton. Susan was studying for her degree at Cape Town University and my other two sisters were preparing to matriculate. My mother felt it best that we stay in South Africa four more years.

My mother was fervently involved with a then relatively docile anti-apartheid movement known as Black Sash. She drove into Cape Town and helped collect 90,000 signatures on behalf of coloured people's rights. She also gave her entire personal wealth to a project called Cafda Village towards rehousing 2000 poor blacks from the Windermere district.

When Granny was alive we had never travelled far from Constantia. Now my mother decided the family should see the Kruger National Park, so, with a couple of friends and all the girls, she headed northeast. I was too young for the long journey and spent the holiday with a schoolfriend, James, by the sea. The memory of an incident at that time will remain etched on my brain as long as I live, as clear a vignette as that painted by Camus with his seaside murder in *L'Etranger*. Making castles in the hot white sand at Betty's Bay, I watched a fat man rise sweating from his beach chair and trudge slowly into the breakers with a surfboard. He ducked and porpoised to less broken water further out, and I forgot him until his wife awoke and found him missing. I can see her homely face now as I pointed for her. Her husband was by then only a dark speck in the sea. A rescue boat was launched but they brought the man back dead, for he had let go of his board. Perhaps he had had a heart attack. When I smell seaweed or feel the heat of a long white beach I sometimes hear again the racking sobs of the woman as she knelt by the sandy body of her man.

Once away from school, James and I were no longer friends. We fought and threw rocks at each other, so his mother telephoned my aunt in nearby Kommetie Sands. This Aunt 'Utcha' was Granny Florrie's daughter by her first marriage, to an Englishman who fell off his horse while hunting and died in her arms. Utcha lived with her thirty-year-old son Michael on a chicken farm, and I went to stay with them. Michael would wake me at 5.00 a.m. and let me hold the kerosene lamp as he moved about fascinating sheds full of the weirdest chicken smells. The woods about Wenga chicken farm were wild and tangled all the way down to the empty dunes beside the Atlantic. Sometimes, resting on hot afternoons, I could hear the thunderous boom of breakers above the happy cluck-cluck of the free-range hens.

The girls, back at Broughton after their holiday, bubbled with stories of hippo, impala and kuda, of lion and elephant. I sulked, for nobody cared a jot about the wonderful Wenga chickens, nor even how I had hit James's head from ten yards with a rock and made him bleed. Susan was the worst, for she had entered the boyfriend stage with a vengeance and made it plain that little brothers were to be neither seen nor heard when her men were at Broughton – which was most of the time. Two of her boyfriends, probably on her instructions, rolled me all the way down the stairs in a linen-basket and, one afternoon, locked me in the upstairs bathroom. Down in the Vlei, I exhorted the valley gang to ambush these boyfriends, but even one-armed Archie, who feared nothing, failed to react. At only seventeen Susan became the youngest student on record to obtain a Bachelor of Arts degree from Cape Town University. She left home for a tour of Europe with a Rathfelder cousin and then to stay with family friends in England.

In 1952, when I was eight, I became a boarder at Western Province Preparatory School. My cousin Nicky Taylor went with me. In later years he became the Elvis Presley of South Africa, though he was not popular with the government because of his political lyrics.

At school it is best to conform and try to blend in with the herd, as any individualistic trait is a red rag to the bullies. I found it immensely embarrassing that, by parental order, I was to study Latin while my peers learned to chatter away in Afrikaans. The school was proud of its cricketing record, but I soon found that my eye was almost as slow as my reactions. Mathematics were utterly beyond my grasp, but I excelled at Divinity and I could fight rather better than most of my contemporaries owing to my Vlei experiences.

I enjoyed the weekly official game of 'Skop die Blijk' or 'Kick the Can', in which two large teams attacked each other inside a forest adjacent to the school. The school staff also organised an indoor, nocturnal version called 'British Bulldog'. All the boarders were divided equally between two classrooms at either end of a long concrete corridor. Each team formed offensive and defensive patrols and, in the pitch dark, attempted to imprison in its room as many boys from the other team as possible. After thirty minutes, the masters switched on the lights and congratulated the winners after a head-count of prisoners. During the nightmarish half-hour all side-doors were locked to prevent reluctant boys from creeping into a haven. This vicious struggle in the dark produced an impressive crop of cuts, bruises and worse, and was intended to be character-building. Had he but known of it, Kurt Hahn would doubtless have included this activity in the Gordonstoun programme.

For a treat on my ninth birthday I was allowed a gang battle in Tokai woods, using the great sticky fircones called donnerballs as ammunition. One boy was struck at by a rat-snake, but we all agreed it was the best party we could remember. Afterwards at Broughton my mother arranged a more normal celebration with an iced cake and candles.

Despite Mark Charnock's eye, my mother was patient with the valley gang and my rowdy schoolfriends. However, she was allergic to guns of any sort. Three times during our Constantia years she caught me pointing a toy gun at someone and without ado beat my backside with a cane. But the worst occasion did not involve a cap-gun. One day, annoyed with Christine the cook for withholding chocolate cake, I took my father's wartime pistol and threatened her: her life or the cake. Instead of complying, our plump cook backed up against the Aga, her eyes bulging. Ella Fitzgerald would have been proud of her sound-effects. Shocked, I escaped to the woods, where a posse of women – my mother, Celia, Gill and Christine – quickly brought me to justice. The penalty for this armed hold-up was six hard strokes of the cane and no supper, let alone chocolate cake. Also 500 lines: 'Never, never let your gun pointed be at anyone.'

With Archie and the others from the Vlei – eight in all plus two mongrel dogs – I often wandered for aimless hours through vineyard and wood. We called ourselves the Mealie Gang because our favourite meeting place was in a high field of Indian maize or 'mealies'. If anyone in Constantia objected to our ethnically mixed and barefoot band of local boys with their curious customs, they showed no sign of it. Apartheid did not seem to touch pre-teenagers, at any rate not inside the valley.

One afternoon at grape-picking time, Archie ran into the clearing by the Vlei huts where the gang played marbles. 'They are taking the dead thief to your mum, Bay. You'd better go quick.' My sisters were out riding, but I found my mother, flanked by Christine and Mary, near our boundary gate listening to a large coloured man with a knobkerrie stick. Beside him a colleague held the bloody neck of an unfortunate coloured tramp in an arm lock. Blood welled from the open wounds on the tramp's head and cheeks. Each time the knobkerrie man's voice rose, his colleague dashed their prisoner's head against our wrought-iron gate as though to emphasise the point. Christine told my mother that the tramp had stolen clothes from a nearby hamlet and that all the inhabitants had gone out into the countryside to find the thief. These two had just caught him hiding in our wood. My mother must call the police. This she did and the thief was taken away, still bleeding freely. My mother must have been shaken by this glimpse of the valley's less serene face, but she never admitted her concern in front of us.

Every century in Cape Town a magnificent festival is held to celebrate the founding of the Dutch Cape Colony under Jan van Riebeek in 1652. I was taken to Cape Town in 1952 to see the exhibitions and funfairs. A Scottish friend of my mother's, a stout-hearted widow who brooked no feebleness in life, devoted her day to giving me a good time but was disgusted when, terrified, I refused to take a ride in a rickshaw pulled by a giant Zulu clad in ostrich feathers, cow-horns and beads. Afterwards the good lady had serious words with my mother. I was obviously spoiled or over-cossetted and, as a result, of a timid disposition that would do me no good when the time came to face the world beyond my mother's apron strings.

In 1954 Celia matriculated with the highest possible grade and my mother took us all on a holiday within the Cape. She drove our battered Chevrolet through the dusty Karoo and the dark mystery of the Titsikama Forest. We stayed for a while in picturesque spots called Allan and George, and spent the first week of May in and around Ceres, the most beautiful countryside I have ever seen. Streams and rocks, fern and oakwood graced the mountain valleys. There were hidden pools rimmed with canna and arum lilies, where bees droned and honeybirds darted. On the lower slopes glades of glorious protea bloomed above a mat of morning glory. The distance south to the sea was blue with haze and green with vines. Inland the Drakensberg range underpinned the huge sky with its western ridges.

We idled east to Assegaibosch, the lowest valley in the country, where the mechanic's wireless in a roadside garage announced that Dien Bien Phu had fallen the previous day and that food rationing was about to end in Britain. At Outshoorn, where the land was Karoo dry and the air clogged with dust, we gaped at the burly Boers who could carry 300-pound tins full of honey around the Bee Farm. Next door at the Ostrich Farm, signs in English and Afrikaans warned: 'Keep clear of the big chickens' legs. They kick worser than a donkie.' In a special corral brave Celia paid a tikki and rode a saddled big chicken round and round in the sawdust.

Back at school, John Stansbury, the severe-faced headmaster who beat me from time to time for good reason, awarded me the Divinity Prize. I decided to become a priest. But in September that year all saintly notions ended when the weekend filmshow ran a Pathé News account of the ascent of Mount Everest. Somehow I was left for years with the muddled impression that Mr Hillary and a Chinese friend had been sent up this great mountain, higher even than Table Mountain, as a wedding present for the English Queen. I, too, would become a climber of mountains and stick the British flag into fierce features of far-flung landscapes.

My mother had been brought up in another era and in different circumstances. She had married at nineteen and left her protected family environment without knowing how to boil an egg or iron a shirt. When Granny Florrie died, my mother was on her own for the first time, with nobody to turn to for advice. She could not count on the family finances to deal with life and education. Memories of my father were too strong for her to accept the various eligible proposals that came her way, but she must have often wondered whether she could continue to cope alone with the future.

In 1954 we left Constantia. On the last night, with the house stripped of its furniture, I looked up from my bedroom window to the high slopes north of the valley and saw red tongues of fire about Tokai – summer conflagrations that blackened the woods for thousands of acres and scattered ash on our vines.

I promised to write to Archie and the Vlei gang, but I don't think I ever did.

A cluster of cousins came to see off the English great-grandchildren of Johannes Rathfelder. They understood my mother's need to go home now that Florrie, her only link with South Africa, was dead. We travelled in the liner *Winchester Castle* with all our belongings, including Gill's horse Quita. Southampton was drab, grey and filled with more men and machinery than I had ever seen.

My godfather, Sir Ernest Gowers, drove us deep into Hampshire to a cottage he had agreed to let us rent temporarily for a nominal sum. Our household, the Broughton furniture, went into storage until my mother could find somewhere permanent for us to settle. Everything was strange and different, including the way people spoke. I dreaded the day when I would have to face the unknown terrors of a new school and of English boys.

2

Coming Home

A manner rude and wild is common at your age.

HILAIRE BELLOC

I n the autumn of 1954 my mother took me to Waterloo Station. I wept bitterly in the lavatory of the Horseshoe Grill and clung to her arms with desperation as she said a _proper_ goodbye before we walked with my suitcase to platform ten for the Salisbury train. There we went through the motions of a _public_ goodbye after she had introduced me to the master-in-charge, a mere wave, with my eyes quickly averted lest a flood of tears disgrace me in front of the chattering faces that appeared and disappeared, puppet-like, in the carriage window. Like the others I wore a purple blazer, purple cap and grey flannel trousers. There was, thankfully, one other new boy, called Lawson.

From Salisbury we drove in coaches over the bare downs of Cranborne Chase to Tollard Royal. Sandroyd School stood in its own grounds, a squat grey Georgian prison, or so it first seemed to me.

I slept in an attic room called Wigwam with Lawson and a podgy lad named McAlpine, whose father was a king-pin in the building business, and I cried myself silently to sleep all too often during the first lonely weeks.

By term's end I found a friend, William Hillary, of my own age and, more importantly, of similar incompetence in the classroom and on the games field. Sandroyd was transformed from a hostile planet to an exciting playground. By the time the winter holidays were at hand, I experienced a wonderful end-of-term feeling; quite the best sensation of all my schooldays.

That Christmas holiday in our rented Hampshire cottage was a tribute to my mother's ability to cope as mistress of her own household. Being young and selfish I paid little heed to my mother's health and money troubles. My godfather lived in the main house over the hill, and I played with his grandchildren on the farm all day, teaching the assembled band of good English children how to make spears from hazel saplings and regaling them with tales of deepest Africa. I loved every aspect of my first cold Christmas: a smattering of snow, stockings, mistletoe, an over-decorated tree. And carol-singing in the nearby Norman church of Trotton with my godfather playing the organ.

During my second Sandroyd term school was exciting and fun. I was less homesick, and other new boys moved into Wigwam to sob into their pillows. My new dormitory was a bigger, lighter room overlooking some fields and a beech wood. On 1 February Mr Ozanne, the headmaster, proudly told us it was the coldest day recorded in Britain for sixty years – and still we went for our afternoon walk on the downs.

My mathematics master soon regarded me as one of those juvenile brick walls against which it would be pointless to knock his head. I was willing, but totally unable, to comprehend his instruction, although I do remember that he always announced end-of-class with the words 'Yes, we have no bananas'.

A pretty young music mistress, an angel named Miss Wheatcroft, taught me to play *Ba, Ba Black Sheep* on the recorder and to make models of galleons from balsa wood and cotton thread. On Sundays groups of younger boys sometimes donned leather gloves and collected stones from the fallow fields, piling them in cairns to help the ploughman. Or else we walked the unspoiled countryside all about the school in the centre of Cranborne Chase in long straggly crocodiles. Sometimes a few of us were able to sneak ahead. We would climb up the steep sides of the downland and kick at the grassy tussocks made by moles until they came free. Some weighed half a hundredweight and, given a push at the right moment, would career down the slope on to the unsuspecting crocodile. I joined the Sandroyd riding school and enjoyed the long winter rides, with cold hands and chapped thighs, through woods and valleys which the crocodiles never reached.

William Hillary persuaded me to write the script for a puppet play of the Dick Whittington story. We made the puppets from papier maché down in a cellar normally used as a photographic darkroom, keeping the play a secret – which was half the fun. Later, I spent the summer holiday with William's family at a rented house in Seaview on the Isle of Wight, where the sound of cannon announced the daily dinghy races.

In the dormitory, I discovered that my South African years were an unsuspected asset. What little the other boys knew of Africa came from the dramatised pages of *Eagle* or the *Beano*. Their minds were open and receptive to tales of derring-do. One owl-faced boy named John Knox was so renowned for his creepy ghost stories that boys would risk Mr Ozanne's cane to sneak into his dormitory simply to hear his tales of the unexpected. I only told my stories on Saturday nights, mainly because we were given our weekly chocolate bars on Saturday afternoon. I charged a square from each listener. I would spend the entire week working out the next Saturday's instalment in detail. One term's story was entitled *The Curse of the River Kwa*.

Life was magical at Sandroyd in 1955. Mr Ozanne handed over headmastership to Mr Buckland. This affected me little – though, because the new boss beat the harder, our mischief had to be better planned. Old Mrs Richardson read stories to us under an oak tree after lunch. I was most bewitched by the tale of *The Little Grey Men* by 'B.B.', although it didn't seem the same when I read it again thirty years later.

Mr Jones-Davison, I always remember, dressed in black football shorts, rugby shirt and neatly turned white socks, with an umpire's whistle permanently in place like Andy Capp's fag-end. Because of J.-D., I joined the wolfcub pack, Woodpigeon patrol, and promised to 'obey the Scout Law'. He also eased me into football, and I made the school second eleven, cherishing the attendant perks, such as coach visits for away matches where there were delicious cakes and trifles. But even J.-D. could do little to improve the ceremonial summer drudge of cricket. Having once been hit on the nose, I feared batting. I was scared of close fielding for the same reason and of bowling because of the derision I attracted. I invariably threw the ball as though it were a spear, which made J.-D. livid. For me, the only pleasurable position on the cricket field was that of Long Leg since I could at least accurately throw the ball quite far. It was at length accepted that this position was mine and nobody else's. There I spent many happy hours ignoring the distant *thwack* of the game as I fashioned complex daisy-chains.

The only sport at which I achieved any above-average success was swimming. Everybody wore very brief cloth pants called blue-bags unless they achieved a certain prowess in the pool. I discovered a liking for the breast-stroke and, even as a short and scraggy eleven-year-old, achieved the dizzy award of a pair of red-bags. After that I spent every possible moment in the pool or, to be more accurate, in my prestigious new pants.

Our swimming master also ran the school plays, and many exciting evenings were passed at rehearsal. One term we did *Oliver's Island*, a pirate fantasy, in which I sang, in high treble:

> Education. Education. You are nothing but vexation.
> Stupid pupil, harassed teacher. Each is an unhappy creature.
> Source of gloom and desperation. Education. Education.

The chief pirate was acted by a ginger-haired Irish boy, Barclay, the Earl of Kingston, who was known as 'Thuggers' owing to his boxing skills. He made a magnificent Captain Morgan.

One holiday in 1955 I spent with my mother visiting Celia, who was studying medicine at Trinity College, Dublin. She lodged with five septuagenarian sisters in a tumbledown mansion on the banks of the River Liffey. These Hamilton sisters were known as 'The Hams', and their friendliness was as warm as their house was draughty.

My sisters and I had all developed the Afrikaaner way with English vowels, but English schooling soon eradicated this. Now I noticed Celia spoke with a distinct Irish lilt. She had also developed quite liberal views, although she was moderate in comparison with many of her contemporaries. It was a time of dawning nuclear awareness, especially in student committees. The government had announced plans for twelve nuclear power stations and for the manufacture of hydrogen bombs. Twelve hundred scientists from seventy-two countries attended a Geneva conference on peaceful uses of atomic energy, leading world scientists issued an appeal for the renunciation of war, and the Pope made an official plea for the end of all test explosions. At eleven years I certainly listened, but the alarming talk of nuclear war and its dangers found no place in my field of interests. Despite the psychologists' dire warnings, I cannot believe I worried even subconsciously about the nuclear threat, Soviet rockets or Calder Hall fallout. Nor do I know a single contemporary who did.

About the time of my twelfth birthday my mother purchased St Peter's Well, a long, low house that had once been three cottages on the eastern edge of the village of Lodsworth in Sussex. In one end there was but a single level which made a high, light room with a wide fireplace and a view up to the rooftop beams. All the other rooms were small and dark, their windows studded with leaded diamond panes as Tudor as the bread oven, low doorposts and the natural curves of the long, tiled roof. There was a little hedged garden fringed by an acre of wild orchard stiff with apples, plums and, later on, cobnuts. Best of all, right across the front garden wall, as far as the eye could see, stretched a paradise of fields, valleys and forest. My life was now happy both at home and at school.

Early in the summer term I took steps to correct what seemed to me a serious omission in the school's general make-up. There were no true gangs. Certainly, there were cliques who built exclusive forts deep in the woods, but these bands did not make animated contact with each other as they would have done at Forres or Western Province. While wolf-cubbing one weekend I discovered a sunken rock garden complete with a slimy cave, creepers, giant ferns, rock slides and even a six-inch lizard. No long-lost Inca ruins could have pleased me more, for this was an ideal hideout. Morrell, Sutcliffe and I formed a gang named Acnuleps after the Latin word for cave, *spelunca*. We wrote out the rules, signed them with blood and hid them in a Players tobacco tin in the cobwebbed roof of the cave. The tin may still be there.

New inductees to Acnuleps were required to endure odd tribal rites. A string was tied around one little finger and the other end pulled hard until the skin broke, leaving a scar which looked like a ring around the finger. Next, the boy's back was beaten by existing members with sprigs of holly and his arms and legs slit from top to bottom with sharp slithers of flint. Finally, a steep comb was pressed into the back of one hand to leave a line of bleeding imprints. One by one we located the forts, destroyed them and put their occupants to flight.

All, that is, except for the Mainwairing gang's fort. Mainwairing and Leslie were powerful characters who had long commanded a magnificent fort fashioned from woven hazel saplings. Having learned of Acnuleps' tactics, they instructed their band in the manufacture and use of hazel spears and whips. Boys from forts we had destroyed joined the Mainwairing gang, which eventually numbered two dozen on Saturday afternoons. Finally, Sutcliffe and I learned the fort's whereabouts. The very next Saturday afternoon, our twelve Acnuleps, armed with six spears each, headed for the Mainwairing fort. Even the best South African set-to paled into insignificance compared with the affair at the Mainwairing fort. Neither group could be said to have won, but the beautiful fort was reduced to driftwood and its occupants to long mornings queuing up for matron's attentions. Acnuleps members were forbidden to have their cuts and sores looked at. Instead, Sutcliffe applied stolen Dettol to all abrasions down in the puppetry cellars.

The full weight of Mr Buckland's authority was brought to bear on this new and sinister threat to the good reputation of Sandroyd School. Being an excellent headmaster, he did not sack Mainwairing or me, but he impressed his will and the cane on both of us to such an extent that Sandroyd returned instantly to its previous gangless existence and stayed that way as long as I remained a pupil. Suddenly mindful of the importance of the Common Entrance exam to my future, I devoted my last two terms to academic strivings, mainly at Divinity, which I loved.

My mother moved the Broughton furniture from storage into St Peter's Well and home was truly home once more with the old carpets underfoot and Granny Florrie's grandfather clock ticking gently in the red-tiled hall. The homely smell of cooking wafted about the house as my mother's kitchen confidence slowly bloomed.

At twelve, I was more able to enjoy my sisters' companionship than when I was younger. Gill, whose horse Quita died, and I would bicycle on weekdays some three miles to Lickfold, where we picked apples for eight hours for a salary of one shilling and sixpence (about 8p) an hour. For a farthing I could buy a large mint bull's eye, so my wage packet seemed a hefty treasure trove. The older pickers, mostly local women wearing thick socks, baggy trousers and headscarves done up under their chins, cracked dirty jokes and shrieked with mirth as they poured tea and ate cheese chunks on homemade rolls. I felt extremely grown-up sitting beside Gill on an upturned apple box, trying to comprehend the light ribaldry.

At home, we chopped at the long grass in the orchard with sickles, following vague directions from my mother. Celia came home from Dublin to join us for a while. There were pears, plums and apples to pick and, in the nearby woods, a bounty of blackberries. We could buy a dozen large brown eggs for a shilling from Farmer Smallridge, whose farm was but a short walk up the lane, through a sunny, unkempt graveyard full of flowering shrubs. The grassy banks and old stone walls of our steep lane bustled with the colour and noise of butterflies, crickets and frogs in summer, and at dusk they gleamed with the soft magic of glow-worm colonies. Soon, the local council would spray the verges of the local lanes, and the glow-worms would disappear, along with the frogs, the crickets, various types of small bird and many species of wildflower. But then, in 1956, the Lodsworth valley and its immediate countryside still retained the friendly unplanned variety of shape and shadow of pre-war days. Hedges, ponds and copses abounded, fields were small and seldom square, with oaks still permitted to survive in their midst.

The River Lod ran along the bottom of our valley, deep in woods, and on its far side a forested hill rose to an isolated hamlet called River. The Lod wound happily past oak and birch, bogs of myrtle and bulrush, glades of bracken, or in spring bluebells, until mid-way between the town of Midhurst and Petworth it reached the mill at Halfway Bridge where our policeman lived. One day Gill and I took a canoe and sandwiches down the Lod to where it joined the River Rother, paddling through the domain of dragonfly, swan and kingfisher until we passed through a cleft in the South Downs and reached the Arun river and, at length, by Arundel Castle, the sea itself. My mother collected us and the canoe in her bull-nosed Morris Minor. She owned this car for twenty years and to the best of my knowledge never once exceeded thirty miles per hour.

A twelfth-century village church overlooked our orchard and the Glebe Path wound through our apple trees to reach the old vicarage. Sundays were filled with a clamour from the nearby belfry. Masters of the bells were the ancient vergers, Messrs Simpson and Newman, assisted by a cheery spinster named Peggy who, when the two vergers were away ill, could ring four bells by herself. Her fame for this amazing feat of campanology reached far beyond Lodsworth: Southern Television once sent a crew to record her. Peggy had fashioned herself a clever harness with which she bound all her legs and arms, inextricably it seemed, to her chosen bell-ropes. Then, with the ginglymus movements of an accelerating devil-dance, the bells to all appearances took control of Peggy. At times her trousered legs shot way above her head, at others she levitated horizontally and then, on the slower chimes, she appeared to be controlling traffic or saluting an invisible Führer with one rigid leg and one stiff arm.

A month before our own arrival, a family of five settled in the hamlet of River, a mile from Lodsworth, in a house very similar to ours. Mr Thomas Pepper ran a chalk pit, as had his father and grandfather, at Amberley, where the River Arun cuts through the South Downs on its way to the sea. The Peppers had three children, two sons about my age and a daughter of nine, three years my junior, and they asked us to tea, as was and is the country custom. 'You *must* put shoes on, Ranulph,' my mother said sharply. 'People do not expect visitors with bare feet, especially on first acquaintance.'

'I don't want to go to tea with two boring boys and a silly girl. Can't I go down to the river this afternoon?'

Exasperated, my mother was firm. 'They are our neighbours. We can't be rude, and how do you know they are boring or silly since you've never met them?'

So we went to tea at the Peppers'. There were excellent cakes which made up for lost time by the river. After the meal my mother left and told me to be back before dark.

George and Charles were not boring. I followed them up to the attic where, on an enormous table, their father had set up an urban panorama in miniature, around and through which a selection of trains and carriages could be raced or shunted from a central electrical control. I first watched and then joined in. I had never owned electric trains and this was great fun.

A pin pricked my knee under the table and I knelt to spot the cause. I had quite forgotten the boys' sister, Virginia. Her brothers ignored her in a pointed fashion and I had done likewise.

Now I saw that she had been playing all along underneath the table and had fired a spring-loaded toy cannon at me.

'Stop it. That hurt,' I told her.

She screwed up her nose at me.

I went back to the trains rather hoping that she might fire another pin. But she didn't. At 6.00 Mrs Pepper said I should be getting home and the brothers announced they would go as far as the river with me. I looked sideways at the girl to see if she would go too. I noticed that her eyes were very blue, almost violet, and that her eyelashes were long. Soon afterwards, I returned to school.

At Sandroyd I made friends and learned to live happily away from home. My upbringing in an all-female environment required balancing; boarding school filled that need.

Common Entrance came and went. I passed with just sufficient marks to make it into Eton. My mother was proud and delighted and so was I, for luckily I could not foresee the immediate future.

3

Eton

*There is no end to the violations committed by children
on children, quietly talking alone.*

ELIZABETH BOWEN

My great misfortune was to be a pretty little boy. I can hardly blame Eton for that, yet my memories of the place are tarnished because of it.

My mother drove me to Eton, the Morris Minor laden with suitcases, a colourful rug and two framed prints of spaniels. Accustomed to Sandroyd with its 100 pupils, I was awed by the thought of over 1000 boys, many of them eighteen-year-olds and over six feet tall. Some, I was told, used razors like men.

At Sandroyd my baronetcy and my South African background had proved to be good PR. Here there were numerous ex-colonials, and baronets were trashy nonentities eclipsed by a welter of earls, lords and viscounts. Scions of the great families of commerce abounded, including two Vesteys and a Sainsbury.

There were three others at Mr Parr's House tea party for new boys. Our parents met in the housemaster's study and fingered thin sandwiches while we summed each other up in a nearby room over an iced cake and chocolate biscuits. I never again saw an officially sanctioned iced cake in Mr Parr's House and wonder whether that first and only goodie was a symbolic goodbye to childhood fare.

The noisiest of my three new colleagues was Dave Hart. He was stocky, sallow-skinned and Jewish, a heavy cross to bear at Eton. Gilbert Woods, willow-thin and sharp featured, was the son of an Oxfordshire MP. He formed a close and lasting friendship with the other new boy, Desmond Sanford, who came from Kenya. Any idea I may have nursed of popularity through jungle tales was dashed by Sanford's presence.

We were all, even noisy Hart, in an understandable state of apprehension that made for a common bond of friendship during the first few days, as together we faced the great unknown.

My mother said as she left: 'If you have any problem, you tell Miss Grieve. I'm sure she will look after you, for she has such nice eyes.' Miss Grieve, a middle-aged spinster, was the matron or, in Eton terminology, the Dame. Every House has one, and most pay special attention to new boys until they find their feet.

I watched my mother disappear in the Morris Minor. It was a moment of dark panic.

At first the customs, the colloquialisms, the local geography and the complex schooling schedules, the residue of 500 years, left me bemused. Those first weeks were like an attempt to gain a set of daily changing objectives blindfolded in a swamp, with a host of hostile custodians shouting instructions in a weird language.

The fagging system was an ever-present bane to my existence – and to that of any boy junior enough to be faggable. The system could easily be abused by the bullying type and there was no complaints bureau. Basic fagging duties involved such things as cleaning shoes and cooking tea for a specific fagmaster in your House. Any other work that might occur to your current overlord throughout the day would also come your way. After a while this sort of fagging settled into a daily routine and was at least predictable. But more general fagging duties could have a catastrophic effect on a fag's day-to-day life.

The six senior boys in each House, including the House captain, had only to stand at their doors and scream the single word '*Boyyyyy!*' This was the mandatory summons for every eligible boy within earshot (and that in theory meant 'currently inside the House') to drop whatever he was doing and head at maximum speed to the source of the scream. He who arrived last was fagged. If there were two tasks to be done, the second-last in the queue was also dispatched. Even those who were not fagged had interrupted their studies and they were well aware that another call could sound the very next minute from quite a different part of the House. This did little for concentration but no doubt heightened powers of constant alertness.

If you were lucky enough to be allotted a well-placed bedroom in terms of access to the bedrooms of the senior boys and the Library, which was their 'headquarters', you would of course fag far less than those living at the ends of cul-de-sac corridors. Those senior boys who had not yet been elevated into the Library but had been elected to Debate, the sub-prefects of each House, could not scream for fags. But they could seek them out. They were the fledgling vultures of the system, and if they disliked a particular junior they could, of course, pick on him for fagging jobs time after time.

Trying to come to terms with this amazing new world, I had little time to be homesick and even less for leisure. But I did find myself attracted to the Drawing Schools. Officially each boy spent one period of forty-five minutes per week at the Schools, but they were open to all comers every day for painting, pottery and puppetry. The senior master was a kindly soul named Wilfrid Blunt whose younger brother Anthony, an ex-colleague of Philby, Burgess and Maclean, was then in charge of Her Majesty the Queen's paintings.

I was to spend many hours completing watercolour paintings under the guidance of Willy Blunt. Two of my fellow painters were Tom Gibson and 'Prog'. They have both followed successful artistic careers until the present day, one as the owner of Thomas Gibson Fine Art in New Bond Street and the other, HRH Prince Richard of Gloucester, as an architect. The latter used to spatter paint-brush water all over me and my works, but not without retaliation.

Willy Blunt recently published his Eton memoirs and explained their revealing nature in the foreword: . . . I felt that some account of the problems that face a homosexual schoolmaster could possibly be of help to others similarly handicapped through no fault of their own.'

He also stated that he had never so much as kissed a single pupil under his charge. I am sure none of us had even a glimmer of suspicion that dear old Willy was that way inclined. He recalls in his book:

> The fact that practically the whole school passed, however briefly, through my hands means that over my thirty-six years of schoolmastering, I must have acquired not far short of ten thousand pupils. Most of these have some recollection, however vague, of me; but the reverse is, unfortunately, not true, and when I am accosted in Piccadilly by (for example) some

ancient white-bearded bishop who addresses me as 'sir', I am not always able to recognise what remains of some cherub of the twenties. Occasionally, however, when the name of one of them catches the headlines, I recall an infant who more often than not showed no obvious sign of future distinction. For example, there was a bright little new boy at Eton in the fifties named Sir Ranulph Twistleton-Wykeham-Fiennes. 'I can't call you all that,' I said. 'Will "Fiennes" do?' 'Just call me Twinkletoes' came his charmingly improbable reply. I would never then have guessed that Twinkletoes might one day conquer a Pole, let alone two.

Twinkletoes, the watchword of a then in-vogue comedian, Bernard Breslaw, was the nickname Woods had bestowed on me. This was preferable to the sobriquet I later received from *Private Eye* – Twizzywick-Piston-Steam.

Although Dave Hart was difficult to get along with, the other two new boys in my House were friendly and lively. In my class there were a good many boys from other Houses whom I envisaged as friends-to-be. Mathematics classes were as impossible as ever but there were luckily two or three other dolts with equally impenetrable skulls. All in all I was as happy as a sandboy.

Quite when and how the horror started is now lost to me since the mind does its best to heal the deepest sores. But I believe I had been at Eton about a month when Woods and Sanford entered my room just before lunchtime.

'They say you're a tart, Fiennes. Did you know?'

'What', I asked them 'is a tart?' – since they were obviously not talking about apple pies or the street women of Mayfair.

They giggled together with much uplifting of eyebrows. 'Not the sort of thing we had expected you to be.'

Afire with curiosity, and knowing my contemporaries would be as ignorant as I, I asked an older boy for the definition of a tart. More sniggers.

I know it took me some days, days of increasing pain, fear and humiliation, before I learned fully what I was in the eyes of my erstwhile friends – for friends they soon ceased to be as one by one they learned of my new status. No leper or spy can have suffered so long or so sharply as I did as I struggled to live cheek-by-jowl twenty-four hours a day for two years with the shouted taunts and the subtle cruelties of my fellow Etonians. There was no leper colony or traitor's prison where I could hide my face from the sadism of my untainted peers.

I visited the school library and found a thesaurus in which a tart was likened to 'Bawd, pimp, white slave, whore, bitch or slut'. I learned that in Eton slang a tart is a boy who sells himself for sexual activities in return for favours, be they cash or kind. I realised there could be no lower form of life than a tart. I must prove my innocence at once. But how? Best to start with close colleagues and hope they would spread the truth to counter the dreadful lie.

'Tell them I am not a tart,' I pleaded with Woods, who I could tell was basically a decent sort. 'Tell them in your class and maybe they will tell people in their Houses and in other classes.' Of course Woods could have made no impact at all once the word was out, even had he wanted to. As it was, his own position, and that of Sanford and Hart, was enhanced by my degrading, for that is the indisputable law in any jungle. In their shoes I would have behaved as they did. Curiously enough, the least unpleasant tart-taunter was Hart, who in every other respect was to become my *bête noire* for the four years until his expulsion.

It never struck me that perhaps many boys at Eton neither knew nor cared who I was or whether or not I was a tart. Nor did I realise that, of those who did hear that Fiennes was a tart, many were aware that any and every pretty boy is a tart whether or not he actually indulges in sexual acts with other boys. In nearly five years at Eton I cannot remember a single boy called a tart who was not considered either pretty or sexually titillating. The Eton tart gossip is based not on what actually happens but on what the gossipers would like to think has happened.

There was no one for me to run to. I could not conceive of pouring out my nightmare to Miss Grieve, the Dame, much less Mr Parr. I could not write or phone home, for how could I make my mother understand such things? I had lived a sheltered life in an all-female family where the straight facts of life had been imparted in the standard Birds and Bees fashion. There had been no reference to gay Birds or queer Bees and I was totally unprepared for the way in which the world fell apart about me. My skin was paper-thin, my imagination fertile and my ability to fight back nil. Perhaps if some male relative had warned me of the impending problems adolescence at Eton would involve, I might somehow have forearmed myself. But I had no brothers, no uncles and no father. The only alternative to counter-attack was to escape, but there was something in my make-up which precluded the option of running away from school. This course simply never occurred to me. Crying hopelessly at nights, I contemplated the option of suicide with growing seriousness, having left a detailed note of accusation naming each and every one of my torturers. In retrospect, this last detail would not have been possible since I was daily troubled by new faces to which I could put no name, boys who pinched my bottom in the crush outside morning chapel, who pursed their lips into a kiss while nudging their companion as they passed in the street, the wolf-whistles and 'coo-eees' from the windows of Houses all about as I passed below.

It seemed to me that 1100 boys stared and sneered, and I loathed the lot of them. The plan that I settled upon was to jump off the bridge over the Thames between Eton and Windsor. Once my mind was made up to do this, I at least had the assurance of instantly available escape and revenge. Subconsciously, I suppose, I knew I would never self-destruct. The ten commandments had been clearly explained by my mother. All human life was sacred. Nor would I have wilfully made my mother suffer.

Beyond the mental self-defence of the suicide plan, there were other aids, such as an ugly scowl, which I practised daily in front of my mirror to lessen the scourge of prettiness. I wore this scowl like a mask as others might apply cream to hide shameful pimples.

Increasingly, any conversation I tried to open was met by ribald responses. So I learned to talk to no one, never to go into an older boy's room, never to look at anyone, only at the ground or my desk or the pavement. And, most important of all, I learned to switch off, not to think of tomorrow or the taunting gauntlet of the next boys' lunch or the 600 pairs of staring eyes at chapel. This lesson was invaluable for subsequent rigours in hostile climes, and I have Eton – or, to be more precise, my fellow Etonians – to thank for that.

At last that first term – or half as Eton terms are called – came to an end and the prison gates, Mr Parr's front door, clanged behind me. Any resolve not to tell my mother crumbled in a long pent-up tidal wave of grief on the way home. She was devastated and, in passing the burden of my problem to her, the beginnings of hope re-stirred for me. I was again able to love and be loved after the long months wrapped up in hatred for those about me. She promised she would do something to make it better, but in the mean time I must try to forget about it all and enjoy the holidays.

*   *   *

Lodsworth was another world. During that first holiday I replenished my solar batteries in readiness for the next dark tunnel. Of course the very knowledge that the holiday would end laid a mantle of increasing apprehension and gloom over me. But I could still enjoy life by the moment, and I did so.

Two people in particular put new colour into my existence – Peter and Ginnie. Ginnie was the girl from River, the Peppers' daughter, whom I saw from time to time riding her pony in the woods. She was always escorted by a friend or one of her father's employees and I only watched her from behind bushes. I had never seen such an appealing face and my heart beat hard whenever I heard a horse pass by our house or, when wandering in the woods, the leaf-muffled beat of hooves. By the end of my first Eton year, despite the fact that no words passed between us, I yearned like some love-sick poet for this ten-year-old girl.

Peter was the son of George Tooth, who, as local chief woodsman, looked after a wide area of forest between Lodsworth and Liphook. Peter was twelve years old, a year my junior, and a down-to-earth character whose favoured holiday pursuits were at one with mine. We bicycled everywhere, fished in the Lod and the Rother, haunted the woods, earned money digging in old people's gardens and, at night, slipped out of our respective homes and indulged in our favourite sport – roof-climbing in Lodsworth or Midhurst. Our all-time record was twenty-six rooftops in one night. What a relief it was to have a friend with no ever-present fear of the cruel jibe or innuendo.

We never read books, listened to music or watched television (not that our parents owned sets). In stormy weather we sometimes plagued my mother by playing in the house, which was full of hiding places. At one end of the house a narrow gallery with a rickety balustrade overlooked the only largish room, and here my mother had hung Granny Florrie's portraits of Fiennes ancestors, heavy oils set in gilt frames. A favourite wet-weather game was for one of us to defend the balcony using an air rifle and lead pellets while the attacker below was armed with bow and arrows. One day my aim was poor and an arrow sped past Peter's ear, burying itself in the left cheek of Gregory Fiennes, the 14th Lord Saye and Sele. Today he hangs in our sitting room in London and I much regret his patched-up port jowl.

As the holiday drew to a close my mother could see the dread of Eton wrapping itself around me. She hated to see me so miserable. 'Can you think of *anything* I can do to help?' I had not meant to suggest it but now, with return to hell imminent, I blurted out the only idea that held any promise. If only my mother would see Mr Parr and plead with him that I be allowed out of bum-freezers, the short cutaway black jackets worn by Etonians under five feet four inches in height. I knew I was small for my age, certainly not the regulation height, but if I could only wear tailcoats like the bigger boys, the taunting might lessen. The short black bum-freezer jacket was cut off sharp at the waist like a male ballet dancer's tunic, leaving the outlines of buttocks naked, or so it seemed when wearing them, to the lewd gaze of the older boys.

Mr Parr was a kindly man despite his rather severe appearance and he understood exactly what my mother was getting at when she awkwardly tried to describe my problems at school. He had probably heard it all before from the parents of previous pretty pupils. To our delight he agreed to bend the bum-freezer rule and things did improve. Not much, but enough that in the next term I gained a few friends in my class if not in my House.

Despite my fear of fist-fighting, I decided an excellent adjunct to my permanent scowl would be a reputation as a ferocious boxer, since no more macho, un-tart-like sport existed. The boxing instructor was an ex-professional welter-weight who took great pride in the school boxing team and in any young recruits. Reg Hoblyn was an oasis of solid friendship despite the stern discipline and training schedules he imposed throughout the spring and winter terms.

But neither the new tailcoats that hung protectively over my backside nor my well-practised scowl nor even a gradually growing reputation as a pugilist could alter my girlish face and shape, so the verbal torment continued day after day, term after term.

I was involved in the world of Eton's sexual fantasy. Boys had crushes on me and imagined me in their beds. All over Eton boys talked about me to each other, comparing my allure with that of other tarts in other Houses. Fortunately, time was on my side. Each new term brought a fresh crop of pretty faces and, selfishly, I smiled inwardly whenever I heard my colleagues direct their jokes, whether from camaraderie or malice, at some new unfortunate. So detailed was the gossip about this and that tart and client that even I caught myself looking at other little boys and wondering if perhaps they *had* behaved as rumoured.

However, only twice during my four and a half years at Eton was I approached in an obvious way. Once during my first term a boy a year or so older followed me into the upstairs shower in the school gym and tried to undo my shorts. I fled. As I was walking down Judy's Passage after boxing training a boy from my own House groped at me from behind and I put my index finger in his eye. That was the sum total of my experience of physical assault or, in today's parlance, unwelcome bids.

I desperately wanted a friend at Eton. After the first year, by which time I was thirteen and a half, there were a number of boys in my class and even in Parr's House who were friendly enough, until someone would spark off a new round of mockery; then for a while everybody kept their distance again. Nevertheless, I began to enjoy events, certain lessons, boxing matches. Life was no longer *all* bad.

History was my favourite subject, especially the study of British sailors and explorers. At that time an attempt to complete the first crossing of Antarctica was in progress, led by Sir Vivian Fuchs and the Everest hero Sir Edmund Hillary. My history master traced the course of the expedition on an ancient chart of the frozen continent. He also made clear to us what was going on in the world at the time, calling it 'history in the making'. That spring Khrushchev was elected Soviet prime minister and Lord Russell launched the Campaign for Nuclear Disarmament, little knowing what a hardy perennial it would prove to be.

I prided myself on my knowledge of Britain's naval heroes and explorers but one attempt to show off rebounded when I shot my hand up to the master's question, 'What did Stanley say at his famous jungle meeting?'

My instant reply, 'Kiss me, Livingstone', was greeted with the derision it deserved.

Gradually my skin thickened, but never enough to ensure peace of mind, because, in the words of writer and playwright David Benedictus, 'The boys at Eton looked for vulnerable spots and once they found them, they applied the dentist's drill'.

Because of our holiday activities Peter Tooth and I became known by the good folk of Lodsworth as 'Tooth 'n' Nail'. My mother, on a shopping spree in the Lodsworth stores, overheard a neighbour remark to Mr Clark, the proprietor: 'They were on my roof again last night, those little devils, Tooth 'n' Nail. If George were still alive he'd scare them off for good with his shotgun.'

Most Lodsworth boys between the ages of eleven and sixteen joined the Bailey gang that held sway in the oak and hazel woods between Lodsworth and the high ground called Twelve O'Clock Knob. Peter and I would taunt them because, though a dozen in number, they took no pride in moving lightfooted and unseen, hiding under leaves or in high foliage as we did. So we flitted about their woods giving mocking whistles as they searched for us with their hazel whips. Only once did we risk contact with two of their members outside the safety of the woods. Wacker Wakeford and Rodge Kingshott bicycled down the steep lane beside my mother's house and, seeing there were only two of them, I jabbed a stick at one wheel. There was a most satisfying collision. Badly grazed, they called on my mother (a tactic which was not permitted by the local Geneva Convention) and I was forbidden local leave for a week.

I was once asked by Lord Cowdray to join a pheasant shoot in Cowdray Park because I was the same age as his son Michael Pearson. Since my father's pair of twelve-bore shotguns were in store I turned up with my 4.10, the pride of my life, although its effective range was thirty yards at best.

I had never seen so many pheasants. All of them seemed to recognise the weak link in the line of guns. I did my best, but it was cold and wet and my fingers fumbled attempting to eject and reload. Birds poured screeching overhead and somehow I managed to score a round zero by the end of the shoot when Land Rovers took us back to Cowdray House. The other guests were disapproving – twelve tweedy caps, scowls and plus-fours are all I remember of them. Lord Cowdray never again risked diluting his weekend firepower.

Back at Eton, I was selected for the boxing team and lived from weekend to weekend in eager anticipation of the next match. Looking back at *Eton Gazette* reports on those matches, it seems my style was not classical.

THE SCHOOL VS CHARTERHOUSE
Fiennes beat Goodman. He was not quite so wild as usual but persists in using his head. If he can overcome these two faults he will do well as he is very strong and courageous.

THE SCHOOL VS BLOXHAM
Fiennes beat Fowler. This was a wild brawl and Fiennes must remember to use neither his head nor the inside of his glove for disabling his opponent. This will not only enable him to see, but also to score the odd point or two. This was a close win for Eton.

There was a younger boy in Parr's named Roberts whom I liked. One afternoon I was drinking tomato soup with him when a tussle started and a bowl of hot Heinz fell off the windowsill. In the courtyard below, Mrs York, one of the boys' maids, was hanging sheets out to dry. She and her sheets were sprayed with soup and she complained to the Dame. That was the first time I was beaten at Eton and it was an occasion well worth recording. The stage-management of the event, as with all House beatings, ensured maximum suspense.

Every evening before boys go to bed the housemaster holds a short evening prayer with everyone present. When he is finished he leaves the room and, if the current captain of the House has decided to beat someone that evening, he must then walk out behind the housemaster to ask his permission for the beating to go ahead. The scene is thus set. Everyone in the House knows that within the hour there will be a beating in the Library. Often enough, news of the relevant sin has already spread to all levels of the House so all eyes swivel towards the perpetrator – whose mouth has gone very dry and whose legs are already feeling weak.

On the evening of Mrs York's 'souping', Higham, the House captain, did walk out. Roberts and I glanced at each other. Up in our rooms we sweated in anguish for thirty minutes, quite unable to concentrate on anything at all, let alone homework for the morrow. There is a passage by Poe which runs: 'There was an iciness, a sinking, a sickening of the heart . . .'

This summarises my feelings when I heard leather soles striding up the long concrete corridor towards my room. Then the sharp knock on Roberts's door and the dreaded summons: 'Roberts. Get your clothes on and wait outside the Library.'

Next, the knock on my door and the hard face of the youngest member of the Library as he shouted the well-used command at me. Together we walked downstairs to the Library making as little sound as possible, but knowing that the occupants of every room we passed were listening to each and every sound of the ceremony.

We stopped outside the door of the Library. Inside the room someone put on a long-playing record, one of Beethoven's more dirge-like works. For ten minutes nothing happened, then the music stopped; a dreadful sound.

'Come in.' The voice of the House captain.

We entered. The six denizens were all slouched in armchairs in a wide semi-circle facing the door and, beside it, a heavy table on which lay newspapers. The table, I knew, was the execution block.

'You are despicable. You have both been here long enough to know better. Mrs York is our best boys' maid. She deserves our gratitude, but what do you stupid little shits do? Pour soup all over her and think you are clever. Have you anything to say?'

There was, we knew, no use in protesting our innocence. We had not intended the soupbowl to end up on top of Mrs York but the fact remained that it had. We kept silent.

'Very well. I shall beat both of you. Wait outside.'

For another interminable ten minutes we listened to Beethoven. Suddenly the music stopped and my heart thudded against my ribcage. But it was only some sadist changing the record. Five minutes later, during which period any resolve to be brave wilted quite away, the music stopped again.

'Roberts. Come in.'

The door slammed behind him but I could hear every sound.

'Bend over and put your head under the edge of the table . . . Get your hands out of the way.'

I counted six strokes of the cane and I heard no noise from Roberts.

'Get out.'

Roberts exploded from the room and scurried away down the corridor with both hands held to his buttocks. I did not see his face.

More music. This time only for a minute.

'Come in.'

I bent over as ordered and flung up a quick prayer to God that I would not cry. I bit my lips and clenched my hands together but still gave vent to a strangled squeal as the first stroke bit into my bottom. I had only experienced such pain at the hands of a wart-remover in Cape Town but this was worse owing to the humiliation and the fear of breaking down and crying. By the second stroke I had controlled my mouth better and made no further sound. Four, five and six took for ever, but then it was over and I was flying back to my room and the pain was turning to a feeling of smarting heat.

Next morning at breakfast all eyes were again on Roberts and me. What were they looking for? Red eyelids?

I was beaten five times at Eton (once by a future CO of the SAS Regiment) and the rituals never changed, although the House captains did.

*   *   *

I am not in a position to say Eton is, was, or ever has been more sexually active or brutal than any other boarding school for young men. John Graham, a distinguished journalist, gave me the following account of Eton in the late 1950s:

There was a lot of sexual activity at school both outside and inside. We lived in boarding houses, we each had our own bedroom. Any boy could easily slip along to another's room and the boys did sleep with one another. We slept with each other not because we were homosexual but because we were at a highly sexual time of our lives and there were no available girls.

We talked and dreamed about girls. Our rooms were ablaze with pin-ups, Brigitte Bardot, Mansfield and Monroe. Had there been any girls around, we would have been as heterosexual, as straight, as anyone. But there were none.

Schoolmasters may say you can sublimate all your excess sexual energy playing football or learning French verbs but that is baloney. A lot of our surplus energy expressed itself sexually and since our only potential partners were of the same sex, our encounters were naturally homosexual. We were in bed with each other and had a very nice time.

In the holidays we chased girls as fast as we could and we certainly did not consider ourselves bent or gay. Perhaps ten per cent of Eton homosexuals remained so after leaving school and they would have ended up gay whatever school they attended.

I know of no instance of physical cruelty or torture but you don't have to engage in torture to be cruel at that age. You do it by taunting, teasing, cold-shouldering and picking on someone. A prefect can pick on a small boy and make his life a misery unless that smaller boy delivers some sexual favours.

The Eton fagging system meant that a small boy became a personal servant to a senior prefect and the boundary between being a personal servant and being a slave is a narrow one. 'I won't send you on errands; clean my boots and so on if you come to bed with me' . . . rather like serving girls and Regency beaux a couple of hundred years ago.

Even now in the 1980s, thirty years after my time there, Eton still has its gay problems. In the early part of this decade there were blackmail rings, one of which made headlines when a couple of young boys were exploited by a bunch of older ones and then threatened to tell. Money and sex and ugly scenes. Does the system cause this or would it have happened at any school? Difficult to say but a day school or a co-ed school would be less prone, I think.

There was very little supervision by masters at Eton. It was largely left to senior boys. All you needed was a few self-indulgent prefects and you pretty soon had anarchy about regulations, about sex, about anything at all. . . .

In the spring of 1960, just sixteen, I trained hard to box in the lightweight division (under nine stone, nine pounds), although my natural weight was over ten stone at the time. My health suffered and I began to experience air hunger. Even the deepest of breaths would not suffice and there were sometimes shooting cramp-like chest pains. I was sent to a specialist in Dublin who diagnosed rheumatic fever. My heart would be in danger of permanent damage unless I took a complete rest for six months. What a magnificent remedy! Ahead of me, like an endless green meadow to a starved cow, stretched the spring holiday, the summer term and the summer holidays.

Those were the happiest days of my youth and the sun shone week after week on the

Lodsworth fields, still ribboned with poppy and cornflower where the creeping nitrates had not yet reached. Every week my mother drove me to Brighton where the priest of St Paul's Anglican church prepared me for confirmation. At Eton I would have been unable to concentrate, to understand the messages of the faith, but merry Father Favell spoke with power and the points that he made have remained with me ever since – a simplified version of the words of Jesus on the Mount.

Peter Tooth had found instructions in some magazine for making explosives. I studied these for several days and experimented with growing quantities in the shed of old Mr Simmonds, the gardener who had recently retired. As the mixtures, mainly granulated sugar and weedkiller powder, began to react more impressively, we used increasingly sophisticated containers and fuses which gave us more time to retreat after lighting up. After weeks of explosions around the house, a thirty-foot-high mushroom-shaped cloud which followed the shattering of my mother's best brass flower vase finally decided her. A halt was called and there were no further bombs. At least not for several years.

Celia graduated and became a fully fledged doctor. Gill, after one or two heartbreaks, met the younger son of the lady who had in Cape Town accused me of cowardice in the face of the rickshaw Zulu. They were married in Trotton church, a lovely Norman place, and I stood in for our father. My collar was too tight and I fainted some minutes after giving Gill away.

During the summer term Peter spent the weekdays at Midhurst Secondary School so I was a good deal alone in the woods. Time and the nastiness at Eton had largely erased my memories of Ginnie, the girl from River.

I went one Saturday to the Lodsworth Village Flower Show where my mother had great hopes for her marrow entries. The village hall was full, so, not vastly worried about the chances of our vegetables, I wandered off to see if Peter was about. He wasn't, but I noticed a slim girl of about thirteen wearing a blue and white skirt and a sports shirt with short sleeves. I was sure God had never designed any girl so perfectly. I sat on an onion display and watched her. I saw her smile and I smiled involuntarily with her although she had not seen me. I had to find out at once the identity of this angel with the shoulder-length hair, hair that turned up at the ends and framed an elphin face of freckles and grey-blue eyes. But I was rooted to the spot and soon the vision disappeared from the hall.

'Isn't it wonderful?' It was my mother.

'Oh. Yes,' I said with enormous feeling. My mother looked at me surprised and pleased, for I did not normally enthuse over her vegetables. She had won a prize and so, both elated, we headed to the Morris Minor. She stopped to chat with the occupant of the next-door car, an Aston Martin. It was Mrs Pepper from River and beside her sat the vision.

'This is Virginia, remember her?' Mrs Pepper said. 'She's back from Eastbourne for half-term.' The girl smiled politely at my mother and looked briefly at me with total unconcern. Hurt to the quick, I watched as they drove off. That evening I told Peter about her.

'You would *not* believe it,' I sighed. 'She has changed. She looks exactly like Brigitte Bardot at thirteen.'

'Does she like you?'

'I think she couldn't care less. I might have been a concrete gnome from the look she gave me.'

'Ah,' said Peter, knowingly. 'That is an excellent sign. They get taught at school nowadays that the best way to attract the man they want is to ignore him.'

'So what do they do to the men they don't want?' I asked.

My parents on leave during the Second World War

With much love from Ranulph.

Above *My father in uniform as ADC to the Governor-General of Canada*

Opposite *Grandparents Eustace and Florrie at the races after the First World War*

The author in South Africa, aged six or seven

Ginnie, aged ten, with her two brothers

Eton boxing team, 1961. The author is seated at right

Two Country Life *pictures of Ginnie, one taken when we were engaged in 1968, one in March 1987*

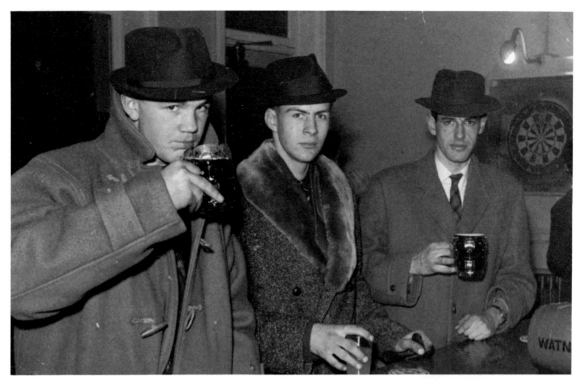

Three Al Capones at Mons Officer Cadet School. Aged seventeen, the author is in the middle. On the left is Tony Brassey

Fifteen-kilometre British Army Langlauf *Championships, 1968: the author is in front trying to keep the lead*

The author's father after Alamein, with Royal Scots Greys tank and crew

The author with Royal Scots Greys tank and crew, 1965

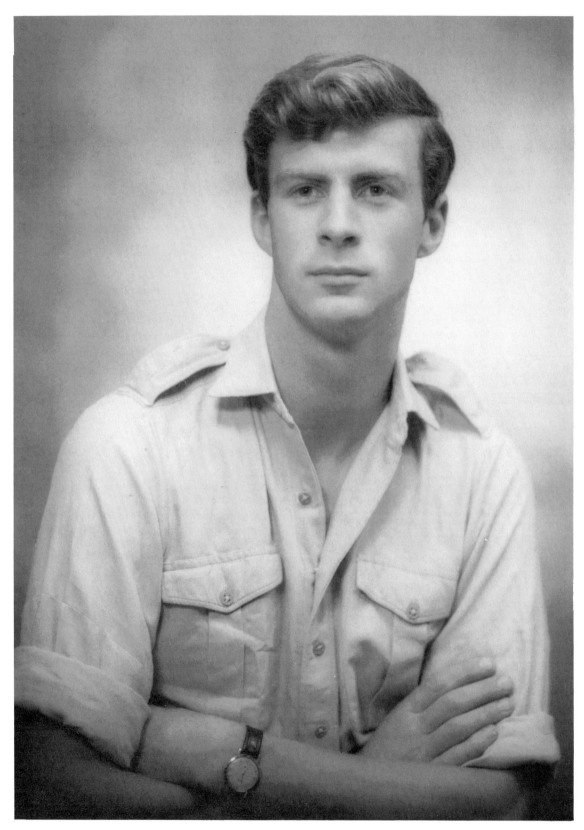

The author as a second lieutenant on joining Royal Scots Greys, 1963

'Well, they ignore them too, but in a different way. But. . . .' He paused. 'You may have a problem, come to think of it. Her father doesn't like you, remember?'

I did recollect vaguely that the previous year a furious Mr Pepper had visited my mother and told her he would horsewhip me if I ever set foot on his land again. The cause of his fury was a rather well-made whip with my initials burned into the handle. We had lost this wandering around at night and must have left it in Mr Pepper's orchard. The wooden handle was nailed to a three-foot plaited lash and two four-inch nails protruded from the knot in the lash-end.

When the summer holidays began Ginnie Pepper moved home and my life entered an entranced state, as though I were permanently high on magic mushrooms. There was a catchy popular song then, entitled 'Ginnie Come Lately', and I played this to myself on Gill's abandoned gramophone. On Sundays I sleeked my hair back in a parting, to the delight of my mother who had long since abandoned all hope of getting me to look presentable. One never knew, *she* might be in church. I began to accompany my mother shopping in the village or further afield in Petworth or Midhurst. *She* might be shopping.

I grew to know when she was likely to go riding and I would be there, up some tree or other above the paths that wound through the wood. Once the man called Vic, who worked for her father and usually rode with her, was replaced by a dark-haired handsome youth of my age. They were in animated conversation and I was desolated.

I told Peter, who said without sympathy: 'If you want the girl, you've got to *work* for it. How do you expect her to like you when she never sees you?' He was right, but her parents never asked me around. This was not surprising after the whip incident, but that was nearly a year ago. My mother gave a small dance-party for me, my first, and she invited all three Pepper children. I danced twice with Ginnie who wore a knee-length white dress with a yellow flower over her heart. I suffered from temporary paralysis of the Adam's apple and said nothing. At close quarters she was devastating. I waited for an invitation to the Peppers' but none came. At nights I lay awake listening to the beat of their generator from over the valley.

That summer Peter and I obtained six fixed-wheel bicycles and mounted some local friends with borrowed and sawn-off polo sticks. Practising on the nearby Ambersham Polo Ground, we became quite accomplished and I invited both the Pepper sons to join the team. They turned out to be enthusiastic players and we challenged the Midhurst Young Conservatives who were led by Jeremy Barber, a well-known exponent of real polo. The Pepper parents watched the match and to my great delight, just before play began, I saw that *she* too was in the Aston Martin. I played with great recklessness and lost twenty-one spokes in one wheel. The Young Conservatives beat us by five goals to one, but what did that matter?

When the summer holidays were halfway through the Peppers went abroad. By then the dread of return to school was already on me and I felt I could face Eton far better if only I had *her* photograph with me.

Late one evening Peter and I went to the Peppers' house and found it dark, empty and locked up. Peter mounted guard and I searched the rooftops until I found an upper window-light loosely fastened. I searched the house feverishly for a photograph. There were a number of framed pictures but not a single photo so I retired empty handed.

Eton life closed around me once more and soon I forgot about Ginnie as a flood of day-to-day school problems left no time for romantic yearning.

Hart was worse than ever, aggressively unpleasant 60 per cent of the time and overbearing the rest. Yet such was the system that I had to sit next to or opposite him every meal every day for four long years of school. The non-stop catty bickering, at which I was hopelessly inept, must have played merry hell with my digestive system over those years.

I had grown six inches in as many months while away from school and my body had filled out in every direction. My chest pains were gone, my voice was quite broken and I weighed eleven stone. Moving up to light-heavyweight, I trained harder than ever with Reg Hoblyn's good advice. I went to hospital for three days with double vision, two of my teeth were chipped, my nose was broken and the joints of both my thumbs became swollen from misplaced hooks with the inside of my gloves. Nonetheless, I lost few fights and no longer heard the old 'tart' taunts of the fifties. To help matters, my face had lengthened and grown encouragingly unattractive even without the scowl.

Academic life was also improving. French with a new master, David Cornwell, had taken on a new lease of life. He kept the language interesting and the lessons enjoyable. He left Eton quite soon, sadly for us but fortunately from his own point of view, as his income rocketed thanks to the books which he wrote under the name of John le Carré.

At a certain stage, Eton boys are appointed to a particular master to specialise prior to taking their 'O'-level exams. By good luck I found myself 'up to' Dave Callender. He taught me how to enjoy using words, both in English and German. His specialist classes were held in his home and his attractive wife sometimes brought us cups of tea.

My newly squashed nose and lost looks increased my self-confidence and the advent of Mr Callender, together with boxing team successes, made Eton bearable. But I only began actively to enjoy life at school after meeting Michael Denny. Michael was in the Library at Mr Crusoe's House, the House nearest to Eton's tallest and most imposing building, School Hall. Since neither Denny nor I was an experienced climber and since we shared no other common interests, it is difficult to conjure up quite why we began to climb together, but somehow the partnership was formed and, as a result, my last eighteen months at Eton included a good deal of nocturnal excitement.

There is nothing new about stegophily, the dictionary term for the practice of climbing buildings by night. Adherents are said to have an edifice complex, an apt description since the more you do it the more compulsive its appeal becomes. It has nothing to do with the more normal sport of rock-climbing. Indeed, since I have *no* head for heights and easily succumb to vertigo, day-time climbing is anathema to me. The beauty of night-climbing is that the thrill of danger is present without the full visual impact of the drop down below.

At Eton the night-climber knows he will be expelled if caught so he learns to be extremely stealthy and silent, to move by way of the smallest shadow and the least cover along lamplit streets and courtyards. Part of the pleasure comes in the planning of each climb, the furtive meetings and the smuggling of the item to be hoisted. There had not been an active stegophily cell at Eton for many years when Denny and I first cast covetous eyes at the high dome of School Hall, so the authorities were at first caught off guard.

Once we had agreed on the date and time of our very first sortie, there was no going back, but I nonetheless had to struggle with my better judgement when the time came to sneak out of my bedroom, along the long, well-lit corridor and down the stairs to the main ground-floor lavatories. I wore a dressing gown over my night-climbing clothes but any senior boy or Mr Parr would have rumbled me at once. I eeled out of a lavatory window and left my dressing gown under a drain cover. From the moment of leaving the house I was liable to expulsion from Eton.

That first time we wore black gym-shoes, rugger zephyrs and trousers, but later we graduated to dark tracksuits specially purchased for the purpose.

At Mr Crusoe's House, Denny had left a narrow ground-floor window open and, when I tapped, he squeezed out. His House was directly behind School Hall and a drainpipe or two enabled us to reach a concrete ledge abutting from the wall some seven feet below the base of the Hall's great dome. With delicate footwork and scrabbling fingers we made the ledge and then the foot of the dome. However, an hour of repeated attempts to scale the smooth face of the dome itself proved fruitless. We could manage about twelve feet before we slipped back exhausted.

A week later we headed not for the Hall but to the other end of Eton, to the School of Maniacs (or of Mechanics). By way of a window Denny had left unfastened that afternoon we entered this lofty hall of lathes and, from a rack of numbered tools, removed a pair of furniture clamps. Back at the dome we used the clamps in a leapfrog fashion to ascend one of the ribs which held the dome's lead slatting in place. Above us now was a mere fifteen-foot climb to the lightning conductor summit of the Hall. Next time we would leave on it a token of our visit. For ten minutes we sat atop the dome high above the roofs of Eton and felt infinitely superior to every one of the 1100 boys in their cosy beds below us.

At about this time in early 1961, I joined forces with Jeremy, the son of William Deedes, former editor of the *Daily Telegraph*, in a business venture to increase my pocket money. I had, and unfortunately still have, an amazingly demanding sweet tooth. I crave chocolate and sweets as others need cigarettes, but, throughout my Eton days, my statutory pocket money for each term was £4, banked with the House Dame. The previous Christmas, farthings had ceased to be legal tender – a fact which to all habitués of sweet shops was nothing short of disaster. A round of price rises followed immediately and my £4 was no longer adequate. Just as addicts are driven to crime to obtain drugs, so I sought out Deedes and his friend Chris Cazenove. Cazenove, even then an aspiring actor in the Eton Dramatic Society, was to become a fellow night-climber, but Deedes had his feet firmly on the ground. Our business was based on the older boys' demand for cigarettes and alcohol, both taboo at Eton. Deedes became treasurer and salesman and I became delivery director. A secret attic in their House was used as an interim store.

No Etonian is allowed out of bounds, and that included all of Windsor except for the High Street as far as the mainline station. All sources of alcohol and cigarettes were forbidden territory, and boys dressed in undertakers' uniforms – for that is what Etonians wear – cannot easily walk anywhere unobserved.

By good luck I knew Sheila Burnell, the young daughter of the owner of the White Hart Hotel, near the station. This made things easy. Deedes and I, for we both delivered when we had a full order book, walked openly in our tailcoats to the news-stand by the station entrance as if to buy a paper, then, checking there were no Eton masters around, slipped through a hole in the station wall and into the old stables behind the White Hart. Here we donned workers' boilersuits and cloth caps and followed a narrow alleyway across Pescod Street to the tobacconist who sold the exotic cigarette brands, such as Black Russian and Abdulla, preferred by our customers. On down a further backstreet to the Victoria Wine Company to collect the drinks, usually Scotch or cherry brandy.

Back at the White Hart we wrapped the bottles in newspaper and stuffed them down our tailcoats. We initially charged 3d commission per cigarette packet and 1 shilling per bottle but soon increased this. The first term's revenue after splitting profits with Deedes and Cazenove came to £6, which was a handy addition to my pocket money. All was squandered on Mars bars.

I turned seventeen that spring and found my mind greatly troubled by pretty girls. This was unfortunate since I had failed all but four of my 'O' levels and needed to study extra hard to make up lost ground. My ability to concentrate was ruined by a daydreaming tendency and, worse, this growing desire for female company. At Eton this was more or less impossible. Dave Hart did somehow manage but he was expelled as a result. Together with Chris Cazenove I wandered down to the Windsor horse show where we met up with two girls of sixteen and took them to tea. One was Georgina Simpson, whose father owned Simpsons of Piccadilly. She later married Anthony Andrews, star of *Brideshead Revisited*, but it was the memory of the budding charms of her friend Linda that ruined my concentration for the rest of that term.

Towards the end of term the school boxing championships took place in the gym. Three or four hundred boys turned up to watch and scream their support for their favourite gladiators. I had quite a following owing to the unintentionally colourful style I lapsed into when I lost control.

Light-heavyweight involved most of the biggest boxers at the school and, after a number of exciting qualifying rounds, I ended up in the finals opposite Daniel Meinertzhagen. This was unfortunate since he was extremely skilful, aggressive and one of the select few who had earned a school boxing cap.

I thought that I would get the very best out of myself if my mother was watching the fight. I wanted her to be proud of me, as she was of my father; and, were she to be present, I would have to win. So I wrote to her. She replied saying she was grateful to be asked and of course she would come, if it was really necessary. She hated violence and blood and feared there might be both. I assured her to the contrary and confirmed that her presence was vital.

Since light-heavy was the penultimate event of the evening, my mother had to sit through a good few bloody noses and red sponges.

Meinertzhagen was fit and fast. I had over the years watched him floor many able opponents with his sudden two-fisted attack. During the first round he chased me around the ring and definitely won on points, but in the second I executed a sudden three-blow move, copied from Reg Hoblyn. A feint with the left followed instantly with a right to the face and, bending low, a sharp left-fist jab to the stomach. This stopped him and I took advantage of his temporary fuzziness to try to kill him.

The final round was vicious and greatly approved of by the onlookers. The noise was deafening, almost drowning the final bell. I was relieved to have lasted the fight at all and amazed when the referee, after collecting the judges' cards, waved his winning flag at my corner. A week later I was awarded a boxing cap and told by Reg that I would be school boxing captain if I stayed on for another four terms.

Michael Denny and I celebrated with a School Hall climb. By then we had hoisted on separate occasions two heavy metal dustbins and a lavatory seat to the summit conductor and watched with secret pleasure the hundreds of boys clustered in the streets and courtyards pointing up at the dome as expensive steeplejacks with ropes and long ladders unlashed our offerings. The lavatory seat was our finest hour because School Hall was under close scrutiny all night by duty masters assigned to the task in the knowledge that the morrow was St Andrew's Day, a major Eton holiday, when an attempt on the dome was anticipated. By then we were able in our dark suits and stockinged feet to reach the top with no sound at all. But then we went too far.

After the lavatory seat we grew bored with the dome and decided to look for other target edifices. But the authorities flung down the gauntlet by calling in builders who fixed barbed-wire obstacles around the only pipes and ledges that gave access to the dome. Denny and I met in a dark corner of the cloisters. I asked him whether the twin cupolas of Lupton's Tower might not be viable.

'Don't be silly. We must do the Hall again.'

'But why? We agreed to turn elsewhere. Why go back?'

'That,' he said firmly, 'was before they put up the wire and started night watches. Listen, there is no moon next Thursday week. I will get the clamps, you get something to put up.'

I felt more apprehensive than usual, so I decided to ease our chances by taking some soft, easily portable item. A war-time black-out curtain from Caxton Schools found its way into my possession. We painted it red and, the following week, fixed it to the dome's lightning conductor. The climb had been easier than usual because the new barbed wire provided more handgrips just where they were needed.

Denny and I sat on top of the dome, sharing, as had become our custom, a flask of cherry brandy. Over our heads a strong wind caused our flag to dance and crack like a whip. 'Christ,' Denny exclaimed suddenly, 'they've rumbled us.' As he spoke a powerful torch-beam illuminated us and, as I flung myself flat along our tiny platform, I noticed two other torches bobbing far below. With considerable apprehension we slid with sweaty palms to the base of the dome.

'Use the rope and go over the back parapet,' Denny hissed at me. 'I'll go to the front. They may not expect that. See you tomorrow.' Denny's slight figure disappeared over the ledge and I ran crouching right around to the rear of the dome.

Fixing our rope to a drainpipe bowl, I flung it over the parapet and slid down, burning my hands. Someone with a torch bore down on me and I struck out at him. A heavy hand caught hold of my football shirt but I wrenched clear and fled via back gardens to Judy's Passage, a narrow lane that eventually led to Mr Parr's House. I had never run so fast; I knew there would be a fire alarm in all Houses and by the first bell I must be back in bed with clean hands.

All was well. There was no fire alarm. But only because Denny got into trouble. Seeing his retreat cut off, he had desperately dropped twelve feet on to concrete, holding a bag with the clamps in his mouth. One of his ankles twisted and he fled, limping, closely pursued by a master whom he recognised. This was Raeff Paine in a nightgown and pyjamas.

Denny flung himself through our normal window and Raeff Paine was halted, unable to fit through the narrow space. He battered on the front door, woke Mr Crusoe and roused all the boys. When every boy was accounted for, the Library members, including Denny, were told to search the House for an intruder. Wet gym-shoe marks led to Denny's room, but friends, including the future actor Ian Ogilvie, laid other wet marks to other rooms and of course no one was found. It was Denny's undisguisable limp that rumbled him. That and his shape were identified by Raeff Paine and Denny was interviewed, prior to seeing the headmaster, Dr Robert Birley, by the provost of Eton.

The provost, Sir Claude Elliott, had himself been headmaster until 1949 and his hobby happened to be mountain-climbing. Denny stood before the ancient oak desk in the provost's office, aware that an awkward interrogation was upon him.

'Who,' the provost demanded, 'was your climbing colleague last night?'

There was a long silence.

'I was by myself,' Denny said at last.

The provost nodded with a slight smile as though Denny had passed some unspoken test. Then, with the behaviour of a stamp enthusiast greeting a fellow collector over a rare album, he moved to a scroll on the great oaken desk. This he unrolled with reverence and Denny found himself looking down at a faded architect's drawing of School Hall.

'How did you go about the climb, my boy?' the provost asked Denny, rubbing his hands together in anticipation. Denny told him.

The provost made marks with a pencil and chuckled to himself. He then told Denny how in his day as an Etonian he had hoisted his own first offering on to the dome. Still uncertain of his fate, Denny did not relax his guard but began to feel safer when the provost invited him to join a climbing party in the Pyrenees that summer. After the provost had briefed the headmaster, Denny was summoned in front of the latter.

'You are aware that you have committed an offence for which the punishment is expulsion. . . . You are, however, anyway due to leave Eton at the end of this half, so, after speaking to the provost, I have decided that you may remain at Eton until that time. You will also complete five Georgics.'

Thanks to Denny my participation remained unknown to the authorities.

I was unaware that, at this time, my mother visited Mr Parr to discuss my academic future.

Although, like most children, I had wished to be a train driver, a spy and many other glamorous things, there had really only been the regimental choice. One day I would be commanding officer of the Royal Scots Greys, like my father. That was the summit of my ambitions and to that end, a year previously, I had joined the Eton College Corps and enjoyed every moment of the training.

There were still officers and men in the Royal Scots Greys who had served with my father eighteen years before and remembered him by his nickname 'Colonel Lugs', on account of his slightly prominent ears. But family connections were no longer a pass into the Army. Now, to enter the Royal Military Academy, Sandhurst, you needed at least two General Certificates of Education at Advanced Level, including mathematics or physics, and five Certificates at Ordinary Level. This effectively precluded any chance of my becoming a professional officer by the normal route. But there was a possible alternative: to obtain a short-service commission through Mons Officer Cadet School and, once in the Army on a two-year commission, to try to extend. Even for Mons, however, I would need a minimum of five Ordinary Level passes and nearly five years of Eton had as yet only gained me four.

My mother, by visiting Mr Parr, had hoped to assess whether my chances of entering Mons would be better if I stayed another year at Eton or moved to a specialist crammer school. Mr Parr was obviously honest about my academic failings for, in the 1961 Easter holidays, my mother told me I could leave Eton, if I wanted, at the end of the summer term. If so she would enter me for a specialist language school at Aix-en-Provence since French and German were my better subjects. The news was wonderful. I voted without hesitation for Aix, for only boxing and climbing held me to Eton. I could box elsewhere and Denny was gone.

My last half at Eton gave me the merest taint of a notion of what people mean when they reminisce about their halcyon schooldays or those never-to-be-forgotten summers at Oxbridge. Even, perhaps, how warm and splendid Eton must be for that happy band who, in their time there, become her *crème de la crème*. It was not that I tasted the faintest tinge of success myself or even trod the bottom rung of Etonian achievement. Far from it. But in those long summer days, the twilight of my school years, I lingered sometimes between ancient cloister and silent classroom or, in my rigger scull-boat, rested a while beside long upstream stretches of swaying willow. At such times I looked about me and realised there *was* something special, almost hallowed, about the place. I won't miss this, I thought, but neither will I forget it. Things were peaceful for me at last. The ever-nagging Dave Hart was gone. Since the Meinertzhagen fight there had been no hint of the old taunting. There was no boxing, no training, few contraband deliveries since our customers drank less in summer, and little chance of climbing since the nights were seldom dark for long enough.

On 4 June, the date of Eton's major annual festivity, I felt confident enough for the first time to invite a girlfriend for the day. She was sixteen and, beneath her straw boater, she looked young and sweet and correct. Together we paced around the hallowed cricket field where the school heroes were busy trouncing or being trounced by the Eton Ramblers, the old boys' team. I thought of daisy chains. Hundreds of other couples moved about with us, black-tailed boys and frilly, boatered girls. Many strolled in groups loud with hoarse laughter and awfully aware of themselves. After dark we followed the excitedly murmuring crowds to the river-bank area known as Fellows Eyot and spread the contents of the picnic hamper, prepared with loving care by my mother, on the grass. All about us champagne corks popped and strawberries in double cream disappeared to the rise and fall of Britain's noblest Adam's apples. We watched and cheered as, boat by boat, the school's best crews, eight oarsmen and a cox to each, paused in a floodlit patch of Father Thames and stood to raise their oars and doff their boaters. Cheers or jeers for each, depending on how wobbly their knees. Then ten costly minutes of high cascading fireworks that brought to ghostly life the walls of Windsor Castle like some flickering House of Usher on the hill. I had suffered four previous Eton June 4ths. This one I enjoyed and felt a part of.

If Denny had been around we would have left our mark on high the previous night. Whether or not the excitement of the 4th brought back to me the long fallow thrill of the night foray, I argued to myself that I owed to Denny at least one attempt on the unscaled heights of Lupton's Tower. So I visited Chris Cazenove and, in Crusoe's House, the new occupant of Denny's room, Hughie Pryor. After two trial outings we found a way up via a borrowed ladder, a complex of drainpipes and finally over the crenellated buttresses immediately below the twin towers.

The wood and lead cupola over the belfry of our chosen tower was rotting and devoid of good handholds but we struggled up to the spire above and impaled a wicker dog basket on it. This had belonged to my mother's late-lamented poodle. She had brought it to Eton for me in the Morris Minor some weeks earlier for reasons now forgotten.

The basket was rapidly removed by the authorities, so we scaled Lupton's again a week later, for it was a satisfying climb. This time, with Chris Cazenove as look-out, we stretched a rope between the two rooftop doors from the twin towers, locking them both. The dustbin we had arranged for a third boy to plant at a certain street corner was not there so Hughie returned to Crusoe's to find an alternative trophy to hoist. He came back an hour later with a tailcoat.

'We can't leave that,' I expostulated in a hoarse whisper. 'What will you wear tomorrow?'

'It's a spare,' Hughie soothed me.

After another high struggle with the cupola we descended to the battlements to survey the fluttering tails with pride and some cherry brandy.

Then an awful thought struck Hughie. 'My name tab. God, it's probably still got my name tab in it. I checked inside the collar but, thinking about it, there may well be a tab in the inner pocket.'

There was no way I was going up twice in one night. The skin on the inside of my arms was already raw and my thighs bruised. So Hughie, gallantly, though with little alternative, edged painfully round the overhang and, clinging above the void, picked off his name tab. That was my last climb at Eton for, a month later, I bid my friends and Mr Parr a tearless farewell and became, for the rest of my life, an Old Etonian.

I wonder if I would be a different sort of person now if I had missed out on those early years of hell. In one sense it proved the perfect preparation for the trickier vicissitudes of life since nothing would ever be so bad again. I arrived at Eton with two built-in and mutually fatal flaws – prettiness and an inability to be aggressive even in self-defence. Others may have big ears or the wrong accent or 101 other characteristics that set them apart from the accepted Eton norm. No matter, so long as they have the capacity to bite back at their persecutors, they can usually get away with it.

I was full of self-assurance when I first went to Eton, buoyant from happy days at Sandroyd. Public school and three long years of remorseless nastiness squeezed every last trace of confidence from me. It would take a long time to get back to a balanced state. I still find myself overly sensitive to the least criticism, a direct hangover from Eton days.

To summarise my old school: Location hard to beat. Facilities excellent. Staff above average. My only complaint was the nature of my fellow inmates, and all schools have their share of nasty little boys. The acid test must be: If I had a son, would I send him there? I cannot honestly say that I would not.

4

Wild Oats

All the live murmur of a summer's day.

MATTHEW ARNOLD

T wo years of excitement, young love and perhaps even learning at Aix-en-Provence: an enticing future for a seventeen-year-old to anticipate. Then, with French and German 'A' levels behind me, two years at Sandhurst Officer Cadet School. From there to the Royal Scots Greys and a steady climb towards the summit of my ambitions, command of my father's old regiment. My future was neatly mapped out.

The Eton College Corps held an annual fourteen-day summer camp and, although I had left the school, I was eligible to attend. The Norwegian Army training base in Kvamskogen, north of Bergen, was deep in mountainous country. The captain of Parr's House, Neville Howard, led the enemy patrol and lived rough in the mountains throughout our fortnight at Kvamskogen. He was to become commanding officer of the SAS in later years. Sodden clothing and bruised bodies helped all 300 fledgling officers decide whether or not to plump for careers in khaki.

Rather than return to England with the rest, I hitchhiked back with another boy as far as Copenhagen. There we squandered dwindling funds at Tivoli, sat in sunny parks staring with longing at the abundance of leggy blondes, and wound up at the Tuborg factory tour-guides' office. There were two types of tour ticket, one for German nationals and one for the rest of the world. Our non-Teuton group went first and polished off the bountiful supplies of free lager. These were not replenished for the Germans: war-time memories were still bitter.

Unable to cope with the lashings of alcohol, I misplaced my equally befuddled companion and did not see him again for several months. I continued alone through Denmark and Germany.

That was my first expedition and, as I explained to my mother back in Lodsworth, its success proved I was quite ready to face whatever challenges Aix might have to offer.

My first cousin, Greville 'Gubbie' Napier, lived in Midhurst, at the other end of Cowdray Park, where he managed the grandly named antique shop, Keil's of Knockhundred Row. His mother, Lady Napier and Ettrick, was a widow and my only remaining aunt. Gubbie's eldest brother was soon to become, and still is, head of Princess Margaret's household, but Gubbie himself was not at all grand. Being five years my senior he was worldly-wise about those very beings public school had hidden from me but which now loomed enormous on my seventeen-year-old horizon – girls.

'France is *the* place,' he told me one day, sipping tea in the cluttered backroom at Keil's. 'French girls cannot say no or even *non*. They are unparalleled in both beauty and naughti-ness.'

The night before we had been to a dance near Midhurst and, as usual, our friendly approaches towards the opposite sex had been firmly repulsed. Gubbie's cross-channel rhapsody was merely a reaction, but it led to the decision that we would pillage Paris without delay.

'How do we get there?' I asked. 'I have £15 in the world.'

Gubbie waved his tin of Keil's Beeswax in the air. 'Absolutely no problem. You are an expert on hitchhiking and I am an expert on seventeenth- and eighteenth-century French furniture. We will have a wonderful time.'

I failed to see the relevance of this but, a week later, we set off after an enormous lunch at my mother's and the hitching went well all the way to Dieppe. Thereafter, despite or because of the Union Jacks on our packs, our thumbs prodded the air in vain. Nobody stopped.

'Now,' Gubbie explained, as we sat on the packs in a steady French drizzle, 'is the time for Anglo-cunning. The French adore all Scots. It's historic, a sort of bemused admiration.'

We had both agreed to bring kilts and now donned them in the ditch in place of our jeans. For some reason the French in the Dieppe area had not heard of the *Entente Cordiale Franco-Ecossais* and roared past us as determinedly as they had when we were mere English hikers.

Again Gubbie sat on his pack, lit a cigarette and deliberated. In a while he slapped his knee with delight. 'I am brilliant. Keil's do not know how lucky they are. We have scarves, do we not?'

I nodded.

'That's all we need. Over the head and under the neck and we become Scots lassies. At least from behind. The French adore Scottish girls.'

This time he was right, after a fashion. There was a squeal of brakes and a lorry stopped beside us. The driver was from Yorkshire and by the time he saw we were male, for we had whipped off the scarves, he had stopped and we were aboard, overwhelming him with gratitude.

Half an hour later we realised that hitching a lift was only half the battle. The other half was to head in the desired direction, and this our driver was not doing. He was heading northeast for Lille on the Belgian border, not southeast to Paradise.

Gubbie checked the driver's map. We were going quite the wrong way but it was warm and dry in the cab. We spoke in undertones and agreed to stay aboard until it stopped raining and we had dried out. These conditions both materialised by the time we reached Arras.

From there the headscarves assured good hiking to the centre of Paris and, close to the Place de la République, we found a kindly madame in the Hôtel Mondia who gave us bed and breakfast for £2 per day. We visited all the well-known sites and for good measure one or two low-down dives heady with garlic and Gauloises. We walked along the Madeleine and around Montmartre. We ogled the street ladies but declined their offers on the grounds that our exchequer was down to the bread-line.

After four magnificent days, Gubbie announced that we possessed no money at all and could not get back to Sussex. 'But,' he added, 'I have thought of a way out. We could sing in restaurants as Noël Coward did in similar circumstances.'

I argued with him over this for I knew for a fact that Mr Coward had not sung in restaurants. He had hung around coffee bars and pinched the tips left on tables for waiters. However, since I was not prepared to risk French gaols I agreed to try singing.

With our kilts and a mouth organ fashioned from my comb and some Hôtel Mondia lavatory paper, we regaled the late diners at the Cervantes and other restaurants around the République. Gubbie had schooled me in a number of Scottish ditties until our joint repertoire was up to a five-minute stint in each venue.

We made the franc equivalent of £9, just enough to travel by bus to Dieppe, where we called upon the British consul for a £10 loan to get us back to Sussex. He agreed, providing we told him a dirty joke. Amazing though it now seems, neither of us in our hour of need could remember a single joke, clean or dirty, but the consul relented and we were able to buy ferry tickets.

'My God,' I said to Gubbie, 'I have forgotten the date. Chris will need instructions by next week.'

I exchanged my leather belt for a Dieppe postcard stamped for England and, scribbling a note, addressed it to Chris Cazenove at Eton College. The card showed a Michelin-type woman making love to a minuscule Frenchman wearing only a beret and cigar. The caption was beyond our powers of translation.

I returned home to find that Peter Tooth was mostly away from Lodsworth, studying to become a mechanic. I was not due in Aix for two months and my mother kindly bought me a Vespa motor scooter for Christmas. I was now mobile and felt very adult, although still one jump behind Gubbie who had recently graduated from scooter to Baby Austin. Fairly short-sighted, Gubbie nonetheless flung his new acquisition recklessly along the winding lanes of Sussex and, to be precise, the border country with Hampshire where we discovered an ample supply of girls in their late teens.

The current passport to success in society, much more important than 'A' levels, was an ability to twist. Attired in narrow striped jeans and black cotton shirts, we both learned to limbo and cavort in this early form of flash-dance.

Somewhere along the commuters' daughters' belt of Liss and Rogate I stumbled my way to learning to kiss girls on their lips rather than their cheeks. A life of kissing sisters and mothers out of family love interfered with my zeal to kiss out of desire. Some senior lady with little patience at a barbecue in Hook prised my teeth apart with her tongue and, after the initial shock, I learned less formal ways.

A fortnight after returning from France, Gubbie had involved himself with a fuzzy-haired beauty with long legs so I went alone to a Liss party on my Vespa. Two of the girls decided to raid their old school, a nearby mansion where Dame Margaret Rutherford had recently filmed *The Happiest Days of Your Life*. The entire party, armed with fireworks and smoke bombs, drove an assortment of motorbikes, sports cars and old bangers to Bycylla School for young ladies. The raid was a noisy success but my girlfriend of the evening was a bad scooter passenger and, by the time we tailed the marauding cavalcade to the gates, the lodge-keeper had collected his wits and taken my number.

Two days later the police called at Lodsworth. The evidence, they said, was irrefutable and I was to be prosecuted for 'malicious damage resulting in costs of £8 3/6d'.

None of the other raiders was caught and, at the Midhurst Court sessions, the proceedings were dropped after I had apologised to the headmistress and paid her £8.3/6d to replace an eiderdown burned by a smoke bomb. However, the national newspapers were hard up for news and made tasty headlines out of the mixture of Bomber Baronet, Screaming Young Girls in Nightdresses and Margaret Rutherford. My mother was at her wit's end, ashamed of her only son and wondering where it would all lead. I was a liability and not to be trusted in England. What might I not get up to if let loose in France? She decided to find a language school rather nearer home.

*　　　　*　　　　*

Chris Cazenove, 1980s star of stage and screen, was as bad an influence at Eton as I ever was. The term before I left we had together plotted to 'blow the place up'. In reality our plan was all bark and no bite but, had it come off, all resident Etonians would certainly have had a memorable night. I had selected suitable reprobates in each of the twenty-five Houses, boys with rooms overlooking the main entrances to their respective Houses, and briefed them that the following term they would each be given a parcel one evening. In it they would find a bomb and a note with a precise time when they must light the fuse and drop the bomb from their window.

For months on corps exercises I had stored thunderflashes until I had over 100. I lashed them together in bundles of four, with a single ignition fuse. These I left in a tin buried under Masters football field in a location known only to Chris Cazenove. We agreed that, on leaving Eton, I would muster a number of car drivers to make our Big Bang appear like an outside job and would let him know by mail the exact time the following term when the twenty-five boys should light up.

A single untreated thunderflash, detonated under a tin helmet, can send it 100 feet in the air. Four of them lashed tightly in cardboard, cloth and string make a highly satisfactory sound. But, sadly, my Dieppe postcard, on which I had written *'Arrangez les garçons dans chaque maison pour 070130,'* and signed James Mortimer, an old climbing alias, put paid to the whole plan. Chris's housemaster intercepted the offending postcard and summoned him to his study. 'What does this card mean, Cazenove Major?' Chris stared at the message slack-jawed, needing none of his already marked acting prowess in order to appear astonished. He was amazed, not so much at the message but at the unparalleled stupidity of my method of conveying it to him.

'I have no idea, sir. No idea at all.'

'It is addressed to you, is it not?'

This was undeniable.

'And who is it from? Who is James Mortimer?'

At this point Chris suffered a mental blockage. His imagination deserted him. Mr Coleridge's steely glare mesmerised him into a rabbit-like state of compliance. Thinking that, as I was outside the jurisdiction of the school, no harm could come to me, he gave my name, but said he had no idea what the card meant. Mr Parr was called and told that I was up to some form of skulduggery involving Cazenove. He in turn phoned my mother who said that I had been in France but she knew nothing of any untoward plot. I scootered to Mr Parr to apologise and to assure him that never again would I send vulgar postcards to current Etonians. My luck was in, for he did not delve into the cryptic contents of the postcard. We parted friends and I felt a definite sadness when, some years later, he died of a heart attack.

My mother discovered a school or, to be precise, a crammer, which was within scooter distance of Lodsworth and which professed a high rate of success in language tuition up to 'A'-level standard. Davies's in Hove would plunge me into French and German courses for a year and I would emerge with two 'A' levels or, at worst, the fifth 'O' level I still needed to enter the Army as an officer cadet. I was to lodge at the Lewes home of another Old Etonian, William Knight, who was also cramming languages.

Before this I went with my mother to a family funeral at Broughton Castle. Cousin Ivo Fiennes had died and his son, Nathaniel, named after our parliamentarian soldier ancestor, became the 21st Lord Saye and Sele. I had splashed the family name over the national media with the Bycylla smoke bomb and was the black sheep of the clan. Nothing was said, but I felt ashamed. I promised my mother I would mend my ways. And for a while I managed to behave.

Lodsworth had lost its charm because my teenage companions were gone away and because, like most of England, the very essence of a once lovely tousled countryside was for ever transformed into tamed land. It must have happened slowly, hedge by hedge, since the 1940s, but only then, in the spring of 1961, did the drear nature of the new Lodsworth present itself as an unpleasant reality: the stark geometry of council house rows, the widening and straightening of the little lanes, the new blue road signs, the ugly fences and, in the loveliest of valleys, the swathes of glinting power lines. On our highest hill, overlooking the unspoiled forest panorama of Blackdown Hill, was a 200-foot space-age erection crammed with BBC antennae and, everywhere, there were extra electricity lines to cope with the power now replacing village gas-lights and generators. Between our house and the churchyard, where blackthorn and bramble once housed brimstone butterfly and a family of wrens, a concrete, brick and tarmac sewage pump was installed. Nitrates sprayed on field and laneside verge ensured the disappearance of glow-worms, crickets and many wildflowers. Draining down streams to the river, fertilisers and effluents killed off the newts and tadpoles as well as the eels for which the Lod was once well known.

Even the softwood copses and spinneys in our local valley were cut down to enlarge the fields or to replant with larch and pine. Only the eastern wood remained untouched, covering the land which rose from the Lod to the village of River where Ginnie Pepper lived. Her brothers, like my sisters, had left home to work abroad or to marry. Ginnie herself, as I overheard in the village shop, was away at boarding school in Eastbourne.

Hove, a western extension of Brighton but without the bright shopping zones, the promenade and the pier, is a place where old folk go to die peacefully alongside their poodles. Not exactly Aix-en-Provence; but Davies's itself, situated in the epicentre of this undertakers' nursery, somehow managed to thrum with vitality. There were 120 students, of whom only forty or so were British. Most of the rest were teenage blondes from Scandinavia or the Mediterranean countries. I arrived at the height of the miniskirt period when Carnaby Street dictates were pushing hemlines higher daily and the lady students of Davies's vied with one another in the extremes of thigh-high fashion: creations known as micro-skirts or, in Hove parlance, pussy-pelmets.

My natural inability to concentrate was not improved during French and German classes by the non-stop visual battering of nubile legs on every side. I struggled with Maupassant, Brecht, Goethe and Voltaire, but whenever my brain began to latch onto the wanderings of Candide or Goldmund, a bronzed thigh would twitch at the next-door desk, quite ruining any thread of concentration.

There were a number of French and Italian stallions at the crammers and the carefully planned attempts of William, myself and the other dowdy Brits at dating the sexy foreign girls were invariably blocked by these dark-skinned, hairy-chested Casanovas. For the first time I began to wish that I was handsome, the natural follow-on from pretty. But no; fate had decided not to follow through and, between fourteen and seventeen, my features grew increasingly skew-whiff.

A month before arriving at Davies's, after a party in Hampshire, I had fallen asleep while driving my Vespa home at fifty miles per hour. The lane bent left but the scooter drove straight on into the hedge. I landed in a pile of gravel, denting my helmet and cracking the glass of my goggles, in which I later found lodged a tuft of bloody eyebrow. Unable to see much, I limped moth-like to a nearby light source. By good luck this turned out to be the window of the Liss Surgery and the duty nurse patched up the cuts on my face. For some months my nose resembled a stick of pink Brighton rock and interfered with my chances of romance.

I met a quiet English girl of sixteen in the Davies's canteen. Maggie Rayner did not wear miniskirts, although her legs were nothing to be ashamed of, and she lived ten miles from Lodsworth. I took her to the cinema and down to the beach at nearby Climping Sands but I did not kiss her because she was too well mannered to look as though she expected to be kissed.

So my sexual frustrations grew. To let off steam I introduced some of the students to the delights of stegophily. Over the next twelve months, the Sussex newspapers reported a rash of flagged spires. On especially complex climbs, my old Eton friend Michael Denny, who lived in East Sussex, would join us and, in his car, we drove as far afield as Marlborough College (which has a particularly interesting spire). My finest climb was Hove Town Hall, in the company of one Julian Moulton. That Victorian building, Hove's tallest monument, housed the police station and soared to a sheer slated 110-foot spire with no handgrips and no drainpipes. With binoculars we had spotted a one-inch lead lightning conductor and, wearing wet wool gloves and cotton socks, we reached the 'summit' hand-over-hand, praying the thin lead strip would not break.

The following day the borough surveyor told the *Evening Argus*: 'An attempt has been made by the Hove Fire Brigade to remove the flag but their escape could not reach it. No further attempt will be made to remove it. The spire is unclimbable.'

During leave from Davies's, William was expected to spend a month at a French château near Blois. My mother decided I should go to improve my French. We drove to the champagne vineyards of Epernay in William's Mini and south to the Massif Central until he crashed into a Panhard and we retired to Blois. By then my French was fluent but my grammar atrocious. I failed both my 'A' levels and was rescheduled to try again in six months' time.

At Christmas, carolling with Maggie, Peter Tooth and other friends from Lodsworth, we drove out to River and sang outside Ginnie's front door. I kept to the back of the throng for I knew her father still disliked me. When the door opened Ginnie was there in a dressing-gown. She was fifteen by then and much changed from the elfin girl of my adolescent dreams.

That brief Christmas glimpse of Ginnie haunted me. I sent her five Valentine cards that February of 1962 and, in the icy spring leave, took a job at the Hornet in Chichester, one of her father's eight Sussex goods yards. I must have thought she would visit the yard. Of course she never did. One day I unloaded a lorryload of drain junction pipes and stacked them the wrong way up. They filled with rainwater and, during the next frost, most of them cracked. My third week's pay packet was my last. Then I tried a new tack.

Ginnie kept two ponies at her father's chalk quarry at Amberley and my sister Celia, home on leave from Gloucester hospital, drove me to the quarry in the Morris Minor. She had Ginnie's mother's permission to exercise the ponies. This we did several times and, on leaving for Gloucester, Celia asked Ginnie's mother if I could continue to ride at the quarry.

One thing led to another and at length Ginnie's mother, probably forgetting her husband's dislike for me, asked me to ride with Ginnie at River. At first she was stiff and talked little. I wondered if she even slightly suspected how I had yearned for her or how often I had watched her in the woods and dreamed of her through the long miserable years at Eton. But of course she knew nothing of this. How could she? I was that odd boy from Lodsworth who played bike polo with her brothers and, more recently, had been in trouble with the police. Her father had warned her to keep away from me ever since the spiked whip had been found in their orchard.

We rode by way of woodland paths and long fallow fields, which we both knew well, from River Common to the manor of Pittshill with its solitary fool's tower and its hidden tunnels. Then we continued north along the bounds of Petworth Park until we came to the Victorian folly. Here we climbed over the high gate and sat in the grass.

'Do you remember when we danced together three years ago?' I asked her. 'You were wearing a white dress with a yellow flower. I thought you were the prettiest girl at the dance.' She looked up quickly with a half-smile but said nothing.

We stayed for a while listening to the wind and the creak of the shutters high up the folly. We rode back a different way in silence, but before we passed the fields of Tanner's Knap, where River village starts, I gave Ginnie a scarf I had bought, especially for her, in Paris. I watched as she opened the wrapping and, when I saw her smile, the whole world danced. She liked it.

We left the ponies in a paddock close to her house and went in for tea. I learned that Ginnie was going back to school in Eastbourne the following day, and offered her a lift. To my delight, Ginnie and her mother agreed. 'I'm not sure what her father would say, but so long as you go straight there, no stopping *en route*, I can't see any harm.' I agreed to pick Ginnie up the next afternoon.

She had a small suitcase which fitted on the rear seat when Ginnie kept well forward. I felt her pressed against my back and her hands lightly around me. I was definitely in heaven. In fact, if heaven is half as good as I felt that day, it will be worth the struggle to attain.

All went well as far as the school in Eastbourne, called Moira House, where we dropped off her case. She agreed to have tea with me in town and, on our way back, I swerved to avoid a bicyclist. I do not remember the accident, nor the next fifteen hours. When I woke up in hospital, I rang for a nurse.

'Is she all right?' I asked.

The nurse told me my passenger was in bed at her school, my scooter was in good nick and the bicyclist, whose fault it had been, was unharmed. Apart from concussion and abrasions to my face, I, too, was undamaged.

Ginnie came to see me the following day and gave me a bunch of flowers she had picked after school. She limped slightly and told me her legs were bruised all over from the crash.

I was fined £4 for riding a scooter with no L-plates and carrying an unlicensed passenger. Ginnie's father was furious and forbade her to see me again. Thus encouraged, we agreed by post to meet by night in a bathroom at the school, a room on her second floor, easily reached by a stout drainpipe.

The scooter journey from Lewes to Eastbourne is an easy thirty-minute drive, and I arrived at midnight when all the teachers and girls except Ginnie should have been asleep. For two hours I sat in the bath and Ginnie, in her nightdress, sat on the loo. My cautious suggestions that we could perhaps make ourselves more comfortable were discouraged and I was determined not to risk alarming her.

Twice more I called on Ginnie in the bathroom and each time I brought her a gift of apples or chocolates. Towards the end of that term I scootered down on a Friday afternoon unannounced and watched the girls play lacrosse. When they all walked back to the school I waited by the roadside and Ginnie, in a bunch of other girls wearing blue games skirts and carrying 'lackey sticks', put her hand to her mouth as she recognised me, despite helmet and goggles. She dropped behind the others and we hid in a patch of rhododendrons.

'You are wicked,' she laughed. She was breathless. We kissed for the first time and I felt that I would love her for ever.

The following term Ginnie was moved to another dormitory on the fourth floor. She sent me directions by way of the rooftops to an attic window which gave access to the 'Tad' or art-room. Those were wildly happy times, days and nights of dizzy electricity between us. An all-but-tangible excitement filled our lives, whether we were together or not. Neither of us had ever made love, nor did we allude to the possibility of such. The present was pregnant with unfulfilled longings and each kiss a moment of sensual wonder. I wished it would never end.

One night a history mistress, an attractive woman in her early thirties, heard my approach somewhere along my complex four-storey route of drainpipes, window-ledges and roof-slates. She appeared without warning in the art-room and asked me what I wanted. I explained that I had been passing the school on my scooter and thought I had seen a fire on the roof. Having climbed up to extinguish it, I found there was no fire, so . . .

The mistress nodded wisely. 'In that case, I might as well let you out, don't you think?'

Much relieved, I agreed and followed her downstairs. I did not return for a week and when I did I climbed up by a different route.

In the spring of 1962 the last national servicemen were leaving the Army but the current system of officer selection was not yet in force. To gain a commission – either from the ranks as a professional soldier or fresh from school – it was necessary to pass the Regular Commissions Board at Wilton, near Salisbury. To attempt the Board an applicant needed at least five 'O' levels. Although still at Davies's attempting 'A' levels, my previous failure had at least netted a German 'O' so, with four 'O's from Eton, I just made the grade.

With twelve other hopefuls, all male and each wearing a numbered bib so the panel would be judging numbers not names, I was put through a series of aptitude tests. Luckily, these were more taxing on the imagination, ability to converse with reasonable fluency, and general physique, than they were on intellect.

To my delight I passed but, shortly after my eighteenth birthday, failed my French and German 'A' levels for the second time. I had blamed miniskirts for the first fiasco. This time I ascribed my failure to Ginnie.

I packed up my things at Lewes and scootered home. That weekend I thanked my mother for sending me to Davies's. It was a far happier place for me than Eton and much nearer to Eastbourne than Aix was.

The next step after RCB was an officer cadet school. For a regular commission, I would have to spend two years at Sandhurst, but lack of 'A' levels meant I could apply only for a short-service commission (two years as an officer) and must pass through a five-month course at Mons Officer Cadet School in Aldershot. There were two companies at Mons, Salerno and Kohima, both containing three platoons. Each platoon was ruled by a Guards sergeant-major and an Infantry captain but there were various other mini-Hitlers for different activities such as physical training and camp guard. Day after day, week on week, we learned drill movements with and without 303 rifle, submachine-gun and sword; how to attack machine-gun nests from the left flank, right flank or head-on under cover of smoke. Route marches, jogging and walking alternated with frenzied uniform cleaning sessions with brasso and blanco. The white blanco paste invariably smeared the gleaming brass buckles or the brasso ruined the pure white strapping. The tiniest smudge on either brought instant retribution and extra guard duties, the most dreaded of punishments since sleep was at a premium.

After the first two months, physical training sessions were slightly curtailed and the number of classroom lessons correspondingly increased. We learned about tanks and bridge-layers, Soviet tactics and armaments, divisional and brigade formations, Giant Vipers and Ferrets, kiloton and megaton damage, and flash-to-bang time. Soon our brains were reeling.

In Salerno Company I met a dashing young cadet, later to be associated with the jet-set and the likes of Baroness van Thyssen, who specialised in hanging upside down bat-like from the barracks beams longer than anyone else. He made a good deal of money this way. The Honourable Richard Wrottesly, known to all as Rotters, wore a monocle at all times and drove a green E-type Jaguar. We discovered a mutual interest in night-climbing and determined to scale the west wing of nearby Heathfield Girls' School, which he said was a challenging climb. With a coil of climbing rope, we left Mons at midnight and parked his Jaguar outside the Heathfield fence.

Three-quarters of the way up the highest part of the school, where my mother and sisters had once boarded, we were disturbed by a clamour from below. Rotters, above me and on the same drainpipe, looked downwards and the beam of a powerful torch flashed off his monocle. Excited shouts broke out.

'We've been spotted,' Rotters hissed at me and, gaining the horizontal guttering, he swung himself across to a fire ladder that disappeared around the back of the building. But there was no escape, for there was a police squad surrounding the school. When we reached the ground, a uniformed officer and the school bursar, a hefty man in his sixties, frogmarched us towards the main entrance. Without warning Rotters lashed backwards with the rope coil and shouted 'Break'. I ran straight for the nearest rhododendrons with an officer and an Alsatian in hot pursuit. Through the shrubs, I scaled the eight-foot fence with wings of fear and sped to Rotters' car. I found it locked and decided to hitchhike back to Mons. First parade at 7.00 a.m. could not be missed.

The first car that stopped for me was a police van and I decided to play innocent. They took me to Ascot Police Station and there I found Rotters demanding his rights and complaining about police harassment of an innocent ornithologist in search of the little-known and nocturnal lesser-spotted wall-twat. He showed no signs of recognising me so I responded likewise.

The police officer from the patrol van looked me up and down. 'Sir,' he said with heavy irony, 'you are wearing black Army gym shoes, red Army PT shirt and you have the haircut which can nowadays only be found on young Sandhurst cadets. Our bird-watching friend over there whom you have never seen before is wearing identical clothing with the sole exception of a monocle. He has a similar hairstyle. . . . Do us a favour and tell us what you were both up to.'

An hour later the van dropped us off at Mons. Heathfield had agreed with our commandant that charges would not be pressed providing both cadets were suitably dealt with. We were summoned before Brigadier P. W. G. Pope, god of Mons, our company boss Major P. Marnham, and a number of other stern-faced officers. The *Sunday Express* the next day quoted the brigadier as saying: 'We are not at all amused by this unscheduled piece of initiative. I have had them disciplined for their activities.' Rotters, who had physically assaulted the bursar, was given the boot and took his leave of Mons at once. I was awarded fifty-six days of RPs, Restrictions of Privileges, which was two days longer than I was meant to remain at Mons.

Every Friday night at 6.00 p.m., when the other cadets had leave, they would sign out at the guard room and many would wink at me as I stood to attention for two hours in my best uniform and boots. My platoon sergeant-major informed me with what I thought was a tone of slight respect that I had chalked up the record number of RPs since Mons was first formed.

Rotters later joined the Parachute Regiment as a trooper and was much loved by his fellow-soldiers despite his monocle and E-Type. He excelled for many years on the Cresta Run at St Moritz. One year in Ireland he drove into a tree to avoid a flock of sheep and died instantly.

I played polo for Mons and ran for the cross-country team, but neither helped my record as the day of reckoning approached. Cadets who do not pass exams are either failed or, at best, suffer the indignity of re-coursing, which entails another five months of purgatory.

There were three major exams: Military Knowledge I and II and Signals. The results of our efforts were published a week later and a crowd formed to check the three lists. Out of some ninety cadets only three were destined for the Scots Greys. Hamish Macrae was intelligent but Anthony Brassey, whose father like mine had once commanded the Greys, was as thick as I was. The results on all three lists were horrifyingly similar. Rows and rows of cadets' names, and finally either Fiennes and then Brassey – or Brassey and then Fiennes. Only Mahmoud, a Somali, kept us from placing last in each exam.

Brassey was re-coursed. Macrae and I were passed out by the Queen and so became commissioned officers. My platoon commander informed me unofficially that he suspected the authorities were not prepared to risk my presence at Mons for another five months. Otherwise, in his opinion, I should have been back again with Brassey.

In the summer of 1962, four free months were available between Mons and tank training camp and I realised this was my only chance of seeing the world, something many young people try to do if they have the time, the inclination and the money between school and career.

An old school friend, Simon Gault, agreed to accompany me to Norway for a canoeing expedition. The idea had been mooted during Eton Corps Camp when we had patrolled beside a number of wild rivers. On a map we had noticed a riverain route by which we could follow rivers from the high western Jotunheim region all the way to the east coast and Oslo.

The only problem, since we both had funds enough for transport and food, was our lack of a canoe. The cheapest suitable model cost £80 and I set to work to earn the money. I sold my scooter for £25 and took on three local jobs. At 2.30 p.m. daily I walked through the Lodsworth graveyard to the polo pony stables in the converted barn where once we had collected brown eggs from old Mrs Smallridge. For £2 I rode a polo pony and led two others to Cowdray Polo Ground where I handed them over to the likes of the Earl of Brecknock and Hanut Singh. More often than not there was an additional ten-bob note to be had by way of a tip. Then I walked via Cowdray Castle into Midhurst and The Angel Hotel where I washed up the dinner dishes. I kept two glass jugs by the sink and filled them with red and white wine left over by the dinner guests. Apart from my wage there was a free staff meal at 10.00 p.m., which I washed down with one of my wine jugs.

Gubbie's flat abutted the Midhurst Grammar School close by the Angel and I slept on his kitchen floor until 4.00 a.m. when I slipped out and, 100 yards down the High Street, let myself into the Southdown Bus Depot where for seven hours I hosed down the Greenline buses, nine double-deckers and two coaches. The coaches were used by school parties and, for reasons I never discovered, the passengers were frequently sick. That was the bad bit. The bonus was coins, often to be found in certain catchment areas which I always checked. At 11.00 a.m.,

Southdown allowed me a free ticket back to Lodsworth where my mother gave me a lunch before the next pony delivery.

In three weeks I had the money and ordered the canoe. Maggie from Davies's joined us and we arrived in the Jotunheim with my double canoe and Simon's single kayak. For three miles we negotiated minor rapids with ease. Then the river dropped into a canyon so I asked the other two to wait while I went ahead to film them in the rough stuff. The film, which I still possess, shows the canoe, my hard-earned canoe, hitting a rock and splitting in two. Maggie was caught underneath a spar but Simon rescued her further down the gorge. The canoe was not insured.

We returned to England the same week. Simon had fallen in love with Maggie and I had learned two lessons. The value of reconnaissance in unknown places and the futility of paying for expeditions from one's own pocket.

Determined to mount a successful journey during the three months that remained before tank training camp, I picked a route from the map after watching an old film of Lawrence of Arabia. To cross the Anatolian desert by camel would take three weeks, and two ex-Mons cadets, including Hamish Macrae, my fellow Scots Grey-to-be, agreed to come. Maggie was also keen on the idea so I worked out the price of three weeks' rental of four Turkish camels. Stupidly, I notified the Army of our intentions, and two weeks before the intended date of our departure a curt note from the Ministry of Defence advised me that permission was not granted for Her Majesty's officer cadets to exercise in Anatolia, owing to the political climate. I was unaware that the Anatolian desert suffered from a political climate but, far too timid to enter an argument with the MoD, I reached for my atlas.

Camels had been the main attraction of our plan so I substituted the European version, mules, and a week later the four of us headed for the Pyrenees, intent on crossing them astride four mules. We arrived on the French–Spanish border on 6 August.

According to the Spanish Embassy in London the average mule cost £10 in pesetas. The three potential sellers in Puig Cerda all wanted over £50, which was well beyond our means, and their mules were so small our feet touched the ground when astride them.

We settled for a mean-looking creature which cost £60 but was at least pony-size. Since we could now only afford one mule we agreed that Maggie could ride with the baggage and we would walk behind. Hamish checked the mule's teeth while we all held its mouth open. Emerging from the evil-smelling mouth Hamish announced that the animal was twenty-two years old and male. 'He is very obviously male,' I exclaimed. 'I can tell that without checking his teeth, and mules don't live to twenty.'

It transpired after heated discussion that Hamish was something of a mule expert and that mules had been known to reach thirty. My comment that he would go far in the cavalry was ignored.

Laden with all our rucksacks, tents and food bags, the mule's knees touched and its hooves splayed outwards, but nonetheless it advanced when prodded. Maggie decided not to mount up for fear of being the last straw.

The journey was idyllic. There were spectacular thunderstorms, we were abused by locals whose maize was eaten by Moocho (the mule's name according to Hamish) and we were eaten by mosquitoes.

A passing car so frightened Moocho that he reared. Maggie was at the time between mule and road-edge. We heard her scream and rushed to the verge. Twenty feet below Maggie lay comatose in a thornbush which grew out of the cliffside. We retrieved her with Moocho's grazing tether and took her to a doctor in the village of Seo de Orgel. On his advice we hospitalised her in the local inn where the doctor extracted long black thorns from all over her body.

Three days later Maggie pronounced herself fit. By then we had purchased a two-wheel cart big enough for our baggage so Maggie could sit on Moocho. Hamish tied a GB sign to the cart's rear and we plodded south, looking down on the valley of the Rio Segre, until the mountains fell away and, two weeks later, we reached the plains and Lerida. Poor Moocho was sold to a friendly butcher and Maggie cried.

Back in England Hamish and I joined twenty or thirty cavalry officers, one or two from Mons but most of them from Sandhurst, including three bound for the Greys.

The tank gunnery school at Lulworth is carefully situated so that even the stupidest officers cannot knock off Dorset villages or main roads with wrongly aimed high-explosive shells. Any mistake will only send the missiles harmlessly over cliffs and out to sea where, by the law of averages, they are unlikely to land on a fishing trawler.

I remember one gunnery sergeant explaining that a reasonably proficient Centurion tank crew should be able to destroy three Soviet tanks 1000 metres away within ten seconds of sighting. My own range results indicated that any number of Soviet tanks could safely picnic 600 yards away. Despite this I passed the course eight weeks later: I suspect no one is ever failed.

Next we were sent to the driving and maintenance camp at nearby Bovington where, they said at the introductory briefing, we would become adequate at driving, operating the radio and (I laughed negatively to myself) understanding the guts of the Centurion Mark VII battle tank. In theory, a cavalry officer should be able to take over from a disabled signaller, loader, driver or gunner. I tried hard at Bovington but my results remained worse than those of all my brethren.

During wintry evenings we took boots full of firewood to the clifftops of Durdle Dor and flung the logs down to the beach close by a sandy-bottomed cave. Maggie often visited and we swam in the wintry sea, then ate sausages by the fire in the cave. I generally behaved as I thought befitted a second lieutenant, but there were some wild characters on the tank course who led me astray once or twice.

Two of us stole a piglet from a nearby farm and greased it with LG 320 tank grease. Then my colleague drove to Camberley. I sat beside him holding the piglet in a knitted bag and feeding it from a bottle. We drove to the annual ball at the Camberley Staff College and took the piglet to a rear window of the huge ballroom where Britain's finest young men cavorted in Mess dress with lovely young things in magnificent ball gowns. Wishing him luck, we put the piglet through the window and held our breath. A fusilade of terrified screams was followed by sounds of pandemonium. Forgetting the prudence of flight, we crouched mesmerised in wonder that one small piglet could cause such havoc. What, I mused, could Soviet saboteurs not do with two dozen greased piglets strategically inserted?

As we kneeled in the flowerbed below the window a most amazing thing happened. The sounds of panic inside came to a crescendo as, with a small squeal, our piglet literally flew out of the window and landed in my lap. I bagged it and we fled to the car. Two weeks later we returned the piglet ungreased and overfed to its owner.

On another night, Macrae and myself, with many others, drove in appropriated Army Land Rovers to the caravan camp above Durdle Dor. The inmates live there more or less permanently, so even in November the camp was crowded. With blue lights flashing and megaphones in hand we warned the caravanners that, as they would have seen or heard through the media that day, the notorious Weasel, the Great Train Robber, had escaped from gaol and (this bit was not true) had been reported as spotted in Lulworth. For an hour we thoroughly searched some twenty luxuriously appointed caravans, accepted drinks from the curious but grateful owners and finally departed, officially declaring the camp Weasel-free.

In February I was to join the Royal Scots Greys in Fallingbostel near Hamburg. I spent the Christmas before this in Lodsworth. Ginnie came home from school and we met many times in the woods. We walked in the snow and sat by the frozen river on a mossy rock beneath Eel Bridge. Soon after Christmas there was a blizzard and more snow was recorded throughout England than in any year since 1881.

The night before I left home to join the Army I placed a letter for Ginnie in a hollow tree outside her house. I was sad to leave her, I said, but one day I would be commanding officer of the Royal Scots Greys.

5

SAS and Doctor Dolittle

Nothing succeeds like success and certainly nothing fails like failure.

MARGARET DRABBLE

My father Ranulph had joined the Royal Scots Greys in India, after Eton and Sandhurst. After a spell as aide to the Governor General of Canada he had risen to second in command when war came. He was charged with disposing of the regiment's 600 grey horses and training the men as tank-soldiers. The first major clash with Rommel was at Allam Halfa in August 1942, by which time Ranulph was commanding the Greys. At Nofilia, he led a 'frontal cavalry charge' against the Panzers from a turretless tank and was badly wounded. Altogether he was wounded four times, and he was awarded the DSO. I keep a letter written to my mother by one of his troopers: 'I knew Colonel Lugs as a sympathetic and understanding, fair and just, loyal and fearless, leader of men.'

At El Alamein, Ranulph led the Greys through two major minefields during the main attack. At one point he spotted two wounded Italians in no-man's land and rescued them, although his tank was hit in several places. In June 1943 he came home on leave and I was conceived. When he left, my mother was never to see him again. He commanded the Greys at Salerno and through southern Italy. Reconnoitring a bridge over the Pescara river unarmed and alone, he surprised three Germans in a cave and took them prisoner at the point of his briarpipe. Two Greys troopers, escaped prisoners, reported that their interrogators had wanted to know the correct pronunciation of the names of three commanding officers of the regiment, Twisleton, Wykeham and Fiennes.

Not far from Naples, checking out a possible route of advance, Colonel Lugs trod on an S-type mine and, on 24 November 1943, four months before my birth and nine months after the death of his father Sir Eustace, my father died of wounds and jaundice in a Naples hospital. My mother never married again.

They were together for only ten years unbroken by war, but for her their love has lasted undiminished down the long years since. From childhood I have wanted to be as he was.

In February 1963 I made my way to Germany to join the Royal Scots Greys. I was eighteen and had just bought my first car, an elderly Peugeot 403, for £150.

Most of the Greys had still not arrived from Aden when I joined their advance party in the dismal barracks of Fallingbostel on the Westphalian Plain. The camp had been built for Hitler's Panzers twenty years before and was sited close by the main tank-training ranges of northern Germany, the British defence sector or British Army on the Rhine (BAOR).

My new fellow officers were Hamish Macrae and Thuggers Kingston (the aggressive Earl of Kingston I first met at Sandroyd) and three others I did not know. Until quite recently newly joined officers, like Victorian children, were supposed to be seen but not heard by their seniors, meaning all other humans in the Officers' Mess. This practice was still prevalent in some regiments, but not in the Scots Greys. So long as you were not blatantly noisy or disrespectful you could get a civil answer to a sensible question. For this I was thankful, since it was altogether a new world and I had plenty of questions to ask.

Regimental Sergeant-Major Rowan, a big man with bristling moustache, swagger-stick and high blood pressure, patiently taught his new officers the Royal Scots Greys' drill with swords and submachine-guns. We were instructed in regimental customs, history and taboos.

A month later the bulk of the regiment turned up in dribs and drabs including the CO, Colonel Jock Balharry, an entirely unfrightening sort of boss. As in my father's day, the lion's share of the officers were Scotsmen, as were over 90 per cent of the troopers and NCOs. Only two Greys remained who remembered my father from eighteen years earlier, but the fact that he had commanded the Greys and that Fiennes, pronounced Feens by all the Jocks, was thought to be a Scottish name, saved me from most of the mickey-taking suffered by a number of the more obviously English Greys.

Few officers were wealthy but most were comfortably off, with a private income to supplement their wages. My allowance was £200 per year and most of the 1963 dollop had gone on the Peugeot. After regimental deductions my monthly wage was between £15 and £25, which left little for extra-regimental activities. I was to find this more and more irksome, especially when fined for misdemeanours.

One of the Sandhurst officers who joined with me, Paddy Earp, was a friendly soul, no taller than most twelve-year-old boys. When he drove around camp it seemed as though his car was on auto-pilot, for his head was invisible through the rear window. His nickname was Grubscrew, since that is the very smallest item in a Centurion tank. Playing cricket in the bedroom block corridor one Sunday with tennis ball and coal shovel, I missed the ball. The steel shovel-head flew off its wooden handle and shot down the corridor. Paddy Earp, emerging from the gents doing up his flies, was struck on the mouth by the shovel. There was much blood but the Grubscrew was brave and told nobody.

A while later, with helicopter pilot Louie Parsons, I was engaging in .22 rifle practice in the same corridor when an NCO crossed the passage without warning. Frightened by a bullet that missed his torso and ricocheted off the wall, he told stories in high places. I was summoned before the adjutant, Prince Edward, Duke of Kent, who gave me a serious warning with a pointed reminder that a few years previously a friend of his had been thrown out of the regiment for shooting his brother officer in the backside with a .45 revolver.

Keen to play polo, I struck a deal with Peter Loyd, one of the other troop leaders in my squadron, that we would each pay for half a pony and share its use. Unfortunately the two of us went to Hamburg in my Peugeot to a farewell dinner for our squadron leader, Major Brian Booth. The party, at the fabulous Vier Jahreszeiten Hotel, included a great deal of alcohol and operatic performances by officers on the tabletop. One Baron Franckenstein, who had followed me from Mr Parr's House to the Scots Greys, sang *Figaro* to the music of the Four Seasons orchestra.

Disorientated by fine wines and port, neither my passenger nor I could remember where my Peugeot was parked. After two hours of useless wandering and reports to the *polizei* we took a taxi back to camp. By selling my half of the pony I managed to purchase an ancient Citroën from an older officer, and took up singing in the garrison choir, a less expensive hobby.

There were no girls in Fallingbostel. Years of incidents between local Fräuleins and the garrison incumbents had caused the parents of all pretty, and most plain, girls to shut them up out of working hours and to resist all attempts at familiarity by British males with short haircuts. In four years at Fallingbostel the only officer who ever succeeded with a local Fräulein was the Grubscrew and he probably managed it by sneaking underneath the parental radar.

This local dearth left only in-house attractions and they were few and far between. A handful of Army education teachers lived in the garrison, but they were singularly unattractive and known by all as screachers. Our regimental paymaster's daughter, Susan, came to stay from school in England. She was dark, sixteen and a classic beauty. I played tennis with her and took her to one or two dances but nothing came of it. Her voice was as intoxicating as her looks, so I had joined the choir to listen and watch. Baron Franckenstein was another keen attender but I never found out whether he came for love of Susan or the sound of his own voice.

Ginnie's parents would not allow her to visit, but Maggie came out for one or two weekends. Driving her back from Hamburg in a borrowed Mercedes, I went to sleep at ninety miles per hour on the *autobahn*. Maggie screamed a warning as we homed in on the tail end of a truck. Somehow I swerved in time.

On other occasions seven or eight of us went at weekends to the notorious David, Herbert or Winkel Strasse and paid ten marks apiece to watch two ladies performing naked rites with bananas. Few if any of us spent time with the prostitutes who beckoned from ill-lit windows in the sin-streets. Whether this abstinence stemmed from moral inhibitions or fears of syphilis I could not say. Senior officers told us there was a Hamburg nightclub where the ladies made love to well-endowed mules and another where, if you left coins on the corner of your table, naked waitresses would remove them entirely by adroit application of their thigh muscles. One officer said he had pre-heated a coin with his lighter and sent a waitress into orbit. Despite numerous weekend sorties to see these wonders for ourselves we never located the relevant dives – if indeed they existed.

The reason for BAOR's existence, as for the American and French armies further south, is to defend Western Europe against Warsaw Pact invasion. Since an attack could theoretically be mounted with only a few hours' warning, all BAOR personnel and vehicles have to be in a permanent state of war-readiness. To test this without warning, regimental commanders hold 'crashes' from time to time and woe betide the troop leader who does not get his three battle tanks, fully crewed and armed, to their pre-designated battle positions within the allotted six-hour period. Indicative of NATO's strategic intentions, the drill was to position each tank in a snug protective hollow with vehicle facing west in readiness for retreat and gun pointing east to knock out a Soviet or two before fleeing. For four years, almost without exception, our training concentrated on withdrawal practice except when acting as 'enemy'.

Each squadron consisted of four troops with three tanks each. Three troops manned standard fifty-ton Centurion tanks and the fourth, of which I was troop leader, crewed the great seventy-ton Conquerors, which were unwieldy but lobbed their shells a good deal further. The Conqueror Jocks referred to Centurion tanks as 'bubble cars'.

Immediately after the war, tank-training was conducted in a cavalier fashion, with little respect for the vanquished farmers, whose crops were crushed and barns destroyed with impunity. By the 1950s 'Huns' were being referred to more often as 'German citizens' and, after the Berlin airlift, as 'our German allies'. Year by year training rights were curtailed until, by the early 1950s, training areas were barely large enough to cope with more than two tank regiments at any one time. For brigade or divisional exercises, which moved over whole areas of German countryside outside the designated zones, a complex scale of compensation was laid down and upgraded each year. Slight damage to a twenty-year-old pine tree could earn its owner £100 and a crushed gate-post £50. Often enough smiling farmers would stand by open gates waving invitingly at oncoming tank commanders. A poor crop could be turned into a small fortune if a British tank could be persuaded to drive over it once or twice.

The main training zone, a quagmire of muddy couloirs, criss-crossed the pine forests of Luneberger Heide, the flattish region between the Elbe borderline and the main cities of Hamburg, Bremen and Hanover. The tanks of a good troop leader moved in slick orderly fashion, never getting lost or bogged down, and leapfrogging so that one always covered the progress of the others. In most American tank units, and we trained with a number, the troop leader did the map-reading and his NCOs went wherever he led, quite unaware of their location. All British tank commanders used their maps at all times and often were told to take over as troop leader for a given exercise or cross-country movement. This led to a testing time for young officers whose map-reading was slow or uncertain. Often enough their troop sergeant or corporal was an old-hand on the Luneberger training zones and knew most of the area by heart.

There are few more embarrassing situations known to military man than to take a wrong turning when acting as lead tank for a squadron move. Twelve steel monsters lumber behind you, each with a commander who is aching for you to make an error. When you discover you have gone wrong, panic takes over. There are many dead-end tracks on Luneberger Heide, and the experience of having all the other tanks turn around in a forest of narrow lanes just wide enough to take a single tank is the stuff of nightmares. The fault may have resulted from a muddy blotch on the map as one squinted through blinding rain or choking dust, but try explaining that later to an angry troop sergeant.

As a rule I found the troopers and most of the corporals good solid characters and easy to get along with. However, as soon as they became troop sergeants and therefore competitive, the sparks began to fly. I disliked my first two troop sergeants as bitterly as they, I am sure, returned the sentiment.

For two years I waged a private war on my own sergeant, Barchi Leader, and on his co-sergeants, Scabby Harris and Big John Audis, in two of the other troops. For reasons I have never pinpointed, my bad feelings seldom extended to the other squadron officers. Even the smallest matter concerning efficiency in the field was grist to the mill of the sergeants. They always maintained outward politeness in terms of addressing me as 'Sir', saluting and obeying outright orders, just as I never shouted at them and always called them 'Sergeant'. But underneath this necessary veneer we loathed each other and scored points whenever possible. Sadly, I lost at nearly every turn, for I was a novice and a slow learner.

There were many incidents on many exercises, but that which hurt the most was the Night of the Shovels. Every year a squadron CIV (Central Inspection of Vehicles) takes place, when every tool is checked and those that are lost are charged against the wages of the man responsible. Naturally a good deal of thieving takes place prior to each CIV, mostly between different troops, but sometimes, in desperation, within a troop.

The week before the 1964 CIV was spent on exercise and my troop was on guard duty within the squadron leaguer position the night before return to camp. My tank crew had identified themselves with me as unfairly treated underdogs, endlessly persecuted over the last two years by Barchi, Scabby and Big John.

They were a colourful bunch and I loved them as brothers, even lapsing within the steel confines of the turret into their Glaswegian effing and blinding against the injustices we jointly suffered. Certainly there was no stiffness between officer and men. The radio operator, tall and ungainly, was called 'Scratch' Sherville owing to an intermittent crutch-itch. 'Zeebo' Stevens, the gunner, had lank spiky hair and was always dirty, while Ian Durrand, the driver, was canny and by far the best mechanic in the squadron.

Our tank's tool supplies had dwindled during the previous nights of exercise, not because we had carelessly lost them but because of silent raiding parties while we slept. 'The worst items,' grumbled Stevens, as we scraped the evening's bully beef and peas from our mess-tins, 'is the shovels and picks. We've none left.'

'That's no yer fockin problem, Zeebo,' said Durrand. 'The shovels are on *my* fockin signature.'

Scratch poked the log fire with his fork. 'The bastards did it on guard-duty, the theevin fockers . . . They must a' done.' He looked up and added, 'What's soorce for the fockin goose, d'ye ken?'

At this the others glanced up too. They were all looking at me. I nodded. There was no alternative.

The next dawn, when Durrand woke me with a mug of tea, he muttered, 'We're OK, Mister Feens, I put the fockers onder the turret floor.'

As I completed the morning check on the gun's alternator, metadyne and Mullins ejection gear with Zeebo, he squinted up at me from his gunner's seat. 'Don't you fret nay mair aboot the shovels. I fetched us two fra Scabby's tank'. His white teeth glistened in the turret gloom.

This meant we now had four shovels hidden in the ammunition bins. I began to sweat.

Scratch Sherville's long legs dropped through the other turret hatch. He said nothing but squashed out a fag-end on the C42 radio and then laid a single finger against his long nose and winked with a look of evil satisfaction.

All around the leaguer, invisible in their mantles of cut foliage, the Morris generators and main engines of the squadron tanks coughed into roaring life. Blue smoke belched in the crisp air of late autumn. I stuck my head out of the turret to check the readiness of the other two tanks and saw, with a sick feeling of imminent doom, a cluster of green denim and white NCO stripes. A deputation of sergeants had brought the squadron leader Major 'Horsey' Anderson, to see me. That had to mean bad news.

'Ranulph,' said Major Anderson, his neat moustache a'bristle and his leather whip tapping the knees of his boiler suit like the twitching of a tiger's tail. 'I am told there is reason to suspect your men have abused their role as squadron guard . . . They have stolen shovels from First, Second and Third Troop.'

Mesmerised with alarm, I could only stare, mumbling, at the empty shovel-holder clasps on the sides of my tank.

'Not there, Mister Feens, not there.' The gravelly tones of Scabby Harris. 'They will be *inside* your tank.'

Barchi Leader, loving every moment of it, glared at me in righteous indignation. I had besmirched the honour of his troop. Big John Audis, whose nose was a scaled-down model of Mount Ararat, lowered his bulk beside Scratch Sherville.

'Out, Sherville,' he said, as though addressing a dog.

The Conqueror's gun barrel traversed slowly left and right as the sergeant gained access to one after another floor bin. As he did so, shovels appeared one by one, handed up to the smug Scabby Harris and down to the squadron leader. Burned into the handle of each shovel was the tank number of the previous owner. My crew had not had time to re-brand them with our own number.

I was severely admonished and given extra orderly officer's duties, but the shame for the four of us was much worse. The taunting went on for months – indeed, was still remembered with much laughter over leaguer fires five years later. We were dubbed Ali Feens and the Fourth Troop Thieves.

Each winter regimental boxing championships were held in the garrison gym to a capacity audience. It was after all a rare chance to watch troopers smashing officers to the floor. I had grown since Eton days to six feet two inches and weighed twelve stone, so I entered the Heavyweight class and fought through three bouts to the championship finals. To my genuine horror I was woken one morning by the Grubscrew, who usually knew everything before anyone else did. 'You're up against The Beast,' he said, 'Trooper Reid 66.' (Since there were many Reids in the Greys the last two figures of their Army number was always appended for differentiation.)

The Beast was not a true Grey. He was a REME mechanic attached to the regiment. Nor, in my mind, was he a true human. He weighed over fifteen stone and stood taller than me. Worse, he was notorious as the most dreaded fighter in Fallingbostel.

I contemplated 'flu – but there was none about. Or falling off my tank turret – but that seemed too obvious. Somehow the time ticked by until the awful moment when I entered the ring to the deafening howl of the assembled Greys, their appetites for violence whetted by the previous bouts of lesser weights. I hardly dared take a look at the grinning bulk of The Beast, fearing I would disgrace myself then and there.

The first round was awful. Twice a glove like a moon-rock contacted my head and my vision exploded in starbursts. Once a sledgehammer swing caught my chest and I hit the floor determined I was done for. Then, realising that roughhouse tactics could only favour The Beast, I cast my mind back to the long years of Eton training and the feint-and-cut tactics of Reg Hoblyn. This paid off and The Beast began to bleed. His bulk made him tire in the third round, his guard dropped and I was able to damage his face. I won by a narrow margin.

I grew to love the Greys as much as I had loathed public school, but for all the wrong reasons. In lieu of a war the Army provides excitement, and therefore hopes to hold on to its more venturesome members, through the medium of adventure training. A certain budget is made available for journeys away from the garrison at times when no tank exercises are anticipated.

Since many of my fellow officers were avid polo players or hunting fanatics there were few contenders for adventure training and sporting activities. I joined the cross-country running team and when Sergeant Ernie Newport, our leader, slipped on ice down Minden Hill and suffered a nasty compound fracture, I took over the team. The training often involved dragging a scented sock across country and over hedges in lieu of a fox for the regimental draghunt to follow.

Since many of Europe's great rivers flowed within easy reach of Fallingbostel, I asked our colonel if I could form a canoe club. He agreed, and forty-eight Jocks each paid 165 Deutschmarks at a rate of 10DM per week in order to purchase one-quarter of a two-seater canoe. I ordered twelve fibreglass Gmach canoes from England. They weighed sixty pounds each and were soldier-proof since they could be endlessly repaired *in situ*.

Each week the entire regiment was paid cash wages in the main canteen. By closing all exits except one, beside which I sat with a millboard and cashbox, I extracted the money over a period of six months. Then the Canoe Club thrived.

For three months each summer I took two separate groups of Jocks down different rivers. An Army lorry with a driver and a cook drove ahead each day to an agreed spot to set up a night camp. Over the years, we descended the Elbe, the Oste, the Weser, the Rhine, the Danube and the Rhone. By the time each summer was over the best four canoeists sported calloused layers on their hands and backsides and invariably won the BAOR Canoe Cup for the main touring canoe section.

I soon discovered that some Jocks had joined merely for the women and wine to be found in riverside towns. Since canoeing 100 miles a day is tiring, I instituted a rule that each canoeist had to sign out after the evening meal and be back again by 10.00 p.m. or forego a week of camp-leave. This was very unpopular and the stronger characters determined to buck my system. A war of wills followed and several Jocks on return to Fallingbostel asked for their 165 Deutschmarks back. I sold their shares to other applicants and gradually weeded out the trouble-makers, but not before the aggrieved ex-canoeists had passed the word around the regiment that the club was in reality 'Mister Feens's Concentration Camp'.

In the village of Oste where we camped, one trooper dropped a thunderflash into the cistern of the newly opened village toilet and blew it to bits. I gave the local mayor eight boxes of Army tinned food to soothe his feelings but the next night my canoeists drank too much at the annual Oste *Schutzenfest* and went on the rampage with broken-off chairlegs. They emptied an entire marquee of 300 villagers and a brass oompah band clad in *Lederhosen* and leather bibs. My corporal came back in a taxi to warn me and together we cajoled the eight drunken Jocks, complete with chairlegs, out of the marquee and into the taxi. That cost six more food boxes and, subsequently, a hefty cheque from the regiment for damages. Our colonel took the matter at face value and I escaped reprimand. But later that summer he had another reason to be unhappy with me.

On a windy day off the Danish town of Snaptun I took twenty canoeists to the leeshore of an island to learn capsize drills. Some of the men started to shiver in the cold offshore wind. Soon the sea between island and mainland was rough with spray and tossed spume. Two canoes went missing for an hour and a well-meaning Dane at Snaptun, misunderstanding some of the Jocks, telephoned the Danish Emergency Service. A well-practised, slick and very expensive operation followed, involving two motor launches, a helicopter and the Press.

Somehow the reporters learned that a canoe was still missing. This was after a launch had picked up one canoe, despite the protests of its perfectly safe occupants, and in lifting it aboard had smashed the fibreglass shell in two. It made for dramatic photographs and erroneous stories of wreckage. The international Press, including the *Scotsman*, picked up the story, alluding to a missing canoe. Anxious parents phoned the regiment, which of course knew nothing. The absent canoe was in fact mine, for I had returned to the island to search for the canoe which had been picked up by the launch. The colonel was not amused. But a month later there was more mayhem.

After the Denmark camp, I had obtained four-weeks' training rights for forty canoeists and twenty trekkers in Schleswig-Holstein. The agreed training zone was along the Schleie River above Eckernfjörde but, for a major night exercise with sixty men, it was a useless area. We had four Army lorries and two jeeps, so we drove south to the Kiel Canal, strictly forbidden for Army training but, since it offered an ideal series of easily controllable checkpoints, by far the best place for an exciting exercise for the Jocks. Besides, the authorities were unlikely to find out about our trespass since the exercise was to begin and end the same night.

The men were dropped off in two groups fifteen miles apart, half with canoes on the Kiel Canal and half on foot in a forest. Their goal was a ruined house with a crate of Carlsberg upstairs and a web of tripflares below. To get there, each group of two trekkers had to locate their designated canoeist partners and cross the Canal by midnight. Although there were only eight 'enemy', including myself, the canal made it easier to locate the Jocks. Identification meant disqualification.

Being crafty, some of the canoeists waited for a merchant ship or tanker to pass by them. Then, braving the powerful wash and backwash between hull and canal banks, they tucked in close behind the stern of their chosen host vessel which sucked them along, making for less work and good camouflage from the watchers on the bank.

I had forbidden my 'enemy' Jocks to fire Very flares close to any ship but, keen to identify canoeists glimpsed in the wash of a giant tanker, one over-zealous corporal landed a red phosphorus flare on the ship's rear deck. He could not have chosen a worse target, for it later transpired to have been a Soviet tanker with a liquid chemical cargo so volatile that the crewmen wore rubber soles so as not to risk causing a single spark.

Our flare hissed and burned away fiercely on the boat deck and in a short while the klaxon and red light system, which is installed along the Kiel Canal banks right across Europe, began to honk and flash as though World War Three was about to erupt. Loudspeakers crackled and a disembodied male voice spoke to us with British Rail-like lack of intelligibility. I understood only two words with crystal clarity: 'Englander Soldaten'. A British-style beret or cap comforter must have been spotted on a canoeist.

I contacted the lorry drivers and the other enemy posts and ordered the immediate end of the exercise. Somehow, within two hours all but four of the men were assembled by the ruins. All grey berets were removed and mud smeared on the vehicle number plates. Those soldiers who were temporarily with us from other regiments were told to keep their black berets on and to sit prominently beside the drivers.

We sped on our way north back to our own training area but the driver of my open jeep (or *champ* as they were known) grew sleepy so I told him we would change places. Officers were forbidden to drive MoD vehicles but I felt sure I was doing the right thing to avoid a possible crash. A short while later I woke from a drowsy trance to find myself driving straight towards a German pine tree. I jerked the steering wheel around but it was too late. I sheered the off-front wheel clean from its axle, flung both my passengers into the dark undergrowth and generally re-designed the shape of the jeep. I seemed to be unhurt but for a bruised ribcage and forehead. The Jocks were bloody but healthily voluble.

Back in Fallingbostel, I was ordered to report to the divisional commander, General Miles Fitzalan-Howard, shortly to become Duke of Norfolk. For my misdemeanour, the crash, I was fined £25 and given a stern warning. Luckily, there seemed to be no MoD central filing system which cross-checked the growing number of incidents I had accrued and, more fortunately, the Russian tanker mishap had not been blamed on the Greys.

Telegrams had flown to all regimental commanders. My own had quite rightly protested innocence. It appeared that because of the flare all canal traffic across Europe had stopped for five hours, an expensive delay. Six months later some busy-body forester found a Greys' beret by the canal and handed it to the *polizei* who gave it to the local British Army liaison officer. Within twenty-four hours my CO had summoned me and this time I saw a different general, received a heavier fine and a dozen extra orderly officer duties. Did I realise the possible consequences had the Soviet tanker exploded? I assured the general that I did but I had acted in innocence and with only the interests of training in mind. I persuaded myself that the matter would be forgotten and that I had as yet done nothing which might slow down my progress towards command of the regiment.

One odd side-effect of the canoeing journeys was that I ended up, after a couple of years, as the possessor of some 2000 of Her Majesty's Forces contraceptives-male-rubber-for the use of. Each journey, by Army orders, I drew from the quartermaster an exact number of contraceptives (the number of canoeists multiplied by the number of days' travel). This was to protect the locals from an outbreak of wee Jocks and to protect the Jocks from collecting hostile pox. After 100 miles of paddling and with only four hours' local leave per evening, canoeists had little chance to utilise contraceptives, so they rarely signed them out. The quartermaster's accounts were happier without quantities of returned prophylactics so they mounted up month by month in my bedroom.

Macrae and others learned of my collection and from time to time 'borrowed' a dozen or so. These would be filled with water and left in more senior officers' rooms as cunningly placed booby traps. The most annoying application of these limp waterballoons was prior to squadron tank parade. Once a week every officer would don his smart khaki service dress and drive from the Officers' Mess to the tank park. Then he would march to his position in front of his men prior to squadron inspection. On one such morning, leaving breakfast at the last moment as usual, I leapt into my old Citroën and started up. Without warning a grey jelly-fish-shaped UFO slid from its hidden perch on the driver's sun-flap and landed on my lap where it burst. There was a great deal of suppressed mirth among my troop as I halted in front of them and saluted, the area all about my crutch sodden wet from Macrae's flying jelly-fish.

When I left the Scots Greys I took the johnnies home in a suitcase and left them for years in my mother's attic. One day a plumber found them strewn all over the place by mice who had used them for several generations of nest linings.

For three months every winter I trained the regimental cross-country (or *langlauf*) ski team, six men including two reserves, in the mountainous country around Wertach village in Bavaria. We lived in a *gasthaus* or cooked for ourselves in a farmer's cottage.

As with the canoeing, there were no competing claims for the post of *langlauf* officer because those who did want to ski made up the downhill team. During the early 1960s the Royal Scots Greys ski team included Prince Nicolas von Preussen, the Baron Franckenstein and Charles de Westenholz, but this did not stop some of the onlookers at the annual Oberjoch Championships from shouting 'Go it, Jock' as our heroes flashed by.

Cross-country skiing was hard work and held none of the glory of downhill racing. During our first year in Bavaria no one in the Greys could *langlauf* except a stocky English corporal named Jones. He was a sadistic fellow, the only active Scots Grey ever to have served in the SAS, and he had learned *langlauf* in Norway. Six days a week for three months he took half a dozen of us around cunningly sited ski circuits through forests, down giddy gulleys and up sharp inclines. And always against the clock. The last man to complete each circuit would do twenty press-ups in the snow.

The start of each day saw us parade in blue cotton jackets, knickerbockers, Noddy-hats and skis at the shoulder. Then we marched through Wertach village with one of our number playing the bagpipes and 'Jonesey' railing at us from the rear. The piper, then Second Lieutenant Jameson, became CO of the regiment in 1986. But in those days he sweated and froze alternately like the rest of us at the whim of the gimlet-eyed monster Jones. We hated him but we did become above-average *langlaufers*.

In July 1963 Ginnie turned sixteen and the following November I returned for my six weeks' annual leave. She had left Eastbourne for a small school in Bath. Still *persona non grata* with her father, I drove there by night and she met me in the school garden. Together we slipped out to a quiet lane and, in the battered Peugeot, we whispered and laughed and loved and life was perfect. The late November moonlight slowly swung the tree shadows over us and we listened to 78s on Radio Luxembourg until Bryan Hyland was interrupted by a news flash . . . President Kennedy lay dead in Dallas.

The following July, a year later, I met Ginnie briefly at a little guesthouse in Dartmouth. She was learning to deep-sea dive at a school nearby. We spent two wonderful days and nights together, then I returned to the Greys. Two months later Ginnie's father decided to lift his long-enforced embargo and invited me to stay three days at the Normandy hotel where the family were on holiday. I drove through Germany, Belgium and France like a cat on hot wires and we spent two days on the beach and wandering the dunes of the Ile de Glénans. My bedroom was between that of Ginnie and her parents and, on the second night, soon after we had all had dinner and retired to bed, I was surprised by a knock on my locked door. Since Ginnie was not in my room I opened it at once.

Ginnie's father looked angry. 'Where is she?' he stormed. Before I could reply he shouted, 'I knew it. You are abusing my hospitality', and then, addressing the darkness of my bathroom: 'Get back to your room at once, Virginia, and wait for me.'

Unknown to me, Ginnie, in a light dressing gown, had arrived via the communal balcony, to return some beach gear to my bathroom, at the time her father had visited her to say good night. Finding her absent he instantly expected the worst and was proved right. I was packed off within the hour and told never to go near Ginnie again.

By my following Christmas leave, Mr Pepper had relented and I was allowed to take Ginnie to a local party given by mutual friends. There were only a dozen young people present, including Simon Gault and Maggie Rayner, whom I still saw from time to time. They were dancing together and the lights were turned low.

We walked in the garden through ankle-deep snow and joined some guests in a snowball fight. Then on tea-trays we bounced down a toboggan run close by. When Ginnie touched me in the dark, just her hand on my shoulder, and laughed with the excitement and the cold, I felt dizzy with longing. We went into the house and upstairs in an empty bathroom I towelled her dry and marvelled at the slim and supple way her arms joined her shoulders. I tried to unbutton her shirt but she shook her head and took away my hand. Down in the sitting room we sat together in an armchair and watched the slowly weaving couples.

The door burst open and the lights glared. Mr Pepper stood in the doorway in his overcoat. He saw Ginnie on my knees with her arm around my neck. 'Come home at once, Virginia.'

Ginnie left, crying in silence.

We did not meet again until spring 1965, my third year in Germany. Ginnie wrote to tell me that over Easter she would again be in Dartmouth at the diving school and staying at a hotel. I drove back from Germany and signed into the same hotel under a false name. We spent four days together in that friendly cliffside town, enjoying candlelit meals, nights of love and rowing-boat trips across the harbour to picnics on grassy shores.

I went back to Germany via a holiday in Spain with Gubbie and a six-foot model girlfriend of his whom he called Palm Tree. Three was not the ideal number for a hot Spanish spree and I yearned for Ginnie. Back in England her father had grown suspicious when she had returned home from Dartmouth with a gleam in her eye and treading on air. Mr Pepper's business was going badly through no fault of his own. There was a countrywide building slump which only the major companies survived. Perhaps this helped to turn him a touch paranoid about his beloved daughter and, in his efforts to protect her, he was determined to leave no stone unturned. He hired a Securicor agent and gave him a photograph of me which he found in Ginnie's room.

The agent soon established that a man named Andrews, definitely the man in the photograph, had stayed for three nights in the same Dartmouth hotel as Ginnie. Further enquiries among the chambermaids, a snoopy bunch, confirmed that Mr Andrews was believed to have spent a good deal of time in Miss Pepper's room; indeed, his bed had never been slept in at all.

Mr Pepper now had to face the unpalatable fact that his efforts to keep us apart were not proving successful, and that his daughter was nearly eighteen. He decided on the carrot-and-stick approach. The carrot consisted of telling Ginnie she could see me again with his blessing if she kept right away from me for the next six months. The stick involved the continued hire of a Securicor agent to dog Ginnie's footsteps and a telephone call to my commanding officer in Fallingbostel to reveal the entire tale of my predatory iniquity. Since Ginnie was well over the age of consent, my colonel clucked soothing noises at Mr Pepper and delivered me a mild scolding, during which he was unable to keep the twinkle from his eye.

In the autumn I was sent to Berlin for a month with my troop to man three tanks which, in the event of hostilities, were intended to repel the Warsaw Pact from Hitler's Olympic Stadium. While my tanks šivelled their guns about defiantly outside the giant arena, I sneaked into the empty Olympic swimming hall and dived off the high competition board, scaring myself silly in the process.

That winter my short service commission with the Greys was to end. I took and passed a lieutenant-to-captain promotion exam but was still, due to my Mons background, a second lieutenant, and my many months of adventure training rather than concentration on field training had not improved my qualifications.

I was about to apply for a one-year extension, the longest then allowed for someone in my position, when I spotted a three-line advertisement in regimental orders. 'Officers wishing to apply for secondment to the 22nd Special Air Service should obtain the relevant form from the Orderly Office.' Only a week before, I had listened spellbound to a Mess story of SAS patrols in Borneo, the only war zone where the British Army was still in action. Here was an open invitation to a three-year secondment with this little-known but élite regiment, after which I could apply to extend my commission with the Greys.

In November 1965, I was told to report to SAS headquarters the following January for a selection course, so I signed on with the Army for three years as a prospective SAS officer. During the intervening months it seemed sensible to de-cavalry myself. I found Corporal Jones, the only ex-SAS man I had ever met, and asked him how best to prepare myself. His response was a touch sarcastic but I extrapolated from his badinage the basic facts that map-reading and extreme fitness with a heavy backpack were important. He added, 'In Bavaria, you told me you hated heights. You're not going to be much use parachuting, are you?'

By chance a two-week course in parachuting was then available in the South of France and the colonel let me go at short notice. The parachute school was at Pau near Lourdes. A fellow French student explained that this was no accident. 'You see, those men who are crippled here at Pau can seek speedy recovery in the holy waters.'

I was the only non-Frenchman in a class of eighty would-be parachutists. The instructors for the most part spoke quickly and, to my ear, unintelligibly.

The first jump, from a Nord Atlas transport plane, was by day. I tried to cure my terror of heights by the simple method of keeping my eyes firmly closed as I threw myself into space. A few seconds after exit, my parachute opened and tugged my body harness up sharply between my legs, jamming my family jewels in a painful position. But at least the canopy had opened. I looked up expecting to see a neat array of rigging lines from my shoulders to the periphery of the silk chute. Instead there was a single knotted tangle of lines which met in a bunch behind my neck. I experienced instant panic. What could this mean? Surely I would be unable to control the lines for a safe landing? The ground was already uncomfortably close.

In fact I was merely experiencing a common problem called 'twists', usually caused by a poor exit from the aircraft. The instructors had probably explained 'les twistes' but I had failed to comprehend what they were saying. The normal process of elasticity slowly unwound the tangle but I was spinning like a top on landing and hit the ground with a wallop.

The next four jumps went well but the sixth and final sortie was a night jump which went awry for me, due, as before, to the language problem.

On the instructor's large diagram of the dropping zone was a watery feature which served for water-jump practice. We were taught in gymnasium simulators how to escape quickly from our parachute harnesses just prior to landing in water. I assumed the last jump was to be into the lake by night.

The night was moonless and cold as we leapt into space from 2000 feet. I peered down and soon spotted a dull, white surface which must be the lake. I headed directly for its centre and began the correct procedures, striking the heavy steel release so that only the grip of my right hand held me to the parachute harness. Trying to remember to let go as soon as I touched down, I in fact fell away from my chute what must have been a full second before I reached ground level. As I did so I realised my error. This was not the lake at all, merely a ground mist. That landing was the worst of my life. It seemed every bone in my body was dislocated and my tin helmet left a blue-black bruise on the bridge of my nose.

Next day Inspector-General de Quénetain pinned French parachute wings to the proud chests of eighty young Frenchmen and one bruised Brit.

I left the Royal Scots Greys in December, assuring my friends that I would be back in three years' time. After spending Christmas at home, I went to Dartmoor and the Brecon Hills and trained alone with a forty-pound backpack and Ordnance Survey map. Then, in early February, I drove to Bradbury Lines in Hereford and through a security gate to the SAS barracks, a battered huddle of low huts or 'spiders'.

Altogether 124 would-be troopers and twelve other officers, the youngest being three years my senior, congregated in the barracks for the selection month. For the first week, officers were tested separately. The first night's activities included a naked swim across the River Wye in temperatures below freezing. There was a great deal of map-reading and fast cross-country movement and very little sleep. Our packs weighed only thirty pounds, but this was soon to be increased.

SAS staff with binoculars seemed to be everywhere. Any form of cheating led to dismissal from the course. Two officers twisted their ankles on the third day and one decided he was not cut out for the SAS. Then there were ten of us. On the fourth day another fell by the wayside. I was selfishly delighted with each new drop-out for we all knew more than 90 per cent of applicants would be failed by the end of the month.

After a night in wet clothes tramping through woods without torches, we were ushered into a classroom and doled out question-sheets involving complex military problems. I never discovered how I fared at this test – which is perhaps just as well. That evening we missed tea and went feeling famished on a fifteen-mile night-march to reconnoitre an isolated reservoir.

Back in the classroom, both hungry and tired, we were questioned one at a time by an intimidating group of SAS veterans and senior officers including Major John Slim, son of Field Marshall Slim. Fortunately my short-term memory is good and I remembered every detail of the reservoir, down to water-height, construction materials and the type of countryside on all sides for over a mile away.

At 10.00 a.m. on the sixth day, I returned from a twenty-mile trudge over the Black Mountains to find a brown envelope on my bed – instructions to carry out a theoretical but detailed raid on a specific bank in Hereford and to brief the SAS staff on its execution by 6.00 p.m. that evening. I gauged that there were two hours in hand to grab some precious sleep, set my alarm and crashed out.

The alarm clock failed to rouse me, and the other candidates, each detailed to a different Hereford bank raid, naturally avoided waking me since their own chances of success would improve with my failure.

I woke at 2.00 p.m. and rushed down to the relevant bank. Too late, for it had closed an hour before. I knocked on a side window and shouted at the girl who appeared that I had an appointment with the manager. She must have decided my short haircut and tweed coat looked harmless, for she opened up and took me to the manager.

Thirty minutes later, after checking my passport, military ID card, German bank account and SAS course papers, as well as speaking to my London bank manager, he accepted that I genuinely wished to open an account. The only untrue frill that I added was the large amount of family silver I wished to store with him. He was quick to assure me how secure his bank was and thoughtfully explained the excellent alarm system.

I felt there were a number of devices I had not been shown but the SAS staff would surely not know everything. So I thanked the manager for his help and left to make detailed plans for the robbery, including a scale drawing of the bank rooms, offices and security devices which I had been shown.

The paper was ready on time and handed in to the staff. That evening was the only free period of the week so three of us drove to a nearby town for a mammoth meal. I had kept a carbon copy of the bank raid plans and this somehow slipped from my coat pocket in the restaurant. Later the Italian restaurateur, being a solid British citizen, reported the papers to the police.

The first I knew of this turn of events was upon reading the headlines of the national newspapers on the following day, 14 February. These included 'Big Bank Raid Mystery' and 'Ministry Enquiry into Bank Raid Scare'. Two days later the headlines had changed to the *Daily Mail*'s 'Army Initiative Upsets Police' and comments in *The Times* that 'the Services are letting their zeal outrun their discretion'.

A weekend-long security operation had stopped all police leave because every bank in Herefordshire had been surrounded, owing to the lack of a specific address on my plans. On Monday the correct bank manager was traced and all was revealed.

Future SAS selection courses no longer involved theoretical bank raids.

I was summoned before the SAS adjutant. It was instantly clear to me that he thought I had planted the plans in the restaurant out of misplaced mischief. This appealed to the SAS sense of humour so I received a warning but not dismissal. Had they known the plans had been misplaced, I would have been sent packing without delay.

By the end of the first week, at which point candidates of all ranks came together, seventy men and six officers remained. Week two saw the departure of forty more men and two officers. I was still around, a lot thinner and craftier.

The third week included a fully equipped run up and down the steep slopes of Pen-y-Fan three times in under eight hours. Each day involved not less than fifteen hours of marching, so sprains and blisters took a heavy toll. Finally, less than thirty applicants survived for the final test known as Long Drag. This was a forty-five-mile cross-country bash carrying a fifty-pound pack (checked without warning by staff), twelve-pound belt kit and eighteen-pound rifle without a sling. This exercise is the equivalent of three consecutive marathons when the steep terrain and the burdens carried are considered. If you take over twenty hours to finish you are failed. And sometimes, for no given reason, some of those who succeed are failed anyway.

During most of the selection course I moved alone for greater speed, but on Long Drag I set out with Captain Fleming, one of three other officer survivors. We decided that the only way we could beat the clock on this last dreadful test was to fool the SAS staff and to complete the whole course, from Pen-y-Fan onwards, by car. Since the observers were more alert on Long Drag than at any other time we would need to use prodigious cunning. We hired the services of a local farmer with a black Ford Anglia for the rest of the day and that night. Luckily the weather was truly foul, with non-stop driving sleet and pockets of mist.

At Pen-y-Fan we were lying sixth, about a mile behind a Scots Guards officer, the son of Britain's chief scout. We needed to maintain that position to avoid suspicion so, with adroit use of the Ford, binoculars and mist cover, we managed to arrive at isolated checkpoints, some of them several miles from the nearest feasible access point, always a mile behind Lieutenant MacLean.

I felt guilty afterwards but not badly so since subterfuge was very much an SAS tactic. I passed the selection, but, sadly, Fleming, who finished Long Drag alongside me, was failed.

In late February 1966 the SAS CO, Lieutenant-Colonel Mike Wingate Gray, awarded three officers and twelve men their buff-coloured SAS berets and sea-blue stable-belts. Since all SAS officers are ranked captain or above I missed out the rank of lieutenant and became the youngest captain in the Army at that time. But not for long. 'Pride came,' in the words of my CO, 'before a bloody great fall.'

* * *

'You are not in yet,' Staff Sergeant Brummy Burnett warned us, 'so don't get cocky.'

He was understating the facts. The selection course proved merely a warm-up to the next four months of intensive training. Mental stress took over from physical toil and a moment's carelessness could undo all the previous effort. A Maltese ex-sergeant was dismissed two months into this period of 'continuation training'. I asked Brummy why. 'Cocky, wasn't he?' was the only reply.

Three of the best men fell down a cliff-side one pitch-black night and all were seriously injured. The eleven survivors of the initial 136 entrants were treated no less delicately as time went by. It seemed the authorities would care not a jot if the whole batch were eventually to fail.

Over the weeks we picked up eight personal skills which were basic to any beginner sent out to join his first SAS unit. Fast response shooting-to-kill, static line parachuting in six-man 'sticks', demolition, signals using Morse, resistance to interrogation, CQB (close-quarter battle), field medicine and field survival techniques. Failure in any one of these separate subjects was not permitted.

The CQB included self-defence against an assailant with knife, pistol or blunt instrument, and in each case we learned a two-step response again and again until our movements were karate quick. Get it wrong and the other man, an SAS staffer, made certain you paid for it. I was black and blue with bruises by the end of the week. The first step of each response instantly disarmed and the second disabled, often permanently.

Field medicine was not my favourite subject as I became squeamish easily and was afraid I would faint at the sight of the gruesome colour slides of gut and eye wounds. Some of the lecturers were fresh back from Borneo and taught us only such practical tips as we were likely to find useful.

'When your mate's shot, treat him for shock. Give him liquid if you have it except when the bullet enters between nipple and knee. Don't forget that, 'cos a bullet going in above the knee might end up in the stomach and the poor feller won't want liquid then, will he now?'

The colour slide would then flip from perforated intestines to a smashed mouth. 'Now, lads, what if your mate cops it through the jaw? What then? Often as not bits of bone and other such crap will end up down his windpipe and choke him . . . Right? Got the picture? OK, so you get your spoon and you fish the muck out. If that's no good, then slit his throat neatly just below the jolly old Adam's apple and stick a tube in to by-pass the obstruction. A biro casing will do. Then he'll breathe like a baby. No problem.'

The next slide showed a sight which is hard to believe until first seen – the pressure of blood escaping from a severed artery. 'Ahh,' said our medic, looking up with enthusiasm. 'Yes . . . We must not forget the main arteries, must we? When one of them goes, you act fast.' He screamed the word at us. 'No time to think. If you can't catch and splice the loose ends to stop 'em spurting, then grab your field dressing and burn it. Cram the ashes in the open wound then bind it hard and bind it fast. Forget all that claptrap about tourniquets. That went out with rock 'n' roll.'

Signals training began in sound booths until we were Morse proficient to five words per minute and knew the basic Q and Z codes by heart. Then, on all field exercises, we were expected to communicate to Hereford HQ from wherever we happened to be in the British Isles. The transmitter and receiver sets fitted easily into the two hip pockets of a combat jacket. Morse was no longer in use in most of the Army but with the primitive SAS gear we could transmit quick bursts of coded message thousands of miles with little likelihood of direction-finding equipment locating our positions.

Our shoot-to-kill training was supervised by Brummy Burnett who was recently returned from jungle confrontations with Indonesian special forces. Most days he took us to a nearby range with standard FN rifles or the light Armalites much favoured in Vietnam. 'When you meet the enemy in jungle it is normally head-on. The two opposing lead scouts will probably see each other at the same moment. Then it is who reacts first that counts.'

Brummy's demonstration belied his 250 pounds. As an electric target snapped up in the bushes ahead, Brummy's fingers instantly clicked forward the safety catch and squeezed off a single round in the rough direction of the target. As he did this, he dropped to one knee and, within a second of the first unaimed shot, had fired a second bullet which, on subsequent inspection, invariably hit target centre. Nowadays Brummy sells insurance, but I would still not wish to cross him on a dark night.

Other sergeants taught us demolition, from the mathematics of fuse-burning rates to the tensile strengths of suspension bridge targets. We demolished old buildings, steel girders, railway tracks and pear trees, and by the end of three weeks I possessed a boot-full of detonators, fuse wire and plastic explosive, the result of demolishing my set targets with less than the issued amounts. I should of course have returned this volatile booty to the stores but I did not. My motives were acquisitive rather than criminal. I did not intend to blow up anything in particular but fancied the notion that I had the capacity to do so, given a suitable target.

I later stored the explosives in old biscuit tins and buried them by the river at home . . . for a rainy day.

Survival skills were taught by a tiny Welsh corporal who slit the throat of a sheep on our classroom table and watched over us as we skinned the animal, dug out its entrails and boiled the mutton. None of the meat was wasted and he stressed that no sign or scent of the butchery must remain. He allotted each of us a gorse patch near Sennybridge and let us loose with a dozen rabbit snares apiece. We boiled and drank various liquid stews containing nettles, worms, grubs, grasses, mushrooms and berries. Theft from farms in winter, leaving no trace of our visit or, if necessary, making it appear that hen coop deprivations were in fact the work of foxes, were dealt with in minute detail. At the end of the Welshman's week, I felt confident of surviving anywhere short of the Gobi Desert.

Resistance to interrogation was taught alongside escape and evasion, and nobody passed that two-week course who was not in a peak state of fitness. The distances travelled by day and night were greater than Long Drag though the weight carried was less. Navigation needed to be spot on. The only rations issued for days would be a pair of live broiler chickens left at some obscure contour line miles from anywhere. Should a fox reach the chickens before you did there was nothing for it but to curse, carry on and wonder whether you had in fact misread the coded signal giving the chickens' grid reference.

Our faded SAS smocks, combat trousers and camouflage-pattern scarves, together with a quickly cultivated expertise in moving at all times in whatever cover was available, made us difficult to locate. Capture by the staff or the RAF regiment soldiers whose job it was to find us was a serious sign of poor operational procedures. We never slept under any sort of cover, whatever the weather. Barns, ruins, copses, even outcrops of gorse were strictly off bounds since these were the places which were first to be searched. Instead we rested, always by day and as little as possible, in low reedbeds or shallow clumps of heather with just enough cover to protect us from helicopter surveillance.

Soggy boots were removed only long enough to wring out socks and apply foot powder. Bergen backpacks were kept full and ready for instant flight. A waterproof camouflaged groundbag was the most important item and a metal mug for boiling in and drinking from. We never slept close to streams for they too would be obvious search-lines for patrols.

No single item of gear gleamed or stood out. Maps were stashed in green-drab, watches carried in pockets or under black wrist covers and faces blotched with cam-cream and filth. Tea was boiled only in deep cover using a hexamin block which gives off minimal smoke. Any form of wood fire was taboo.

In fourteen days, moving through hundreds of miles of open Welsh countryside between fixed checkpoints, none of us was even glimpsed by the troops detailed to locate us.

Signalled instructions caused us to come together into three groups of three or four which, at separate specific timings, were to 'infiltrate and sabotage' the isolated nuclear power station at Trawsfynydd. After a two-day forced march my group found itself three miles from our goal with only half an hour in hand before our required target-entry time. One of our patrol, a little Scots paratrooper, noticed on his map that a single-track quarry rail curved up the mountainside towards the power station. This could save time so we ignored the standing rule never to follow obvious routes and jogged up the narrow gauge line.

In the gloom I almost tripped over a rail-trolley parked on the line. Hardly believing our luck, we placed our weapons, demolition packs and bergens in the centre of the trolley and climbed on to the tiny platform, two to each end and facing inwards. Each man held on to the centrally pivoting crank-handle and pumped it energetically back and forth. We climbed the rail at a good pace until a solid-looking chock lever blocked our further advance. Picking the trolley up bodily, we put it back on the rails above the lever and continued up the steep gradient to the terminal buffers near the power station.

We stealthily avoided the security guards, whose patrol timings we had memorised two weeks earlier along with the labyrinthine layout of the power station. Then we retired, thankful to be rid of the heavy demolition packs, by a different route.

Although we did not know it then, one of the other two groups, who laid their charges an hour later, decided to leave the area quickly by means of the rail-line. They too found the trolley and set off downhill at a very fast, indeed almost uncontrollable, pace. Alas, they spotted the chock lever too late and hit it hard. The four men, their bergens and rifles were catapulted into the air and came to rest over a wide area of bushes and heather.

Later that night we were ordered to meet an 'agent' by a cottage. A Land Rover then drove us into a trap and a large body of Irish Fusiliers detained us with another captive group in a derelict farmhouse.

Stripped to our underpants and handcuffed in a long line, the hours ticked by slowly in bouts of frantic shivering. To maintain body temperature we lay on the concrete floor in a closely huddled heap, each man praying he would not have to pee. Nonetheless, from time to time some poor sod gave in to the urge and then all eight of us rose up cursing his guts as we shuffled to the far corner where a bucket stood half-full of frozen urine. Twice the current offender stood over the bucket and desperately tried to pee. Nothing happened for embarrassment had overcome the earlier urge – until, that was, we were all once more back on our cold concrete bed.

The interrogations which followed were beneficial to Britain's small band of professional military interrogators, for they were able to use techniques far closer to war conditions than they could with standard troops. Part of the process of degrading the prisoner was total nudity except for a blindfold and an anal search for such contraband as a button compass or miniature fire-stick.

Next our group was sent to Abingdon airfield near Oxford for a standard parachute course under RAF sergeants. The training was similar to my French experience, but different in that this time I could understand the instructors. This served to undermine, not – as I had hoped – to increase my confidence, since for the first time I learned the many dreadful things which could go fatally wrong should a student fail to follow instructions.

Initial jumps were made from a wicker basket beneath a balloon tethered 800 feet up, in many ways more unpleasant than from an aircraft because the ascent and the waiting are more cold-blooded. You feel the void more closely. But for the wind in the rigging everything is silent, and every creak of the basket, each comment from your colleagues, makes you more nervous. Jumping from a transport plane, your body is swept sideways in the 120-mile-per-hour slipstream. From a balloon you plummet straight downwards.

The British used Hercules C130 transport aircraft, which were different from the French Nord Atlas, so I re-learned the exit techniques. On my seventh jump, prior to gaining the much coveted SAS wings, I felt an uneasy pain in my stomach and visited the camp medic. A blood test revealed that I had glandular fever and my spleen was swollen.

'No more jumping for you,' said the medic. 'In fact you are a lucky man. Any sharp jolt to a swollen spleen is liable to burst it, which causes the speedy internal loss of five pints of blood. The quickest way of bleeding to death without any outward mess that I know. You must go straight home and rest until you lose all signs of the fever.'

The SAS reacted predictably. Despite my French course and seven Abingdon jumps, I had not completed the British course and so must take it again once recovered. Then in July I would join the others for a six-week jungle training course in Brunei and Malaya.

At home my various glands swelled up in picturesque fashion and I fretted in bed with the blinds drawn against strong sunlight. I longed to slip out of bed after dark and to visit Ginnie but it was painful to walk. Ginnie had three months previously spent a month in bed with glandular fever and, since we had seen each other by night during my rare free weekends away from Hereford, I assumed I had caught the fever from her.

Her father, an artiste at blowing hot and cold, now decided Ginnie could officially see me again, not that he was aware there had been any unofficial meetings. I was delighted and surprised when my mother, who had always liked Ginnie, announced a surprise guest and ushered her into my room. She wore a light summer frock with a fashionably high hemline which can't have been good for my swollen glands.

'I picked these for you in the wood.' She gave me a bunch of late spring daffodils. She was no longer the little girl that I had loved for so long. At nineteen Ginnie was tall, shapely and much sought after by a number of eligible West Sussex suitors. While in Hereford I had kept wary tabs on my competitors through Gubbie, now the manager of an antique shop in Midhurst.

For the first time I was able to take Ginnie out and about openly. As soon as I could walk and my strength began to return, I drove her to the Rex cinema in Haslemere and afterwards to the George Hotel for dinner. At this and subsequent outings things were somehow awkward between us for the first time. We found little to talk about to fill the long silences.

Until now the fascination of our covert rendezvous, the possibility of discovery and the hostility of her father had all added spice to our assignations. Long separations had always ended in whispered nights of passion and increasing sensuality, as our adolescence matured with passing time and our needs and awareness grew more demanding. But now, confronted with the normality of an orthodox young-man-dates-girl affair, we were each reduced to a more honest reappraisal of the other. Now we must get to know each other on a less exhilarating plane. It was a testing time and a flicker of warning for the future.

By the end of May I was back at Abingdon for another parachute course. Then, awaiting the jungle course in Malaya, old habits unfortunately took hold like an addiction. With Michael Denny and other old 'climbing' friends, I drove down to Eton in an old 2.8 Jaguar.

David Benedictus, ex-captain of Mr Parr's House, had recently published a controversial book about Eton – *The Fourth of June*. I decided to hoist him to the top of School Hall wrapped in a blanket and flagged with the inscription '*Malescriptus Benedictus*'. Elaborate plans to lure him to Eton by taxi came to nothing, so Denny and I merely hoisted a standard dustbin for old time's sake. Then we walked through the fields to the Brocas where we donned frogsuits and underwater apparatus. Helped by the others we laid a 300-foot length of rope underwater, opposite the grandstand seats erected in readiness for the festivities the following night.

We pegged both ends of the rope to the river bottom, then swam to Luxmore's Island where, beneath the cover of weeping willows, we cached our underwater gear.

Next day we wandered the standard festivities alongside hundreds of other old boys and proud parents and, at the right moment that evening, our small group parted from the ambling throng and slipped into swimming costumes. An obliging girlfriend took our clothes to the boots of our cars parked on a nearby cricket field. Nobody worried when three of us began to swim around, for the evening was hot and close. Soon, unnoticed, we disappeared beneath the willows of the island.

At length, as the river banks on either side filled with the audience of thousands, floodlights focussed on the river. There came a great hush from the watchers as the first boat of the night procession appeared from upstream. The treble tones of the cox sounded and, one by one, the colourfully clad crew of eight stood up on their seats, lifted their oars to the vertical and, shakily, doffed their hats towards the grandstand VIPs. Then, greatly relieved, they sank back to their seats and rowed off. Unseen, we submerged at that point and made for the tethered line.

The crowds on both banks, whether Etonians or general public, had one thing in common, apart from wanting to see the fireworks at the end of the evening; that was to watch a boat or two overbalance and soak their precious little occupants.

Then it happened.

Another eight had arrived and raised its oars when the boat gave a sudden lurch. Its crew teetered, striving to fend off disgrace – but too late. Straw boaters bobbed like ducks and the crowds roared their approval. Sounds of 'bravo' and 'encore' only died away when the next boat appeared as though nothing had happened. No one was worried since the boats could not sink and all the occupants were strong swimmers. Once they reached the edge of the floodlit area they were picked up by waiting rescue boats. Then, to the enormous delight of the watchers, the second boat tipped over and, just when excited parents were whispering that nothing like this had happened since the 1920s, an uproar announced the dunking of yet another crew.

Careful observers then witnessed a strange happening. Amid the flotsam of straw boaters a black shiny head like that of a seal popped up and began to swim hastily away from the floodlights. A rowing boat crewed by schoolmasters spotted the seal and, angrily, gave chase.

All had been going well and I had just been relieved by a fellow frogman when, with no warning, my breathing apparatus went haywire and tried to force air, compressed to 160 pounds per square inch, straight into my lungs. I shot to the surface and soon found myself fleeing from a rowing boat, the crew of which included my old schoolmaster, Dave Callender. He did not recognise me through my facemask but, to avoid capture on reaching the bank, I abandoned the cumbersome air bottle and fled the hue and cry which followed me over the nearby field and under the friendly gloom of Fifteen Arch Bridge. With seconds to spare I dropped into the stagnant pool beside the arches and lay there submerged as my pursuers rushed by in full cry.

A nasty thought crossed my mind as I lay in the mud. The oxygen bottle I had abandoned on the far riverbank was stamped with a serial number and it belonged to Ginnie. The police would track me down easily once they found the bottle.

I sneaked via shadows to the Jaguar and tore off my wetsuit. Dressed as before, I drove fast over Windsor Bridge then left along the road to Windsor Locks. A glance at the river bank revealed a new problem. The bottle was not on this bank at all; it lay on the far side of a long, narrow island in mid-river.

Perhaps a bridge connected island and lock station. Groups of people strolled with torches along the riverbanks on their way to watch the fireworks which were due to start in half an hour. I ran to the lock-keeper who said there was no way to the island but by boat. At that moment a powerful searchlight swept over us.

'That's the river police launch. Why don't you hitch a lift with them?' He was joking, but he gave me an idea. The police were heading slowly downstream, combing both banks with their searchlight. In minutes they would spot the bottle. The lock-keeper lent me his torch, a powerful four-battery affair, and I flashed the launch with urgent signals. The helmsman responded instantly and nudged the bank with the bows of his launch.

I jumped aboard and, producing my most Etonian accent, explained to the police captain that Dave Callender and Chiefey, the head Eton river-man, had sent me over to collect an oxygen bottle which they had spotted abandoned by the fleeing frogman. No questions were asked and the bottle soon appeared in the searchlight beam. 'Shall we drop you on the Eton bank?' the captain asked after we had retrieved the material evidence. I shuddered at the thought of the police launch and Dave Callender's boat meeting in mid-river.

'Thanks, but my car is on this side. I'll take the bottle back to Mr Callender by road.'

They dropped me back at the lock where I returned the torch and, once in the dark, fled as though chased by devils.

Social trends and the cost of the fireworks that followed the boat procession meant this was the last year of the traditional ceremony but at least we had helped the final night procession to be a memorable one.

Why, I now ask myself, did I do these things? Out of rebellion against the system? For the pleasure of seeing authority fall on its face? Revenge after the bad years at Eton? None of these possible motives strikes me as remotely accurate. My only explanation is that of sheer devilment as congenital, inevitable and unfortunate as an inherited malady. I am not trying to excuse my behaviour since most of us are born with devils of one sort or another and if they are anti-social we struggle to quash them. Obviously I failed to struggle hard enough.

*   *   *

Later that hot glorious June I was asked by my old Eton friend, William Knight, to join a party for an annual charity banquet in Bath. There would be sheep's eyes and belly dancers so I accepted.

After the banquet William made an unusual proposal. I was due to fly to Malaya with an SAS squadron for jungle training on the morning of Monday, 27 June, on the very same day an unfortunate event, as William described it, would upset the tranquillity of rural Wiltshire. William was responsible for supplying wines to the pub in the picturesque village of Castle Combe, between Bath and Chippenham. He had overheard locals in the bar there complaining bitterly of the damage being suffered by their village at the hands of the American film company 20th Century–Fox, who would begin shooting a film that same morning.

William was not alone in objecting to the abuse of Castle Combe, recently voted by the British Travel Association as 'the prettiest village in England'. The Royal Fine Arts Commission had attacked the local county council for allowing the film-makers to alter such 'an exceptional English village'.

William's aim was to publicise the depredations of the moguls by disrupting their first day of filming. *The Adventures of Doctor Dolittle*, starring Rex Harrison and Samantha Eggar, was centred around a rustic pond, complete with plastic fish, constructed by damming up a trout stream that meandered through the village centre. 'The dam,' William explained, 'is made entirely of sandbags and will be easy to destroy. Unfortunately Fox are aware of local feeling and maintain a twenty-four-hour Securicor patrol around the filmset.' William's plan involved a diversion to draw away the security men and their dogs for long enough to allow him and a friend to destroy the dam. With no lake, there could be no Puddleby-on-the-Marsh, home town of Dr Dolittle, and therefore no filming.

To ensure publicity William asked me to leak his plot to a friendly journalist. To provide a diversion, I could utilise some of my explosives. We would be striking a blow for Old England since, if successful, the ensuing publicity would cause an uproar among conservationists and Fox would be forced to restore the village to its former rustic charms.

I phoned a freelance journalist acquaintance, Gareth Jones, a part-time trooper in the 21st SAS Territorial Regiment, naïvely assuming that all SAS men would be loyal to one another. He agreed to go to Castle Combe on the night in question to record on camera whatever might happen there. He would tell no one until after the event, at which point he would release his photos and blazon his story across all the dailies. He must of course forget the source of his tip-off.

Jones decided he would do better financially by shopping me and the others to the *Daily Mirror*. The *Mirror* in turn decided it was their duty to inform the police, which they did late on the Sunday evening. The police telephoned my mother and asked her to have me cancel whatever plans I might be nursing for an imminent disturbance of the peace. But by then I had left home bound for Bath, and my poor mother, although she tried hard, could not contact me. So the police ringed Castle Combe with patrol cars at each of the access lanes and sent more constables to the village.

Quite unaware of this reception committee I drove to William's cottage and parked my Jaguar facing downhill, a necessary precaution since the car would not start without a push or two. It was not a good getaway vehicle.

After a meal and last-minute plans, the four of us, three wine importers and one SAS officer, departed for the Puddleby dam. We left our cars in a pub car park two miles from Castle Combe and walked across country towards the dam, unwittingly circumventing the police checkpoints.

William headed for the dam itself while Ben Howkins and I laid plastic explosives and petrol flares with time fuses at three strategic points around the village. Designed to shoot ten-foot-high flames into the night air at fifteen-minute intervals, the flares should lure the security men well away from the dam.

Once the fuses were lit, we withdrew to the wall of the dam to help William, but no sooner had I set foot on the first sandbag than a shout went up from the darkness of the far bank, closely followed by a pandemonium of excited cries and canine joy.

Having but recently learned all there is to know about evading capture by various types of hound, I jumped immediately into the stream beside the bank, and submerged all but mouth and nostrils. The water was too shallow for swimming: the dam saw to that. So I trudged cautiously south along the waterway until it passed beneath the London-to-Chippenham road. Approaching my Jaguar from the bushes behind the car park I found that Ben's car was gone. He must have escaped the police. But William's Mini was still in the park and, since my Jaguar would start only with a good tow, I must wait for him. Meanwhile I changed into smart clothes, dried my hair and waited in the bushes.

William did not turn up but a police car did, sliding quietly and without lights into a corner of the park. After twenty minutes with no William and no movement from the police I decided I must make a move or I would miss the plane to Malaya. Retiring up the lane some distance, I then approached the park whistling and, after surveying the dimly lit cars, spotted the police and went over to them. There were two officers and, when I hailed them, one put a finger to his lips. In a low voice I explained my car would not start and could they kindly give me a tow-start. Realising that their ambush would be better off without my presence, they agreed.

'Which car is yours, sir?' the driver asked. I pointed at my Jaguar.

'You must be Captain Fiennes, then.' It was a statement not a query. 'I think you had better come with us.'

I was only later aware of Jones's treachery but the game was quite obviously up, whatever the reason, so I decided to cut my losses. Time-wise there were two flares as yet undetonated so I told the police and, with them, defused both devices. They drove me to Chippenham Police Station where I spent the night in a clean and well-appointed cell with William as my neighbour. They recorded our fingerprints, photographed our faces and gave us cups of pre-sugared tea. The blow we had struck for Old England was not appreciated by the local law. Next day we were released on bail of £100 apiece.

My mother had spent the previous night in London with a friend doing church work, unaware quite why the police had called her. She learned the answer on the mid-day train from Waterloo to Haslemere when she read to her growing horror the headlines of her fellow passengers' newspapers: 'Bomber Baronet captured in Prettiest Village'. Somehow she made it home to Lodsworth before fainting on the sitting room floor.

An Army bomb disposal unit in two Land Rovers, red and green with blue flasher beacons, drove me to Lodsworth to retrieve the rest of my pyrotechnics supply. I had admitted to having buried biscuit tins full of plastic explosive and detonators in the local bog and the authorities wanted them as evidence.

I blanched at the thought of what my mother's neighbours would say at the sight of the Land Rovers, military police sergeants and demolition men parked in our lane, the nearest vehicle access point to the relevant bog. Then I realised my escort would not know the lay-out of our woods so I directed the little convoy to the Halfway Bridge pub between Midhurst and Petworth and walked them through a mile and a half of swamp until we reached the quagmire where my tins were hidden.

The bog was in fact a mere six-minute walk from my mother's house but the soldiers did not complain. The chief engineer decided the explosives, which were sweating freely, were far too dangerous to move and must be detonated *in situ*. On his instructions I left the bog, having assured him there were no more tins, and walked home to face my mother. When I reached our lane I heard voices and hid behind the hedge. It was our neighbour Hariette Hurst and a friend. As they approached, the ground shook to a major explosion from the direction of the woods. 'Glory be!' exclaimed Mrs Hirst. 'That must be young Sir Ranulph back from the Army and up to his tricks again.'

I found my mother in bed and only then did the full gravity of my situation sink in. She was ill with the worry and shame of it all. I loved her dearly and yet I was hurting her as she had never been hurt before. I swore then and there that I would never again do anything to worry or shame her.

She contacted a neighbour, Bryan Walter, who was prosecutor for Hampshire. He agreed to act as barrister in my defence against the public prosecutor. He warned my mother as gently as he could that I was to be prosecuted at the next Salisbury Assizes on six different charges, just one of which, should I be found guilty, held a minimum gaol sentence of seven years. The charges included malicious damage and the theft and possession of explosives. Quite apart from these civil charges, my military career was in danger. I realised, watching my mother's worried face, that at the very least I would no longer achieve my dearest wish. The Royal Scots Greys might not want a convicted arsonist for their commanding officer.

6

Hopeless Love

Those eyes of deep, soft, lucent hue–
Eyes too expressive to be blue,
Too lovely to be grey.

MATTHEW ARNOLD

The first blow, although expected, came only a week after the Castle Combe incident. I was expelled from the SAS and at the same time demoted to second lieutenant.

I drove to Keil's Antique Shop in Midhurst and drank coffee in the cluttered backroom with Gubbie. He was relieved that for once he had not been involved. William Knight and the others had been sacked from their jobs.

'What will you do,' he asked, 'if they find you guilty at the Assizes?'

'Go to jail, I suppose,' I replied with forced bravado, 'and learn to pick locks.'

'I mean afterwards. When they let you out after a few months for good behaviour.'

'Difficult to say. There's no Fiennes family business and I have no qualifications. An ability to attack Soviet forces with sixty-ton tanks is not highly sought after in most jobs.' I lapsed into gloomy silence.

Gubbie was as always constructive. 'Self-employment is the only answer and you must set something up now, before Her Majesty detains you – if she does.'

Lengthy discussions ensued, interrupted only by the occasional antique hunter, and a five-year plan evolved entailing the formation of a limited company. With Gubbie and I as £1 share owners and directors, we set this up right away through a local accountant and soon afterwards we bought a two-acre bog in Inverness-shire. As soon as I emerged from prison I would begin work on our Highlands Adventure Training School with Scots Greys ex-troopers, preferably my old tank crew, as instructors. I felt much better, ready to face the worst.

There were no more Wiltshire Assizes until October so I was kept in suspense four months. During that period my mother received letters of sympathy from friends and relatives, which only served to rub in her sense of shame. My probation officer visited her and told her that I would be sent to Ford Open Prison, not to a closed penitentiary. As far as he was concerned, the fact that I had not yet been found guilty was irrelevant. I had committed arson on public property and used high explosives. There could be no doubt about the outcome.

Since the Army was still paying my salary and had no wish to waste their money, new orders arrived with a temporary posting to the 14th/20th Hussars, a tank regiment garrisoned at Perham Down in Wiltshire.

I did not see Ginnie at all while with the Hussars. She was another casualty of the Castle Combe affair. The day after my arrest Mr Pepper had summoned Ginnie from her secretarial job in Midhurst in a fury. A month before there had been a major theft of dynamite from his chalk quarry in Amberley. He put two and two together and made five. Either Ginnie or I had removed the dynamite which, as he heard misreported on the BBC news, had been used to blow up a dam at Castle Combe. Now he was desperately worried that the police would trace the explosives to his Amberley stock and arrest his daughter. The obvious answer was to send Ginnie abroad beyond the long arm of the law. A young cousin of Ginnie's was working in Spain, so Mr Pepper made instant arrangements to pack Ginnie off to Madrid for at least a year. She was to teach English to the children of a wealthy porcelain manufacturer.

Informing Ginnie of her imminent exile, her father warned her under no circumstances to contaminate herself further by even telephoning me. He then rang my mother and frightened her with dire consequences should I try to contact his daughter again. Our long-lived affair was to be over once and for all. Much concerned about my mother's health, I assured her I would stop seeing Ginnie at once. When, two nights after the débâcle, Ginnie phoned me with her news about Madrid, I explained my own dilemma caused by her father's threats and my mother's health. She must know I loved her but I could not risk killing my mother. For the next year we must not see each other, so perhaps her exile would be the best thing for both of us. Ginnie wept bitterly. I knew I was the worst sort of rat: I had made the two people I most loved miserable.

'When I am away,' I said to Gubbie, 'please be sure to look after Ginnie.' He assured me that he would. I was fortunate to have a cousin who was also a trustworthy friend.

On 5 October 1966, together with my three co-conspirators, I appeared at the guildhall in Salisbury to attend the case of *Regina*, in the person of Mr Justice Nield, *versus Fiennes, Knight, Howkins and Fraser*. My barrister, Bryan Walter, had taken on the services of Sir Peter Rawlinson, QC, to appear on my behalf. Witnesses for the prosecution included various police officers and the commanding officer of the 22nd SAS Regiment. Judge Nield listened carefully to the evidence, and then sentenced us.

'The Court is satisfied that none of you intended or desired any hurt or injury to anyone . . . but the use of explosives is indefensible . . . It is clear to me beyond any sort of doubt that my public duty does not require the imposition of a prison sentence . . .' The rest of the sentence was lost on me for an intense surge of relief was succeeded by a feeling of euphoria. I had been expecting a prison sentence and merely hoping for a shorter rather than a longer one. Immensely grateful to the law in general and to old Judge Nield, Sir Peter Rawlinson and Bryan Walter in particular, I swore to myself that I would never again act illegally.

My fines, on three separate counts, totalled £500, plus court costs of £450. Together with the £700 fee for Sir Peter Rawlinson, I had frittered away one-quarter of my entire worldly wealth, the capital held in trust for me following the death of my grandmother Florrie, in the course of a single night's activity.

Put in the economic context of the day, I could have purchased a brand-new E-Type Jaguar and fuelled it for a year for the money I paid out as a result of the Castle Combe attack.

Immediate reactions to the Assizes were mixed. The media made hay again, raking up various dramatic descriptions of the original events. The *Daily Express* headlines proclaimed, 'The Four Just Men are Fined'. *Time* magazine used the title 'Muddle in Puddleby'. David Frost, alluding to my hyphenated surname, referred to me as TW3 which was also the nickname of his popular programme *That Was The Week That Was*. Public reactions, especially from local inhabitants, as indicated by my mailbag, were all on our side. Comments such as 'Regret to read you are the victims of gross rough justice' and a £10 cheque with the scribbled comment 'A savage sentence – Allow me to help' were typical. One £5 cheque was enclosed with a note, 'I am all on your side. Good show', signed Terence Alan Patrick Milligan, alias Spike. Fifteen years later I accosted the great goon himself at a TV Breakfast Show but he had forgotten the event.

More apposite to my worries about the Army council was a letter from General Sir John Hackett, then commander-in-chief of BAOR, which included the sentence, 'Let me only add, looking into the not too far distant past, that I followed certain events in Castle Combe with the greatest interest, having had some fishing on that water a few years previously.'

To my great relief, soon after the Assizes, I was ordered to report back to the Royal Scots Greys in Fallingbostel. The commanding officer, John Stanier, could easily have refused my return, especially since the Army council had as yet made no decision on my future. I will always remain grateful to him for accepting me back.

So I left the Hussars and the comparatively idle life of soldiering in Britain to return to Fallingbostel and the same old tank troop of Scratch Sherville and Zeebo Stevens.

Things had altered. Colonel Stanier was the most feared and respected CO in the cavalry. He checked the tiniest detail and forgot nothing. He expected dedication and efficiency and was ruthless with the most senior officer or the newest recruit when they let the regiment down. Poor Paddy Earp, the Grubscrew, fell foul of the colonel when his three tanks became bogged during a divisional exercise and, worse still, his troop lost radio contact for several hours with the rest of their squadron. Paddy was posted away from the Greys.

Luckily for me, the colonel realised that a peace-time regiment needs success in sport as well as in its military role, so I was encouraged to resurrect the canoe club, the *langlauf* ski team and other competitive groups. That Christmas leave, with Gubbie, two Scots Greys lieutenants and a girlfriend named Vanda, I went skiing in Aviemore. Gubbie was by then in frequent correspondence with Ginnie and, when she next returned from Madrid, he told her I was no longer interested in her but was carrying on with Vanda. He was correct as far as Vanda was concerned but not about my lack of interest in Ginnie. Ginnie was left in no doubt as to the truth of Gubbie's assessment when William Hickey's *Daily Express* gossip column announced that Vanda and I were officially engaged and on holiday in St Moritz. We had spent a week in that ski resort and, on the way back to England, my Jaguar's engine had blown up so we had hitchhiked the rest of the way. There was no question of an engagement save in the Mitty minds of the Hickey columnists. But the damage was done.

On her holidays from Madrid, Ginnie would often visit Gubbie at his cottage in Treyford beneath the South Downs where she and I had met for many a happy tryst.

They liked each other. That I knew, for we had long been three close friends. But now I feared they might become more than friends and I had nobody but myself to blame. Gubbie was behaving quite openly and hiding nothing from me. I had after all asked him to look after her, and I had instigated the separation from Ginnie, whatever the reason. This did not stop me from being consumed with jealousy and misery in faraway Fallingbostel. But the memory of my mother, grey with worry and humiliation, was still too fresh for me to chase after Ginnie, although I had no doubt at all but that she was properly mine. Throughout the winter of 1966 I tore myself apart thinking that Ginnie and Gubbie might be growing close or, when she was in

Madrid, who her dark, handsome friends might be. Whether or not my fears were based in fact made no difference.

I took my worries out on the Jocks in my teams, cajoling and bullying them on to ever greater efforts and longer training sessions in their spare time. Since all were volunteers I had to limit my zeal according to their individual interest in the relevant sport. If I went too far, they would simply resign, but many were as keen as I to win. The squadron boxing team collected the annual trophy, the regimental orienteering team won the divisional cup, the cross-country running team easily took the brigade championships. In the summer, after three weeks' hard training on the Rhone, our tourer-canoe team were outright winners of the BAOR Cup and in the process beat all but one of the racing-canoe class, despite the thirty pounds difference in craft weight. The Jocks involved were all original members of the Canoe Club with four active summers and many river journeys behind them.

That August I spent my three-week leave on an unusual project in Norway. Simon Gault had not forgotten our unsuccessful canoe journey with Maggie Rayner. He had recovered from his frustrated love affair with her and was keen to try another journey in the rugged Jotunheim. This time our plan was to follow an ancient cattle trail or *drift* over Europe's largest glacier, the Jostedalsbre, in Central Jotunheim, then to canoe down the glacial waste-waters to the east. Three Scots Greys officers agreed to accompany us and so did Vanda.

To start the journey we agreed to save valuable days of leave by cheating. We would hitch a lift on a charter plane and parachute onto the 8000-foot-high glacial plateau with all our gear. Sergeant Don Hughes, a founder member of the SAS free-fall parachute team and a pioneer of the sport in Britain, agreed to 'throw us out at the right moment' so we would stand a good chance of avoiding the 6000-foot cliffs which rim the plateau.

The drop went as planned: although no one was injured the experience was decidedly hairy. But other aspects of the journey failed. We did not follow the complete course of the cattle trail because the combination of heavy packs, altitude and thick snow proved too much for some. Only Simon accompanied me on the thirty-mile hike down the Faberg Glacier and on to the fount of the eastern river system. Finally the rivers were too rough for our canoes, which were all smashed to bits. I learned on that little journey to lead by physical example rather than rhetoric and also to choose, for challenging endeavours, a selection of chiefs and Indians, not a gaggle of the former. A by-product of the trip was a good deal of coverage in the Norwegian press, all of it favourable to the British Army. I was awarded the brigade Tie of Merit, a sure sign of forgiveness for previous sins and a welcome boost for further regimentally-based expedition plans.

The distractions of canoes, parachutes and skis did nothing to alleviate the background knowledge that Ginnie no longer loved me. Her absence from my life left a vacuum which confronted me daily except in moments of intense physical competition. Then one day in late August, over a year since we had last spoken, she telephoned me in Fallingbostel. My throat dried up and words deserted me. How was she? She was well. And me? Fine, thanks. I thought she sounded hoarse and hoped desperately love had made her nervous too.

In a while she came to the point in a simple fashion. Gubbie had written to her to ask if he could come to Madrid and stay with her for a week. She presumed I did not mind this but thought it best to check.

The long year of emptiness ended for me at that moment. All my fears that Ginnie had left me vanished. Did I mind Gubbie visiting her? Yes, indeed I did. I objected violently to any male so much as looking at her. She was mine. None of this came out in words. Instead I told her she must see Gubbie if she wished but it would be nice if she didn't. However, could she come and see me? I had no leave from the regiment for several months as I had used it up in Norway, but my three-month winter ski camp would begin that November. Would she fly to Munich, then stay in our team lodgings? She agreed to think about it and I spent the next three months anticipating our reunion.

The *langlauf* Greys that year were better than ever. The other three members were all corporals from Edinburgh: Scott, Campbell and Skibinski (the last being ethnically what we called an Oatmeal Pole). The only reserve was a little trooper named Jack McConnell. He and Skibinski were, years later, to be involved, none too pleasantly, in my post-military career.

The five of us trained hard six days a week in all weathers and by the New Year of 1968 reached a peak of fitness. We narrowly missed winning the BAOR patrol race due to a broken ski and I lost the individual combined ski championship by faulting a single gate on the giant slalom course. In the Army biathlon twenty-kilometre race I came third despite poor shooting on the range due to numb fingers. I was not to know it but the months of dedicated ski training for the Greys were to serve me well for the future, just as the years of preparation in battle tanks subsequently proved about as useful as learning Latin.

During our final week in Bavaria, Ginnie came over from England. She was finished with Madrid and her father was no longer worried about us. She was nineteen now and he was preoccupied with bankruptcy and his marriage, which was sadly breaking up. I took a room at the local Sonne Hotel, all carved wood and thick carpets. Outside, the February snow lay deep and skiers hissed along the double-track circuits in preparation for the daily races at Oberjoch some miles further uphill by the Austrian border.

We skiied together and drank hot chocolate by log fires in mountain *Gasthausen*. We talked of a thousand things that had happened to us – details which would have meant nothing to anyone else in the world – and it was as if the year since Castle Combe had never happened and Gubbie and Vanda did not exist. We laughed and talked, threw snowballs, and Ginnie learned to *langlauf*.

Then she left for England and our team returned to the drear mud plains of Westphalia.

A section of the regimental bridge layer fell onto a Jock corporal I had known for four years and crushed him from the hips down. He died soon afterwards and my troop corporal, Tony Smythe, was killed in our squadron Land Rover when a loose radio set smashed his skull. My old troop friends left one by one, even Scratch and Zeebo, and an annual round of canoeing, skiing and tank withdrawals became less and less of an appealing prospect.

It would have been different had I felt there was even a faint chance of personal achievement to be had within the regiment. I liked most of my fellow Greys but the system was against me. I was not Sandhurst-orientated; I knew I would never pass the inevitable hurdle of staff college even if I was deemed academically eligible to go there – which was doubtful. And, more to the point, I had scored an own-goal of the sort which, although apparently forgiven, would never be forgotten. The Army council, six months after my return to the Greys, had ruled further punishment unnecessary, but my Whitehall file was marked in indelible red for caution. I might somehow wriggle my way up to major over the years but I would go no further. I had no wish to mark time in khaki mediocrity and so made up my mind to call it a day as soon as my three years' contracted service were up. Such was my state of mind when a letter came from Major Richard John, who had shown me around on my first day with the Greys and was on secondment to the

Sultan's Armed Forces in Oman. Although Richard was several years my senior he had always been friendly and he knew I was on the lookout for a change. Why not, he suggested, volunteer to serve in Oman? Postings lasted two years for seconded officers and the pay was marginally better than in BAOR. More important, there was sun, sand and excitement aplenty, none of which was to be found in or near Fallingbostel. Service in Oman did not further cavalry career prospects but that aspect of life no longer concerned me. I wrote to Richard by return and applied to the regimental orderly room for an application form. The commanding officer approved my application without delay – in fact, I reflected, with indecent haste. There was no flattering interview to suggest that I think things over before taking such a drastic step. I was to leave for a three-month Arabic course in England in two weeks' time.

Since, when my two years in Oman were over, I would leave the Army, my time in the Greys was now up. I pondered this with a tinge of reluctance. This was a final farewell to my lifelong ambition. How pleased my parents would have been – and I include my father, for I believe in life after death – to see their son continue in the footsteps of 'Colonel Lugs'. I was intensely proud of my father, and wanted so much to achieve as he had done, to know that he approved of his only son.

The Greys' traditions stemmed back over 300 years and occasions such as regimental mess dinners were steeped in ritual and etiquette. The loyal toast to the Queen was drunk seated – without the naval excuse of rough seas. At a certain point the regimental pipe sergeant-major and two senior pipers would enter in their tartan finery and pipe their way, in slow and quick time, around the long table heavy with its antique silver. The music, which always thrilled me, was stunning within the close confines of the narrow dining room.

In this same room Hitler's Panzer officers had, two short decades before, followed their regimental rites. Some would call it jingoism or mumbo-jumbo: to me it was a chance to hear the communal heartbeat of the timeless regimental family and to think for a moment of my father and of three centuries of our predecessors who held their own mess dinners before Sebastapol, Balaclava and Waterloo.

After the close of my last mess dinner, as the clink of departing spurs sounded from the hallway, I walked deep in thought from the billiard room. I was startled from reverie by the pride of the Mess, a six by five-foot oil painting entitled *Forward the Greys*, which fell from the wall where it had hung peacefully for at least four years and, knocking the whisky tumbler from my hand, landed heavily beside me. I denied any evil intentions when notifying the Mess secretary of the damaged painting and my innocence was accepted. The regiment, I decided, was, through its resident poltergeist, saying goodbye.

Twenty-four years old, with two false starts behind me, I reported to the headquarters of the Army Education Corps in order to learn Arabic. Eight other officers from various regiments were on the same three-month course.

'If you pass the end-of-course exam,' our captain informed us, playing his trump carrot up-front, 'you will receive £100 tax-free.'

With our enthusiasm assured, he handed us over to our three instructors. Until very recently we would have been taught at the Middle East College for Arabic Studies in exotic Beirut, but government economies had changed all that. Our place of instruction was a high-rise concrete block overlooking the golf-course of suburban Beaconsfield.

By the third month we were constructing lengthy but simple sentences and conversing with the instructors. I made a serious cultural error with Mr Nasser, a strict Muslim. When told to produce a sentence containing as many words as possible, I tried: '*Ahib ashoof al noohood yaasar min bint maalak, waalaakin fee akhdar*', or, roughly translated, 'I like to watch the left breast of your girlfriend, but it is green.' Or that is what I intended it to mean. Unfortunately, Nasser's understanding of the word *bint*, as I later discovered, was daughter not girlfriend and he left the classroom, mottled with fury. I followed him out and apologised profusely in English, assuring him I would never again mention any part of the female anatomy. Since this was not his gripe, I remained his *bête noire* up until the final exams, at which he invigilated. The eight other officers passed. I failed.

All weekends were free from Beaconsfield and, since Ginnie's father was wrapped up in his business, we were free to enjoy life as and where the spirit led us. Mostly we wandered the woods, where we had grown up, through daffodils and bluebells. We spread picnics on the springy moss in a nook above the river that we had first discovered years before by moonlight. We took a tent and little else for one glorious June weekend to the white sand dunes of Climping, beside the mouth of the Arun.

My cousin Gubbie did not hold it against me when Ginnie came back to me and soon afterwards he fell in love with Juliet, daughter of Alexander Durie, the director-general of the Automobile Association. I went with Ginnie and our mothers to the wedding, as the groom's best man, and afterwards watched Gubbie and his bride driven to the reception in a vintage open jalopy with the registered number AA1. A far cry from our days of hitchhiking in headscarf and kilt.

My old world was breaking up, as is the way of things. Your friends fall to brides and you too scent the hearth. Later they die and you contemplate death.

I felt no urgency to marry and settle down. Far from it; I had a powerful urge to do and see things and be free as I had never truly been. I thought not at all of married life but a great deal about Ginnie. I knew I could have easily lost her after Castle Combe and, soldiering in remote Oman, might risk her again. Sitting in Ginnie's battered Mini van in a Midhurst side street, the tarmac shining from a summer shower, I asked her to marry me. She nodded and hugged me with her head on my chest. I saw, when she moved away, that she had been crying silently.

We made no announcement except in confidence to our mothers, both of whom were happy. They even gave their blessing, two weeks before I went to Arabia, for Ginnie and I to spend a week in Portugal. We flew at once to the Algarve to an almost empty hotel. The Atlantic breakers were uninviting but the white sands were hot and deserted except for the two of us.

At the end of June I left England for Arabia.

7

First Blood

From shadows and types to reality.

JOHN HENRY NEWMAN

In the late 1960s few people had heard of Oman or knew of its close links with Britain. A trickle of British volunteer officers had been fighting there since 1965, and the Labour government in London was well aware of the growing Marxist threat of subversion and invasion from Soviet-led South Yemen. But it was, if anything, embarrassed by the few British officers already in Oman and happy with the lack of media interest. Only in 1971 were SAS units sent to Oman.

Oman lies along the east side of the Arabian Peninsula between the Indian Ocean and the great sand desert of Saudi Arabia. The northern sector of the Sultanate is peopled by Omanis but a southern portion, the size of Wales, contains tribes of African origin known as Dhofaris who were ruled, very feebly until the 1970s, by the Sultans from Muscat and Nizwa, the capital cities of Oman.

So long as the British ruled neighbouring Aden, the Sultans could easily contain internal troubles. But in June 1967, with Harold Wilson at the helm, the British finally withdrew and, within three months, the Russians took their place. For the first time Marxism had a firm base in Arabia. Dhofar was the first natural target since it shared a common border and since only Oman blocked the way between Aden, now the People's Republic of Southern Yemen, and the Straits of Hormuz, gateway to the Persian Gulf, through which two-thirds of the free world's oil needs were daily tankered.

Soviet propaganda, through the 1000-megawatt Voice of Cairo and Radio Aden, beamed a seductive message to the transistors of Omanis. Their Sultan, a reactionary dictator and a friend of the British imperialists, had long oppressed them and ensnared them in poverty. They must now rise up as had their fraternal brothers in South Yemen and throw off the yoke of the Sultan's Army. This should not prove too difficult since there were less than a thousand poorly armed Sultanate soldiers, half of whom were faint-hearted mercenaries from Baluchistan. No outside intervention was to be feared since the Sultan's sole ally was Britain, which was still smarting from memories of Suez and would not risk involvement beyond the loan of a few volunteer officers.

In 1964 the first Dhofari rebels were merely nationalists who wanted Dhofar for the Dhofaris. Under the lead of a disgruntled oil company employee, Musalim bin Nuffl, they mined lorries and killed oil workers. After a year's training in Saudi Arabia and Iraq, bin Nuffl and forty followers returned via the desert in seven Dodge jeeps, quite a feat in itself, and caused further trouble by killing a few soldiers and their British officers. But the Sultan's little force destroyed all the jeeps and seized the rebel arms' dump. Demoralised, they turned, via South Yemen, to

Russian and Chinese mentors, and for a while all was quiet as a wounded bin Nuffl remained abroad and various new factions of both old nationalist and new Marxist guerrillas prepared for the fray.

Meanwhile the ageing Sultan, Said bin Taimur, fearing coups and assassins in Muscat, retired to a beach-side fortress in Salalah, the capital of Dhofar. He ruled largely through a few trusted Britons, ex-colonial administrators from the Indian Empire and, when they nagged him with warnings of the growing Yemen-based threat, he reminded them that he could hardly afford his three existing regiments, his navy of one old wooden dhow and his air force of two BAC Piston Provosts. The existing arrangements would have to cope.

So nothing was done to prepare for the impending storm. At the time I joined the Sultan's Army, there were but 200 fighting men in Dhofar under a dozen British officers and their standard weapons were bolt-action rifles dating back to the Second World War.

With the other seven officers from Beaconsfield I flew via Rome to Bahrain in an RAF VC10. I had never been anywhere hotter than temperate South Africa and was impressed by the totally new experience of an Arabian summer. The wet heat was exhausting, even during short outings from the air-conditioned cool of our hotel.

Back in England BOAC went on strike so we were marooned eight days in Bahrain, a lucky if brief chance to acclimatise to this new and debilitating hothouse. On the seventh day a BOAC hostess with a boyfriend in the local forces hospital told us with relish that a British officer had just been flown out from Muscat with one shoulder and a portion of his chest shot away by the Communists.

I asked her his name.

'Major John,' she said. 'Major Richard John. They say he was on a stretcher in the mountains for ten hours before they evacuated him. Your Sultan uses mules instead of helicopters. What a place to volunteer for!'

Richard was the only friend I had in Oman. Ironic that his tales of sun and sand had tempted me out here. I decided not to visit him in hospital, as I feared the sight of his wounds might taint my mind when my time came to face enemy bullets.

The vintage Fokker to Muscat staged via Sharjah where we took on our first real-life mercenary. The Sultan hired freelance officers as well as seconded Brits, which was a sensible insurance against Harold Wilson getting cold feet or, in the words of one of my Beaconsfield colleagues, 'bad advice from that woman, Folkbender, to remove us all overnight'. Most of the mercenaries, or contract officers as they preferred to be called, were ex-British Army and enjoyed a better salary than the rest of us. But once the bullets started flying, any petty differences soon disappeared.

The new arrival, Captain David Bayley, was from Hove so we had common ground to discuss. He had recently spent three interesting years fighting for the royalist guerrillas in the mountains of North Yemen. Nerve gas attacks by Egyptian aircraft on his cave headquarters, he explained, were the most dreaded events.

We skirted the silver blue rim of the Gulf of Oman and sneaked through pig's-tail canyons to Bayt al Falaj airport, nerve centre of the Sultan's forces. The heat, once we left the Fokker, was incredible. The tarmac lines between the concrete slabs of the runway hissed and bubbled. The glare was intense. An open Land Rover halted beside us, its driver hidden by a cloud of fine dust. 'Hop in,' shouted a disembodied voice. 'You must be the new chaps. Sling your kit in the

Dhofar and Oman

back.' Our driver dropped us within the walls of a white-washed fortress, straight out of *Beau Geste*.

Next day we were individually briefed by Brigadier Corran Purdon, a kindly man with well-ironed sleeves rolled up over bulging biceps. He did two hundred press-ups a day. I was to join the Muscat Regiment, stationed an hour's drive inland from Bayt al Falaj, where I would command the Reconnaissance Platoon. In a few months the regiment would go to Dhofar, some 600 miles and three days' driving to the south. Each regiment did a year's stint in the Dhofar war zone and two years in the almost peaceful north.

Night fell suddenly upon the fort as I left with my burden of kitbags. The whine of mosquitoes and the ululation of Muslim prayer from unseen mosques mingled in the hot air, as did the smell of unguent hair oils from nearby billets and the odour of excrement from the bushes all about the camp. The men did not use lavatories, but this caused no disease as the heat quickly dried up the filth.

The following day I was taken to the garrison of BidBid by the second-in-command of the Muscat Regiment, John Cooper, a sinewy major with sun-blackened skin and the features of a Greek bandit. He was armed only with a holstered pistol and drove his own Land Rover unescorted. John had fought with the Yemeni royalists. Before that he had served against Rommel as desert driver to Colonel David Stirling, the founder and first commanding officer of the Special Air Service. John stayed with the SAS through the years of sabotage raids in occupied France to postwar campaigns in Malaya and the Radfan. He was also Oman's only ham radio operator, speaking from time to time to King Hussein of Jordan on the other side of the Empty Quarter.

John drove fast along a gravel track, the main road to the interior. Stark mountains closed about us, soaring 10,000 feet to the Mountain of the Sun. This was the Hajar Range where, John explained, no European had been until 1835, when two British lieutenants from the Indian Army first climbed it and were lucky to escape alive from the tribes that lived on the hidden plateau above. As recently as 1950, Wilfrid Thesiger, the greatest of European travellers in Arabia, was unable to enter the Hajar or Inner Oman.

After forty miles the mountains fell away where a wide river valley, the Wadi Sumeil, crossed our track. We bounced through a ford of pools and pebbles where, in monsoon seasons, a rock-rolling deluge roared. Above the date palms of the valley, on a bare sandstone outcrop which commanded this pass to the interior, there squatted the wired-off barracks of BidBid, headquarters of the Muscat Regiment and my home until the move to Dhofar.

John showed me my room, one of six in a block, a tiny bare-floored place with fly netting windows and an inactive air conditioner. The Officers' Mess was opposite, a sitting room with magazines and a dining table laid for six. Spicey cooking smells and the crunch of bare feet on cockroaches came from the kitchen beyond.

There were five other officers, including John, at dinner. They were polite enough to me and I kept quiet, listening hard to their chatter, most of it of mines and deaths down south, of sex with the oil-girls in Muscat and of trouble brewing in a nearby district called the Sharqeeya. Omani words I failed to recognise punctured their talk and, after coffee, they sat on drinking quite heavily but with little visible effect.

At Bayt al Falaj I had been warned about *bidbid* tummy but was unprepared for the vehemence of its sudden arrival an hour after dinner. There was no time even to say good night. I stumbled crouching from the room and vomited with violence into the nearest monsoon ditch. For the next two days I was forced to keep close to the Mess lavatory, the only one in the camp since the soldiers were accustomed to using stones rather than paper, and no known flushing system could cope with this habit.

In dire need of a shower after stumbling from the ditch to my quarters I pulled aside the plastic curtain at the back of my room and screamed as a large spider jumped on me. It slithered down my neck and the back of my shirt. Terrified into immobility at first, I then lost control and tore my shirt tails from my trousers, clutching wildly for the loathsome insect. Knocked off, it jumped on to the wall and with great speed reached the furthest corner of the shower cubicle. I slammed at it with a clenched fist. The body was surprisingly tough and leathery but it fell stunned to the concrete floor where I trod on it. The span of its black hairy legs was a full seven inches and its mouth was a curved bird-like beak. I slept badly despite having searched the room for other unwelcome inmates. In the morning an Arab brought me tea.

'You kill this?' He spoke English.

I nodded.

He shook his head and made a tut-tut sound. 'No good thing to kill such an insect. A chapter in the Holy Book is given to his honour.' He glanced at me with disapproval and took away the corpse on his tea tray.

The Commanding Officer, Peter Thwaites, detailed his adjutant to show me round camp. We went first to the barrack room of the Reconnaissance Platoon. Just outside the adjutant stopped me with a warning.

'Your platoon's make-up is not exactly what it should be and that is going to be your main problem. You should have five Land Rovers, each with a driver, signaller and five soldiers. But,' he shrugged his shoulders, 'recruiting has lapsed of late and now there are only fifteen men in all. Some are Omanis, others are Baluchi mercenaries. Basically they dislike each other although they're all Muslim. This can lead to bad trouble, even mutiny, if you let it. *Never* show favouritism for either race.'

We came to a hut by the compound wire. Inside flies and wasps swarmed where dates lay on dirty tin plates. The place smelled of sweat and tobacco. Open hair oil bottles from India lay about and giant wasps called *dibbees* waded drunkenly through the scented grease. A rifle hung unattended from a bedstead and a Baluchi soldier squatted by a Singer sewing machine chewing a wad of grass and picking his nose.

'Well, over to you,' the adjutant grinned. 'In six months you will be let loose in Dhofar and, between you and me, it would be suicide to go anywhere near *adoo*-held territory with this platoon in its current state.'

'Who is *adoo*?' I asked him.

'Arabic for enemy. A year ago, when I was last down there, they were hard to find. But things have changed following the British withdrawal from Aden in November. Now they have a safe base and are multiplying like bacteria. In their own mountains, they are the finest guerrilla fighters in the world. That is our misfortune of course.'

His glance lit briefly upon the glaze-eyed Baluchi. 'If you set foot in the Jebel, the Dhofar mountains, with ill-trained soldiers, you will be asking for trouble. The *adoo* move like invisible gazelles. They know every *wadi*, every cave, because it is their homeland, and they can smell an army presence a mile away upwind. The moment you arrive in the Jebel, you are under observation. Then, one wrong step, one careless move and they cut you off. Call for reinforcements? You'll be lucky. We have 200 men to cover an area larger than Wales and, as you will have heard, no means of evacuation except for six mules.'

A bundle of clothing stirred on a nearby bed and from it there materialised a little Arab who swung his bare feet to the floor and rubbed his eyes awake with the corner of his grimy headcloth, red-and-white chequered like a Kashmir shawl. 'Ya-wallah,' he exclaimed in alarm as he saw us, and jumped to attention. He was all of five feet tall with pointed Puck-ears and a bulbous nose set among crinkles of good humour.

'This is Private Ali Nasser,' the adjutant introduced me as the two shook hands in friendly greeting. 'Ali is from the Hajar where they breed them small but tough.' Ali shook my hand, 'Hello, Sahb.' That, I learned, was the limit of his English repertoire. He bade us stay for coffee, which he heated with a paraffin burner on his trunk. When it was ready he filled a set of small china cups from his battered *dhille* coffee pot, brass with a curved beak spout. The coffee was strong and good. Then he proffered dates.

'Be careful of the *dibbees*,' the adjutant warned as I tried to remove a date from the attentions of the striped wasps. 'Their sting is as bad as an African hornet's.'

A tall man with an outsize beard entered the room. His eyes were grape-black and his features finely cut. This was Mohamed Rashid, chief machine-gunner of the platoon. I came to know Mohamed as a true gentleman of Oman, trustworthy and brave. He came from a village near Ziki at the foot of the Hajar cliffs and was known to all as The Beard.

Other Recce-men arrived and joined us, each with elaborate greetings. All were Omanis. No Baluchis came near although I noticed a group of them in another part of the room.

The adjutant left and the conversation died. Ali Nasser offered dates. Everyone declined. I racked my brain for words but all that came to mind was 'Your daughter's left breast is green, Mr Nasser.'

None of the Omanis spoke English or Baluchi, and few of the Baluchis, who also spoke no English, knew much Arabic. This, I realised, might hinder my ambitions, rapidly formulated that very morning, to turn this rabble into a cohesive fighting force, a term I remembered from Mons.

Triumphantly I formed the question, 'How many of you are there in the platoon?' They all answered at once, and all, it seemed, gave a different figure. So I nodded and said, '*Ab hamdu lillah*'. This vital phrase means 'To God be the praise' and can be repeated as often as you like and in any context. Nonetheless, after several *Al hamdu lillahs*, a pregnant silence hung heavily about the billet. I felt my shirt and the crutch of my trousers wet with sweat and I left, shaking hands with all the Omanis. The Baluchis did not look up, so I left them alone despite a strong feeling that this was quite the wrong thing to do.

As I left, a paunchy but handsome out-of-breath staff-sergeant approached. '*Salaam Alaikum*,' he greeted me and then switched to excellent English. 'I heard you come to visit, Sahb. I am pleased. We are all in Recce very pleased. For many months we have had no officer and when I ask the major-sahb for new equipment and more men I get nothing. Now you are with us, all will be well, *Im'shaalah*.' His name was Salim Abdullah.

He took me to the vehicle lines. Of our five Land Rovers only three appeared to exist and two of these had been cannibalised to maintain the third, the only working vehicle of my unit. The drivers were a shabby crew, most of whom seemed to be called Mohamed.

Under the shade of a flowering fig tree, the staff-sergeant spoke to me earnestly. He held my hand, anxious that I should understand. I repressed a smile at an unbidden image of my Greys sergeant, Barchi Leader, holding my hand. 'You will understand, Sahb, that it is best I speak to you now. In the new season, the Muscat Regiment will move south and the word is about among our men that many hundreds of *adoo* will come from other lands, from Yemen and Iraq and Egypt, to fight us. It is said that the *Shooyooeen*, the Communists, have sent them new *automatiqueeya* guns and many instructors from Russia and China. They will be strong and we of the Sultan are few.' He pointed his long and elegant fingers towards heaven and then prodded my stomach. I felt he was coming to the point. 'The companies of the regiment will be safe, God willing, for they are 100 men each with mortars and Vickers machine guns. But we of Recce can only survive by stealth and cunning. This means good training and good heart. But, Captain Sahb, this Recce Platoon has neither. They are rabble, they are too few in number and, worst of all, they quarrel bitterly among themselves.'

I said nothing when he paused so he continued, his voice now lowered. 'Why, you may ask, is there bad feeling? One reason only, Sahb. In the past the Recce Platoon was of the best Arabs in the regiment, men who could drive well, signal well and shoot with a straight eye. They preferred to serve in Recce for two good reasons. Number one, because in the companies the men must walk and carry guns, food and ammunition. In Recce there are Land Rovers. Number two . . . ,' his voice lowered still further, 'because in Recce, there used only to be Arabs.' He shook his head in sorrow. 'But now, Recce is like the companies. We too have wretched Baluchis. Baluchis who moan like women at pain or discomfort, who must drink twice the water an Arab needs, who are unhappy if they have nothing to complain about.' He ended by wiping his mouth as though cleaning away dirty words.

How, I asked him, did he think I might get rid of Recce's existing Baluchis at a time when the platoon was at mere half-strength? If anything, I must surely try to attract more men, whether Baluchi or Arab. Anyway, as a staff-sergeant, should he not treat all our men equally, without favour?

His eyelids did not bat. 'Sahb,' his right hand rested on his heart, 'I treat all the men with a remarkable fairness. I see them only as fellow Muslims under God, all of whom are naturally afflicted with some evil. But the Baluchis, praise Allah, are more gravely afflicted.'

In northern Oman, the patrol area of my platoon covered the entire region south of the Hajar Range, west on to the Empty Quarter and south to the Sharqeeya and the Wahiba Sands. My first patrol was to the Sharqeeya. The entire region of the Sharqeeya was ruled by one sheikh, Ahmed Mohamed Al Harthi, whose ambitions were a growing threat to the Sultan. An armed patrol was sent in by way of the Wadi Tayyin every year to establish, however fleetingly, the Sultan's right of way and to maintain his recruiting rights.

The two weeks of preparation for the patrol were a nightmare. My stomach eventually accustomed itself to BidBid water but the sweltering heat grew as June became July. Because of my lack of Arabic I had to rely on the staff-sergeant, Abdullah, to effect any change within my platoon. Abdullah, far from keeping order, was shouted down by the Baluchis and by a couple of arrogant bedouin corporals who turned up soon after my arrival. Only after a number of petty but violent quarrels between the factions, which took a patient day to disentangle, did I separate the group into three ethnically mixed Land Rover patrols. The bedu corporals threatened resignation: I prayed they were in earnest.

I selected Murad, an Omani Baluch, the only mixed-heritage man in the unit, as my driver. Murad was an excellent mechanic and I learned to my relief that he responded with intelligence and pride to any specific task he was given. Somehow, perhaps to the detriment of the company Land Rovers, he managed to resurrect two of our inoperative vehicles in time to have three Land Rovers ready for the Sharqeeya patrol.

Weapons were cleaned and oiled. Some were in a filthy state and the two-inch mortar had gone missing altogether. I could not believe it. In the British Army there would have been a major enquiry and heads would have rolled. I set out to find a replacement. Richard John was still away recovering from his wounds and there was no other British officer in his company at the time so I 'borrowed' a mortar and, for good measure, a machine-gun from his armoury. Over the next two years neither was missed by its previous owner and they saved our lives more than once.

We camped first at Naqsi in the Wadi Wasit. Then we entered the Tayyin, the soldiers bouncing on their bundles of bedding and rations and clutching their weapons. Often they chanted together, their palms beating the hot metal sides of the vehicles. Only the darker faces of the Baluchis were sullen as the wild tunes of the Arabs followed the wind. Creeping down the furrows of the jagged Hajar moonscape we came to isolated villages cut off by the rim of their local watershed. Here grew clover, vines and cress in water meadows. Melons, figs, mangoes and pomegranates ripened outside the shade of date groves. Houses were made from local clay or from *barusti*, the dried branches of palm trees.

We called at a great many villages. Some were relatively well off. Others, like Mazra 'Ain, were no more than a clump of withered palms by a stagnant pool. At Mazra a toothless woman offered us a pomegranate and a cup of green water. Her husband lay sick but mouthed the customary greeting *'Tafuddel'*. 'You are our guests. Eat what we have.'

At each stop I followed the Arabs to meet the headman. The Baluchis preferred to stay and guard the vehicles. Over coffee and dates I asked each *wali* a list of stock questions. How many goats? Date trees? Any trouble? How many of his village served in the *Geysh*, the army?

Until we came to the narrow valley of Zayyan there was no trouble, but there, deep into the Sharqeeya, we hit a wall of resentment. The Zayyanis watched us from the *wadi* cliffs in silent groups high on their she-camels. Five-foot muzzle-loaders hung from their shoulders and six-inch soft lead bullets held by criss-cross bandoliers of goat leather festooned their bony chests. Word of our coming had preceded us via the *wadi* telegraph.

We stopped short of the boundary trees and Abdullah sent the men out on foot across the *wadi*, the bedu with a machine gun to one flank and The Beard with his to the other. Abdullah and I glanced at each other. 'What do you like us to do?' His English was not as good as usual.

'What's the normal form when this sort of thing happens, Abdullah?'

The ball was back in his court but he seemed non-plussed. So I added, 'Just tell them we are friends and want to ask them some questions on behalf of the Sultan.'

This he apparently did and, by the length of his oration, added some remarks of his own, through which I learned that we of Recce Platoon were but the first unit of an entire regiment coming up to Zayyan.

A thickset man in a mauve *dishdash* robe shouted back and brandished his gun. Others joined in. Tempers were rising.

Abdullah turned to me. 'Sahb. These are bad people. They will answer no questions and say they want no Sultan's men on their land. They are for Al Harthi only and he hates the Sultan.'

He shrugged. 'I think, Sahb, we would do well to end our patrol here, for these people are not worth our time and trouble.'

I agreed but, thinking to impress these potential troublemakers with our superior firepower, I told Abdullah to arrange some shooting practice. This clearly pleased the men. Even the Baluchis brightened up and there was much noisy cocking of weapons.

A nearby space was cleared of goats and two empty jerry cans were placed 100 yards from our vehicles. Our ten riflemen, including the drivers and signaller, somehow managed to let off fifty rounds between them without hitting either can.

A crowd of Zayyanis had gathered close by and growing mutters on a jeering note made me doubt my decision to show off our proficiency. However, there were still our machine-guns, .303 Brens, and these I knew could not fail to pepper the cans.

The clear fire orders of Abdullah silenced the Zayyanis. A wild burst of fire issued from the bedu's Bren and wisps of rock dust rose from a ledge some twenty feet above and beyond the cans. Ricochets pinged above us and the Zayyanis ducked in alarm. The bedu were jubilant, the more so when they noticed The Beard's Bren had jammed.

The men withdrew to the Land Rovers in high fettle, quite unabashed by the undamaged jerry cans and the derisive sneers of the onlookers. God help us in Dhofar, I thought.

We turned around and headed back west to camp beyond the friendly village of Ghiyazah.

Miles later at Hindarut village, they knew of our reception by the Zayyanis. I never did discover the local telephone system. Drums often beat in the villages, so perhaps that was how they did it.

We visited the off-shoot hamlets we had missed on the outward patrol and always ate dates with the *wali*. The food invariably crawled with insects and I grew to loathe the black and yellow *dibbees*. Sated flies rose in swarms from the faeces about the huts and settled on the *wali*'s plates of fruit.

I had little appetite but refused nothing when the watchful eye of Abdullah was upon me. We sat barefoot on the *wali*'s carpet with legs tucked uncomfortably underneath us so our soles could not point at another man – an insult to a Muslim.

Coffee was always poured to guests in order of importance. I came after all the others for, being a *Nasrani* or Christian, I rated lower than the poorest Muslim. But this was not always the case. In villages of the Sunni sect, less strict than the Ibhadi Muslims, I came higher on the coffee list than even the *wali*, because I represented the Sultan.

After coffee, the sick people came to the vehicles. We had first-aid satchels but no medical orderly. A grey-beard with puffy eyelids thrust his face at me to show his ailment. Pressing one thumb against the corner of his eye, he caused a surprising amount of white pus to exude from beneath his lower eyelid. This he repeated with the other eye and I felt queasy.

'Give him an Aspirin and he'll be happy,' shouted Murad.

There was Optrex in the satchel so I squeezed some into the loose sacs below the man's eyes once I had swabbed out most of the poison.

The population was riddled with eye trouble, including trachoma. Even young children were affected, usually in only one eye, which was glassy and grey like faded marble. 'Hundreds of our people go blind each year,' said Abdullah. 'There is nothing to be done about it. To God be the praise.'

The filth-bearing flies buzzed about, massing at the backsides of naked babies and crawling about the eyes and lips of children who scarcely blinked, much less bothered to brush them away. These same flies fed on the suppurating sores of the ever-present pi-dogs. The racking cough of TB-riddled lungs was common. Enlarged spleens and other signs of malaria and chronic anaemia were in evidence. Leprosy was endemic.

There were three hospitals in all Oman and eight out of every ten babies born died within a year. The Sultan would not allow foreign units such as Save the Children Fund into his country. 'Why,' I asked Abdullah, 'are there so few hospitals? I have never seen such suffering. Something should be done about it.'

Abdullah was not impressed. 'The government has little money. We are not a wealthy country. There are more pressing matters. Anyway this is a poor area with miserable people. Illness comes to those who sin.'

We left the Tayyin and I never went back. It was a place of beauty and mystery tucked well away from the twentieth century. We returned to BidBid and, the next weekend, to Muscat. To oil terminals and bustle from a place where progress meant nothing and time had stood still for 800 years.

Sultan Said bin Taimur seemed determined, as far as I could make out, to perpetuate his country's backwardness and poverty, content that the conservatism of the Ibahdi hierarchy would continue to strangle all strivings for change, to smother all revolutionary mutterings. He and a chosen few lived well with the first fruits of oil wealth while the mass of Omanis and Dhofaris lived out their narrow existence in squalor.

My conscience was increasingly ill at ease: I was clearly a part of the military machine that upheld the Sultan in denying 800,000 Omanis their rightful inheritance, the benefits of progress, schools and above all hospitals. Away from Muscat, Muttrah, Nizwa and the other large towns, the people did not know what they were missing in life and local *walis* feared change as a threat to their authority. But ownership of cheap transistor radios was spreading and discontent increased alongside awareness.

All around us the Arab world was in ferment – from Egypt to Jordan, from the Sudan to the Yemen. Oil revenue was changing lifestyles radically for our nearest neighbours in Kuwait and the Trucial Coast. Until now the Persian Gulf, known to Omanis as the Arabian Gulf, the Indian Ocean and the western sand barrage had absorbed the shockwaves of Arab militancy, buffering Oman against contagion. But no longer. I, too, listened to Aden Radio – it was good for my Arabic.

> Throw off the harness of British imperialism. Take back the wealth that is yours but is stolen by the Sultan. Why does he hide from you in distant Dhofar? Because he is ashamed that he has betrayed you. Here in the People's Republic of Yemen, the revolution has already provided schools for our children, hospitals for our sick. With the help of our Russian and Chinese brothers we are building a great future for our people. The only road to success is revolt. Our programme will show you how to achieve success. Tomorrow, at the same time, Said Massoul, leader of the gallant Omani freedom fighters here in Aden, will speak to you . . .

For two centuries the Sultan's family, the Albu Saeedi dynasty, had ruled Oman, surviving the loss of the richest slaving empire in the world. But a family feud and the secession of Zanzibar from the Omani empire caused a collapse and a shrinking. Then only dates and limes provided Oman's income, together with annual aid of £1 million from the British. Now the Sultan had been receiving oil revenue for three years, yet there were not even rumours of development plans beyond a water and electricity project in Muscat.

In the furnace-heat of summer evenings I often walked with Abdullah among the palms of Fanjah village close to the camp. I taxed him with the failings of the Sultan but received little reassurance. After all what could he say to defend policies that denied his own people a better life?

Towards the end of July Abdullah announced that, due to family problems, he must leave the Army. Our training of the platoon, partly because of the 120° heat, was not going well, so I was relieved when Abdullah promised to stay at least until my Arabic improved enough to manage reasonably well without him.

Our plans for training were frustrated on 1 July when the CO summoned me to his office. 'You and David Bayley are to fly south tomorrow to join the Northern Frontier Regiment for a month in Dhofar. They are short of officers and you could do with the experience before I let you loose down there with our Recce Platoon.' He smiled at me from behind wire-rimmed spectacles. 'Things are hotting up in the south, so be careful.'

Next day we flew south over a 500-mile gravel desert that shimmered without a shadow, save that of our Beaver, to the unmarked border of Dhofar. For the first time in hours the pilot spoke over the intercom. 'We are now over the Qara Jebel. It's as green as England below the clouds but not as friendly.' He chuckled and switched to VHF for landing instructions from RAF Salalah.

I peered below but the Dhofar mountains were invisible, swathed in a cloak of cloud. However, I knew from colour slides back in BidBid that, unlike the rest of Arabia, these hidden Jebel, the spinal mountains of Dhofar, were covered in jungle, lagoons and grassy downs. The cloud that covered the mountains also hid from us the Plain of Salalah, a flat gravel shelf caught between mountain and sea. In the centre of the plain's seaward edge there sprawled the capital city of Salalah with its royal palace, safe from guerrilla raids as yet, due to two installations a mile or so inland. One was the Army headquarters, the other a threadbare airbase manned by an RAF garrison with very little to do. The wily Sultan allowed RAF use of remote but strategically desirable Masirah Island, vital to Britain since Aden's demise, only on the condition that they maintained a presence at Salalah. This gave him a guarded base for his own two-plane airforce and assurance that, should the guerrillas ever attack Salalah, the British would respond positively if only through worry about their own personnel.

The Beaver eased low over the monsoon surf. A flash of palm trees and mist-shrouded hovels. Then fencing and radar installations. We landed close by a sandbagged hangar to be met by a Land Rover with no hood or doors. The two occupants wore faded khaki streaked with black and green dye. Each carried a Sterling submachine-gun slung at the waist. A loaded magazine was taped upside-down to the magazine already clipped into the driver's gun so that sixty-four nickel-nosed 9mm rounds were immediately available. Green *shemaghs* covered their heads, the loose ends hanging about their shoulders and deeply tanned forearms. Dust filmed their goggles and every item in the vehicle.

The driver indicated the rear compartment. We climbed in with our bags and he set off at high speed through the camp and out over the plain. 'We're headed for Umm al Ghawarif, our HQ. It's only a couple of miles,' the driver shouted back at us as he struggled with the leaping vehicle. He was avoiding the main tracks. 'Mines,' he screamed at us. 'They lay them by night. Mark Seven anti-tank mines left in Aden courtesy of Harold Wilson. Make a real mess of a Land Rover.'

86

My thighs squeezed together involuntarily despite the reassuring sight of sandbags on the floor and under our seats.

Seen through mist and dust the camp reminded me of the East German frontier – searchlights in stilted towers, heaped clusters of barbed wire and sandbagged trenches along the perimeter fence. Soldiers, dressed like our driver, but with green berets rather than *shemaghs*, moved purposefully about the camp. Bedford lorries laden with ammunition crates passed us on their way to a tiny airstrip just beyond the wire and Pakistani mechanics battered a mine-mangled chassis back into shape in an open workshop. A light and fitful seabreeze fanned the dusty camp. When it died the heat was oppressive.

Our driver drew up by a larger replica of the BidBid Officers' Mess. He unwound his headcloth, detached his goggles and lit up a briar pipe. A good-natured person, I judged by his initial grin. 'I'm Bill Prince, second-in-command of B Company to which you are both attached. We are glad to have you.'

Bill introduced us to the six other officers and to the men of his company. Most of the officers spoke fluent Arabic and some had a good grasp of Urdu. All seemed slick and keen. Security was tight. Convoys for outstations on the plain left the camp silently by night without lights. They drove at snail-like speed, for noise could carry to listeners on the Jebel eight miles to the north.

The CO was not like our own gentle colonel. Mike Harvey of the Northern Frontier Regiment operated his companies on a close leash with an iron fist. His nickname was Oddjob because his hobby was karate. Serving with the Gloucesters in Korea he had won the Military Cross extricating his company from the Imjin River trap by a frontal assault on the Chinese. The rest of the Gloucesters were killed or imprisoned. He hated Communists and his tactics were thought by many to be ruthless. At first I concurred with this view.

David and I were issued camouflaged clothing and headcloth, three blankets, 100 bullets and a bolt-action Mark 5 .303 rifle. Also a set of maps of the mountains on a weird scale I had never seen before, 0.63 inches to the mile. There were few place-names and many of the existing ones had the words 'position approximate' in brackets beside them. We were each given command of a platoon in Bill Prince's company.

Our work was simple and unpleasant. The colonel's policy was to subdue the people of the plain and the foothills into refusing food supplies to the guerrillas. Arrests, harassment and interrogations would in theory cow the locals. In practice our patrols served only to increase their hatred of Army, government and Sultan.

As the mists on the Jebel grew thicker and a ceaseless drizzle soaked their hovels, more and more Jebalis descended to the relatively easier conditions of the plain. The mountain soil was of ochre clay that slid from under their bare feet. Gradients became mud-slides and the bushes everywhere teemed with a billion monsoon tics which sucked the blood of man and animal and drove one mad with the violent itch of their serum.

Our task was to scour the *wadis* and cave-riddled cliffs and arrest every able-bodied male who might conceivably be an *adoo*. Then, in a lorry, we took them back to Umm al Ghawarif where they were interrogated and entered into a filing system. Each was given an identity card to proffer if arrested in future. While their menfolk were so detained, many families came close to starvation.

I wondered increasingly why we should be involved here at all. The Dhofaris had fought each other for centuries; why not let them carry on? I could think of no good reason for bolstering the

Sultan. What was in it for Britain? All oil discovered to date was in northern Oman, not here. The RAF garrison could look after themselves or, if attacked, a temporary task force from Bahrain could sort things out.

I resolved to resign from the Sultan's forces without delay. This resolution lasted until dinner the same evening when I realised that other officers might mistake my motives. I remembered Mess gossip about officers I had never met who had terminated their Dhofar service. Without exception they were referred to with disdain. The inference was invariably cowardice. I knew such talk spread quickly to regimental Messes in BAOR and England. Recalling the undeserved stigma of tart, I knew I could not face that of coward. No, I must delay any mention of resignation until my month down here in this dangerous region was over.

I grew accustomed to the routine: daily patrols on the plain or dawn ambushes in the foothills. The purpose of foothill ambushes was to discourage the *adoo* from visiting and feeding from the semi-permanent camps of the goat and camel herders there. The camps consisted of low brush hovels roughly cemented with clay and sited in the zone of thorn brush and giant anthills where the plain began to rise to meet the *qara*.

These camps were hard to find, let alone to ambush, but Bill Prince knew the plain well. He led us silently on a northerly bearing for four or five hours until we reached the scrub. Then in single-file we crept between the murderous spikes of camel-thorn brush, seeing little but the man ahead and the weird silhouettes of ant-hills. Suddenly and for no definable reason, Bill would decide we had arrived. Then we fanned out and waited. No smoking. No coughing. No light. We shivered, strained our ears, fought off sleep and cursed the mosquitoes, the biting ticks and the never ending drizzle – until dawn, clammy and grey, sneaked into the scrubland and one by one the ant-hills reared up about us. Then a whisper from one side or the other. Somebody touched me and I rose to advance, cursing the cramp and feeling for grenades and rifle.

For an hour or sometimes only minutes we moved forward, avoiding the thorns that spiked headcloths, tore at skin and threatened eyes, trying not to skid on the wet clay and, most importantly, not to lose the man on either side, mere shadows in the gloom.

We came one memorably miserable morning to a group of hovels in a clearing and rifle shots sounded as we breasted the last bushes. The source of the firing was muffled by the mist and no one knew who fired or at whom. Still, it was my first confirmation that the *adoo* actually existed.

We closed to search the *rondaavals* and soon found the portioned meat and entrails of a freshly butchered goat. All male villagers were arrested but no weapons were found except the usual vintage matchlocks. Beneath a nearby bush a soldier found two spent .303 cases in the mud. But the *adoo* had gone, melting through our cordon in the brush.

The .303 cases meant *adoo* militia, not the hardcore guerrillas who were armed with the latest fully automatic Russian rifles. In any sudden contact in close country it is the side with the greatest initial firepower that usually comes off best. Our rifles had to be cocked anew after each shot and this had a dampening effect on the morale of the Sultan's soldiers.

I watched Bill Prince closely. I saw how he handled the men and the sergeants, Arab and Baluchi, how he controlled seventy men in thick bush by night and a great many minor things that I might need to know in the days ahead.

We were unaware of a new *adoo* group, the strongest yet to enter Dhofar, which at this time crossed the Yemeni border seventy miles to the west.

*   *   *

Reunion on ice after seven months apart

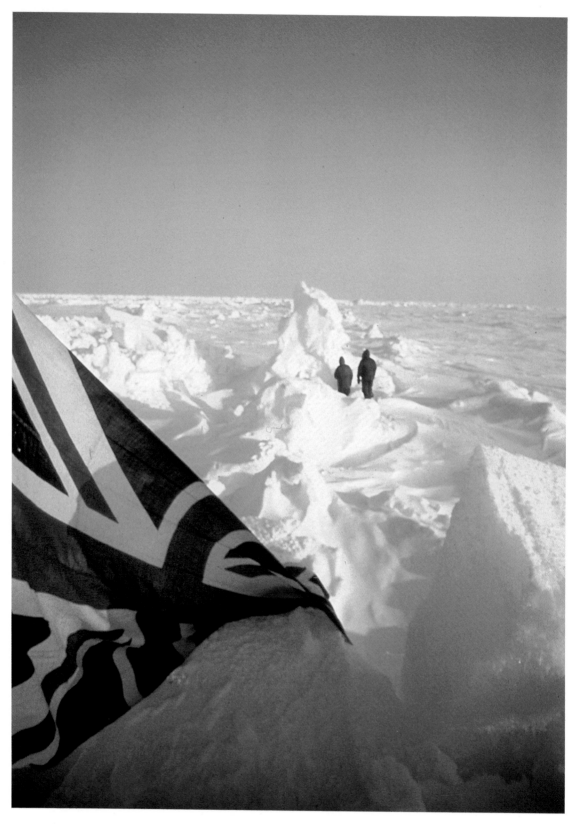

Easter Day, 1982. The author and Charlie Burton become the first men to reach both Poles overland

The author with Browning machine-gun in ambush position in the Qara mountain range, 1968

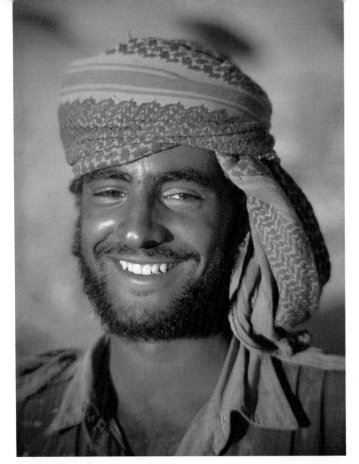

Left *Fat Hamid, Omani member of Recce Platoon*

Opposite above *The author removing an anti-tank mine carefully because of a possible grenade beneath*

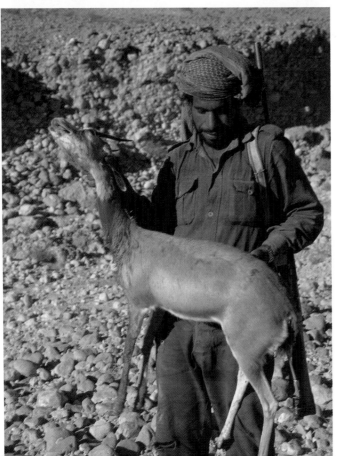

Left *Ali Nasser with the evening meal, a Thompson's gazelle*

Opposite below *Bringing field-gun up a gulley in the Nejd desert*

Overleaf *Night guard on the edge of the Empty Quarter*

Dead adoo *(Communist guerilla) with Kalashnikov rifle following battle of Mirbat fort*

Cave ambush above the spring of Arzat

Muscat Regiment soldiers after an operation in the foothills

The British officer is Captain 'Tom Greening', Dhofar intelligence officer

Ginnie while living in the harem of Sheik Hilal, 1974

Ginnie (in my harem), 1982

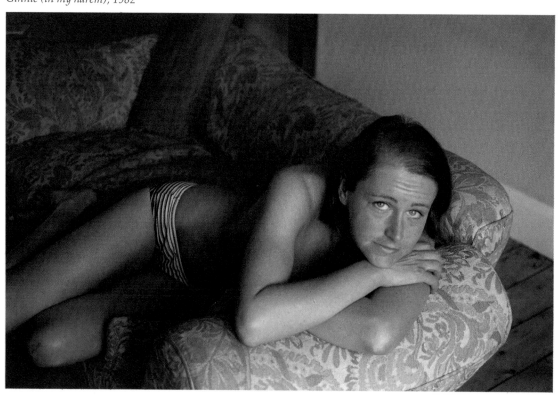

David Bayley and I arrived in Dhofar in July 1968. The *adoo* leader in Hauf, Al Ghassani, had, on 20 July, completed preparations for an attack on RAF Salalah. Together with his chief strategist Abdel Tahir, Al Ghassani had mustered 400 Russian-trained guerrillas armed with modern Soviet weapons and Chinese fieldguns which were each portable by twelve men or four camels.

As the monsoon mists settled over the entirety of the Jebel and the slippery infiltration trails, the guerrillas left Hauf and, on 1 August, split into two equal groups. Abdel Tahir's unit moved on east to the government outpost of Marbat while Al Ghassani's men headed for the foothills immediately north of Salalah and the RAF base.

During the last week of July the South African intelligence officer in Salalah, whose attentions were normally focussed on collecting wild flowers, surprised himself and everyone else by producing a snippet of intelligence. Under cover of the monsoon, he declared, the *adoo* were planning an attack on one of the two towns east of Salalah, Marbat or Taqah; he was not sure which or when.

Each town was garrisoned by Omanis in an isolated fort whose sole lifeline, in the event of attack, was an Army signaller.

Colonel Mike Harvey was away from Dhofar at the time but his stand-in, a major, sent the only company on the plain off to search Taqah, the nearer of the two towns. Only one track led east to Taqah and, twenty-five miles further on, to Marbat. This was a narrow gravel road, running parallel to the seashore, which the *adoo* frequently mined.

After a four-hour drive, with many halts to check for mines, we reached Taqah and placed machine gun sections all around the town except on the seaward flank. Monsoon breakers dashed against the sand and then sucked backwards with a roar of sound, deadening the clatter of rifles and boots as the platoons hurried to their positions.

The cordon was quickly in place, for Taqah was not much larger than the area covered by a football stadium. Most of the houses, single-storey clay-brick buildings, were hugger-mugger about four narrow streets with a patchwork rim of gardens on all sides. Withered fig trees and indigo bushes, from which the tribes obtain dark blue pigment for their cloth, bordered the strips of cultivation. From time to time the mediaeval fortress of Taqah floated into view beyond the town. Then fresh banks of mist closed over the high butte above us and the vision was gone.

The *wali* of the fortress, who owned a separate house in the town, greeted us with an extravagant display of silver coffee pots and fresh fruit. Extravagant but sincere, for these were tricky times to be *wali* to a lonely garrison in a town full of Dhofaris. Any show of Army strength could only bolster his confidence and that of his twenty *askars* – northern Omanis doing a two-year stint of duty as civil policemen. Aged from twelve to twenty, they could not have held their fort against a determined attack without the assurance of speedy Army back-up. Their only protection was the fort's high thick walls and their own paltry fire-power.

The pleasantries over, the *wali* and Bill Prince left to supervise an arms search in the town. This was completed by dusk. In a makeshift intelligence centre, money was exchanged for market gossip. But everything was vague. Rumours of rumours. We returned to Salalah none the wiser.

At 7.36 a.m. on 7 August a Baluchi duty operator at Umm al Ghawarif Signals Centre picked up a faint but insistent message. He recognised the call-sign of Marbat Fort and the twin treble-dash in Morse of an Operations Immediate message. For five minutes he scribbled furiously, translating the broken code into English which he could not understand.

Five hours later our Beaver circled above Marbat but could see too little through the mist to assess the situation. Then both of the Air Force jets strafed the high ground inland of the fort. They could see no people but the red flag of the Sultan still flew so, hoping for the best, they parachuted ammunition crates between the fort and the sea.

Our company commander ordered an immediate move to Marbat so Salalah was again denuded of an effective defence unit. Our convoy made good time to Taqah but soon afterwards an ammunition lorry overturned in a *wadi* and scattered its volatile load down a rocky slope.

There were two deep, narrow gorges *en route* to Marbat and we came to the first at dusk. Bill Prince sent me forward with a platoon and, long before reaching the lip of the defile, I smelled cordite fumes mingled with the scent of flowering shrubs. The *adoo* had blown up the track at its narrowest, steepest point. Two soldiers with mine detectors edged down the track and the rest of us gazed at the dark holes of caves. A good place to prepare for a killing.

The company commander wisely left all the vehicles beside the sea and ordered us to continue the eleven miles east on foot. If the Marbat garrison were desperate by now, they would have to hold out at least another nine hours.

To give warning of possible ambushes at the two deep *wadis*, Bill told me to move ahead with two machine gunners and a transceiver. Slowly, for there was no moon, we traversed the first gorge and, on the far side, I clicked the pressel switch of the walkie-talkie twice. Bill's reply came back at once, three quiet clicks. Under cover of the machine guns, the ninety men of B Company clambered to join us. The crash of the monsoon surf drowned all noise.

We trudged east for eight hours in the soft sand of the dunes and, losing contact with the main body, continued without them to the mouth of the Wadi Marbat.

Not being heroically inclined, I stopped with the four machine-gunners in a cave close by the ruins of a mosque. With the advantage of hindsight, my action was most unfortunate since, during the very two hours I lay low awaiting Bill and the rest of B Company, the guerrillas withdrew their dead and wounded only a few hundred yards to our front beyond a rough patch of hillocks.

Soon after dawn the company arrived. They had marched along the soggy beach itself and the going had been painfully slow. Together, in battle order, we advanced into the mist and over the last low hills to Marbat.

The scene which unfolded jolted my memory. It seemed to have happened before but perhaps only in Technicolor in the Midhurst cinema. Shredded by shrapnel, the Sultan's flag fluttered from the battlements of the white fortress. As we breasted their horizon the turbaned *askars* who manned the turrets raised their rifles and cheered. I thought of the US Cavalry, in this case arriving too late in the day. We stepped through the bric-à-brac of battle and I noticed the black holes in the fort walls where 3.5 rockets had blasted through the solid masonry.

Askars, clasping one another with joy and pent-up relief, streamed out of the great wooden gates to greet us. A boy of twelve pulled two soldiers by their sleeves towards a corpse, evidence of his prowess the day before. I went over to listen and photograph the boy with the body. 'They attacked with ladders when they thought we had spent our last bullets. But I found three bullets by my bed. I came to the wall and saw this *adoo* below me. Many bullets came close and my cousin Nassir was hit. But I shot the *adoo* dead with one bullet. Look!'

The corpse was right below the battlements. The boy kicked at it and a cloud of flies rose buzzing. It must have lain there since the first night of the attack and could hardly have been shot from directly above since the entrails were partially exposed with a wound in the small of the back. The stomach gases had escaped through the wound and the belly was not swollen. The lad levered the body over with his bare foot.

'I killed two more last night but they took them away.' He beamed at us with pride, quite unaffected by the sight of the dead man's face, puffed and split by the heat. I wanted to vomit for the smell grew intense when the body slumped over.

We congratulated the *askars*, amazed at their survival and their luck. Fate had given them some warning. An *askar*, relieving himself on the beach, had heard noises of stealth and the clink of steel. He had crawled back and raised the alarm. The *wali* then opened the armoury and shared out the paltry stocks – just in time for the initial jarring crash, as the first rocket entered the compound. Eighty *adoo* attacked in groups with ladders under cover of heavy fire. By the time the two aircraft arrived with supplies, the garrison was all but out of ammunition.

We found evidence of a mortar baseplate position on a rooftop just east of the fort so we cordoned off the town with orders to search every house in the warren of streets. There were over 300 buildings, from wattle shacks to mud-brick two-storey houses honeycombed with dark rooms and cellars.

We searched in groups of four with lanterns and mine detectors. For days afterwards the stink of the houses clung to my hair and the bites of fleas covered my skin. In many cellars, *oomah* sardines dried out on racks or clipped to strings. Outside on the beaches they lay in great heaps but there the stench was not so confined.

We found curved *khanjas* and swords and bags of Maria Theresa dollars dated 1780, still used as a local currency. Even in the poorest houses there were teak chests of perfumed clothes and silver ornaments, some exquisitely worked. Crude urinals of clay were built into the flat rooftops, their waste pipes leaning over the edge of the buildings.

We found three modern rifles, ammunition and a case containing faded photographs of Arabs in uniform. These were confiscated to give to the South African intelligence officer to puzzle over.

The storekeepers of Marbat told us that times were worse than they could remember. The traditional barter with Adeni merchants had, after centuries, dried up the previous year owing to the hostilities. They had a fine stock of frankincense and the skins of wildcat, hyena and wolf but there were no buyers. What could they do? They had long since despaired of any help from the government.

Dispirited, on the second evening at Marbat, I went to the beach and undressed alone in the dark. I stripped off and tried to wash at the edge of the surf. The salt water made my clothes sticky but at least my flea bites stung healthily and stopped irritating.

On the eve of the third day we left Marbat after replenishing the *askars'* ammunition stocks. By midnight we reached Kohr Rawrhi creek near Taqah and camped at the ruins of Sumhuran. Over 2000 years ago this was the greatest city of southeastern Arabia, peopled by worshippers of the Moon God, Sin, guardian of the frankincense stores. From here camel trains loaded with incense marched to every part of Arabia and the Roman Empire. The first taxed and policed caravan route was agreed between the Yemeni Queen of Sheba and her northern neighbour King Solomon of Jerusalem. When the creek became blocked by rock falls the seaward trade and the mother city died. I walked between the lorries to the ruins and by the clifftops found the mouth of a deep well.

From the west I thought I heard the boom of a distant explosion above the din of the sea.

Others followed, clearer now, and I hurried back towards the lorries. A rustle sounded in the scrub ahead and I switched on my torch, startled. A black snake, five feet long, uncoiled and hissed at me. I hit at it with my rifle, splintering the stock and missing the snake. Still hissing, it disappeared under rocks.

There were no more explosions so I fell asleep under a lorry. A minute later, it seemed, David Bayley woke me. 'Come on Ran. We're off. A message has come through. Salalah's under attack.'

We dispensed with the normal precaution of mine clearance but kept all vehicle lights switched off in case of ambush. Drivers could only avoid overturning by staying on the main track. Even then it was only possible to see the vague outline of the trail by looking skywards but concentrating on the lower rim of vision. Our luck held and by 2.00 a.m. we reached our camp at Umm al Ghawarif.

All was quiet. The worst had not happened. A mortar attack had been mounted against the RAF camp but the expected follow-up had not materialised. Exhausted, we slept – but not for long.

Bill Prince shook me awake at 9.30. He was weary, unshaven and, though his briar was in position, it was unlit.

'The *adoo*,' he grunted, 'have sunk to an all-time low. It seems they have attacked two RAF lorries emptying sewage near the foothills. Almost certainly against the Geneva Convention. We are to go and inspect the damage.'

Pining for breakfast and smelling of Marbat, I dressed, pocketed two grenades from my pen-tray, and went to the lorries. Sleep-bemused soldiers, tucking shirts into trousers, scrambled aboard. Only two platoons of fifteen men each, and a mortar section, were going. Within twenty minutes we were past the RAF camp and heading for a thin plume of smoke by the foothills.

We halted some way back from the burning lorry. Bill set up his 81mm mortars and told me to take the platoons forward to check the lorry and search for signs of the enemy's fire positions. Both of us, I think, assumed the *adoo*, with their normal hit-and-run tactics, had long since departed. The men were clearly annoyed by this pointless task after their exertions in Marbat. They advanced in a line, listless and close together, my sergeant Seramid's men to my left and the platoon of a staff-sergeant I did not know on my right. The ground was flat and without cover all the way to the ant-hill line some 400 yards ahead. No birds rose in alarm as we closed on the scrub. No grazing camels loped away.

For some reason we were spared annihilation by the *adoo* themselves. Perhaps a sweating finger pressed in error too hard against the hair-trigger of an SKS. Perhaps the leader, whoever he was, decided that 300 yards was close enough to kill and not be killed. Had they waited just another minute our slaughter would have been assured. As it was, the first shock wave of high-velocity bullets passed slightly high with a crackle that sent us instantly to the ground.

The signaller beside me fired wildly, his eyes tightly shut. The blast from his first round removed an inch of skin from one of my fingers and filled my eyes with dust. I squinted but failed to see any identifiable target beyond the vague outline of low sangars of clay, protective works dug between ant-hills.

The weight of fire was stunning and interfered with my thought processes. Fear was tugging at my mind. A rock the size of a football would have been enough to shelter behind, but there was nothing.

My signaller lay behind his radio set, his face pressed into the earth. Bullets cracked by, closer now as the *adoo* adjusted their aim by the spurts of mud kicked up all about us. To my astonishment the staff-sergeant on my right screamed 'Advance!' and ran forward. Well behind him his men followed suit.

Automatically I shouted to Seramid's men, 'Rapid covering fire – 300 yards.'

The staff-sergeant's a lunatic, I thought. To advance will simply hasten our plight. But at the same time I felt a stabbing guilt. I was being yellow – shown up as a coward by an Arab in front of Arabs. I thought of my father. I kicked the signaller to help fuel my courage level and yelled at Seramid. Weaving low, as I had years before on Aldershot heath, I went forward until parallel with the staff-sergeant's men. Then I dropped to the ground. More than enough heroics for the day.

But no, the little staff-sergeant was up again yelling at his men who seemed to be stuck to the ground with Superglue.

'Stop!' I screamed at him. 'Get down!' But he did not hear. Suddenly he jerked to a halt in mid-air, his rifle flying away. He fell to the ground and lay still. 'Thank God,' I breathed to myself. I grabbed the headset and spoke to Bill Prince.

As he answered, the first brace of mortar bombs exploded in the ant-hills. 'That will shake them. I've signalled for the Provost. How many *adoo* do you reckon?'

I could not tell. I had only spotted three sangars but *adoo* muzzle flashes were visible over a front of 600 yards.

Without warning a Provost fighter dived low directly above me and headed for the ant-hills. I switched on my Sarbe pocket beacon. This operated to any aircraft on the international distress frequency of 121.5 megacycles. I tried to speak to the pilot but there was no reply. The ground shook as a 250-pound fragmentation bomb exploded over the ant-hills. Metal chunks whistled by.

Now we must advance. I rose to move but a wasp's nest of bullets warned me off. I wondered why I had not yet been hit and what it would feel like.

The Provost had climbed for another run-in. The pilot now came in on my Sarbe radio. I knew the man, a middle-aged Scotsman, dour but kindly, with a Conquistador moustache. Despite our mortars, a stream of *adoo* tracer was plainly visible pouring up at the Provost as it dived. The second and last bomb fell well behind the *adoo* sangars.

The Scotsman climbed out of his dive as bullets slashed through the fuselage. One jammed the joystick control hard back with the ailerons fully elevated. The Provost climbed steeply. Realising he was about to flip or stall, either course being fatal, the pilot slid back and jettisoned the cockpit cover prior to a parachute exit. But he could not get out of his seat. The joystick jammed his escape. Struggling for his life, he managed to force the lever forward and the aircraft instantly levelled off, almost throwing him from the open cabin. Through brute force and the luck of the devil the Scotsman landed safely at the RAF strip three miles away.

Bill's mortars were now ranged on the *adoo* sangars and the guerrillas withdrew. We advanced with caution and found well-sited sangars for fifty or sixty men. There were scattered heaps of empty cases, machine-gun clips and bloodstained cloths, but no bodies. By a miracle our dynamic staff-sergeant was only wounded: a bullet had passed through one of his thighs.

'We'll not be so lucky again,' said Bill as we walked back to the lorries. 'Automatic weapons are new to them now, but their shooting can only improve.'

*　　*　　*

Six miles to the south in the confines of his beach-front palace, Sultan Said bin Taimur had for the first time heard the sounds of fighting and this, unlike months of prompting by advisers, persuaded him to re-equip his army. He ordered 3000 7.62 FN rifles and a million rounds of ball and tracer at once.

My month on loan to the Northern Frontier Regiment over, I flew back to BidBid.

At mid-day on 10 August, Radio Baghdad reported the clash between Al Ghassani and Bill Prince. Their version claimed 'the destruction of one Hawker Hunter and the death of forty-nine British imperialist troops for the loss of only six dead and ten wounded martyrs.' The BBC said nothing. This was not surprising since most of the British public had never heard of Dhofar.

8

Recce

Whatever you do, do cautiously, and look to the end.

GESTA ROMANORUM

My decision to leave Oman had not wavered while in Dhofar. Back in BidBid, I decided to visit the men of the Recce Platoon before seeing the colonel to tender my resignation.

Driver Murad suggested a coffee party to celebrate my return and hustled me round to the billet. Everyone joined in, even the normally reserved Baluchis. There were remarks about my improved Arabic and proprietorial pats on my back. Little Ali Nasser commented on 'the battle of the sewage truck'. Mohamed Rashid of the Beard said simply, 'We are pleased you are back, Sahb. Now we will begin to train and become strong, God willing.'

Staff-sergeant Abdullah joined us. He greeted me with warmth. 'I smelled Murad's coffee from the other end of camp and knew we must have an important guest.'

Sitting on beds, tin trunks and the cool concrete floor we sipped the hot black coffee. I knew that I liked these men. I felt they could become an effective little group for the fighting in Dhofar.

Later I spoke with Abdullah and, trusting his discretion, told him of my intention to resign. He shook his head as I spoke. When I was finished he gripped my arm. 'No. No. Sahb. You are very wrong. I understand your words but you must see other sides to the problem. I have met Communists, from abroad, here in Oman. They have silken tongues but their talk of revolution is without sound base. They try to turn us from God and that must never be. Communism must not come here, Sahb.' His voice rose with the urgency of his words and his grip tightened on my shoulder. 'Perhaps it is true that the Sultan gives us nothing, Omanis as well as Dhofaris. But he has stopped the fights and feuds that plagued Oman under previous rulers. With peace between the tribes our life has improved.'

He relaxed his grip but his eyes were fixed on mine. 'You must not feel the British do wrong here, Sahb. They do not meddle with our way of life or our religion. Listen to me.' He lowered his voice. 'It is said in the *sooq* that Qaboos, the son of the Sultan, will rule before long. With oil money, he will give us those very things the Communists are promising but without taking away our religion. If you British leave before that can happen, then the Communists will take over without a doubt. They will force us to denounce Islam or they will kill us.'

I was impressed by Abdullah's sincerity but unconvinced. It was several days later, in the BidBid garden, that I finally came to justify my own role without misgivings.

Captain Tom Greening*, from whom I had taken over the Recce Platoon, had returned briefly

---

*The captain, whose real name I have not given, is now a brigadier and HM Sultan Qaboos's personal representative in England.

from an intelligence course to see old friends in BidBid before going to a different part of Oman. He had, I knew, a special relationship with the Sultan's son, Qaboos bin Said. They had been at Sandhurst together and, when Qaboos was kept under house arrest in Salalah, Tom was allowed to visit him. This seemed harmless enough to the old Sultan who was unaware that they were plotting a coup to oust him. I knew nothing of this but recognised Tom's extensive knowledge of Oman and the current crisis. He talked with authority and feeling and I listened absorbed.

Afterwards I felt both reassurance and a personal sense of purpose. Change was inevitable in Oman. Either the Sultan must use his new oil revenue for progress or a more enlightened ruler must take over. The critical period was now – until one or other improvement occurred. Unless the British ensured the status quo during this dangerous time, the Communists would, via Dhofar, take over all of southeastern Arabia. Once Dhofar fell, Oman would follow and if Dhofaris were not soon given aid or support by their existing government, they would continue to swell the ranks of the People's Front for the Liberation of the Occupied Arabian Gulf (PFLOAG).

From Tom's summary it was clear to me that I must stay and do all in my power to help keep PFLOAG at bay, at least for as long as it took Tom and others to remove the Sultan and replace him with Qaboos.

The matter was straightforward. Some 2000 Soviet-inspired terrorists were attempting to bring atheistic Communism to over half a million people against their will and their disposition. Arabs are individualistic with keenly developed ideas about religion, morals and the inferiority of other beings in general and women in particular. In short their whole essence is diametrically opposed to the Communist ethic. Arabs do not take naturally to regimentation whether Fascist or Communist and it was up to us to see that the Omanis and Dhofaris were subjected to neither. I had further qualms from time to time but never again considered resignation.

Weekly reports were signalled from Dhofar. In September the monsoon clouds began to disperse and the few available army units moved into the mountains. Subsequent clashes indicated that newly trained *adoo* bands with modern weapons had arrived in many regions of the Jebel. Their tactics were imaginative, their shooting accurate.

Weapons such as heavy 81mm mortars and Russian machine-guns were now in *adoo* hands. It was no longer safe for Army units to travel on the Jebel at less than half-company strength, some sixty men. Recce Platoon, even if I could recruit successfully, would number only thirty men and, being vehicle-borne, would be especially vulnerable to the *adoo*.

As the last monsoon mists lingered over the Jebel, four Land Rovers of the Northern Frontier Regiment Recce Platoon were ambushed in a gulley between three *adoo* machine-guns. The leading two vehicles and their crews were shredded. Total slaughter was averted only by a shift in the mist cover.

The CO summoned me and gave me 8 weeks to prepare Recce for operations in Dhofar. We must cover those camel caravan infiltration routes from the Yemen left unguarded following the NFR ambush. The training started at the hottest time of the Omani year. Beyond the camp compound, where gravel hills formed mirages, a choking dust rose under foot and no one liked playing soldier with heavy steel gear too hot to touch except through a cloth.

At 9.00, sticky wet and streaked with salt, we stopped for an hour's breakfast. From 10.00 until 1.00 we worked at ambush reaction drills and again for two hours in the evening when the heat was more bearable. During the afternoons everyone slept and, away from the protection of local shadows, the air burned into nostrils and lungs. The men complained, but not to my face.

Abdullah came to my room in the evenings to sip *loomee*, a drink of sweetened lime juice, cooled with ice. After a polite pause the day's woes came out, a filtered and censored version of the verbal attacks he had himself suffered earlier from the men. Some requested compassionate leave with heart-rending tales of their family's plight. This I refused as the men had already received their annual quota of leave. Two of the Baluchis and three Omanis applied for transfer to the companies, all of which I granted. The two bedu asked for discharge from the Army, and I passed on their request to the colonel happily.

I took care to allot nasty jobs evenly between Baluchis and Omanis and this meant the latter no longer received the preferential treatment they had grown to expect. On the other hand, they all suffered daily from the same pressures, so for once their grumbles were in unison.

My five years with Centurion tanks had done little to prepare me for an infantry Recce Platoon, but I did find my SAS training useful. One of the few hard and fast Hereford rules was movement by night whenever feasible and my brief visit to Dhofar led me to apply this maxim to Recce Platoon. In the SAS, four men form a basic operational group, not two dozen, so I worked on my own system of control by night. The resulting drills were not to be found in any textbook but they emphasised speed, simplicity, silence and common sense.

All our training involved use of live ammunition and some of the men acted as *adoo* to represent the sort of emergencies I expected to meet in Dhofar. Only when each man reacted instinctively to twenty simple hand-signals did we begin to train at night, still using live ammunition. Total silence of movement would be essential in Dhofar but here it took weeks to eliminate clattering pebbles, stifled coughs, loud whisperings and the clunk of rifle butts on rock.

Advances over broken ground by night, with frequent switches from single file to line abreast and back to file, were practised time after time. Whispers were no longer necessary once reactions to hand signals were perfected. Any error could cause chaos and, in Dhofar, death.

If the moon shone, the men spread out automatically to twenty-yard intervals and so never presented a worthwhile ambush target. When it was dark, they closed up enough to identify and pass on the hand signals which dictated the types of formation in which we would move through changing terrain.

Abdullah laid trip flares in defiles to simulate night ambushes. As for a daytime ambush, our section leaders reacted by falling flat and flinging a phosphorus 83 grenade towards the *adoo* position. In four seconds a dense cloud of white phosphorus smoke would give us cover for withdrawal or counter-attack. If the *adoo* were positioned among rocks, the descending shower of phosphorus would fall on them, whereas the shrapnel from a Mills grenade would merely bounce off the rocks.

Our clothes quickly rotted from the salt of our sweat. Sharp rock and camel thorns cut through our shoes and equipment. Some men wore socks but most used only canvas gym shoes, however rough the terrain. The regiment's quartermaster was a good-natured Englishman, but his equipment stocks were limited and he kept a tight rein on them so that only a quarter of Recce's requirements were met. Luckily, during the hottest months, most of the British officers went on leave and Pakistani or Omani junior officers took their place. I made friends with many of these men, exchanging occasional gifts of cigarettes or fruit for supplies. The quartermaster sergeant, an amiable Pakistani, was most generous with equipment once the quartermaster himself was away. Two new signallers and three new BCC 30 radio sets came from the Indian signals lieutenant and a generous supply of spare Land Rover parts from the MT sergeant. By late October Murad had all five vehicles in working order. Now I only needed the men to fill them.

Of the fifteen soldiers in Recce when I arrived, seven had left disillusioned and Abdullah was due to de-mob in a month. Only eight men, not including drivers, remained. I told the CO. I needed eighteen soldiers, three signallers and a medic. His eyebrows shot upwards but he agreed to my asking for five volunteers from each company. He warned me this would be unpopular. Company bosses would only allow their least capable men to transfer. I knew that, but the time of year was again in my favour since two of the three company majors were on leave.

The very next day I set off with a Land Rover filled with my selection panel. Abdullah, Ali Nasser and Mohamed Rashid of the Beard were joined by a Baluch Moolah or priest to vet Baluchi entrants. After five hours we came to the city of Rostaq with its crumbling fort dwarfed by the sheer walls of the Jebel Akhdar.

The company commander was Captain Guy Sheridan, a colleague from Beaconsfield, and a Royal Marine. Years later he led the raid which re-captured South Georgia from Argentinian forces. Now he was acting company commander in his major's absence and was quite unconcerned when I told him of my mission. 'Go ahead. I'll get the sergeant major to put the word about. Any keen young fellows wanting a couple of years with Recce Platoon. It might help their promotion prospects. I'm sure the major would approve.'

We were given an empty desk with a bench on which Abdullah, the diminutive Ali Nasser, Mohamed, Murad in dark glasses and the giant Moolah all managed to squeeze on either side of me, presenting a formidable array of black beards to any would-be applicant.

The word which Abdullah put out must have been a much-twisted version of my original, fairly honest propaganda, for a gratifyingly long queue formed outside our room.

First to enter was a small man with a wild mop of hair. He greeted and shook hands effusively with all the board members and then, placing himself centrally, stood rigidly to attention, eyes fixed on the ceiling.

'Your name?' Abdullah asked.

'Saif Musabbah.'

'Tribe?'

'Hawasena.'

At this I noticed a certain warmth among the board. All but Murad and the Moolah were of the same ilk or of tribes allied to the Hawasena.

'Why do you wish to join Recce?' I asked.

'Yes, I wish to join.'

'But why?'

'God be praised.'

'Is it because of the comforts of Land Rovers or because you have friends already in Recce?'

'God be praised, Sahb.'

I gave up. He seemed a strong, honest type. I told him what to expect with Recce: how much more training than with the companies; how little use would be made of the Land Rovers and how much of our feet; how we would have to move in the Jebel without help from the companies; and how there would be no discrimination or segregation between Arab and Baluchi.

Quite unmoved, the little man replied: '*Im shaalah*, all will be well and I shall in time receive promotion.'

Abdullah told him to wait outside.

Three tough-looking Omanis arrived late and out of breath, a swarthy pirate-face with a lopsided mouth, a thin mortar crewman named Said Salim who carried a stiletto in a sheath and a gentle-faced ox named Hamid Sultan. All three stated firmly '*Ureed Recce, Sahb*', 'I want Recce', after listening to my tale of predicted woes.

Hamid Sultan came back a second time, propelling a Hawasena corporal with the bearing of a Scots Guard sergeant major and quick disarming smile. Abdullah whispered to me with excitement, 'This man is known for his bravery. All men like him. He is Salim Khaleefa of the Benni Hinna. If you cannot find a sergeant when I go, this corporal will surely be all that you need.'

The five successful applicants went to pack their simple belongings, a metal trunk and a bedding roll, and to take leave of their friends. I thanked Guy and we left for BidBid with our human booty.

The following day we visited Ziki camp and another company. Alarmed at the all-Arab influx from Rostaq, our Moolah toured the billets with his own line of patter. The Recce Sahb, he said, was scrupulously fair to all and had even rid the platoon of the two hated bedu who had long made life miserable for the Recce Baluchis. In the Companies, he added, there were British officers who loved Arabs only and gave Baluchis the dangerous work. This, he promised, would never happen in Recce.

Two tall Baluchis applied and were accepted. Sadeeq Jumma and his friend were inseparable, spoke good Arabic unlike many Baluchis and were, unknown to the Moolah, hasheesh addicts.

A six-foot Zanzibari with a handshake that crushed my fingers and a head of fine black fuzz wished to join us for original reasons. Recce Platoon, he observed, had more machine-guns per man than the companies. Mubarreq Obeid had been unable to obtain the post of machine-gunner in his company. With such a weapon, he said, his thick lips compressed in a snarl, he could kill many Chinese *Shooyooeen* in Dhofar and that was his main desire in life.

I protested that there were no Chinese Communists in Arabia, but Mubarreq was adamant. 'You are wrong Sahb. They are behind the troubles everywhere. Soon there will be many like locusts in Dhofar. In my house in Zanzibar, the Chinaman talked to the African of how he must throw out the Arab. Then, seven years ago, they rose and murdered all the Arabs they could catch, slitting many throats of people still asleep. Some of us escaped to the *dhows* but my parents were chased along the beach by a crowd, though my mother was African. They ran into the sea to swim to us in the boats but some of the crowd followed, caught hold of their hair and drowned them. So I, Mubarreq, have no parents because of the Chinese rats.'

When he had gone, I looked at the others. All nodded their assent.

Once I had thirty men I divided them into five sections of six, allotting to each a Land Rover driver and signaller. The Baluchis, a third of the total, were evenly spread through the sections, and in the billet their practice of sleeping as a group was stopped. Now they must identify themselves by sections and not by race. I gave expensive prizes to the best section in skills competitions.

Abdullah lived in a separate room so Corporal Salim Khaleefa was effectively in charge. I gave one section to a Baluchi and the remaining two to Ali Nasser and Mohamed Rashid of the Beard whom I promoted.

Each section commander carried a radio transceiver with a two-mile range. Three sections also carried a BCC 30 backpack set with a 200-mile range. By day or night the men were allowed to talk on the sets only in a whisper.

In mid-October five Land Rovers bulging with men and weapons left BidBid at dawn for a six-day exercise. Murad drove along a *wadi* bed, corkscrewing into the bowels of the Jebel Akhdar until a boulder barred the way. He pulled up, patted my back, grinning, and said, 'Have a good time up there, Sahb. I will be back here in six days. It would make me most happy to come with you but sadly these other foolish drivers need my guiding hand.'

Our six days were to be spent 10,000 feet up the Jebel. Corporal Salim knew the way, leaving the *wadi* trail by a certain tamarisk shrub and following a track often visible only by a slight shine to the rock. We ascended a near sheer ravine where no breath of wind alleviated the blistering heat. At 5000 feet we rested and sucked limes picked *en route*. We did not drink: it is bad practice to drink often on the march. Finally we stopped at the spring of Salut where the Beni Riyyam water their camels. There we drank and refilled out *zamzamia* bags.

Nights on the Jebel Akhdar were blissfully cool. There was no moon. We moved through countryside unknown to us towards a deserted village eight miles over the broken plateau. By dawn we reached the village. We had marched in ever-changing formations, using only hand signals, never a word. The men were pleased with themselves and friendly banter began as to which section was the most efficient.

'What will keep us alive by night?' I asked them.

'Silence,' they shouted. 'No coughing, no snoring, no sneezing.'

Beneath us the mountain fell away in giddy tiers of irrigated steps. Each layer was fed by artificial water channels which came together in a terminal pond. This overflowed in a single cascade to the step below and so on for 2000 feet of tiny fertile orchards. Figs, pomegranates, nectarines and peaches flourished alongside almonds, walnuts and berries of several types. Sugar-cane groves bunched on the lower tiers and lucerne spread a green carpet at every level. Butterflies and small highly coloured birds enjoyed the sunlight and the bounty. Above us massive crags formed chimneys and buttresses.

On the sixth day we descended again to Salut where, not far from the spring, a steep scree chute falls away towards the Wadi Muaydin for more than 1000 feet. With Mubarreq and two of the Arabs, I slithered at speed down the loose slate of the scree. It took fourteen minutes, followed by an hour's wait for the others who descended by the orthodox track.

We returned five more times to the mountain plateau and each time the pace improved. Three Baluchis and an Arab found life too difficult and we replaced them. Soon our regiment was to depart for a year in Dhofar with no home leave so, for two weeks, we drove to the far corners of Oman, stopping in remote villages to meet and eat with the families of the men.

At the end of November we returned to BidBid and, four days later, left for Dhofar. Abdullah had seen me through the difficult times. Now I was confident. He stood alone by the camp gates and waved as the five Land Rovers of singing men left the compound.

For two months we patrolled the Gat'n deserts north of the Dhofar Jebel, ranging north to the edge of the Empty Quarter and west to the Yemeni border. I enjoyed the life and found the men good companions so the time passed quickly: it was a period of quiet before the storm.

I was due my regulation six weeks' annual leave so, putting Corporal Salim Khaleefa in charge, I returned to Britain.

*   *   *

While at Beaconsfield I had begun plans for an expedition to ascend the Nile from mouth to source with two Land Rovers and, as an afterthought, two mini-hovercraft. With a touch of optimism I had decided the journey would take less than six weeks and so would fit neatly into my leave period from the Sultan's army.

From BidBid I had written to European manufacturers requesting free goods but the response had been poor. Back in Britain I went home to Lodsworth. Ginnie's family had moved away and she now lived there with my mother. I felt guilty that my leave would not be spent at home with them.

There was a great deal to prepare in the ten days before we were due to leave for Egypt. Ginnie correlated and waterproofed 400 maps of the Nile. Two Hoverhawk two-seater hovercraft had been promised me but only now did I discover that the maximum distance one had ever travelled non-stop was four miles round and round a gravel pit. My cousin Gubbie's father-in-law, director-general of the AA, responded to my appeal with the loan of a pensioned-off diesel Land Rover painted bright yellow. All efforts to borrow a second vehicle failed.

My worldly wealth, until now raided only to pay the Castle Combe fines, consisted of £8000. I would need this one day to marry and buy a home. But the Nile arrangements could go ahead only through private investment on my part since, to obtain a Land Rover and travel reservations to Egypt, I would need £6000.

My mother was adamant. The money would be lost and I would end up with nothing. It was not fair to Ginnie whose father, once a millionaire, was now bankrupt and unable to leave her a penny. I argued that, once de-mobbed, my only career potential lay with expeditions. The £6000 was therefore an investment needed to lay the ground for bigger, more ambitious journeys to come. This appalled my mother, who could see no end to my lunatic approach to life and my failure to settle down to a worthwhile profession.

Since there was no alternative, I frittered away my private fortune in purchasing a brand new petrol Land Rover, there being no available diesel models.

To tow the two half-ton hovercraft behind the Land Rovers we obtained trailers specially made by a company with a flourishing business in babies' perambulators.

The expedition team were chosen without any check on their characters. The first member was Nick Holder, an old Mons Cadet School colleague. His place on the team was assured because the idea of the expedition had been his. He had read a book called *The White Nile* by Alan Moorehead and persuaded me in Bahrain to put things together for a voyage up the river. After three years with the Parachute Regiment, Nick had become a razor salesman for Gillette. They posted him to Bahrain, a difficult mission since 95 per cent of the male inhabitants were bearded and the females happy with hairy legs. Unable to alter one of the fundamental facets of Islam, Nick had left Gillette and was unemployed.

Peter Loyd was selected chiefly because we needed somebody who could handle a hovercraft and, unable to find such a person, I decided the next best thing must be a helicopter pilot. Peter had just completed an army helicopter course. Like Nick Holder, he had been a member of the Norwegian parachute expedition the previous year.

A volunteer movie cameraman and Mike Broome, a photographer, also joined up. We now needed only a hovercraft mechanic. The owner of our sponsors, Hoverhawk Ltd, an elderly but spirited lady, summoned her son the sales director, Charlie Westmorland, and told him that he would accompany us. Charlie, thirty years old, displayed neither dismay nor surprise at his mother's announcement. I was to learn that Charlie never showed any emotion other than pleasure. He was ideal expedition material apart from his laugh, which was hysterical and uncontrollable.

The team met up at Dover in mid-February during a blizzard and drove through France and Italy, then by car ferry to Alexandria, Egypt. A few perfunctory sandbags rested against shop windows, the only visible sign of the war then raging with Israel.

The British consul handed me a letter from the embassy in Cairo. This had been sent too late to my home in England and then forwarded by my mother to Alexandria. 'The Egyptian Ministry of Tourism have turned down your proposed expedition. This must be a disappointment to you but I am sure you will realise that . . . due to the war . . . foreigners are suspect . . . Under normal circumstances you would have been welcome.'

We set out at once to Cairo to remonstrate. Close by the pyramids a tyre burst on a trailer and the wheel nuts would not budge. Two hours later we discovered they were French nuts and unscrewed the wrong way. God knows how the Concorde functions.

The British military attaché in Cairo believed that we had arrived in good faith unaware of the official refusal. But, he told us, a state of emergency had been declared that very morning. Citizen forces were to be armed, civic buildings sandbagged and blacked-out by night. Patrol centres had been hurriedly established at each Nile bridge to watch for Israeli commandos in the guise of tourists. No hovercraft had been seen before in Egypt and ours could easily be mistaken by an excitable home guard as weapons of war. Hovering on any part of the Nile within Egypt was out of the question. However, the attaché agreed to accompany us to the first checkpoint in the village of El Wasta. Nothing ventured, nothing gained. A crowd of curious *fellahin* closed about our trailers with the cry of '*tayyara abyad!*', 'white aeroplanes'.

At the barrier pole, seething with uniforms and heavy with body odour, we sat for an hour. At length a little policeman came to the cab window. 'You are the helicopter trade party from England going through Africa, yes?' I nodded vigorously.

'You are lucky,' he said. 'All others we turn back but you have the Ministry of Tourism to thank. We give you an escort south.'

Months later we discovered that we had the hovercraft to thank. One of the Egyptian ministries, perhaps of Agriculture or Defence, was interested in their potential.

All went well for several days until our escort abandoned us without explanation in Luxor. He assured us another escort would meet us 'somewhere south'. The town was short of campsites but, beside the police station, we found what Charlie called a lawn. All Luxor's dogs used this patch of waste-ground, as did any local with garbage to dispose of. After dinner on the lawn, by the light of a sixty-watt street lamp, we sipped Horlicks and decided to take stock. Peter unrolled our main river map. This was an impressive sight for it was eighteen feet long, some eighteen inches of which we had so far travelled. With a wax crayon Peter carefully marked our journey to date with camp sites and dates.

Our schedule was a week behind the timetable set in London to keep us just ahead of the sandstorm season in Northern Sudan and the flood season in the Sudd swamp region.

At Shellal, just south of Aswan and the site of the Nile barrage, the southerly road ended, submerged by the new reservoir. We bought tickets for the 200-mile ferry trip down the predictably-named Lake Nasser bound for Wadi Haifa and the Sudan. Throughout the long hot journey passengers from the main deck wishing to reach the dining saloon had to climb over both hovercraft or crawl under a Land Rover.

Nick unpacked our steriliser bottles and treated the scummy green water known to contain the

The Nile

103

flatworm parasites of bilharzia. This bug lives in the blood and bladders of many African riverfolk and kills thousands annually. Even spray from a canoe paddle can contain the worm which, landing on human skin, will burrow into a pore to escape the hot sun.

Early in March we landed at Wadi Haifa, Arabic for grassy valley, now a sprawl of wood and tin shanties in the sand. We had entered the Sudan, Africa's largest country, via the Nubian Desert.

The mighty dam had already caused the river here to rise an incredible 470 feet, with a further eighty feet still to go before the villagers could build permanent homes beside the new banks.

Ibrahim, the temporary commissioner of Wadi Haifa, gave me a telegram from Khartoum where the commercial attaché at our embassy, guessing at our likely arrival date, had arranged for a public hovercraft demonstration. The president and entire supreme court of the Sudan would attend. We had just eight days to hover 1000 miles of Nile. I told Ibrahim we would set out as soon as the hovercraft were ready.

Twenty-four hours later we left the Land Rover team of Peter, Nick, and our photographer, and, with much revving of engines, slid down the beach and away over the dawn-chilled waters of the lake with hardly a ripple to mark our passage. The machines were nicknamed Baker and Burton after Nile explorers. I drove Baker with fifteen spare gallons of fuel while Charlie shared his cramped cab with Anthony Brockhouse, our ciné cameraman. Burton was the newer but slower craft.

Wadi Haifa's low shacks soon disappeared. The lake was so wide and the enclosing granite hills so uniform that I could identify no break in the horizon to head for. Burton soon fell behind, a fast diminishing speck only visible when the rays of the morning sun reflected from the white fibreglass hull.

Rather than lose Charlie for the rest of the day and unable to slow down without unsettling the temperamental setting of engines and skirt, I circled slowly to the east and north until I headed back towards him. Now the gap between us closed with surprising speed for there was no sound and no sensation of movement, just the faint pull on the steering wheel as a breeze caught the fins. It was a novel feeling, quite unlike any other dimension of propulsion, and exaggerated by the vast and lonely lake.

We intended to camp at Akasha, a village above the flood level, where we would await the Land Rovers and more fuel. But one of Baker's engines began to overheat. I attracted Charlie's attention and made for the nearest beach. Repair work would take some time so we made camp.

We made radio contact with Peter. His news was also bad. Thirty miles to the east, the Land Rovers were bogged down in a trackless desert bowl surrounded by mountains. Their guide, a pitch-black Haifan, insisting he knew the way, had led them far from any usable trail into soft sands where a clutch had burned out. Peter was not sure how far they were from Akasha or whether they could find a way back to Wadi Haifa through the surrounding maze of sand dunes and rock bands. The wind had obliterated their tracks behind them. If they could replace the clutch they would attempt to return to Wadi Haifa. We had sufficient fuel so I told Peter we would also head back once Baker was repaired. There was always the railway which might still get us to Khartoum in time for the exhibition. Charlie announced that Baker had blown a piston head which would involve at least twenty-four hours of improvisation work to replace. On the second night Anthony was woken by a low primordial roar from the lake: he froze with horror in the dark as the sound of emerging bodies left the waves and began to ascend the beach. He stumbled to higher ground and, straining his eyes, made out three alligator shapes in the sand.

At dawn, as the wind-whipped lake turned slowly orange, Anthony discovered that his nocturnal visitors were horned lizards some four feet long. Before the sun rose they returned to the water.

Once the repairs were completed, our journey back to Wadi Haifa was enlivened by the winds which covered the lake in a sand cloud. Charlie used compass and drift estimation to land us quite near to our old campsite and there, a day later, we rejoined the others.

The weekly train to Khartoum left the next day and Ibrahim cabled for two open wagons to be sent. These would carry our vehicles at little extra cost.

That evening the local football team, who doubled as the town band, agreed to a song-and-dance show in our camp. Between the Land Rovers we built a log fire and, unaware of any danger, Peter lit it with a match. Downwind and on the far side of a vehicle Mike had decided to make firepots to provide more light for the dancers. He filled three tins with sand which he soaked in petrol from a jerry can. There was a sudden thud of exploding ignition followed by shrill screams.

Peter and I peered around the Land Rover and found Mike blindly pawing himself as a ball of flames enveloped him from knees to head. There was a nightmarish second of inactivity, so sudden and unexpected was the event. Then we jumped on Mike and rolled him in the sand, heaping handfuls of it on to his face and hands which were soaked in fuel. The fire kept re-igniting but at length we extinguished the last flame and Mike stopped screaming. He lay curled up like a grotesque foetus and stared moaning at the layers of blistered skin that hung in shrouds from his arms, stomach and thighs. Raw and bleeding flesh showed through where we had rubbed sand on burning skin.

I gave him a morphine jab and applied loose paraffin gauze dressings to the open wounds. Not having piped water, Wadi Haifans had to defecate on the beach and the dirt was spread about by minute sand flies, so Mike's wounds were likely to be infected. The local doctor, who arrived two hours later, administered penicillin pills and gentian violet. Then Mike slept and the Nubian drum-dancers arrived.

We left Wadi Haifa the next day on a great steel train made years ago in Birmingham. We stripped to our shorts because it was so hot. Nick opened a window but dust and soot poured in. So we sat on the wooden seats dripping in sweat, as though the carriage were a sauna. Mike's sweat ran into his wounds and the salt added to his discomfort. I fed him bananas, aiming with care at his mouth as the train jerked spitefully.

At Khartoum Station the British military attaché met us and took Mike to hospital prior to the next flight to London. I cabled Ginnie to meet him with an ambulance and to arrange things with the Burns Unit at Roehampton. He was to spend eighteen months having skin graft operations before he fully recovered. After the night of that fire I always took my own expedition pictures.

We had twelve hours in which to prepare for the well-advertised hover demonstration and drove to Gordon's Palace which faces the confluence of the Blue and White Niles opposite Tuti Island. On a wide grassy bank beside the river we laid out radios, water sterilisers, tropical gear, medical kits, weapons, mini-rations, both Land Rovers and Baker. Sales brochures were placed on folding tables and the attaché promised a police unit to marshal the expected crowds.

The next day, we staged our show, the largest commercial demonstration ever held in Khartoum, with Peter and Nick manning the equipment and Charlie thrilling the crowds that packed the banks and beaches overlooking Tuti Island. The president and his three-minister supreme court arrived in a purple Rolls Royce and with a chauffeur in purple uniform. I shook the eminent hands and gave the ministers a quick tour of our equipment.

The president was small and short-sighted so Peter radioed Charlie to bring Burton close inshore. The craft approached the palace at speed and proscribed a succession of 360° skids right beneath the Rolls Royce. Then Burton swung across the broad river and headed straight for the sandy shores of Tuti Island at thirty knots.

The president and the hushed crowds seemed alarmed . . . there would be an accident. But no, bucking like a thoroughbred, the little machine, accelerating still, left the water and roared over the undulating dunes between logs and other jetsam. A sudden spray arose as Burton hit the water on the far side of the island and a rapturous cheer of wonder erupted from the spectators. For half an hour Charlie charged around the arena in fine style and the crowd never failed to produce a deep-throated 'Oooo-ahh' at each transference from water to land and back.

The Army commander-in-chief took the radio from Peter and, speaking direct to Charlie, ordered him around the island in a series of tight loops. Other officers and presidential staff were all eager to 'have a go' but, luckily, the president took his leave after wishing us a safe journey, so Peter retrieved the radio and Charlie made good his escape.

The British Embassy staff were delighted. A flood of enquiries for sales details followed the show and our arrangements to travel south into the Great Sudd swamp and the war-zone were smoothed by the presidential pleasure. A month later the *Daily Telegraph* reported that our 'expedition was doing much to improve the friendship and goodwill between Britain and the Sudan.'

The humidity increased as we headed south. The seven-month rainy season was due and the land simmered in sultry expectation. We felt clammy and irritable. Clouds of flying, biting ants attacked us in the grasslands south of Khartoum. Scratches and sores tended to infection despite antiseptic cream. Two months earlier, during a training exercise at night, a Baluchi soldier had stomped his rifle butt on my hand and half-severed a finger. This had become swollen and reopened where the stitches had been.

We had followed the Nile for 2000 miles but the river ran on for the same distance again. Any day now the rains would come and waterlog all tracks within 100 miles of the river. These rains annually rendered impassable an area of Sudan larger than Great Britain, a fact which I pondered as we camped by the camel beach of Ed Dueim. All our refuelling points in southern Sudan were beside the river and well off the main north–south track; easily accessible only until the grass prairies turned to marsh.

South of Ed Dueim we hovered without problems until we met the northern outriders of water hyacinth, a modern scourge of the Nile. This purple-flowered water-cabbage floats on a buoyant tuber and grows six inches high. Triffid-like, the bulbs multiply and cover huge areas of river, obstructing all river traffic, including hovercraft. We smashed our way through many wind-blown islands of hyacinth, some of them sixty feet wide and all but covering the river from bank to bank.

I took over from Peter as a Land Rover driver for several days and I was able to see the countryside, impossible from the hovercraft, as we headed into the fringelands of the Sudd. For 100 miles either side of El Jebelain the track was rutted with hummocks so high they could only be crossed by unhooking the trailers and hauling them over manually. Red dust clogged our nostrils and goggles.

The Nile around Malut, where we changed over driving roles, was free from hyacinth so the hovercraft made good headway. We saw herons fishing from floating islands of weed and otter-like animals which stood on their hindlegs to watch us pass. Hippopotomi scowled at us but I saw no crocodiles. Storms broke with brief intensity and I prayed that they were not the first broadside of the rains.

After each squall the river boiled for a period – a seething cauldron of spinach soup. Swirling eddies toyed with islands of rotting papyrus and half-sunken logs lurched sideways in the grip of whirlpools, making navigation tricky. We sweltered in the cockpits, trying to ration our water, and stopped only at refuelling points.

I was glad to be hovering on the day we came to Malakal, capital of the Upper Nile Province and of all the Shilluk tribal lands. The river here was just as described in books of Gordon's day. Avenues of shady palms hugged the eastern bank along which the townsfolk promenaded. Arabs in white robes and yellow turbans strolled by hand in hand. Shilluks, their faces and shoulders pocked with tribal cicatrices, bore bundles of hippo hide, while gangs of naked children, wide-eyed and hands held high, stopped their play to see the hovercraft slide by.

Ancient paddle-steamers, some aground, lined the banks, their cracked lattice shutters swinging with the storm-swell. From the windows and low rotting passenger decks there plunged and screamed the shiny naked bodies of happy Shilluk, young and old, enjoying their poor man's funfair. Red cloaks and spears lay discarded on the roofdecks.

The Malakal police chief appeared within minutes of our arrival and introduced us to the local Army commander. They had been expecting us for three weeks and, with the other members of the local junta, had organised and advertised a 'hoverplane show' like the Khartoum one he had heard vividly described on his radio. 'Can you do the show tomorrow?' he asked. When we agreed, he summoned runners who went off, excited, to pass the news.

Charlie and Peter located a suitable launch site on a muddy slope between two steamers. From there, out of curiosity, they hovered upriver for some miles towards Lake No where the river becomes known as the Bahr el Jebel, the Mountain Sea, and the true Sudd swamps begin.

Our demonstration was to start at noon, but by sun-up, the tribesmen were already arriving from outlying villages. The commissioner, chiefs and dignitaries brought shooting sticks. Everyone else crowded about the muddy arena, kept back by police with rhino-whips.

I shouldered my way through the heaving, shouting throng, coming into frequent contact with the bouncing bare breasts of excited female spectators. The ostrich feathers of the soldiers' bush hats were dyed according to the colours of their regiments, three of which had arrived by steamer that morning from the war-zone.

All was ready at the riverside by noon. The shouts of the crowd were full of anticipation. I felt apprehensive. Our audience included Shilluk, Dinka, Nuer, even the light-skinned Azande. Many had scaled lofty trees by the waterside, others, on the steamers, clung to running-boards or to the hafts of spears which they had plunged into the woodwork. Many children, pushed forward by those on the banks, stood up to their waists in the muddy shallows.

The hovercraft slid away to a roar from the watchers and accelerated through small isles of hyacinth. Charlie then launched Burton into a series of figure-of-eights perilously close to the steamers. The thousands of bunched Malakalis loved this and screamed their approval.

Then the show turned sour.

A dozen militia-men were trying to keep our landing ramp free, lashing out with their whips. A tangle of hyacinth snarled Baker's skirt and Peter switched to full throttle to charge the ramp, intending to clear away the weeds. The hovercraft surged out of the water at twenty knots to climb the bank. A sign of wonder at this amphibian magic sparked a sudden scrabble at the rear of the throng. The resulting pressure at the front, quite unstoppable by the police, pushed a mass of naked children down on to the ramp just as Baker roared up it. I caught a glimpse of Peter's face, mouth frozen open, as he swung the wheel in vain to avoid the human wall.

There were screams and shrieks of pain ahead and bellows of confusion behind. I fought my way down the bank as the hovercraft slid back into the Nile, sucking an unknown number of children into the mud under its skirt. Peter cut both drive engines. The propellers feathered to a standstill. With the quick reactions of a helicopter pilot, he left the lift engine running. Better to risk its blades cutting into a chance limb than allow the half-ton machine to sink into the mud and crush the trapped children.

Nick and I scrabbled in the mud, stretching our arms downwards as far as we could with our nostrils still above the slime. A policeman grasped a flailing limb and we lifted the skirt a few inches until a small body, all blood and filth, came clear and was passed none too gently into the screaming crowd. Two more bodies were removed soon afterwards.

'Are they alive?' I shouted. Nobody answered.

Carefully, we edged Baker out from the mud to deeper water where Peter switched off and the hovercraft's lower hull sank slowly into the water. The accident area was now awash with policemen prodding the mud with spear-butts and shouting to each other.

Nick grasped my arm. Clenched fists and shaken spears accentuated the growing anger of the chanting crowd. It was not difficult to divine that we were the source of their displeasure and I was relieved when police reinforcements appeared alongside a battered ambulance. A uniformed inspector beckoned to us and, with the others from the hovercraft, we retired under escort to the Army compound.

That night a government official arrested Peter and took him away to police HQ. I thought of our schedule, the imminent rains and the vast swamp to our south. We could ill afford a long delay in Malakal as prison visitors.

Some hours later a thoughtful officer came to tell us how things were progressing. The Malakal magistrate, a Nubian, was well aware he must be seen to dole out stiff justice to foreigners in the south just as he would in the north. The two sectors of Sudan had long been at each other's throat, the largely Christian south resentful of the Muslim government in Khartoum. Sudanese law was tough on traffic violations and manslaughter was punishable by a long gaol sentence. By good fortune the judge received a hospital report on the victims before he reached a decision about Peter. One child had lost an ear and two had internal injuries. Otherwise none was seriously hurt. I sent a silent thank you heavenwards on hearing this.

After hours of waiting, Peter was summoned to the old judge who told him: 'Our law is still that of the British administration and I have found no clause which covers your offence. You were driving neither a boat nor a road vehicle and there is no legislation at all concerning vehicles which hover, an omission about which I will inform Khartoum.'

Since Peter had transgressed no written law, no charge would be pressed. He received a severe warning and was dismissed. Charlie bustled us into action. The rains were coming. We left at dawn knowing that in a short while the only southerly track through the Sudd would be submerged.

The Sudd, which means 'block' in Arabic, is a meandering labyrinth of dank waterways. Only the best river-pilots, who have traversed the region many times as apprentices, can afford to be confident in the swamps because the navigable channels are always changing. A single storm can alter the geography of the terrain overnight by breaking up whole islands of stinking vegetation and piling uprooted banks of reed one upon the other, crushing and suffocating any trapped creature. Dead crocodiles and hippo float bloated in newly-formed streams after such storms and elephants wander starving around islands which were previously part of the swampy mainland.

We travelled in the Land Rovers mile upon mile through drenching rain. Progress was possible only in first gear and four-wheel drive. Often we de-bussed to push and pull. Mud clogged our boots like snowshoes.

We came to Mogoch, a miserable patch of high ground with only five villagers, at midnight. These people were of the Twae or Thunderbolt sub-tride, sister-clan to the Than people who lived on remote islands in the Sudd, eating only fish and hippo flesh. The next day we skidded and pushed our way to the Duk, a north–south ridge of high ground mere yards above the high-water level and, once on it, made better progress.

Bor forest lay ahead, scene of many a fatal ambush by the secessionist Anya Nya guerrillas. Nick handed out our loaded guns.

Black clouds spat forked lightning across the southern horizon and, as we entered the confines of the forest, the heavens opened. The storm broke with deafening force. Thick branches cracked and split above us and cascades of red slime splashed up from the track. The forest was a gloomy place straight from the pages of Tolkien or Peake, with thick foliage closing above the track where grotesquely mildewed branches entwined.

We crossed many gulleys over turbulent floodwater, praying as we went that the hap-hazardly laid bridge-planks would not give way. We strained with ropes and makeshift levers each time the deep mud bogged our trailer. We became more fearful of being cut off by floods than of ambush. Baker came unlashed and fell down a rocky gully *en route*. With a struggle the hovercraft was reloaded and we pushed on. At last we came to Bor where the Nile was briefly narrow and high-banked. We slept at once, too tired even to erect mosquito nets.

In return for signed entry permits to the next province, an active war-zone, we donated Baker, damaged beyond repair, to the district commissioner of Bor. He was a keen gardener and positioned the hovercraft in his Nile-side marrow patch as a hippo-scare. Some day I must return to Bor, if ever the interminable civil war allows, to see if it is still in residence.

With only one machine between five of us, we agreed to let Charlie, with a triple fuel load, hover south in Burton. We would hitch a lift with the vehicles on the weekly ferry between Bor and Juba. All roads south of Bor had long since been washed away by floods or destroyed by guerrillas. They had been closed to traffic for the past four years.

Sandbagged machine-gun positions decorated the stern and roofdeck of the tiny tugboat which powered two flat-top barges lashed like saddlebags to its hull. We strapped a Land Rover to each barge and fixed our mosquito nets on poles above the cargo of flour sacks.

Charlie was quite prepared to take Burton on alone to Juba but the very real threat of Anya Nya ambushes made this course inadvisable and he agreed to compromise. So Burton hovered in long slow circles, never quite out of sight of the ferry's machine-guns, and Charlie grew hourly more frustrated. His boredom was alleviated by the occasional hippo and crocodile and sometimes he showed off his hover-skills by inducing skid-turns around hyacinth islands.

The ferry pilot managed to steer upriver only by bouncing his barges off the outer bank on each bend, a slow and giddy process which recurred hundreds of times during the three-day journey to Juba. Charlie estimated that, given a free rein, he could have hovered to Juba in less than one day. Nevertheless, we arrived at the Nile-side town, nerve centre of government operations in the war-zone, with a sense of relief. From Juba we could only reach Uganda by road, for the river now became a seething rush of turbulence, unnavigable and narrow. This was a nuisance because Charlie was rightly adamant that we should take Burton to the source of the Nile, Lake Victoria, rather than abandon the hovercraft in Juba and continue with only the Land Rovers.

Fortune intervened in the shape of Ahmed el Sherif el Habib, commander of operations in Equatoria, who came to look at Burton. I told the general about our transport problem. That night we were invited to a dance at the Juba Officers' Mess. There were no women, so staff officers danced together or with guests such as ourselves and a Japanese salesman. Jiving was the 'in' step and the favourite tune was *Yellow Submarine* by the Beatles. After dancing with a portly colonel and the Japanese salesman I felt my duty was done. So apparently did the general, who winked, as I bowed my farewell, and said simply: 'All will be well for your journey, young man. I will see to it.'

We left the very next day, Burton riding high on an Army truck, by river ferry to Gondokoro on the east bank. A twelve-man platoon escorted us through the forests to the Ugandan border. We crossed many river bridges, each of which was protected by a troop of armoured vehicles. All habitation between Juba and the frontier had been destroyed in a brutal earth-scorch operation some years before.

Late one night our escort unloaded Burton on to the dust road at Nimule, six yards on the Sudan-side of the border-post. Peter and Nick drove away at once in the diesel Land Rover, already three weeks late back to their respective jobs.

Ninety miles from Nimule we found a merchant with a pick-up truck who agreed to take Burton south to Kampala. Back at the border post, with the help of the customs-chief and his wife, we lifted the hovercraft on to the flat-back van, the suspension springs of which turned concave.

On 3 April, three weeks behind schedule, Charlie proudly took Burton over the yacht-club lawn at Gaba on to the clear surface of Lake Victoria. The East African Press turned out in strength to witness the advent of Uganda's first hovercraft and, as in the Sudan, agents were found on behalf of Hoverair to process sales orders. Businessmen and government ministers came in droves from Kampala and nearby industrial Juba. The British military attaché introduced me to a fat corporal in the King's African Rifles named Idi Amin. The corporal was obviously of an ambitious nature since he requested a hovering lesson. Charlie, eyeing his bulk, tactfully refused.

Substantial export orders for Hoverhawks followed the expedition and the UK Ministry of Technology, impressed by the evident toughness of Burton, arranged a sales tour of Canada and the USA. Within two years, £20 million in export orders from those countries alone had been placed for the little machines which, like all small hovercraft, had previously suffered from the stigma of unreliability.

We had not been able to hover up the length of the Nile, but then neither did the early explorers manage to follow its entire course. Like them, we had glimpsed the colourful interior of the countries through which the river flows. There are less rewarding ways of spending an Army leave.

I sold the petrol Land Rover in Nairobi and earmarked the funds for future expeditions.

Charlie took Burton back with us by RAF Hercules from Nairobi and the little hovercraft retired to demonstration circuits around Peterborough gravel pits.

The poison in my injured finger had infected my arm so, while Nick received deep stomach injections against bilharzia, I took a course of less painful penicillin jabs. The medic at Chelsea barracks recommended a month's inactivity, but a letter came from the temporary adjutant of the Muscat Regiment in Salalah. There had been alarming increases in *adoo* strength. Some of our soldiers were on the verge of mutiny and all absent officers were sorely needed. The letter was vaguely worded, as though the writer felt embarrassed, but the meaning was clear enough. I decided to return at once, finger or no finger.

9

Ambush

And we are here as on a darkling plain
Swept with confused alarms of struggle and flight,
Where ignorant armies clash by night.

MATTHEW ARNOLD

When I landed at Salalah the earth was baked dry across the plain and the foothills. Only the *khareef* or monsoon belt of the Jebel remained fertile.

The RAF camp bristled with barbed wire and newly erected searchlights. There had been mortar attacks during my absence, one of which had scored a direct hit on the Officers' Mess. A camp tannoy system had been installed to broadcast emergencies. As I left the camp a metallic voice announced the maiden flight of Concorde in Britain.

At Umm al Ghawarif, Colonel Peter Thwaites gave me my new orders. He did not comment on my overdue return from the Nile. This was generous of him since his three companies were overstretched with increasing *adoo* attacks. The Army was for the first time outnumbered and vulnerable, except on the plain where the existence of the Sultan's two jet fighter planes, coupled with lack of ground cover, discouraged *adoo* daytime movement.

The colonel needed the Recce Platoon as a mobile ambush group on the Salalah side of the Jebel but could not move our Land Rovers over the only mountain road until at least two companies were available to clear mines and provide protection. In a month that should be possible. Until then he wanted Recce to complete three missions near the Yemeni border.

The Beaver flew me to the desert base of Thamarit, from where Recce was operating local desert patrols. As the plane taxied in by the rusty oildrums which formed a makeshift stockade around the camp, soldiers ran out from the shade of the huts. They surrounded me, grabbing my bags and gun and pumping my right hand in greeting.

I felt moved by this unexpected welcome. I sensed the men's pleasure that my Arabic was now fluent and that I knew all thirty by name despite the fact that seven were Mohameds, three were Hamads and six were Salims. They called me *Bachait bin Shemtot bin Samra*, for reasons which I never discovered. The nearest English equivalent is John, son of rags, son of the thorntree.

For a week I trained with the men inside Thamarit. Searing hot winds from the Empty Quarter blew sand through the air day after day so my eyes were bloodshot and sores formed where I tossed and turned at night, sweating on a gritty blanket.

The camp, a long-deserted oil prospectors' base, was right beside a well, where bedu of the Bait Kathiri called with their thirsty camels. I went to greet each new arrival with Corporal Salim Khaleefa and we gave out flour or aspirins in exchange for information about the *adoo*. It was a one-way trade: all aspirins and no information.

Since Thamarit was the only Sultanate camp for 200 miles north of the Jebel, it had a permanent garrison, consisting of twelve Arabs and a British captain with a Hitler moustache, baggy khaki shorts and knee-length socks. His favourite topic was the defence of Thamarit, although the likelihood of an attack was remote because the Jebel was forty miles away. Nevertheless, he prepared diligently for the worst and any attempt at sarcasm on my part was met with a muttered comment about foolish virgins or closing stable doors. He sounded a gong daily to rehearse his men at defence. One night our Land Rovers returned late from a desert patrol and, as we reached Thamarit, a cascade of green flares lit up the camp and an unmistakable English voice shouted, 'Halt. Who goes there?'

'Only me,' I replied *sotto voce*. I was ordered to advance slowly.

The captain stood stiffly by the Burmails (Omani for oildrum, a corruption of Burmah Oil). His moustache bristled with aggression above voluminous shorts and, to my disbelief, a drawn cavalry sword. 'How do we know you aren't an invasion force from the Yemen?' he complained. 'In future you will warn me by radio whenever you intended returning after dark.'

From Thamarit the CO ordered me to the Yemen frontier to verify a suspected *adoo* infiltration route by locating camel tracks. We drove 200 miles along the southern edge of the Rubh al Khali, the greatest sand desert in the world, which stretches from the Oman coast northwest into Saudi Arabia. In it there is nothing but the wandering bedu with their camels and goats. All day we passed by rock, sand and bunches of dwarf palm or acacia scrub. Mostly the surface was good, gravel based or caked pans of gypsum. Mirages of lakes were common and faraway outcrops appeared, inverted, as nearby features. Sand devils rose like lamp genies and spiralled in tornadoes through the wasteland only to disappear as though they too were mere chimeras.

Driver Murad had been twice before to the frontier and knew of a spring in the *wadi*. Ali Nasser shot a Thompson gazelle which Said Salim skinned with his stiletto after slitting its throat as Islamic ritual demands. As the meat boiled on a fire of dead acacia, Said rubbed the pelt with rock salt and rolled it into a tight scroll. 'Tomorrow I will dry it for you, Sahb,' he said. 'When you have ten such skins, you may join them for a rug.'

We drove all night when the sand was cooler and harder. At dawn, the sky pricked with fading stars, we stopped and squatted around a fire in a nook among tall white boulders. Ali Nasser prepared sweet tea and chupattis fried in butter and we watched in silence savouring the relative cool. The sun climbed fast and shadows soon fled. Within two hours the temperature was 115° in the shade.

A signal diverted us into the Wadi Habarut where a Sultanate fort, like that in Mirbat, guards the only oasis along the Dhofar–Yemen border. We were to evacuate an injured *askar*.

The Omani fort was built, à la Foreign Legion, by a London architect in 1966. It stood exactly opposite a similar fort built decades earlier by the British-officered Hadhramaut Bedouin Legion. This now housed a well-armed garrison of the People's Democratic Republic of South Yemen. From our fort's crenellated tower I stared through binoculars at the tricolour of the PDRSY and beside it a bearded officer who was watching me through binoculars. I waved at him and he waved back.

The chief *askar* of our fort took me to the sick room. As we entered I saw a man limp quickly to a stretcher on to which he lowered himself with dexterity. This must be the 'injured' man we had come to collect.

Three miles up the *wadi* I found a narrow airstrip consisting of 300 yards of gravel, cleared of stones. Once machine-guns were sited all around, I called in the Beaver from Salalah. 'He is a malingerer,' I told the Rhodesian pilot.

He laughed. 'So are most of the fellows I fly back to Salalah just before the Ramadan fast. And who's to blame them? I'd prefer to fast in a hospital bed than in this fly-ridden spot.' The little plane rose off the runway with fifty yards to spare and spun away east over the forts.

We left Habarut for the uncharted and waterless steppes to the south. Searching for a fresh west–east camel trail in a labyrinth of dry canyons was not the soldiers' idea of sensible Ramadan work.

About one in five British soldiers admit to a belief in God; one in fifty might regularly attend church. But the Omanis had fewer material distractions and a stricter upbringing. Religion formed a secure base to their lives, socially and mentally, and the fasts and feasts of Islam were of special importance. Ramadan means 'to be hot'. It is the ninth month of the Muslim year, but each year it is later by fourteen days since its advent depends upon the first appearance of the new moon at that season. The fasting consists of no drinking or eating during daylight hours and lasts for a month.

We followed a wide valley that cut deep into the southern steppes. We nosed the vehicles along storm gullies, between giant boulders and pushed them through rifts of soft sand. On the second day Corporal Salim Khaleefa suggested we stop early for the night. 'Tonight the new moon will come. We should stop well before the Gat'n where there may be *adoo*.'

Mohamed Rashid of the Beard shot an ibex so there was good eating for all. Afterwards everyone climbed a hill above the camp and watched for the moon. Said Salim stood beside me and picked his nails with his stiletto as the gruff voice of the Moolah cited the Koran into the void beneath us.

'Before Ramadan can begin in any Muslim country,' Said whispered, 'three Moolahs must sight the moon. In Muscat it is already in force: the signaller heard so this morning.'

'In Pakistan,' muttered Sadeeq the Baluch, 'three chief qadis fly up in an aeroplane to see the moon arrive. Once they report by radio, it is Ramadan for all.'

Hyenas called in the *wadis* but the men fell silent.

'I see the moon.' Corporal Salim stood on the highest rock and craned his neck to the west.

A sigh came from the men and all of them knelt to pray. I remained standing but I also prayed since it felt appropriate. I prayed for my mother and sisters and Ginnie and that the Nile photographer might recover from his burns.

For two days we pushed south, shedding broken-down vehicles and their men to fix their own repairs since we had too little water to wait for them. Huge boulders blocked our way and the *wadi* narrowed to a winding corridor as dark as a Manhattan alleyway. The men began to complain. The Army had never been in these parts before. It was Ramadan, no time to be pushing heavy vehicles through soft sand until the forehead veins bulged. The Baluchi Moolah was especially vociferous but I told him we must obey our orders. I too had drunk and eaten only during the sunless hours so my arguments did not seem unfair.

When we were unable to drive further I left Murad and the drivers and took the other men with *zamzamia* hemp-bags full of water. For six hours we zigzagged over a high plateau, twice crossing deep canyons. By noon I could clearly see the ridge line of the Qamr mountains and the high bald mesa called Gant's Hill on my map. With my father's old telescope I checked the ground ahead minutely. A wide *wadi* ran south in serpentine loops and was not, as far as I could see, penetrated by a single westerly access valley. As certain as we could be, given our water supply, that there were no penetration routes between the Qamr and Habarut, we turned back.

Back at the Land Rovers we discovered that Murad needed a half shaft before we could move. Four hours later the Beaver parachuted the spare part and told me I was five miles on the wrong side of the border. This later reached Muscat as gossip and Colonel 'Oddjob' Harvey described me as a 'misguided missile'. My own colonel eliminated the entire steppe area from his subsequent block and ambush strategies on the basis that no camel could gain access from the Yemen there. He ordered me to go into the western mountains to cover an attack he planned to mount.

After two days' driving we came to Deefa camp, high on a bald escarpment just above the monsoon belt. Two of the companies converged on Deefa in readiness for a southerly night move to attack a group of *adoo* thought to operate there. Their major was a six-foot six-inch Royal Marine who was afraid of nothing.

I watched the companies leave Deefa at dusk. There was no moon but, for twenty minutes after their departure, we could still hear the creak of rifle slings and the plunk of gravel under the hooves of the machine-gun-bearing mules. Unknown to our colonel at the time, some 600 *adoo* with heavy weapons and Soviet pack radios were awaiting the companies' arrival in the thickly wooded valleys far below.

I felt thoroughly useless guarding Deefa camp and listening to the thunder of guns, bombs and mortars from below the escarpment. After two days the company returned bearing their dead and wounded on stretchers.

Mubarreq Obeid brought me tea that evening and spoke in a whisper. 'The new major has a *djinn*, a bad spirit. Many of his men say they will not leave camp again behind him. Also the Baluchis hate him for he favours the Arabs. They say they will shoot him. He throws stones at men who march slowly. That is proof he has a *djinn*.'

The major treated his men as though they too were Royal Marines, trained on the tough commando course at Lympstone in Devon. He was fit and fearless but no good at making allowances. His authoritarianism went down badly with the Arabs but his downfall was his rotten luck. The *adoo* seemed to outwit him at every move and the soldiers were quick to notice. Over the next few weeks there were more deaths in his company and this was to lead to mutiny.

We spent the last night at Deefa manning the heights of a ravine while the second company men laboured across it. I saw how they were tired but still spirited, unlike the Marine's men. One soldier grinned at me from a stretcher. A morphine label lay across his beard like a price tag. A bullet had passed through his upper thigh and genitals but he was uncowed.

This was the last time we penetrated the western mountains. The *adoo* grip on Dhofar was tightening from the west.

One of my colleagues from Beaconsfield, Patrick Brook, took two platoons on a local ambush party in the western Jebel. They surprised a patrol of twelve armed *adoo* and shot one through the head. On their way back through dense thornbush they moved in file, Patrick leading with his compass. They ran into a close ambush and Patrick was flung to the ground. A Simonoff bullet passed through his left upper arm and another smashed the radio strapped to his right hip. He crawled back to his Bren gunner but a bullet had passed through the man's skull and out of his ear. The next soldier, a sergeant, was unconscious, one of his eyes a bloody mess with a shattered socket. The third man was also wounded so Patrick had been lucky.

* * *

Early in June we left Thamarit for Salalah. Two companies were positioned at key points along the track which crosses the mountains but we drove fast because jungle-clad ravines nudge the escarpment along which the road runs and provide cover for machine-guns.

In Salalah I was briefed by the CO and an Australian mercenary named Spike Powell, later killed in Rhodesia. He specialised in weapons and evaluated intelligence reports concerning *adoo* with twenty-foot-long metal tubes. These, he said, were 140mm rocket launchers much used by the North Vietnamese. Each rocket weighed seventy pounds and had a range of 9000 yards, enough to reach Salalah from the Jebel. Once the *khareef* settled with its cover of mist, the *adoo* could bombard Salalah with impunity.

'But,' the CO emphasised, 'the *khareef* makes the Jebel so slippery, these weapons can only come in along the foothills – and that you must prevent.' So for many months we harried the foothills.

Until the end of June the grass of the previous year's *khareef* lay flat and withered. One-third of all the herdsmen's cattle starved to death and the *adoo* no longer paid for the milk they took. In the Wadi Naheez we met a Bait Qatan herder who had lost two sons and half his cattle from malnutrition. He said he hated the *adoo* but the Army was no protection so he had to give what he could whenever the *adoo* visited.

Corporal Salim gave the man flour and rice and was told we could do worse than ambush a certain cave in the Naheez where *adoo* had been seen visiting the local bedu for milk and for sex with their women.

The cave turned out to be spectacularly large. It was set into a cliff behind a long-deserted village. Fallen pillars indicated age and past wealth. We set up the machine-guns on the floor of goat and bat droppings. Dry wings scrabbled above us in the gloom and the air thrummed with a high-pitched whistling. Further into the cave in wattle huts were families of bedu and their animals. Goat fleas infested the dung and small ticks dropped on to us from the rocks. We stayed two days in the cave but no *adoo* came. Afterwards I was sick, perhaps due to the tics.

Not all ambushes were unpleasant. Once, deep inside the Wadi Dut, we lay hidden above a chain of pools where fresh camel prints spattered the sand.

From my cave I could just see Ali Nasser and his men hidden in the flowering lianas which fringed the pools of Dut. To my delight I saw a large hyena pass close by Ali, presumably upwind of him.

Mubarreq Obeid touched my knee. I followed his gaze and saw three dark shadows in the indigo shrubs beyond the pools. Said Salim adjusted the range setting on his rifle but soon we saw they were only bedu girls, probably of the Bait Jarboob that graze the Dut.

A breeze blew showers of scented pods from the giant tamarinds about the pool and the girls' laughter came up to us as their sarongs billowed in the wind. They unwound the cloths from their shoulders and hitched them about their hips. Long black hair fell about their breasts as they waded about and splashed each other. They washed using handfuls of fern and afterwards they squatted beside the pools while the sun dried their skin. Hummingbirds as large as English kingfishers whirred in the shrubs.

Two of the girls left by the way they had come. The other dallied, arranging her hair and plaiting reeds. Suddenly the girl rose and ran into the indigo shrubs. She clasped a black skinned Jebali around the neck and rubbed her nose against his. I glanced at Mubarreq but he had not seen the man come. The two Jebalis climbed the mossy incline towards us and lay down together beneath the tamarind trees. The man was already half naked. He flicked aside the girl's blue cloth beneath which she wore black leggings. Unlike European tights, the Dhofari version end at the upper thigh and do not cover the genitals. There was much movement but no noise for a minute or so, then the man stood up and adjusted his loin-cloth. He stooped once to touch the girl then left, quickly blurring into the foliage.

The girl lay still for a while then walked with languid steps to the pool. She washed her face but not her body and disappeared behind the rocks in which Taj's men lay hidden.

I looked at Mubarreq. He rolled his eyeballs heavenwards. I was glad no *adoo* came to the Dut that day.

Sometimes a Jebali *seeyasee* or informer came with us as a guide to find a specific village or cave. The chief *seeyasee* was Said bin Ghia, a sheikh of the Bait Qatan who had defected from the *adoo*. He had a keener ear than many gave him credit for, perhaps because they were fooled by his merry face and formidable girth. He was not able to predict *adoo* movements in advance but he did have Jebali contacts and knew of most events in the Qara within a few days of their occurrence. He stopped me in the camp one day late in June and warned me that the *adoo* of the central mountains had taken two of the bedu whom I had been cultivating with food and medicine to the Yemen.

He also told me the *adoo* were satisfied that the Sultan's three companies were a quantifiable danger since they were under permanent surveillance and normally advertised their patrols by easily detected noise and movement. But as Recce moved only by night to ambush a wide and unpredictable front, we were not so easy to avoid. We were also known to be in contact with the people of the foothills who were more susceptible to the persuasion of our food and medicine than the mountain clans. Bin Ghia warned that a specially appointed *adoo firqat* (tribal band) had been sent to deal with us during the course of our operations. I thanked him, but paid little heed to his advice at the time, since *seeyasees* were known to be alarmist.

Early in July an intelligence transcript of a Radio Aden announcement made me think twice about bin Ghia's warnings. 'The freedom fighters of Dhofar have located a group of British propaganda specialists who are attempting to bribe and seduce the plainsfolk of Dhofar. We are following the movements of these specialists and will soon eliminate them.'

From then on, during most of our operations, I positioned the sections with two separate aims, to ambush *adoo* patrols and to ambush locations likely to be used to ambush us.

Since we never patrolled with soldiers suffering from noisy complaints such as coughing fits, we were often thin on the ground. A week before the 1969 monsoon arrived, the platoon was down to only sixteen soldiers, two sections of eight, and six machine-guns. Each man carried thirty pounds of gear in his backpack. Our chief surveillance target that week was Darbat and I intended a three-day watch from caves above the village, a known hideout of Bait Maashani *adoo*.

To reach the fertile plateau of Darbat without using a track involved climbing a thickly wooded escarpment. There was no moon, so the men moved in close single file with slung weapons, leaving their hands free to haul upwards from bush to bush. Then, from further up the slope we heard a crackle of twigs. The noise grew louder. There seemed to be a host of people descending the mountainside directly towards us. Behind me a soft click sounded as my signaller eased off the safety catch on his submachine-gun.

The noise was soon all about us and a black-and-white cow crashed past me. I relaxed then and felt my heartbeat ease. The rest of the herd followed past, and we heard the sharp tac-tac of the herdsmen's sticks tapping trees.

Someone halted above us and waited as though listening. Then came the falsetto cry much used by Dhofari camelmen calling their beasts. None of us understood Jebali but we heard from far above us a faint reply, the warbling trill of a woman.

When the man was gone, Said Salim whispered, 'He smelled us, Sahb. The wind blows from the sea towards Darbat. We must cover ourselves.'

We smeared the liquid green spattering of the cows on our shirts and trousers and smelled satisfactorily unpleasant.

'They heard the Land Rovers,' Said muttered, 'and sent the cowmen to find us. The Qara move their cows only by day except in the late monsoon. We must be more careful.'

We eased slowly, furtively, up to the lip of the escarpment. As was our habit, we then divided into four groups, each with at least one machine-gun.

Mubarreq, the signaller, and Said Salim stayed with me to the east of the village. From above our hide a wildcat snarled, startling me. Once our packs were quietly removed from our backs we began to place rocks about us in a protective sangar, hoping that no spiders, snakes or scorpions nested beneath them. An animal screamed close by as our sangar neared completion. Mubarreq grabbed his machine-gun. 'That is no *senoor* cat, Sahb,' he whispered. 'That is *adoo*. The Darbat *adoo* are Zingibaris like me. Their night signs are from the rainforests of Usumbara and Ukambani.'

I had not seen Mubarreq frightened before.

Said Salim was calm. 'They know where we are, Bakhait. If they move above us this will be a bad place to defend.'

I had seen nothing to suggest we were detected but Mubarreq's fear was contagious and I trusted Said's keen senses. I touched the pressel switch of my radio four times and waited. Corporal Salim replied likewise and soon materialised with the other men.

I told them that our presence was known. Although we now overlooked the village, there were *adoo* who had moved behind and above us and into our only line of retreat to the plain.

To our south lay the sheer abyss of Dahaq, along the clifftop of which the village cultivation began. Our only chance was to head east through the crops between the clifftop and the village to where another steep escarpment descended plainwards.

Corporal Salim had switched his transceiver off before coming close to me to avoid any electronic 'feedback' screech should one of us activate his radio by mistake. So it was a shock when, quite clearly in the tense silence, a rapid whispering sounded from my radio.

Mubarreq seized it and put his ear to the speaker but the whispering had ended. 'Zingibaris,' he muttered.

We did not wait. In file we eased from bush to bush down towards the clearly delineated lip of the cliff. Mosquitoes rose from the scrub to the hypnotic scent of our sweat. The man behind Corporal Salim was a seventeen-year-old bedu named Kamis Ali, a good soldier and full of common sense. I could see his silhouette in the other file the moment he flung his rifle down and screamed. I rushed across to him but Corporal Salim and Mubarreq reached him first and flung him to the ground.

This is all we need, I thought; a *djinn* attack with dawn imminent. Twice on exercise in Oman I had watched normally calm soldiers become 'possessed by *djinns*' or demons.

Streams of froth swung from the bedu's chin. He fought with surprising strength for one so

118

slim but Mubarreq's ham fists clamped his jugular so, although the unnatural spittle continued to ooze, there was no further sound. Corporal Salim bound the bedu's threshing limbs with two *shemagh* headcloths and Mubarreq forced a shell dressing in his mouth. His pupils, bulbous and filled with terror, darted about beyond his control. 'Hurry,' said Mubarreq, 'I will take the bedu. Dawn is coming.'

We zigzagged along the hard rock areas to the very rim of the abyss, where soon the monsoon floodwaters would cascade 500 feet in a chute visible from faraway Taqa to form the only perennial river in Eastern Arabia. We ran crouching over the rock. In the morning not even Jebalis would find our spoor. The smell of burning dung was strong from the village now, cancelling our own body odours. The cliff of Dahaq, for centuries a site of sacrifice, was immediately below us. By day its base, when dry, shines white where truncated stone stalactites meet a dark confusion of huge castor-oil plants that curl and sway as though alive. Soon we would be seen by the *adoo* behind us. We must hide in the thick vegetation of the hillock immediately east of the village. This hill was not itself overlooked and commanded a good view of our escape route to the escarpment.

Again we split up. Said Salim joined me from the rear. No one, he said, had followed us. Crawling on hands and knees, we dragged the guns and ammunition beneath a web of liana and thorn close to the crest of the hillock. We slept in turns.

I woke at noon to a foul stench and the loud buzzing of flies. Some dead thing lay close by and the sun was now directly overhead. We ate corned beef from a tin, wiping off clusters of flies from each mouthful.

The village below, seen through my telescope, appeared peaceful. The Bait Maashani wore loose body-cloths and leather thongs bound their shaggy hair. They were finely-featured Qara folk, but most of the Darbat villagers were Negroes, escaped slaves or freedmen from Salalah. Their houses were quite unlike other Dhofari dwellings, being the conical shapes of the African *kraal*.

Twice that day goat flocks swarmed over our hillock and each time the women herders searched each thicket and hollow as they passed. But the goats avoided our cave, put off perhaps by the smell. The hag who drove the second flock came close to us, examining the ground about our refuge and casting covert glances directly at our hide. She moved above and behind us and her shadow fell across the latticework of thorns. Then she screamed at her goats and went.

Corporal Salim had watched our prospective escape route all day, the scrub between our hillock and the escarpment. Only a large herd of cattle were there, a good sign since Jebalis always kept their cows away from a planned *adoo* ambush area. But it was unusual for them still to be there so late, because there were wolves and cow-thieves about at night. They should be back in their byres.

We waited and watched during the four hours of moonlight. An hour before midnight there was a commotion among the cattle and Said Salim picked out, with my 'scope, a dozen men herding the animals towards the escarpment. We had again been compromised. For a second time our escape route was cut off.

We quietly conferred. Then, leaving four men and two machine-guns on the hillock lookout, we moved north towards the high Jebel, making more noise than usual. For an hour we kept this heading and left clear tracks in sandy places. Then we wheeled around 180° and returned by a more easterly route towards the still visible hillock. Once the feature was to our direct flank I

119

gave a signal to the four men left behind. They headed due east until we hissed at them. Said Salim was quietly elated. 'Had we moved south from the hillock, the *adoo* were ready. Two hours after you left us, the cattle returned and with them many men. They moved all over our hill then, finding nothing, they went north following your scent.'

We fled like the wind, reaching the plain in two hours. Three green flares fetched Murad from his vehicle hide at Mamoorah. The men were happy and proud. We had sprung no ambush but we had played a close game of chess with experts and avoided defeat.

With the coming of the *khareef*, many Jebalis in our operations district experienced a new turn of events. Young men of their own kith and kin came home from courses in Russia. The long hair and the beards, symbols of their belief, with which they had left home, were now gone, crudely shaven. They were as strangers to their families and tribes and they preached against Islam. Many older Jebalis tried to incite their communities against the new Marxist doctrines but this ceased after two vociferous sheikhs of the Eastern Mahra had their eyes burned out in public.

Bin Ghia told me the *adoo* mistrusted the Eastern Mahra and would wipe them out given provocation. To ensure confusion within suspect tribes, the young people were taken away for training so that only the old and feeble remained. Even young women were recruited for military training, although for a woman to fight alongside men was previously unheard of. Normally the female sex were treated as useful chattels of secondary importance to the family camels.

Only once did Recce knowingly become involved with she-guerrillas. During the first week of the *khareef*, with nine others, I spent four days in a cave above the sweet water spring of Arzat, source of the Sultan's private water supply and recently a popular target of *adoo* saboteurs.

Early on the fourth morning the aqueduct was broken in two places and the *adoo* responsible were spotted by another observation group, who radioed for a jet and for a detachment from Salalah. Major Simon Sloane, from the Argylls, arrived in an antique scout car. I joined him in the foothills beside the spring and noticed four Jebalis in dark cloaks springing away from the aqueduct towards a steep gulley. All carried large bundles and continued to run when we shot at them.

Jumping into the car, I used the turret-mounted .30 Browning. Through the sights I watched the glowing tracer kick dust either side of the fugitives. They were soon out of range. Then the jet dived, firing Sura rockets at twice the speed of sound. Simon took some men up the gulley and returned with three bodies on stretchers. Curious to see the saboteurs we had awaited for so long, I went over to the silent group around the stretchers.

Some bedu from a cattle herd nearby bent over the bodies. A herdsman clutching a tattered shawl to his chest removed the army blanket from one corpse. 'She is my wife,' he muttered without emotion.

Simon's lips were tight. His voice trembled as he said, 'They should have stopped when we first fired. Everyone on the Jebel knows it is foolish to run if you are innocent.'

The bedu shrugged. It was the will of God.

Simon swore quietly. 'Bloody war. How could we know they were women?' Up the gulley he had found the smashed bodies with their clothes blasted apart. One had a breast sliced off by shrapnel. Three of Simon's Baluchis had been sexually aroused by the sight and he had only restrained himself with difficulty from striking them. 'What a way to earn a living.' He shook his head and walked away to his car.

I found a rough notice stuck to a tree by the sabotaged aqueduct. 'Socialist people for the emancipation of the Arabian Gulf . . . to our brothers opposed by the imperialist colony who are aggressive against the people . . . We will fight a long war until we are victorious.'

We took the women's bodies to Salalah for burial.

I treasured letters from Ginnie and fretted if a month went by without one. I daydreamed about her during the interminable ambushes and on long vehicle patrols when mines were at any moment liable to blow us to bits.

That month she wrote: 'Prince Charles has been invested at Caernarfon, I am now twenty-two – in case you forgot – and they've done away with the ha'penny.' She worked for the Scottish National Trust, taking tourists around the mountain trails above Loch Torridon.

Sometimes for many days my mind was filled only with thoughts of how to trap and kill *adoo*, which trails or waterholes to ambush, which soldiers to take. Ginnie was then out of sight and out of mind. But as soon as a lull came in activities, when we were resting in Umm al Ghawarif or when the men were all hidden and my machine-gun was ready above the relevant killing ground, then I invariably thought of her.

Within eight weeks of the *khareef*'s arrival, a flood of accurate information about *adoo* movements reached the Army via the intelligence officer who succeeded the South African. The new man was 'Tom Greening', the captain who, in BidBid, had persuaded me not to resign from the Sultan's forces. Nobody knew the source of his information but its value was appreciated by an army hitherto ignorant about its enemy.

At the time Tom was working secretly with his old Sandhurst friend Qaboos, the Sultan's only son, to arrange a bloodless coup. The Sultan himself allowed Tom to visit Qaboos, since he trusted the British. He feared a coup of Omani or Dhofari inspiration.

Tom's co-conspirators ranged from Bareik, son of the *wali* of Salalah, to Omani bankers, oilmen, senior Army officers and Foreign Office contacts in Whitehall. He was the key to the various threads of the plot and he knew that timing was vital. In August 1969, arrangements were far from ready, yet to act too late would be disastrous since the *adoo*, with growing Soviet aid, would soon be ready to attack Salalah.

Early in August I escorted an English visitor to Salalah Palace to see the Sultan. As we drove past the house where Qaboos was kept under house arrest I saw Tom emerge and head towards the nearby court of Bareik.

We parked within the courtyard and I escorted the English civilian to the royal quarters. White dustcovers hid the six armoured cars of the Sultan's guard and a ciné camera whirred quietly from a window slit above us. We passed through heavy doors of sandalwood, finely carved, to a labyrinth of passages and anterooms. The Sultan had two wives, one being the Dhofari mother of Qaboos, a native of the village of Darbat, but there were also ninety comely Negresses within the palace walls and a room well-stacked with bottles of Chanel – performance awards. Close by the perfumery was an armoury of rifles, machine-guns and sufficient ammunition to withstand a long siege.

I waited by a door of scented wood, watched impassively by a turbanned slave built like an ox, whose massive black forearms crossed one another above the silver curl of his *khanja* dagger. At length the Sultan emerged with his guest and retainers. I saluted. He nodded with a slight smile and shook my hand, his turban at the level of my shoulders. The men of Recce stood ramrod stiff in the courtyard.

'These are your men?' The Sultan's English was cultured and without accent.

'Yes, Your Majesty: the reconnaissance unit.'

He shook each man's hand and looked into their eyes. To divine loyalty? It was only a year since soldiers he was inspecting had attempted his assassination.

There was an aura of dignity about the little Arab and I felt both respect and loyalty for him. Although the Queen of England, not he, was my liege and paymaster, I knew I was ready to fight for him and if necessary die in his service for all that I disliked his shortcomings. Yet many times weekly I blackened his name when we were refused extra food to take on patrols and cursed him when there were only Aspirins for dying bedu.

But, after meeting him and seeing the kindness in his fine old face, I found it difficult to associate him personally with the misery and poverty prevalent in his country. So much of it could surely be alleviated. Or could it? My feelings about the man and his viable options were most confused.

The monsoon mist covered the plain and the Jebel by the middle of August. Visibility on a good day was 100 yards, the two jets and the Beaver were grounded and no ship could land in the churning seas which lashed the coastline. Dhofar was cut off from the outside world; the mountain track to Thamarit and Oman was already a quagmire impassable to vehicles. One night the RAF radar sweeping the plain detected movement from the area of the abandoned sewage truck. The Army camp was alerted and its perimeter defences manned. The suspect zone was shelled but no *adoo* attack materialised. A herd of camels or cattle had probably been blown to bits due to the radar's inability to tell men from animals.

Our ambushes were now uncomfortable affairs. To gain high ground quietly became a matter of skill and patience. A man who missed his grip or his footing would slide downwards, crashing through undergrowth, his gun, ammunition and primed grenades flying into the dark.

One night our colonel accompanied Recce on an ambush north of Taqa. He had only one kidney and the going was doubly hard for him. The *adoo* detected our presence and ambushed us as we left the next day. Only one of the men was wounded and we withdrew in fast coordinated groups, slithering through the scrub. In the withdrawal we lost the colonel's backpack which contained two desirable tins of sardines. Being extremely partial to these, I volunteered to retrieve them. With two others I sallied forth over the ground we had just lost, but a hail of bullets sent me back empty-handed to the colonel. A week later he took eight British, Omani and Indian officers to a barbecue on the white sands of Sumhuran. Three Recce sections mounted machine-guns in the ruins above. The sea was too rough to swim in, but the picnic was a pleasant touch of other-world normality.

Three days later, with another officer, I removed a newly laid anti-tank mine from the main track between Taqa and Sumhuran. The *adoo* were hoping for another picnic.

With the *khareef* for cover, *adoo* minelayers grew bold, lacing the tracks of the plain with Soviet TM6 plastic mines and British anti-tank mines. Most of the drivers who became mine casualties had their feet or legs amputated and recovered. Others' spines were snapped and they died.

Each week we drove unavoidably over fifty or sixty miles of track in the course of patrols and twice picked up the bits of other vehicles destroyed where we ourselves had been only hours before. We seemed to lead a charmed life and everyone held my driver in great esteem, even though we all knew only God was responsible for our continued unscathed existence.

Murad never drove along tracks by day or by moonlight but, on dark nights, he had no option. The other four Land Rovers followed his tyremarks and, as a result, became highly proficient drivers. One misty day we returned from a three-day ambush in all five vehicles, well spaced out. Halfway back to camp I halted, but only three vehicles closed up behind mine.

'Where,' I shouted to Ali Nasser, 'is Mohamed of the Beard?'

'Perhaps he has broken down, Sahb.'

I checked on the radio. There was no reply.

'They have a new driver this week,' said Murad. 'Perhaps he is in difficulty.'

Sending the others on, I returned with Ali's men and we found the missing Land Rover beside a narrow trench. The vehicle was upside-down with deep skid-marks indicating where the driver had obviously tried, too late, to avoid the sudden drop of the gulley. Only Mohamed Rashid of the Beard and the driver were unhurt. Mohamed looked at his vehicle vacantly, his hands clasping and unclasping, his rifle nowhere to be seen.

I heard groans from beneath the Land Rover. We flung ourselves at the chassis and heaved until it returned to an upright position. An Arab with a smashed leg and gaping chest wound was dragged free but Hamid Sultan, he of the friendly pirate face, lay crumpled and still. His face was a dented pool of blood, recognisable only by his wispy beard. He seemed so much smaller than before. I felt his pulse and, tearing his shirt back, pressed my ear to his sternum. He was dead. Four of the others were badly injured. They were flown to Muscat and never came back to the platoon.

Normally the Arabs and Baluchis mourned only casualties from their own race but the Baluchis Recce showed their grief for Hamid Sultan. Perhaps the platoon became more closely knit as a result of his needless death. In Umm al Ghawarif the regimental sergeant major, an Omani, referred to the platoon as *qabila recce*, the 'Recce Tribe'.

On a fine day when the mists had retreated for a while I lay along a rock cranny high up the face of a crumbling cliff which overlooked the seaside springs of Mugshayl. An *adoo* arms caravan was expected to pass by the springs that night.

Five hours after dusk the mist cleared briefly and we marvelled at the fire of bursting waves, for the spray was alive with phosphorescence. The moonlight silvered the sea and hung suspended in the spring below. For the first time, and unknown to us, a man walked on the surface of the moon that night at the sea called Tranquillity. I told this two days later to our Dhofari guide, Naseeb, and he became angry. 'The blasphemers,' he growled. 'How dare they trespass on holy ground.' A week later Naseeb was assassinated by the *adoo*.

From Mugshayl, where no *adoo* appeared, we moved to the site of a long-term ambush above a spring to relieve a group led by David Bayley. I met him on the plain on his way out from the ambush caves. He was exhausted, his face, arms and ankles a mass of red spots, many bleeding, which he scratched at as we spoke. 'The little bastards eat you alive from dawn to dusk,' David warned me. 'Those caves are a living hell.'

By our second morning in the caves, which smelled of the faeces of previous ambush groups, even the imperturbable Said Salim was slapping at the teeming monsoon ticks, or *bau'ooth* as Jebalis call them: flying bloodsuckers, small enough to penetrate the mosquito netting we draped around our bodies. Once fed, they burst at the least pressure but first they injected their itch-inducing serum. Two of the Baluchis were reduced to silent tears and our relief was great when, at dusk, the ticks went and mere mosquitoes took over.

We could only lie down or crouch in the tick-caves and when we departed on the third night our legs were weak from inactivity. Edging along a six-inch ledge to descend from our cave, my legs buckled and I fell, still carrying the barrel and tripod of a Browning .30 machine-gun.

I bounced off rocks in the dark, making enough noise to announce our presence to any nearby *adoo*. There was pain in both my knees when I tried to pick myself up and for a while I could not walk. The others took my load and Mubarreq Obeid gave me his shoulder for a crutch. I was flown to Bahrain where an RAF doctor diagnosed strained ligaments in both legs. For two weeks I did nothing.

Tom Greening persuaded the Sultan to allow us food and medicine for Jebalis in need, so our visits to the foothills increased and we began to gain information which we passed back to Tom.

For visits to the Wadi Naheez we always took the chief guide, Said bin Ghia. The Qara hated him as a traitor, but they knew he could tell when they lied. Aware that the *adoo* were annoyed by our food patrols, we tried to lure them into making a move. A Qara goat-owner was known to consort with the *adoo* and one day Said bin Ghia led us to this man's cave.

They rubbed noses in greeting and kissed each other's cheeks. I did not get this treatment: the Qara looked me up and down and asked Said bin Ghia where he had brought 'this kaffir' from. When we left the cave I told Said to announce we would return in four days with more food.

We did return but only after laying a careful trap the previous day for any would-be ambushers. The ruse failed and this made us careless.

With twelve men – the others all had monsoon-coughs – I took a food patrol into the mouth of the Wadi Thimreen by day. Once into the bushes Corporal Salim and three men disappeared to the left, Ali Nasser's men to the right.

Said bin Ghia, who knew our target village, moved by my side. After an hour of slow, silent advance, I smelled dung fires. On the transceiver, Salim and Ali confirmed that they too had reached the settlement.

Sparse foliage and ant-hills appeared, then a clearing and thorn cattle enclosures. There was no one about; not even a cow. I checked with the telescope. Said bin Ghia grimaced with unease, sweating freely. He plainly had no desire at that moment to continue in a forwards direction.

Crouched behind the last of the thorn-bush cover, I heard Ali Nasser's brief response to my two-finger pressures on the transmitter switch. Somewhere along the northeastern rim of the clearing his men crept forward. Corporal Salim's men to the west were invisible. I gave Ali five minutes, then signalled to Mubarreq who rose, cradling his light machine-gun, a camouflage net over its gleaming belt of bullets.

As we left the tree fringe and stepped into the clearing a murderous rattle of Bren gun fire came from the west, momentarily stunning my senses. Two hundred yards ahead a ripple of earth spurts exploded like hailstones in a pond.

Then the 'woodpeckers' opened up from the other side of the clearing. These were Soviet RPD automatics, nicknamed due to their rapid rate of fire and the sound of their high-velocity bullets. I felt and heard the shockwaves pass by very close. Said bin Ghia screamed and fell to the ground.

I twisted away from my rice-filled rucksack and lurched back to the nearest ant-hill where Mubarreq struggled with the Browning.

Bin Ghia rolled over and over, quickly for a man of his girth, and flour spilled out of his pack, red with his blood. He reached an ant-hill one step ahead of the woodpeckers. It would have been suicide to move a muscle behind our mound. Mubarreq clasped my back and pulled me towards him with the big gun between us. He grinned and rolled his eyeballs in mock horror.

The *adoo* bullets dug into our ant-hill. A bullet ripped through my loose shirt tail. I flinched and the first nudgings of fear began to gather. Earth showered us, kicked up from the mound, and the vibration of bullets eating deep into the soil thudded against our cheeks. My signaller was back with Murad at the mouth of the Wadi Thimreen, but I knew he would have heard and called for a plane.

We had so far survived a well-laid ambush thanks entirely to the skill and alertness of Corporal Salim and his three men. Outflanking the *adoo*, they had seen our predicament and opened fire just as we entered the clearing. But Corporal Salim was now in danger. His voice came through, high with excitement. 'This is Five Two. They are closing, Sahb. Twenty or more have moved behind those in the village, to get around us. They know we are only four men.'

Our hope lay with Ali; his three soldiers each had a Bren gun. I told him to fire and move in. His reply was a whispered 'Five Four. *Im'shaalah.*'

His men opened up as one and the woodpeckers stopped as though switched off. Mubarreq at once jammed the Browning's steel tripod on our mound. One great hand fed the snake of bullets into the chamber, the other panned the gun and squeezed the trigger back. Instant destruction reigned in the thorn huts and in the scrub beyond.

Then we ran across the clearing. I forgot the pain in my knees; it was dispelled, along with fear, through action.

Only bloodstains and empty cases remained where the *adoo* had been.

Corporal Salim's jubilant voice came over the radio. 'They are running, Sahb. Shall we follow?'

I said no. They would not run for long if we exposed our total number.

Bin Ghia's wrist tendons were slashed by a bullet. As we dressed the wound he swore dramatic vengeance, his belly heaving. We all ducked as a stray bullet splintered the butt of my rifle.

One of the Sultan's two Strikemaster jets roared overhead and Sadeeq the Baluchi laid out a long fluorescent panel pointing to the likely position of the *adoo*. The jet returned along the line of the panel and loosed off four 80mm Sura rockets. Two malfunctioned and exploded close by Ali's men.

Two weeks later, Tom's intelligence sources confirmed that six *adoo* had died in the Thimreen clash.

We continued our work in the foothills but with far greater caution, entering villages only by night.

The days cooled as the *khareef* clouds slowly withdrew to reveal a world of green mountain, waving grass and steaming jungle. As the Army stirred its units to move into the newly accessible heights, unpleasant incidents, indicating an altogether more sophisticated *adoo*, occurred.

Along tracks and in rock sangars often frequented by our patrols we found plastic mines no larger than pocket-torches but powerful enough to blow a man's leg into his stomach, to tear off his scrotum and to blind him with the shrapnel of his own bone splinters. For the first time *adoo* killer groups came down to plains villages to carry out local executions. Tom Greening told me to watch Arzat village after dusk. Night after night for two weeks I ringed the coastal village with machine-guns and trip-flares but nothing happened . . . until four nights after we were moved away to another task.

Six men moved at a fast Jebali lope from Darbat to Arzat village, all with Soviet weapons and no back-packs. Their leader, Said bin Mistahayl, moved with confidence for he knew the way; he had spent most of his life in Arzat. Avoiding those wattle *barusti* huts where he knew there were dogs, he came to the house of Naseeb, the Army guide. Outside he gestured his men into the shadows and then rapped on the door.

In a while the door opened and Naseeb's face appeared in the light of a paraffin lamp. Naseeb's parents watched from within the hut as their son Mistahayl murdered his own brother in the name of PFLOAG.

Six days later two Chinese, experts with explosives, demolished the long wooden ramp where the mountain road from Thamarit climbed up from the desert. At specific points along the road, ten heavily armed *firqat* groups laid ambushes in the dense monsoon scrub for they knew the track was now dry and firm enough to take vehicles. Their timing was excellent. Only a day later, on 17 September, the Army launched an operation to secure the road.

From the north the tall Marine major, at the head of his company column, arrived by the wooden ramp to find it destroyed. His men repaired the damage quickly so as not to delay the carefully synchronised plans of our colonel.

From the plain, the other two companies approached the Jebel with the Recce Platoon Land Rovers up ahead. We found huge craters where the road was at its narrowest and boulders the size of jeeps straddling hairpin bends. Soldiers filled up the craters with earth while others levered away the boulder barriers. We leapfrogged ahead on foot to give cover to two men with mine detectors.

Spike Powell, the Australian mercenary, stood in the middle of the road in white slacks and khaki shirt. He seemed to be lifting two fingers at the unseen *adoo* and saying, 'Here I am. Grade One target; white officer. Shoot me if you can!'

Once the various obstacles were cleared, we nosed cautiously along the high winding road. We were to stop at the southern rim of a deep pass called Ambush Corner and wait until the Marine major's company reached the north side. Only then would men move down into the ravine. The trouble which followed was partly due to the fact that we arrived too late, but afterwards the Marine's mutinous men blamed everything on him and his jinx.

Having dealt with the sabotaged ramp, the Marine, nicknamed *Taweel*, 'the tall man', dropped off men at vantage points beside the road all the way to Ambush Corner, by which critical point only one platoon and a single small field gun remained at his disposal. At the final approach to the great ravine, *Taweel* and his men were pinned down by two machine-guns. His twenty-five-pounder gun crew swung their weapon round and, treating it like a kingsize rifle, pumped a single shell in the *adoo*'s general direction. As they re-loaded an *adoo* behind them mowed them down like skittles.

Taweel watched his men being picked off all about him. Any move on his part brought a hail of bullets from three directions. Some of these, he noticed with alarm, were Shpagin 12.7 high-explosive projectiles. One such bullet set the artillery lorry on fire and the flames rapidly spread towards a rack of twenty-five-pounder shells. The Baluchi driver leaped on to the truck and beat frantically at the burning debris. Then he arched backwards with a bullet through the head and toppled off the lorry. More soldiers were killed before the *adoo* melted away. Two hours later the companies met and lorry convoys from northern Oman began the post-monsoon re-supply. Recce dug in above Ambush Corner and I watched as truck after truck rolled by in low gear down the curling track. The convoy would take three days to complete its work and on the first night, with nine men and a guide, we descended into the forests of the Wadi Naheez. For four hours we avoided open places of new grass, movement through which leaves a tell-tale swath that can be spotted by Jebalis from afar. We stopped in a clump of rocks and hid beneath flowering shrubs. I was woken in mid-morning by our guide.

Beneath us, through his binoculars, I saw three thatched huts between great fig and tamarind trees. Children played and women gossiped in the shade. Then an armed man emerged from one hut, soon followed by four more.

We were separated from the village by 600 yards and the *adoo* looked all set to depart. Sura rockets or twenty-five-pounder shells would make short work of the huts. I reached for my radio to summon a rain of steel on to the target but something held me back. Artillery shells are not selective in dealing out death and mutilation: women and babies would be hurt. But here was my chance to avenge yesterday's dead. I picked up the hand microphone but still could not bring myself to speak.

The men watched me, tense and eager like cats observing mice. The guide frowned.

'We will wait,' I explained to him, 'till we are sure there are no more *adoo* to appear before I call up the big guns.' He raised his eyebrows and shrugged.

I knew he was right but did nothing. Forty minutes later fifteen men in dark brown uniforms and khaki hats emerged from the hut with packs and weapons. Then, too late, I called the artillery.

The second shell landed in the trees behind the *adoo* but they scattered out of sight in seconds and subsequent shots were mere guesswork on my part. I had blundered badly. No innocents were dead but that was no consolation at the time. The men and the guide were sullen for a while, but they soon forgot my stupidity: it is after all the will of Allah that guides even Christian minds.

Back in Umm al Ghawarif, Corporal Salim, who adored gossip, told me that *Taweel* had been removed from company command. The slaughter at Ambush Corner had been blamed on the Marine's *djinn* or evil spirit. The mutineers had forced the major to leave their camp and threatened to shoot him if he ever returned.

A week later the colonel ordered me to go north of the Jebel to the region called Nejd, a narrow band of steppe-country between the monsoon belt and the true desert. The Nejd is a crazy land of crumbling cliffs, snaking escarpments and a thousand secret ways by which heavy-laden camels can pass from western to eastern Dhofar. There were no army units in the Nejd, indeed no people at all, apart from bedu with herds of goats or camels wandering the *wadis* between scattered waterholes.

David Bayley's men were also moving from the plain so we approached the Jebel together. Nearing the foothills we came under heavy fire and leapt from the Land Rovers. For an hour we leapfrogged in sections towards the *adoo*, supported by fire from David's soldiers, and killed six of them. There was further trouble before we crossed the mountains and three of David's men were wounded.

Tom Greening's spies discovered the location of an *adoo* cave where a heavy Russian Shpagin machine-gun was secreted. I was ordered to infiltrate and ambush the Arbat valley east of Ambush Corner. One of the companies would then sweep down the Arbat from the north and catch the Shpagin men between our two groups.

Things turned out rather differently, for at least sixty guerrillas guarded the Shpagin with a well-sited ring of automatic weapons. The company was forced to withdraw with its dead and, by mid-day, Recce was alone in the bottom of the Arbat valley, twenty men in four separate groups.

In the afternoon two young girls came close to the knot of scrub where we lay. I saw Said Salim slip his stiletto from his sheath and I knew we must silence both girls if they found us.

The girls saw us while still outside our hide. Their eyes widened in fear. I smiled at them and beckoned through the foliage. They stood still, uncertain like young does. Behind the bush I sensed Said Salim creeping towards them.

'Ish Kish. Ish Kish,' I whispered through the leaves – the Jebali assurance that all is well.

The girls held hands; one had a semi-shaven scalp and a silver pendant about her neck. Perhaps they heard Said's stirring behind the curtain of leaves. With a flick of their grubby little cloaks, they were off, scurrying through the undergrowth to their village. Said was after them like a flash but I whistled and beckoned him back.

I reasoned that the girls might think we were *adoo* from another area. After all there were *adoo* with yellow faces and slit eyes and Arabs from the Mediterranean with paler skin than mine.

But such theorising ceased when I heard excited male voices from further along the *wadi*. We sweated in the dappled heat. We were too few to be in the epicentre of the mountains, in the heart of *adoo* territory. Said Salim pressed his head to the ground. 'They are coming this way, Sahb. We must move.'

We brushed the place with our *shemaghs* and Mubarreq obliterated the latrine area so there would be no sign of our presence. For half an hour we crept through low undergrowth until there were no more voices.

I prayed the little girls had not compromised us. Like spiders reacting to the tactile message from prey caught within their webs, *adoo firqat* could very quickly plug off any part of the Jebel area.

Night came at last and we moved through open meadows to the wood appointed as a rendezvous. Corporal Salim and Ali were already there. They shook my hand in greeting. Men smiled up from the dark rim of the trees and our retreat began. Each section leader held a phosphorous grenade as did the rear man – the Moolah.

For nine hours without a rest we traversed defiles strewn with boulders, crossed endless minor valleys and skirted clusters of thorn huts with names like Gurthnod, Habdoomer and Erikob. We reached the safety of the barren Nejd soon after dawn.

The mountain road was used only once again that year; the *adoo* grip tightened along its length, their growing strength and heavier weapons now a match for all but a full regimental group, more than the colonel could spare. The *adoo* now held the Dhofar mountains from the Yemen border to the Arbat valley. Only the lands of the Eastern Mahra around Bait Fiah territory were to any degree independent of the *adoo*. Once they were subjugated, the plain of Salalah would be cut off, with its back to the sea.

10

Leopard Line

The night has a thousand eyes.

F. 'V. BOURDILLON

To stop the flow of heavy weapons from the Yemen into central Dhofar, our colonel devised the 'Leopard Line' – a loose blockade running north from the coast over the Jebel to the sands of the Empty Quarter.

One company manned the line on the plain and in the foothills, and David Bayley's men were scattered along the mountain ridge called Raydah, where the foliated Qara are at their narrowest and so least favourable to the *adoo*. In an elastic sort of way David's company blocked movement across a line running south from the Nejd. In theory, the thirty men of Recce were to block the Nejd all the way to the Sands, leaving the *adoo* camel trains no entry point to central and eastern Dhofar. In practice, since the *adoo* were already present in strength throughout the entire Jebel, the Leopard Line must expect attack from the rear while preventing incursion from the west.

Since Recce would need to live in the desert for many months and be as self-contained as possible, I was assigned a three-ton lorry in which to carry water, any firewood we could collect and twelve goats. Every fifteenth day a section would return to Thamarit with the truck for more goats. Sultan bin Nashran, a sheikh of the Bait Shaasha bedu, accompanied us as desert guide.

In late September we left Thamarit and followed the only available vehicle track leading into the Nejd, a vulnerable route to the pools of Ayun which passed directly beneath *adoo* territory for ten miles with no cover. Each time my truck returned to Thamarit for more goats, the escort would be in considerable danger. There seemed no way around this problem, nor around the fact that the *adoo* would at all times know whether Recce was bottled up in the Nejd or had emerged via the Ayun pools track and returned to Thamarit. On this side of the Jebel we were cut off from all other Army units.

The guide Sultan led us to the remote waterhole of Thint. There was little sign of life or water, as there had been no rain for fifteen years. From Thint we walked along canyons and up mesas to a ridge known as Pasadena, then north to a gravel bowl, a dusty amphitheatre through which snaked a well-used camel trail called the Dehedoba. This baked plateau became our base for many months. Back in Salalah, where I was referred to by British officers merely as 'The Fiend' or, by sergeants, as 'Captain Fiend', the headquarters map was marked from the Qara to the Rhubh al Khali, or Empty Quarter, with the word 'Fiendforce'. The little plateau became known as 'Fiendfield'.

I was determined no arms caravans would penetrate our area. To achieve this with only five Land Rovers in so vast a region meant non-stop patrolling and the finding of new access routes. It also involved recognising *adoo* signs if and when we chanced upon them. For this our guide was invaluable. Water points dictated the route of camel travel and he knew the location of most if not all springs in the Nejd. By kneeling beside the prints of a lone camel, he could glean a mine of information. Sometimes he knew the name of the camel's owner by the shape of the hoof, where and when it had last drunk by the amount and frequency of its droppings, and, by their texture, in which *wadis* it had last eaten.

The Nejd looked both lifeless and harmless. In reality it was neither: every crack in the crumbling surface concealed something that crawled or slithered. Normally I wore no shoes once the soles of my feet were hardened, for it was so much cooler without them. For patrols I wore only suede desert boots bought in London.

Two hours east of 'Fiendfield', in a deep canyon, the spring of Ayun bubbled into pools surrounded by boulders. Reeds and flowering lianas rimmed these lagoons and the diving screech of swallows echoed off the soaring cliffs above. Here, on the way back from goat-meat collection, the relevant section would fill our water barrels from cans carried laboriously up a winding track. Then the men would wash their clothes and bodies, keeping a watchful eye out for the five-foot long water snakes that lived in the pools.

Tom Greening sent a message to check the sands north of the Nejd. It was just possible arms were circumventing us that way. Running the gauntlet of the Ayun trail with two sections, we left the Nejd and patrolled the sands from the Yemeni frontier to the old oil camp sites of '455' and Fasad for two weeks.

In the Nejd we always whispered by night, but in the sands we were at ease. The men talked into the small hours, squatting with fingers sieving the pure sand or simply watching the stars. They never spoke derisively of one another or tried to score over a neighbour as British soldiers do. Each man had his say and the Baluchis sat at peace among the Arabs. They were happy to talk for the sake of communicating, needing no alcoholic stimulus or swearwords to help express themselves. I thought of other nights by other fires: of the Jocks in Germany, the clatter of beer cans, the filthy language with every sentence and the crude laughter as someone rose to urinate into the fire.

I felt happy and at one with these Muslim soldiers – a way I had never felt in the Greys or the SAS. There was no ever-present barrier of self-consciousness, no artificial officer–soldier gap designed and maintained to prevent familiarity gnawing at discipline. Such a gap was unnecessary with the Arabs. Their morals and manners were built-in, as was their respect for authority. In time their traditions would doubtless be eroded by contact with an outside world in which both social and individual standards had degenerated, but, until then, they would remain the best companions any man could want.

Very few bedu came our way in the Nejd. A scrawny Bait Ghawwas sold us goats and accepted bribe money. His only information was that our movements were being watched: by whom and from where he would not say.

One morning we lay in ambush above the Pass of Qismeem south of Ayun when two unarmed Jebalis scurried along the track through our killing-ground, a fifty-yard stretch of a well-used footpath. Said Salim crept down, intercepted them and brought them to our hide. Both were from the Arbat Valley and one was an old friend whose family we had often fed: Ahmed Sehail of the Bait Tabawq. He shook hands with the five of us but said, 'I must go. If we are seen we will be killed. There are many watchers.' He gave a signal and Said Salim took the other man back to the track.

The Tabawqi then continued: 'There are twelve armed men with binoculars whose work is to watch the movements of your men. It is known you guard the Dehedoba but not what else you do in the Nejd. They learn first how you move then they will use mines or, when you go to Thamarit, they will kill you east of Ayun.'

As he spoke the man twitched his neck about. 'Do you want medicine?' I asked.

Throwing back his dirty cloak, he revealed a jigsaw-puzzle of purple wheals over his back and chest. One crossed his right nipple which was broken and swollen. Accepting a packet of penicillin tablets, he refused a dressing of any sort, saying the *adoo* would notice.

'But why did they do this to you?' I asked.

'I sold goats to the Army at Hamrir and the *adoo* found out. They beat me with wire and tied me to a tree. For a day no one dared cut me down.'

Close to Ayun, Ali Nasser disturbed two armed *adoo* but, mutually surprised, neither group opened fire and the *adoo* disappeared. Ali thought they were mine-layers.

South of the Nejd David Bayley's company was attacked by *adoo* leader Bakhait Ahmad. He shot two soldiers from a distance of ten yards, seized their weapons and was gone. It was only a matter of time before we received similar attention and, since our patrols were normally only ten strong, we could expect to be outnumbered. I resolved to find some other route from the Nejd other than the Ayun to Thamarit track.

We split into three groups: one to stay at the Dehedoba, one to patrol the sands and the third to locate a safe route to the desert. I warned each group to be erratic in their routine and never to relax their guard.

It being the turn of my section for sands patrol, we undertook two tasks on the Yemen border. The first, to capture ex-*adoo* leader Musallim bin Nuffl, failed, for he did not cross the border as expected by intelligence. The other mission involved driving to the fort at Habarut where I exchanged messages by runners with the commander of the Yemeni fort across the *wadi*. He agreed to a meeting in no-man's land.

With an eye to Yemeni treachery I positioned our machine-guns, mortar and all the fort *askars* in a state of open readiness before our mid-day meeting in the *wadi*. The Yemeni officer did likewise, so both skylines bristled with gleaming barrels. Awaiting noon, I sat unarmed in the *wadi* with Murad and Said Salim beneath a withered heliotrope and watched 500 camels shuffle by the nearby pools.

Said Salim nudged me. Three men appeared to float over the white stones towards us. Behind us the *askars* and Recce men readied their weapons. At this time of day the blinding glare favoured the riflemen of neither fort.

We stood up in the centre of the *wadi* as the Yemenis approached. Two were tall soldiers of the Hadhraumi Bedouin Legion – now the Aden Federal Army. They walked on either side of a little man with yellow skin and a khaki baseball cap.

We all shook hands and sat in a ring on the hot pebbles. After the greetings, there was silence. Then Murad produced 200 Rothman cigarettes from his shemagh roll. I prodded him and he found 200 more. I offered them to the Yemeni who took them without the customary feigned refusals with which Arabs precede the acceptance of a gift.

He spoke classical Arabic. 'Men of your Sultan's village have wounded a man of our village. We are bound to protect our villagers. You understand?'

His name was Said Allowi bin Ali, commander of the easternmost garrison of the People's Republic of South Yemen.

'*Na'am ya ra'ees*,' I said with politeness, 'but His Majesty the Sultan wants only peace. We apologise for the trouble which was the work of troublemakers unknown to the Sultan. They will be punished.'

He said nothing. I saw that he had acne.

I continued, 'Any attack on the Sultan's fort or the villagers on his side of the *wadi* by your men must be considered an act of war and will be met with strong retaliation. We hope you agree this will be unnecessary.'

'Your apology is accepted. You deal with your troublemakers; we with ours.' His features softened as he added, 'We have no luxuries such as Western cigarettes in the Republic. I have nothing to give you save the wish for peace.' He rose and the six of us withdrew from the unmarked border.

Soon afterwards the Yemeni garrison filled with PFLOAG *adoo* who attacked the Sultan's fort and razed it to the ground. The Sultan's Air Force then bombed the *adoo* camp at Hauf in the Yemen. A cross-border war was averted only through diplomatic moves within the Arab League.

We travelled northwest to the well of Shahan, speeding over black plains and skidding sometimes as our tyres punctured the thin veneer of gypsum and sent up plumes of white dust. By dusk we were all powder-grey. We camped in a bowl of sand and lit kindling under our cauldron, battered by many journeys. Then men washed with sand and spread their prayer mats to face Mecca.

Wolves howled in the east as the Dog Star pulsed low. The nine of us lay in the still warm sand but huddled together about the fire, for we knew the night would be cold and heavy with dew. Someone explained to me why there are shooting stars. When angels catch devils spying at the gates of heaven – to glean information about the future – they throw burning lamps to scare them away. The Prophet learned this when he went to heaven by camel.

Some areas of the Nejd were featureless wastes of gleaming rock as far as the eye could see: yet even here Sultan could locate others of his nomadic tribe with uncanny accuracy. Once he pointed suddenly to the north and Murad swung the wheel. For fifteen minutes we sped over undulating gypsum flats until a single dark mound appeared amidst a sea of yellow folds, like the mole on the chin of Chairman Mao.

At the mound we found a family of Shaasha, a ragged herd of goats and one she-camel. Sultan and his kinsfolk kissed and rubbed noses, expressing great happiness. The greeting sputtered on for a full ten minutes.

The headman of the clan milked the camel into a tin and the frothy warm liquid, too salty for my taste, was passed around. From a long *dhub* lizard skin, he then revealed a supply of salted shark guts resembling chopped-off thumbs. They tasted fishy and rotten but not as bad as the stench had led me to expect.

The bedu's close dependence on the elements – for they died easily at Allah's whim, at the drying up of a well or the death of a camel – made them deeply religious. They had no education but the Koran and the harsh tutorage of the desert. They are rightly proud people. Sultan once said to me of Moses, whom he called 'Kalamu 'illah', 'the man who spoke to God': 'He too was an Arab and like all bedu he was of Allah's chosen people.'

The Shaasha family appeared to own nothing except their camel, their goats and the contents of a few leather bags. They carried a meagre supply of water in a lorry's inner-tube. They had given us milk and meat that would have lasted them many days and they were a long, long way from the nearest water. They were not to know that we would supply them with flour and water.

When bedu eat they share their food and their last cup of water with any stranger who happens upon them. Perhaps this explains the bedu saying, 'Visit seldom and you will be welcome'.

Determined to locate a safe route from the Nejd, I left 'Fiendfield' with three sections and, less than a mile east of Ayun, followed an old camel trail north and west. The plateau we climbed was one we had tried several times before without success, but now Murad persevered further than most drivers, or the vehicle manufacturers, would have considered advisable.

Holding our breath, we roared up a 45° mountainside, gravel flying as the tyres skidded and screamed. There were three successive inclines and the last was the worst. The Land Rover seemed bound to topple over backwards but we finally reached the summit. The other vehicles, crammed with nervously cheering men, bounced up behind us.

For a week we ranged north into a wild new land where ibex and gazelle were in abundance. We saw two wolves, great shaggy beasts much larger than their Alaskan relatives. Said Salim found the prints of a big cat, twice the size of the wildcat spoor of the Qara, possibly a leopard since the mountain lion was thought to be extinct in Dhofar.

Each day took us deeper into a country of huge mesa. It was like travelling along the hedgetops of a maze. We drove cautiously via narrow ridgelines, some no wider than our vehicles, with cliffs falling away on either side. Some were cul-de-sacs which caused nerve-racking retreats in reverse. We followed many false trails which ended on pinnacles with fine views of the Nejd and the shimmering but unattainable sandsea below – our gateway to safety.

Before we could find any way down from the plateau a radio call came from Corporal Salim, whose men had arrested an unarmed *adoo* courier at the Ayun pools. The man carried bundles of Yemeni money in his *dishdash*. He might be moving ahead of an *adoo* group so we followed our tracks back to the ramps and to Ayun.

There was a full moon above the pools. I lay in the reeds close to the only approach track and quietly squashed mosquitoes. Towards midnight Salim whispered over my radio. 'Come quickly, Sahb. It is Salim Mayoof. He will kill us all.' Mayoof was a Negro soldier who had replaced one of the men injured when Hamid Sultan was crushed to death.

Leaving four men in the reeds, I crept away with Said Salim and Fat Hamid, a merry character who had taken a liking to my .30 Browning machine-gun and had joined my section. Quickly, we climbed the track to the clifftop where Corporal Salim's men were positioned. As we first glimpsed their silhouettes, there was a scream, a high keening noise. Fat Hamid stopped abruptly behind me. I turned to find him lying on the ground behind his gun. He was tense, his eyes wide with fear in the moonlight.

'Come on, Salim.' With Said Salim's help I heaved him up.

But he clamped his hand on my shoulder. 'No, Sahb, there is something *zift* up there, something evil.'

There was now no sound at all from Corporal Salim's section and I pulled the fat man along by his gun. He came grudgingly and kept behind Said. We followed the very rim of the cliffs and stopped as we reached the cluster of rocks of the section. Puffs of cloud passed the moon, and their shadows slid over the rocks.

The others came abreast of me and then I heard a low hissing, as of mating cats, from within the rock cluster. The moon emerged to reveal a voodoo-like vignette.

Brave Corporal Salim and four of his men cowered together between two boulders, their rifles pointed at the figure squatting above them. Its teeth and eyeballs glinted as its head shook with a sibilant hiss. I pulled myself together. It was Mayoof, his outline somehow distorted and enlarged by the moon directly behind him.

Fat Hamid dropped to the ground, loaded the Browning on its squat tripod and took aim at the ape-like figure. I kicked sand in his face and tore the honeycombed barrel from his grasp. 'Don't be a fool, Hamid. It's only Salim Mayoof. He must be drugged.'

But as I spoke, Mayoof, a big Zanzibari, rose up on his boulder and, clawing the air as though he would tear the moon to pieces, began again to scream. The sound, more animal than human, rose on a single frantic note which mingled with its own echoes coming back from the cliffs of Ayun.

'Get his gun, Said Salim. Make sure he's not armed.' I felt sure Said would not let me down. But he did. He cowered behind his rifle and made no move. My mind raced. I felt the atmosphere of the place take an uncanny hold on me. Soon it would be too late to fight the mounting fear. My mind raced back to Abner, our South African gardener, who died because he believed in witchcraft, and to my mother's words that evil cannot touch those who believe in Christ. I went to Mayoof's rock but saw no rifle.

'Shut up, you fool, you'll have all the *adoo* in Dhofar here in no time.'

He stopped screaming and looked down at me. I saw the foam and slobber about his mouth. He began to giggle, holding his ribs as though they hurt and slowly lowering himself until his head was near mine. His protruding eyeballs were more than I could stand and I moved back.

Said tugged at my shirt and hissed at me. 'Come away. You don't understand. He is Malik, leader of the *taghut* and keeper of hell. He is inside the soul of Mayoof. Come away. You can do nothing.'

Two things happened simultaneously. The giggling ceased and Mayoof crumpled sobbing as a single shriek sounded behind me. I reeled backwards, affected by the terror of the others. Fat Hamid lay spreadeagled among the rocks, his limbs jerking like those of a puppet.

Said's grip tightened on my arm. 'See. The *djinn* has flown to Hamid. An Arab soul is better than a Sambo's.'

I knew Fat Hamid well – a quiet, cheerful man and no actor. His transformation from mere fear to control by incubus, if such it was, had been instantaneous. I did not wish to believe in ghosts or evil spirits. This was undoubtedly a hallucination brought about by the eerie nature of the place, the white cliffs and the pools. The showy ritual of Islam overlaid centuries of Semitic practice in fetishism, animism and blood sacrifice. Perhaps the soldiers' monotheism was a skin-deep veneer, a coat of bright paint through which the scabby rust of superstition readily erupted at times such as this. Yet a coldness played about the rocks, an atmosphere so pregnant with malaise that the flesh puckered along my back as I watched Fat Hamid's limbs and eyes thresh at the whim of his unwelcome visitor. Nothing would have induced me to approach him.

At length he was quiet and lay still. Only the muffled sobs of Mayoof disturbed the silence.

Next day Hamid remembered nothing and was as cheery as ever. Mayoof however, was inconsolable, wailing again and again that his soul had been stolen by persons unknown. Since this behaviour was bad for morale I sent him back to Salalah on the next goat-bearing Beaver.

A week later the adjutant in Salalah sent me an agitated signal. 'Salim Mayoof says your driver has stolen his soul. Please return it at once.'

I asked Murad if he had taken anything at all from Mayoof before he had left us. He had not. I told the adjutant this and Mayoof was sent north for medical treatment.

I returned to Salalah for a course of penicillin injections because my armpit and crutch glands were swollen with poison from festering desert sores on my legs and hands. Idling in the Officers' Mess, I noticed that all beer and Coca Cola cans were taken in sacks to Spike Powell's office where he had set up a production line to manufacture anti-personnel mines. He used equipment easily obtainable from regimental stores: torch batteries, electric wire, detonators and plastic explosive.

The *adoo* had of late blown the legs off a number of company soldiers with cleverly planted British Mark VI anti-personnel mines, but the Sultan's Army had nothing with which to retaliate. Hence Spike's beer can factory. All three Leopard Line officers, including me, laid 'Muldoons' along their local infiltration trails. I surrounded mine with barbed wire so that, although the barriers were obvious to innocent bedu, the narrow Dehedoba trails were effectively sealed.

A few months later a Baluchi soldier went to urinate in a minefield. Apparently the men had only been told in Arabic where the 'Muldoons' were placed. His officer, an old SAS friend of mine named Eddie Viturakis, entered the minefield and dragged the mangled soldier clear without tripping other mines. Some weeks afterwards, Eddie's orderly, a drug-taker, entered his tent and shot him as he slept to avenge some grudge. Then he fled to the *adoo*.

After ten days of penicillin and no flies I returned to 'Fiendfield'. The men looked weathered and hard compared to Salalah inmates. They welcomed me with a dinner of gazelle and pulled at my plasters to see if my sores had healed. Then came a barrage of questions.

'How is my brother Ahmed?'

'Is Hillal still alive?'

'Has Mayoof found his soul?'

'Did you bring my bananas?'

At first they would not admit to there being any Recce news. Then, over the embers of a veritable feast of gazelle, rice and dates, Ali Nasser broke the news, for it was his to tell.

Not much taller than the squatting Mubarreq, Ali stood by the fire to address us, his voice loud enough for even the outer sentries to hear, although everyone but I knew well enough what he had to say. 'Soon after you left, my patrol travelled hard for five days from Murad's new ramp. We came to a country where no bedu had been before and no man has seen.'

Ali took a deep breath of oratorical pleasure and picked his great nose with care. 'Allah was good,' he continued, 'to show us the way and I was always correct in choosing the right route. On the evening of the fifth day we came to the very top of the world where we killed two ibex.' More nose-picking for effect. 'After eating, I moved apart to pray behind the rocks and, below me, many hundreds of feet down, I saw a great white *wadi* running north. At once I ran down without delay – after my prayers were ended – and found a ledge of rock which led down to the *wadi*. This ledge, Sahb,' he glanced down at me, 'is, *Im'shallaah*, big enough for the vehicles of Recce.'

Ali, dazed by his own delivery, sat down to much good-natured cheering, and I congratulated him. The next day all but the Dehedoba guards followed Ali's trail, a circuitous way via many dizzy ramparts, until we reached his 'ledge'. On seeing it, my hopes sagged. Only a madman would drive a Land Rover down so precarious a gully and he would never get back up. But here at least was a possible safe way to Thamarit.

For several days two dozen of us levered boulders down to widen the natural ledge. Finally Murad slithered his Land Rover to the bottom. Since the *wadi* might prove to be a cul-de-sac no more vehicles descended until, after three more days, we had perfected the ramp. Then, to wild cheering, Murad drove back up to the top.

Next day we all descended and nosed north into the valley below, until it forked northeast and led us to the Wadi Yistah and at length to Thamarit. I signalled Salalah of the new safe route from the mountains and, soon afterwards, David Bayley's men withdrew their artillery by way of our track.

From then on our movements in and out of the Nejd went undetected by the *adoo*; a factor soon to prove critical.

I was on patrol at the Yemeni border when an Operations Immediate signal summoned Recce to Thamarit at once. We drove east to Ayun to collect two of the sections, then continued, via our secret track, to Thamarit. Suspecting some lengthy mission, I bade all the men, except for the drivers, to sleep.

Late that afternoon Tom Greening landed in the Beaver, accompanied by a small, dark-skinned Mahra whose handshake was weak and wet. In an empty shack with a table, Tom laid out his map. The Mahra squatted on the floor and picked his nose.

'This man,' said Tom, 'comes from a village south of Qum, some five miles into the Jebel.'

I knew at once that Tom was talking of a no-go area, a centre of *adoo* activity. His finger traced a line from the desert where it met the Jebel at the spring of Obet, then south over a bewildering complex of deep valleys and into the foliated upper reaches of the Wadi Sahilnawt.

'Two nights ago,' Tom explained, 'this chap, who calls himself Sahayl, a son of Sheikh Musallim of the Bait Howeirat, walked forty miles solely to ask us to kill three *adoo* to whom he has taken a dislike. These three arrive every morning, regular as clockwork, to get milk and a quick bump with the girls of his village.' Tom glanced at me to see how I was taking his story: then continued, 'As soon as the *adoo* discover Sahayl's missing, they will be all over his village. That is why I want you to be there by dawn tomorrow. Leave here as soon as you can. I believe two of the three *adoo* he hates are important. Get them back to me alive.'

Tom left as I digested the details of his job. Normally I distrusted *adoo* informers, with the exception of the old and trusted guides like Said bin Ghia, Sultan and the murdered Naseeb. But Tom seldom made errors of judgement. Here was a man with fresh information from an unknown *adoo* area. Tom had taken Sahayl straight to our colonel and asked for an immediate patrol to capture the three *adoo*.

No large Army group, Sahayl said, could hope to infiltrate the area, for it lay inside a network of *adoo* camps.

'Where, on my map, is your village?' the colonel asked him.

The Mahra's bony finger hovered for a while, then lighted on a barren part of the Empty Quarter. 'This is our *bayt*, and here,' he indicated some sand dunes, 'are the *adoo* camps.'

This evidence of Sahayl's reaction to maps suggested to the colonel that he should not be used to guide an aerial attack. The only central Jebel company was surrounded, under daily mortar attacks, many miles from Bait Fiah. So, since Sahayl's information must be acted on at once, the colonel sent for 'Fiendforce'. For once the firm ruling – a minimum of half a company on the *adoo*-held Jebel at one time – would be broken.

Since Recce had been a semi-autonomous desert unit for many months, no one back in Salalah was quite sure how many active men made up my group. But, as two troops of Oman gendarmerie had recently been sent from Muscat to strengthen our desert ambush points, the colonel was under the impression we were some fifty in number.

This was unfortunately not so. I had left fourteen gendarmes along the Dehedoba and, as soon as word had spread in the platoon of an impending 'deep' patrol, an epidemic of coughs, dysentery and lumbago broke out. So, when we assembled to leave Thamarit, we numbered twenty-four. We were the only Army unit whose current presence was unknown to the *adoo*. As far as they were concerned, we were still boxed up in the Nejd north of Ayun.

Battle rations and ammunition were given out and our twelve machine-guns checked over. I called the men together. They sat around in the dust, their grim faces staring balefully at Sahayl; many remembered company friends whose deaths in ambushes had been attributed to double-dealing guides. I explained the mission and we left Thamarit.

Five miles from the Obet waterhole at the Jebel's edge we stopped for prayer. With engines revving as quietly as possible despite soft sand, the vehicles left us and returned north. At such moments many patrol soldiers pray that they too may soon pass their Land Rover test and become drivers.

On the high peaks ahead of and above us the *adoo* scouts would be settling for the night, their keen ears alert for the wind-borne whine of motors. Tonight they would have no such warning, for the sounds of engines, coughs and rattling pebbles would head north with the southerly breeze.

All guns were cocked and grenades primed. Then the rear man, the Moolah, gave the 'move' sign. I prodded Sahayl and pointed south. He grinned.

Tom had said the journey would take eight hours 'at Jebali pace'. If Sahayl's pace was the basis of Tom's reckoning, we were in trouble, for he moved far too fast to be followed by men with heavy loads. I ran after him and gestured for him to slow down.

Childishly sullen, he lapsed into a ridiculously slow pace. I cursed him silently, wishing I had a compass bearing to follow instead of this mercurial Mahra.

The climb up the cliffs from Obet was steep and took us an hour. At the top Ali came to me whispering, 'Look back, Bakheit, over the Gat'n.'

At first there was nothing. Only the twinkle of a billion stars, the sound of a cricket and the wide gloom of the desert. As suddenly as summer lightning, a green signal flare shot up. Then a second and third: there was no telling how far away. 'That is the second time,' Ali whispered. 'Altogether six flares now. Either *adoo* in the Gat'n have heard us and signal to those on the Jebel. Or it is Murad in trouble.'

There was no Army presence in the Gat'n to explain the flares. Time was short but I could not ignore the flares. Leaving half the platoon on top, I retraced our steps to where Murad had left us. He had not returned and there were no further flares. A waste of time. Back up the bloody cliffside.

With two hours squandered, the men further dispirited and those who had made the ascent twice already tired, I began to feel that this was not my type of mission. The men were jittery. All knew the gamble we took. Unable to move south to the plain through the *adoo* heartland and unable to retreat back north to the Gat'n, we would be surrounded and picked off in the Bait Fiah grasslands from the moment the Jebali detected our presence. Any wounded man would be abandoned if a sudden retreat became necessary, since there were no stretchers, mules or helicopters. The nearest surgical team was in Bahrain, 2000 miles away, and the nearest company not itself under siege, at least two days' march from us. We only had water enough for two static days.

For three hours we stole through thickening scrubland fractured by valleys. Here Sahayl came into his own. No compass could have taken me along the confusing route of interconnecting paths, up and down deep gullies, where no white man had hitherto been fool enough to wander. Once inside the thick screen of creeper and thorn which crammed each new defile, the men closed up for fear of taking a wrong turning.

Sahayl had effortlessly avoided caves, thorn houses and even the temporary bedu camps which scatter the Jebel. Dawn was due in three hours. I now urged Sahayl to go a little faster. He grinned knowingly.

Corporal Salim came forward carrying three rifles. 'Some men are tired, Sahib. Two are already saying they must rest.'

I snapped at him. 'Tell them if they rest they die. We must be in position by dawn. You know that.' I regretted my temper as soon as Salim left. I was on edge. At any time I expected the sudden hell of an ambush; the flares were fresh in my mind.

Valleys a mile wide now fell away to our flanks, their rims visible only as dark shadows as we moved over the grassy shoulders between them. For an hour we stumbled through a region of skull-sized stones that slowed us down, but at 3.00 a.m. we cleared the broken ground and entered an inhabited valley. Dark shapes blobbed the upper slopes, fig tree clumps and cattle kraals of thorn. Twice we passed the acrid tang of burning dung from villages until, on a high knoll, Sahayl knelt without warning and looked about him. Again I smelled dung. To the southeast a patch of spreading grey suffused the sky. Dawn.

A faint bird-like prattle came to us on the breeze – the voices of Jebali women. Sahayl's hands closed over my shoulders, thrusting his face close to mine. He was smiling again. We had arrived. He pointed down the slope to six dark hummocks: a Mahra village.

As I turned to signal for the section leaders, a pinpoint of light pulsed from high ground further east. It lasted only a moment. I might have imagined it.

The village was badly placed for a safe ambush; wooded slopes rose sharply on both sides but too far from the huts to be useful. The only good cover was itself overlooked by these high woods. With little time for finesse, I positioned Corporal Salim and Mohammed of the Beard with their men well back from the village to give cover to the other sections. Ali Nasser's men wormed into a clump of rock and thorn 300 yards from the huts.

With Sahayl behind me, my section jogged east from cover to cover, chased by the dawn. I found a good dominating spot but noticed a thicket still higher up and, remembering the light signal, sent Said Salim ahead. He gave me his gun and left like a ghost to enter the thicket from behind. We heard a brief scuffle, then Said's whistle.

The thicket was hollowed out, with a ruined thorn hut inside its shell and a floor of loose stones. Said held a tall Jebali by his hair and pressed his stiletto into the side of the man's neck. A Martini Henry rifle and cartridge belt lay on the ground.

Fat Hamid, who had carried the .30 Browning all night, collapsed, exhausted. He picked up a tiny wallet which we found to contain a flint and tinder. 'This man is adoo,' Hamid whispered. 'He has been making signals.'

Sahayl, entering the clearing, clasped the Jebali and, ignoring the latter's awkward position, rubbed his cheek with his own and muttered a spate of greetings.

Said Salim said, 'They are brothers, Sahb.'

I was totally confused as to the implications of this so, to play safe, I had Mubarreq bind the two Mahra together back to back and gag their mouths.

We quietly made sangars of rocks for protection, sighted our weapons and left Said Salim on guard. Then we slept.

The sun was well up when I woke. Said Salim fell asleep within a minute of waking the rest of us. A hummingbird whirred in the chintz ceiling of our hide. Warm sunlight came dappled through the thorn and dust-filled shafts played on the strained faces within. I saw that Sahayl's brother had only one eye.

I looked south, at the scattered huts below and the rolling green wonderland all about us. In the distance the plain of Salalah stretched mistily away to the Indian Ocean.

Four armed men in dark brown uniforms moved quickly from the huts below into nearby scrub and out of sight. Fat Hamid and the others were instantly alert. In two years of ambushes we had never had so easy a target. But the penalty for a single shot would be the failure of our task. Our only safety lay in concealment. Our three *adoo* commissars, if they appeared, must be captured silently or we would stand no chance of escape.

Jebalis were at work all about us – women cutting grass and tending goats, children playing in the long grass which cows grazed contentedly after the long months of drought. Two young men approached our thicket carrying long flintlock guns. They were Bait Kathir and they would soon spot us. One cry of alarm would give us away. I moved half out of the bush and beckoned to them while Mubarreq let them see the snout of his machine gun.

Surprise showed briefly on their handsome faces, but they came quietly and Said took their rifles.

Over the next two hours, as the heat mounted, seven more Jebalis, including a woman and two children, came by the thicket, saw us and wisely joined our somewhat cramped quarters.

Three uniformed *adoo* came into the village from the south and sat talking by the hut farthest from our vantage point. From time to time they glanced in our direction and then left the way they had come.

I followed their path through binoculars until they disappeared and then carefully scanned the hills beyond. I felt my chest tighten. Some sixty or seventy figures moved about along the high scrubby ground south of the huts. Most were in uniform and the intermittent glint of metal suggested many were armed. They were positioned as though expecting some form of attack from the south.

I could not tell what lay to the north of our thicket as our hill continued to rise a few feet higher to its knoll. The likelihood that we were already cut off from the Nejd weighed on my mind.

Since waking I had experienced the stab of stomach pains. This was nothing new, for they came often in the desert, caused by the water or the meat. But usually I could find a bush or rock to squat behind for relief: then the sick feeling would abate, leaving me weak and sweating. Now there was nowhere to go but outside the thicket and that would put everything at risk. The pains grew worse, extending to my rectum. I stifled a groan and knew I could wait no longer.

The space within our hide was overcrowded. The last two bedu to arrive were standing, for there was no more room to sit. I built a parapet of small rocks around my backside, between me and the others, and lowered my trousers as my insides gave way in a flood. For minutes I grimaced in pain. At once flies swarmed into the thicket. I used pebbles instead of paper and collapsed the little 'cubicle' on to the results of my personal crisis. I fastened my trousers. Not a moment too soon.

Sensing a movement outside the hut, I wiped the sweat from my eyes. My rifle was beneath Mubarreq who was still studiously and politely trying to ignore my presence. Urgently I hauled the gun back towards me and released its safety catch.

A narrow goat trail ran between our thicket and the top of a steep grassy slope. Two tall men were approaching quickly along it. I saw their dark clothes and the glint of weapons in their hands. The second *adoo* wore a shiny red badge in his cap, not the Mao button badge worn by many of the PFLOAG militia, but the hexagonal red star of a political commissar.

These were our men. I was sure of it. There was no time to think. They were fifteen short yards away. Soon they would see us.

The first man stopped abruptly, appearing to sniff the air. His face was scarred, his hair closely shaven. I watched the Kalashnikov, its round magazine cradled in his elbow, swing round as he turned to face us. A touch of a Kalashnikov trigger will squeeze off a magazine of hollow-nosed 7.62 bullets that rip bones apart and blow guts aside like papier mâché.

Inch by inch I lifted my rifle. The sun outlined the man. Only his shadow falling upon the thicket shielded my eyes, stinging with sweat, from the glare. He peered directly at me now. I remember thinking, He has seen us. He is weighing his chances.

My voice seemed to come of its own volition. 'Drop your weapons or we kill you.'

The big man moved with speed, twisting at the knee and bringing the Kalashnikov to bear in a single movement.

I squeezed my trigger. He was slammed back as though caught in the chest by a sledgehammer. His limbs spread out like a puppet and he cartwheeled out of sight.

Behind him the commissar paused for a moment, unsure what to do. I noticed his face beneath the jungle cap. He looked sad and faintly surprised. His rifle, a Mark IV .303 was already pointed at my stomach when a flurry of shots rang out. Mubarreq and Said Salim, forcing themselves free of encumbrance by the Jebalis, fired simultaneously.

The man's face crumpled into red horror, the nose and eyes smashed back into the brain. Further bullets tore through his ribs and a pretty flowering shrub caught his body at the top of the grassy slope.

Said Salim crawled on his belly from the thicket. There might be other *adoo* behind these two. He searched the copse, bringing back rifle, ammunition and a leather satchel stuffed with documents. He handed these to me and began to crawl back with a .36 grenade in one hand. He would jam this beneath the body with the pin removed. I hissed at him, without knowing why, 'Forget it, Said. Come back.'

My signaller repeatedly called Salalah for fighter support. Sahayl gazed at the corpse on the thorn bush. He did not look happy.

I glanced south. The brush scurried with movement. There was no time for balanced decisions; the other sections would be awaiting orders, knowing we were compromised. I flicked the radio switch, no longer bothering to whisper. 'All stations Five. Withdraw now . . . over.'

Salim, Ali and the Beard acknowledged and, fatigue forgotten, the sections broke from their hides to fan out in a long straggled line. Speed was our only hope and we moved with the wings of fear.

Shots sounded from behind and bullets passed overhead, but my fears of a northern cut-off group did not materialise.

For four hours we fled, keeping Sahayl and his brother ahead of us. We reached the cliffs and the safety of the Gat'n with two jet fighters strafing the hills to our rear. The *adoo* never quite caught up with us.

Back in Thamarit the soldiers slept like dead men but I found sleep elusive. I had often shot at people hundreds of yards away; vague shapes behind rocks who were busy shooting back. But never before had I seen a man's soul in his eyes, sensed his vitality as a fellow human being, and then watched his body torn apart at the pressure of my finger. I tried to force away the image of his destruction but his scarred face kept watching me from my subconscious. A part of me that was still young and uncynical died with him and his comrade the commissar, spreadeagled on a thorn bush with his red badge glinting in the hot Qara sun.

Sultanate intelligence garnered much from the captured documents. From Sahayl and his brother, during the next few months, I learned basic Mahra and heard sad stories of his tribe. Whether he had hedged his bets with the *adoo*, whether he escaped from his village or was set loose to bait a trip, I never determined, but he took us on subsequent missions without problems until the *adoo* caught him and his brother and shot them both.

I also learned that the green flares had been put up by the pilot of a low-flying Beaver sent from Salalah to recall me from the mission when the colonel had discovered we were only half as strong a force as he had expected.

The death of the two Communists in the centre of an *adoo* command area had far-reaching effects, as Tom Greening had hoped. Other Jebalis in the east took heart from Sahayl's successful example and came over to the government. More importantly, the *adoo* were everywhere less confident in their own territory. They could no longer discount the possibility of sudden ambush at any time or place. They became more inward-looking. The impetus of their plans to attack the plain was spoiled by a fierce purge of suspect Jebalis. All this, during the key months of early 1970, gave Tom Greening the breathing-space he needed to prepare for his palace coup.

Once Qaboos, on 23 July 1970, became Sultan, he began at once to defuse PFLOAG. He was himself half Dhofari and the amnesty he declared triggered a trickle of deserters that soon became a flood. The deserters were re-armed and re-directed against their former colleagues under the direction of SAS men from Britain. By 1975, with help from Sadat's Egypt, Jordan and Iran, the tide was turned and the Marxist threat removed from Dhofar.

The old Sultan, exiled to the Dorchester Hotel in London with a group of retainers, died there in 1972, a sad but charming old man. In three short years, Qaboos heaved Oman from the Middle Ages into the twentieth century. He used his blossoming oil revenues to maximum effect and in doing so whipped the carpet from under the feet of the revolutionaries.

In the spring of 1970 my Army contract ended. I left 'Fiendforce' on the little plateau guarding the Dehedoba trail. On a makeshift airstrip I said goodbye to them.

Mubarreq grasped my hand and pressed it to his forehead. He tried to speak but did not. His face was averted. He clung to his machine-gun as though it were all he possessed. 'God stay with you', I said.

The Beaver circled and descended.

Ali Nasser and Mohamed Rashid of the Beard came down from their hillocks, as did the Moolah and the Baluchis, smelling faintly of hair grease, and Fat Hamid, for once without a smile. I wondered how the future would treat them in their uncertain world of *Im'shaalah*.

'We are your brothers, Bakhait. Do not forget us, where you go to.' Said Salim came with me to the plane. Twelve goats were unloaded and I climbed in beside the pilot.

Corporal Salim looked up from the cockpit step. 'I will look after the men, Sahb. Perhaps one day you will come back to us.'

Dust cocooned the Beaver. It shuddered violently as the engine roared to maximum pitch. Then away up the strip, banking sharply once airborne to avoid jagged rocks. The plateau grew smaller below the spiralling plane. The dark waving figures on the hillocks blended with the ground and the plateau with the whole wild moonscape of the Nejd. I felt then a keen sense of loss, an emptiness that mirrored the wastes of the desert below.

11

Hell on Ice

I do not believe that any man fears to be dead,
but only the stroke of death.

FRANCIS BACON

On 2 March 1970, the day Ian Smith proclaimed Rhodesia a republic ruled by whites, I flew back to England. I was twenty-seven and my chosen career was ended. I must find a new life that suited my startling lack of qualifications and London was obviously the place to begin the search.

For a while I stayed at home in Lodsworth, which was most relaxing after Dhofar. But inactivity palled and my mother insisted that I must not delay in finding a job.

Ginnie had left Scotland and now worked for Leslie Whiteside, the vicar of the church of St Edmund the King in Lombard Street, an old friend of my mother's and known to our family as Uncle God. She shared a Kensington flat with three other girls and they kindly let me sleep on the sofa.

At this time I received an advance of £400 to write a book about the Nile journey. Ginnie had arranged this in my absence by contacting a literary agent, George Greenfield, who handled such authors as John le Carré, my old French master, Enid Blyton and David Niven. More to the point, his hobby was major expeditions for which he obtained the book rights and news coverage which made such endeavours financially viable. He had already dealt with Vivian Fuchs, Francis Chichester, Edmund Hillary and Chris Bonington, all supremos in the expedition world.

If Ginnie had consulted me before approaching this doyen of literary agents on my behalf, I would have told her to forget it: such a man would not be interested in a nonentity with no major expedition or book to his credit. But, acting on impulse, Ginnie did telephone him and must have caught him in a receptive mood, for he agreed to a meeting. *En route* to his office, she tripped and fell down an escalator in the Holborn Underground and badly bruised one leg. She limped to the appointment and so impressed Mr Greenfield with the likely literary ability of her absent fiancé that he agreed to act as my agent, providing I first produced a reasonable manuscript.

I was thankful to both of them and set to work on the book. In her spare time, Ginnie researched Nile history and I wrote non-stop for six weeks, working in her London flat.

I could not afford to take Ginnie to theatres or restaurants so we normally stayed at home. She slept in the attic room with one of the other inmates, a girl named Sarah Salt. Since Ginnie's name was Pepper, the two were referred to by all as the 'Condiments'.

The book was ready on time and George Greenfield sold the rights to Hodder and Stoughton.

Although the total revenue was under £600, it seemed I might be able to make a basic living out of expeditions. I joined Foyles Lecture Agency and went the rounds of dingy town halls, earning £25 a talk. A rough-and-ready income tally led me to believe I might survive on the breadline, providing I could plan and execute an expedition every year between June and October and then write and lecture about it from November until May.

From Ginnie's flat I set about organising my next project – an unambitious summer journey in central Norway. My only firm business rules were to spend no money on mounting the expedition and to ensure that any income accruing from it came only to me. Team members would only be accepted on the basis that they were happy with my one-way financing system.

For the first time Ginnie and I were living together in a normal way. The romance of secret meetings and imminent partings to which we had grown accustomed, and which we had unwittingly allowed to become the very essence of our mutual attraction, was no more. We were engaged to be married but never broached the topic of wedding bells – she because she felt it was for me to lead the way and I because I treasured my freedom.

After a lifetime of school and Army, I was for the first time tasting the pleasure of open options. Admittedly, cash restraints reduced these options drastically. The charm of being my own boss was not at that time tarnished by cramping realities, since my Walter Mitty plans did not have to be put into immediate effect. I would become a great explorer and a successful novelist or, if those paths proved impossible, a politician and minister.

I had no itch to become wealthy – which was just as well – and absolutely no desire to marry and settle down. It never occurred to me to ask myself why on earth I had proposed to Ginnie if I never intended marrying her. The thought of any other man marrying her was unthinkable and, prior to two years in Arabia, I had simply staked my claim with a diamond ring. Analysing all this in retrospect, it is clear I acted from purely selfish motives. Ginnie had become engaged, not to be married but to be stored in a larder with a vague expectancy of consumption in the indefinite future.

But she was not a person to be used or misused easily, even by someone she loved. At first she put down my failure to talk about marriage to the stress of writing my first book. However, when the book was finished I began to talk to her, and to others in her presence, of ambitious future plans that covered just about all aspects of life other than marriage.

The final straw came with a letter from my old friend in Dhofar, the coup-plotter and intelligence officer, Tom Greening. He offered me a two-year job working as a contract officer, a more likeable term than mercenary, with a band of western Mahra along the Dhofar–Yemen border. I leapt at the chance and told Ginnie what a wonderful opportunity it would be to strike at the *adoo* in their own safe bases. I wonder now at my total lack of sensitivity but, at the time, I was shocked and surprised when Ginnie's long pent-up grief gave way in a night of sobbing and anguish.

If I was not prepared to set a date for our wedding, even a distant date, what was the point of remaining engaged? Did I really love her? Did I want children by her? As I listened to her tears and saw the hopelessness in her eyes, I felt like the worm that I was. Through the twin urges of guilt and compassion I must have come very near to promising Ginnie a marriage date. But the more I allowed myself to contemplate the likely actualities of married existence, the stronger my aversion to the notion grew.

'If I was to marry anyone, my love,' I told her, 'it could only be you. But I'm just not ready yet.'

144

Why, oh why, Ginnie wept bitterly, had I not told her that two years before, instead of dishonestly trapping her heart.

There was no answer: I was truly ashamed but could not bring myself to put matters right. Painfully but steadfastly, Ginnie made up her mind. If I would not promise her marriage, she would return her engagement ring and go away – from me and from London and from all her past hopes.

It seemed to me, the day Ginnie left, that we had never been more in love. There was no anger – only sadness and a sense of inevitability in our parting.

I went to a car auction in Hammersmith and bought a Mini van for £200 which I left with Uncle God to give Ginnie. She left for Scotland the following week and I returned to Lodsworth. My mother had grown attached to Ginnie and was sorry to hear of our break-up. As usual she was comfortingly fatalistic: 'Life must go on. You won't find another Ginnie but it's not the end of the world.'

I immersed myself in organising the Norwegian expedition and tried to forget that Ginnie was no longer a part of my life.

The general purpose of the expedition was to tackle a physically difficult task and to succeed, so that subsequent, more ambitious schemes would more readily gain sponsorship. The specific purpose was to survey the Fabergstolsbre Glacier on behalf of, and at the request of, the Norwegian Hydrological Department. Norway's glacier expert, Dr Gunner Ostrem, warned me that this would be no easy task.

In 1966 the Hydrological Department had made photogammetric charts of twenty-seven of the twenty-eight glaciers flowing off the 10,000-foot-high Jostedal Ice-cap. By comparing these with similar air photos taken in 1955, Dr Ostrem learned whether the glaciers were receding, advancing or surging. Only the Fabergstolsbre had eluded the survey due to an error made when the aerial dye-bomb markers were dropped.

A land-based survey party to cover the omission would save a great deal of money, avoiding costly flights with specialist equipment. To survey the glacier by means of theodolites sited on the ice-cap above, we would need clear visibility, but the ice-cap is known for its storms and mists. Only in mid-August is there a fair chance of blue skies.

To avoid wasting a week humping heavy gear up the ice-cap, I approached the Norwegians and the British MoD for helicopter support. None was available. Remembering our 1967 parachute descent, I tracked down the relevant sea-plane charter company in Bergen but discovered our previous pilot had died in a plane crash. Another man in the same company agreed to help us for a minimal fee so I set to work recruiting eight amateur surveyors, a doctor, a film-team and, to get us to Norway, three Land Rover drivers.

Once the survey work was done we would have to descend on foot from the ice-cap with the expensive and delicate survey gear. The simplest route appeared to be straight down a glacial tongue and from there to the nearest roadhead via a glacial river in light boats. This would present no equipment problems but it did mean all the team members must learn to parachute, ski, river-boat and climb. Advertisements in university magazines and exploration clubs attracted no one. I approached all the male members of my 1967 Norwegian expedition but none could make it this time.

Finally, on a rainy spring day, Johnny Muir, now an accountant, once a top Army skier, agreed to learn to parachute and come to Norway. Patrick Brook, who left Dhofar soon after I did, was a cross-country skier and liked the sound of the expedition. Oxford University produced a qualified Army surveyor, Roger Chapman, who had recently been awarded an MBE for trying to save the life of a drowning SAS man on a Blue Nile expedition. To lead the survey team I recruited Geoff Holder, one of Britain's leading free-fall parachutists.

A geologist from Leeds University, Peter Booth, met me in London to discuss the Nile problems before leading an expedition there. He became attracted to the Norwegian idea, shelved his Nile project and took a course in surveying. Henrik Forss, a Finnish doctor and veteran of many ski expeditions in Arctic Lapland, joined us as ice-climbing adviser and medic.

At the Army Parachute School in Netheravon, I showed the team-members air photos of the ice-cap and explained that, in 1967, we had jumped from a stable aircraft in perfect conditions and with minimal equipment. This time our survey work and its timing would control when and how we jumped. Close to our Faberg Glacier work-area, and easily visible in the air photos, was a small bowl-shaped depression that, unlike most of the ice-cap, was free of crevasses for some 100 square metres. Unfortunately this uncracked zone lay adjacent to a 5000 foot cliff, one of the ice-cap retainer walls, which could suck an unwary parachutist into its thermal wind currents with potentially lethal consequences.

A free-fall expert would improve our chances by timing our plane-exits with precision and Don Hughes, our jump-supervisor in 1967, agreed to help me again. Some of the men turned out to be aerodynamically unsound. The key to free-falling is to control your body's flight, when dropping at a speed of 120 knots, so that it does not cartwheel or spin. Johnny Muir consistently did both. On his second drop he narrowly missed electricity lines and landed in the vegetable garden of a council house two miles from the drop zone.

His third attempt was his last, for he chose a windy day and came down heavily backwards, dislocating his thumb and confirming his fears that, if the grassy fields of England could produce such experiences, a 6000-foot-high ice-cap surrounded by cliffs might prove nightmarish. He left the survey team but stayed on as road party leader.

Patrick Brook, at the time an Army undercover agent in Belfast, qualified at a parachute school in the city outskirts.

Following our final jump at Netheravon we were addressed by the chief RAF sergeant-major. In the presence of a grinning Don Hughes, he told us, 'Thank God I'm not responsible for yous lot in Norway or wherever it is that you're off to. Never, in twelve years of instruction, have I seen such a collective abortion as your last effort.'

By way of river-training, Roger Chapman took us over some rapids on the Dee at Llangollen and then dragged our two rubber boats on to a lawn beside the river to give us 'dry training'. 'In Norway,' he said, 'an enormous weight of water pours down the glacial valleys between boulders. In the event of capsize you must locate the handles sewn into the underside of each hull, grab your paddles which are tied on by cords so they cannot go missing, then fight to re-right the boat as fast as you can.'

A sense of competition soon mounted between the two three-man crews doing practice re-rights on the grass. Roger timed us from the moment of theoretical capsize until we were all back aboard with our paddles.

The day was hot, the more so inside our clinging wetsuits, and, following a struggle to turn the ninety-pound boat upright, I could see very little due to sweat in my eyes. I located my paddle but its cord snagged so I tugged at it viciously, not wishing to let down my crew.

Somebody struck my shoulder and shouted. Squinting backwards I found the team's biologist clawing at his neck, his face a mottled puce and his tongue thrust out of his mouth.

The thin sharp cord of my paddle had twined itself under a davit and round the biologist's neck during our struggle with the boat and I had then done my best to garotte him. He later became Britain's leading aerobatic ace and captain of the Rothmans' display flight: it would have been a shame to have throttled him.

At weekends I jogged in the Welsh mountains with an eighty-pound backpack and a compass. For four years I had brooded about my time with the SAS, not my sacking which I had deserved but the fact that I had never really passed the selection course. True, I had been judged as suitable SAS material by the selection staff, but only because they failed to discover my deceit on the final Long Drag march, the key endurance test.

On applying to join the Territorial Army soon after returning from Dhofar, I discovered that there was a curious anomaly known as Reserve Squadron ('R' Squadron), 22nd SAS Regiment, which was neither Regular nor Territorial in its Army role. About two dozen civilians made up the unit. The role of 'R' Squadron is to provide re-enforcements for the Regular SAS in time of war and is entirely different from the SAS Territorial Army.

Applicants to join 'R' Squadron had to pass the regular SAS selection course. Here was my chance to put the clock back and banish a ghost which would otherwise always niggle at my conscience.

Thanks to my Welsh jogging stints, I found no difficulty in keeping ahead of the 100 or so Regular Army applicants. I passed into 'R' Squadron, but only as a trooper. No matter, I had completed Long Drag without help from a local taxi.

The sergeant-major in charge of my new unit turned out to be my old SAS training sergeant, Brummy Burnett. After six months with 'R' Squadron, desirous of more pay, I asked Brummy if I might get a commission to captain. He looked down at me. 'If you're very lucky, Fiennes, you might make corporal in five years. But no promises. Pigs might fly.'

Many of the old and bold SAS sergeants, though not I think Brummy himself, held a grudge against me then and for many years to come. They never forgot that, following my indiscretions in 1966, the Special Investigation Branch had raided all private lockers and rooms in the SAS and uncovered a number of illegal goodies. But, far more unforgivable, I had caused a shaft of public scrutiny to fall on a unit with an obsession for secrecy and obscurity.

In years to come Harold Wilson was to use the SAS as a public relations tool in the struggle against IRA terrorism so, for the first time, the British public became aware of the élite regiment's existence. But my own indiscretions occurred when, to most people, 'SAS' merely meant Scandinavian Airlines System.

Between weekend SAS exercises in Europe and the expedition work, I purchased a Triumph Tiger 250 cc motorbicycle for £75 and discovered that girls liked motorbikes. There were a great many pretty, unattached girls of my age around and my SAS pay enabled me to go to London three or four times a week. I began to see Vanda Allfrey again and she agreed to come to Norway because she had enjoyed the 1967 journey there. Ben Howkins, my fellow conspirator at Castle Combe, shared a basement flat near Sloane Square where there was normally a spare bed or two and, if warned, he would leave a sash window open by night.

The Scots Greys Paymaster's daughter, Susan Duncan, whose adolescent beauty I had so admired in barren Fallingbostel, was now studying anthropology at Cambridge. She agreed to tour Turkey and India for a month on my motorbike once the Norwegian journey was over.

I learned via the grapevine that Ginnie, back at work with the Scottish National Trust, had become good friends with the son of the Lord Lieutenant of Ross-shire and his family. Norwegian preparations were all in order and I lived off my earnings from SAS weekends. With no precise plan in mind, but aware that whatever happened I must not let Ginnie get too involved with this Scotsman, I decided to go to Ross-shire, north of Inverness, and be with her on her birthday.

The Trust caravan where Ginnie lived was parked beside a homestead close to Loch Torridon and her Mini van was there. Not stopping to think what I would say, I parked the Triumph Tiger and knocked on the door.

When Ginnie's little face peered, startled, through the misted window, I saw quite clearly that I must marry her; if necessary that very week in Torridon kirk – assuming there was one.

'Hello,' I said.

'Why have you come?'

'I brought you a birthday card for next week.'

'Couldn't you have posted it?'

Silence. I saw the futility and stupidity of my journey from her point of view and realised I might already be too late. Why should I stand another chance after the pain and grief I had already caused her?

She opened the door reluctantly. 'You look tired. Would you like coffee?' Her voice was cold and expressionless.

It was late. Could I sleep the night close by? I had a sleeping bag.

She shrugged. 'Suit yourself. I have to work tomorrow.'

Gradually over the next two days she thawed out a bit. On her birthday she drove me to Applecross and we walked north along the deserted coast which looks west to Skye. She let me hold her hand as we walked along the white beaches to the cry of gulls. But when I tried to kiss her and tell her I could not exist without her, there were bitter tears, and she said I must leave and stay away for ever.

I promised to go the next day and that night, when it rained, Ginnie let me into the caravan where I slept on the floor beside her narrow bunk. Before leaving for Inverness I asked if she would drive down to Newcastle in early August to see me off on the ship to Norway.

'Maybe,' she said. I could not tell what she was thinking.

A month later Vanda, Johnny and his fiancée drove our three Land Rovers to my mother's house to load up the results of my calls to sponsor companies. The vehicles themselves were on loan from British Leyland. At dawn the next day all sixteen members of the team wedged themselves aboard and we drove to Newcastle.

Simon Gault, who lived and trained as a ship designer in the city, met me at the quayside. 'You've got a visitor staying at my flat. Have you time to come and say hello?'

The visitor was Ginnie. Simon left us alone in his sitting room. 'Slam the front door when you leave,' he said, 'and, Ran, don't get killed in Norway. I won't be there to look after you this time.'

I told Ginnie that, if she would only agree to marry me, we would hold the wedding within ten days of my return from Norway. She looked happy but she shook her head and refused to give me an answer.

The time came to leave. Ginnie drove me to the quay and met the others. I told Patrick Brook, who knew Ginnie from Beaconsfield days, that she had turned down my proposal. He took her aside and spoke to her with much gesticulation.

The gangplanks were cleared and I said goodbye to Ginnie. As I kissed her, she whispered 'Yes' – which was the most precious single word of my life.

On the way to Bergen I told Vanda, who took the news in good part and became a close friend of Peter.

'What did you say to Ginnie in Newcastle?' I asked Patrick.

'Only that, if you were to fall down a crevasse in Norway – which is quite likely – she would never forgive herself for having said no.'

Leaving Don Hughes in Bergen to seek out the Cessna float-plane which was to drop the team, we drove north for eight hours, crossing the Sognefjord by ferry and reaching the Nordfjord by nightfall. We booked into the Hotel Alexandria at Loen, a village that nestles in a wide valley beneath the Jostedalsbre Ice-cap, and slept soundly.

At 8.00 a.m. my alarm clock buzzed and I telephoned Don Hughes back in Bergen. The forecast was clear both ends but the Bergen Weather Centre predicted a low front reaching the ice-cap by mid-day, preceded by high winds and low clouds. Once in place, this low was liable to remain for at least a week. 'Is there a ski-plane available right now?' I asked Don. 'If so, perhaps we could put everything forward by a day and jump this morning.' He agreed to find out and phone back in an hour.

To advance our whole schedule by twenty-four hours might be simple, but the knock-on effects could prove troublesome, even deadly, to those involved. I had planned to spend a whole day prior to the jump with binoculars checking out the Briksdals Glacier, our proposed route down from the ice-cap. Roger Chapman was likewise to reconnoitre the fast river running down from the glacier to the nearest road-head. Armed with sketches and foreknowledge of the glacier and the river, we would feel safer when the time came to descend them. If we jumped today, the subsequent descent would have to be a blind one.

Such ifs and buts became irrelevant when Don telephoned to announce that he would arrive on the lake beside the hotel in two hours' time for an immediate take-off for the ice-cap. An hour before noon Don arrived in a six-seater Cessna sea-plane and bade the pilot tie up to the hotel's wooden jetty. 'Loose clouds are already over the western end of the ice-cap,' he told us, 'and heading this way fast.' He checked our parachutes and gear minutely, fixed smoke cannisters to Roger Chapman's ankles and then taught us one by one how to jump out of the Cessna's side door.

The obvious way was to reach out for a wing strut and then leap into space. This, Don explained, would almost certainly cause the body to be blown by the slipstream straight into the metal float rudders, which could prove fatal to aircraft and jumper. Instead, we must reach out for a narrow wing-bar well away from the hull and then, gripping it, lurch both feet towards the nearest float-top. Once there we should throw ourselves sideways and outwards, consciously fighting the fierce inward drag of the slipstream.

Everyone practised jumping from the Cessna's door on to the float. Then Don marshalled the first group of four into the fuselage, glancing as he did so at the approaching screen of cloud which already filled the sky to our west.

As the Cessna's engine roared, I licked my lips. My stomach felt furry-lined as squadrons of butterflies free-fell within it. I would be first to jump and did not relish the idea. However, the other three men looked unconcerned as the alloy floats surged out over the lake so I put on a mask of nonchalance. I found myself staring at Patrick's fingers, drumming on his knee, but he noticed my glance and was still. Stiff upper lips but thudding pulses were the order of the day.

The Sunday Times described the occasion as 'The World's Toughest Jump', but then they had paid £1000 for coverage rights and wanted their money's worth. Their photographer, an ITN ciné-man and other media people were already hovering high above the ice-cap in press helicopters.

I looked down at the holes and slits of crevasses big enough to swallow a regiment of parachutists without leaving a trace. My hands were cold as I feared to wear gloves which might mute the feel of my chute release-handle when the time came. I caught a whiff of body sweat. They are all sweating, I thought with satisfaction. They are just as frightened as I am even if they don't look it.

I had seen no area suitable for a drop-zone, only cliffs and serrated crevasse-fields. The ice-cap surface was 6000 feet high and we would drop from 10,500 feet, a safe height which would enable us to get well clear of the Cessna, orientate ourselves and steer towards the drop-zone.

We levelled out 2000 feet above the ice and the pilot set a circular course over the target area. Don taped a pair of clear-glass goggles into place and thrust his face into the doorway. His skin sucked taut against his skull and his lips drew back in a fixed snarl as the slipstream tugged at his head. One hand jerked out and deftly released a furled streamer which jinked away, its orange fabric tail unrolling as it fell. Its flight path acted as an anemometer, telling Don the speed and direction of the various wind currents between us and the ice. He must remember the exact position of its release relative to its landing spot and form a mental picture of the landscape below, knowing thereby precisely when and where to release his human loads to give them a fair chance of landing on smooth ice.

Although the drop would take place from this noted position along the oval of the Cessna's course, we must first climb another 2000 feet. From that height we would jump and count each second out aloud, up to fourteen, as we fell. Then, at the height where Don had ejected the streamer, we must pull our ripcords. From there to the ice-cap we would behave like the streamer unless the wind currents had changed.

There should be little danger of overshooting the ice-cap unless a jumper pulled his ripcord prior to falling free for fourteen seconds. Peter was prone to premature pulls and I sensed his apprehension as he sat waiting for the engine sound to ease off. We had stopped climbing and turned into the final up-wind run. Don urged us to get ready.

Awkwardly, careful not to brush our packs against each other, we levered ourselves into kneeling positions facing the door. This was the moment of truth from which there could be no honourable withdrawal. I knew not to look down nor out into space but to concentrate fiercely on my watchstrap or even a stud on the fuselage ceiling. My greatest fear was not so much the act of jumping as the thought that one glimpse of the black peaks below, or the cold space beyond the aircraft door, would activate the vertigo I invariably experienced.

A rough hand shook my shoulder. Don was shouting at me, his words whipped away by wind and engine roar. He prodded his index finger meaningfully at the exit as though to say 'Get the hell out'.

But something was wrong. I had been subconsciously awaiting the sound of the engines cutting back, the necessary preliminary to any free-fall jump which slows the plane down to just above stalling speed and minimises the suction of the slipstream. The Cessna was still plainly at maximum speed. I pointed at the pilot but Don simply repeated his 'shove off' gesture.

I forced one arm through the slipstream and grasped the wing strut. Then I lunged my legs, tightly clenched together, outwards, aiming for the float. As my boots scrabbled for a foothold, my hands lost their grip on the strut and I was sucked bodily into space. Out of control, I passed close by the fuselage and struck the side of the float with the back of my hand.

'One thousand and one. One thousand and two . . .' I heard my voice inside my helmet churning out the seconds and I opened my eyes. I will freeze solid in this ridiculous position, I thought, for coldness was the first sensation. Then came fear as I recognised the early signs of body-spin. I stretched my arms and legs out and back and thrust my stomach forward . . . but the spin became more, not less, pronounced. 'One thousand and five, one thousand and six . . .' I craned my neck to the side and spotted the cause of my instability: my left leg was running, kicking out like a trapped rabbit, trying to lever me back into a stable position but only succeeding in compounding the error. The leg had acquired a mind of its own and only through an effort of will did I control and force it to remain rigid. 'One thousand and nine.' Five long seconds still to go.

For a moment I sensed neither movement nor urgency. I was floating in a void, a most pleasant sensation I would have liked to prolong. I was now flying at 120 miles an hour, my terminal velocity, and every limb must remain perfectly positioned in a star-shape for my body to remain stable. Without warning I began to keel forward into a nose-dive. 'One thousand and twelve . . .' Then sudden panic.

Both my arms snapped inwards to locate my ripcord but a camera had come loose inside my anorak and lodged itself against the ripcord bar. Now my body position was bunched and beginning to tumble.

Grovelling in the folds of my anorak, I found the red handle and ripped it outwards. Then I snapped both arms back to the star position to arrest a rapidly materialising somersault. A second or two later, with a whipcrack sound and a breath-taking jerk, my orange canopy deployed fully, a beautiful sight from my point of view.

Down between my legs, the icescape passed by at twenty knots. The jagged edge where ice met clifftop was 1000 feet away and moving parallel to my present course. Reaching up I tugged on a steering toggle. In nil-wind conditions my chute was designed to advance at five knots. Now, in response to the toggle steerage, I tacked across the wind and swung towards a high peak, the Lodalskapa, which I knew to be a boundary marker to our drop-zone.

Two fissured crevasse fields passed beneath my boots. Rock and ice rushing up now, everything close including crevasses. The ice surface provided no perspective, no clue to its proximity. I braced my legs, knees bent for the impact . . . when it came I hardly knew it as my landing was cushioned by the softness of a snow-bridge spanning an old crevasse.

Surface winds caught at my parachute and dragged me over the ice. I hauled in on a single cord until the wind spilled out of the canopy. The adrenalin dispersed and I felt suddenly cold.

Patrick and Peter picked themselves up from different corners of the drop-zone. Patrick planted flare-sticks – markers for Don's next drop. Clouds already obscured the mountain ranges to the west and south.

Don and the Cessna pilot worked fast, dropping the rest of the team without preliminary streamers to save time. To aid the photographers in the press helicopters, Roger ignited the smoke flares attached to his ankles and Geoff, jumping next, used a camera installed in his helmet to film Roger as they dropped. Geoff landed seventy-five yards from the edge and was dragged by the ever-strengthening surface winds to within eight yards of a sheer precipice. He cracked two ribs and split open the bridge of his nose on the steel aiming-sight of his helmet camera.

Nigardsbre

JOSTEDALSBRE

Crevasses

Crevasse field

Ice-axe found

Lake

Fabergstolsbre

To Kvamme

Briksdalselve River

Galdhoppigen Range

Ice-camp

Briksdalsbre

Lodalskapa (2079m)

Drop Zone ✕

Lake Loen

Loen

Nordfjord

area of main map

Trondheim

Stockholm

Jostedal

Oslo

Bergen

Jostedal Glacier

SAS training in North Wales

The Nile. Our hovercraft ploughs over the Nile at Malakal watched by a curious crowd. The accident occurred shortly after this picture was taken

Below *Hovercraft, parked on the shore of Lake Nasser, south of Wadi Halfa, Sudan*

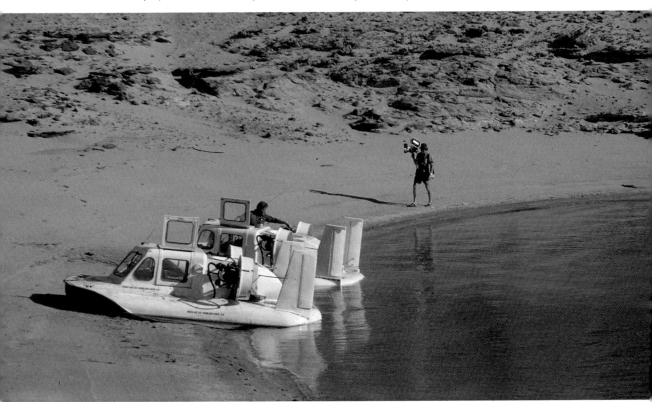

Opposite *Training in England for the parachute drop on to Europe's highest glacier*

Apprehension before the first ice-fall of the Briksdals Glacier

Using Dexion shop shelving as an ice-ladder. Our crampon spikes often caught in the bolt holes

Roger Chapman, Bob Powell, the author, Geoff Holder and Patrick Brook

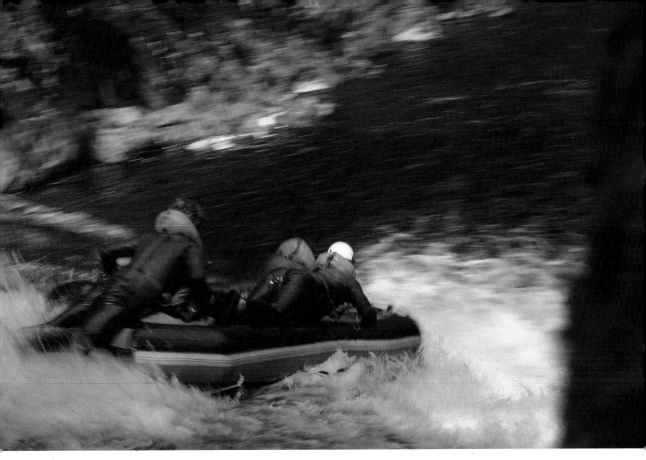

Training with the inflatables in Wales

Canadian rapids

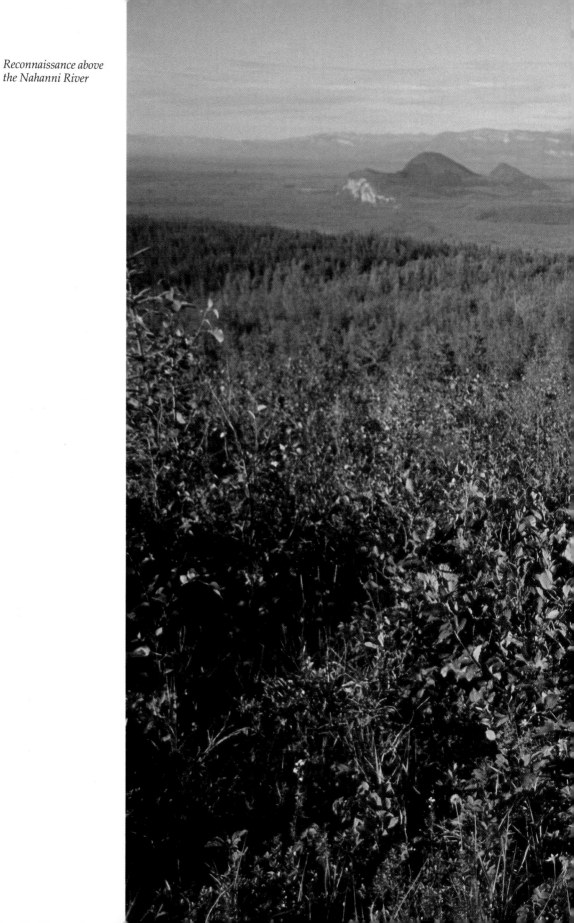

*Reconnaissance above
the Nahanni River*

Above *The author and Stanley Cribbett stuck in a log-jam*

Opposite *Pulpit Rock and the Nahanni River. This rock alone is 300 feet high*

Below *Arrival at Virginia Falls, twice the height of Niagara*

Rough water in the Bridge River rapids

The author attempting to contact Ginnie by radio during the crossing of Sifton Pass

We spread around the perimeter of the drop-zone and, when Don began to drop equipment loads soon after dusk, we rushed hither and thither, grabbing at the billowing silk canopies as they careered towards the cliffs. Nothing was lost and none of the survey gear broken.

Separating into groups of two, we bedded down on the parachutes with blocks of snow for windbreaks around our cotton tents.

At dawn we loaded our two sledges with 500 pounds apiece of survey gear, inflatable rubber boats and 1800 feet of rope coils. Personal kit and tents filled our rucksacks and Henrik gave us each a pair of *langlauf* skis and sticks.

To the southeast of the drop-zone and some four miles distant, the ice-cap poured down, via two deep canyon glaciers, to the Faberg Valley below. Our task was to survey the northernmost of these glaciers, the Fabergstolsbre, and we needed to pitch camp at its crest by nightfall. At first the metal sledge-runners ripped hissing over firm crust. After four hours Roger stopped, frowning. 'By my reckoning we should have reached the top of the Faberg Glacier half an hour ago.'

Not everyone agreed and a heated discussion ensued. All ice sloped downwards to our front and, if we took the wrong route, we would sooner or later have to climb back up with full loads. A compromise route was selected, down which we slid at an ever-increasing pace. Henrik stopped and so, with difficulty, did the two skiers harnessed to the sledges.

We fixed rear-retaining ropes as brakes to each sledge and continued more warily towards a cluster of rocks which marked the upper crest of a glacier. Reaching this feature, we peered downwards and, sure enough, found it to be the hinge point of the northern side of a glacier. From the rocks all ice poured downwards in a slowly moving tongue between enclosing granite cliffs. This ice-river flowed for a mile or more, dropping thousands of feet in a series of ledges or ice-falls. But the memory of the Faberg Glacier which Simon Gault and I had briefly glimpsed in 1967 was different from the ice now ahead of me.

While the others rested I went northeast with Patrick, a strong skier, and, forty minutes later, breasted a rise above another, very similar, glacier. I scanned the far, northern cliffs of this new ice-tongue and knew for sure that *this* was the Fabergstolsbre. The others were now at the top of the Nigardsbre, a glacier which earlier in the century had surged down its captor-valley crushing houses and farmsteads in its path. To cross in a straight line from where we were to the far, northern side of the Fabergstolsbre would entail crossing a wide crevasse field. Yet our camp must be on the north side of the glacier's crest for survey purposes.

When the others reached us with the sledges, we debated for or against a long uphill detour around the crevasses. Exhausted by the heavy work, nobody could face the thought of the safer but more tiring way, so we set out to cross the zone of fissures. Our route zig-zagged around open holes and cracks by way of 'gangplanks' where the snow from last winter's blizzards still bridged the gaps. The problem was knowing which of these bridges were several feet thick and which were on the point of collapse.

No more than ten yards of forward progress were possible between the slits and sometimes less than half the length of a sledge would fit on an ice-ledge between two fissures.

Patrick went ahead to lay a trail. Geoff, in harness, fell through a snow-bridge and his sledge very nearly followed him. Two of us hauled him up by his jacket, fully aware that, had the sledge broken through, he could have been crushed. We became adept at avoiding the weaker snow-bridges and took long detours in order to find gangways of snow not yet rotted by summer rain and sunshine.

By late afternoon only a steep slope of blue ice separated us from a rock cluster which marked the northern side and summit of the Fabergstolsbre where we hoped to camp. The sledges would not budge up so steep an incline nor could we climb it on skis, so we detoured around and above, unladen, and then hauled the gear up with ropes.

By six the four two-pound tents were staked into a snow patch among the rocks. I jammed the pole of our Union Jack between two rocks above the camp. From this point, over the next few days, groups of two or three must establish commanding points on the surrounding heights and equip them with survey gear. The work must be finished by 21 August since there were only two available guides who knew our desired descent route and they could only work with us on two specific days.

Although two of our control points were on the ice-cap within three hours' march of our camp, the third was on a separate mountain range four miles east of the Fabergstolsbre and separated from it by the main Faberg Valley, in which Johnny Muir and our road party were camped. Geoff and one other surveyor decided to descend to the valley right away and I left with them to help carry gear.

We passed the night in Johnny's campsite and left at dawn for the eight-hour climb up the far side of the valley. I parted with Geoff at an existing Norwegian Trig Point, marked by a stone cairn. He was in pain with two splintered ribs but he knew, as I did, that the map could not be made without him.

I returned again to Johnny's camp 3000 feet below, collected radio batteries and rations and trudged back up the Fabergstolsbre by way of its northern rock flank. Halfway up I switched on my radio and listened in to a lively exchange between Roger and Geoff – the supervisor of the survey programme – as to the exact location of their respective positions. Glancing up, I was not surprised. Sheer black cliffs reared to the north and south, their upper walls invisible in mist. Alongside and above me, the glacier itself, within its container cliffs, rose to meet the mother ice-cap and the grey sky at an opaque, indefinable rendezvous.

From somewhere up on my side of the glacier Roger spoke frustratedly. He had picked up the distant flares of Geoff's location and marked the azimuth on his chart, but the position of Henrik, Patrick and one other – directly across the glacier – had eluded him.

'You must be blind,' radioed Patrick. 'We have erected fluorescent panels on a backbearing of ten degrees from your location.'

I moved on, weary from the heavy pack, as thunder rumbled continuously along the valleys. Storm-clouds burst over the ice-fields with a spectacular show of lightning and, three hours later, the weather reached the cliffs up which I inched towards our camp. The whole glacial valley was now awash. Ankle-high water rushed between the rocks and boulders and the entire valley rumbled to the roar of the deluge.

Two hours after dusk, slightly disorientated, I reached the uppermost rocks. The sleet lashed at my face in the dark and I came quite by chance on the Union Jack lying in a puddle. I replaced it as a marker and slithered down to the camp. It was a sorry sight. The original snow-patch was now an incline of grey mush. The tents had blown down and, worst of all, sleeping bags and clothes were strewn sodden about the ice.

This was alarming. Two teams were still out in high-exposure risk conditions without their safety gear. Without moonlight, I could scarcely see five yards. There was little sense in mounting a solo-search so I re-erected two of the tents, wrung out four sleeping bags and anoraks as best I could and hung my torch from a tent pole. I fired three flares into the storm. I listened but heard nothing except my own teeth chattering and the enormous sound of rushing water. I crawled into a wet sleeping bag inside a tent and switched on my radio. I called but there was silence. I left the radio switched on and lay back, shivering, to contemplate a situation pregnant with unpleasant possibilities. What had happened to them I learned later from their diaries. The northern survey group, Peter and Roger, dismantled their theodolite as the mist reached them. It dawned on them then that they had made a stupid mistake. The golden rule in such a place, given bad conditions, is to stay put, erect a shelter, and crawl into it. Since the weather had been excellent when they left camp and the weight of their gear had been crippling, they had dispensed with tent and sleeping bags. Now they must try to reach safety and warmth, but there was one large snag. Between them and camp, along the direct route they had used on the outward journey, lay a 600-foot gorge. There was, however, an eight-kilometer ice-traverse flanking this gorge; their only chance of survival . . .

The glacier surface was melting at an unbelievable rate. On level ice they walked through slush up to their calves but, on any slope, black streams rushed by at torrential speed. One cataract moved so fast that to have slipped and fallen into it would have taken them straight over the cliff edge . . .

Sometimes they fell over in slush pools and disappeared up to their waists. After two and a half hours, according to Roger's calculations, they should have reached the camp. They had not. Both began to wonder if they had made an error. If so, they were in deep trouble. At 2030 hours they hit rock. They left their compass bearing and cautiously groped across boulders, not knowing where the cliffs dropped away. There was no sign of the camp . . . Roger wondered whether it had been washed away. To find the tents was by now the be-all and end-all of their lives. To sleep in a wet sleeping bag seemed the ultimate luxury . . .

Then they saw the dim light of my tent. Numb with cold they awkwardly stripped off each other's clothes, and crawled into a single bag to benefit from each other's meagre warmth. I produced a flask of brandy.

They knew nothing of the other group. 'Henrik can't possibly have tried to lead them across the crevasse field: not in this blizzard,' said Peter. 'It would be suicidal . . .'

With Henrik were Patrick Booth and Bob Powell, a tough Territorial parachute officer. At 6.00 the weather on their part of the ice-cap had deteriorated with no warning. They agreed to return to camp with haste. Thirty minutes later they were in sight of the glacier but by then the conditions were appalling. Mist covered the ice-cap so they tried descending the cliff to the glacier itself. But they could not traverse the deep *bergschrund* which dropped away between rock and ice . . .

They had fallen into the same trap as Roger. The morning had seemed so bright and clear, they had left without protective gear or rations. Now, in the blizzard, they faced the prospect of either huddling together under groundsheets or blindly traversing the Fabergstolsbre crevasse-field . . .

Bob favoured locating some shelter but Patrick argued that, with no tent and a freezing wind, they *must* attempt the crossing. Henrik, undecided, was swayed by their lack of gear and food, and agreed with Patrick . . .

For four hours they crept through the crevasse field in the white-out. Only a few safe crevasse bridges remained.

Bob began to get stomach cramps, possibly through having drunk mineral-free glacier ice-water. But he could not stop, being roped behind the others. The cold was biting and they could not risk a halt . . .

Bob could see only the line of his rope leading forward into the dark and he marvelled at how Henrik kept to his compass course since they spent most of the time in crazy detours around crevasses. He lost all sense of direction.

Towards midnight they came to a steep gradient. Could this be the final slope? They shouted . . . no answer. About 100 yards up the slope they screamed again and heard my faint answering cry followed by the gleam of my torch. As they turned, elated, Henrik plunged through a snow-bridge to his armpits. The last 100 yards took fifteen minutes to traverse.

We all drank whisky in the tent. Bob shivered uncontrollably for the five hours until dawn; nominating that night as the most miserable of his life . . .

Two days later the storm cleared and the survey work began in earnest. In four days many hundreds of theodolite readings were recorded. The work was cold and boring but allowed no lapses in concentration since even the slightest slip could render the resulting figures unacceptable and the whole project a failure.

Geoff finally announced that the survey was complete. Peter and one other left us to commence geological work further down the valley. They took the survey paperwork and as much gear as they could manage. Had the terrain allowed we could have followed them down to the valley then and there, but many porters would have been needed and many hours of good weather if we were to get the heavy and bulky equipment carried down the tortuous tracks to the valley 5000 feet below. All being well, our Norwegian guides would lead us to the Briksdalsbre down which we would simply lower our gear, since it was very different from the Fabergstolsbre – steep, narrow and straight. From its snout we would place all the gear straight into our inflatable boats and paddle down to the road-head. No porters. No sweat.

The only niggle in my mind was our failure to reconnoitre the Briksdalsbre or its glacial river due to having jumped a day early. Still, we had 1800 feet of rope, enough to see us over even the worst ice-falls. I told the others that they should leave with Peter if they did not like the idea of the descent, but no one volunteered to drop out.

In promising me the very best Jostedalsbre guides, the Norwegian Tourist Board had described David Mindresunde and Jan Mickelbust as 'superb'. They knew the ice-cap better than anyone. At the time of our rendezvous the guides were nowhere to be seen and when they did turn up, four hours late, their clothes were wet through and they shivered as they unstrapped their skis. Neither spoke English but Henrik translated for us.

Geoff woke me at 4.00 a.m. A thick mist lay over the ice-cap, tamped down by rain. We ate a good breakfast, took the tents down and prepared the sledges. Henrik talked to the guides as they packed their gear. He came over to me, frowning. His words came as a shock – as an ultimatum from our paid guides which I felt was unwarranted. He said that they had spent a poor night and were not prepared to take us, in dangerously thick mists, on the forty-kilometre ice-cap journey to the top of the Briksdalsbre. On skis with light packs they could do the trip in eight hours. Pulling heavy sledges, they reckoned we would take two days, if indeed we could get that far, overloaded as they deemed us to be.

We gave the guides hot soup to improve their morale but they were adamant.

Henrik said, 'Mindresunde has skiied the entire Jostedalsbre but never in such weather. The

Briksdalsbre Glacier

only safe route is to zig-zag along the upper spine of the ice-cap and that can only be done in conditions of reasonable visibility. Mickelbust says the Briksdalsbre has never been descended and, in these conditions, will be riven by tons of melting, falling ice. He says we must abandon the gear and descend by the Faberg route.'

I tried to cajole the guides. I could see they were loath to let us down but their inborne sense of caution, their respect for the nature of these ice-fields, held them back from what they considered to be sheer folly. Both were giants of men with rugged faces; reliable characters with the sense not to bite off more than they thought they could chew. They knew that none of us except Henrik had previous climbing experience.

At length we reached a compromise. They would ski along the ridge for thirty kilometres, at which point they would leave one of our ice-axes pointing in the direction of the Briksdalsbre. They would then veer north to descend a little-known track to the Kvamme Valley.

Following the guides' tracks we toiled at the sledge traces for five hours. Up and down had no real meaning in such white-out conditions; the heavy sledges were dead weights and slid neither forwards nor backwards if left untended.

At mid-day the mist lifted and the plateau stretched mile after mile into the western glare. Towards evening, mist and falling sleet slowed us up again. The guides' tracks snaked on, becoming increasingly hard to detect, for a wind had sprung up and blew the sleet over the spoor. After eleven hours of non-stop haulage, we came to the ice-axe marker.

Henrik grasped my arm: 'From here on it will be downhill so the five of you will easily manage the loads. I will give you my medical gear for I will follow the guides' spoor down to Kvamme. I will make sure Johnny makes camp at the base of the Briksdal and keeps the radio open. Take great care.'

Later he gave his reasons for ducking out of the descent as appalling conditions and maximum avalanche danger, poor equipment (we were using Dexion shop-shelving instead of ice-ladders) and the considered opinion of the guides that our descent plans were suicidal.

Roger asked him to stay as far as the top of the glacier but he was determined. We watched him ski off into the mist.

The wind blew sleet horizontally and I regretted the loss of my goggles the previous day. It was too cold now to stop, with an icy blast coming up from the massed crevasse fields between us and the cliffs to our right flank. Explosions of falling ice sounded close by, and I knew the sloping shoulder which we traversed fell away to plummeting cliffs somewhere in our immediate vicinity . . .

As it grew dark we entered our first crevasse field and gingerly threaded a maze-like route through wicked-looking fissures. We knew we should be roped up but were too tired and cold. Each new chasm forced us off our chosen bearing. We advanced between the cracks in the ice along a narrow but solid isthmus. From every side now came the booming echoes of avalanches. With numb fingers we erected two tents and pegged their guy-ropes to ski sticks. Next morning the mist cleared at dawn and we saw the first ice-fall of the Briksdals Glacier directly below us.

The descent was sudden and, in minutes, one of our laden pulk sledges slid out of control and careered into a crevasse. Alarmed, we donned helmets and roped up to each other. About 100 yards further down the yawning incline, our second sledge turned turtle, dragging Roger and Patrick behind it. Using a sawtooth sheath-knife, Roger slashed through the harnesses and saved their lives. The pulk disappeared down a crevasse. All our skis were lost for we had, minutes earlier, donned crampon boot spikes. Our only remaining gear was in our backpacks, including one two-man tent between the five of us.

I winced at the thought of the thousands of pounds' worth of lost gear, of angry sponsors and the effect on my future expeditions. But there were more immediate worries to hand: 3000 feet of near-sheer ice. Most of it was as yet invisible from above but immediately beneath us lay a great field of jagged ice-blocks; a nightmare in blue and white.

Our packs weighed sixty pounds each, so, descending narrow rock chimneys, we lowered them ahead of us on ropes. We reached the base of the rock at noon and stopped beside a waterfall. Just above the waterfall a chance ledge of ice-blocks formed a temporary causeway from rock-face to ice. Since the entire glacier was moving slowly down within its *bergschrund* sheath, the gap between rock and glacier, the causeway was liable to be dislodged at any moment. Clearly, there was no other route onwards and downwards save via this unstable ledge.

Roger viewed the teetering bridge alongside me. 'Any further movement from above will remove that, you know.'

Roger switched on the radio and this time Johnny's voice came through at once. The news was bad. He could not understand why no one had warned us before but the Briksdalsbre was generally known to be a killer. Of the twenty-eight glacier tongues that pour off the Jostedalsbre, it was the only one as yet unclimbed by Norway's ace glacier-climbers.

'You must go back up and come down the Kvamme trail as Henrik did,' Johnny told us. But getting this far had involved a steep rock descent with ropes which I knew we could never reverse. Since none of us was a climber, we needed gravity on our side. Downwards lay our only chance. Then I thought of a helicopter.

'No,' said Johnny, 'we've thought of that. There are helicopters but Jan Mickelbust here warns against their use. The noise and downdraught will dislodge avalanches all around you. You must understand this is the worst week of the year. Everything's melting. From down here it's like listening to Tchaikovsky's 1812. Through binoculars I can see whole areas of the face break off and fall away. If you can't go back, at least take care.'

Roger switched off the radio and I edged warily over the causeway. In places only thin wedges spanned the gap with nothing between them save a glimpse of rushing water far below. Twice I froze as lumps of ice, disturbed by my passing, fell away like rotten planks from a foot-bridge.

Once across I made the rope firm and one by one the others joined me.

I noticed blood on the ice and discovered that my fingers were bleeding. There was no pain, for my hands were numb, but the coarse-grained ice had worn away both the wool of my gloves and the skin from my fingers. The others found the blood-trail a help when we passed through piles of loose ice-boulders.

The ice plateau was riven by the biggest crevasses I had seen, but we crossed twenty by leaping across without rucksacks and clutching our axes. A twelve-foot crack that stretched across the entire glacier finally foxed us. We were forced back on to the rockface deep inside the *bergschrund*, difficult because the ice ran very close to the rock at that point and the latter was polished smooth as glass. Streams of icy water ran down our backs and a knife-like wind whistled down the dark cranny. The roar of subterranean torrents rushed below us in the nether regions of the *bergschrund* and I prayed I would not slip from my fragile holds on the wet rock.

When we emerged from the cavern we had by-passed the crack but evening stars were already visible. We must quickly find a flat ledge away from ice movement and big enough for our tent.

Patrick, I noticed, had collapsed and he refused to respond to my shouts to hurry. I swore at him and this set off ice-falls further up the glacier. This did chivvy the exhausted Patrick who rose teetering under the weight of his pack.

Geoff found a ledge at the very point where our *bergschrund* rock route reached the level of the glacier ice. Uncertain how we could cross from rock to ice, a distance of twenty feet, we agreed to camp on the rock ledge.

With bloody fingers we erected the tent, designed for two six-foot soldiers, and the five of us crawled in. We melted ice and made weak tea. There was only one twenty-four-hour ration pack to be shared by all. This worked out at a single spoonful of curry gruel each and two 'sips' of tea. Patrick was allowed two spoonfuls and three sips after he announced that it was his birthday.

Breakfast was exactly three-quarters of one Army biscuit and one gulp from a tin mug of steaming hot water boiled with yesterday's two teabags. If anyone's Adam's apple jerked more than once as they drank, Bob's large hand descended at once and removed the mug.

Bootlaces, zips and rope coils opened up the raw patches on my fingers. Blisters squelched and Bob's lips bled. Geoff nursed his ribs but did not complain. Once the tent was packed he lay along the ledge and decided our only escape must be by rope down the cliffside. He fed out a 300-foot coil, secured to a boulder, and we slid down one by one. I had wrapped socks round my hands, which were blood-soaked by the time I finished the descent.

Next we faced a wet rockface which descended sixty feet to a possible causeway over the *bergschrund*. When Patrick saw the rock route, he snorted his reluctance. I must have spoken angrily, for I sparked off a tirade. He accused me of being totally unaware of the perils of our situation and of having abused his friendship by falsely luring him into the team with promises of fishing, a little skiing and minimal physical discomfort other than a night or two in a tent.

There was an element of truth in his charges so I said nothing and moved off down the wet rock. We clung like limpets to every tiny hold, cursing the outward pull of our packs and sweating at the thought of what lay below. We were not roped up at that point for fear of one man unseating the rest.

We made the causeway and regained the glacier. Avalanches sounded every few minutes and the ice under our feet kept sliding away. For an hour we were forced to climb over temporary platforms of avalanche rubble. At some point I heard a scream from behind. Roger and I could not move due to loose ice underfoot but we could see the others fifty yards behind. Patrick had fallen through the platform and hung dangling unseen somewhere below. Bob held fast to his rope while Geoff tried to remove the ice-blocks that had fallen into the hole above Patrick.

Geoff's urgency disturbed many heavy chunks, a further risk to our hanging colleague, but at length he re-exposed the hole. Bob and Geoff hauled together on their ropes and Patrick's head appeared in the 'plug-hole' between them. He was numb with cold but unhurt. There was no time to rest so we continued over the rotten platform until, two hours later, we reached the top of the glacier's bottleneck. Here all avalanches from above were channelled into a 100-yard front.

Back at the camp Peter Booth wrote in his diary:

Henrik came down from the glacier and joined me below the snout of the Briksdalsbre. There were many local guides and farmers with us watching the dark figures high above us on the ice. Watching the painful progress of the climbers down the glacier was an exciting experience. There was the feeling that at any moment falling ice would obliterate them. They were at the glacier's mercy whichever route they selected and the crowd of Norwegians and tourists watched in tense silence.

Through binoculars I could identify the individuals. It was like a ciné-film. Suddenly there would be a tremendous cracking noise followed by a rumble: huge lumps of ice would roll down the glacier, shattering and bounding as they went and triggering further falls. On either flank avalanches raced down with regularity at a speed I found frightening to watch. Within seconds of the first crack, tons of ice would bounce down the near vertical walls . . .

We surveyed the bottleneck with dismay, looking down its length to the final ice-falls and the terminal lake. Not a minute passed but some part of the tongue was temporarily covered by an avalanche.

Geoff fixed our longest rope, a 400-foot coil, to an ice bollard, and threw it downwards. Henrik's voice came over the radio then. The rope had snagged. Geoff tried again. This time it fell clear to its full length, spanning the most lethal stretch of the glacier. We abseiled down wearing rucksacks. Bob joined me after a safe descent, but flying rubble caught the others halfway down. Geoff lost his grip and slid 100 feet, saved only by the friction of the rope against his waist clip. One of Patrick's crampons raked down Geoff's leg, scraping along the bone. Roger, who was unhurt, tore off his shirt tail and bound up the wound. We knew we could not delay in this volatile spot and Geoff, despite this new injury, was as keen as the rest of us to hurry on.

Again Henrik's advice by radio proved critical. We were now no more than fifty yards from the final ice-cliff that ended in the lake, but cut off from it by a group of wide crevasses. A sheer gulley ran down between the left-hand cliff and these crevasses and Henrik bade us cross it. 'It is your only way, but go one at a time and watch above as you traverse. Every few minutes since mid-day an avalanche has crashed down the slipway.'

Alluvial mud oozed slowly down the slide like lava flow. We grouped beside the gulley and tensed as several tons of ice hurtled by with the effect of a passing express train. One by one we cramponed across this skittle-alley as fast as the loose surface allowed. Bob came last and, hampered by one broken crampon, lost his grip and hung for an edgy minute held only by his ice-axe and our side rope. Within moments of his crossing, the whole grey slipway shuddered under a deluge of ice-spoil.

Our very last rope, another 400-foot length, took us down the rock cliff to the lake where Johnny, Peter and Henrik awaited us in a spare Avon boat which they had carried up from the road-head far below.

Ten days after returning to England and with Gubbie as best man I married Ginnie in Tillington church, a mile to the east of Lodsworth and River.

12

Fast Water/Bad Blood

The Canyon has been called beautiful. If this is beauty,
it is the beauty of nightmare.

BRUCE HUTCHINSON

I did not marry Ginnie because I had decided she was more important than my freedom, but because it appeared possible to have both. Since the day Isaac Newton, or some such sage, proved that cakes disappeared when eaten, all attempts to fly in the face of this unfortunate truism have led to frustration or worse. In our case they led to many months of married hell.

I thought it would be interesting to drive through Eastern Europe for our honeymoon. Two years had passed since Soviet tanks crushed Dubcek's Czechoslovakia and _The Times_'s holiday supplement advised me to expect a welcoming atmosphere and excellent value for money.

I did not consult Ginnie about our honeymoon programme since my understanding of tradition was that bridegrooms do not interfere with marriage arrangements nor brides with honeymoon details. She was therefore unprepared for the fact that I had asked my friend Simon Gault and a female companion of his to come too. My idea was that we would each take a car and subaqua gear and camp beside the Black Sea for ten days before Ginnie and I moved further east.

I sold my Triumph Tiger and purchased an MGB sports car on the never-never. We left our Tillington wedding reception with the standard bric-à-brac lashed to our axle and a potato shooting out of the exhaust pipe. Relieved that the service was over, I told Ginnie about the delightful journey on which we were about to embark. There followed a stoney silence and an unbecoming scowl, from which I gathered that Eastern Europe would not have been her first or even last choice and that, much as she liked Simon, I should not have invited others on our honeymoon.

That night in a Victorian bridal suite in Kent I unpacked a bottle of Veuve Clicquot removed from our reception party and offered the only available toothmug to Ginnie.

'What about you?' she asked.

'I'll drink from the bottle. It tastes just the same.'

'My God, you are uncouth,' she growled.

I wrote wedding gift 'thank you' letters by the bedside and that drove her wild.

I had never known her like this. It must be the aftermath of the wedding – at which she had fainted on her brother's arm. She would be back to her normal cheerful self in the morning. But she continued to bristle on the car ferry to Le Touquet, talking to Simon and openly ignoring me.

I drove at a steady 110 miles per hour along the German autobahns, but on the second day, just short of Munich, after a long silence, my young bride exploded: 'I thought you would have the decency, having driven all the way from Le Touquet, to let me drive today.'

I explained, patiently at first, that it was my car. When we travelled in her old Mini, then of course she could drive. If we sold one of the cars, as we probably would, then she could take herself wherever she wanted in the MG. But, when we were both aboard, I would always drive. I was the male member of the family and, in my book, driving was a male prerogative just as housework was her preserve.

Ginnie's blue eyes flashed like short-circuit sparks. 'Marriage is all about sharing. Didn't your mother ever warn you? You . . .'

'Don't bring my mother into this,' I interrupted. Now I too was riled. 'Marriage is also about the facts of life, which include male dominance. Why do you think the woman promises to love, honour and obey her husband?'

'If you had been listening,' she spat back, 'you would have noticed that Father Young only asked me to love and honour. He very sensibly omitted any reference to obeying.'

This evidence of priestly duplicity left me astonished. All I could manage was: 'Well, I don't intend you to wear the trousers in our marriage, now or ever, and that means I drive.'

Silence. Until a large blue sign flashed past proclaiming 'Munchen, 6km'.

'Take me to Munich Station,' Ginnie said, quietly.

'What do you mean? We're going to cross the border into Italy.'

'I am going straight home. You can honeymoon and drive by yourself when and where you want but I have had enough. Turn off here or I throw my bag out and, if necessary, myself.'

I followed the Stadtmitte and the Hauptbahnhof signs and helped her unpack her luggage in the central station car park. Only when I saw that this was no bluff, that she really did intend heading home, did I give in. She took the wheel and for a while the air between us was lighter.

A few hours later, with driving sleet slashing across our headlight beams, Ginnie tried to pass a lorry on a bend high in the Alps. I had told her it was clear to go. Since the road curved to the right and I sat on the left as we overtook, I was first to spot the lights of an oncoming car.

'Slow down, Ginnie. You can't overtake. Get back.'

She did nothing and, panicking, I swung the wheel inwards, thinking that we were just behind the rear wheels of the truck's flatbed.

Unfortunately the wheels I saw were not the rear wheels and the front of the MGB on Ginnie's side was crushed by some hanging steel appendage under the flatbed. She swerved away into the centre of the road, just avoiding annihilation by the lorry's rear wheels but ending up immediately in front of an oncoming Fiat. By the grace of God the Fiat halted mere yards from our front bumper. The driver was, rightly, livid.

We quickly moved off the road, apologised to the Italians and spent two hours hammering at the bodywork of the MG until the front near-side wheel was free of buckled metal.

'If that's your idea of sharing the driving,' Ginnie muttered, 'you had better not try it again.'

We waited for a week at a hotel in Split on the Yugoslav coast but Simon, along with our subaqua gear, never turned up. He told me later that the attractive girl he had brought along, soon after leaving Le Touquet in our wake, had mentioned that she never stayed at any hotel with less than four Michelin stars. Simon had acknowledged this with a sickly smile and curtailed his holiday a few days later on some business pretext.

In the east of Yugoslavia, *en route* to Rumania, the MG's exhaust pipe fell off. The remaining fortnight was as unpeaceful for us as it was for the villages through which we passed.

The officials at both ends of Czechoslovakia were painstakingly unpleasant, the Bulgarian and Hungarian police hounded us due to our noisy exhaust and the East Germans screwed every pfennig from us at the obligatory campsites. Thankfully, after three weeks, we came in from the cold and sped to Vienna where I was determined that Ginnie should enjoy herself, if only with my eye on defensive ammunition in readiness for future tantrums.

With our funds dangerously low, I decided on two 'memorable events', both quintessentially Viennese – the Lippizano Riding School and the Opera House.

The horses were away in Spain on holiday and the last show at the Opera House was due to start in an hour. Rushing Ginnie away from the first comfortable hotel room of the entire honeymoon, without time for bath or meal, we made it to the Opera House and attached ourselves to the end of one of the ticket queues. Ginnie looked happy and excited.

'You wait in the queue and I'll buy a couple of ice creams.' I rushed off to a nearby shopping mall under the central plaza and purchased two magnificent twirls of chocolate ice cream in giant cornets.

I must have emerged from a different escalator into the square and noticed for the first time that the Opera House was as similar on all sides of its circular facia as is the Albert Hall. There were many open entrances with ticket desks and dwindling queues, and I could not find the right one. The cornets began to leak down my trousers so I licked at them both as I ran.

Ten minutes later I located the correct entrance and a half tearful, half furious Ginnie. The queues had dispersed, the show was barred to further entrants and the ice cream cornets were mere sodden suppositories.

Our obligatory period of joyful bliss ended, we spluttered back to England where I looked up honeymoon in the *Concise Oxford Dictionary* and was surprised to find an apt explanation for the word: 'Holiday spent together by newly married couple: a period of waning affection.'

With no home and my only hope of income resting on a contract for a book about Norway, I agreed to go north to Ginnie's beloved Wester Ross where a friend had offered her three months' lodging for a peppercorn rent.

I sold the MGB, which improved our financial position, and became Ginnie's passenger in the Mini I had given her a year before. She drove like a maniac and so terrorised me that the arguments, which were fast becoming a feature of our life together, petered out as soon as we hit the road.

The cottage where we spent the winter of 1970 was set back beside a spinney of Scots pine overlooking the wide valley of Lochmaree. The shadow of snowclad Slioch shivered in the black loch below the cottage and the glen of Grudie tumbled past us from high moorland lochans. We could see no habitation in any direction and, during our first month there, not a soul called except for a London-based revenue officer come to claim back-payment of £168 on National Insurance stamps.

A sitting room, two bedrooms and a kitchen became our isolated home. I rose at 8.00, lit a fire and spent all day in front of it writing. At 4.00 I went for a five-mile run, followed by a swim in the loch. Then more writing until 8.00 p.m.

If Ginnie talked or played her radio, I could not concentrate. She had never learned to cook, so day after day we ate 'Irish stew' or scrambled eggs. I never complained, since I liked both. We began to learn about each other and only bad points seemed to emerge. Whatever was good we had already served up.

As soon as we were married Ginnie felt like a caged animal. Rather late in the day, she now began to express the worries I had nursed all along about lost freedom.

She looked slim, sweet and incapable of spleen but, with increasing frequency, she turned into a vicious spitting thing with mercurial moods. She was as proud and as stubborn as an Omani mule. The troubles between her parents when she was in her teens had made her slightly paranoid. She thought all the world was against her; especially me.

From Ginnie's point of view, she felt consigned to a monastic order, chained to a silent writer with a rigid schedule to his daily existence. She went for many a lonely walk as I sat and wrote through the winter of 1970.

Simon Gault drove north and for two days, with heavy rucksacks, we tramped the wet highlands above the Fionn Loch. Why, Ginnie asked me, had I not included her in our tramp?

'We enjoy pushing ourselves. We move fast for the sake of it. You would not keep up.'

'How do you know?' she retorted. 'I've spent a year in these mountains taking National Trust parties on tours.'

As always, I tried to close the touchy topic by shutting up.

We spent Hallowe'en, the eve of All Saints' Day, in silence, following a major altercation about nothing much. I pushed Ginnie backwards in the kitchen and she hit her head against the wall. I was instantly contrite and Ginnie, luckily unhurt, was furious.

I found a female kitten on the kitchen window ledge at dawn the next morning and invited her in. We named the kitten Slioch after the mountain that brooded over the loch. There are no buildings for many miles from Grudie except for the hotel, three miles along the loch, and Miss Moodie, the manageress, was not missing a cat. The kitten was well fed and totally tame: her origin remained a mystery but she became a healing part of our family scene, a pint of oil in a troubled lake.

One day I received a telegram from the William Morris Agency asking me to go to London to audition for the part of James Bond. Sean Connery had retired, his successor George Lazenby had been pensioned off, and the prime mover of the Bond films, Mr Cubby Broccoli, was on the lookout for a new 007. I drove three miles to the nearest phone box and was told by a William Morris woman that Mr Broccoli was looking for 'an English gentleman who really does these things'.

'What things?' I asked.

'Shoot rapids, climb drainpipes, parachute, kill people, you know . . .'

'Hey. Wait a minute. I don't kill people or climb drainpipes.'

My protest went ignored.

'We have been told you sound suitable.'

'I cannot act. I have never acted.'

'That's OK.' The voice went silky. 'You'll be great.'

About to refuse, I realised a free trip to London might be on the cards. Would they pay my fare? They would, so I went.

The interview lasted ten minutes, sufficient for Mr Broccoli to decide I was too young, most un-Bond-like and facially more like a farmhand than an 'English gentleman'.

But the journey was not fruitless, for it led indirectly to my next expedition. I happened to meet Nick Holder who, after our Nile journey, had joined the Royal Scots Greys. He was active at Adventure Training within the regiment and only recently had proposed an ambitious scheme called Exercise Arctic Moose to the CO. We discussed his plans in detail but, on leaving London, I forgot all about them.

Within hours of my return to Grudie and a loving welcome, Ginnie and I were back on our war-like footing, with periodic truces to draw breath.

At the New Year I went south by train to visit my mother. Heavy snowfalls stymied British Railways and kept me in Sussex for ten days, during which time I visited one or two houses for sale. There was a four-room brick bungalow called Stickledown in the suburbs of Midhurst which cost £7000. My worldly wealth was £4000, but I received a mortgage for the balance from my mother's bank.

Back at Grudie I announced the glad news: our very own house would be ready for us within three weeks. Ginnie was not as overjoyed as I had hoped. Half our troubles, I had assumed, were caused by Grudie's isolation and the fact that no friends called. In Midhurst things must surely improve. They could certainly be no worse than life at Grudie.

From the start Ginnie hated Stickledown and I was too insensitive to understand why. The bungalow was my choice – with my mother's assistance, and without reference to Ginnie. The fact that my mother lived a mere four miles away did nothing to help, for Ginnie wanted, as do most new wives of men with loving mothers, a clean break from the old environment. She accepted that the bungalow was a bargain and knew we must stay there until I managed to improve my earnings, but this did not stop her bitching about it.

The town hall and civic centre lecture season was in full swing, so I plied the circuit three or four evenings a week with Ginnie as projectionist.

For a while I continued to train with 'R' Squadron, 22nd SAS Regiment in Hereford as a trooper, but the long drives, low pay and lack of promotion prospects sparked a call to 21st SAS Regiment (Territorials) in London, whose CO agreed to take me on straightaway as a captain. With tripled pay packets, I spent most weekends with my new unit.

In February a letter arrived from Lieutenant-Colonel Norman Arthur of the Royal Scots Greys, on whose list of reserve officers I still figured. Nick Holder's original Arctic Moose scheme had been turned down, but the Canadian authorities had proposed an alternative.

On 20 July 1871, British Columbia, a land mass equivalent to twenty Switzerlands plus Great Britain, first joined the Canadian Confederation and transformed Canada into a single transcontinental federation. Now the province intended to hold ambitious centenary celebrations and their planning committee liked the idea of a river journey to commemorate the early pioneers, most of whom were Scotsmen. These men had travelled by river because the alternative land routes were hostile and thickly forested.

The centenary committee suggested that a river journey by Scotsmen from the Yukon to the United States would be a feat to match those of their forebears. If successful, it would also be the first recorded transnavigation of British Columbia.

The Ministry of Defence passed the suggestion to Scotland's last remaining cavalry regiment, the Greys, who liked the idea, especially since in June they were due to lose their identity and their famous grey berets through amalgamation with a Welsh regiment – part of Harold Wilson's Forces-pruning policy. The expedition would be a fine last fling. But they were currently overworked, with squadrons in Ireland, Cyprus and the Middle East. There were no officers, including Nick Holder, and few soldiers to spare for such a lengthy project as this. Nick had told the CO I was free, so the 'Arctic Moose' file duly arrived at Stickledown with a promise that,

ALASKA

YUKON

NORTHWEST
TERRITORIES

Virginia Falls
S. Nahanni R.
(Headless) Deadmen Valley
SPLITS
Liard R.
Nahanni Butte

Hyland R.
Cranberry
Rapids

Fort Liard

Ft Nelson R.

Fort Nelson

ALBERTA

R. Stikine

Kechika R.
Skook's Kingdom
Gataga Forks
Sifton Pass
Fox Lake
Fort Ware
Deserter's Canyon

Fox R.

ROCKY MOUNTAIN
CASSIAR MOUNTAINS

Williston Lake
Finlay Forks

Finlay R.

TRENCH

Skeena R.

BRITISH
COLUMBIA

Parsnip R.
McLeod Lake

Crooked R.
Pack R.

Summit Lake
Giscombe
Prince George

Edmonton

Fraser R.

PACIFIC OCEAN

Quesnel
Alexandria

Williams Lake
Moran
Gang Ranch
Clinton
Canyon
Fountain
Lillooet
Bridge River Rapids
Lytton

Thompson R.

Boston Bar
Hell's Gate
Black Canyon
Vancouver

Point Roberts   USA

0   100   200 miles

British Columbia and The Yukon

167

should I agree to take on the project, the regiment would provide 'two or three soldiers and some supplies'.

I warmed quickly to the proposition, which was more ambitious than the Nile or Norway journeys. Sponsorship in the form of equipment was becoming less difficult to obtain, since each expedition obtained publicity which the equipment manufacturers used for promotion purposes. I determined to find a film-team and a newspaper photographer to come to Canada along with the soldiers.

Ginnie agreed to join the team as road party leader and radio operator, and to start at once on research into the British Columbian rivers. She could work in the Royal Geographical Society libraries since we were both 'Fellows' of that institution.

We sold Ginnie's battered Mini van and obtained from the Midhurst butchers a white Morris Minor van which had delivered meat and fish about the locality for many years. No amount of scouring and scrubbing with ammonia rid the vehicle of its rank smell, but it served to collect all manner of gear from sponsors around Britain. Ginnie would return from a day on the road, stack the goods in the Stickledown garage, then soak all her clothes and body to get rid of the odour of mackerel and porkfat.

Brian Branston, BBC-2 director of travel and exploration, offered me a lead part in a film for his *World About Us* series. The subject was 'Under London' and involved a journey beneath the city pavements by way of the sewer system and other subterranean by-ways. The pay was excellent so I accepted and, for two months, alternated between the Ministry of Defence and the sewers.

Ginnie would arrive most evenings in our friends' London flats covered in dust from the book vaults of the RGS or smelling of fish from the butcher's van. This odour mingled to evil effect with the sewer stench emanating from my clothes.

The BBC crew proved understanding when I rushed to a telephone every hour to check with my MoD desk: I could not afford to miss sponsors' calls. I used telephones down in the silver vaults, in the GPO Holborn nuclear-proof exchange containing the Hot Line, in the Abbey Mills sewage pumping station, and in the Billingsgate deep-freeze fish cellar at −40 degrees. My most frustrating morning was spent being filmed behind Winston Churchill's desk in his War Room. Everything remained precisely as on Armistice Day: the wall-charts, the chunky desk with cigar-cutter and bell-push, the tiny bedroom and the multi-coloured battery of telephones. None of the telephones worked, not even to the Ministry of Defence, so I spent a fruitless morning.

I drove to the Scots Greys' headquarters in Edinburgh where the colonel promised me my 'pick of the regiment'. He then revised this to 'any three men in headquarters mad enough to volunteer'. Even this largesse proved less generous than it sounded since only one-quarter of the regimental strength was in Britain and these were the pipes and drums, the bandsmen, the cooks and the engineers.

Two members of my old ski team from Bavaria, now working with the regimental headquarters, volunteered and I accepted both at once. One was an ex-butcher's apprentice, an Edinburgh Scotsman named Joseph Skibinski; the other, Jackie McConnell, was a skilled radio operator and an ex-runner from my Fallingbostel cross-country team. My last acquisition was a small tank mechanic from Devon, Stanley Cribbett, who, according to Skibinski, could repair anything from a clock to a sputnik.

The Observer agreed to sponsor the expedition and to send their top photographer, Bryn Campbell, on the journey. *The World About Us* sent a two-man team, consisting of their producer Richard Robinson and cameraman Paul Berriff.

I obtained three rubber boats, fourteen feet long and powered by outboard engines. Bryn and Stan Cribbett would travel with me, then the two Jocks, and finally Richard and Paul with their cameras. To steer their boat while they filmed, they recruited a Yorkshire policeman named Ben Usher, whose rubber boat experience came from off-duty work with the RNLI detachment in Bridlington (about which Richard and Paul had recently made a documentary film).

Ginnie's research revealed a possible riverain route down the Rocky Mountain spine of British Columbia, all the way from the Yukon border to Vancouver and the USA, a journey of about 1100 miles, only ten of which could clearly not be travelled by river.

Since Ginnie's route involved grade nine rapids and none of our team had white-water experienced, I included in our schedule a month's acclimatisation of rough Yukon rivers prior to the main journey. Northern Canada's annual spring floods subside in mid-July, when I planned to begin the expedition.

By the end of April our garage was full of gear and Slioch had kittens curled up in an inflatable boat. The team met for the first time at the Snake's Tail Rapids on the River Dee, where Roger Chapman had trained us for Norway the previous year. The various characters appeared to gel together quite well. Even Ginnie, who has a sharp eye for personalities, spotted no likely hang-ups, no warning signals.

The soldiers were business-like and quickly learned how to handle the boats. The two BBC men were as inscrutable as Chinamen, said little and gave me the feeling they were unimpressed by boats and crew alike. This, I felt, mattered little. I was confident of our abilities and the film-men would soon learn we could cope. Bryn Campbell was a delightful extrovert and Ginnie agreed we were lucky to have him.

The national Press turned up on the second day of our rapids training. A caption under a front-page photo of the soldiers completing capsize drill stated they were out of control. How, if we could not cope with a Welsh stream, would we survive the British Columbia cataracts? This touch of mis-reporting caused our boat sponsors to withdraw. Frantic searches for a month obtained one twelve-foot C-Craft and two sixteen-foot RFD inflatables.

On a fine day in June we tested the new boats, fully laden, on the Thames by Battersea bridge. They made good headway against a five-knot current with one forty-horsepower outboard per boat. Dragging the boats ashore at low tide we slithered past the carcass of a bloated dog and several dead birds embalmed in oil. The virgin rivers of British Columbia beckoned welcomingly.

An RAF Hercules flew us to Edmonton, Alberta with 9000 pounds of equipment and a ten-year-old Land Rover which had seen service in Aden, Cyprus and Germany. The Army had declared it 'Beyond Economical Repair' and the Greys' Quartermaster had sidetracked it from the knacker's yard. The Canadian Army lent us a four-ton lorry which was driven by an English corporal attached to the Scots Greys, whom I had cajoled from the CO rather late in the day.

Our two-vehicle convoy drove northwest through 600 miles of prairie where, two short centuries ago, there roamed some twenty million bison. Most of the way west the rain rolled down in sheets and we began to discover the meaning of the Army term 'Beyond Economical Repair'. The Land Rover's wipers only functioned manually and little Stanley, perched on an extra cushion, steered with one hand while twiddling the wiper control endlessly to and fro with the other. I sat between Stanley and Ginnie on a metal battery cover. Acid fumes began to rise between my legs and the battery temperature needle swung to the danger level. My backside grew unbearably hot so we halted for two hours, dodging leaks in the canvas roof.

Our destination was Fort Nelson where Ginnie and Wally, the driver, would stay for a month while the boat crews completed a 400-mile trial journey. If we could cope with this, then in August the main expedition would begin. I had chosen the trial journey with care as a true test for men and boats. The goal was to reach the little-known Virginia Falls, twice the height of the Niagara Falls and 110 miles up the South Nahanni River. American river-runner and author Colonel Snyder, described the South Nahanni as 'the fastest river in North America and the most dangerous in five continents'. To reach the Nahanni involved a further 290 miles of river travel down the Fort Nelson and Liard rivers. Afterwards we would return by the same route using pre-positioned fuel caches. *En route* to the falls we would pass through an interesting area known as Deadmen Valley. In the early 1900s, three headless skeletons were found in the valley. Since then thirty-two other people had died or disappeared there.

Our main expedition had to reach the US border by mid-October, before winter. This curtailed our Virginia Falls journey to just four weeks. I was not happy therefore, on arriving in Fort Nelson, to be told by the Mounties that the river was dangerously high, with worse floods than they could remember. The day before, the big road-bridge at the southern end of town had been crushed and swept away by a log jam.

While waiting for the floodwaters to subside, we prepared the equipment and slept in a hangar at the local airstrip. A pilot took me on a firespotting flight. Below us in every direction was thick forest: we might just as well have been flying over the Amazon and the jungles of Brazil. Somewhere, lost in the northern haze, thundered the Nahanni, Indian word for 'Over there and beyond', fed by the high glaciers of unnamed mountains.

In the hangar we inflated the boats and stowed them with enough dehydrated food for three weeks. Eighty-foot Terylene coils were attached as bowlines and Karabiner snap-gate rings fixed to all external safety lines. Malayan panga knives in greased sheaths were taped to the forward dodgers – easily to hand in emergency. All perishable goods, from food and first-aid equipment to film, clothing and tents, were packed in airtight plastic buckets, then stowed in 'mummy bags'. These tailor-made neoprene containers with waterproof access zips were lashed to the floorboards. Each boat had six separate air compartments and should float fully loaded even with three punctured tubes. Above the equipment loads we lashed four-gallon jerribags and ten-gallon barrels. Each boat carried ninety gallons of fuel as well as 1100 pounds of gear.

After two days the floodwaters began to abate. Local rivermen told me to wait a week but, looking at a map of what we must do over the next four months, I grew impatient and decided we must leave at once.

The sun blazed down but the sky was pallid, with thunderheads rimming the eastern horizon. The four of us who were of the Royal Scots Greys wore our grey berets with their silver eagle badges as we left. This was out of respect for our famous regiment which, four days previously, had ceased to exist after 300 years as Scotland's own cavalry regiment. My father had seen the last of the grey horses; I wore the last grey beret of the Greys.

The three boats slid away, spinning in eddies as we each tried to find somewhere to sit. Then, edging the current, we gathered speed. A Mountie, two Indians and a group of Press from Vancouver waved us off. Ginnie stood alone, small and forlorn in her dusty jeans, soon a fading blur in the willows.

The river was 300 yards wide, both banks were thickly wooded and the world passed by quite silently but for the rush of water, the soft plunk of paddles and the sudden boil of converging eddies. An hour from Fort Nelson things changed with a vengeance. 'The current's racing along,' Bryn mused, 'as though there's a waterfall ahead.'

'There's no rapid on this river,' I assured him.

From up ahead I heard a sound as of breakers lashing a shingle beach; the same dull double boom and the rushing hiss of undertow. The channel ahead curved right but the local current sucked us left. The other boats were out of sight.

Along the left-hand bank fallen trees rose and fell in the water. Torn down by the force of the floods upon the elbow of the river's curve, their gnarled roots clung to the bank and their trapped trunks threshed to the pulse of the rushing water. If a boat was sucked into this chaos of tangled roots, the tubing would be torn and punctured. We stabbed deep with our paddles, straining to move into mid-river. Before Stan could reach the outboard, a branch lashed across his face, bringing blood. A splintered root dug into the hull behind Bryn and ripped it open. The port air tube wrinkled and subsided and the boat shuddered as we struck a grounded log. We bounced off. If the boat had been of wood, we would probably have foundered and been sucked beneath the mass of heaving vegetation.

For a moment we were free, spun away from the bank by an eddy. This was merely a brief respite, for the shock of our narrow escape was soon eclipsed by the horror of the scene ahead. Now we could see the source of the earlier wind-borne roar, an island in mid-river on which, it seemed, every log borne downriver by the recent floods was impaled. The whole force of the current, channelled by the acute bend, ran full tilt against the upstream apex of the island, and every piece of flotsam, from floating stumps of juniper to eighty-foot logs, was ensnared where the current split in two against the island.

We could not go left because that channel was a moving mass of tangled debris. So we swung right, sweating over the paddles. Stanley wrestled with our outboard, swung its drive-shaft down until it locked vertically and tugged hard on the ignition cord. Again and again he pulled at the cord and twice the engine spluttered hopefully. Bryn stopped paddling to look over his shoulder, distracted by the shocking sound of log crashing against log.

The water about us was disturbed now by back eddies surging around the jam. We were sucked inexorably backwards to where the river rushed under the sieve of logs. I thought to myself: 2000 miles to go and here we are drowning on the first day. Then we smashed into the logs, sharp branches whipped at us and the boat up-ended. Someone screamed and a heavy object rammed my chest. I felt a branch rip down my back and the shock of cold water.

For a moment the boat was held by a branch and I scrabbled up from the floor to the mid-tubing. The branch broke and our bows disappeared, sucked inch by inch under the churning debris. Water poured over the mummy bag and the lashed drums.

A branch flailed at Bryn and tore him away. He disappeared underwater, his hands clawing the air as he went.

The boat was about to go under. We must get on to the logs while there was a chance or we would all drown. I shouted to warn Stan and tried to scramble on to the nearest log above us. But it was too large and too slimy to grip. Then the boat shuddered and I fell back among the drums. Stan shouted with excitement. He had started the engine. All this time he had single-mindedly tugged at the cord, not noticing the disappearance of Bryn. Now he engaged gear and the forty-horsepower engine roared in reverse cavitation.

There was hope. We both jumped up and down on the half-submerged craft to vibrate the trapped bows loose. A lashing line snapped, a ten-gallon drum broke loose and the bows shot free. Stanley grabbed the tiller and, with painful slowness, we edged away from the log jam.

Despite the knowledge that Bryn must have drowned, I felt only relief and gratitude to Stanley for saving us both through his doggedness. We broke free of the island's drag and shot away into the right-hand channel.

Then I saw Bryn, or rather his mop of black hair. An underwater surge had spewed him up further down the log jam and his smart denim 'ranger' jacket was caught up on a branch. As we watched, his head sank a few inches. The full force of the undertow was dragging at him from the waist down.

We donned lifejackets and Stanley nosed the boat as near as possible to the downstream end of the birch. I jumped on to the slippery log and edged along its bucking length towards Bryn. Sometimes the tree spun through half a turn. Reaching Bryn, I held his jacket scruff firmly and, with our combined strength, he came clear of the water. He was white, cold and shaken, but managed a rueful grin. His frail stature and normally immaculate garb belied a tough and resilient spirit.

The other crews both managed to keep clear of the great jam. We learned our lesson about the danger of snags and thereafter warmed our engine for a while each morning and started it at the first sign of any likely threat.

The BBC crew wished to camp an hour before dusk each evening to sort out their tent and bedding gear in the light. My own policy was not to waste good river-time so I stopped only when I could no longer spot floating snags. They were annoyed by this.

Each evening Ben Usher erected two two-man tents for himself, Richard and Paul, and cooked a meal from special rations. We put up a single four-man tent into which the five of us squeezed, for Bryn mucked in like the others. Joe cut willow swatches and laid them on the wet mud under our groundsheet.

A grizzly bear had recently killed two young girl campers in their sleeping bags. We slept with four loaded pistols in the tent. 'A bullet woodn'a get far,' Jackie muttered in the dark. 'The air's so thick with mosqueeters.'

At a narrow beach called Nelson Forks we carried 140 gallons of fuel above the highwater level and hid the drums under dead leaves. In a month's time, on our way back, this cache would be important.

At Fort Liard we were met by 100 Indians. There were a handful of whites including a saintly and enormous nurse with a surfeit of moles, a long lean Mountie with a crewcut, an eccentric French priest with a heavily pocked-marked face and sledgehammer hands, and a clean young Scotsman who ran the Hudson's Bay Company store. This shopping centre had a single sign proclaiming 'HBC 1886'.

'The Company was here,' the Scotsman told us, 'long before anybody white except perhaps the missionaries. Locals say HBC stands for "Here Before Christ". In truth we ruled this country long before Britain established British Columbia as a colony.'

The mosquitoes, he warned us, would be far worse in Nahanni country. 'The upriver Indians say the air is so thick with them, you canna starve. Simply keep breathing with your mouth open and you will receive your daily food ration.'

That night the two hundred village dogs sang to the moon. There were five dogs to every adult male Indian and they worked hard in winter, when the rivers become frozen highways through the white forests.

The French priest, Father Mary, gave us moose stew for supper and advice about the river. 'I know the rivaire well, my friends, and I tell you. Your rubbaire boots . . . Piff! They never take you to the falls. You *must* have a flat-bottom rivaire boat like mine. Thirty feet long and solide. Hire one pleeze, I tell you, at Nahanni Butte. From here to there is OK in your rubbaire tubs. But not on the Nahanni.' He doled black moose gravy and carrots on to our plates. 'At this time the wataire is high. You have 140 miles of big fast rivaire. One mistake and woosh! The most bad place is the Devil's Whirlpool where the German died eight year ago. Aftaire that is more difficult encore. The Nahanni races down like the galloping horse. Incroyable!'

There were two rapids north of Fort Liard but both lay dormant, only rippling the veneer of floodwater into a gentle swell above their hidden teeth. Flotillas of new islets and clumps of wind-rustled willow passed by hour after hour, until the Nahanni mountains grew from a blue blur to chunky features.

In the hour before dusk the forest was quiet and the mountains reared close above the river. When the Liard bent east to join the Mackenzie and the Arctic Ocean, we nosed west up a backwater through islands of swamp-grass until we came to the green swirl of the Nahanni River. Even where there were no rapids this new and powerful river moved at ten knots, faster in narrow gorges or splits around islands. The racing water drops well over 1000 feet in its passage from the Virginia Falls to Nahanni Butte, the river's junction with the Liard.

Two boat teams had tried for the falls in the 1960s – one with tragic consequences – and eight expeditions had set out in 1970. All of these turned back short of the falls except for a Mr Mikas, who borrowed an Indian scow at the butte and succeeded.

A hunter at the butte named Brian Doke told us to go carefully. A moose-hunter he knew had capsized only twelve miles up the Nahanni, lost his kit and twisted an ankle. They found him nine days later half-starved and demented by insects. The previous year another hunter friend had turned around in the bush to see a black bear, normally harmless to humans. His body, half-eaten, was found alongside his loaded rifle. A helicopter pilot went in to destroy the killer bear, which attacked him only minutes after he had landed. He stepped back into the revolving heliblade and scalped himself.

Thirty log cabins housed the Nahanni Indians. Snowshoes, furs and outboard engines hung under the eaves and battered sledges lay upturned in alder clumps. Old men and children stood about, their hands in the pockets of their faded jeans. Over a hundred dogs were chained to stakes about the clearing.

I hired a thirty-two-foot riverboat made by a local Indian for $50 and a bottle of our sponsored Black and White whisky. With two outboards this craft should provide a means of carrying extra fuel and a more solid platform for the BBC crew, whose inflatable we left at the butte.

Richard, spokesman for the team, cornered me the night before we left the settlement. He sought certain assurances. Was I certain we would finish the expedition by mid-October? I tried to explain that I could not be 100 per cent sure since there were so many imponderables, but he would settle for nothing less than a firm date. He and Paul had won an international award for their film of a Grand Canyon canoe expedition the previous summer and they judged me and my plans by direct comparison with that experience in Colorado.

Both expeditions involved fast North American rivers with the film-teams working from a powered inflatable, but there the similarity ended. The Grand Canyon journey entailed a ten-day descent by a dozen kayaks and two thirty-foot inflatables down a portion of the Colorado River which, though dangerous, was descended by 8000 tourists, including many an eighty-year-old grandma, annually. The expedition was run by a university team who had been through the canyon twice before, with cargoes of T-bone steaks, salads and milk in freezer boxes. They could predict their arrival time at journey's end to within an hour or two.

Unable to shake Richard's conviction that I should be able to furnish him with a schedule, I asked for his other complaints. There were many, but the most memorable was my failure to take into account that the film-team needed to stop for lunch on the riverbank and not, as was my practice, simply eat on board as we travelled, thereby saving an hour or so of good travel time. Furthermore, we should get up later to allow a full eight hours' sleep and, as he had already requested, stop with an hour's daylight in hand. Otherwise Richard and Paul could not be expected to make a film.

Sometimes I felt an expedition leader should lay down the law and stick to it, however much muttering and hostility this might cause. At other times I was prepared to plump for a more mellow middle course of diplomatic appeasement. When I suspected I was dealing with natural, indeed professional, moaners who thrived on the sheer joy of hearing themselves whinge, then I reverted to ignoring all complaints in order to avoid chasing my own tail in my efforts to please.

As we loaded the hired boat with fuel – we named her the *Torrey Canyon* – Ben noticed that the rear transom was cracked and partially rotten, a critical failing since the full wrench of two forty-horsepower outboards would transfer directly on to this board. After floating fully laden for a single night, the *Torrey Canyon* had filled with eight inches of water. We bailed her out and caulked what leaks we could find with Bostik.

Passing an island ten miles out from the butte, we squeezed through a fast channel almost blocked by threshers, fallen trees that rose and fell like gnashing fangs, water cascading through their branches as they rose clear of the water. Bryn was particularly nervous as we ran the gauntlet. A dull roar sounded above the outboard noise as the river forced its way through forests of submerged roots. Then, quite suddenly, the delineated riverbanks fell away and we entered the Splits, a vast floodplain strewn with sandbars, wooded shingle islands, huge drift-piles and broken-off tree roots sewn across certain channels like dragons' teeth. Father Mary had warned against camping anywhere in the Splits, a twenty-mile watery maze, for the water level in the canyons further upriver can rise sixty feet due to a distant rockslide or storm and deluge the whole floodplain with no warning at all. We prodded with sapling poles to sound the shallows but nonetheless had to stop three times to replace propellers with buckled blades.

At dusk we reached the Twisted Mountain and a high safe beach for the night. We lay in our tent listening to the boom of thunder and the crackle of lightning against a background of Bryn's rattling adenoids. Remembering Mike Broome's burned body, I forbade smoking on the boats, because we refuelled the outboard tanks on the move and this led to unavoidable spillage and fumes.

Twenty miles from the Twisted Mountain we entered the first canyon of the Nahanni, the gorge of the Tlogotsho Mountains. At the canyon mouth we stopped to swim in warm sulphurous springs by the riverside. Although in winter the temperature along the Nahanni drops to 70° below freezing, the sulphur pools support a tiny sub-tropical micro-climate where brightly coloured butterflies flit among the columbine that colours the wood and where hummingbirds from Brazil spend their summer. But meanwhile the river and the Virginia Falls themselves freeze over.

The river rose eight feet overnight and filled with debris, including tree trunks. We entered the canyon. The towering walls acted as an echo chamber to every gush and twirl of the current, the sky narrowed to a faraway strip of blue and we shivered in deep shadow, three waterbeetles struggling weakly against the flow in a sheer-sided drain.

At the first narrow bend the *Torrey Canyon* wallowed in back-swell from the cliffs, unable to advance even with both engines at full throttle. Unwilling to turn around for fear of capsizing when broadside to the current, Ben reduced power and slid back into an eddy.

After we had spent three hours ferrying drums of fuel upstream by inflatable, the lightened riverboat ploughed through the bottleneck, taking on water from waves on each side. Richard bailed like an animated bilgepump and Paul filmed his producer at work.

My diary for the day records: 'The river has an unpredictable power which must be watched all the time. There is little inclination to relax and enjoy the incredible scenery . . . to do so would be as suicidal as studying the Arc de Triomphe while driving around it.'

High above us soared sheer red walls with successive pine-clad tiers of rock teetering atop the lower cliffs, a wild jumbled place where exposed pressure lines of many-hued mineral strata zigzagged to a faraway skyline. The sun seldom touched us as we inched along the gloomy corridors of the canyon.

Echoes of turbulence often reached us ahead of the rougher stretches but, at Lafferty's Riffle, there was no audible warning, only a high-flung spray cresting the river's horizon where Lafferty Creek entered the main river and corkscrewed the normal flow into a series of rapids. Our rubber boats bounced, bucking madly, along the ceiling of the turmoil, but not so the *Torrey Canyon*, which almost foundered at the lower edge of the riffle.

We tried to tug the riverboat upstream on tow-lines with the eight of us hauling knee-deep in icy shallows. Ben, the strongest of us, was built like an Aberdeen Angus and, when he slipped, we all went under. The rope ripped away, tearing free of my numbed grip. Next time we lined her, the jockey-light Stanley stayed aboard and cleverly reversed the boat upstream as we took in slack on the ropes.

The next rapid, George's Riffle, was larger, but Ben found a dead patch between breakers where a freak midstream eddy enabled the *Torrey Canyon* to limp her way through the wild water.

The following day we entered a valley of wide white-stoned creeks and pine-clad hills, the legendary Deadmen Valley, tucked between the Headless Mountains and the Funeral Range. Joe caught three fish and shot a rabbit, all of which made for an unusually tasty supper. In readiness for the faster water in the canyons ahead, Stanley battered the buckled propellers back into shape and Ben stripped naked to wash in our cooking pot. Unlike the others he shaved each day and always looked smart despite heat and mosquitoes, a credit to the Yorkshire constabulary.

Canadian newspaper articles put the death-toll of Deadmen or Headless Valley visitors as high as twenty-nine but, after careful research at the Royal Geographical Society and through Royal Canadian Mounted Police records, Ginnie had traced only seventeen unexplained deaths or disappearances, plus three straightforward drownings and one plane crash.

We left Deadmen Valley safely. The next day the transom of the *Torrey Canyon* split in two and, but for skilled handling by Ben, the riverboat would have sunk in minutes. Somehow he manoeuvred the stricken craft back to the beach near our earlier camp. Stanley cut out a replacement transom board and bolted it to the broken original. Owning no drill, we fired 7.62 rifle bullets through the wood as required to take the bolts.

My fuel estimates began to indicate we would run out well short of the falls, so I asked the BBC crew to make room on the *Torrey Canyon* for Jack and Joe together with their deflated inflatable. There was much dissent so I started to haul the rubber bundle aboard myself. The incident marked the start of a vendetta between me and the film-crew but it also enabled our convoy to carry on, saving one-third of our fuel – just enough to make the falls.

The river poured through the second canyon with a show of raw power, using even the smallest rock outcrop or curve in the canyon walls as an excuse to form violent eddies. There was nowhere to camp, only low sandbars which might overnight become submerged. That night we found an island and lit a brushwood fire, for all our clothes were soaking from spray and a sunless day.

Almost immediately after the second canyon fell away from the river, the cliffs of a third and greater ravine loomed ahead and we came to the very heart of the Nahanni, known as the Gate. Above this womb of rock, sheer ramparts of scarred limestone climb in a single giant slab to well over 2000 feet, dwarfing the 300-foot shark's tooth Pulpit Rock that juts up sentinel-like in mid-river. Even at full throttle we made little impression on the Gate's current, merely swinging about in the grip of the eddies which boil the water's surface and move almost as fast as the main current, but in a sideways direction.

Our slow fight through the Gate used up precious fuel, but by devious zig-zags we won through and came at length to the Devil's Whirlpool. Three members of a German expedition in 1963 had drowned in this rapid, so we climbed above the feature to study it before going any further. After ten minutes of discussion we agreed there was no certain way to bypass the danger. Two distinct whirlpools rotated between sheer cliffs on an acute bend in the river. The outward cliff accepted the full force of the river but turned much of the water back on itself in turmoil. The base of the cliffs on both banks was cut away by wave action, forming dangerous overhangs.

Stanley decided on a mid-river course away from the cliffs and between the whirlpools. This would have been easy had each vortex remained constant in size and location but, as we watched, the twin maws gyrated across the whole width of the river, sometimes slowly, sometimes quickly, so that the surface water tripped over itself, forming subsidiary whirlpools and great erupting boils that spread away from the central violence like tidal waves from an undersea eruption.

To lighten the riverboat we reflated the C-craft, Jack and Joe's boat, and they went first into the Devil's Whirlpool. They did not reappear, so Stanley powered us up the river's centre line and bounced the boat through the downriver turbulence. We saw the right-hand whirlpool dead ahead and veered off to the left at right-angles. I lost my grip and sprawled in the bilge water. A pocket of spinning waves tossed us sideways and for an age, it seemed, we lurched between the whirlpools in a no-man's land of eddies converging from either side.

The stern slipped left in an unseen grip and we were swung into the outer convolutions of a whirlpool. Stanley wrenched at the helm and we nosed straight towards the left-hand cliff overhang. Our momentum carried us clear of the eye of the whirlpool and, once beyond its drag ring, we veered to our earlier course, missing the overhang by a narrow margin.

By noon the other boats were safely above the whirlpools and we each had some ten gallons left in our tanks. Against such a powerful current we could average only one mile per gallon and the falls were still a dozen miles or more further west. A close call.

Up ahead rose a canyon named by Father Mary as Galloping Horse Rapids, a series of snake-like corridors. Soon the mountain walls were tight about us and spray soaked us as the boats lost headway in a millrace of churning combers. Stanley fought the tiller to keep our boat straight to the flow as we wallowed about. A gash in the cliffside remained beside us for ten minutes – we were using up fuel and gaining no headway. Stanley tried a new approach, tacking between the waves and straightening out at the last moment before each successive wave broke. Bryn and I paddled hard but to little effect. Our progress was snail-like but the new tactics did pay off as we gradually made ground. Three miles into the galloping waters, I became aware of a background noise to that of the waves and our motor – a sound of continuous thunder.

In less than a hundred miles we had climbed over 1000 feet. This final canyon was an impressive display of water-force, the river powering past us as though racing to eternity. I felt completely insecure, possibly due to the prolonged effect of the struggle, the noise and the dwindling fuel supply. Each time the boat raced down the back-end of a curling hydraulic I wondered if the next wave would bury us in its own deep trough.

A pocket of converging currents held us in a watery vacuum, a mass of water crashed over us and the boat, too heavy now, lost ground. Together with Bryn I jumped on to the bows and, responding to the slight change in trim, the propeller blades gripped with greater effect, the shrill whine of cavitation changing to a deeper note. We inched up the wall of water in the eddy-trap and water poured out of the butterfly valves in the bilges, lightening the tilted craft. Stanley zigged the tiller and, shouting with relief, we crested in an explosion of spray. After that, everything seemed possible and shortly before sunset we rounded a massive buttress, the final bend of the third canyon.

The roar of pounding water intensified to an overall boom and from the heavens, or so it seemed from water-level, there issued a waterfall of Olympian grandeur beneath a halo of high-flung spray. As the sun set we watched our waterfall, twice the stature of the Niagara, and even the dour features of Constable Ben softened with pleasure at the majesty of the place.

The current whisked us back to Nahanni Butte where Bryn and the film-team caught a bush-plane to Fort Nelson. They were to film firefighting in British Columbia where 131 major conflagrations were currently ablaze. A forest ranger in Fort Nelson had warned us of the power of the outback fires. They can jump two-mile-wide lakes in minutes and boil the surface water of creeks.

As we headed back along the Liard the sky darkened for a day and ash settled on the river about us. We feared a nearby blaze but need not have worried since the source of the smoke was in fact over 200 miles away, the Tee zone, where 300,000 acres of prime forest were destroyed and thousands of animals incinerated. A change of weather, not the efforts of firefighters, finally subdued the blaze.

The trial journey over, we drove north-west up the drift highway to the Yukon border and launched the boats on our 1500-mile attempt to transnavigate British Columbia. Only Bryn was absent: *The Observer* had sent him to Paris to cover the riots there.

No sooner had we rejoined the BBC crew again than I sensed an overtly hostile atmosphere. I could not put my finger on it, but I sensed I was in for trouble.

The Hyland River took us gently over the Yukon border into the Liard and all went well as far as the Cranberry Rapids, where the Jocks overturned and Stanley ripped our own boat open on a snag. Jack's morale was dented by the experience, for he was sucked below by undercurrents, despite his lifejacket, and battered against submerged rocks.

Not far beyond the Cranberry Rapids and above the Rapids of the Drowned, we entered the Kechika (or 'Big Muddy') River which greets its rare visitors with a rash of minor rapids close to its mouth. The river and the wild lands which it cleaved were uninhabited for 200 miles but for a single camp 100 miles upstream. This was the 'Kingdom' of Skook Davidson; *Skookum* being Indian for 'the tough one'. Skook's camp is for big-game hunters and all his clients, guides and stores are flown in by float-plane to the river beside his ranch. Since the Kechika flows due north from its high tributary in the Rocky Mountain Trench, we would have to struggle against the current all the way.

The Kechika sourced from a high swamp known as the Sifton Pass and every authority I had consulted assured me our inflatables would not penetrate very far upriver, in fact probably no further than Skook's ranch. From that point on I planned to canoe or to walk with rucksacks. With this in mind I had brought from England two portable canoes which, when dismantled, would be divided between our four backpacks.

The film-crew approached me when they learned that Skook had pack-horses for hire. 'Since we have to manage heavy camera gear as well as our personal kit, it makes sense for us to follow you with the help of ponies. Then we won't hold you up.'

Richard's suggestion seemed sensible on the face of it but the ethics of the expedition, after all a river journey, to my mind excluded outside support. Either we travelled by river or, where we ran out of waterways, we walked.

Richard tugged at his fine black beard in frustration. 'You can walk if you wish. I am suggesting pack-horses only for the film-team.'

'But,' I persisted, 'I can hardly expect the soldiers to stumble on with heavy backpacks when there are ponies a few yards behind us which could happily take all our gear as well as yours.'

Richard was angry. So were Paul and Ben. I was being wilfully obstructive for no good reason as far as they were concerned. From that moment my fate was sealed in terms of portrayal in their documentary films. Richard decided they would ascend the Kechika to Skook's, then charter a float-plane south over the Sifton Pass to Fort Ware, an Indian settlement where there was once again a navigable river. There they would await our arrival over the pass.

I planned to send the boats back from Skook's ranch to the Alaska Highway. Ginnie would then take them south to reposition them at Fort Ware. To make this possible Ginnie and lorry-driver Wally were to come by boat to Skook's with us. Once there they would leave us and return down the Kechika to the Alaska Highway with the inflatables.

All went as planned for some eighty miles up the river to a red rock feature known as Moose Licks. At this point I realised my fuel estimates were low and we would never reach Skook's ranch. I took most of the fuel drums from the C-craft and sent the now empty boat back to the highway with Wally – much to the ire of the Jocks, both now housed in the riverboat. The best tactical move is often the least popular one and rumbles of discontent were audible at the campfires that evening.

In two boats we would go no faster than before but the extra fuel would see us to Skook's . . . just.

For two days we were lashed by thunderstorms. I wore three thick sweaters under my anorak but shivered a good deal, for there was no room between the tiller and the high load of fuel drums to take exercise. The land was endlessly forested on both banks and on the fourth day we passed the Little Muddy River, once the path of a glacier from the Cassiar Mountains. Soon after the Little Muddy confluence we entered a burnt-out region of utter desolation, with river banks so low we could see many miles. The land rolled black and silent to faraway mountains, empty but for the ranks of charred and mostly branchless pine. Nothing stirred but a few high-wheeling specks which dropped like stones from time to time, the sharp-eyed birds of carrion. The strength of the grizzly, the speed of the cougar, the camouflage of a million tiny field mice, even the brains of the lonely trapper – nothing is proof against a racing forest fire.

The river slowed down for thirty miles of dead snyes, shallows and islands until, at dusk, we came to Skook's. Mooring the boats, we found a trail marked by a confusion of hoof-prints and a sapling fence. After a mile a fire-branded board proclaimed 'Diamond J. Ranch – No shooting'.

In a clearing with a panoramic view we found the family of log cabins which constitutes Skook's big game-hunting headquarters. The great man welcomed us from his bed, an old gnarled pioneer crippled by arthritis. He fumbled to light a candle. 'Sit down, darn you,' he barked. 'You folk from the old country never seem to know what the Lord gave you asses for.' Candlelight revealed a row of medals nailed to a log. Skook had done a stint as a sniper in the 29th Vancouver Battalion during the First World War.

Skook was over eighty. Leaving Scotland as a teenager with £10 to his name, he became the finest rodeo rider in British Columbia and settled in his valley in 1939. Now he looked after twenty big game-hunters a year for $150 a day, specialising in grizzlies, bighorn sheep, cougars and mountain rams.

The boats went back downstream with Ginnie and the film-team flew south by Cessna 150 miles to Fort Ware.

I asked Skook about the country to the south.

'When you can canoe no further,' he advised, 'you'll find my old trail beside the river – all the way to Sifton Pass.'

The Rocky Mountain Trench and the Kechika both lie north–south and, on the far side of the Sifton Pass, a new river, the Tochika or Fox, flows south all the way to Fort Ware. Skook's memories of his trail from thirty years ago were difficult to check and I found it ominous that surveyor Hugh Pattinson, whose book I had studied, described the trail – only six months after Skook had made it – as 'requiring much work every season if it is to be kept open, due to washouts, rapid growth and windfalls'. Skook's Indians still travelled along the trail once a year, but he admitted knowing of no white man who had been along it since his own last journey decades ago.

I asked Frank George, an Indian guide. 'You'll be all right,' he said, 'so long as you don't follow a game trail by mistake. They're all over the place.' When asked how we were to recognise the real trail from the game trail, he replied: 'Why, you just do. I been along that way most years since I was a kid and you just get to know the right way after a while. But you watch out for bears, man. Last month a female grizzly came for me and I dropped her with my .303 not far from Gataga Forks. You surprise a grizzly on the trail or with her kids and she can get real mean.'

The four Scots Greys left Skook's in fine weather and paddled up to Gataga Forks. Then the stream became too narrow and too powerful so we collapsed the canoes and lashed them to our packs. Each rucksack weighed 110 pounds. In England each of us had selected his own from the two Army types available. I had a Bergen which is bulky but tough, the others had all chosen Tripack frames, lighter but apt to buckle. We carried enough dehydrated food for eight days, but expected to reach the Sifton Pass in six, averaging fifteen miles per day.

On leaving Gataga Forks we followed a trail blazed with old tree-slashes, definitely the only trail within a mile of our side of the river. Everyone, including the guide Frank George, had been quite clear that the trail was east rather than west of the river.

We were wet with sweat and biting horseflies took advantage of our captive hands. Jack fell off one tree-bridge and landed spreadeagled in a thicket of thorn and dead branches. He lay face upward and pinioned by his rucksack. Removing my own pack, I released Jack from his predicament but that incident alone cost us half an hour's delay. Mentally I revised my fifteen-mile-per-day schedule downwards.

After a frustrating afternoon Jack and I came to three deserted log cabins by the Frog River. Little Stanley Cribbett, who was not much larger than his rucksack, stumbled along an hour later and tottered over beside us, his face pale and sweating profusely. He winced from a spasm of coughing and spat a gob of bright blood onto the grass. He said that his groin pained him and he has tasted blood for some time. He was our only trained medic.

Another hour passed before Joe arrived. He had fallen off a log and wrenched his back, which now hurt him badly. Unable to carry his pack he had hauled it along the trail lashed to two saplings. Fallen trees made this impractical and over the last two miles he had almost abandoned his load in desperation.

Reluctantly but unanimously, we agreed that both Stanley and Joe should return to Skook's by canoe and radio for a plane to take them to Fort Ware, to rest and recover with the film-team. They assembled their canoe and left, wishing us luck.

An hour later the track ran out altogether so we followed a blazed trail which veered east away from the river, hoping we might pick up the correct southerly trail further along. We camped under a polythene sheet a mile inside dense forest. The trees dripped all night and heavy animals moved about in the undergrowth.

Next day we continued deep into the forest, hoping always that the track would bend back to the south. Instead it began to head northeast. Towards noon the undergrowth closed in and several small paths, none of which looked hopeful, veered off in various directions. I remembered Skook's words: 'There's only one trail to Ware, dammit, and than runs south clear as a bell beside the river. The trees are well blazed so you can't go wrong, not even if you're an Englishman.'

Somewhere we must have overlooked a southerly turning. We had wasted eight hours but Jack was philosophical. He never complained. We turned back, reached the Kechika by nightfall and drank thirstily, for we had long since emptied our water bottles.

In the morning rain lashed the trees and our meagre cover. We coaxed some dry kindling into a fire and dissolved our daily ration of four oatmeal biscuits into two mugfuls of boiling water to form a glutinous porridge that we laced with salt and gulped down with relish. Then we helped each other into the rucksacks and tottered about for a while, getting re-acquainted with bruised muscles and taut blisters. Starting along the river bank and working inland we spent two hours searching through the wet foliage. We found many game trails but no trace at all of a southerly blazed track. We discussed our predicament. As the sun rose we stopped shivering and began to feel better. To force our way through trail-less brush with our packs jamming at every step was positively the last alternative.

In the hope that yesterday's trail, the only marked route, eventually returned to the Kechika – perhaps close to the Sifton Pass – we wearily set out again, in the wrong direction but knowing there was no alternative. For three long, wet days we slogged through swamps, up steep hills and down slippery slopes. Jack missed his footing on the second morning and fell off the pathway down a muddy forested incline. I found him badly scratched and bruised. His ankle was sore and began to swell, so I bandaged it.

Rain fell all day every day so that the trail became a stream and deep pools formed between the knee-high roots that criss-crossed our route. We trudged in silence, sometimes losing the trail altogether until one of us spotted another faint tree-slash or sawn-off branch.

When lodgepole pines blocked the route we took off our packs and dragged them behind us, pushing our way backwards through tangles of wet branches beneath the fallen giants. Each night it seemed colder and, on the third morning, thin slivers of ice fell off tree branches as we disturbed them, many landing between our shoulders and packs where they melted.

At night we slept close together under our polythene sheet. However wet the forest, there was always moss and old bark to be found under windfalls, enough to kindle a fire and dry our skin.

With four days' rations left we began for safety's sake to cut down our daily intake and decided to shoot anything edible that came our way. The thud of hooves or paws of heavy animals was audible from time to time and twice the fresh spoor of a wolf showed on our path, but the trees were too close and the foliage too dense to see any game. Our morale was temporarily boosted when a Spruce or Franklin's grouse landed on a branch a few yards ahead. My rifle was lashed to my canoe canvas so Jack carefully drew his 9mm pistol and took aim at the pretty dappled bird. He missed but it stayed put, clucking with indignation and fixing Jack with a stoney glare. This may have embarrassed him, for he missed two further shots. Since we had little spare ammunition and I was mentally bewitched at the thought of roasted grouse meat, I grabbed the pistol from Jack and toppled the poor bird with my third and last shot.

On the fifth day the trail gave out in a region of many creeks, numerous wooded valleys and, immediately to the east, a high-walled canyon. We could struggle for ever through these gloomy forests and never find Skook's elusive trail. We agreed to be bold: to cut due west by compass until we reached the Kechika; then, if there was still no sign of the trail, to wade along the river itself. The only alternative was to admit failure.

Jack's ankle was badly swollen so I took the radio from him to lighten his pack. As we inched west we climbed until we reached the treeline. At first we were pleased to be clear of wet leaves but, out in the open, the wind lashed through our wet clothes.

A snowstorm caught us on a high mountain slope so we sheltered in a narrow space between rocks. Jack, his face gaunt and wan, shivered and rubbed his bad ankle.

When the snow stopped we climbed higher to a ridgeline, and for the first time in days we were able to take stock of our location. I clutched our map against the wind. To the south an armada of jagged pinnacles floated black above a sea of cloud. Ahead, to the west, an unbroken line of bald-topped mountains and, beyond them, a glimpse of the razor-edged Cassiars. To return towards the Kechika River in a direct line would mean climbing this western ridge which, by my map, was nowhere under 6000 feet and was separated from us by numerous forested valleys. Depressing as it seemed, our only sensible choice was to return to our starting-point, and this meant relocating our own outward trail.

Descending to the tree-line, we passed the night at the head of a tiny creek, then pressed on in the general direction of our earlier track. We waded through mushy swamps, climbed over tangled deadfalls and swore as our compass needles swung confusedly in response to unseen mineral deposits. We could no longer see mountains or other useful features, in fact nothing but the immediate tangle of vegetation. In the morning we found a sheet of ice beneath our ground sheet.

A few days later we struggled clear of forest and found our progress barred by the terminal wall of a canyon. That evening we ran out of rations. We had to find our way back quickly to

Skook's, collect more food and try again. Jack nursed septic ankles where his boots chafed against burst blisters. My shoulders were raw in places where the pack had rubbed against them and a rash of swollen boils across the small of my back did not help.

One swamp took eight hours to cross and we sank to our knees in the spongier veins. This sapped our will to keep going. What would have happened had we chanced to take any other route or follow a different bearing is difficult to assess, but our chances of making it to Gataga Forks through uncleared forest would have been slim in our weak state. The labyrinth of entwined valleys made a mockery of direction-finding: we were forced to follow their meanderings rather than a compass bearing in order to avoid mountains and ravines.

We emerged from an open swamp along a wide game trail and I remember thinking how strange it was to find footprints in this wilderness. We must have trudged along for a full five minutes before common sense began to assert itself through the fog of exhaustion and hunger.

'Hey, Ran,' Jack mumbled, 'd'ye no think these bootprints could be oors?' They were. The relief was great. The blazed trail, which had earlier seemed so difficult, was now like a motorway.

We came to Gataga Forks on the last day of the month and paddled our canoe the thirty miles back to Skook's. He could not understand how we had missed the trail and again stressed that there were no other blazed routes. The Irish doctor strapped Jack's ankle and we packed a fresh supply of rations. For a day we rested and feasted on moose steak and blueberry pie.

Next day, in ten degrees of frost, we set out again – this time without our canoe, rifle, ropes or radio. After three miles Jack was lagging badly. Normally he kept close. I waited for him, but I could see it was hopeless. His ankle was worse than ever and we would only court disaster to tempt fate further. We argued the toss and Jack finally agreed. I saw that he was crying with frustration. He gave me his pistol and we shook hands.

I followed the trail back to the Gataga River junction and tried to wade the river, but found it too swift and deep. Fashioning a raft from logs, I stripped off and swam the raft across, keeping my clothes and pack dry. I slept in the least dirty of the Frog River cabins and, in the morning sprinkled penicillin powder on the raw places along my shoulders and back. Once more I came to the place where the blazed trail left the riverside, but this time I carried on into the undergrowth beside the river. The going was in every way as bad as before but it was warmer beside the river than in the mountain forests and for three days there was no rain. By night the temperature dropped below freezing but I kept a fire going until I slept. There was a moment of panic when I saw the dark cloud of a forest fire to the east, and again when I lost the river and ran out of drinking water. Twice I became jammed on my back having fallen off giant tree-trunks spanning thick undergrowth. On the fifth day my sores wept poison and I ran out of penicillin. Dizzy bouts affected my judgement and, after two days wading up the river itself, I found myself hemmed in by rapids ahead and sheer rock walls either side.

I laid out my orange lifejacket on a tiny beach and lit a bonfire to attract attention from the air. I was losing my grip. Then, through thoughts of failure, a niggling idea struck me. What if Skook had been wrong all along? What if the Indians had moved his trail to the far side of the Kechika? I had food enough for two more days and there was no alternative. So I waded back downstream to a place with access to the western bank.

Six hours later I picked up the clearly marked triple slash which in the territory of Sikanee Indians, the nomads of these parts, indicates a nearby trapline. In a while there were further signs and I knew for sure that I had found the trail. Forgetting sores, hunger and blisters I covered the next twenty miles in two days to the headwaters of the Kechika, high in the flats of the Sifton Pass, a cheerful place of flowering plants and berry bushes. This was good trapping country, flush with beaver, marten, mink and otter. Now the Indian trail became easy to see, no longer a will o'the wisp passage through undergrowth but a trodden path with blaze marks every few yards.

Late in the afternoon after crossing the Pass I rounded a bend to find Jack and Joe hunting squirrels. Both men seemed rather quiet. Jack winked at me but gave me no explanation. I followed them four miles to the cabins of the McCook Indians at the side of Fox Lake. Close by the cabins was the film-team's camp: their blue two-man tents and a hung tarpaulin lent by the McCooks. Everyone was subdued. There was no welcome of any sort. Jack brought me tea and a pot of stew and in a while made a sign when the others were not in the vicinity. I followed him into the bushes where he told me what was going on.

'They are reel bitter and twisted. When I got in, I saw Joe and Stan were up-tight and would'na talk. Joe has always been my friend but now he's cold and sour. The Beeb are out to get yoo's, Ran.'

'But why?' I asked. 'I can understand the film-team being paranoid after I vetoed their mule train but what have I done to upset Joe and Stan?'

Jack did not answer at once. He shook his head: 'I canna say for sure. My guess is that the Beeb and Ben have talked them into hating yoo's. They get them sittin round the fire and drinkin their beer. Then they start diggin into yoo's for this 'n that until the boys feel that ye have done them doon. And all the time they have their tape-recorders going.'

'Do you think I've done badly by them?'

Jack laughed. 'Of course ye have. Yoo're a bloody terror and a slavemaster. I told the Beeb how ye whipped me all the way up the Kechika.' He turned serious. 'But they've got their knives oot for yoo's and they're makin a bad, bad film from yoor point of view. When I got in, they were at me rait away, wantin to ken if ye'd forced me on or, when I told them no, if ye'd tried to get rid of me.'

We talked for the best part of an hour. Then we heard Joe calling and Jack went back alone. It was better for him not to have been seen talking to me or, as the Jocks say, brown-nosin' the officers.

I sat on the bole of a hemlock in a glade of tamarack floored with wild strawberries. My earlier elation at breaking through the pass was gone, a pricked balloon.

I had counted on a fair BBC film of our journey, a fair reproduction of our struggles, not an artificial *Mutiny on the Bounty* stirred up, then recorded, by the film-team. If *The World About Us* with its audience of eight million gave me a bad name for brutality, inefficiency and glory-seeking, the damage would be irreparable, because the sponsor companies on whom my future totally depended would blacklist me. They were as crucial to my expeditions as creditors to a small business. There was nothing unusual in my sensitivity to the feelings of sponsors; it is the ingrained and ever-present worry of all expeditioneers without funds of their own. It can affect the judgement and the ability to make correct decisions and was, in the years ahead, to come within an ace of destroying my career.

I analysed the BBC team's plot as it appeared from Jack's gleanings. To press their point that I was cruel to the others, they had filmed the diminutive Stanley staggering about under the weight of his rucksack. That I was inefficient was stressed by a recording made around their Fox Lake campfire of an angry Joe declaring that I 'could'na organise a piss-up in a brewery', referring to the size of our overland pack loads. And, by way of proof that I was a glory-seeker, the suggestion was laid that I had encouraged Joe and Stanley to drop out, and subsequently Jack too, so that I could cross the Rocky Mountain Trench all by myself. To this end I had previously ensured that the film-team were not present by unreasonably vetoing the idea of pack-horses. On top of which, I was plainly a lousy navigator if I could not find the Indian 'highway' over the pass which Skook and his guides had told the BBC was easy to find.

After the journey was over both Joe and Stanley, spending a week with me at the London Boat Show, expressed their regrets that they had fallen under the film-team's thrall after their Kechika injuries. Joe pointed out that the aura of romance of the film-team had exercised a certain influence over him. The BBC crew were special people, the winners of international film awards – the men who made entertainment for millions. But the damage was done: the campfire invective, cleverly married up with film-clips such as wee Stanley tottering under his giant pack, proved damning.

All that was now needed to ram home my ineptitude was that the journey should fail somewhere along the 800 miles of violent rivers to our south. Then the BBC could make a fascinating meal: an in-depth study of leadership failure.

To date, I consoled myself, the expedition had completed every foot of the way from the Yukon border. There had been no unethical support. The only cost of this was of course the fact that I had laid myself open to the accusation of egoism. This I could have scotched by flying out along with Jack and continuing from Fort Ware as though nothing had happened. But I had a fixation about cheating, a physical aversion to it that surfaced whenever I thought back to my successful duplicity on the SAS Long Drag.

The journey from Fox Lake to Fort Ware, where Ginnie was waiting with the inflatables, entailed a further forty-mile walk to the south along the well-used McCook family trail. The film-team and the injured Jocks declined my suggestion that they accompany me along the trail but Jack, despite his still swollen ankle, was determined to come.

In twenty-four hours we reached Fort Ware where the Tochika River flows into the more powerful Finlay River. The village consisted of a single line of low cabins close to the high river bank. The trek was over and, a day later, Bryn Campbell flew in on the weekly mail plane fresh from various camera assignments in Europe. He brought copies of Canadian newspapers with headlines reporting Jackie and me lost in the Rockies.

Ginnie was also on the float-plane. She was worried about the tensions in the team. 'Don't let things get worse,' she counselled.

I shrugged. 'There's little I can do. The film-crew seem determined there should be trouble. Let's not talk about them.'

We spent an hour together in an empty mosquito-free warehouse. It was the first anniversary of our wedding. She gave me the maps which she had waterproofed and marked with warning comments learned from Mounties and game wardens she had contacted. Not all the news was rosy. The Fraser was by all accounts infinitely rougher than the Nahanni and riven with whirlpools, sinkholes and twister-waves. Before we could reach the Fraser we must cross wide lakes jammed with logs and navigate rivers too shallow for outboards.

Ginnie's friend Sarah Salt had arrived with a borrowed Land Rover, so our road party was now in the hands of Salt and Pepper. Bryn called them the Condiment Convoy. Wally and the borrowed lorry had returned to Alberta.

The hum of the outboard and the slap of waves against our hull felt good. Stanley and Bryn were friendly and I began to forget the troubles. Not for long, however.

I noticed Ben puffing a chubby cheroot and I saw red. Stanley throttled back and I waved Ben down.

'Put that cigar out, will you? I have told everybody not to smoke in the boats. How can you expect the others, all smokers, to refrain when you do it?' The rock-faced policeman glared at me, his cigar clenched firmly between his lips. He wore a white stetson bearing the heavy silver badge of the North Yorkshire Constabulary. I addressed Richard, the nominal boss of the trio. 'If I see him smoking again he can shove off back to England on the next plane.' This plunged the atmosphere into new depths, for I had previously only defended myself against Richard's complaints. Now my voice had been raised on the offensive.

In retrospect I regret nothing nor, were I to select the men for that journey all over again, would I have chosen differently. Ben was highly efficient at the helm, and he enabled Richard and Paul to make films that were visually excellent. The three of them were good at their specific jobs and their presence, painful though it was to me personally during and after the journey, did not hinder our chances of eventual success. To select the perfect expeditionaire is nearly impossible. There is no foolproof selection process, and the longer, the more ambitious the endeavour, the more often each person's failings will rise to the surface. The most I hope for is to find at least one true companion on each journey. In Canada I was lucky. Jack became a loyal lifelong friend, a man I would ask again on any expedition and trust whatever the stresses.

At the end of the Finlay River, where once the un-navigable rapids of Deserters Canyon blasted south, we came up short against a jostling carpet of logs that blocked our way for three miles or more, caused by the world's largest earth-filled dam, 600 feet high and a mile and a half wide. The dam itself was hundreds of miles away but the waters of the Finlay were still backing up into its boundary forests and whole trees daily detached themselves from the lake floor, spearing to the surface like corks and adding to wind-driven log jams.

Another hazard, Ginnie had warned me, was the risk of mountain mud-slides, which caused tidal waves that swept across the lake without warning. We moved through loosely-packed logs but, after an hour, a wind caused the jam behind us to shift and the pack to contract. I signalled wildly to the others. Ben reacted with speed and skill and found a way to the half-submerged forest which boundered the jam. The C-craft also reached safety, but we were too far into the log maze and a sharp log, rising from below, struck the boat and ripped through two hull compartments below the waterline. Seconds later another unseen snag surfaced under the outboard and struck the propeller. The 200-pound engine leapt out of the water, straining violently at its transom hinges. Stanley swore as the engine cover struck his wrist.

Minutes later logs from both sides squeezed the hull concertina-like and began to ride above the punctured tubing. I used an oar for a lever but it snapped in half.

The hull rubber screeched in shrill protest as a web of branches crept over the tubes. We climbed out of the sinking boat on to the tree trunks and both hauled together at the safety lines on the undamaged side of the hull. A branch snapped and, with a sudden upsurge, the boat came free. Logs knit together beneath her like frustrated jaws. Remembering cinema films of loggers riding tree trunks through rapids, we set about dragging our stricken boat over the spinning, grinding jam, wishing we had spikes on our boots, for the wood was wet and well polished by ice action from previous winters. At length we found an open channel and, thankfully, slid the boat back into the lake. Stanley jammed wedge-shaped rubber plugs into the hull and we pumped in air before lowering and starting the outboard.

For hours we nosed through semi-submerged trees, a gloomy half-drowned forest through which our slalom course proceeded, bouncing off islands of matted vegetation. Gradually the log jam thinned and by mid-afternoon we emerged into clear water. The three crews, keeping a wary eye for floating debris, sped down the centre of the lake at twenty knots. A storm blew up by Finlay Forks, where the lake was five miles wide. High-crested waves responded to the wind and obscured our view of snags ahead. Soon we were soaked with spray and, sighting a deserted log cabin, we went ashore for the night.

Attempting to locate us further south, Ginnie and Sarah drove along a narrow track close to the lake. Finding a cabin soon after nightfall, they opened the door and shone a torch around inside. The beam alighted on an Indian sleeping naked on a rug. Ginnie yelped and awoke the Indian who, in drunken fury, gave chase without a stitch, followed by a clutch of yelping huskies. The girls fled back to their vehicle and never again knocked up lonely log cabins by night.

The lake narrowed by the logging and pulp boom town of Mackenzie, where we spent two days while Stanley repaired our boat. Then on to the mouth of the Pack River via a loose log jam that stretched five miles along the widened course of the old Parsnip River. The mouth of the Pack was elusive, hidden by many islands of poplar and stunted alder.

At first the Pack was a delight, not unlike the Thames in summer, but with cottonwood in lieu of weeping willow. Then, after an hour, we struck sub-surface rocks and, thereafter, mile after mile of shallows forced us to nudge upstream, questing at a snail's pace, and eventually to ship the outboards and wade ahead with tow-ropes. Often there were unseen sub-water shelves so that the lead-man on each boat would suddenly disappear up to his neck or hips after a stretch of shallows. For sixty miles we crept up the Pack until, with relief, we came to its source, McLeod Lake, famous for its rainbow trout, carp and Indian sapi.

Hidden at the south end of McLeod Lake, we found the mouth of the Crooked, our eighth river since leaving the Yukon border and the last before the mighty Fraser. This was a fast, shallow and confusing waterway which twisted and turned through myriad ox-bow lakes and split-side channels. For many days we bumped and pulled our way along and tempers frayed. One night Ginnie waited in a thickly-forested musky swamp beside the river. I had asked her on the radio to be there at dusk with spare propellers. Our schedule proved impossible to keep due to delays on the river, and Ginnie waited four hours in the dark. The batteries of her torch died and strange noises sounded all about her as the night hours advanced. Muskrats and beavers, raccoons and deer all came to the water and, finally, so did a black bear. The bear did not see Ginnie until they were near one another. Ginnie lost her nerve and screamed. The bear came closer and she pulled her .38 Smith and Wesson out of her anorak pocket. Somehow she pressed the trigger before the gun was clear and a bullet passed through the outside welt of her rubber boot – within a couple of millimetres of her foot.

The bear departed and so did a terrified Ginnie. Next time I met her she was furious. Why had I not made the rendezvous? Why did she have to wander through stinking woods and portage heavy gear? Nobody ever thanked or acknowledged her.

I did, I pointed out.

'No, you don't. You just use me. You couldn't care less what happens to me so long as I'm in the right place at the right time.'

There was no consoling her. Luckily, Sarah was a kind companion and, despite many difficulties along muddy tracks, changing wheels in deep mire and becoming hopelessly lost in a maze of unmapped forest tracks and fire breaks, they somehow always fetched up when needed and Ginnie was invariably on the radio listening whenever a key spare part was wanted in some remote swamp.

Sometimes the Crooked River was so shallow we could not even float the boats along on lines. In such places we dragged each craft over the rocks yard by yard, cursing the weight of the forty-horsepower engines we could seldom use.

As we dragged our boat up and over a beaver dam, Bryn missed his footing, the hull tilted and the propeller hit Stanley's head. His eyebrow was deeply gashed, blood streaming colourfully on to the engine and tubing. We patched him up and, at the very next bend, I spotted on the southern horizon the high bump of Teapot Mountain, northern marker of Summit Lake. We reached the lake by twilight – 2400 feet above sea level and the upper limit of the Arctic watershed. That night, as we camped beside the lake, a bear mounted the roofrack of our Land Rover and ate our rations.

From Summit Lake all water flows north into the Arctic Ocean but the Continental Divide falls east for eleven miles of rolling forest to the Fraser River, 200 feet lower than the lake. The Fraser water flows south into the Pacific.

A logging track led from the lakeside to the Fraser, a journey of eleven miles. Just one of our boats required four porters: our necks and shoulders became cramped because, with three of us over six feet tall, the boat's fourth corner – supported by little Stanley – was inclined to droop and bounce unevenly.

We launched the boats onto the Fraser River late on 20 September and within minutes swept over the Giscombe Rapids wearing black frogsuits and lifejackets.

From Giscombe, the river, lifeline but also grave to so many pioneers, flowed for 850 tempestuous miles to Vancouver and the sea. Simon Fraser and Sir Alexander Mackenzie used the river in their search for the West Coast and both treated it with respect, portaging their boats around the great canyons and fearsome rapids.

Between Prince George, British Columbia's most northerly city, and the Fraser-side town of Lytton the river drops 1200 feet, four times the height of Niagara Falls and, within the canyons, it rises up to eighty feet in spring: then the power of the whirlpools, boils and hydraulics is greater, but the danger of hidden rocks causing endless rapids and razor-sharp snares becomes less.

Seventy miles south of Prince George the river penetrates a deep trough valley, many hundreds of feet below the surface of the surrounding land mass. The river responds to the new resistance of the enclosing walls by seeking a sinuous route through a succession of nightmare canyons, livid with foam and mad with the roar of boiling water to the exclusion of all other sound.

The uncertainty of not knowing the state of the river ahead wore at our nerves, especially Jack's. Each day the cataracts grew more powerful and more frequent. In a small rubber boat even a twelve-foot wave can seem awesome. When they are legion and they explode from every side, some boiling up from beneath the hull, they can make any traveller edgy. In the back of my mind lay the fear that around the next corner, or the next, we would come without warning, without chance of extrication, to the impossible maelstrom or the bottomless whirlpool of some half-remembered nightmare.

The maps were not valid: they could not possibly be, for rapids change year by year with new rockfalls, and season by season with precipitation. My chart clearly showed a place called the

Iron Rapids. After seventy miles of recurrent rough water we reached the supposed position of these rapids and the place was relatively tranquil. Elsewhere we sped through long corridors and bottlenecks where the boats were hidden from each other in a welter of high dashing waves, yet the map would indicate calm water.

After careful research in London and Vancouver, Ginnie had discovered that only one expedition had ever travelled the Fraser from Prince George to the sea without portaging their craft, a five-man group of Vancouver river-runners using large inflatable rafts.

Ginnie and Sarah came close to the river when that was possible. On one occasion Ginnie, alone, drove up a logger's track on Pavilion Mountain with a rock cliff above and below. The steep track curved sharply upwards, its surface churned red mud. Carrying four 450-gallon fuel drums in her trailer and with her Land Rover heavily laden, Ginnie was slowed to a crawl by the mud. On an especially nasty bend the vehicle began to slide slowly backwards, its wheels spinning to no effect. Ginnie, frightened, could do nothing. As the trailer, jack-knifing, neared the cliff-edge, a logger drove his truck-cab into the Land Rover's rear bumper and saved the day.

The river moved with lithe power and we progressed at twenty-five knots through the canyons of the Caribou region. This called for vigilance and constant checking of my river-map. At Frenchman's Bar the rapids were clearly marked between cliff-bound narrows so we were taken by surprise when the boom of white water and churned-up spray was suddenly evident a mile or so short of the narrows.

There was little time to think. The standard drill is to locate the 'V', that dark smooth chute that cannons between the rocks of a cataract. However violent the crash of water against rock to either side of the 'V', the chute itself is safe enough until it drops into the turbulence below where the eye of the rapid is met. A 'V'-chute will lead a boat down to the roughest region of any rapid but via the only rock-free passage.

Standing up in the bows and craning my neck, I caught a glimpse of the 'V' and signalled Stanley to go right. There was no point in shouting since Stanley could hear nothing above the overall din. Nor could he see the rapids ahead over the lurching bows.

This unexpected cataract proved to be the fiercest yet. We entered it from the worst possible approach angle: too far left of the only rock-free route. Stanley hauled two-fisted on the tiller and the boat veered across the face of the rapid. We edged along broadside to its lip and fought the downstream suction in our effort to reach the 'V'. Too late to make it and sideways on to the current, I signalled desperately with my left hand. If we were to slam into rocks, it might as well be bows-on.

The boat spun round and at the same time dipped forward for the descent. Now, at close quarters, the foam and the fury raged below.

Our bows caught against a snag, the hull began to swing sideways, then mercifully the pliant rubber gave and we were falling down into the biggest hydraulic comber I had ever seen. We were under the wave but upright and dry. Then a great weight of water smashed on to us, forcing us down into the heart of the sub-rapid turbulence.

When we emerged, tossed up like a balsa cork, we were facing upstream. A fuel drum was missing but Stanley and Bryn were aboard and the outboard was ticking away.

Having seen our plight, the others made sure to correct their course before entering the fall. Looking back, we saw no other possible entry point either side of the 'V'.

At a lonely shack by the old Big Bar Ranch we beached the boats and I trudged up the canyon trail to search for the girls, who were overdue. I found a world of rolling sagebrush meadows dusted with the first fine layer of winter snow.

A farm truck took me to the main track at Jesmond Ranch where I waited five hours. At dusk the girls arrived, muddy and shivering with cold. They had been lost in a desert region by Gang Ranch, breaking down on a teetering bridge with rotten planking. They changed a wheel on a hairpin bend beside the canyon wall above Dog Creek and Sarah skidded into a deep flood-ditch. Ginnie, unhitching her heavy trailer, pulled the bogged vehicle free, but a dust-storm followed by a snowstorm further confused their navigation. Ginnie and I argued fiercely about camping arrangements for the team and she crouched in the bushes, crying and obviously exhausted. Filled with remorse, I tried to hold her but she shook me away.

That night the film-team and Joe were as sullen as monsoon storm-clouds. My attempts at a cheerful analysis of our progress around the campfire were met with silence and a cynical snort from Constable Ben. Jack played with his shoelaces in obvious embarrassment.

Part of the trouble was the team's awareness that the worst lay ahead. The constant cliff-hanging apprehension of the past weeks rendered nerves raw and tempers inflammable. The power of the Fraser had impressed us all. There was no doubt but that it had controlled us, not we the river. Our survival was largely a matter of luck and every new canyon had surpassed its predecessor in successive displays of unpredictable violence. Ahead lay the Moran Canyon, followed by a series of awkward major rapids.

For three days, based at the old gold town of Clinton in the Caribou, we tried to reconnoitre the Moran Canyon before embarking. Helicopters were way beyond our means, aircraft too fast to be helpful and no trails led to suitable vantage-points. At the southern end of the canyon we found an old ferry trail, but from the ferry beach we could only see, even with binoculars, a mile back upstream. The canyon walls were hundreds of feet high and even a view from their largely inaccessible rims would afford little scope for reconnaissance.

To glean knowledge from locals we visited the Pavilion Reservation's chief who said that, not being crazy, he had never been into the canyon nor would a thousand spirits drive him there. He took us to an ancient ex-chief who remembered a manned railway station, now derelict, that was once beside the canyon clifftops. All he added to the current chief's advice was that many Indians and whites had died over the years down in the canyon and we should avoid the place. There were whirlpools that stretched across the entire river and a metal steamboat had once been dashed to pieces there.

In Kelly Creek we visited the shack of Andy Moses who had spent fifty years beside the river. 'Never been into the canyon,' he said. 'Too many guys drowned in there. Anybody who tries to boat through it is jest plumb crazy.'

After three days in Clinton I feared the men's morale was beginning to plunge so, although I hated to enter the canyon unprepared and ignorant, I knew we must go before any further delay sapped our will.

We entered the canyon, a rushing, rolling alleyway squeezed between black walls 1000 feet high, wherein the current gained momentum mile by mile down to a curving gut no more than fifteen yards wide. The underplay of currents was impressive. Stanley would shake his head in disbelief as the boat shot sideways in total variance to the commands of tiller and propeller. Huge surface boils, bubbling like hot water in a saucepan, twice turned us about completely and thrust us chaff-like against the granite walls.

The hours and the miles passed by unnoticed. We came through three major cataracts and many stretches of clashing wave and whirlpool. Three times we found narrow beaches from which we reconnoitred especially evil water and, by nightfall, we stopped a mile above the great killer-rapid of the Bridge River confluence.

The Press were waiting in Lillooet town below the Bridge River Falls; they sensed drama. Ginnie's morale was low, not helped by hearing tales of others who had attempted the rapid. Four months earlier a muscular Frenchman had arrived in town. He had canoed every major rapid in North America, including the Lava sinkholes of the Colorado. Now he had come to tame the Bridge River Rapids. The Mounties retrieved his battered body from the whirlpools below the falls.

All of us rose early to preview the rapid and, in descending the rocky slope from the road to the river, I slipped and one foot landed on a jagged rock. The rubber sole of my gym shoe was slit and the heel of my foot gashed open. I limped down to the river leaving a bloody trail. Paul bound me up and I squeezed the cut foot into a black rubber frog-shoe.

Our first look at the cataract was off-putting, the boom of the water hypnotic. The Bridge River flows into the Fraser just below Fountain Ravine, itself a cauldron of foam, then jinks sharply south to fall at thirty-five knots over a ledge of serrated rock. The water here is chaotic, with spiralling waves rising high above the maelstrom, then falling back in explosions of spray. Great whirlpools whisk heavy logs into their maw and swallow them whole, while convoluting boils, over six feet high, rush sideways into dark caverns cut into the cliffs that rim both banks.

Stanley pointed at a log, some ninety feet long and four feet in diameter, which entered the rapid. After disappearing for two minutes, it was spewed up some hundreds of yards downstream of the confluence. A lifejacketed body, though equally buoyant, would be a smaller, easier morsel for the down-currents and would almost certainly remain below the surface longer.

We agreed upon a likely route, returned upstream to the boats, and then fought our way through the remaining rapids of the Fountain Ravine. Nerves were tattered. Jack and Joe had a bad time in the ravine and, spotting an especially rough stretch not far above the main cataract, refused to risk attempting it in the knowledge that a capsize there would lead to being swept into the turmoil below. I agreed that their boat should be lined through the rapids and then the two Jocks would continue in the boat of the film-team who were preparing to record the rapid-shooting from a cliff-top.

Stanley took us through the last section of the Fountain Rapids without a capsize and we beached three hundred yards above the Bridge River rapid. One hundred yards upstream of the troubles a rock ledge ran right across the river and sieved the water through shiny black teeth. Should a boat overturn here there would be no time to re-right it before the falls.

The sun was pleasantly warm. I felt drained of energy. The rubber suits were hot and clammy and my foot was oozing red over the rocks. I began to feel faint and lay in an eddy pool clinging to a rock as the water rose and fell in the backwash from the header currents. Gloriously cool water seeped into the frog suit, splashing over my face and helmet. I felt better. But I knew we must go *now*. The temptation to wait and continue to discuss alternative routes was strong. My stomach fluttered wildly. Stanley was deathly pale and sweating profusely. He nodded at me and ground out a cigarette on the rock. He climbed on to our boat as though it were a tumbrel.

Bryn and the film-team waved from a high boulder. They were ready. Joe, idling on the bank, gave us a thumbs-up. Jack was nowhere about.

Stanley whipped the engine to life. I pushed the boat off and sprang aboard. Plucked from the bank like a feather we plunged into the white water below the rock ledge. Twice the propeller crashed into submerged rocks and we scarcely dared breathe as the outboard burred unevenly, threatening to stall. If it did, there would be some twenty seconds in which to re-start it or to man the oars before we hit the main falls.

But the engine, perhaps remembering the Nahanni, the Liard, the Kechika and the Crooked, did not fail us. The rocks were behind and now a short stretch of smooth racing water, too powerful to fight, sucked us straight into the maw of the cataract. Our previous plans were immaterial.

A roar like the thunder of doom rushed at us as we shot downwards. For a while I could see nothing. Then a scene of total turmoil. We became like sodden shirts inside a high-powered washing machine. We entered by way of a broiling flume to be engulfed by a huge hydraulic, in the grip of which we corkscrewed deeper and deeper. There was nothing to see or to feel but solid water; we were awash within a cartwheeling tunnel.

The craft keeled over, forced up the side of the monster wave by centrifugal force. It was a wall of death on the horizontal plane and our hull clung to the inner side of the spinning liquid tube. Almost upside down within this whirling tunnel, I could see only a confused kaleidoscope of moving water.

At the lower end of the hydraulic tube's cyclic action, the boat was gripped by an undertow, dragged around and around, then spat out into a whirlpool. Our engine roared frantically as we swung around the sinkhole, and the cliffs of the river disappeared as we sank deep within the river's bowels. Then the sinkhole closed and thrust us towards the left-hand cliff. Stanley, water gushing from his helmet, tried to steer away from the rocks. He failed and we dashed against a boulder. The hull screamed in rubbery protest and crumpled along one side as the tube split open. But we were through.

We shook hands and felt on top of the world.

Landing where we could, we clambered up to the film-team's vantage point. Jack was silent. The culmination of weeks of fear had come to a head. He knew our boat had remained upright both in and under the falls through sheer good luck. In the temporary grip of unrabid hydrophobia, he decided not to risk this rapid.

'I'll go. Jack can use my camera.' It was Richard, his bushy beard thrust firmly out above his wetsuit. With Joe at the helm and Richard crouched in the bows, our second boat defied the Bridge River Rapids.

That evening the Lillooet doctor stitched up my injured heel and said we had been luckier than we deserved. He had seen three young men who had attempted to shoot the Bridge River cataract off to the Lillooet mortuary.

After repairing the boats we continued south to Lytton and Boston Bar. Here the river flows fast and furious through the Coastal Range to pound down a deep and gloomy gut called the Black Canyon. We fought through nameless rapids hidden from the world by the gorges they had forged. We plunged down the rearing hummocks of eighteen-foot waves at China Bar – a rapid which caught us by surprise with its giant breakers but which gave Jack back his nerve. By the time he saw what he was in for he was committed and he clung to the C-craft as it tossed and dived like a junk in a hurricane. The experience gave him confidence to face the Fraser's final monster rapid, Hell's Gate. The whirlpools beneath the gate had recently sucked down two thirty-foot inflatable boats, folding them in half the better to accommodate them. The Gate was caused by rockfalls from a rail-line which had been dynamited through the cliff-face and, in 1913, by landslides from both sides of the canyon. The river descends through the resulting bottleneck at up to fifty miles per hour. Water drained from an area of 84,000 square miles tears through a sheer-sided alley less than forty yards wide. Thirty-four million gallons pass the point every sixty seconds and the undercurrents are vicious, sucking flotsam down towards the river floor 175 feet below the surface.

We navigated the Gate with ease, a simple affair compared with the Bridge River rapids, but, a mile downstream, came to near-disaster in a vicious rapid about which no one had warned us. Further on at the narrows called Sailor's Bar we slithered through saw-tooth rocks where, a year before, a thirty-foot rubber raft had capsized and the helmsman drowned.

Autumn glowed about the river and burnished the cottonwood glades 1000 feet above us as we came to Lady Franklin Rock, a bare and solitary island. Then the last confining ramparts of the canyon fell away and our three boats moved on through a gentler land of grazing cattle and fruit farms.

Four days later the river split into three wide channels below New Westminster, once the capital but now a sprawling suburb of Vancouver. We passed through the beautiful city with its backdrop of snow-clad peaks and into the river delta. A sea mist covered the marshes so we navigated with care into the Pacific until a police launch met us with a bullhorn, 'This is it, folks. You're in Yank territory now.'

The two BBC films led their sixteen-million-strong British audience to believe that I was a cruel and incompetent publicity-seeker. The innuendoes which helped paint this picture certainly added spice and colour to the films, did surprisingly little to discourage my sponsors in the future and helped me in a small way to develop a tougher skin in readiness for future events which would lay me open to public scrutiny and criticism.

Jack and Stanley left the Army a year after the expedition and emigrated to Western Canada where they both married and now live. Jack started an office-cleaning firm called 'Jock's Janitors' in the far north where he fathered two boys, one of whom he named Ranulph. In the film Ben Usher summarised his experiences away from the Yorkshire Constabulary with the words, 'Although I can forgive, I will never forget'.

A year after we left Canada a great fire raged through the Rocky Trench and the Kingdom of Skook. All the old man's possessions were burned, even the medals of which he had been so proud, and he died soon afterwards. The Indian elements of fire and earth, air and water still hold sway, if not untrammelled, in the wilds of British Columbia and north to the Nahanni – 'somewhere over there and beyond'.

13

False Start

Nature cannot be ordered about except by obeying her.

FRANCIS BACON

I appreciated the comforts of home wonderfully for a week or so after our return. But my jaded senses soon began to forget how tasty home cooking, even fifty-seven varieties of Irish stew, can be compared to dehydrated rations. Bills had stacked up in our absence while royalties from my books had thinned to a trickle, so I started again the dreary rounds of lectures and weekends with the London SAS regiment, while beginning to write a book about Canada.

'You never *speak* to me,' Ginnie would complain. 'You never have time for a normal conversation. Either you are wrapped up in your book or you're away lecturing. At weekends, if you aren't playing soldiers with the SAS, you visit your mother. What about me?'

I found our in-house war a strain and my heart began to 'flutter' to an irregular beat. A London doctor told me to do nothing for a month and to avoid all strain. Ginnie meanwhile grew gaunt and developed a psychosomatic lump in her throat, making it difficult to swallow.

During a night-time lull in combat, Ginnie shook her head as we lay together. 'How,' she whispered, 'can we do this to each other? We are destroying our love bit by bit.' Neither of us could produce a rational explanation.

The best time to end a long-running period of hostility and silence was first thing in the morning by making breakfast and bringing it to Ginnie on a tray. After finishing the cereal and toast, I would reach for her hand and peace would often return, providing no reference was made to the recent blaze – for even an apology could metamorphose in seconds into recrimination and a renewed war footing.

Six months into our marriage Ginnie had told me she wanted a baby, my baby, above all things in the world. As gently as I knew how, I had explained that it would be better to wait two or three years until we were in a stronger position financially and fought less. This merely provided a new point of friction between us.

Some three months after returning to Sussex, Ginnie was stirring the stew when she came up with a weird suggestion. 'Why don't we go around the world?' She had mooted the idea once before, during a brief Highland holiday, and I had ignored it as impractical. She envisaged a perpendicular route – through the Poles – which was, I knew, neither physically nor administratively possible.

My mother sometimes drove over from Lodsworth, only four miles away, to give us vegetables or apples from her garden and to share a cup of tea. On one occasion she arrived without warning and Ginnie blew a gasket. It was the age-old and understandable mother-in-law syndrome at work and I was too insensitive to understand Ginnie's reaction. She urged that we move to London and out of reach of our respective mothers. We drove the butcher's van to town and purchased a dark and dingy basement flat in Templeton Place, immediately behind Earls Court Station, which proved to be a place of evil smells and constant noise.

Two days before we left Bepton, with the carpets rolled up and the china half-packed in crates, we fought bitterly over the wisdom of starting a family. Ginnie wrenched at my hair and I smashed a walnut table into small pieces. When our anger subsided, Ginnie wept and decided to leave me. Anything must be better than this. She packed and drove north to friends in Torridon. I gave our cat Slioch to my mother and completed the move to London alone.

By the time Ginnie phoned me a month later, I was desperate for her return. I begged her to come back and, two days later, we took counselling from a Cowley Father friend, Bill Slade, whose religion was a mixture of Christian and Buddhist ethics. Our fights continued in much the same format as before, but the high-tensile fury was no longer present and post-battle hostilities simmered for hours rather than days.

Once my Canadian book was finished, George Greenfield obtained a contract for the story of my Dhofar experiences and Ginnie agreed to handle the research in the relevant London libraries. She purchased a scooter from Sarah Salt and was away from the flat most days.

The summer of 1972 was hot and fetid. The dustbins of all five flats above us were stored in the stairwell outside our front door. The smell was foul and bluebottles, fat and drowsy, thronged in response. We dug out the tangled heap of bric-à-brac from the twelve-square-yard sunken space at the rear of the flat, and Ginnie planted geraniums, busy-lizzies and fuchsia in moss-baskets.

Within three months Ginnie had transformed the flat inside and out, but I had grown to hate the place and my book hardly progressed at all. Since we shared flat or garden wall-space with no less than seven neighbours, there was a good deal of scope for argument. Although Earls Court was known in those days as Kangarooville because of its large population of transient Australians, my neighbours came from a variety of backgrounds.

The sunken brick-walled square that we called our garden bloomed with fuchsia and geraniums, with a jasmine climbing over a white trellis frame in the corner. My hopes for a nook of countrified tranquillity foundered along with the discovery of seven used condoms, numerous fag-ends and half a toupé in our flowerbeds.

Wild, unmelodious strains of sexual ecstasy and screams of aggression from the Templeton Place felines kept us awake most nights. We counted nineteen cats, without including the burgeoning kitten population being spawned non-stop at rooftop level.

Sad old ladies fed the cats in the warren of back streets behind Earls Court. They carried tired canvas bags which stank of mackerel and talked to themselves when not chatting to their foster-cats. The queen cat-woman lived in a second floor flat in Spear Mews at right-angles to our street. She owned no garden but climbed down a ladder daily from her back window to a fenced-off patch just beyond our sunken garden.

At 7.00 a.m. punctually the Irish cat-woman's bottom would appear in her window, a billowing Rubens posterior clad in pink Damart combis: a very close fit through the window frame. She would then descend ponderously, with an offal dish in one hand, into the seething feline mass from which issued a single voracious miaow.

I contacted the RSPCA and joined a three-month waiting list for an official cat-trap. When it came I was required to sign a number of forms, one of which was returned to me a week later when I told them that persons unknown (probably Damart-bottom) had smashed the trap. The small-print which I had stupidly ignored held me liable to pay for damage to my loaned trap. The net result was a £12 cheque to the RSPCA and no improvement to our situation. Desperate, I purchased a catapult and steel ball bearings.

The Rumanian Embassy officials' crèche two gardens away held Kindergarten lessons. There were two dozen youngsters and their favourite game at play-time (much of the morning) was Al Capone. The elder children were gangsters who, armed with machine guns (branches torn from the only holly tree not ravaged by previous Capone generations), mowed down their opponents – the younger children. These latter were made to bury each other neck-high in a spacious sandpit. The bodies were then exhumed so that the whole process could recur – which it did, indefinitely. The rat-a-tat-tat imitation machine-gun noise of the Capones, the screams of the dying and the groans of the buried drove me to near distraction and one morning I decided to kill two birds with one stone. When the Irish cat-woman was singing in her kitchen with the window open and a Rumanian mass burial service was in full swing, I put a ball-bearing smack through her kitchen window. Immensely satisfying. Her Celtic temper was majestic, her vocabulary amazing and her lungs as impressive as her bum. The Rumanians fled, but for the buried ones, and for a month my morning writing was comparatively undisturbed.

One late-summer morning Ginnie gently woke me and pointed at two cats curled up on my desktop. I leapt out of bed in fury. A wild struggle ensued among Ginnie's geraniums. One cat escaped over the wall, but as I was about to carry the other inside and phone the RSPCA, I heard cheering. Looking up I saw a sea of faces and waving arms protruding from upstairs windows. When I noticed with horror that I was still quite naked, my hands shot down to cover myself, and I dropped the hissing cat in the process. 'That is it,' I told Ginnie, as she swabbed my scratched arms and chest. 'I will not put up with this place a minute longer.' My pride was badly dented, the more so when I noticed a broad grin on Ginnie's face.

I phoned two estate agents and put the flat on the market. In the evenings we took the butcher's van around neighbouring Hammersmith in search of a less colourful area.

I continued work on my Arab book in the autumn, but found that I needed information from two specific Dhofari ex-Communists, now fighting for the Sultan's Forces against their former colleagues. I therefore seized the chance to go to Dhofar when ITN boss Don Horobin asked me to take one of his film-teams to Oman for an interview with Sultan Qaboos, who had bloodlessly ousted his father. When the new Sultan approved the appointment, I received a crash course in TV news reportage from Peter Snow, the ITN newscaster, and others.

We spent two months in Oman, where Ginnie worked with the Save the Children Fund in various villages. My ITN film-crew consisted of two fine young technicians, each with a wealth of front-line experience from Belfast.

In Dhofar we visited the Sultan's armed encampment of Simba, overlooking the South Yemeni border and the *adoo* infiltration routes. Mortar bombs slammed about our temporary fox-hole and the film-crew revelled in the action. My interview with His Majesty Sultan Qaboos went well, as did our reports of the country's great new plans for fish canning factories and a current purchase contract for a fleet of Short's Skyvan aircraft. For our coverage of the Special Air Service at work training ex-Communist *firqat* bands in the Jebel, we filmed a British officer of the Sultan's Army leading a fearsome band of *firqat* warriers charging downhill, with automatics and machine-guns blazing.

*   *   *

Back in England for Christmas 1972, we began to research the possibility of a journey around the world's polar axis via the North and South Poles. Ginnie had suggested the scheme some months before but, believing it would be impossible, I had ignored her.

Now, with no other projects to hand, we visited the Royal Geographical Society map vaults and – grudgingly – I began to accept that her idea might after all be feasible.

Ginnie started full-time library research into the feasibility of the endeavour whilst I began the long search for suitable volunteer participants. To cross the Arctic and the Antarctic we would need a small team of exceptionally able navigators, radio operators and mechanics with reasonable medical know-how. I decided to look for people who were good-natured, patient and fit, then have the Territorial Army train them, free of charge, in the necessary skills.

I intended to select a team of 3 men from more than 100 volunteers put through ten tortuous training weekends for the Welsh 3000 Race each year over a five-year period. This race took place in Snowdonia every June between two dozen Regular and Territorial Army regiments, each represented by a team of their fittest men. The course began on Snowdon's summit and runners followed a tortuous twenty-four mile route between and over the peaks of thirteen mountains over 3000 feet high while wearing Army equipment and carrying a Sten gun.

The SAS regiment was happy enough with the arrangement, providing that our team captured the coveted Welsh 3000 annual Territorial Army trophy. In 1973 we came within a hair's breadth, two minutes after twenty-four miles, of winning the overall Army Challenge Cup from the invincible Gurkhas. By the end of 1973 I had a superbly fit team, but not one of them had a personality remotely suitable for the circumpolar journey.

We moved to a semi-detached house in Barnes, a long stone's throw from Hammersmith Bridge. By the summer my Arab book was complete, though still lacking the details about the two Communists. Another chance came my way to go to Dhofar, so I gained the permission of Sultan Qaboos and his personal confidante, my old friend Tom Greening, to interview the relevant ex-*adoo* wherever I should find them in Dhofar. I was to travel to Brunei for a jungle training course with a squadron of the Regular (22nd) SAS Regiment, the very same course that I had missed owing to my arrest by the police in Castle Combe some seven years earlier. I planned to drop off in Dhofar on the way back.

Ginnie, who had featured in a *Woman's Own* article about female explorers, was asked by the magazine to write about life in an Omani harem. As I drew my jungle kit from the stores at the Hereford HQ with five other SAS Territorials, Ginnie phoned from Baghdad in Iraq, *en route* to Muscat by a cheap charter flight, to say her passport had been removed by the police. By bad luck, Iraqi forces had that very morning joined the Arab–Israeli War and a retaliatory air raid was anticipated in Baghdad at any moment. 'Make sure you get a ground-floor room and, if the bombing starts, get under a stout table,' I advised Ginnie somewhat lamely.

Luckily the Israeli bombers' range proved to be just short of Baghdad, but the Iraqi police locked Ginnie into her hotel room and only freed her two days later. The British Embassy had been gutted a month previously, and when she tracked down the burned-out British consul in a backroom at the Swedish Embassy he was unable to do more than loan her his car and a handsome Iraqi chauffeur. Back at the airport police office, Ginnie waited five hours until the duty officer left his office to relieve himself; then she removed her passport from his desk and caught a bus to Basra. A friendly truck driver secreted her in a load of rubble and drove her past the Iraqi guards on the Kuwaiti border. Reaching the rubble dump, he pointed to a group of houses away over the desert. 'Kuwait,' he said. She tipped him with her last Iraqi coins and, in Kuwait, borrowed enough funds from the British consul to buy an air ticket to Muscat. Five days late, she arrived at the house of Hillal bin Nabhan, Sheikh of Ullyah, under the Green Mountain.

Meanwhile, an RAF Hercules flew our SAS contingent to Brunei, with an eight-hour stop on Gan Island in the Maldives, where I fell asleep sunbathing on a pleasant beach. When I awoke, six hours later, I was lobster-red and tender as under-cooked lamb; by the time we landed in Brunei, my stomach and hips were rubbed raw where the burned skin had chafed against my trousers. The squadron quartermaster sergeant, Wally Poxon, was totally unsympathetic.

Each man packed three weeks of SAS rations into a Bergen backpack, coated his SLR rifle with animal fat against rain and rust, and embarked in sticks of six by helicopter to a jungle training camp. Each of the five Territorial soldiers was attached to a four-man squad of regular SAS men accompanied by a veteran jungle NCO. For a week I really struggled to do what was asked of me. The Bergen straps were painful against my stomach sores, but I took a course of penicillin tablets and the raw places gradually healed over.

The regimental sergeant-major in charge of training, a big Geordie, remembered me from my 1966 misdemeanours. He laid booby traps all over the place to teach jungle students where not to tread.

At first the training centred on a single camp site, where each squad constructed a defensive area. We went daily into the surrounding forest where our NCO, Sergeant Trevor Henry, a highly capable Scot, taught us the rudiments of jungle tradecraft. We learned how to hang a hammock and mosquito net between trees under a camouflaged ground-sheet, out of reach of the ever-present creepy-crawly population, whiplash scorpions, poisonous millipedes, spiders and snakes. Also above the ochre mud of the jungle soil, everywhere sodden twice a day by the monsoon rain. We learned how to spot movement sources and to kill before being killed in close foliage. There were forced marches through dense undergrowth along zig-zag ridges following game trails.

The highest hill in the region, Bakat Latut, became familiar territory. The routes to its summit were long, hot and guarded by hornbills and long-tailed monkeys, which laughed at us from the high forest canopy. Whenever we moved through foliage, a few stinging ants would brush off on to our clothes. Every few minutes, the lead scout of our group would raise his hand, halt and kneel, listening intently. Each man faced left or right as predesignated, and the tail man faced rear. Before selecting a night campsite, the squad's route would describe a wide circle which ended back at a spot from which we could overlook our earlier tracks.

The toughest soldier in my assigned squad went down with *dhengi* fever after a fortnight, probably through drinking tainted stream water. He was removed and I did not see him again. The patrol medic, Roger Coles, was bitten on the neck by a large black and yellow spider as we were demolishing a clearing in the jungle big enough to allow helicopter access for emergency evacuation. The area where it bit him rose in a spongy black lump. The patrol leader, Captain Simon Garthwaite, slipped on a wet rock while descending a steep watercourse and cracked the back of his skull. We patched up his bleeding scalp and he kept going.

I was beginning to feel quite pleased with myself. I had recovered from my initial sunburn and the jungle had lost some of its hostility. The fourth member of our squad, a tough Irish radio operator, saw that I was growing cocky as the others fell by the wayside. 'We've a lot to learn yet, y'know,' he said as he applied a lit cigarette to leeches sucking blood from his ankles, 'before we're jungle-wise.'

The next day, trying a shortcut along the side of a ravine, I slipped and fell down a muddy slope. Trailing lines of barbed *attap* thorn arrested my slithering descent and I came to a standstill caught up by the lobe of one ear. Gingerly, I cut the thorny strand with a penknife, but half the lobe was torn away from the ear itself and bleeding freely. Roger Coles pumped me full of penicillin and patched the damaged ear-lobe with suture band-aids when I refused his offer of needle and cotton.

When our squad returned to the main camp-site we celebrated at a local *kampong* tea-house. Alcohol was forbidden by the government, but beer and whisky were served from a china teapot into delicate teacups.

A year later Simon Garthwaite was shot dead by *adoo* in Dhofar.

The RAF dropped me in Singapore, where my old Dhofar CO, Colonel Peter Thwaites, persuaded the RAF to allow me a passage to their base at Salalah on another Hercules. Despite the written permission of HM Sultan Qaboos, the SAS CO in Dhofar and the Sultan's intelligence officer, Ray Nightingale, prevented me from entering the Jebel. I returned to London empty-handed and cursing the gentlemen of 22nd SAS Regiment.

Fortune smiled on me a week later when I got back to the 21st SAS Regiment. Angus MacLean, the new regimental sergeant-major on secondment from 22nd SAS Regiment, was a Dhofar veteran. So too was Billy Condy, the adjutant. Both of them knew the men I was looking for personally. 'You were wasting your time in Salalah,' Bill told me. 'They are both learning English in Bristol.' I soon met both ex-*adoo* and, with translation help from Angus MacLean, filled in the gaps for my Arab book. Both Dhofaris were subsequently killed back in the Jebel.

Ginnie returned from two months in Oman with yellow henna staining her hands, a brilliant orange dye on her fingernails and a varied collection of Arabian scorpions now on display in the British Museum, Natural History Department (Arachnida section). She had grown fond of Sheikh Hillal's second wife Rayah and her children, with whom she had lodged, and could not comply with *Woman's Own*'s wish to sensationalise her story by stressing their backwardness and quaintness. This was a blow to our finances. However, potential polar sponsors found her harem stories romantic, which made them more receptive to our requests.

We agreed early in 1973 to set up an office in London for our venture, which we christened the Transglobe Expedition.

For the next seven years we were to work non-stop and unpaid to launch the endeavour, during which we often despaired of eventual success. Luck and hard work saw us through. At weekends and on free evenings we lectured in civic centres, borstals, ladies' luncheon clubs and men's associations. We attacked the problem with total dedication and a determination that every item of equipment, every last shoelace and drawing pin, must be sponsored. We opened no bank account and possessed no chequebook, so there was no danger of the expedition overspending.

In the beginning, I approached my 21st SAS Regiment CO, Colonel Paul Wilson, to see whether the SAS group of regiments (the Regulars at Hereford and the two Territorial units) would sponsor the expedition. The director of SAS, a brigadier, at first refused to consider the idea because of my involvement with the Castle Combe raid. 'This expedition,' the brigadier expostulated, 'is unbelievably complex and ambitious. That Fiennes is not a responsible person. I can tell you straightaway that the SAS will not attach their good name to a plan such as this under a fellow like Fiennes.'

We were disappointed to hear the CO's account of his meeting but, a week later, he summoned us to his office. The brigadier had consulted the veteran SAS major, Dare Newall and others, and had evolved a workable solution. Brigadier Mike Wingate-Gray would make an excellent overall commander of the Transglobe Expedition, the SAS director advised me, and if I accepted his loose supervision, then the SAS group would nominally sponsor the whole venture and provide us with office space in the Duke of York's barracks just off the King's Road, Chelsea. We were in business. Over the next two years, our new office, a high attic which had earlier served as a .22 rifle range, filled with sponsored equipment, and its walls became papered with maps showing the more remote stretches of our proposed 110,000-mile journey. The expedition principle was that at least some members of our team must travel over the entire surface of the world via both Poles without flying one yard of the way.

Early in 1975, Ginnie, who was to be chief radio operator and mobile base leader, joined the Women's Royal Army Corps to learn about radios, antenna theory and speedy Morse operation. Oliver Shepard applied to join us. I remembered him vaguely from Eton and had decided he was definitely not Transglobe material. But he joined the Welsh training weekends and proved to be more determined than he looked. He resigned his job and slept on a floor in the barracks, breakfasting on expedition rations and working evenings in a nearby pub, the Admiral Codrington. Oliver introduced me to an out-of-work friend named Charlie Burton, who had spent four years in an infantry regiment. His rugged face bore a pattern of rugby and boxing scars. Charlie passed the Territorial SAS selection course and joined our Welsh mountain training sessions. So, too, did Geoff Newman, who gave up his career with a printing firm. Finally, a part-time secretary, Mary Gibbs, joined us as nurse and generator mechanic.

The six of us seemed to work well together, despite the strain of the tiny office and single telephone. By the autumn of 1975 we were sponsored by over 800 companies.

Andrew Croft, an Arctic explorer of note, advised me: 'Three men is a good number if you all get on. Two men is relatively suicidal. Four men can create cliques of two. *In extremis*, with three men, two can gang up against the leader. My advice is that you should decide whether to have two or three companions only after you have seen your potential colleagues in action in the Arctic.'

The expedition we were to attempt involved crossing Europe and the Sahara, descending the Atlantic to its ice-bound extreme, crossing the Antarctic continent via the South Pole, ascending the Pacific from the southern ice to the Arctic, boating over 1000 miles of the Yukon and Mackenzie rivers, traversing the Northwest Passage and 500 miles of icebound archipelago to the north, skiing 300 miles over Ellesmere Island's ice-caps and crossing the Arctic Ocean via the North Pole. It was important to choose compatible colleagues. I did not seek out old friends because the three-year duration of such an expedition would be bound to cause friction between its members. I was certain any existing friendship would be destroyed or at best soured.

From the moment Ginnie and I started our joint struggle to launch Transglobe, we began to grow together. Our continued dedication to the venture survived even our total lack of know-how in all polar matters, the assurance of experts that our plans were impossibly ambitious and the long will-sapping years of negative response, lack of funds and stonewalling refusals from various government bodies, including key offices such as the US National Science Foundation and the Foreign Office Polar Desk in Great Britain.

For four or five years the British Antarctic Survey and the Royal Geographical Survey (without whose blessing it would have been impossible – short of being a millionaire – to enter Antarctica) genuinely believed the projected journey to be hopelessly ambitious and probably impossible, as I had done originally. Our prospects were summed up by one of Britain's polar godfathers, Sir Miles Clifford, an ex-director of the Falkland Islands Dependencies Survey. 'You are saying, Fiennes, that you will, in the course of a single journey, complete the greatest journeys of Scott, Amundsen, Nansen Peary, Franklin and many others. You must understand that this sounds a touch presumptuous, if not indeed far-fetched.'

If we had read about the journeys of the polar pioneers at the outset, Ginnie and I probably would not have hitched our star to Transglobe. To us, the Arctic and the Antarctic were simply white spaces on the six-inch tin globe from which our first route plan was drawn. We chose to follow the Greenwich Meridian around the world's axis. We would start at Greenwich and head south to Antarctica. Then up the other side of the planet, over the North Pole and back to Greenwich. A simple plan on the face of it: by the time I started to read detailed accounts of previous polar journeys and to appreciate the unique difficulties inherent in life and movement at either Pole, we had already mortgaged a year or two in getting under way.

Sir Vivian Fuchs advised me that we could not hope to achieve Transglobe without polar training, so I began to plan two separate trial journeys. The first, to the Greenland ice-cap in 1976, would train us for similar terrain in Antarctica. Next, in 1977, we would try to reach the North Pole itself. Throughout 1975 and 1976 the six of us raised funds and equipment and received specialist training in Britain in readiness for our two trial trips.

The new CO of the 21st SAS Regiment, Colonel Richard Lea, expected us to put in training time with our squadrons commensurate with the considerable support the expedition was receiving from the Territorial Army. So Oliver, Charlie, Geoff and I joined the annual two-week SAS camp in Scotland in September 1975. Each twelve-man troop began the exercise with a night parachute drop on the moors about Carrbridge in the Cairngorms. Then for nine days each troop made its silent way, unobserved by locals, to a set military target.

My specified goal was RAF Lossiemouth and the target penetration was to take place over a set forty-eight-hour period. The garrison commandant had been alerted to expect us, and saturated his entire five-mile perimeter fence and his Phantom bombers' hangars with over 400 guards. All camp personnel had their leave restricted for the weekend and were drilled to trust nothing that moved, including each other.

I was arrested by a keen-eyed guard about eighty yards from the floodlit hangar. Under interrogation, I signed a form with the signature Elizabeth Regina and answered erroneously all questions asked of me, including my number, rank and name. Wrong. Resistance-to-interrogation rules demand that SAS men sign nothing under interrogation and say nothing save their number, rank and name, which should be given accurately. The reason I had erred was purely because I had never completed 'continuation' for the 21st SAS Regiment and it was nine long years since my 22nd SAS Regiment 'continuation'. All I could remember was not to yield any accurate information.

A mild admonishment might have closed the matter but for the intervention of my training major who disliked me intensely. Twice before, by tagging on to the rear of my squad, he had done his utmost to expose me as incompetent, once on a night attack on a Southampton arms depot and more recently on the approach march to Lossiemouth. The major, whom I shall call only by his nickname of Patsy, was a professional hardman with an invisible sense of humour. He fought with cunning and distinction in Dhofar, was awarded medals by the Queen and commanded the SAS raid on the Iranian Embassy. Militarily perfect, he was nonetheless the bane of my existence. I could not work out precisely why he loathed my guts and indeed those of Nick Forde, another captain in my squadron, but by blatantly, if unwittingly, disobeying resistance-to-interrogation rules I had laid myself open to his venom.

Nick Forde let himself down at the same time during his troop's attempt to kidnap Sir Fitzroy MacLean from his castle in West Scotland where, throughout the specified weekend, the laird was guarded by a group of Regular SAS men. One of these guards slammed Nick Forde on the bridge of his nose with a revolver butt and later gave a poor report on the whole failed kidnap attempt. Nick was dealt with separately but Patsy told our CO that I could realistically be removed from the regiment.

I was placed on Commanding Officer's Orders and marched in to the CO's office. Colonel Lea was above all a fair man and, after listening to my defence, decided not to throw me out of the regiment, but rather to enrol me on an imminent resistance-to-interrogation weekend organised by the 21st SAS Regiment and the RAF Regiment. After spending ten hours naked, blindfolded, wet and cold, being dragged alternately through nettles and dog messes, and long spells of physical jerks of a less than comfortable nature, I was rehabilitated. My SAS file recorded that I had 'a bad camp' but was otherwise mediocre. 'He is physically and mentally very tough and has a great deal of drive and initiative. He gained a good report from jungle training in Malaya but his personal commitments make his attendance erratic. Otherwise he would be a natural choice as a squadron leader.'

I loved the SAS training which was a breath of fresh air from the interminable hours in our dingy office and be-suited talks with sponsor representatives. The majority of SAS-men I met over the years were friendly characters and for the most part softly spoken, intelligent people who would not have hurt a fly unless it was necessary in the course of their work. But Patsy is not a man I remember with affection and I was delighted when he left the 21st SAS Regiment. I suspect the CO was equally relieved.

Shortly after the Scottish camp, Ginnie went to St Theresa's Gynaecological Hospital for an operation which was supposed to help with the child she had wanted for two years. Six hours after returning home, though still in pain, she spent two days and nights preparing a beautifully typed, twenty-five page logistics plan with various complex annexes for the Ministry of Defence. Her work gained us permission for our first polar training, and after four years in our barracks office, the RAF flew us to Greenland in July 1976 with 30,000 pounds of equipment.

We landed at a US Forces airbase in the northwest of the great ice-bound island. Local Americans denied that its nickname – BMEWS – stood for 'ballistic missile early warning system' but said it was christened by the first 'poor sods' to man the site as 'barmy men existing without sex'. Along with two similar sites, one at Fylingdales, Yorkshire, and the other at Clear in Alaska, this base formed part of a radar screen across the top of the world. Hills of grey gravel enfolded the base and we could see the rim of the ice-cap which covers all of Greenland save for the lower rock-girt fringes of the island about eight miles inland, a hazy pink in the evening sun.

One of the few original Thule Eskimos who had not been moved north to the remote settlement of Qanaq when the airbase was built in 1950, a local lady who remained on Dundas peninsula a mile or two from the radar site, took our measurements and made us a set of fur parkas, which fitted us to perfection, from twenty-four timber wolf skins. The redoubtable polar traveller Wally Herbert had advised me that fur parkas are unbeatable for Arctic winter travel.

Wally also recommended that the ice-covered parts of our journey would best be attempted by machines rather than by dog teams. He had once written that 'the partnership of man and dogs is the safest form of surface travel in the Arctic Ocean when beyond the range of light aircraft . . .' But because he also stressed the need for everyone to have a year or two of intensive dog-handling training, we looked instead at the only alternative means of travel – by ski or by snow machine.

At Thule we found that our sponsored snowcats (which we called Groundhogs), fitted with home-made buoyancy bags, would float, swim and steer reasonably well between the cruising islands of pack-ice. We spent our first night out as a team at an abandoned camp called Tutto by the edge of the ice-cap, a miserable, shivering, sleepless experience. Altogether, we intended to travel for 250 miles over the ice-cap and then 100 miles into the interior, passing through known crevasse fields. Each Groundhog towed two 1000-pound sledge-loads separated by long safety lines.

During the first week a two-day blizzard kept us tent-bound and we learned simple lessons which would have been second nature to seasoned polar travellers: which way not to position the tent's entrance hole; how not to leave anything anywhere except on a Groundhog or inside the tent; how to string the radio's antenna wires to ski sticks rather than laying them along the snow surface where, after a blow, they become hard to dig out without damage.

Due to disorganised lavatory arrangements, uncoordinated with the collecting of snow for melting into drinking water, we ended up with unwelcome foreign bodies in the tea so we instituted a rule that the loo was to the left and 'drinking' snow to the right of the tent door.

The Groundhogs, which started easily at temperatures down to −10°C, thereafter revolted and failed to respond to the electric circuit or the manual crank. Oliver poured the two Thermos flasks of hot chocolate prepared for the day's travel over the Groundhog starter motors, and both engines roared into life. Over the next month these machines caused non-stop trouble. Brittle cracks and splits led back from Oliver's fingernails as a result of his long hours wrestling with the engines and the sprocket wheel system. The vehicle manuals were all in German, which did not help.

I learned that neither my jungle nor my desert experience helped me much as ice-cap navigator, for the cold made my hand compass frustratingly slow to settle, while all manner of new problems cropped up to confuse and hinder accurate use of the theodolite. My first computed result in Greenland, following altitude shots of the sun at noon, was wrong by some sixty-two nautical miles.

As our Groundhogs twisted their way through narrow valleys beneath the coastal mountains of Harald Moltke and Pitugfik, I used obvious features such as the rock hillock called Freuchen Nunatak for compass backbearings. Later, we climbed on to the inner ice-fields of the Hayes Peninsula, passing between heavily crevassed slopes above the Savigsuaq Glacier. Blizzards pinned us down, inclines overturned the heavy sledges, throttles jammed, carburettors blocked, fuel lines leaked, a gearbox gasket blew and sprocket tyres shot off – landing up to sixty feet away.

Finally, within four miles of our set goal, a high point due north of Norujupaluk Island, we ran into serious trouble. On the final approach I decided to travel by night while good weather lasted: a bad mistake. Both Groundhogs plunged into crevasses and we spent three precarious days tunnelling down to and under the stricken machines to retrieve them with pulleys and aluminium ramps.

By the time we emerged from the upper ice-fields through dense mist, we were working well together. Oliver's mechanical procedures were slick and we could strike or break camp in under an hour – compared with six hours a month before. Although no polar veterans, we had mastered deep snow ice-cap travel in temperatures of −20°C. The next step, a different game in every sense, was apprenticeship to Arctic Ocean travel in temperatures of −40°C.

I arrived back in London weighing thirteen stone. Over the next three months I lost sixteen pounds without dieting or exercise and grew my first grey hairs, as every possible political hurdle that might hinder our Arctic Ocean plans was raised by the authorities. With limitless funds, we could have bought our way around most obstacles but we were, in Oliver's words, 'skint as squirrels'. One day we had to call a meeting just to work out a plan for raising £100 to send Oliver to Austria on a snow-machine engine course. We finally agreed to buy six premium bonds at £1 each. Oliver did not have £1 so he borrowed from Charlie.

In desperation I explained our immediate requirement – £60,000 to charter a ski-plane for re-supply flights over the Arctic Ocean – to Tom Greening, my old friend from Dhofar. He introduced me to Doctor Omar Zawawi, a wealthy international Omani businessman, who kindly agreed, in conjunction with colleagues of his at Tarmac International, to sponsor all our charter-plane costs.

In early February 1977, a chartered DC6 flew the six of us into the polar darkness, heavily laden with all our gear from Thule (except the Groundhogs) plus new specialist equipment from London.

Alert Camp, the world's most northerly settlement, is supplied only by air since there are no roads for hundreds of miles and all sea access is permanently frozen over. Sixty Canadian soldiers and scientists manned the base, none of whom stayed for more than six months at a time lest they become 'bushed'. They spent most of their time in their heated offices or mess-hall because the outside weather, except for a short two-month 'summer', is hostile in the extreme. On the day of our arrival the temperature was −48°C and the night was pitch black. There would be no sign of the sun for a month.

Our own camp, a deserted huddle of four wooden shacks, was perched along the very shore of the frozen sea some two miles north of the army camp. Between our huts and the North Pole lay nothing but miles of jumbled ice and smoking seams of open sea; 425 nautical miles in all. To stand a chance of reaching the North Pole an expedition must set out on or close to 3 March, the day the sun reappears at the latitude of Alert.

Of our first night at Alert, Oliver wrote: 'The huts are deplorable. Two are just habitable, the remainder full of ice. No heater and so, so cold. I slept wearing ten layers of clothing. It is impossible to get warm.' The next morning, we awoke to find the daylight hours as dark as night. Torches with new batteries went dead after six minutes' use outside the huts. Flesh glued itself to metal and, if you tore your hand away, the skin remained behind. Ginnie went outside to our makeshift lavatory, and knocking the wooden seat aside by mistake, made contact with one side of the steel-rimmed bucket. She received a painful cold-burn down one cheek of her bottom and rushed into our hut to warm up against the oil-fired stove. She stood too close and singed her other cheek with a hot-burn. This must have been some sort of a record.

With only two weeks to our departure date, we worked around the clock, making frequent visits to the kitchen shack for flasks of hot tea. We could manage about an hour outside in a stiff breeze before retreating to thaw out. When a thirty-knot wind was blowing, twenty minutes was the limit.

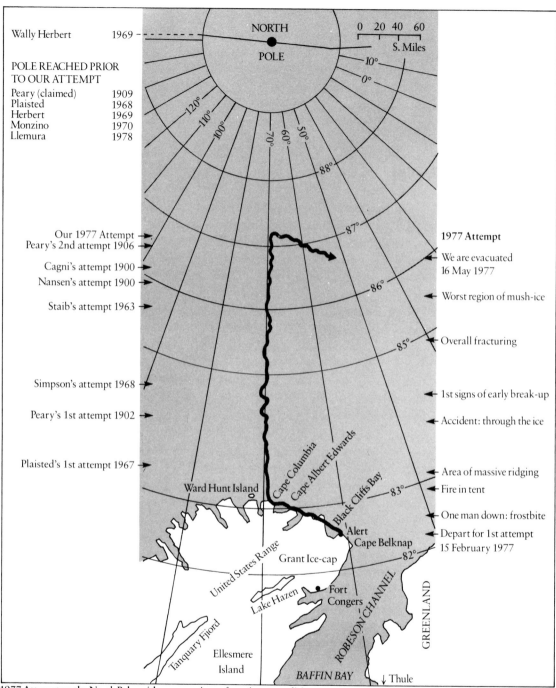

Wally Herbert   1969

POLE REACHED PRIOR
TO OUR ATTEMPT
Peary (claimed)   1909
Plaisted   1968
Herbert   1969
Monzino   1970
Llemura   1978

NORTH
POLE

0 20 40 60
S. Miles

10°
0°
120°
110°
100°
70°
60°
50°
88°
87°

Our 1977 Attempt →
Peary's 2nd attempt 1906 →

Cagni's attempt 1900 →

Nansen's attempt 1900 →

Staib's attempt 1963 →

Simpson's attempt 1968 →

Peary's 1st attempt 1902 →

Plaisted's 1st attempt 1967 →

Ward Hunt Island

1977 Attempt

← We are evacuated
   16 May 1977

← Worst region of mush-ice

← Overall fracturing

86°

85°

← 1st signs of early break-up

← Accident: through the ice

← Area of massive ridging
← Fire in tent
83°

← One man down: frostbite
← Depart for 1st attempt
   15 February 1977

Cape Columbia
Cape Albert Edwards
Black Cliffs Bay
Alert
Cape Belknap

United States Range   Grant Ice-cap
82°

Lake Hazen   Fort
              Congers

ROBESON CHANNEL

GREENLAND

Tanquary Fjord

Ellesmere
Island

BAFFIN BAY   ↓ Thule

1977 Attempt on the North Pole, with a comparison of previous expeditions

Oliver and Charlie prepared our new snow machines, called skidoos. Much lighter than the Groundhogs, they were powered by 640 cc two-stroke engines and steered by way of handlebars controlling a single short front-ski. Skidoos are the snow traveller's motorbike: they provide scant protection from the elements. In the meantime, I practised with my theodolite in a twenty-eight knot wind at temperatures of −45°C, fairly average conditions for the time of year.

One night the shooting of a single star took an hour and fifty minutes. In England I would have shot a dozen in twenty-five minutes. My eyelashes stuck to the metal of the scope and my nose cracked with the first symptoms of frosting. If I directed my breath on to the scope, it froze; if I then wiped its lens with my bare finger, this brought on circulation problems. Each time I tried to turn my head, my beard-hairs were tugged by the ice that meshed them, my eyes watered and more ice formed on my lashes. I persevered all week, for my ability to keep track of our position on the Arctic Ocean, whether by the sun or stars, would be key to our survival. An error of four seconds would put my position wrong by a mile.

We set out on 1 March and travelled five miles along the shoreline west of our camp before driving on to the sea-ice to cross Black Cliffs Bay. A mile later we camped at −51°C, two men to a tent. Geoff tried to send a message back to Ginnie, but his Morse key froze up and his breath simply froze inside the fine wire mesh of his microphone. Then the main co-axial power line cable cracked when he tried to straighten it out from its coil. Next morning, after an unforgettably evil night, none of the skidoos would start.

Over the next four days of mechanical delays we all learned the nature of tent life at −50°C. A useful lesson for the future. Geoff found the extreme cold especially difficult and, in a demoralised state, allowed six of his fingers to go numb while driving his skidoo. At the time he was wearing silk gloves, woollen gloves, heavy quilt gauntlets and thick leather outer mitts, but the numbness nonetheless quickly turned to frostbite. We limped back to base and Mary sedated Geoff who was obviously in pain.

With cobbled-up heating systems for the skidoos, we set out again, this time without Geoff, on 8 March. The torture of the cold at night was such that we could not sleep without taking Valium tablets.

The sea-ice was at first only slightly fragmented and for four days we followed the coast to the west, gaining slowly in northerly latitude. At a mountain called Cape Albert Edwards, I set a course due north. For a week we struggled through our first pressure ridges – walls of broken ice-blocks, many over twenty feet high.

The heavy sledges overturned, as did the skidoos. We sunk to our hips into deep snow, cut passageways for the machines using heavy axes, shovelled for hours to form snow ramps, sweated in our fur parkas when it was −52°C and, on relaxing, felt the raw coldness rush through our clothes and our bones to our bodies' core. All day we ached for the protection of our tents but by night, shivering out of control in our damp bags, we only wished to be moving again.

Oliver wrote: 'What a night! I had to thaw out my bag which was solid with ice and the zip was frozen. The cooker would not start so the tent was unbearable. When I did start it the fumes stung our eyes. I shivered all night and woke with a frozen nose. I hate this f. . .ing place . . . The cold is so intense and my hands are letting me down badly. The pain is indescribable and non-stop. I cannot sleep because of it.'

*   *   *

During the two months of our North Pole attempt, the chartered plane, an Otter with skis, visited us eight times. But there were other days when we were far out to sea and the pilot returned to Ginnie with a glum face and a negative report: we were nowhere to be seen. Ginnie sat at her radios for ten hours a day, often longer, knowing we were passing through areas of unstable, breaking ice. She never missed a schedule and at times of major ionospheric disturbance, when even the Canadian radio experts at the camp were blacked out, Ginnie would tirelessly change antennae on her high masts, hop from frequency to frequency and yell out her identification sign hour after hour in the hope we might pick up her call. Out on the ice we were dependent on her ability. Hearing her faint Morse signal or, in good conditions, her voice in the tent was the happiest moment of any day.

One morning the wind blew at a steady forty-five knots, with gusts above fifty knots. The wind chill factor was −120°C and the natural liquid in our eyes kept congealing, making it difficult to navigate through the broken ice-blocks. Vision was all-important. To progress at all meant choosing the least nightmarish route through the rubblefields and ice-walls. We never tried to drive skidoos and sledges north until we had first prepared a lane with our axes. After each section was cut we would clamber up a nearby ice-slab and peer north. I always hoped to see a sudden end to the rubble beds, but my hopes were always dashed. A chaotic jumble of blocks, large and small, invariably constituted the entire 180° view; that and the sky.

We dreaded axe-work because of the body sweat it caused and, later, the shivering when sweat particles inside our clothes turned to ice, which cascaded down our underwear when we moved. A typical stint of axework would last nine to eleven hours and clear a skidoo lane of between 500 and 3000 yards.

At first, aware of the danger from polar bears, we each carried a rifle, but soon dropped the practice through sheer exhaustion. Slipping, sliding and falling into drifts made it difficult enough to manage a shovel and axe. The work was thirsty and, with nothing to drink all day, we ate balls of snow. I once axed off a tantalising, lolly-pop-like chunk of ice from a block and crammed it into my balaclava's mouth-hole. There was a fizzing sound and a stinging sensation. I felt around with my mitt and removed the ice which was stained red. I tasted the blood for an hour and my tongue was raw for days. 'You should eat more ice,' Charlie commented. 'It keeps you quiet.'

Our daily ration of two frozen chocolate bars each wreaked havoc with our teeth. By the time we returned to London, we had between us lost nineteen fillings.

Without Geoff in my tent I noticed the lack of his body heat, but the absence of his companionship was the greater blow. Little things took on great importance. Some nights everything went wrong and I felt at the end of my tether. For long minutes in the dark I thought of nothing but my eyes. The pain was a live thing. I squirmed. I pressed against my eyeballs with the wet mitts. I knelt and looked downwards but the feeling of sharp grit moving about under the lids persisted. And the tent always grew quickly colder. I can remember no dentist, no limb breakage, nothing in my life so painful as 'Arctic Eye'.

A week later, I moved in with Charlie and Oliver – a tight squeeze, but less intensely cold with the warmth of three bodies. The ends of Oliver's fingers had gone black, with layers of skin peeled off all but the little fingers. Deep cracks edged back from his cuticles and criss-crossed the tender sub-skin revealed by the frost removal of his epidermal layers. Most of his mechanical duties involved work with petrol and cold metal. My nose and one ear were frostbitten and I could sleep only on my back or on one side as a result.

It is difficult to avoid outbursts of temper and hours of silent hostility in such conditions. For three years in London and four months in comparatively temperate Greenland, relations between the three of us had been idyllic. But the Arctic put an end to the harmony. Any outside observer would have thought we were a close-knit group, but the new level of strain was beginning to get to us. Apsley Cherry-Garrard, describing Scott's 'winter party', wrote: 'The loss of a biscuit crumb left a sense of injury which lasted for a week. The greatest friends were so much on one another's nerves that they did not speak for days for fear of quarrelling.'

Over the weeks we inched north until the pressure ridges were no longer an unbroken mass. We began to find flat 'pancakes' where travel was easy and quick flashes of hope, even elation, would then upset my determined cocoon of caution. I experienced the exhilaration as the ice flashed by, my skidoo making a jarring thud as it bounced off ice-walls, or quick relief as my sledge, leaping behind like a live thing, settled back on its runners instead of overturning.

The fear came when my skidoo rolled over, down thirty-foot ramps of hard, sharp-edged ice-slabs, and I flew off to land yards away, the wind knocked from my lungs, my head buried and my goggles stuffed with snow. Was I hurt? Would I be able to carry on? The ridge and rubble zones were most exhausting. The three of us together would slowly drag, shovel and haul an overturned sledge or a bogged skidoo from a drift to the tired, endlessly-repeated chant: 'One, two, three – pull.'

With only coffee for breakfast and only two Mars bars for day-time snacks, we felt hungry and thirsty all the time. I would wake in the night to find my body liquid sucked away due to stomach rehydration of our dehydrated supper, leaving a raging thirst and no water at hand to assuage it.

During the second week of April the pack showed the first symptoms of break-up. The temperature soared to −36°C within twenty-four hours and nights of creaking, rumbling thunder gave way to mornings of brown steam-mist, a sure sign of newly-open waterleads. For days we crossed open ditches and lakes of *nilas*, which is newly-formed dark grey sludge-ice. As long as the temperature remained below −20°C, the delays caused by the fractures were a matter of hours not days, for the open water re-froze steadily providing no wind blew to provoke further movement of the pack.

Geoff, his fingers still bandaged, joined one of our Otter re-supply drops in mid-April. He told us over the radio: 'There is a great deal of open water ahead of and behind you. The minor floe you are on is floating free.' A shift in the wind pattern closed the pack overnight, forming new high walls of rubble where the floes, some weighing over a million tons, crunched against each other.

Winds picked up surface snow and filled the air with the glint of freezing ice-particles. White-out conditions resulted when clouds blocked the sun and then we travelled slowly, for navigation was awkward without shadow or perspective. No hole in the ice was visible until you fell into it; no hummock or thirty-foot wall evident until you collided with it. One of us would walk ahead with a prod, feeling the way forward for twenty yards, before the skidoos slowly followed. Axe-work was hazardous in white-outs, since we could not see where our blades struck until they landed. We cut our way through high rubble knowing that, somewhere to the left or to the right, a clear passage might well detour north involving far less work.

Our words were swept away by the wind, so more often than not we communicated by hand signals. Around us the ridge-walls, like giant sails, caught the wind and strained to respond. Floes split under the resultant stress and the eerie boom and crack of unseen fractures flayed our nerves. Open water, being black, was clearly visible but new ice, mere centimetres thick, was quickly covered by spindrift and formed traps for the unsuspecting. We prodded ahead to avoid falling in. Conventional wisdom has it that 'white ice is thick and grey thin'. I discovered that this was not always true while gingerly exploring a recently fractured ice-pan. The ice felt spongy underfoot at first, then more like rubber. Suddenly the surface began to move beneath my boots, a crack opened up and black water gushed rapidly over the floe, rushing over my boots and weighing down on the fragile new ice. As the water rose to my knees, the crust under my feet cracked apart. I sank quickly but my head could not have been submerged more than a second, as the air trapped under my wolfskin acted as a life-jacket.

The nearest solid floe was thirty yards away. I shouted for the others, but of course there was no-one about.

Each time I tried to heave myself up onto a section of the submerged crust, I broke it again. I crawled and clawed and shouted.

Under my threshing feet was a drop of 17,000 watery feet down to the canyons of the Lomonosov Ridge. Sailors in the World Wars, I recalled, survived one minute on average in the North Sea.

I began to tire. My toes felt numb and there was no sensation inside my mitts. My chin, inside the parka, sank lower as my clothes became heavier.

I began to panic. After four, perhaps five minutes, my escape efforts had weakened to a feeble pawing movement when, ecstatic moment, one arm slapped down on to a solid ice chunk and I levered my chest on to a skein of old ice. Then my thighs and knees. I lay gasping for a few seconds, thanking God, but – once out of the water – the cold and the wind bit into me. The air temperature was −38°F with a 7-knot breeze. At −20°F and 19 knots, dry exposed flesh freezes in sixty seconds.

My trousers crackled as they froze. I tried to exercise my limbs but they were concrete-heavy in the sodden, freezing parka. For fifteen minutes I plodded round and round my skidoo, which I could not start. My mitts were frozen and the individual fingers would not move.

Oliver came along my tracks. He reacted quickly, erecting a tent, starting a cooker, and cutting off my parka, mitts and boots with his knife. Twenty-four hours later, in spare clothes and a man-made duvet, we were on our way again.

I was lucky to be alive. Few go for a swim in the Arctic Ocean and survive. The fact that I wore animal leather all over my torso and hands, with heavy felt boots, was my saving grace.

During the latter half of April we pushed hard to squeeze northerly mileage out of each hour's travel, speaking to each other hardly at all except inside the tent. Lack of sleep made us lightheaded. We had lost weight and strength and lived in a dream-world of whiteness and weird shapes, intense glare and hard ice. The only certainty was north. We must go north. Every minute spent gaining northerly paces produced satisfaction, every delay frustration.

Only three teams in history had undisputedly succeeded in the entire journey. By 20 April we had exceeded the records of the Swede, Björn Staib, the Italian, Cagni, and the Norwegian, Nansen. By the end of the month, we had surpassed all but the journeys of the three Pole conquerors, Plaisted, Herbert and Monzino.

On 29 April we were brought up short by what Oliver called the escalator, an 800-yard-wide river of moving mush-ice fringed for a mile on either bank by an unstable concoction of part-open pools and compressed pancake ice formed from broken pieces of *nilas* and ice-rind. A local storm must have devastated the pack all around the open river, for the floes were nowhere bigger than a dining-room table. Slabs leaned crazily in all directions and the thunderous crunch of fragmenting floes surged and receded all around. A river of porridge-like *shuga* sludge moved across in front of us at two miles an hour and every feature on the far bank was, on closer inspection, also floating past from west to east.

We first attempted to cross the escalator in an inflatable rubber dinghy we carried, but a wave of ice-sludge climbed over the upstream tube of the inflatable, threatening to pour into the boat like lava and submerge us. We camped two days and nights, awaiting a freeze-up. In the end we crossed the moving surface of the jellied river well before it reached a thickness we would normally have considered 'safe'.

Every day we confronted more zones of swamp-mush and webbed fissures of open water, for the sun's ultraviolet rays bored down into the surface pack, rendering it rotten and susceptible to the slightest stress from wind and current. On 5 May we passed by 87° North, a mere 180 miles from the Pole.

The transpolar drift stopped us. The two major currents of the Arctic, the Beaufort Gyral and the Trans-Siberian Drift, meet and diverge somewhere between 87° and 88° of latitude, causing surface chaos, tearing floes apart in places and jumbling others up to heights of thirty feet. On 7 May there were wide canals and slush-pools every few hundred yards. The entire region was in motion, slowly swirling and eddying. At this point the engine of my skidoo blew a head gasket and we could not progress without a re-supply drop.

Finding a safe floe, we waited with mounting frustration while Ginnie tried to cajole a ski-plane from the nearest charter company, 600 miles to her south. When she succeeded, three days later, temperatures rose to −15°C and mist banks caused the plane to miss us altogether. On a second attempt they found us. By the time we fitted the new skidoo engine we had drifted sixty miles to the south and east and a six-mile belt of sludge surrounded us. We waited for a further week hoping for a freak temperature drop but, on 15 May, with the temperature at 0°C, I decided to call it a day.

Our funds ran out with the flight that extricated us from the floe and took us back to Alert. There Ginnie gave me a radio message from London: Prince Charles had agreed to become patron of the Transglobe Expedition.

Back in the London office we carried on much as before. But the Arctic journey had humbled me; my first expedition failure. I had learned a good deal about myself as well as the others. Soon afterwards, Mary and Geoff were married and left the expedition. Mary's place as Ginnie's base-camp companion was then taken by a young Cumbrian named Simon Grimes.

By the end of 1977 we had over 1500 sponsors, and sixty tons of equipment were stored in various parts of the Duke of York's barracks. After a four-year search for an aircraft, the Chubb group loaned us a second-hand Twin Otter ski-plane. A scruffy-looking man with a black beard applied to join up as a ship's deck-hand. Anton Bowring was quiet and unflappable. He listened impassively when I explained there was no ship as yet for him to be a deck-hand on. But his first job, to keep him busy, could be to find one. A year later he located a thirty-year old strengthened vessel, once called the *Kista Dan*, and persuaded the giant insurance brokers, C.T. Bowring, to buy her on our behalf. This they did, with an eye to the fact that they had sponsored Captain Scott seventy years previously with his ship, the *Terra Nova*. Bowring's sister company in New York, Marsh and MacLennan, paid for half the vessel and Mobil Oil provided all the fuel for the ship, aircraft and snow machines.

On a summer weekend in 1978, visiting my sister Gill's farm in Yorkshire, Ginnie's pet terrier drowned in a slurry pit. For weeks Ginnie was inconsolable. I chanced to tell Peter Booth, who kindly gave Ginnie a Jack Russell puppy with which she instantly fell in love. We called it Bothie in honour of his donor, and Ginnie informed me she was not coming on Transglobe without him.

In the spring of 1979 Prince Charles opened the Transglobe's Press launch in the presence of 900 supporters. He arrived at the controls of our Twin Otter on an appropriately snow-bound runway at Farnborough. He announced that he was supporting the expedition 'because it is a mad and suitably British enterprise'.

Aiming to set out in September 1979, we worked hard through the summer with the help of many volunteers. Anton recruited sixteen crewmen for his ship, which he christened the *Benjamin Bowring* after an adventurous ancestor. I was lucky enough to obtain the services of Britain's most able Twin Otter pilot, Captain Giles Kershaw, and flight engineer Gerry Nicholson.

In July and August we packed and labelled over 3000 heavy-duty boxes bound for eighteen different remote bases around the world. A year before, I had finally opened an expedition bank account, and the day we left England with a mind-boggling array of equipment for the 110,000-mile journey, a team of thirty, a ship and an aircraft, we were in credit to the tune of £81.76.

Late in the afternoon of 2 September 1979, the *Benjamin Bowring* left Greenwich with Prince Charles at the helm. He wore a black tie, because his uncle, Lord Mountbatten, had been killed three days before. There were many people lining the pier. I spotted Geoff who was shouting rude messages at Oliver, and Mary, smiling through her tears. At the end of the jetty Gubbie held up one of his daughters who was busily waving her arm at the nearby *Cutty Sark*.

14

The Axis

*Sooner murder an infant in its cradle than nurse
unacted desires.*

WILLIAM BLAKE

On the day we set out from England, Prince Charles commented, 'Transglobe is one of the most ambitious undertakings of its kind ever attempted, the scope of its requirements monumental.' *The New York Times* editorial column, under the heading 'Glory', stated, 'the British aren't so weary as they're sometimes said to be. The Transglobe Expedition, seven years in the planning, leaves England on a journey of such daring that it makes one wonder how the sun ever set on the Empire.'

Our initial plans were mundane enough. With three Land Rovers we would cross Europe, the Sahara and West Africa. The ship would take us from Spain to Algeria and again from the Ivory Coast to Cape Town. Departure from Cape Town had to be timed precisely in order to enter Antarctic waters in mid-summer, when the ice-pack should be at its loosest. This was the reason we left England in early September and why we had to leave South Africa by late December.

Anton Bowring's crew of volunteers were a wonderful bunch, professional at their posts but fairly wild when off-duty. They included Quaker, Buddhist, Jew, Christian and atheist, black, white and Asian. They came from Austria, America, both ends of Ireland, South Africa, India, Denmark, Britain, Canada, Fiji and New Zealand. Most of the crew were Merchant Navy men who gave up promising careers, at a time of growing unemployment, to join a three-year voyage with no wage packet.

Ginnie was not the only girl aboard, for Anton had selected an attractive redhead, Jill McNicol, as ship's cook. She soon gained a number of ardent admirers from among the crew.

In Algiers the port officials showed ominous interest in our three-year supply of sponsored spirits and cigarettes. When the first wave of officers departed, promising a second visit in an hour, our skipper decided to make a run for it and quickly unloaded our vehicles and gear. As the crew waved us goodbye, the *Benjamin Bowring*'s thirty-year-old variable pitch control jammed itself in reverse. So the vessel retreated out of the harbour and out of sight steaming backwards.

We drove through Algeria to the sand-dunes of El Golea, a sticky-hot hell-hole dubbed 'El Gonorrhoea' by Oliver. We were pleased to leave the sweltering sands and head south to the Hoggar Mountains. At 8000 feet we reached the Pass of Asekrem, haunt of French monks. We savoured views of vast mountain ranges disappearing to Chad and the centre of Africa. From Tamanrasset we rattled down ever-worsening trails to lonely Tit and thence over trackless miles of sand and scrub to Tim-Missao and the Touareg lands of the Adrar des Iforas. Wide starry

Transglobe Expedition, 1979–1982

nights and wind-blown dunes brought back memories of the Dhofari Nejd and desert days long past.

From the Forest of Tombouctou to Goundam on the Niger we roared through veins of 30-foot-high sand in low gear to the cheer of barefoot donkeymen in sampan hats driving cavalcades of pint-size mules along the trail.

At Niafounke we learned that extensive flooding barred our planned route to the Ivory Coast, but a 700-kilometre westerly detour took us at length to Loulouni and the Ivorian border at Ouangolodougou. For a week we camped in thick jungle beside the Bandama Rouge River, an excellent collection point for bilharzia-bearing water-snails, then south to the lush and hilly coastline. In Abidjan harbour, we were met by the *Benjamin Bowring*. Simon and two members of the crew were weak from malarial fever but we pressed on and sailed across the Equator close by the Greenwich Meridian.

The Benguela Current coincided with a Force Seven storm. The electrical system of the stern refrigerator room broke down and a ton of sponsored mackerel turned putrescent. Brave hands

SOUTH PACIFIC

Brunei
Borneo
Sydney
Auckland
Christchurch
Campbell Island
SOUTHERN OCEAN
Scott Base
South Pole
ANTARCTICA
Sanae, Ryvingen
(winter 1979–80)
Antarctic Circle
Equator

3000 km
2000 S.miles
0° longitude

Transglobe Expedition, 1979–1982

volunteered to go below and clean up the mess, slipping about, as the ship rolled and heaved, in a soup of bloody fish bits. They fought their way up the ladders and tossed the sloppy bundles of rotten fish overboard. Then a forklift truck burst its lashings, crushed valuable gear and spattered battery acid about the cargo hold. Nowhere on the bucking ship, from cabins to fo'c'sle, could we escape the fumes of acid and mackerel. We were in the tropics and there was no air-conditioning system. With each roll to port our cabin porthole spat jets of sea-water on to our bunks. All night the clash of steel on steel and the groan of hemp under stress sounded from the cargo holds.

The old ship struggled on at a stately eight knots and delivered us, slightly dazed, to Saldanha Bay, near Cape Town, on 3 December. Jackass penguins squawked from the rocky shoreline, hundreds of thousands of them, as we anchored to take on fresh water.

We stayed two weeks in Cape Town to mount an export sales-orientated exhibition of our equipment, one of eight such events to be held during the course of the voyage. On a free

213

evening I drove to Constantia with Ginnie and visited our old house, built by Granny Florrie twenty-five years before. Nothing was as I remembered it. The valley was no longer the wild and wonderful place of my dreams. Residential expansion had tamed and suburbanised the woods and vineyards. The vlei where I had roamed with Archie and the gang was now a row of neat bungalows for foreign embassy staff. Our own house, Broughton, was a transitory post for US Marines on leave and nobody had tended the garden in years. There was no longer a view of the valley, for Granny Florrie's shrubs had flourished unchecked and the four little palm trees named after my sisters and me were now roof-high.

We wandered in silence through the old vegetable patch. No trace remained of the summerhouse, a place of bewitching memories. My mother's rockery, tended with so much care and love, had run amok. Up the valley, beside a building lot where caterpillar trucks were at work, we called on my cousin Googi Marais, whose rifle bullets passing over the roof at night had once caused our English nanny to pack her bags and flee. Googi was now crippled with arthritis, but he and his wife gave us tea and filled me in on the past quarter century of happenings in 'our valley'.

Over the next ten days I was reunited with twenty-two other cousins, one of whom, an alderman of Cape Town, showed me a family tree which proved he and I shared a close relationship with Karl Marx. I regret not having taken away a copy to shock the family back in England.

We left South Africa three days before Christmas, passing by Cape Agulhas, the last land for 2400 miles, and set a course south to Antarctica.

Bothie, our Jack Russell, appointed himself as ship's mascot and, respecting no privacy, left calling-cards in all cabins. Ginnie tried hard to remove all his indiscretions before they were discovered by the crew but it was an uphill struggle.

The Observer, covering the expedition, sent Bryn Campbell to Antarctica with us to record the ship's arrival. A four-man film-team was also on board – provided by millionaire octogenarian Dr Armand Hammer, a friend of Prince Charles – intending to film the entire three-year journey by joining the team in the more accessible areas. Richard Burton was to provide a background commentary.

Swelling the ship's complement still further were a number of oceanographers. At certain stages of the voyage there were eight scientists on board and at all times our own resident boffins, an Irishman and a Cape Town University girl, worked with their bathythermographs and nets to study current patterns and the interaction of water bodies at sub-tropical and Antarctic convergences.

Christmas spirits were dampened by a Force Eight storm which tore away the Christmas tree lashed to our mast and made eating rich festive fare a risky business. Giant Southern Ocean rollers forced the ship to list 47° both ways and, fearing the worst, I asked Anton if the ship could cope. His eyes glinted evilly and he proceeded to tell me a number of Antarctic horror stories.

As the old year slid away, we entered pack-ice and the sea slowly settled. The skipper sent a look-out up to the crow's nest to shout directions to the fo'c'sle through the antiquated intercom. The loose pack-ice yielded to our steel-clad bows and only once did we need to halt and slowly ram a new path through the floes.

On 4 January 1980, we sighted the ice-cliffs of Antarctica and the same day gouged ourselves out a nest, in the thin bay-ice of Polarbjorn Bite, where we could climb straight down a ladder on to the ice. The unloading of over a 100 tons of mixed cargo, including 2000 numbered boxes and the 1600 fuel drums, began at once.

To ensure that the ship could leave before the pack solidified and cut off her escape, we raced to carry every item two miles inland to more solid ice. Everyone helped, even the film-team. Our only tow-machine apart from skidoos was a Groundhog rescued from Greenland but, in only eleven days, the complex operation was complete.

Halfway through the unloading a storm broke up the ice and I watched from the bridge as eight drums of precious aircraft fuel sailed north on a floe. It was as if the bay-ice were a completed jigsaw puzzle dropped onto concrete and shattered.

Our steward, Dave Hicks, drank too much whisky and fell off the gangplank. He floated belly-up between the hull and the ice-edge, in imminent danger of being crushed, until someone hauled him out on a boathook.

One of the engineers slipped and broke three ribs and Bothie lost a fight with an angry Chinstrap penguin. The chief engineer, who had hoisted his Honda motorbike on to the ice for a quick ride, lost the machine for ever during the storm. Otherwise the unloading went well and the three of us waved goodbye to the ship and our friends on 15 January. All being well, they would pick us up again in a year or so, two thousand miles away on the far side of the frozen continent.

Ten days later, in conditions of nil visibility, Ollie, Charlie and I took our skidoos and laden sledges on a 370-kilometre journey inland to set up a base in which to spend the next eight months of polar winter and the long disappearance of the sun. Navigation was tricky, for although there were numerous mountain features spearing the overall ice-mantle, our route through them was confined to those slopes not riven by heavy crevassing. I came close to plummeting 200 feet down a crack at a time when I was not roped up to my skidoo.

We passed through a band of especially-difficult crevasse fields known as the Hinge Zone. From there I followed a series of carefully selected compass bearings which wiggled us between the peaks of Draaipunt, Valken and Dassiekop to the 6000-foot-high Borga Massif.

As we inched south, the Twin Otter crew – after a fifteen-day flight from England – flew Ginnie, Simon and 100,000 pounds of gear to an ice-field below Ryvingen Mountain. There they erected four huts made of cardboard which Ginnie had designed. Once snow drifts covered the huts' outer shells and insulated them they would be proof against the worst Antarctic winter.

Antarctica's 5,500,000 frozen square miles dwarf the United States, yet no more than 800 humans live in this continent. Only about fourteen of these polar denizens are women, so it is a very peaceful part of the earth.

The site of our winter base was chosen because of its height above sea-level and its distance inland, the furthest which the Twin Otter could be expected to reach carrying a 2000-pound cargo load. We hoped, by wintering at 6000 feet, to become acclimatised to the bitter conditions before the main crossing journey the following summer, when the average height would be 10,000 feet above sea-level. Until we reached our winter site we would be simple travellers. But once south of our camp, we would become true explorers of one of earth's last untrodden regions. For 900 miles we would pass through terrain neither seen nor touched by mankind.

We reached Ryvingen without mishap and began a race to prepare our camp for the long winter. The Twin Otter crew completed their seventy-eighth ferry flight from Sanae to Ryvingen and we wished them a safe flight back to Britain via the Falkland Islands and Argentina. Ginnie was to stay with us through the winter.

The weather clamped down on the ice-fields, travel for any distance became impossible and we were soon cut off from the outside world. For eight months we must survive through our own common sense. Should anyone be hurt or sick there could be no evacuation and no medical assistance. We must daily handle heavy batteries, generator power lines and heavy steel drums, but avoid the hazards of acid in the eye, serious tooth trouble, appendicitis, cold burns, fuel burns or deep electrical burns. Temperatures would plunge to −50°C and below. Winds would exceed ninety knots and the chill factor would reach −84°C. For 240 days and nights we must live cautiously and mostly without sunlight.

After a few days the huts disappeared under snow drifts, and all exits from the huts were blocked. So I dug tunnels under the snow and stored all our equipment inside them. In two months I completed a 200-yard network of spacious tunnels with side corridors, a loo alcove, a thirty-foot-deep slop-pit and a garage with pillars and archways of ice.

Since our huts were made of cardboard with wooden struts and bunks and our heaters burned kerosene we were apprehensive of fire. A neighbouring Russian base, 500 miles away, had been burnt out the previous winter and all eight occupants were found asphyxiated in an escape tunnel with blocked hatches.

Katabatic winds blasted our camp and snuffed out our fires through chimney back-blow. We experimented with valves, flaps and crooked chimneys, but the stronger gusts confounded all our efforts. The drip-feed pipe of a heater would continue to deliver fuel after a blow-out and this could cause a flash-fire unless great care was taken on re-lighting the heater.

Generator exhaust pipes tended to melt out sub-snow caverns which spread sideways and downwards. One day Oliver discovered a fifteen-foot-deep cave underneath the floor of his generator hut. He moved his exhaust system time and again but nearly died of carbon monoxide poisoning three times despite being alert for the symptoms.

Without power from the generators, Ginnie's radios would not work, so our weather reports, which Oliver must send out every six hours, could not be fed into the World Meteorological System, nor could the complex, very low frequency recording experiments for Sheffield University and the British Antarctic Survey be undertaken. So we fought hard against snow accumulation in certain key areas of the camp.

At night in the main living hut we turned the heater low to save fuel. We slept on wooden slats in the apex of the hut roof and in the mornings there was a difference of 14° between bed level and floor temperature, the latter averaging −15°C.

Ginnie and I slept together on a single slat at one end of the hut, Oliver and Charlie occupied bachelor slats down the other end and Bothie slept in a cavity behind the heater. The long black nights with the roar of the wind so close and the linger of tallow in the dark are now a memory which Ginnie and I treasure.

There was of course friction between us. Forced togetherness breeds dissension and even hatred between individuals and groups. After four years at work together our person-to-person chemistry was still undergoing constant change. Some days, without a word being spoken. I knew that I disliked one or both of the other men and that the feeling was mutual. At other times, without actually going so far as to admit affection, I felt distinctly warm towards them. When I felt positive antagonism towards the others I could let off steam with Ginnie, who would listen patiently. Or else I could spit out vituperative prose in my diary. Diaries on expeditions are often minefields of over-reaction.

Each of us nursed apprehensions about the future. The thought of leaving the security of our

First press announcement of the Transglobe Expedition, February 1979. Facing Prince Charles is Brigadier Mike Wingate-Grey, who threw the author out of the SAS, subsequently in charge of the expedition. In the background and to the right are Sir Vivian Fuchs and Sir Edmund Irving

Heath Robinson water trials to see if the groundhog swims (Geoffrey Newman)

Groundhog crossing crevasse

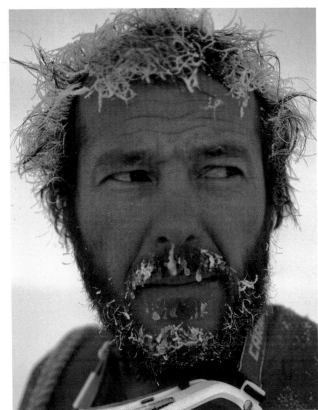

Above *Charlie*

Above left *Ginnie*

Left *Ollie and Bothie at −42°C*

Below *Bothie, the only dog to have lifted his leg on both poles*

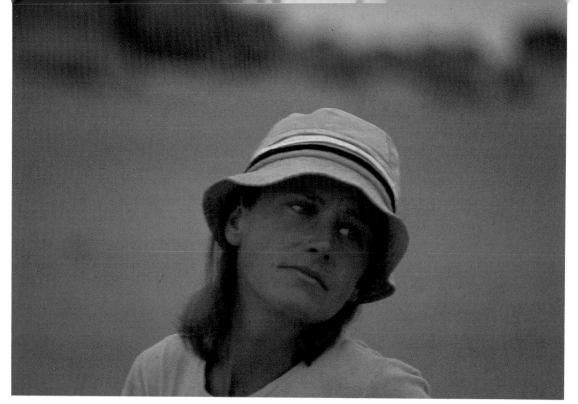

Ginnie at 'El Gonorrhea'

The author, Charlie and Ollie shelter from the sun in the shade of a Land Rover: west of Chad en route to Ivory Coast

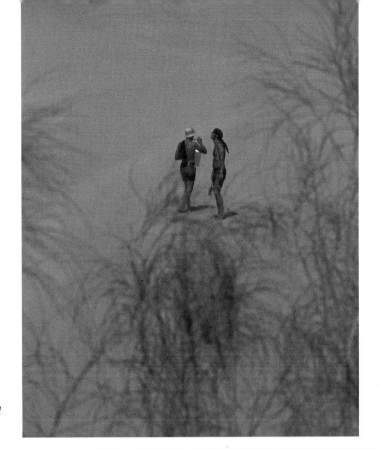

Ivory Coast rain-forest. The blurred back-ground demonstrates that high heat and humidity play havoc with photographic equipment. The camera shutter has opened twice: once for daylight and then a split second later for the flash

Left *The author checking equipment list in No. 2 hold of the* Benjamin Bowring *en route for Antarctica*

Opposite *Off the Yukon Mouth*

Opposite below *The* Benjamin Bowring *leaves us in Antarctica*

Below *A Transglober checking equipment in our ice-hut. Every item for an eighteen-month self-contained sojourn was listed*

Oliver and Bothie during crevasse-trials

Giles Kershaw takes the Twin Otter away from Antarctica before the 1980 winter. Charlie Burton in foreground

Oliver Shepard digs his way out of the cardboard hut at Borga

Overleaf *Borga camp at the return of the sun in 1980, before the crossing attempt begins*

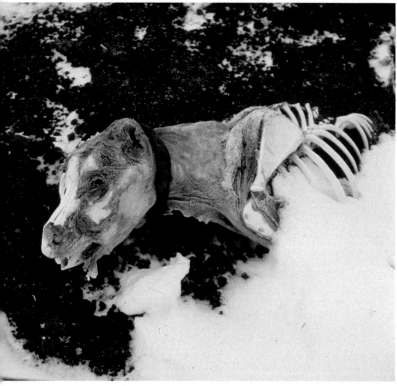

Above *Sledge jammed on sastrugi 800 miles from camp during the crossing of Antarctica. We passed through 900 miles of previously unexplored territory*

Opposite above *Catastrophe. Our store hut, on the edge of the Arctic ice-cap at Alert, is destroyed by fire*

Opposite below *After the fire*

Left *The mummified remains of one of Scott's dogs, preserved in the ice for seventy years*

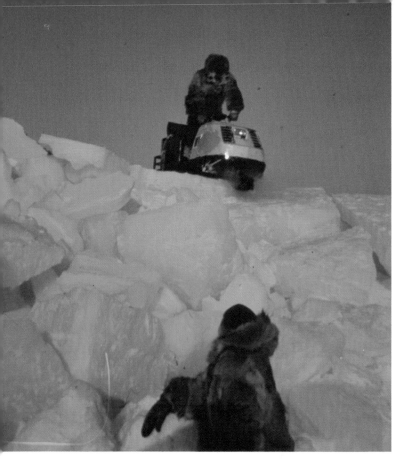

Left *Charlie Burton gets ready to descend a fifteen-foot pressure ridge in the Arctic*

Opposite above *The* Benjamin Bowring, *stuck for ten days at 82° North. The expedition team can be seen beside her*

Opposite below *Success at last, after nine years. The expedition team beside the* Benjamin Bowring

Below *The author struggles to prevent his skidoo falling through thin ice*

The author at home in Exmoor, 1987; with Bothie and Husky, son of Black Dog

In the most northern hut in the world, Ward Hunt Island, 1986, after failing to reach the North Pole unsupported by dogs, aircraft or motorised equipment. We will be attempting this again in 1988. Oliver Shepard is at centre, the author is on the right, Paul Cleary of Central Television is on the left, next to Beverly Hoover and Laurence Howell, our radio communicator from the Transglobe Expedition

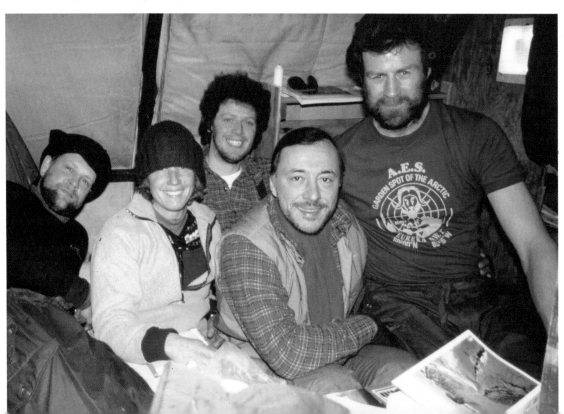

cardboard huts for the huge unknown that stretched away behind Ryvingen Mountain was not something on which I allowed my thoughts to dwell.

On May 2nd the wind chill factor dropped to −110°F. Windstorms from the polar plateau blasted through the camp with no warning. Visiting Ginnie's VLF recording hut one morning I was knocked flat by a gust, although a second earlier there had not been a zephyr of wind. A minute later, picking myself up, I was struck on the back by the plastic windshield ripped off my parked skidoo.

Even in thirty-knot wind conditions we found it dangerous to move outside our huts and tunnels except by way of the staked safety lines which we had positioned all around the camp and from hut to hut. Charlie and I both lost the safety-lines one day when an eighty-knot wind hurled ice-needles horizontally through the white-out. We groped separately and blindly in circles until we blundered into a safety line and so found our way to the nearest hut's hatchway. That same day the parachute canopy covering the sunken area of Ginnie's antennae-tuning units was ripped off, and by nightfall two tons of snow had filled in her entire work area.

Before the sun disappeared for twenty-four hours a day we trained daily at skiing. I taught Oliver and Charlie the rudiments of *langlauf* skiing, for I knew, if we succeeded in crossing Antarctica, that we would meet many regions in the Arctic where only skis would be practical.

On a fine autumn day we left camp with laden sledges for a quick sixteen-kilometre trip to a nearby *nunatak*, a lonely rock outcrop. A storm caught us on the return journey and, within minutes, the wind had burned every patch of exposed skin and frostnipped our fingers inside their light ski-mitts. At the time we were each moving at our separate speeds with a mile or so between us. This was not acceptable by current mountain safety practices but it was a system encouraged on all SAS training courses. The fewer individuals in a group, the faster the majority will reach their goal. This presupposes that the weakest link can look after himself. Oliver was last to arrive back at camp, his face and neck bloated with frostnip. For a week he took antibiotics until his sores stopped weeping.

Ginnie's problems were mostly connected with her radio work. Conducting high-frequency experiments with faraway Cove Radio Station, she was wont to work a 1.5 kva generator in the foyer to her hut. A freak wind once blew carbon monoxide fumes under her door. By chance I called her on a walkie-talkie and, receiving no reply, rushed along the tunnels and down to her shack. I found her puce-faced and staggering about dazed. I dragged her out into the fresh −49°C air and told the Cove Radio operator what had happened. Next day we received a worried message from their controller, Squadron-Leader Jack Willis.

Even in a comfortable environment the operation of electrical radio components is a hazardous operation. In your location the dangers are considerably increased . . . Remember that as little as thirty mA can kill. Never wear rings or watches when apparatus is live. Beware of snow from boots melting on the floor . . . Your one kilowatt transmitter can produce very serious radio frequency burns . . . Static charges will build up to several thousand volts in an aerial. Toxic berillium is employed in some of the components . . .

Only four days later, with all her sets switched off and no mains power, Ginnie touched the co-ax cable leading to her forty-watt set. She was stunned by a violent shock that travelled up her right arm and, as she put it later that morning, 'felt like an explosion in my lungs'. The cause was static, built up by wind-blown snow.

Not being a technical expert, Ginnie used common sense to repair her sets, replace tiny diodes and solder cold-damaged flex. When a one-kilowatt resistor blew and she had no spares, she thought of cutting a boiling ring out of our Baby Belling cooker. She then wired the cannibalised coil to the innards of her stricken radio and soon had everything working again, the home-made resistor glowing red-hot on an asbestos mat on the floor. The chief back at Cove Radio described her as 'an amazing communicator'.

To keep our little community happy, Ginnie listened to the BBC World Service and produced *The Ryvingen Observer*. On 6 May we learned that the bodies of US airmen were being flown out of Iran following an abortive attempt to rescue American hostages, that Tito's funeral was imminent, that SAS soldiers had killed some terrorists at the Iranian Embassy in London and that food in British motorway cafés had been summed up in a government report as greasy and tasteless.

Bothie spent his days following Ginnie from hut to hut. She kept old bones for him in each shack and dressed him in a modified pullover when the winds were high. I fought a non-stop battle with the terrier for eight months, trying to teach him that 'outside' meant right outside the tunnels as well as the hut. I lost the struggle.

Charlie, in charge of our food, rationed all goodies with iron discipline. Nobody could steal from the food tunnels without his say-so, a law that was obeyed by all but Bothie. Our eggs, originally sponsored in London, were some eight or nine months old by mid-winter and, although frozen much of that time, they had passed through the tropics *en route*. To an outsider they tasted bad – indeed evil – but we had grown used to them over the months and Bothie was addicted. However hard Charlie tried to conceal his egg store, Bothie invariably outwitted him and stole an egg a day, sometimes more.

The months of June, July and August saw an increasing workload in the camp, due both to the scientific programme and our preparations for departure in October. The sun first came back to Ryvingen, for four minutes only, on 5 August, a miserably cold day. Down at our Sanae base hut, Simon, overwintering with one other Transglober, recorded a windspeed in excess of 100 miles per hour. July 30th was our coldest day. With the wind steady at forty-two knots and a temperature of −42°C, our prevailing chill factor was −131°C, at which temperature any exposed flesh freezes in under fifteen seconds.

In August Ginnie discovered the oscillation unit in her VLF time-code generator had failed due to the cold. To complete the VLF experiment without the instrument meant manually pressing a recording button every four minutes for unbroken twenty-four-hour periods. Wrapped in blankets in the isolated VLF hut she kept awake night after night with flasks of black coffee. By October she was dog-tired and hallucinating but determined to complete the three-month experiment.

As the sunlit hours grew longer, the ice-fields reacted. Explosions sounded in the valleys, rebounding as echoes from the peaks all about us. Avalanches or imploding snow-bridges? There was no way of knowing.

With departure imminent, I realised how much I had grown to love the simplicity of our life at Ryvingen, a crude but peaceful existence during which, imperceptibly, Ginnie and I had grown closer together than during the bustle of our normal London lives. Now I felt pangs of regret that it was ending. Also tremors of apprehension. As the days slipped by my stomach tightened with that long-dormant feeling of dread – once so familiar during school holidays as the next term-time approached.

'I wish you weren't leaving,' Ginnie said.

In the last week of October it should be warm and light enough to travel at 10,000 feet above sea-level. Then we would attempt the longest crossing of the Antarctic continent, the first crossing attempt to use vehicles with no protective cabs for the drivers. The frozen land mass we must cross was bigger than Europe, the USA and Mexico combined, than India and China together, and far larger than Australia. The ice-sheet was four kilometers thick in places and covered 99 per cent of the entire continent. Four days before we set out, a news release through Reuters quoted the New Zealand Antarctic Division boss as criticising our intended journey as under-equipped and our skidoos as under-powered. The official view was that we would fail: it was 'too far, too high and too cold'.

The Transglobe Expedition's Route across Antarctica

On 29 October we left Ginnie and Bothie in a drifted-over camp and headed south. The wind blew into our masked faces at twenty knots and the thermometer held steady at −50°C.

Clinging to a straight bearing of 187°, we crossed the sixty-four kilometres to the Penck Escarpment, a steep rise of several hundred feet of sheet ice. Spotting the curve of a slight re-entrant, I tugged my throttle to full bore and began the climb, trying to will the skidoo on with its 1200-pound load – a heavy burden for a 640 cc two-stroke engine operating at 7000 feet above sea-level. The rubber tracks often failed to grip on smooth ice, but always reached rough patches again before too much momentum was lost. Renewed grip and more power then carried me on – just – to the next too-smooth section. The ascent seemed interminable. Then came an easing of the gradient, two final rises, and at last the ridgeline. Fifteen hundred feet above our winter camp and forty miles from it I stopped and looked back. The peaks of the Borga Massif seemed like mere pimples in the snow, Ryvingen itself just a shadow.

We pressed south and by dusk there was no single feature in any direction. Only endless fields of snow. Nothing to navigate by but clouds and soon – once we left the weather-making features of sea and mountain behind us – there would not even be clouds.

On the second day, at −53°C, we climbed slowly into the teeth of high winds and a white-out, the true plateau still 4000 feet above us. After four hours Oliver staggered off his skidoo and lurched over to me, his speech slurred. 'Must stop. I'm getting exposure.' We boiled water and gave him tea. He was physically the toughest of us and wore five layers of polar clothing. But the cold was cruel and wore us down hour after hour. We travelled for between ten and twelve hours a day.

That night Oliver wrote: 'Very bad weather. I think we should have stayed in the tent.' I saw his point but Greenland five years earlier had taught me that we could travel in high wind and white-out and every hour of progress, however slow, helped our slim chances of success. We had 2200 miles to go, 900 of them unexplored.

I took a bearing check every ten minutes against the clouds: as these moved slowly and maintained their silhouettes for quite a while, they served me well. At times when partial white-outs hid sun and clouds, all I could do was aim my compass at imperfections in the snow ahead. When the sun shone I navigated by means of the shadows of a series of penknife-scratched lines on the plastic windshield of my skidoo. To check on the accuracy of this crude system and to put some life back into our frozen limbs, I stopped for five minutes in every hour. We always maintained a space of a mile between each of us so, as soon as I stopped, a backbearing on the two specks back along my trail provided a good check on the angle of travel.

For four days and nights the temperature hovered around −50°C creating weird effects such as haloes, sun pillars, mock suns and parhelia.

In the mornings the skidoos were difficult to start. Any wrong move or out-of-sequence action caused long delays. Try to engage gear too soon and the drive belt shattered into rubber fragments. Turn the ignition key a touch too hard and it snapped off in the lock. Set the choke wrong and the plugs fouled up. Changing plugs at −50°C in a strong wind was a bitter chore which no one fancied.

Often the whole day would pass without a word spoken between us. Our routine was slick and included, after camping, the drill of ice-core samples at every degree of latitude, a full coded weather report by radio to the World Meteorological Organisation, and the taking of urine samples as part of our calorific intake programme.

Back at base Giles and Gerry had returned from England with the Twin Otter and took Simon up to help Ginnie. Every 300 or 400 miles we would run out of fuel and Giles would have to locate us from my theodolite position. In ten days' travel we were 404 nautical miles from Ryvingen with a suspected major crevasse field just to our south. Since no man had been there before us, we had only satellite photographs from which to try to detect such obstacles.

On 9 November we ran into our first bad field of *sastrugi*, teeth of ice cut by the wind and resembling parallel lines of concrete tanktraps. Due to the prevalence of east-west winds, these furrows were diagonal to our southerly direction of travel. The *sastrugi* were from eighteen inches to four feet high and, being perpendicular, they often impeded any advance until we axed out a through-lane. The *sastrugi* buckled our springs, bogey wheels and skis. Oliver struggled to improvise repairs.

At 80° South we camped in one spot for seventeen days to allow Giles to set up a fuel dump halfway between the coast and the Pole.

For weeks our progress was painfully slow. Sledges with smashed oak spars were abandoned, frequent overturns caused minor injuries, axe-work through *sastrugi* fields progressed sometimes at a mere 800 yards in five hours, and the ever-present fear of crevasses gnawed at our morale. One morning, stopping on an apparently harmless slope, Charlie stepped off his skidoo to stretch his legs and promptly disappeared up to his thighs. He was parked right over an unseen cavern, with less than two inches of snow cover between him and oblivion.

Close to 85° South, in a high *sastrugi* field, we had stopped for repairs when we heard from Ginnie that a team of South African scientists, operating at the rim of the coastal mountains near Sanae, were in trouble. One of their heavy snow tractors had plunged sixty feet down a crevasse together with its one-ton fuel sledge. One man then fell ninety feet down another crevasse and broke his neck and their rescue party, returning to their coastal base, became lost in the ice-fields. They had, by the time Ginnie contacted us, already been missing with minimal gear for five days.

At this point we learned that there were no rescue facilities available in the entire continent and, since the missing men were more than fifty miles from their base, they would almost certainly die. Already short of fuel and with a recurring engine start-up problem, highly hazardous in Antarctica, Giles nonetheless flew over 1000 miles to search for, and eventually locate, the missing South African scientists.

From 85° South we struggled on, detouring east to avoid a mammoth crevasse field and running into total white-out conditions. Navigation became critical and on 14 December, after nine hours of travel in thick mist, I stopped where I estimated the Pole should be. There was no sign of life, although a sixteen-man crew of US scientists work in a domed base beside the Pole. We camped and I radioed the Pole's duty signaller.

'You are three miles away,' replied a Texan twang. 'We have you on radar . . . Come on in.'

He gave us a bearing and, an hour later, the dome loomed up a few yards to my front. At 4.35 a.m. on 15 December, 1000 miles south of Ryvingen and seven weeks ahead of our schedule, we had reached the bottom of the world.

Six days after our arrival, Giles flew Ginnie, Bothie and Simon to the Pole, complete with the radio station stripped from Ryvingen. Every pound of skidoo fuel that he flew from the coast to the South Pole had used up thirteen pounds of aviation fuel via his complex network of isolated fuel caches.

The temptation to spend Christmas Day with Ginnie at the Pole was powerful, but we had to press on. With each passing day the crevasse systems between the polar plateau and the coast were growing more rotten, snow-bridges built the previous winter were daily sagging and collapsing.

For five years I had tried to discover a straight-line descent route from the plateau to the coastal ice-shelf. The Scott Glacier appeared to be the straightest, but no one knew anything about it and I only had an aerial map to go by. This showed extensive crevassing at the glacier's crest some 9000 feet up, fractures in belts down its course and massed around its mouth where the ice debouched on to the ice-shelf 500 feet above sea-level.

We left the Pole on 23 December. I thought of Captain Scott, whose team had turned back from the Pole sixty-nine years earlier. 'All daydreams must go,' he had written. 'It will be a wearisome return.' They never made it back.

From the Pole we steered north. Every direction was of course northerly but my compass setting was 261° for 180 miles. There were no *sastrugi* all the way and no crevasses, so we reached the plateau edge in only two days. At 5.00 p.m. on Christmas Day I stopped on a small rise and saw far ahead the summit of Mount Howe, guardian of the Scott Glacier Valley and the first natural feature we had seen in well over 1000 miles. It made an excellent Christmas present. That night there was an air of apprehension in the tent, not in anticipation of Christmas stockings but through fear of the impending descent.

My map dotted Scott Glacier with vaguely delineated rashes of crevasse belts, an artist's impression rather than an exact record from which an optimum compass course could be set. I decided to play Scott Glacier by ear rather than compass. Oliver changed all our carburettor jet settings for the lower altitudes and we swapped our one-metre sledge tow-lines for six-metre safety lines.

A series of east-west pressure swelling or *olgives* heralded the first obstacle. We breathed in as we passed over huge crevasses but all were bridged well enough to take the minimal ground pressure of our skidoos. The narrower fissures, from four to twenty feet wide, were the greater danger, for many were spanned by sagging snow-bridges that collapsed under the slightest weight.

Each time I crossed a relatively weak bridge, my sledge, heavier by far than my skidoo in terms of ground pressure, broke through, plunging a cascade of snow down into the fissure below. Charlie, behind me, would have to find himself another crossing-point. So too, later, would Oliver.

The La Gorse range for which I was headed was soon obscured by mist as were all other features, so we camped in the centre of a wide crevasse field. Next morning the white-out was still clamped about us and, impatient, I decided we should move on. This was perhaps a rash decision.

From about this period of the expedition Charlie underwent a subtle change that I cannot, to this day, explain. He radiated a muted hostility which never broke out into rage. Instead it simmered away month after month, nursing itself quietly.

After six years of working together with two men for whom I had no prior affection or common ground – save for the single desire to achieve Transglobe – the vicissitudes of our common experiences had slowly led me to grow fond of Oliver and to dislike Charlie. I disliked being disliked. Hostility bred hostility. I was fully aware that the major part of the expedition, and by far the more hazardous sector, lay ahead and that one of my two companions and I were silently at loggerheads. Since this situation was only known to the two of us and it was never openly acknowledged, I saw no reason why it should impair our chance of success, which was, after all, all that mattered.

Our nightmare trail down the glacier led us into a cul-de-sac, surrounded by open crevasses. We retraced our tracks and tried again via another narrow corridor between blue ice-walls. A maze of sunken lanes beset with hidden falls finally released us, shaken but unhurt, close by the Gardner Ridge and 6000 feet above our ice-shelf goal. In forty-knot winds and thick mist, we followed the Klein Glacier for twelve miles until forced along a narrow ice-spit between two giant pressure fields, a chaos of gleaming ice-blocks.

I knelt to study the map to find a way through, but the wind tore it away. I carried one spare chart with my navigation gear and, using it, plotted a course to the eastern side of the valley. Halfway through the smaller pressure field, a sudden drop revealed the lower reaches of Scott Glacier, a breath-taking show of mountain and ice-flow, rock and sky, dropping 600 metres to the far horizon and the pinnacles of the Organ Pipe Peaks. A crevasse field five miles deep crossed the entire valley from cliff to cliff and halted us short of Mount Russell, so we detoured east over a 1000-foot-high pass and, three hours later, re-entered Scott Glacier – beyond the crevasse field – by way of a wicked ravine. We had travelled for fourteen hours and covered five days' worth of scheduled progress. The next day our mad journey continued. More ice walls and skidding, out-of-control sledges. At the foot of Mount Ruth we cat-footed along the ceiling of an active pressure lane as rotten as worm-eaten wood.

The last concentrated nightmare, southwest of Mount Zanuck, was a series of swollen icy-waves pocked by broken seams.

Beyond the powerful in-flow of the Albanus Glacier the dangers lessened hour by hour until, at the final rock outcrop of Durham Point, there was nothing ahead but flat ice and the Pacific. We had reached the Ross Ice-shelf. Dog-tired, we camped after fifteen hours of travel and awoke next day to Oliver shouting 'Welcome to the tropics! It's *plus* 1° on the thermometer.'

For nine further days I held to a bearing of 183°, which took us well north of the disturbed zone known as the Stagshead Crevasses. On the seventh day we crossed the 180° meridian which, at that point, is also the International Date Line. I experienced a zany temptation to zig-zag north along it singing, 'Monday, Tuesday, Monday, Tuesday.'

On the ninth day, passing the region where Oates groped his frostbitten way to a lonely but honourable death, we first saw the mushroom steam-cloud of Mount Erebus, 100 miles distant but marker to our destination. Beneath the 13,000-foot volcano lies Scott Base where, on 11 January, we arrived at 6.00 p.m. We had crossed Antarctica in sixty-seven days.

Much of our strength, despite our lack of polar experience, lay in our collective ability – remove any one of us and the other three became a far less capable entity. Unfortunately that is precisely what happened. Oliver's wife Rebecca, from whom he had been separated – then re-united for the past few years – had grown sick with worry during the Antarctic crossing. Oliver was faced with the cruel choice of wife or Transglobe. He took the long-term option because he loved Rebecca more than his six-year-long ambition to achieve Transglobe's goals.

Oliver's loss caused wider problems than the mere mechanics of food supplies and weights to be carried in the Arctic. Back in London the committee who represented the expedition, including Mike Wingate Gray, decided it would be irresponsible for us to attempt the northern hemisphere with a team of only two. They were solidly in favour of a third man, probably from the Royal Marines or SAS, being recruited to replace Oliver. A committee deputation was to be sent to meet us in New Zealand.

The *Benjamin Bowring* penetrated the pack-ice again and removed us from Antarctica.

On arrival at Christchurch, New Zealand, I received a warning message from Anthony Preston, the ex-RAF man in charge of our London office and a volunteer staff of eight. He had discovered that an American, Walt Pedersen – one of the 1968 team that reached the North Pole under Ralph Plaisted – was all set to sledge to the South Pole early next year. Determined to become the first man in the world to reach both Poles overland, he had spent twelve years getting his act together. It looked as though he would beat us by four months, since the earliest we could hope to reach the North Pole would be April 1982. I reflected that virtually none of our Antarctic experience was applicable to our coming Arctic struggle. The two places were as alike as chalk and cheese.

In Auckland we held a trade exhibition which the New Zealand Prime Minister, Mr Muldoon, opened – likening Transglobers, in his speech, to old English merchant adventurers. Over 22,000 visitors flooded our show.

Sir Edmund Irving, Sir Vivian Fuchs and Mike Wingate Gray, chairman and key members of our London committee, held long meetings with Ginnie, Charlie and me, but we could not agree to the recruiting of a third man. I resolved to put the final decision to our patron, Prince Charles, and at Sydney, where he opened our trade fair, I explained the whole problem to him in the skipper's cabin.

The upshot of the various discussions was that Charlie and I should carry on alone, but Sir Vivian Fuchs warned me that if things should go wrong, the blame would be entirely mine.

On the *Benjamin Bowring*'s boat deck we gave Prince Charles three cheers and a miniature silver globe, marked with our route, to congratulate him on his engagement to Lady Diana Spencer. Bothie joined the cheering, yapping aggressively until Prince Charles patted and spoke to him.

While we were in Sydney, Charlie married the girl that he loved and Anton married Jill, our ship's cook. The *Benjamin Bowring* was becoming quite a family ship. All in all the Expedition was to witness seventeen marriages of its members to each other or to outsiders.

From Sydney we steamed north over the Equator to Los Angeles, where President Reagan had kindly agreed to open our trade exhibition. Sadly, someone shot him just beforehand so he sent us a message instead. 'My warmest congratulations . . . Now that you are halfway through your polar circumnavigation of the earth we welcome you to the United States . . . You are attempting something which has never been done before which will take courage and dedication. The "can do" spirit your expedition so perfectly exemplifies is still alive in the free world . . .'

Our final exhibition, in Vancouver, was completed on schedule and we followed the coastline north to the mouth of the Yukon River in Alaska.

If the ship had been able to continue north through the Bering Straits – between Russia's eastern tip and Alaska – she would have sailed on to the North Pole, over the top and back to England via Spitsbergen. Because the Arctic Ocean is full of moving ice the best the *Benjamin Bowring* could do was to drop Charlie and me overboard with rubber boats in the Bering Straits, as close as she could get to the mouth of the Yukon.

Eight years earlier we had scheduled our arrival off the Yukon for the first week of June because, in a bad year, that is the latest time when the northern rivers shed their load of ice and become navigable. All being well we would now ascend the Yukon for 1000 miles, then descend the Mackenzie River to its mouth in the Arctic Ocean at the Eskimo settlement of Tuktoyaktuk. From there we would make a 3000-mile dash east through the fabled North West Passage and north up the Canadian archipelago to Ellesmere Island and Alert, our old stamping-ground. It was imperative to complete the entire boat journey from the Bering Straits to Alert within the three short summer months when the Arctic Ocean ice-pack should be at its loosest. We had to reach Alert by the end of September or risk being cut off by freezing seas and twenty-four-hour darkness.

Less than a dozen expeditions had ever successfully navigated this passage in either direction. Those few all used boats with protection from the elements and took an average of three years to get through due to blockage by pack-ice *en route.*

The *Benjamin Bowring*'s skipper tried hard to close with the Yukon mouth but, when still fourteen miles away in heavy seas, the echo sounder showed only six to eight feet clearance below the hull, with a ten-knot offshore wind making the ship's position highly risky.

Our two twelve-foot dinghies slammed up and down in the lee of the ship as we loaded them. Bryn Campbell of *The Observer* was to accompany Charlie and me as far as Tuktoyaktuk and he clambered atop the fuel drums on Charlie's madly tossing boat. I experienced a sudden flashback to the very first day of another boat journey, ten years before, when Bryn had come within an ace of drowning. Bryn's diary on leaving the *Benjamin Bowring*:

> We waved until the ship was out of sight. Soon the waves were breaking over us, hitting us hard from behind. Often we were completely awash . . . As we watched Ran's boat pounded by the sea and disappearing in the ten-foot troughs, we had all too vivid an image of how vulnerable we were. I turned to talk to Charlie and saw him lifted bodily by a surge of water and thrown clean over my head. As the boat capsized, I tugged my feet free of the fuel lines and jumped as far away from the propeller as I could. Then the hull crashed down on me.

I was attempting to keep to a compass bearing despite the silt-laden water smashing on to my boat, stinging my eyes and covering the compass glass. At the top of a breaker I risked a quick glance backwards and to my horror saw Charlie's boat upside-down with no sign of either passenger.

It was a while before I tried to turn round. The secret of survival in such shallow riotous waters was to remain totally alert and keep the bows at all times into the next breaker. In just such rubber boats we had come safely through far worse conditions on the rivers of British Columbia. It was a matter of aim and balance. After a big wave, I whipped the tiller round and the boat sped through 180° in time to face the next attack. In a while I saw Charlie crawl on to his boat's bottom and then haul Bryn up by his hood. I breathed out with relief. They began to try to re-right their inflatable using the hull hand-grips, but they were too exhausted. I flung a rope across to Charlie but a wave ripped the line's fixture point away from my hull. With my propeller threshing only inches from their prancing rubber tubing, I flung the rope over again. Timing the arrival of the next big wave, we succeeded in flipping the boat back over. I slowly towed the stricken boat with its waterlogged outboard back towards the distant silhouette of our ship.

Charlie had lost only his rifle, but Bryn's cameras had sunk and he was decidedly unhappy. Overnight, back on the *Benjamin Bowring*, a Force Seven gale blew up and the hull began to strike the sea floor in the heavy swell. The skipper weighed anchor at once and we headed 200 miles north to another mouth of the Yukon, known as the Apoon Pass. With 120 miles to go and off a dangerous lee-shore, one of the main tie-bolts – which hold the ship's engine in place – sheared. This had happened before and the engineers had only one replacement. After eight hours of toil below decks and anxiety above, the engines re-started and we reached Apoon.

Seventy cold, wet miles in the inflatable boats followed before we came to the river village of Kotlik where we bedded down in the local gaol. The Kotlik sheriff warned us that the summer winds could turn certain stretches of the river into no-go areas.

At Kravaksavak we joined the brown and powerful Kwikpak River, which is the main arm of the Yukon. The banks were thickly forested but we saw fox, bear and river birds. Continuing through half the moonlit night we covered 150 miles to the village of Marshall. The river then narrowed and for days we fought an eight-knot current.

Fifteen miles short of the village of the Holy Cross we noticed dust-storms raging on both banks. With little warning the river erupted into a cauldron which caught us in mid-stream. Pine trees crashed down into the river and whole sections of the banks collapsed. The forest swayed towards the river, its upper canopy pressed flat by the force of the wind. There was no question of trying to land in such conditions. In mid-stream we battled through five-foot-high waves which followed one upon the other with hardly a breathing space for recovery. Once or twice my bows failed to rise from a plunge and the next wave swamped the boat. I thanked the Lord for positive buoyancy chambers.

Then the river twisted to the east and the storm subsided. My long-nurtured idea of the Yukon as a gentle Thames-like river was destroyed.

At Holy Cross, the keeper of the travel-lodge told us we were lucky to be alive. We had been travelling north, he said, in the first big southerly blow of the year, with winds exceeding seventy knots.

For long days of glare and heat we moved on across the face of Alaska towards Yukon Territory and the Canadian border. On 15 July we reached the only river-bridge anywhere from the sea to Dawson City, having boated over a thousand river miles. Ginnie and Bothie met us in their Land Rover, onto which we lashed our deflated boats and gear. She drove us 500 kilometres up the recently-opened Dempster Highway. Floods held us up for four days where this dirt highway was washed out but, a hundred miles from the sea, we reached the end of the road at Inuvik on the Mackenzie River.

Simon awaited us at Inuvik airstrip with a sixteen-foot open fibreglass whaler boat. Jackie McConnell, now a Canadian citizen, joined us for the journey to Tuktoyaktuk. He took the helm of Bryn's boat while the rest of us squeezed aboard the whaler and set out for the mouth of the Mackenzie.

The little whaler was a last-minute idea which had come to me back at Kotlik. I had used the sheriff's radio phone to ask Ginnie to obtain one from a sponsor. Somehow she had, after phone calls to Hong Kong, London and New York, obtained the boat, outboards and a cargo plane flight from Vancouver to Inuvik. While we boated upriver she had worked at a motel outside Dawson as a waitress – in return for free telephone calls and a bedroom.

On the afternoon of 24 July, back on our tight schedule, we entered the harbour of Tuktoyaktuk in the North West Passage. Jack and Bryn flew south. Ginnie and Simon set up a radio base and Charlie and I loaded the whaler for our 3000-mile journey through the passage.

Worried about navigation, I visited a local barge skipper with sixteen years of experience. I was planning to navigate the passage by magnetic hand compass plus my watch and the sun. The skipper said simply, 'You are mad.'

'But I have good charts and a hand-made balanced prismatic compass,' I assured him.

'Throw it away,' he muttered.

'What do you use?' I asked him. He pointed at his sturdy barge-towing tug. 'She has everything. She goes in the dark, out in the deep channels. Radar beacon responders, MF and DF, the works.' He shook his head dismissively. 'You must hug the coastline to escape storms so you will hit shoals, thousands of shoals. Also you cannot go across the many deep bays for fear of wind and big waves so you must hug the coastline which is like crazy pavement. You have to use more gas and take extra days. Most of the time there will be thick fog. No sun means you use your compass. Yes?'

I nodded.

He flung his hands up. 'Ah, but you cannot use a compass. Look . . .' He prodded his desk chart of the passage and I saw the heavily printed warning 'MAGNETIC COMPASS USELESS IN THIS AREA'.

'Too near the magnetic Pole, you see. You stay here in Tuk. Have a holiday.'

On 26 July we headed out into the choppy bay of Tuktoyaktuk. In thirty-five days we must not only complete the 3000 miles of the passage, which traditionally takes three years, but also cover an additional 500 miles further north, attaining some point within skiing distance of our intended winter quarters at Alert before the sea froze, forcing us to abandon the whaler.

Four or five isolated Eskimo settlements and eight defence early warning camps were the sole inhabited points along our route. Five years previously I had set up a complex arrangement with the air company which supplied the bases, to take our ration boxes and fuel cans to these outlying sites. To cover the intermediate distances was just possible (given the maximum fuel load capacity of our whaler), providing I made no navigating errors *en route*.

The coastline, on leaving Tuktoyaktuk, was flat as a board and quite invisible whenever shallow water forced us out to sea. The treeless tundra of the Tuk Peninsula might just as well not have been there. Fortunately the sun was out, so we headed due east until the glint of breakers off Cape Dalhousie showed like silver froth on the horizon. A conical hill, or pingo, stood proud from the otherwise unseen coastline, giving me a rough indicator of our position.

East of the Cape we bucked forty miles through a rising sea which soaked us anew at every crest. A flat tongue of shingle south of Baillie Island was the cache-point agreed a year previously with a government helicopter pilot, then in the area, for two drums of fuel.

The sea was too rough on both sides of the spit to allow a beaching. So Charlie dropped our light anchor overboard and I waded through the surf, back and forth with twelve jerry cans. Three hours later, re-fuelled, we entered Snowgoose Passage via a vicious tide-rip toothed by shoals. Once in Franklin Bay the full force of wind and wave struck us and for fifty miles we ran the gauntlet between fourteen-foot breakers and the wave-pounded cliffs to our west. We were soaked and our teeth chattered in unison. Each wave that broke over the whaler showered us. Salt-water poured down the face-holes of our survival suits, running down back and chest and legs to collect in slowly rising pools inside our waterproof boots. Our underclothes were salty and sodden. Time and again we were forced to swing off our course to face into rolling waves which raced at us from the flank. Once the boat hung almost on its side as a green wall of water surged by in a rush of power.

As dusk approached I saw fires ahead and, an hour later, we passed a section of low cliffs

The North West Passage

wherein the mineral components smouldered and gave off an acrid chemical odour. Dante's Inferno. Sulphur deposits glowing red and yellow, for ever burning. Yellow smoke curled up from deep rock crevices.

The storm grew in intensity but, by a piece of good luck, we penetrated the beach breakers via a ten-foot-wide channel into a tiny lagoon beneath Malloch Hill. Next morning, shaking with cold, we marched up and down the beach in our wet clothes until the blood ran again. Then we set out east into thick mist. 'Surely we should head further to the right?' Charlie shouted.

Knowing how easy it is to be tempted to distrust the compass at the best of times, I closed my mind to his suggestion: 'The compass says this way, so just keep aiming for that darker patch of sky.'

I had a local error of 43° set on the compass, with five more degrees added to cope with the effect of the boat's engine and metal fittings. How great the magnetic Pole's influence was I could not tell but I had, over twenty years of navigating, developed a certain faith in the compass.

To our great relief, after two hours of nothingness and our first chunks of floating ice, Rabbit Island loomed close ahead and, an hour later, we stopped in Cow Cove, a protected beach. The next morning we returned with our camp-kit to the boat to find the wind had boxed through 180° and the whaler, now on a lee-shore, was full of water and being pounded by breakers.

For two days we drained the fuel system and dried our gear; then, in a twenty-knot wind and the usual fog, we entered the narrows of Dolphin and Union Strait. For thirty-six hours without a break we ploughed east. We grew very tired and had to shout and sing to force our brains to stay alert. We determined not to stop, for there was no beach with a stitch of cover from the surf. The evenings, when the mists rolled back, were full of wild beauty which faded from red dusk to purple dawn with no darkness between. But winter was poised. Already the sun at midnight caressed the silent surface of the sea.

For 340 miles we stood in the narrow space between helm and fuel cans until at last, dodging a rash of inlets, we crossed a narrow channel to Victoria Island and left the mainland coast for the first time. We spent the night at Lady Franklin where I set up the radio. Ginnie came through clearly from Tuktoyaktuk. She and Simon were watching live coverage of Prince Charles's wedding. The previous night a storm had sunk many of the local Eskimo boats, complete with outboard engines and fishing gear, so she had been worried about us.

Over the next four days we were delayed by outboard troubles 130 miles east of Lady Franklin but limped on through rain and high winds. Wild storms lashed our passage across the mouths of bays, one wider than the English Channel, and past forlorn capes of twisted red lava domes. There was no shelter, no landing beach until we reached Cambridge Bay Eskimo settlement.

Because Ginnie was losing radio contact with us, she and Simon moved their base to Resolute Bay on Cornwallis Island. On their way north they stopped in at Cambridge Bay and I noticed a black dog, smaller than Bothie, in Ginnie's kit-bag.

'What,' I asked, 'is this?'

'Ah,' she said. 'This is Tugaluk. Two months old and a good dog.'

'Whose is she?' I pressed. Ginnie blustered and I knew she was feeling maternal. If she had left the dog in Tuktoyaktuk, she said, it would have been shot as a stray. Bothie had fallen in love, she added, but he would doubtless get over it in Resolute and then Ginnie would give the puppy to a new owner. The matter was closed, Ginnie was clearly intimating, but the very fact that she had given the dog a name struck me as sinister.

Ginnie and the others flew on and, a day later, we too left Cambridge Bay.

*　　　　*　　　　*

Originally I had planned to strike east across Queen Maud Gulf by way of Jenny Lind Island, but a tongue of pack-ice had recently slid down in a northerly wind and blocked off this route, so we detoured south an extra 200 miles to creep around the pack. The navigation was complex and only possible with total concentration. All day a mist obscured the coastline. We passed through corridors between nameless islands filled with shoals where the sea boiled between gaunt stacks of dripping rock. Hour after hour I strained my eyes through the misty glare to recognise some feature but there were islands of all shapes and sizes and the coastline was so heavily indented with fjords, bays and islets that the fog made it easy to mistake a through-channel for a dangerous cul-de-sac.

After 130 miles of nerve-racking progress between these shoals, a storm came at us from the west and threw great rolling waves over the reefs. I deemed it too risky to continue and we camped on Perry Island in a sheltered cove. After twenty-four hours the storm showed signs of abating so, impatient, we ploughed on east for ten hours, often out of sight of land.

Since the compass was useless and the sun made no appearance all day I kept my nose glued to the charts. At dusk the storm renewed its attack and we plunged through cresting breakers. I prayed we would not strike a reef in the dark.

Close to midnight, a gap in the cloudbanks revealed a low gap along the dim silhouette of the cliff-line. Nosing inland, we were rewarded with a sheltered islet where we spent the remaining four hours until dawn. We shivered uncontrollably in the tent and agreed to broach a bottle of whisky. By dawn the bottle was empty and we were shivering less.

With the first streaks of eastern light we squelched back into the survival suits, our thighs red-raw from the long days of salty chafing. For nineteen hours we weaved our way through innumerable gravel islands, a task made easier when the sun decided to show itself weakly through the post-storm haze.

At Gjoa Haven, the Eskimos or Inuit as they prefer to be called, warned us that pack-ice blocked the Humboldt Channel and the Wellington Strait to the north, my planned route, and we would be crazy to attempt to travel to Resolute Bay without first calling at the last Inuit settlement in the region, Spence Bay, to hire boat guides. I eagerly concurred and, after crossing Rae Strait in fine weather, we entered Spence Bay – the halfway point on our voyage to Alert.

Here we obtained the services of an Inuit hunter with an unrivalled knowledge of the area. He was accompanied by the local Mountie and three Inuit boatmen. We followed our guides whose boats, like ours, were some sixteen feet long and outboard-powered. An hour or two north of Spence Bay the Inuit turned inland and shelved their craft on a beach. We hovered offshore. 'What's wrong?' I shouted.

'There's a storm coming', the Mountie shouted, 'a bad one. Our friends will go no further and advise you to stop here or head back to the village.'

The sky looked clear and my overall fear of winter catching us in the passage overrode any suspicion that the Inuit might be right. I was also suffering from the delusion that I knew better than the Inuit. There was no apparent danger, so why waste precious time?

For a hundred miles we moved north until the storm caught us. The coastline was not blessed with a single nook or cove where we could seek shelter. Committed, and caught between heavy pack-ice and a hostile lee-shore, we had no choice but to struggle on. After six hours of drenching with ice-cold water our eyes were inflamed and our fingers ached with cold. Thankfully, we reached a keyhole-cove named Parsley Bay and turned east – directly away from the wind – to gain shelter.

But the next two miles proved the wisdom of the Inuit and only luck saved us from a watery end. The bay was a boat-trap. Waves followed one another, steep and close, so that our bows plunged off one six-foot wall, down its front and into, not over, the next. The whaler was awash. Waves smashed on to the prow and filled the cockpit. Visibility was difficult. As soon as we opened our salt-filled eyes, more water would cascade over our heads.

Surf pounded against the beach when we finally made the crossing, but we located the mouth of a small river and the boat was flung into its estuary on a surge of flying foam.

Next day the sea was down to an angry but manageable swell outside the bay and we clung to the coastline to avoid the ever-increasing presence of ice.

A day later, some miles past the vertiginous cliffs of Limestone Island, a strong northerly wind sprang up and set the entire ice-pack of Barrow Strait on the move. It became painfully obvious that, inching along a north-facing coastline with no likely place of shelter, we stood in grave danger of being crushed. Much to Charlie's annoyance I decided to retreat until conditions were safer. This involved back-tracking by twenty miles to a shallow bay for protection from the encroaching pack.

On the morning of our third day in the cove a skein of new ice sheened the surface of the bay, a nasty reminder of the approaching freeze-up. Next day the wind changed and we threaded our way out of the cove, now all but beset by crowding bergs. Later we crossed Barrow Strait, forty miles wide, and nudged past pack-ice into the cove of Resolute Bay, capital city of the archipelago.

Resolute is home to over 200 Eskimos and a number of transient Canadians, mostly technicians and scientists. Ginnie was housed in a tiny shack with her radio beside her bunk, Simon lived in the main scientists' accommodation. The black dog from Tuktoyaktuk had grown to almost twice Bothie's size and Ginnie was plainly infatuated. Our outlook from Resolute to Alert looked bleak. In a week or so the sea would almost certainly undergo a general freeze-up, stranding us *in situ*.

The Resolute meteorological station commander proved to me by way of his ice-charts that we were all but blocked into Resolute for the year. The strait east of Bathurst Island was frozen, as was the northern end of Lancaster Sound. All routes to the west and northwest were already solidly iced. We could still attempt a 600-mile detour round Devon Island but its eastern coast was storm-bound and a maze of icebergs. I thanked him and opted for the last course through lack of an alternative.

For four days our whaler, very nearly crushed in an overnight ice-surge, was blocked inside Resolute Bay cove. Then, on 25 August, a southerly wind allowed us to escape east along the coastline of Cornwallis Island.

The seas were rough and high for hundreds of miles and the coast to our north was either teetering cliff or glacier, pounding surf or disintegrating icebergs. With over 1000 miles to Alert and under a week before freeze-up, we slept little.

With high waves breaking violently upon icebergs all about us, we were caught ten miles short of any shelter at nightfall. Two propeller blades broke against growlers. Straining my eyes up at the mountaintops silhouetted against the moonless night sky was not easy, for the boat bucked and danced in the waves. Charlie fought the tiller to avoid icebergs visible only at the last moment. By weak torch battery and wet chart I guessed at the location of Dundas Bay and we nosed cautiously past cliffs against which waves smashed twenty feet high, faintly luminous through the dark. The mouth of the bay was crammed with grinding bergs and only lack of choice made us risk pressing on. Once past the outer ring of clashing icebergs a huge swell took over from the breakers. Soaked to the skin and numb-handed, we secured the boat between two grounded bergs and camped in a long-deserted Inuit hut. For an hour before sleeping we let the tension unwind as we lay on the floor propped up by our elbows, sipping tea by candlelight and chatting of army days long ago in Arabia. Charlie's not such a bad old sod after all, I thought to myself.

The next five days are etched on my memory. I remember a blur of danger, a race against the dropping thermometer and constant cold. The nastier the elements, the further the natural barrier of restraint between Charlie and me dissipated. Our latent antagonism disappeared altogether once the predicament of the moment passed the danger level and became positively unpleasant.

Glacial valleys draining enormous ice-fields created bergs larger than cathedrals, which sailed seaborne from their dark spawning valleys to collect off the coast. Battered ceaselessly by waves containing broken ice-chunks, these bergs disintegrated bit by bit. A course running parallel to the cliffs and four hundred yards offshore seemed the least dangerous.

Waves smashed against cliffs and icebergs in a welter of thundering surf. Our port shearpin split against a growler, a half-submerged chunk of ice, entailing a repair job only possible at anchor. We prayed the second engine would keep going or we would soon be fibreglass matchwood, ground to pieces by rock or ice.

Eventually we found a deep inlet between cliffs. At the only possible landing point a large polar bear sat watching us, so we stopped in rocky shallows and fought to steady the craft among basking beluga whales. I stood in the sea holding the stern while Charlie worked as fast as he could on the propeller. The bear dived into the sea and swam around us. We kept the rifle to hand but only the animal's nose and eyes remained above water as it swam.

After three hundred miles we rounded the northeastern tip of Devon Island and aimed across Jones Sound for Ellesmere Island. At Grise Fjord, the most northerly Inuit village in Canada, we beached the boat in a safe cove and rested for twenty-four hours. Our skin was the texture of etiolated bacon, our faces burned dark by the wind and the glare. We had lost a good deal of weight and various parts of our bodies, especially our crutches, thighs and armpits, were suffering from open sores and boils. The sea was due to freeze over in two or three days should the winds drop and flatten the water.

Back in Resolute, Ginnie, fully aware of the dangers of Devon Island's east coast, had awaited my radio call for twenty-eight hours. At Grise Fjord I fixed up an antenna between Inuit drying frames and, although her voice sounded faint and faraway, I could detect Ginnie's happiness that we had reached Ellesmere Island.

With forty-eight hours to go and five hundred sea miles to cover to the most northerly point we could hope to reach, Tanquary Fjord, we slid into our damp survival suits after emptying the last of our foot powder down the leggings.

The journey to Hell's Gate Channel was a blur of black cliff, freezing spray and increasing pack-ice. The channel was blocked with bergy bits but, through good fortune, the alternative corridor, Cardigan Strait, was partially open and we edged into it beneath the great mountains which guard the western gateway of Jones Sound.

The long detour had paid off, but that same evening the surface of the sea began to freeze, congealing silently and quickly. Twenty miles south of Great Bear Cape we were caught between pack-ice and newly-forming frazil ice, a paper-thin crystalline cover.

Forcing our way back south through the new crust, we spent an anxious night camped at the edge of Norwegian Bay and Ginnie promised to obtain aerial guidance if she could. At noon on 29 August, Russ Bomberry, a Mohawk chief and one of the best bush pilots in the Arctic, flew his Twin Otter overhead for two hours to guide us, by a labyrinthine route, through sixty miles of loose pack to Great Bear Cape. When Russ flew away back to Resolute, we broached our last bottle of whisky. We slept five hours over the next two days and prayed for once that the wind would continue to blow. It did and the surface grease ice did not settle thickly enough to prevent us ascending Greely Fjord, Canon Fjord and finally the dark narrows of Tanqary Fjord, a cul-de-sac deep within glacier-cut mountains.

Tiers of snow-capped peaks rimmed the winter sky as we snaked deep into a twilit world of silence. Wolves stared from shadowed lava beaches but nothing moved except ourselves to sunder in our wash the mirror images of the darkened valley walls. Twelve minutes before midnight on 30 August we came to the end of the fjord. The sea journey was over. Within a week the sounds behind us were frozen.

Alert camp lay a hundred and fifty miles to the northeast of Tanqary Fjord. With the temperature dropping daily and sunlight hours fleeing over the polar horizon, we needed to reach Alert within three weeks. The eastern heights of the main United States Range and the Grant Ice-cap block a straightforward overland route to the northeast. We planned to use skis and snowshoes, rucksacks and light fibreglass sledges to cross the ice barrier, carrying fourteen days' food and fuel from Tanqary Fjord where we abandoned the boat.

Charlie carried his bear-gun and I packed a .44 Ruger revolver into my eighty-pound rucksack. We followed a series of riverain valleys, trudging slowly, for we were weak from the months of boat travel and the salt-chafed places that rubbed as we walked. In one narrow valley a huge ice-tongue, an offshoot from the ice-cap, tumbled into the canyon blocking our advance. Summer floods had cut a tunnel through this icy barrier so, with heads bent and rucksacks dragged, we crept underneath the glacier.

Charlie slipped on ice and his forehead struck a rock. Hearing him shout, I dropped my pack and ran back, thinking a bear had attacked him. Blood filled one of his eyes and covered one side of his face and neck. He felt sick and faint. An hour later, bandaged and dizzy, he carried on. That night we checked his feet and found broken, weeping blisters covering both his soles and most of his toes. He said he ached all over.

Charlie and I seldom walked together. Sometimes we were separated by an hour or more. In a film made later of the Expedition, Charlie said: 'Ran is always pushing himself. He can't do it the easy way. I don't know what drives him but he always pushes himself. I'm not that way inclined. I'm a slow plodder. If I tried to keep up with him, I wasn't going to make it.'

Each time I stopped to wait for Charlie, I became cold and impatient and swore at him. If I had moved at his pace I could have avoided this, and I did try once or twice to do so. But I just could not maintain such a desultory amble.

On the third morning ice crystals lined our tent, although we were merely a thousand feet above sea-level. Snow covered the land and walking was difficult. Skis were not practical due to long stretches of ice and rock. Charlie's left eye was quite closed and puffed up like a yellow fungus. His back and his knees and his blistered feet all hurt him. The blister wounds had gone septic and walking must have been purgatory for him.

In mid-September we passed Omingmak Mountain and Charlie could go no further without a rest. His groin glands were swollen with poison and his knees with fluid. But winter was coming and I urged him to keep going, for we had to complete the journey over the high ice-caps before polar sundown. There seemed little point anyway in waiting for new skin to replace the open sores on Charlie's feet since the first few miles on snowshoes would soon re-open them.

We emptied the contents of our rucksacks onto our light portable sleds and, strapping on snowshoes, set out in a cuttingly cold wind. The temperature fell to −18°C as we passed Lake Hazen. North of the lake I tried to follow a bearing of 130° but the compass was sluggish. Musk-oxen snorted and stamped as we loomed through the freezing fog.

There were no distinguishing landmarks. At 2200 feet above sea-level we camped in a frozen gulley at −20°C, a temperature which remained steady for three days' hauling through deep snowfields where the stillness was immense. No musk-oxen now. Nothing and nobody.

Over the rim of the Grant Ice-cap, spurred on by increasing cold, we limped at last to the edge of the high plateau beneath the twin glaciers of Mount Wood, dwarfed by the blue ice-falls which rose to the sky. A wary hush presided below these 2000-foot ice-formations. A cataclysmic event seemed imminent. Craning my neck back to ease my knotted shoulder muscles, I glanced up and felt momentary unease as the sky-high ice-falls seemed to teeter on the verge of collapse.

Towards dusk we found the narrow entry-point to the upper canyon of Grant River, a winding ravine that falls thirty miles to the sea. The canyon kinked, snaked and was blocked by black boulders, so that often we manhandled the sleds over solid rock for hundreds of yards.

On 26 September, towards noon, the river-bed plunged thirty feet down a frozen waterfall. From the top of this cleft we could see the Arctic Ocean, a jagged vista of contorted pack-ice stretching away to the polar horizon. Nine hours' travel along the edge of the frozen sea, dreaming of warmth and comfort, brought us to Cape Belknap and, by dusk, to the four little huts that we knew so well, the most northern habitation on earth.

We had travelled around the Polar axis of the world for 314° of latitude in 750 days. Only 46° to go but, looking north at the chaotic ice-rubble and remembering our failure in 1978, we knew that the journey to date had been easy compared with what lay ahead.

Five days before our arrival at Alert, Ginnie had flown in with winter equipment, our old Antarctic skidoos and the two dogs. The three of us spent the next four months of permanent darkness in the Alert huts preparing equipment, completing a new series of scientific research tasks and training on the local pack-ice.

In mid-January the Alert met-man warned me his sea-ice recordings showed a thickness of 87cm, thinner than that of any previous January on record, the average being 105cm.

The true cold, which crackles the nose and ears like parchment, congeals the blood in fingers and toes like rapidly setting glue and fixes the sea-ice slowly into a precarious platform to the Pole, finally came in late January. Better late than never. The camp thermometer hovered around −51°C with a fresh ten-knot breeze. One night a fox outside the hut awoke me and I noticed Ginnie's hot-water bottle lying in between her bed-sock'd feet – frozen solid.

We received a radio message from a Californian friend. Walt Pedersen, the American aiming to reach both Poles, had given up his impending attempt on the South Pole due to stonewalling by the US National Science Foundation.

Prince Charles radioed through to Ginnie and mentioned he had heard rumours of a Norwegian team racing us to cross the Arctic. 'No racing,' he said to me with a stern edge to his voice.

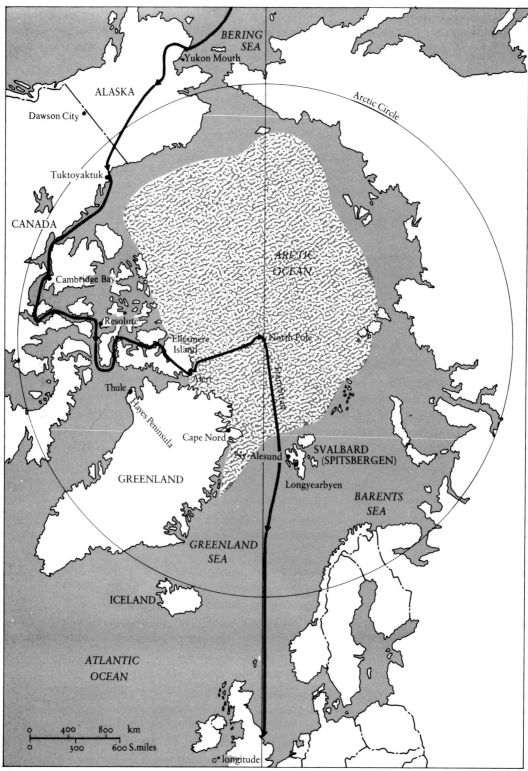

The Transglobe Expedition's Route across the Arctic

By the last day of January I must decide when to set out to cross the Arctic. To start prior to the first appearance of the sun would be to lay myself open to accusations of irresponsibility. On the other hand it was imperative that we reach the North Pole before the annual summer break-up. Once at the Pole we would at least be in the zone of currents which float their ice-cover in the general direction of Spitsbergen or Russia. If we delayed our departure from Alert until after sun-up in March, as in 1977, we would again risk falling short of our target. Whenever we set out we could not be certain that success was attainable, for the simple reason that no man had ever crossed the Arctic in a single season.

On 13 February 1982 I said a quick goodbye to Ginnie. We had spent the previous night in our hut closing our minds bit by bit to reality. Over the years we have found it better that way. The wrench of departure was worse than in Antarctica for we both knew the southern crossing was a mere nursery slope compared with the Arctic.

The weather was clear, although the day was as dark as night, when we pulled away from the huts. I glanced back and saw Ginnie clutching her two dogs closely and looking up at the passage of darkness by which we had left. At such moments we both wished she had never conceived the idea of the journey.

Charlie and I sat astride the open, heavily laden skidoos, each towing six hundred pounds of fuel and gear. Our beards and eyelashes were ice-laden within minutes, for the chill factor was −90°C when stationary, increasing with the speed of our advance. We followed a wild zig-zag way along the dark and ice-girt coast. I remembered the 1977 travels which helped me not to get lost although that year we had of course travelled in daylight. Crossing a high pass somewhere on the Fielden Peninsula, Charlie turned his sledge over on a steep slope above sheer cliffs. He managed to extricate himself some yards from a long drop into the dark.

On 17 February we came in twilight to a canal of newly open water from which emanated dark clouds of frost-smoke. In the depths of winter, long before sunrise and at a point of maximum coastal pressure, this was an ominous sign.

With extra care we skirted the canal and entered the narrow corridor of blue ice between the glacier of Mount Cooper Key and a high wall of ice-blocks formed inland by encroaching ice. Apart from this ten-yard passage there was no other landward route west. We emerged a short distance east of Cape Columbia, that coastal point off which the southerly sea currents split west and east. This makes the Cape a sensible jumping-off point from land-ice to sea-ice. After axeing ourselves a ramp of ice blocks we took the skidoos over a twenty-foot void above the tide-crack. We were now at sea.

We camped 300 yards out from the coast in a field of broken ice. In a way I was glad of the darkness for it prevented a wider and therefore more depressing view of our route north. I pressed a mitt to the raw end of my nose and was silent as a host of vignettes flooded my mind, memories of what had passed last time we tried to pit our wits against the power of the Arctic pack.

During the first day of twilit labour we cleared 800 yards of highway through the pressure rubble. Our axed lane was precisely the width of a skidoo and it followed the line of least resistance, thereby adding 75 per cent of extra distance to the straight course we would have taken were it not for obstacles. To gain the Pole we must cover 825 miles – then much further again on its far side to reach a potential rendezvous point with the ship.

There were two dangers: failure to reach the Pole – and therefore the Spitsbergen current – by break-up time, and the subsequent worry of reaching the *Benjamin Bowring* before the end of summer when the ship must retreat to more southerly waters. We could not hope to achieve either goal without air re-supply from the Twin Otter which was to fly out from England with Gerry Nicholson and a skilled Arctic pilot called Karl Z'berg, the Swiss Canadian who had flown our chartered Otter in 1977.

On February 19th we axed our skidoo lane through 200 yards of twelve foot high ice blocks. With a total of 1000 yards cleared we went back to bring skidoos and sleds up to our new front-line point.

Charlie and I both weighed 185 pounds, so together, by using our joint weight as a fulcrum, we could just shift the 800-pound laden skidoos and the 600-pound sledges over any insufficiently axed blockages.

Damage to equipment was inevitable as the only way to negotiate the switchback lane was at full tilt, bouncing off walls and over iron-hard slabs. On 19 February, halfway along the lane we had axed, my drive axle snapped. That did it: I determined to switch to manpower and abandon the skidoos – at least for the first 100 miles where the pressure rubble would be at its worst.

The previous winter at Alert, preparing for this eventuality, I had tested two lightweight eight-foot pulks and it was with these fibreglass sleds, carrying 190 pounds each, that we pushed north on 22 February. After eight hours of haulage, our underwear, socks, facemasks and jackets were soaking wet or frozen, depending on which part of the body they covered and on whether we were resting or pulling at the time.

My haemorrhoids became worse day by day until I could think of little else. The constant vicious tugging of my shoulder and waist harness, as the pulk jammed against snags, exacerbated the discomfort. Charlie's lower back and his knees pained him constantly but, by the end of four dark days, we had logged eleven northerly miles. This would not sound very impressive except to someone who has pulled a load in excess of his own bodyweight over pressure rubble in the dark and at a temperature of −40°C.

Charlie plodded on at his own pace and, unable to slow down, I stopped every hour for twenty minutes or more for him to catch up. I attempted to avoid freezing solid during these long waits by cursing the Arctic in general and Charlie in particular. Sheer exhaustion overcame any fear of bears or indeed of falling into the sea.

Charlie and I saved time daily by never cooking breakfast. We merely drank a mug of coffee from our vacuum flask, heated the night before. This gave us the courage to unzip our bags and climb into our frosted clothes and boots. For seven months we were to remain in precisely the same clothing without washing.

We dragged behind us, man for man, the same weight as Scott and his team. Their aim was to be first to reach the South Pole, ours was to be first to reach both Poles. Like them, we were racing the clock. On 3 March, at −49°C, the blood-red ball of the sun slid briefly along the rim of the sea. Sunlight, although welcome to improve visibility, was our number-one enemy. Ultra-violet rays would now begin to eat at the structure of the pack-ice and, by mid-April, so weaken the ice that the least pressure from the wind would crack up the floes and halt our progress.

At 4.00 a.m. on 4 March, at −40°C, a fire broke out in our stores hut at Alert. Ginnie rushed out with an extinguisher but, 'It was just one big fireball inside with smoke issuing from the seams in the walls and flames filling the windows . . . There were forty-five gallon drums of fuel stacked by the wall. They had been there for years and were frozen into the ice.' While they watched, eight drums of gasoline exploded, as did fusillades of rocket flares and 7.62 FN rifle bullets.

Until that point the world's press had ignored the expedition. Now newspapers and television screens all over the world carried headlines such as 'Conflagration at Polar Base' and 'Polar Expedition in Flames'. After the night of the fire every action we took – and one or two that we didn't – became news from London to Sydney, from Cape Town to Vancouver.

Seven years beforehand Ginnie had argued that I should lay an equipment cache at Tanqary Fjord as well as at Alert – just in case. With the generous help of the Canadian Coastguard's icebreaker two years before, we had done so. This meant that the expedition need not now be abandoned. Spare radios, generators, ice rations and skidoo gear were available for Karl Z'berg to collect from Tanquary as soon as the weather allowed. I made a mental note to tell Ginnie she was not just a pretty face.

With enough food for eight days we digested the news of the fire – about which we could do nothing – and concentrated on northerly progress, yard by painful yard. Our shoulders and hips were raw from the rub of the pulk harnesses. My nose, weeping blood and fluid for the last two weeks, was now frost-nipped as well. The rough and frozen material of my face-mask chafed the wound and I could no longer wipe away nose-dribble with the back of my mitts, so a sheen of ice, constantly growing in size, covered the bottom half of my face-mask, punctured only by the small hole over my mouth.

At night the act of breathing caused the worst discomfort. Generally speaking, polar travel would be quite pleasant if it was not necessary to breathe. When we tried to snuggle down inside our sleeping bags, our breath formed a thick rime of frost where it met cold air. The resulting frost layers cascaded down our necks whenever we moved. To avoid this I blocked both nostrils up with plugs of Kleenex tissue and tried to position my mouth to breathe out of the bag's hood-hole. This worked well except that my frostbitten nose remained outside the bag's warmth and, unprotected from the tent's average temperature of −40°C, was far colder than a deep-freeze.

A storm blew up and shattered the ice-pack. All about us were vast areas of open sea where, for at least the next two months, the ice should have remained largely solid. On the coast behind us, the five-man Norwegian expedition, which had announced its intention to beat us across the Arctic, were astonished to find open sea and no ice at all in sight. They made camp on the land and waited.

On 14 March Karl and Simon located the two skidoos we had abandoned along the coastline and managed to land the Twin Otter beside them. Later they delivered the skidoos and steel sledges to us on a flat floe. Overjoyed at shrugging off the harnesses, we continued by skidoo and were blessed by a patch of good going.

Still travelling at dusk, I swerved to avoid a sudden canal and drove straight into a trench full of *shuga* porridge-ice. I was flung clear and watched my skidoo sink out of sight within a minute. The steel sledge slowly up-ended but I caught hold of its lashing strap. Charlie ran over in response to my yelling. He attempted to save our tent by removing his mitts in order to undo a lashing buckle. In seconds his fingers began to freeze and, before we could loosen the tent, the sledge disappeared underwater. We saved only our radio and theodolite.

Charlie's hands were in immediate danger. I erected a makeshift shelter from the tarpaulin with which Charlie used to cover the vehicles and started up the cooker. He spent an hour forcing blood slowly back into his hand and so saved his fingers from anything worse than painfully nipped ends. We passed an extremely uncomfortable night at −40°C under the sieve-like tarpaulin with one bag between us.

Two days later Karl found a landing floe half a mile from our location and brought in a skidoo, sledge and gear from Tanqary Fjord. 'Don't sink any more skidoos,' he advised. 'That's your last.'

Forty-knot winds battered the pack and we headed north in a semi-white-out. With no visible sun I followed my compass needle.

On 16 March, with millions of tons of ice on the move all about us, we camped and lay listening to the awe-inspiring boom and crackle of invading floes. The anemometer rose to fifty-five knots and weaker pans fractured all about us, nipped and flaked by their larger jostling neighbours. One crack opened up twenty yards from our tent and cut us off on an island for a day.

Ginnie warned me that the Press were turning critical. In England the *Daily Mail* stated that the Transglobe sponsors were considering finding a new leader since our chances of success were looking bad. One reporter interviewed Paul Berriff of the BBC-film crew who, reminiscing about the Canadian expedition, said the soldiers on that journey had mutinied and threatened me with knives. In Vancouver reporter Moira Farrow pointed out that SAS members Fiennes and Burton had cleverly cut themselves off in the Arctic beyond all possible recall by their regiment for service in the Falkland Islands war.

When the storm died away we packed up in conditions of total white-out and moved off into a curtain of brown gloom, a certain sign of open water. Within minutes I narrowly missed driving into the edge of a river of moving sludge.

Charlie and I took a deep breath and spent two perilous days pussy-footing through a sludge swamp, often crossing lakes of half-inch-thick ice which writhed under our skidoos and broke under the sharp runners of the sledges. God was good to us on both days.

The next two days passed by in a haze. We pushed on our bruised bodies.

My chin was numb one evening when I came into the tent. I must have pulled my frozen facemask off too hard. When thawing the garment out over the cooker and picking ice-bits from around the mouthpiece, I found a one-inch swatch of my beard complete with skin implanted in a bloody patch of iced wool. It took a while to detach this from the mask. Where the skin had torn away from my chin, there was an open patch of raw flesh the size of a penny. In a while my chin warmed up and bled. Then it wept liquid matter which froze once the cooker was turned off.

On 22 March I shot the sun with my theodolite and found the loose pack had drifted us many miles too far east. I applied a 15° westerly correction and we moved on at a good rate. My chin throbbed like a tom-tom by nightfall and, running out of antibiotic cream, I applied some pile-cream.

'He's got piles on his chin,' Charlie shrieked with mirth. It was lucky we shared a weird sense of humour.

During a long axe-session I cut through one mukluk, the blade slicing through the nail of my big toe and deep into the flesh beneath. Charlie bound it up with gauze liberally daubed with pile-cream.

For a week we averaged fifteen miles a day, sometimes travelling for sixteen hours at a time in what we called a 'double-shuffle'. Charlie was frost-nipped along the length of his nose and one of my eyelids puffed up with wind-burn. Navigation was becoming more or less instinctive, with or without the sun.

On 27 March, at −41°C with twenty-three knots blowing in our faces, we had to stop frequently to restore blood to our extremities. Fingers were quickly numbed by axe-work. My neck glands puffed up. The whites of my eyes were blood-red: I could not navigate wearing protective goggles and the glare was intense.

A memorably evil day was 29 March, during which we pushed to the limits of skidoo travel. Streamers of brown vapour wafted through the overall fog and soft squeaking, grinding sounds emanated from the moving sludge banks we passed. To check each apparently weak section, before charging it on my skidoo, I went ahead gingerly on foot with my ice-prod. Charlie advanced halfway between me and the sledges, calling from time to time when I lost sight of him in the gloom.

When we made it at last to solid ice I felt elated. If we can cross that, I thought, we can go anywhere. We stopped at 87°02', within nine miles of our most northerly camp in 1977 but forty days earlier in the season. If our aim had been solely to reach the Pole we could have felt reasonably confident.

As we crept north in early April the movement and noise of the floes increased. It seemed as though we were rushing pell-mell, caught in an unseen tidal race, towards the maw of the world, Poe's maelstrom.

For three days the troubled fissure zone of the convergence, the area where the Beaufort Gyral current ends, slowed us to a crawl. For some time we crossed a no-man's land where floes spun around in limbo, uncertain which way to go. Then the fringe of the transpolar drift began to take hold of all surface matter and we entered a new gyral with a strong northeasterly pull. A great deal of rubble was piled up in pyramidal heaps within the convergence and at 87°48' North we were stopped by the bulkiest wall I had ever seen in the Arctic. Rising to thirty-feet high, the barrier was well over 100 yards wide. It took us four hours to axe and four to cross.

After the convergence we entered a sixty-mile region of fissures and high barriers. On 8 April we crossed sixty-two sludge cracks, often by shovelling snow into the water and then ramming the resulting weak bridge before it sank.

Twenty miles short of the Pole the going improved dramatically. At mid-day on 10 April I carefully checked our noon latitude and each subsequent mile until we were at 90° North. I had no wish to overshoot the top of the world. We arrived there at 11.30 p.m. GMT and passed the news to Ginnie early on Easter Day 1982. We had become the first men in the world to have travelled the earth's surface to both Poles.

Apprehension about what lay ahead overshadowed any sense of achievement that we may otherwise have felt, for the *Benjamin Bowring* was still many cold months beyond our horizon.

I aimed south along a line some 15° east of the Greenwich Meridian. We changed to a routine of travel by night and sleep by day so that the sun would project my body's shadow ahead and prove a natural sundial.

As we left the Pole, the Transglobe crew steamed from Southampton harbour *en route* for Spitsbergen.

Over a thousand miles still separated us from the latitude to which the *Benjamin Bowring* might, with luck, be expected to smash her way when, in August, the pack was at its most penetrable. The *Benjamin Bowring* would not be able to penetrate heavy Arctic pack, being merely an ice-strengthened vessel, but, if we could reach as far down as 81° North, she might – through the skill of her skipper and the eyes of Karl in the Twin Otter – be able to thread her way into the pack's edge.

From the Pole all went well for four days – in reality, nights – during one of which we achieved a distance of thirty-one miles in twelve hours over a freakishly unbroken pan of floes. From 88° down to 86° the conditions deteriorated slowly with an increasing number of open leads. I had grown accustomed to keeping an eye ever open for potential Twin Otter landing strips. But for the last forty miles there had been neither a single floe flat enough for a landing nor a pan solid enough to camp on safely during a storm.

The temperature rose to −20°C and stayed there. New ice no longer congealed over open leads within twenty-four hours, so wide canals with no crossing-points became permanent stoppers, not mere hold-ups. Long foot patrols to find crossing-points became increasingly necessary. Following a brief storm on 23 April we axed for two hours through a forest of twelve-foot-high green rafted blocks and reached a series of winding couloirs of new ice packed with black pools of sludge. Alongside this marsh I tripped and fell. My hands shot out to ward off a heavy fall. My axe disappeared and sank. My arms pierced the surface up to the elbows and one leg up to the knee, but the snow-covered sludge held my body weight. Seven miles later seawater cut us off in all directions except back north, so we camped. The wind blew at thirty knots and chunks of ice, floating across pools and along canals, all headed east.

That night I told Charlie I would begin to search for a floe on which to float south. He was horrified, feeling we would never reach the ship if we did not make much more southerly progress before beginning to float. Stop now and the expedition would fail. I argued with him that wind and current should take us to 81° before winter, providing we could only locate a solid enough floe to protect us during storm-crush conditions. If we waited one day too long before locating such a floe we could easily be cut off on a rotten pan and then there would be no answer to our predicament. Better safe than sorry. Charlie agreed to disagree. But, he reminded me, in the future – whatever happened – I should remember the decision to risk a float from so far north was mine alone.

Two days later we escaped from the weak pan and managed to progress another five miles south on increasingly thin ice. Then came two solid second-year floes which were cut off from the south by a river of grey sludge. At a point where this was only 100 yards wide, I decided to risk a crossing attempt.

Charlie wrote in his diary:

It was not completely open. There was ice on it, bad ice rather like sponge-rubber. We tried to cross it. I gave Ran a bit of a start then followed. But I saw him stop, swing around and turn back towards me and, at the same time, I felt a motion underneath me like being on a roller-coaster. I looked back and saw the ice behind me was actually breaking into waves. I realised the same thing must be happening to Ran. He was trying to get off the river . . . When these two waves meet – mine and Ran's – I thought – I don't want to be on this lead. So I turned in a big sweep and managed to run up on to some firm ice and Ran went past me and got back on to the floe where we'd left it. We chatted about this. We had been on this sort of ice before but we have never encountered such big liquid waves.

With no alternative, we camped. Four days later I thought the river ice had congealed and attempted to cross by skidoo. To my surprise my sledge runners broke through the sludge at a point where I had safely walked an hour earlier. Thereafter the river remained at the same tacky consistency, insufficient for sledge weight. The temperature rose towards 0°.

I told Charlie we should stay on the floe and try to find the safest spot. He searched for cracks and weak points and eventually decided upon a line of hummocks along the impact point of an old pressure ridge. We flattened out the top of this high ground with axes and made a camp there.

During the first week of May I asked Ginnie to send us two light canoes and rations for a long float. She flew with Karl, Gerry and Simon from Alert to the northeast corner of Greenland and at remote Cape Nord set up her last radio base. She told me that the remnants of the Norwegian expedition racing us to cross the Arctic had reached the Pole too late to continue and had been evacuated.

On 11 May, without a sound, our floe split apart 500 yards east of our tent and we lost a third of our original real-estate. Bending over the edge of the newly opened canal, I saw that our own floe was some five or six feet thick. I had hoped for a minimum of eight feet but – too bad – we were committed to this place.

Our tent floor of axed ice was uneven and daily became more sodden with water as the surface of the floe melted down. Soon, all about our slightly raised platform, the floe became a floating pool of vivid blue salt-water, five feet deep in places.

Late in May two members of our London committee travelled to Spitsbergen to visit the ship. Karl flew them over the pack and, horrified at our overall predicament, they returned to London and warned the committee that our chances of success this summer were minimal. We must be airlifted out at once while such a course was still possible or any subsequent disaster would be on their hands. Ginnie queried the committee's follow-up message, a direct evacuation order, and rallied those in London who were against such a course. Only when the order had been softened to a recommendation that we abort the float but that the final decision should be mine, did Ginnie inform me.

I felt, and Charlie agreed, that there was still a strong chance of success without risking an international search-and-rescue operation, so we continued to float at the mercy of wind and current. For five days a southerly storm blew us back towards the Pole and for several days our southerly heading veered sharply towards Siberia, but overall we continued south at a steady rate towards Fram Strait, between Greenland and Spitsbergen.

Karl managed to land on a rare mist-free day. He dropped us off two tents, two canoes and a two-month supply of rations. He warned us that in another week he would no longer be able to take off from our soggy floe. We were on our own.

On 6 June in thick fog our floe was blown against our northerly neighbour and, where the ice touched, a fifteen-foot high wall of broken blocks reared up.

The sense of smell of the polar bear is phenomenal: they can detect a seal from ten miles away. Large males weigh half a ton, reach eight feet tall and tower to twelve feet when standing. They glide over ice quietly, yet can charge at thirty-five miles per hour.

One night in my sleeping bag I was woken by loud snuffling sounds beside my head on the other side of the tent cloth.

'Ran?' Charlie called.

Since his voice came from his own tent I knew with a sinking feeling that he was not snuffling about outside my tent. It must be a bear. Grabbing camera and loaded revolver, I peered outside. So did Charlie, whose eyeballs grew large as he spotted – behind my tent – a large bear. I craned my neck and three yards away saw the face of the bear which was licking its lips with a large black tongue. We photographed the fine animal and after a few minutes it shuffled away.

A week later another bear would not leave and showed signs of evil intent. We fired bullets and even a parachute flare over its head but the bear only grew irritable, swishing its tail to and fro and lowering its head. We agreed to shoot if it approached closer than thirty yards. It did, so I fired a bullet at its leg. The bear hesitated in mid-stride then broke sideways and loped away. There were blood splashes but no sign of a limp.

Over the next few weeks many bears crossed our floe and eighteen visited our camp, tripping over our guy-ropes. This kept us from getting bored by our inactive existence.

The uncertainty of our situation, especially at times when communications blacked out, was a great strain on Ginnie. She had a long history of migraines and spastic colon attacks and her life at Nord was full of pain and stress. She had no shoulder to cry on and no one from whom to seek advice. She hated this part of the expedition but kept steadily on at her job. Late in June Ginnie made contact with the *Benjamin Bowring*. The sooner she could remove us from our floe the better, for we were hastening into a danger area known as the Marginal Ice Zone, the ice pulverisation factory of Fram Strait. Two million square miles of the Arctic Ocean are covered by pack-ice and one-third of this load is disgorged every year through Fram Strait. Very soon now our own floe would enter this bottleneck, where currents accelerate by 100 per cent and rush their fragmenting ice burden south at an incredible thirty kilometres a day. Keenly aware of our danger, the skipper and crew agreed to take a risk. Arctic pack-ice is far more hazardous than the Antarctic equivalent.

All the crew had studied the Arctic Pilot for the region:

The Greenland sea pack-ice is in general unnavigable. In the northern part the pack may be up to six and a half feet thick. As a result of pressure due to wind or current the pack may be hummocked to a height of thirty feet. Typical damage to ships may include broken propeller blades, rudders and steering gear, damage to stern and plating causing leaks and the crushing of the hull. Also the buckling of plating and the tearing out of rivets . . .

On 2 July, after a game attempt, the ship was forced back some one hundred and fifty miles south of our floe. On 10 July the mist cleared at noon long enough for a sun shot. After seventy days on the floe we were at 82° North. That night a chunk of two acres split off our floe. The next-door floe rode up over a forty-yard front and 80 per cent of our pan was covered in slush or water up to seven feet deep. New ridgewalls rose up daily and noisily where we struck our neighbours. Off our seaside edges humpback whales sang at night and huge regattas of ice sailed by before the wind. There was seldom any sign of the sun and the low-hung sky reflected the dark blotches of great expanses of open sea to the south and north of our floating raft.

Hardly a day passed without a bear visit, sometimes two. For a while they came at us from our one remaining dry side but, as this narrowed, they took to swimming across the lake that hemmed us in. At night I would awake, my heart pounding. Was it a bear close by or a new breakage of the floe? By way of an answer, more often than not came the plunging roar of many tons of ice breaking off our floe-rim, followed by the rushing of waves striking the lead-banks.

As we approached nearer to Fram Strait we began to gyrate like scum heading for a drain. To remind us that summer here was short, the surface of our melt-pools began to freeze over.

The *Benjamin Bowring* tried a second time to reach us in mid-July and again they failed, this time putting themselves in considerable danger. Anton recorded: '. . . hurling the ship at six- to seven-feet thick floes which are breaking without too much difficulty. But the ice is more solid and further to the south than before . . . Evening: We are stuck solid at 82°07' north, 01°20' east, 82 miles south of Ran . . . Jimmy has spotted a cracked weld.'

Cleverly the skipper rammed a low floe and managed to lift the damaged bows clear of the sea. Two engineers worked, squatting on the ice, to effect temporary repairs with welding gear.

During the last week of July our floe was daily buffeted and diminished in size. Charlie had chosen our camp spot with great skill, as it was about the only part of the floe still uncracked. But on 29 July he showed me a widening seam close beside his tent. We had been on the floe ninety-five days and our entry into the crushing zone was imminent.

I told Ginnie and she spoke to the skipper. They decided to make a final dedicated push northwards. Karl flew Ginnie from Greenland to Longyearsbyen where she boarded the *Benjamin Bowring*. They set out on the first day of August, our seventh month out on the pack-ice, and – within twelve hours of smashing a straight route through medium pack – they reached a point forty-nine miles to our south.

Late on 2 August after a twenty-four-hour fight northwest through heavy ice and thick fog, the skipper reported sinister signs of a wind change. The pack would close about the ship if the wind rose. Throughout the long night the skipper and crew willed the ship north yard by yard in a potentially suicidal bid to reach us.

At 9.00 a.m. on 3 August Ginnie spoke on my radio. She sounded tired but excited. 'We are seventeen miles south of your last reported position and jammed solid.'

Charlie and I packed basic survival gear into our two canoes. We had hoped the *Benjamin Bowring* would smash her way to our floe, but this was clearly impossible. For us to attempt to travel from our floe might easily prove disastrous, for everything was in motion about us: great floating blocks colliding in the open channels and wide skeins of porridge ice marauding the sea lanes. At noon I took a sun shot which put us only twelve miles from the ship. A southerly wind could easily widen this gap. We left our bedraggled tents and I took a bearing south-east to the probable position of the ship, although this would alter as we moved and as time passed. The wind blew at twelve knots as we paddled nervously through the first open lead.

Having lain in our bags with scant exercise for so long, we were unfit. Charlie was nearly sick with the sudden effort. Every so often I filled my water bottle from a melt pool and we both drank deep.

Makeshift skids attached to the canoes snapped off on rough ice and then we dragged the boats along on their thin metal hulls.

Trying to negotiate a spinning mass of ice-islands in a wide lake, I glanced back and saw two high bergs crunch together with an impact that sent a surge of water towards my canoe. Luckily Charlie had not yet entered the moving corridor and so avoided being crushed.

At 7.00 p.m., climbing a low ridge to scout ahead, I saw an imperfection on the horizon along the line of my bearing. I blinked and it was gone. Then I saw it again – the distant masts of the *Benjamin Bowring*.

I cannot describe the feeling of that moment, the most wonderful of my life. I jumped high in the air, yelling at Charlie. He was out of earshot but I waved like a madman and he must have guessed.

For three years I had always known the chances of success were heavily loaded against us. I had never dared allow myself to hope. But now I knew and I felt the strength of ten men. I knelt down on the ice and thanked God.

For three hours we heaved and paddled. Sometimes we lost sight of the masts, but when they re-appeared they were always a little bigger.

At fourteen minutes past midnight on 4 August at 80°31' North, 00°59' West, all but astride the Greenwich Meridian, we climbed on board the *Benjamin Bowring*.

Ginnie was standing alone by a cargo hatch. Her eyes were full of tears, but she was smiling. Between us we had spent twenty years of our lives to reach this point.

Revelry lasted well into the night. There was no hurry now, which was just as well because the ship remained stuck fast for twelve days, until the wind changed.

From the lonely islands of Svalbard we steamed south through the Greenland Sea and the North Sea. On 29 August Prince Charles joined us on the Thames and brought the ship back to our starting-point at Greenwich, almost three years to the day since we had set out. Ten thousand cheering people lined the banks. Our polar circle around the world was complete.

That night, when all the crew and our friends had gone, Ginnie and I slept in our old cabin. I watched as she fell asleep and the lines of stress fell away from her face. I felt as happy as I have ever been and I thought of the words of an American poet: 'And the end of all our exploring will be to arrive where we started and know the place for the first time.'

15

Almost A Yuppie

Think sideways.

EDWARD DE BONO

Three days after returning home I learned that the expedition had accumulated a debt of £106,000 in my absence. Contracted to write a book, I had no time to raise this money and my fellow Transglobers were fast dispersing to find employment.

Anton Bowring appeared in our hour of need to announce that he considered the expedition completed only when all debts were paid. For the next eighteen months he and Ginnie worked to that end, a thankless task with long hours and no salary. They paid off our debtors and obtained a further £75,000 largely through sales of T-shirts and old Transglobe gear at Camden Lock street market. This surplus was paid out to all the Transglobers early in 1984, by which time Ginnie and I were urgently in need of a new project.

I turned forty that March and one of my presents was a sweatshirt emblazoned with the words 'I'm over the hill'. For a year or so my wrists and hips had suffered arthritic pains and my lower back was increasingly putting me out of action, sometimes for several days. I resolved to find a way of making a living that did not rely on my physical abilities and, for a while, I steadfastly turned down all proposals for new expeditions whilst searching for more sedentary work using a pen instead of boots.

People telephoned and wrote from all over the place, mostly the United States, Australia and Canada, with suggestions ranging from jungle quests for Aztec gold to fun-runs through the Gobi Desert. I regretfully declined them all, and even resigned from the SAS Territorials for it is very much a young man's regiment.

My book about the Transglobe Expedition made the *Sunday Times* Top Ten – the literary version of *Top of the Pops* – and for the first time in over fourteen years of marriage we found ourselves with all debts paid and money in hand. A delirious experience.

The aftermath of the circumpolar journey, which continued for nearly two years, included TV shows and promotion tours in Europe and the United States. I was even awarded an honorary Doctorate of Science and sighed to think of all those futile hours spent swotting up maths, physics and chemistry. *This Is Your Life* did manage to re-unite my mother and my three sisters in the same room for the first time in twenty-five years. Eamonn Andrews tricked me, with the connivance of Ginnie and others, into his *This Is Your Life* programme. He produced as though from a hat, but in reality through his generous travel budget, Jackie McConnell, Chris Cazenove, Gonda Butters from South Africa, Peter Tooth, Peter Loyd, Hamish Macrae and other fellow-expeditionaries including the entire Transglobe team, the history mistress who caught me on Ginnie's school roof and many other faces from the past.

It transpired that Eamonn's programme researcher, concentrating only on the more respectable periods of my life, had been entirely put off any military anecdotes after meeting my ex-Sultan's Forces' CO, Peter Thwaites who, when asked if he could regurgitate any tale of my bravely saving someone's life, replied with vehemence, 'Saving lives?! Fiennes wasn't out there to save lives. He was there to kill communists.'

Lecturing to gatherings of company executives, Ginnie and I travelled to Maui nine times, Hawaii four times, Helsinki, Seoul, Mauritius, Sydney, Acapulco and many other more remote spots. We flew to the USA for thirty-two separate conferences within eighteen months and made twice that many trips to continental Europe.

Bothie, about whom Ginnie wrote an illustrated book, was interviewed by Selina Scott on breakfast television. In the studio waiting-room, remembering the satisfaction of having snapped at Russell Harty the previous week, the terrier had a go at Arthur Scargill's hand when that miner patted him fondly with the words, 'I'm a doggy sort.' Later, escorting Ian MacGregor to a meeting at Claridge's, I mentioned Bothie's brush with Scargill. 'I hope he was injected against rabies,' commented the Coal Board chairman. 'Your dog, I mean.'

To keep fit I had jogged, for an hour, for many years four or five times a week. This practice must have damaged my back little by little and, some two years after the Transglobe journey, I could only walk with a severe list to starboard. After months of hip and disc pain, a brilliant doctor, Bernard Watkin of Wimpole Street, gave me a course of memorably deep injections in the lumbar region, pumping a dextrose solution into my lignacious tissue. This gave me a second life and a timely warning to stop punishing my body while it still functioned reasonably well.

I decided to try mountain walking as a palliative to wean myself from the need for expedition involvement. With Simon Gault, Geoff Newman and Nick Holder I spent long weekends in the Alps visiting the summits of Mont Blanc, the Jungfrau, the Matterhorn and others. This was enjoyable but no substitute for the real thing. As the less comfortable memories of the Transglobe years receded, I increasingly felt the lure of the North. Dr Frederick Cook, co-claimant as first man to reach the North Pole, wrote: 'A passion which has dominated my life – the voice of the Arctic. Something keeps calling, calling, until you can stand it no more and return, spellbound by the magic of the North.'

I determined to ignore this mesmeric polar attraction with the same vehemence as a smoker must shun thoughts of tobacco.

'Concentrate on writing,' Ginnie would say when she sensed my restlessness. 'You could do book reviews and travel articles. Lots of people make a living that way.'

I did receive a commission from *Departures*, the American Express magazine, for an illustrated article about an obscure, but bloody, nineteenth-century battle which took place in Oman between Anglo-Indian and rebel Omani troops. With this as a stimulus, I spent a summer there arranged by Patrick Brook, at the time the CO of the Sultan's Armoured Regiment.

A lone Dhofari officer with a .22 rifle led me along that part of his country's coastline which I had known as the *adoo* heartland, a region where I once feared to venture even by night and with thirty armed men.

Departures turned down my article, mainly because I had failed to identify the correct site of the relevant battle. By the autumn of 1984 I had no book to write and the lecture circuit was alarmingly quiet. As though from heaven, a job opportunity presented itself from an unexpected quarter.

A phone call at 2 a.m. from Los Angeles.

'Is that Ran Fiennes?' The voice was gravelly and brusque. 'This is Armand Hammer.'

Assured that it was me, the good doctor continued. 'I want you to work for me in London.' This was my very first offer of a civilian job. 'You will be my Vice-President of Public Relations in Europe.'

The eighty-seven-year-old Dr Armand Hammer, one-time friend of Lenin and of every Soviet leader since with the exception of Stalin, was Chairman of Occidental Petroleum Corporation, the seventh largest oil company in the United States, and one of the wealthiest multi-interest corporations in the world. He had helped the Transglobe Expedition in many ways, including the provision of a television team to record much of the journey.

'I'd love to work for you, Doctor,' I replied, 'but I'm a self-employed traveller, writer and lecturer with no experience of the oil business.'

'Don't you worry about that. You handled the expedition OK. That's enough for me. You can stay self-employed and carry on with your other activities just so long as you handle my business over there when I need you.'

A silence followed for all of three seconds, then he added: 'Make up your mind and call me tomorrow.' He rang off.

'What was that about?' Ginnie asked from under the duvet. I fetched two cups of tea and, after a half-hour debate, I called Los Angeles and took on the job with the proviso that I could spend up to three months in any year travelling and lecturing.

I did not expect to hold down the Occidental position for long. They would rapidly dispense with my services as soon as my total lack of know-how revealed itself. That I survived for a month, never mind eight years, with Occidental was largely due to the mothering of my secretary Jan Milne, who came down heavily on my errors and hid them from the outside world until I gradually learnt the ropes.

I heard the horror stories of Dr Hammer sacking his executives for a single false move or naïve comment at the wrong moment. He was known to have stopped his Rolls-Royce on a motorway in the middle of nowhere and ordered some poor erring gopher (American for lackey) to 'get out and stay out'. With this in mind I was determined to keep my hand in with the lecture circuit and the publishing world. Otherwise, I could suddenly find myself dropped by Dr Hammer with nowhere to go.

Aged forty, I experienced the joys of commuting and office work for the first time. I swotted up on the totally alien topic of the North Sea oil industry and discovered that 'nine to five' actually meant 'seven to seven'. I wore a suit, a tie and black city shoes. I parked the Mini (soon changed to an Occidental Rover) in a concrete basement close to Victoria bus station and lunched in the office on Coca-Cola and cheese rolls from a nearby Boots. This was what real life was all about. I read magazines for oil news and became an expert on the 'hysterics' of OPEC.

I made dinner speeches in French and German on behalf of Dr Hammer at glittering European functions and filtered hundreds of requests for sponsorship (including many from expedition leaders). I tried hard to sell an unwanted oil terminal on Canvey Island. I lunched and made friends with the energy press and spoke to two thousand heads of the industry at the 1985 Institute of Petroleum black-tie dinner.

Dr Hammer's visits to Europe, the exhibitions of his Leonardo da Vinci Codex and his oil paintings had to run without a hitch despite his penchant for changing his mind, and his schedule, constantly and with little warning. In the course of a single week he had me rushing to

Rome with secret papers for the ex-King of Afghanistan (whom he was hoping to reinstate to Kabul) and making speeches to Raisa Gorbachev in Moscow. I learnt to chat up airport officials to allow me to meet the Doctor's private Boeing 727 with a bevy of rented Rolls-Royces *on* the airstrip to avoid the tiresome business of customs and immigration. This worked everywhere in the world (including Moscow, Peking and Cardiff) except Heathrow, where the rules were totally unbendable and incorruptible, and – when I finally gave up trying to buck their system – I felt quite proud to be British!

The job was a great boon for we had no savings. For the first time we were able to consider our dream of living in the country. Not in Sussex, where we had both grown up, but somewhere less tame and over-populated. On fine weekends we drove to the West Country and eventually found a ramshackle farmhouse deep in the Exmoor National Park at 1500 feet above sea level. No telephone poles and electricity from a forty-year-old Lister generator. Not a man-made feature in sight. The wind, the rain and the mist come clear and fresh over the moors. We fell in love on sight and Ginnie began the long task of turning the place into a working cattle farm. It was lonely work for I was away much of the time: her companions were Bothie and Blackdog, the bitch she had brought back from Tuktoyaktuk in the Arctic.

In between tasks for Dr Hammer I began to mount an expedition to search for the lost city of Ubar in Dhofar. Since 1968 I had launched five separate attempts to locate the place, four whilst serving with the Sultan's Forces and one, in the early 1970s, which was curtailed by the Transglobe Expedition preparations. My previous searches had, I believed, been unsuccessful largely because they had involved desert patrols with no air support. In 1985 my plans included Land Rovers with trailer-towed microlight aircraft capable of operating out in the sand dunes.

Oliver Shepard called me one day with a proposal for the ultimate polar journey, the grail of the international fraternity: to reach the North Pole with no outside support and no air contact. For a month Ginnie and I argued the pros and cons of Ubar versus the North Pole. Ubar had lain hidden from explorers and archaeologists for 2000 years, and no man had reached the North Pole unaided by outside help since the world began to spin.

There was no immediate reason to believe that Ubar would be discovered by others since no archaeologist had been allowed to work in Dhofar since 1972 and I believed the Sultan, whose sponsorship of my previous expeditions had been crucial, would give me the go-ahead if I came up with a reasonable proposal, even if I delayed doing so for a year or two. On the other hand there was a band of enthusiastic young men, increasing in number every year, from Britain, Canada, the Soviet Union and the USA who were hellbent on reaching the North Pole unsupported. Time was not on my side, nor Oliver's, since we were both in our forties and well past the ideal age to take on the enormous physical effort involved. Most of our competitors were between ten and fifteen years younger. If we were to go at all it must be sooner rather than later. This rationale finally convinced me to call off the Ubar search until we could complete our North Pole plans.

In the winter of 1985 Ginnie was due to lecture about her Very Low Frequency work in Antarctica to a conference in Chicago. At little extra cost she flew on to Resolute Bay in the North-West Territories and our old friends at Bradley Air Services let her hitchhike on a twin Otter ski-plane that was positioning sonar buoys in the Arctic pack.

When the plane landed briefly at Ward Hunt Island, the most northerly tip of Canada, Ginnie quickly measured the skeletal steel ribs of an outhouse, one of the four long-abandoned huts of a scientists' summer base camp. Ward Hunt was the ideal spot for our North Pole attempt, being about ninety miles west of Alert, where we had spent many months prior to, and during, the Transglobe journey.

Ginnie reported on the state of the old camp and a canvas-tailor sponsor constructed a tough custom-made cover to fit snugly over the ribs of the Ward Hunt outhouse. Ollie joined us and the dogs on the snow-slopes at Aviemore where we met two technicians from British Aerospace. We then conducted our first manhaul trials with two prototype amphibious sledges which they had manufactured from Kerlar to an original design I had produced, by wrapping chicken wire around ninety days of food and fuel, the main ingredients for our intended journey.

Hundreds of uncontrolled beginners screamed past us in the mists which covered the White Lady piste and Blackdog bit one by mistake. Ollie and I managed to tow the 500lb loads up a fairly gentle slope for half a mile in eight hours, a performance which indicated we had no hope at all of even partial success in the Arctic. But it was a start. Ginnie drove us back south in our rented van and Bothie disgraced us by stealing somebody's mixed grill at a Little Chef.

Ginnie had started to breed from the puppies and grand-puppies of Blackdog. She was also tending six Aberdeen Angus cows, the nucleus of an organic beef herd, and this involved installing troughs, fences and all the other necessities of an efficient smallholding. She could not follow two stars so our many years of expedition work together came to an end. She suggested I replace her as base leader with Laurence 'Flo' Howell, one of the Transglobe team and currently running North Sea oil platform communications for Phillips Petroleum.

In October 1985 Central Television sent director Paul Cleary to join Ollie and me in the Arctic.

Things went badly from the start. Eight six-hour flights of cargo were needed to set up a base on Ward Hunt Island, self-sufficient enough to use as a training centre and launch site for our first unsupported journey the following spring.

The first flight was nearly aborted by a blizzard. Our ski-plane pilot Russ Bomberry, an old friend from previous polar journeys, just managed to land on bumpy sea-ice immediately below the Ward Hunt Island abandoned camp. The weather was deteriorating. We unloaded the crates in a hurry. Film-man Paul and I were left behind. Ollie's last words before slamming the fuselage door were, 'See you again tomorrow with the next load.' The little plane immediately bounced away, twin engines on maximum thrust, into the gloom. Paul and I struggled to fit Ginnie's pre-measured canvas cover over the hut's ribs. At −28°C, with a forty-knot wind, this took time for our hands quickly grew cold. Within an hour we were working in darkness and horizontally driven snow.

The Twin Otter returned with the second load eight days later. In the interim period Paul, who had never worked in cold places before, proved my pre-conceived opinion of 'media man' was an inaccurate generalisation. In the past I had been confined with BBC film people for long periods in remote places and my opinion of them had lowered to ground level. Paul now revived it for he was neither narrow-minded nor self-centred. Indeed, he proved so adaptable that the polar base was soon completed, with wind-generating masts and a complex battery bank erected and all snow shelters finished on schedule, despite Ollie's absence.

Throughout the eight-day bad weather delay, Paul cooked from the single food box dropped off with our arrival flight. This contained only tinned ham and frozen eggs. He produced an impressive succession of egg and ham meals, none of which was identifiable, nor similar to its predecessors.

In hot deserts isolated travellers can be exposed to the lethal effects of heat and thirst and unless their personal planning and awareness is up to scratch, they can soon get into trouble.

Conditions of extreme cold, coupled with an environment of moving ice floes weighing millions of tons, are infinitely more hazardous and require a level of competence seldom needed in other equally remote parts of the world. Usually a novice expeditionary can cut his or her milk teeth and learn lessons the hard way during preparatory forays of controlled duration and limited risk. Out on the Arctic Ocean, especially during the dark period and early spring, learning a lesson can be fatal. Novices should keep off the ice until early March when the sun again shines on the 50,000,000 square miles of shrieking, fractured sea ice.

In darkness and mind-numbing temperatures, the simplest of errors can quickly lead to death by drowning, or the loss of frozen hands and feet as a result of some small oversight. Modern clothing, rations and safety gear do not stop travellers dying. As the polar expert Wally Herbert puts it, 'even a man with perfect circulation and the best clothing designed by man will suffer terribly under the worst Arctic conditions'.

One problem caused by the extreme nature of Arctic hazards is the narrowing of choice when looking for suitable travel companions. To manhaul over polar pack ice involves many hours of great exertion dragging over 300lb in deadweight. You sweat like pigs despite outside temperatures of around −50°C. When you stop for breath, the sweat turns to ice in your underwear. Little people, however bold in outlook and determined of spirit, are simply not built to manoeuvre heavy weights. So you need men, not women, of hefty stature and good pulling power; carthorses not fine racers.

I receive many letters from aspiring polar explorers, but the risks involved in taking an unknown quantity on to the Arctic Ocean are too great to even consider. So, wherever possible, I take only those who have a known history of survival on polar journeys in winter. This is unfair on the young hopefuls, for it causes a chicken-and-egg situation where those needing polar experience find it difficult to make the break.

No such difficulties face the would-be traveller of the world's hot deserts. With basic skills such as photography, first aid or communications to offer, anyone can get in on the act and quickly become an old Saharan hand.

After many previous journeys with Oliver Shepard both in Antarctica and the Arctic, I knew there would be no problems caused merely through ignorance or underestimation of the Arctic's awesome powers. Once the polar base at Ward Hunt Island had finally been set up and Paul Cleary had departed to prepare his film team for the following spring, Ollie and I settled into the most northerly habitation on Earth. Our nearest neighbours, a hundred miles to the east, were eighty Canadian servicemen watching Soviet submarines from their centrally heated base at Alert. Our only companions were Arctic foxes, hares and wolves. All birds had long since left for warmer climes.

We set up scientific recording gear, sledged through the darkness to measure ablation on a floating island of ice and carried out exhaustive tests of prototype sledging gear in temperatures below −50°C over fields of fissured ice blocks up to twenty feet in height. On a number of occasions we became separated many miles from our base and twice I feared for Ollie's life when he failed to return to Ward Hunt Island during long and fierce blizzards that came without warning.

The cost of the expedition was £70,000, payable entirely to Bradley Air Services who operated the Twin Otter ski-plane that had enabled us to set up the base. There were no other costs since all equipment, food and insurance had been provided free of charge in return for promises for publicity. Dr Hammer, in agreeing that Occidental Petroleum would pay the £70,000, had stipulated also that the expedition should acknowledge his help in news and television coverage.

To obtain the interest of a major newspaper and a television film producer we had to achieve a major physical challenge. In the 1980s expeditions to remote areas were two a penny. It was not enough merely to reach the North Pole without support or air contact. We must be the first to do so. This was an unfortunate but unavoidable fact of life and reflected the hard rule of sponsorship in a highly competitive world.

Success in reaching the North Pole depended upon the failure of others to achieve the same goal before Ollie and I could do so. Although we appeared to have a head start, there were dangerous stirrings of opposition from several quarters. American, Norwegian, Soviet, Canadian and other British teams had all announced plans to reach the North Pole with or without support as soon as they were able.

The ability to persuade an individual or a corporate board to give away a large sum of money to an event that is not in itself a charity depends entirely on the publicity factor. In the days of Scott, Shackleton and Livingstone, rich merchants may have been driven to support great endeavours into the unknown for purely altruistic or jingoistic reasons. Not so nowadays. Marketing directors need their pound of flesh. They need to know that they will receive greater media exposure by linking their company name and logo with the expedition than they would through spending the same amount on, say, a two-page advertisement in a newspaper.

So long as we held a demonstrable chance of being the first to reach the Pole without support, I could be confident of finding a sponsor. Neither Ollie nor I was happy with our winter trials. The sledges, when laden with enough food and fuel for ninety days' travel, weighed 460lbs each. Our progress rate with these loads, not a great improvement on our initial Aviemore outing, was one mile in three hours, which meant we would never reach the Pole, 425 nautical miles to the north, in ninety days.

So we played with mathematics. Could the journey be done in forty-five days, giving us less horrendous loads, but half the time? There seemed no obvious answer. The optimum team strength for such a journey is generally believed to be a threesome. All non-consumable goods are, of course, shared among the team, since three people do not, for instance, require three radios. This means a three-man team can carry a smaller pro-rata total than two people require. On the other hand the very nature of an expedition that sets out to be unsupported entails failure the moment any aircraft support is summoned, no matter for what reason, and the chances of three people remaining uninjured all the way to the North Pole would be correspondingly smaller than for our two-man team.

In mid-November we packed up the base, making it snow-proof by applying heated cloth-tape to even the tiniest of holes in the canvas walls and sealing the chimney and vents. Then we placed tins of kerosene-soaked rags at intervals along the plateau to the east of our hut, ready to provide an 'illuminated' runway. Karl Z'berg, the Transglobe Arctic pilot, managed the hazardous, ill-lit landing, and three days later we were back in London.

There followed three months in which to modify our sledges and equipment in response to the lessons we had learnt at Ward Hunt. We must be back there by first sun-up on 3 March 1986. The time passed as a blur for I had a backlog of Occidental work for Dr Hammer and wanted to spend as much time as possible on Exmoor with Ginnie. The farmhouse was almost a mile from the next neighbour. The winter months had been lonely, sometimes frightening for Ginnie. There had been disturbances by night and only the company of Bothie, Blackdog and her puppies had kept Ginnie from going back to London. For weeks cold weather had cut her off without access to the nearest village road, without electricity when the ancient generator refused to start and, often, without water except from the stream when the pipes froze.

I felt guilty when I left her again in February 1986 and returned to Resolute Bay where Ollie, Flo Howell, Paul Cleary and I met up with Paul's camera lady, the American Beverley Johnson. She had suffered severe frostbite in all her toes whilst filming the Transglobe Expedition not far from Ward Hunt Island, but was still by far the best cold-weather camera operator I knew.

Flo brought with him crates of radio gear and complex antennae systems. These were normally erected in his back garden near Aberdeen. He could eavesdrop on more or less any high frequency conversations and there was little that took place in the Arctic about which Flo did not know. He told me of the imminent departure of an American dog-sledge team and a French solo manhauler, all North Pole bound and all *supported* in one way or another. He also knew of at least two *unsupported* Soviet attempts due to commence that very week from the far side of the Arctic Ocean.

A few days after our group landed by ski-plane at our Ward Hunt base, a Twin Otter brought in the French manhauler, Jean Louis Etienne. We agreed to show him the best route through the chaotic pack ice that forms a high wall just north of the Ward Hunt ice-shelf. Although this is in continuous motion and sometimes gives way to many miles of open sea, there had been little change since our trials there the previous winter and we soon found the best passage through the tortuous fields of ice. We shook hands with the diminutive doctor and watched him disappear into the moonlit icescape.

'I wish we had sledges like his,' Ollie commented. The French sledge weighed 4lbs and its load 80lbs. Our own 450lb loads included 70lbs of bare sledge. Jean Louis would be resupplied by air every eighth day and his sledge replaced whenever it was damaged so he could afford to travel light.

As the Steger dogs and Jean Louis slowly battled their way north, each vital day after sun-up found us still floundering about the ice-shelf in fruitless experiments with our giant loads. Even the superior design of our new sledges did little to improve our snail-like performance. We pared down equipment to a bare minimum, even shaving the Teflon runners with Stanley knives. All to no avail. The blow came by radio in late March. Ollie Shepard received an ultimatum from his London employers, Beefeater Gin. Either he returned within four weeks or he lost his job. With a wife and home to look after, the latter course was no option, so with great reluctance he signalled for a Twin Otter to come north by the end of the month.

In England Ginnie immediately began to work to find a replacement to take over from Ollie. This was not an easy task, since we needed somebody who had undergone recent polar acclimatisation and was fresh from a manhauling journey; preferably a heavily built person in good trim. There were only a dozen individuals in Britain whom she knew would be experienced enough, but none had been on polar expeditions for months if not years. The only exception was the three-man team of a South Pole expedition whose leaders were Roger Meare and Robert Swan. The latter was in Cape Town and the third man was in Antarctica. Roger Meare told Ginnie he would consider it, but, two days later, he reluctantly succumbed to book-writing pressures and suggested in his place the first reserve of his expedition, Dr Mike Stroud, of the Emergency Unit of Guy's Hospital.

Mike Stroud was startled by Ginnie's call but agreed to come to the Arctic at once. Four days later, with clothing Ginnie had rustled up from our sponsors, Mike left Heathrow and reached

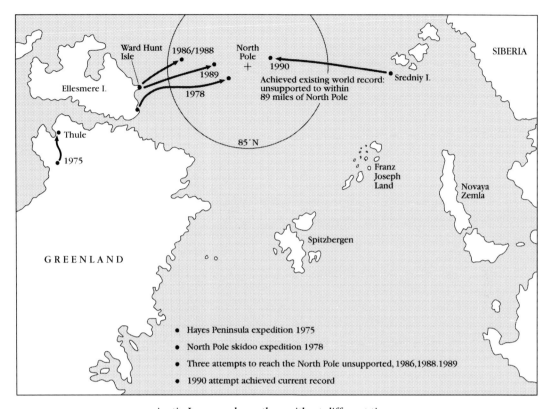

Arctic Journeys by author with, at different times,
Oliver Shepard, Charlie Burton, Geoff Newman and Dr. Michael Stroud

Ward Hunt Island two days before 1 April, which was my deadline for departure for the Pole. Even then I knew we would be cutting things dangerously fine.

I received a shock when Mike climbed off the Twin Otter. Sensibly, Ginnie had not warned me by radio that Mike was small in height for a manhauler, *extremely* small. I am around six feet tall and lean, without visible muscle. Mike's head came to a level with my shoulder but he was built like a brick outhouse, with the biceps, chest and thighs of a bodybuilder. Swallowing my disappointment at the new arrival's appearance, I waved goodbye to Ollie.

Two days later the outlines of Laurence, our film crew and the hut slowly disappeared into the distance of the Ellesmere mountains as we dragged our sledges north. The film crew had dubbed Mike 'Mighty Mouse' after his first trial manhaul on the ice shelf. He pulled like a husky, digging his boots in and leaning so far forward that his nose seemed to scrape the ice. He dragged his sledge completely oblivious to its size and weight – more than twice his body weight – and trudged on relentlessly for hour after hour. For the first two weeks I would stop at the end of each hour and follow my trail back to find Mike. I would help him for a while, and this he was sensible enough to accept. At the end of each day we compared our position with that of the other two expeditions, for Laurence's radio spy system enabled him to keep a precise log of their progress.

Travel through polar pack ice is not merely a matter of brawn and the correct equipment. The greatest bonus is experience, which brings an awareness of the ever changing ice conditions, where to avoid, where easy corridors might best be sought, how to detect zones of open water before reaching them, what colour and thickness of wet ice can safely be crossed even though it screeches and bends at every step. Such knowledge can save hours, even days and is the greatest single factor in the success or otherwise of any expedition, save only for the matter of luck.

Each of us towed a load of 380lbs. Since our expedition was above all else *unsupported* to request *any* aid was to admit failure. At the time of writing, in the spring of 1994, no man has yet reached the North Pole without support, although a number of teams, all of whom received air contact *en route*, have made false claims to the achievement.

At the time Mike Stroud arrived in Ward Hunt Island the world record for human travel without support stood at ninety-eight nautical miles following the near fatal journey of the Simpsons and Roger Tufft in 1968. Subsequent attempts, such as those of David Hempleman-Adams and Clive Johnson in the 1980s, had ended in failure and frostbite less than fifty miles from the Arctic coast.

An exact physical parallel of the task involved would be to drag two heavy six-foot-tall men, tied together, through sand dunes for 425 nautical miles. The terrain includes some 2000 walls of ice rubble up to twenty-five feet high, regions of rotten ice that break up and overturn as you try to negotiate them with your hefty sledge and zones of open water, sometimes as far as the eye can see, which are often laden with treacherous *shuga* ice of porridge-like consistency. Add to these obstacles a temperature that is often lower than a deep freeze and a northerly wind that cuts into exposed skin like a bayonet and it is no wonder that, despite intense international competition, the challenge has yet to be met.

Some seventy miles from the coastline, the highest mountains of which had long since faded from view, we encountered dangerous conditions caused by strong winds to our east. Strange sounds akin to thunder and gunfire wracked the ice and distant daubs of black and brown sky patched the horizon, where newly formed lagoons released warm air into the supercool atmosphere.

Struggling to force the sledges over a field of broken ice blocks, I misjudged the colour of the surface below. My sledge cannonaded off a twelve-foot high mound and knocked me from my hauling position. I hit the ice hard and was instantly immersed. Mike was close at hand and dragged me out, but the damage was done.

'We must get the tent up at once,' Mike shouted above the din of the moving pack. 'At this temperature, your wet clothes will freeze and frostbite will set in quickly.'

He was right, but I knew it would be suicidal to try to camp in a fracturing zone. The chances were too high of instant immersion and sea burial under tons of rolling ice. A lone piece of ham in a saucepan of stirred scrambled egg would have as much chance of remaining on the surface. So we continued to head north in a crazy series of tacks wherever the floating floes provided a route.

Four unpleasant hours later the scenery ahead changed abruptly from blue-white to yellow-white, as wonderful a sight to us as an oasis to a thirsty desert traveller.

Once on firm 'land' Mike erected the tent, since by then my hands were lumps without feeling and useless for such tasks. He helped me into the tent, lit the petrol cooker and unpacked my sledge as well as his. Because mine had fallen into the sea beside me, the lashing straps had been coated in brine, which then froze around them, causing delay.

Inside the tent I struggled to remove my sledge jacket, but since both it and my clumsy mitts were encased in a thick film of frozen sea ice, I had no success. All the while I battered my two boots together in an attempt to force blood to flow, but there was no feeling in either foot.

Mike at last appeared through the tent's tunnel entrance with some four inches of frozen nose dribble stuck to the chin of his balaclava like a gnome's beard.

Unlashing the sledge had quickly made him cold. *Any* pause from the exhausting action of manhauling soon results in a lowered heart rate, so that the blood flow rapidly retreats from the extremities and shivering begins. Sweat caught between layers of clothing turns to ice and there is an urgent need to do one of two things: you can either return to the treadmill of manhauling or, if too tired, erect the tent and eat into the sternly rationed daily quota of fuel to provide life-giving heat.

So as to cut down cargo weight, our fuel ration allowed only for cooking, not for clothes drying or tent heating, so an immersion like mine caused major problems with the vital fuel supply. This in turn could lead to bitterness between team members, since to fall in was, or could be, considered to be the result of stupidity. On all previous expeditions I had gone to considerable lengths to carefully vet every team member but through force of circumstance had accepted Mike sight unseen. That we proved to be totally compatible was remarkably lucky. There was no strained atmosphere, no recrimination, no hint of tension, not even the occasional heated exchange.

Mike managed to remove my mitts and I shoved my hands inside the ski jacket and under my armpits. There was a chance they might return to life, according to Mike's practised eye. My boots would not come off however hard Mike struggled with them. The obvious answer, since it was vital we extricated my toes from their immediate frozen environment with minimal delay, was to cut through the frozen bootlaces with our pin-nosed pliers. Since the laces were completely encrusted, the actual boot canvas would need cutting too.

'If we cut up the boots,' Mike said, looking at me from beneath a fringe of iced-up eyebrow, 'it will mean the end of the expedition: failure.'

I nodded. We carried no spares. To save weight, every item not vital to progress had been jettisoned: no toothbrush, no personal mementoes, and none of those 'spares' normally considered indispensable such as extra mitts or goggles. Since we carried no spare laces or replacement boots, we faced the choice between delaying resuscitation of my feet for at least a quarter of an hour whilst thawing the laces out, and cutting through the obstacles at once to give my feet a better chance.

Ruefully I remembered a day eight years before when I had fallen through Arctic ice and Ollie Shepard had saved my feet by cutting my boots off with an axe. That had been a normal *supported* expedition and an hour of rubbing my feet immediately after their immersion had saved them from frostbite, gangrene and amputation. But now we were faced with the full meaning of our self-imposed puritan regime. 'How stupid!' the armchair traveller might exclaim, or, 'Sheer masochism.' But we were no more masochists than the Everest mountaineer who refuses to use oxygen or the marathon runner who does not use a bicycle. All sports are hedged about by rules and some forms of sport involve sterner parameters than others. If all competitive sportsmen are stupid or masochistic, then so were we.

Reluctantly I asked Mike, by now shivering with cold himself, to thaw the boots out as quickly as possible. I could feel no sensation at all in either foot. The thawing process seemed to take for ever. Once the boots were off, Mike declared my left foot 'redeemable' since it had remained miraculously dry except for the toes and the sole.

'Not so good,' he said, shaking his head, as he examined my other foot. Three of the toes and an adjoining area of skin were parchment-white and devoid of any feeling. Slowly he warmed up both my feet, expending valuable fuel, before applying dry dressings. Breaking the normal rule against using the cooker merely for damp clothes, he dried out my socks and slipped them over the bandages.

Next day we set out on time. I felt no pain throughout the day and was surprised when, back in the tent, Mike swore aloud on removing the dressing. What appeared to be the outer half of my little toe and a segment of flesh had come away with the bandage. A large area of raw flesh and bone was left exposed which felt, as soon as my foot warmed up in the tent and blood returned to the nerve ends, as though it were on fire. For the rest of the journey I dreaded the mornings until, after an hour or so of travel, the foot grew cold enough to deaden the nerves. Likewise the evenings, when the reverse process took place. Nevertheless, despite our heavy loads and my early morning limp, our progress continued to outpace that of the two supported expeditions to our north. After fifteen days we passed the ninety-eight nautical miles point, the existing world record, and celebrated with an extra cup of tea.

Some days the wind blew from the north, making conditions doubly uncomfortable. Our normal schedule involved ten to eleven hours of manhauling with two breaks of four or five minutes each. When the wind was about twenty knots we often hauled for eight hours without a break, to avoid the likelihood of getting frostbitten fingers from trying to drink tea from the two vacuum flasks. These were standard titanium models, to save the extra weight of steel flasks.

In bad conditions we craved for each tea break, yet at the same time we feared the intense cold that accompanied each halt. It could take up to an hour to force the blood back into toes and fingers afterwards, so the halts were a mixed blessing.

One evening Mike announced that he had broken one of our very fragile flasks. Since this cut us down to a single intake of hot liquid each day, I felt distinctly hostile towards him, although I made no comment.

'We have a choice from now on,' Mike said. 'We can use the remaining flask either for tea or for Pre-stress.'

Pre-stress was a specially prepared quick-energy drink that helped to stave off hypothermia and which we normally alternated with tea.

'As a doctor, what do you advise?' I asked Mike.

'We'd better stick to Pre-stress, despite the taste,' he said, giving the reply I had expected.

Two days later Mike was unusually quiet in the tent and after a while broke the news that he had somehow managed to break the second and last vacuum flask. This was a major blow since the conditions were still extremely severe and, after five or six hours of maximum effort, the body cried out for an energy source to stimulate dangerously flagging metabolic rates.

Because we had to manhaul in only two thin layers of clothing in order to minimise body sweat, we were often on the fine edges of hypoglycaemia, a lethal condition in such circumstances. A single energising hot drink often kept us from suffering exposure, especially towards the end of the sledging day. Now, this would be impossible.

I silently swore at Mike's carelessness but managed to refrain from an outburst. He had obviously thought through the results of the breakage before admitting to it, for he immediately followed the news with his plan to make amends. 'It's not the end of the world,' he assured me. 'We still have the pee bottle.'

In the extreme cold the bladder very sensibly contracts and causes frequent stops both *en route* and in the tent. To avoid going outside the tent three or four times a night and allowing precious warmth from inside to escape, we used a one-pint noduline bottle with a plastic rim to which a shrunken member could not stick.

'You must be joking, Mike,' I replied. 'Are you suggesting peeing into it each night and drinking Pre-stress out of it each day?'

'Why not? We can call it Pee-stress. Urine will do you no harm, after all.'

'*Mine* won't,' I retorted. 'But I can't say I fancy the idea of drinking from a container with *your* frozen pee stuck to the outside.'

'I never thought of you as fastidious. But I'm quite happy if you don't wish to share the contents.'

'It's one short step from cannibalism,' I muttered. But the following day I noticed no change in the taste of the Pre-stress.

Only two days later, as Mike changed the bandage on my foot in the morning, the tent was filled with a foul smell which Mike recognised as gangrene. Three days earlier I had finished the last of the penicillin tablets and he had warned me then that only luck could keep the bacteria at bay. The foot was only slightly swollen – and, if anything, hurt less than normal when I forced my boot over the wound – but the writing was on the wall.

Since there are no weather stations on the Arctic Ocean, the Resolute Bay bush-pilots have to rely on the often amateurish summary of expedition personnel. They must be sure of ideal conditions in Resolute Bay, at halfway Eureka and at the pick-up site. It is common enough for seven days to pass by without such usable weather. Knowing this and fully aware of the speedy progress of gangrene, Mike advised an immediate radio signal to Resolute Bay once we could find an area suitable for an airstrip amid the many miles of chaotic broken ice.

The next day we found 400 yards of comparatively flat surface on a well-weathered floe and marked out an airstrip with coloured ration bags. I tuned in our HF radio, after laying out the dipole antenna to face south, and made instant contact with the ever alert Laurence at Ward Hunt Island. By coincidence, one of the Steger expedition, an Alaskan dog-sledger named Bob Mantell, had serious frostbite in his hands and feet. Laurence managed to contact the Twin Otter

pilot as he circled above Steger's camp 200 miles to our north. Four hours later the Twin Otter reached us, bumped perilously over our 'strip' and we said goodbye to our dreams of the Pole that year.

Another of Steger's men, a hefty New Zealander with two broken ribs, met us back at the base. Disappointment showed on his face and in his slumped shoulders.

We had passed the previous best northing by only nine miles and yet were still over three hundred miles short of the Pole. We had learned a number of key lessons which neither of us intended to waste and we agreed to try again as soon as the money could be raised and providing others did not pre-empt us.

The day after our return to Ward Hunt Island my foot and leg swelled alarmingly and a smell of rotten flesh pervaded the hut. Laurence had given Mike all our penicillin supply, the Twin Otter was busy removing husky dogs from the Steger team and my foot's predicament looked as unsettled as before.

Laurence performed miracles with his antenna systems and, after a long correspondence with the bush-pilot base, announced that, weather permitting, we could expect evacuation with a maximum of 1500lbs of cargo the following morning. Working without a break through the night, we packed up the valuable communications and scientific gear along with the ice-core samples from the previous winter. Everything else, including the wind generator system, we left in place for other teams and in the hope that we would soon return.

In Resolute Bay an Inuit nurse did her best, under Mike's supervision, to clean the open wound and I began a new course of penicillin. Two days later we were back in London and Mike contacted the Burns Unit at Roehampton Hospital, where he had once worked. A friendly surgeon agreed to operate immediately and grafted a two-inch square swatch of skin from my thigh on to the remains of the toe and the outer side of my foot. Later that week, along with Paul McCartney for music and Billie-Jean King for sporting prowess, I was nominated for the *Guinness Book of Records'* World Hall of Fame, and described as the 'World's Greatest Living Explorer'. This was especially embarrassing in the light of our recent failure to reach the Pole and I hobbled on to the BBC stage to receive my award from David Frost and Norris McWhirter wearing a black sock over the bandages and feeling very fraudulent.

Ginnie and I were given the Polar Medal by the Queen, with unique bars for Antarctica and the Arctic. Ginnie was the first woman to receive the medal and later that year became the first female member permitted to enter the hallowed male portals of the Antarctic Club. At the Club's black-tie Annual Dinner, where our places had been reserved next to the President, Ginnie's acceptance was to be honoured. However, somehow or other I managed to make a dreadful mix-up in my diary and we failed to attend.

I was constantly aware that I must maintain the impetus of the expeditions and my lectures about them without a break since I could not rely on continuing employment with Dr Hammer, who consistently refused to give me a consultancy contract of more than one year's duration. There was nothing personal about this, he said; it was just the way he preferred to operate. I needed to reach the Pole but in the short term I would have to work hard to keep my job and that meant at least a year without further absenteeism. Consequently, many weekends were spent working full time for Dr Hammer, trying to cope with a plethora of totally unrelated projects. The Doctor was conceited in a frank and amicable sort of way and liked me to carry copies of his biography to give to the many potentates and leaders of industry who punctuated the itinerary of all his London visits. Recently he had produced, through a ghost writer, a fat and glowing autobiography, which I had been tasked to promote in Europe. My own publisher commissioned an autobiography, which amounted to a compendium of expedition stories, and my book and the Doctor's were published in London at roughly the same time.

Driving past a large bookshop in Victoria, the Doctor bade Bob stop. 'That's my book!' he exclaimed, as pleased as any author to see his handiwork prominently on view. I helped him out of the car, for he was a touch wobbly on his legs. By chance the bookshop's window-dresser had filled the window with copies of my book on the upper shelves and Dr Hammer's below. The Doctor turned and looked at me. 'Tell 'em to rearrange it,' he said with a straight face. 'They should learn to get their priorities right.'

Although Prince Charles had been Patron of my polar projects for the past ten years I knew little about him. My work for the Doctor at this time often involved decisions to be made by the Prince. At the time the Prince's image, as portrayed with monotonous regularity by the media, especially the television programme *Spitting Image*, was one of a vacillating, weak-willed princeling inspired mainly by conversations with trees. On two occasions I had found that this was far from the truth.

The United World Colleges was an educational enterprise set up under the aegis of Lord Mountbatten, the uncle and early hero of Prince Charles. I spent a great deal of time on projects devised by the Doctor to raise funds for the UWC and in attending meetings all over the world between UWC trustees and headmasters. After ten years as President of the UWC the Prince had grown somewhat tired of the factionalism in the higher echelons and did not tend to mince words at meetings. At a private dinner given by the Prince at Highgrove for thirty of the senior UWC trustees, the subject of Bulgaria was brought up by the Canadian delegation, who, with the approval of the London headquarters, had been especially keen to encourage the funding of a UWC college in the communist sector.

Privy to Foreign Office briefings and reports of atrocities that never make public reading, the Prince was opposed to pandering to tyrannical regimes. He had made this clear before and now boiled over. Why, if these people asked for his advice, did they fail to listen when he gave it? 'No, no, no.' He thumped the table and the glassware and silver clattered in response. 'If you wish to deal with those people then you must do so under another President.' Sonny Ramphal, the Secretary General of the Commonwealth, tried to remonstrate on behalf of the Bulgarian scheme but the Prince was not to be budged.

On a windy morning in a less than salubrious district of London's Finsbury, so called after the burial site of my ancestor's heart was given to the nation, I sat outside a shabby prefabricated hut waiting for the Prince to finish his business so that I could hand him a large charity cheque from Dr Hammer.

The Prince was on a visit organised by Business in the Community to help find employment for the out of work and often disillusioned youth of the area. Disregarding anxious advisers, he said he wanted a face-to-face meeting *alone* with a representative body of the community. This had led to his entering the hut, which was crammed with angry young Londoners, most of them Rastafarians in torn jeans and berets. There were no police, officials or Royal bodyguards in earshot – merely a clutch of official photographers, the Prince's equerry Rupert Fairfax and me with my white envelope.

Inside the hut, from which I had earlier picked up a strong whiff of beer, wet cigarettes and unwashed socks, we heard a surge of fractious argument and I saw that Rupert looked extremely anxious.

'Had you better not go out and see if everything is OK?' I asked him.

'I know,' he said, gritting his teeth. 'But he specifically said he should not be interrupted and I don't want to upset him.'

Twenty minutes later the noisy meeting ended and the Prince emerged amidst a bundle of Rastas, one patting his shoulder, another giving a clenched-fist salute and all looking happy, especially the Prince.

Rupert Fairfax was one of fourteen successive royal aides that I grew to know. Dr Hammer would often call me a day or two before a London visit to say he wished to meet Prince Charles or Mrs Thatcher, the Soviet Ambassador, Earl Spencer, Robert Maxwell, Edward Heath or, even worse, some unknown with an unpronounceable name whose address he had lost but whom he had met before the war. Ginnie would set to work on the latter type of problem since she had an excellent nose for ferreting and research work, while I would rush to London from our Exmoor home and beg the most influential aide of HRH, Mrs Thatcher or whoever, to grant the Doctor a last-minute appointment in their normally hermetically sealed programmes. To do this meant maintaining a friendly relationship with the aides and we made an annual habit of inviting one or other of the current equerries to Glyndebourne or some other equally solid event.

Wherever the Hammer work took me I needed at all times to keep fit for the expeditions, so my Reeboks and running shorts travelled everywhere. When in the London office, I would join Ollie Shepard at lunchtimes and we would jog for an hour from Buckingham Palace to the Serpentine, twice around the lakes and back. At times of hectic schedules, I needed to remain within Occidental's headquarters. Then I would don a thirty-pound rucksack and run up and down the emergency stairs from the entry hall to the rooftop, eleven floors up.

For two weeks I went with Ginnie and a group of friends to the wildest corner of Britain, the mostly uninhabited peninsula of Knoydart, in Scotland, to fish, climb and windsurf. Dr Hammer was inclined to 'blow a gasket' if I was not instantly available on the end of a telephone at any time of day or night, so he sent Tony Childs, the head of Occidental's London communications department, to set up a telephone system at our remote Highlands croft. Tony hired a fishing boat, since the croft could only be reached by sea, and also installed a fax machine at a tiny inn seventeen miles inland.

A letter reached us on return from Scotland with a summons to the High Court for a long awaited libel case against the Canadian magazine *Macleans* and the journalist Alan Fotheringham. Our barrister had asked the famous polar explorer Sir Vivian Fuchs and my colleague Dr Mike Stroud to appear as witnesses. The jury glowered at Ginnie and me as if they held us personally responsible for interrupting their normal routines. Not one of the twelve gave the glimmer of a smile throughout the two-day hearing.

The article had painted me as a highly unsavoury character on numerous counts and the effect on potential sponsors of future expeditions was likely to be disastrous. We needed an outright apology from the magazine. The only demonstrably inaccurate statement that stood any chance of being nailed as libel was the statement that no expedition of mine was of scientific value. Our barrister showed the jury the scientific report of the Transglobe Expedition, Sir Vivian and Mike Stroud gave evidence of their involvement in our scientific research over the years and the jury unanimously awarded us damages of £100,000 and a full apology. I could not believe my ears.

A week later the Canadians appealed and the damages were reduced to £10,000 despite the jury's decision. We wondered what was the point of having a jury award at all if it could crumble on the very first appeal. Nevertheless the Canadians did print an apology, which meant our main problem was alleviated, and they did pay all the very considerable court costs, which would have broken us for good had we lost.

I mailed copies of the apology to Nordair and other major Canadian and UK sponsors, and all the necessary equipment, transport and insurance came through. This enabled Ollie, Mike and me to try again early in 1988 for the unsupported Pole journey. Laurence Howell was again base leader, this time together with his wife Morag, who was a radio technician in her own right although her accent was initially difficult to interpret even when conversing face to face since she hailed from the Outer Orkneys. The 1988 attempt was beset with appalling terrain and weather and we hardly managed sixty miles before time overtook us. By the end of the spring the rumours of coming attempts by Norwegians, Americans and others convinced us that we must not give up and all agreed to return the next year for a third attempt.

Back in London, through my work with Occidental, I learnt that over one hundred multi-million-pound North Sea oil platforms must by international law be removed once their profitable lives were ended. This was likely to be around the year 2000 and removal costs were estimated at around £6 billion to the UK taxpayer. What outraged me was the clear likelihood that over ninety per cent of the work would go to American, Dutch and Norwegian firms simply because those British companies with the technical ability to complete the highly complex removal operations had not banded together with governmental support (or at least encouragement) to provide a sound home team to bid for the contracts when they came.

With Dr Hammer's approval, I approached all relevant UK companies and the Secretary of State for Energy, and Mrs Thatcher's confidante, Peter Morrison. He was sympathetic and kindly hosted receptions in his office for the fitting captains of the construction (and therefore destruction) industry. I was soon able to form the Offshore Abandonment Group and for a year or so chaired meetings, held in the Carlton Club, which looked most hopeful until the participants including Wimpey, Taylor Woodrow, Offshore Marine and the Bird Group had to 'put their money where their mouths were' and provide the seed money to formally establish a working group. Because the project was by its very nature a long-term concern and British business is traditionally focused on short-term profits, all our work came to nothing. The Japanese would have sympathised with my efforts but laughed at the results.

Through the spring and summer of 1988 I worked for Dr Hammer without a break and found little time to follow up either expedition.

Following a visit to Highgrove to discuss charity work with the Prince of Wales, Dr Hammer was due to go direct to Heathrow, where his Boeing 727 was waiting. About thirty minutes into the flight, the four-seater Bell helicopter which I had hired in Surrey began to smell of burning electrics. I was very keen that the Doctor should reach Heathrow quickly or he would miss the strict departure time limit and have to stay another night in London. I had an expedition meeting that night and I realised that if I brought the smell to our pilot's attention there was likely to be a delay.

Neither the pilot nor Dr Hammer noticed the acrid fumes but after a while, remembering a crash landing in Arabia, my nerve broke and I signalled a warning to the pilot. Quickly he checked the instruments and, with a curt command on the intercom, dropped the helicopter in quick spirals to the nearest green field. This was a parking lot on a caravan site beside the Thames. The helicopter was soon surrounded by chattering locals with cameras. The pilot and I went off to find a telephone and in due course another helicopter arrived which took us just in time to Heathrow.

A week later the drama-loving Doctor wrote to Prince Charles saying that I had abandoned him in the smoke-filled helicopter to near fatal asphyxiation.

By autumn, after a heavy round of black-tie dinners and speeches for Dr Hammer, I had put on a good deal of weight and become disgracefully unfit. The next North Pole attempt was due in a few months, so Ollie and I did a crash fitness course, designed by him, which began with a marathon. Neither of us had ever run for more than an hour or so at a time and we completed the twenty-six miles in a sorry four hours and forty minutes.

I was back in London when an emergency call from Occidental's headquarters announced an explosion on our North Sea oil platform, *Piper Alpha*. Over a hundred of the inhabitants perished by fire or water and Dr Hammer, against the advice of his American colleagues, flew to Britain without delay. Again, against their advice, he gave an impromptu press conference at which he took all the blame upon himself. 'The buck stops here,' he said, and added that he would donate £1 million to the *Piper Alpha* survivors' and dependants' fund. Mrs Thatcher immediately made a similar announcement.

I had ordered Dr Hammer's usual hired Rolls-Royce and his driver Bob Raynor to drive overnight to Aberdeen to take the Doctor around to thank rescuers, see survivors and generally do the best he could. Two newspapers harshly criticised the expense. I tried to protect the Doctor from the ferreting of the British press but twice risked potential 'revelations' of the sort Fleet Street loved to manufacture. The Doctor had long been scheduled to attend London meetings a week or so after *Piper Alpha*'s sad end. Since he had done his level best for the survivors he could see no reason to cancel any of his existing schedule. To do so would benefit neither the dead nor the bereaved.

As part of the visit, eight of the Doctor's colleagues were due to join him for a theatre evening. I had asked the booking agent to reserve seats at the play or musical currently most popular with Americans. The day before, I was sent the tickets, and to my horror I noticed that the play was called *The Deep Blue Sea*. Shuddering at the thought of the play on words the tabloid editors might produce for their banner headlines I cancelled the tickets at once. The following week the Doctor was due to attend a major auction of English paintings at Christie's, so on the Saturday a private preview was arranged. 'Doctor,' I told him, 'a photograph of you entering Christie's at this time would be a boon to the nastier news hacks.'

He refused to cancel the preview but consented to Bob taking the Rolls from Claridge's on such a labyrinthine route to Christie's that even the KGB would have lost us.

The lengths to which the British press would go for some VIP scandal was finally made clear to Dr Hammer that autumn. The occasion was the fortieth birthday party of Prince Charles given by his parents at Buckingham Palace.

Dr and Mrs Hammer were lucky to be included on the tightly controlled guest list of close friends and relatives totalling no more than 300. I dropped them off in the forecourt of the Palace and pointed to the red carpeted entrance. 'Over there, Doctor,' I said. 'Bob and I will be back here in two hours.' 'Whaddya mean?' the Doctor's voice raised ominously. 'You're coming with us.' 'I can't,' I assured him. 'I'm not on the guest list.'

Dr Hammer made a noise signifying disgust and finality which I recognised as a danger signal. I decided, since I was in a dinner jacket, that the best course was to escort the Hammers into the reception lounge, introduce them to someone who would keep an eye on them and then disappear smartly. In the great hallway I noticed a queue of finely attired guests and many a well-known face slowly ascending the long, curved stairway towards the royal reception upstairs. Dr and Mrs Hammer, both frail and in their late eighties, must not join the queue: they would never make it up the stairs.

I spotted Harold Brown, the Prince's butler, and begged him to look after the Hammers.

'No problem,' he said, and led them by a back way to a small lift.

'Goodbye, Doctor,' I muttered, but he gripped me by the sleeve and I found myself heading upwards.

'Here we are,' said Harold as he slid the lift door across, immediately opposite the Queen. Dr Hammer introduced himself with the broadest grin and the Queen was her usual charming self, while the Princess of Wales looked radiant and patted the Doctor's shoulder. In fact all went well up to the point where Prince Charles saw me. He knew precisely who was and who was not on the guest list and must naturally have assumed I was purposefully gatecrashing. If looks could have killed, I would have disappeared through the floor.

The following spring Mike Stroud and I again tried for the North Pole from Ward Hunt Island. The conditions were average but we fell short of the record that we had ourselves set in 1986. I decided to call it a day from the Canadian side of the Arctic. Certainly the journey was possible; our 1986 timings, despite our impossibly late start that year, showed that it could be done given good surface conditions. The problem would remain the impossibility of predicting when a 'good year' would be.

Halfway, during our 1989 attempt, I bruised my foot in a fall from a pressure ridge and soon afterwards the skin graft of three years earlier came away altogether, leaving a wound very similar to the initial one. This time Mike had ample penicillin tablets, which staved off the onset of gangrene. As we left Ward Hunt Island for the last time I asked Mike, who nursed nine frost-damaged fingers, if he would like to try once more, next time from the Siberian side of the Pole. 'Glasnost permitting,' he replied with a grin.

The following spring the élite of the world's polar travellers were ready to tackle the first journey to the North Pole without assistance. Russians, Canadians and Norwegians made announcements that they would commence their various attempts at the first appearance of the sun along the rim of the polar sea.

In Moscow I met Dr Dmitri Shparo, a Hero of the Soviet Union and the proud possessor of the Order of Lenin. His Arctic exploits are revered throughout the former Soviet Union and I was delighted when he agreed to become the organiser of my North Pole attempt that year. He warned me of stiff competition from Colonel Vladimir Chukov of the Soviet Special Forces, who was also about to attempt the Pole unsupported at the head of an eight-man team.

According to Dmitri, Chukov had led a strong polar assault two years earlier. Two of his men had died in the attempt and two had become so weak that a helicopter had evacuated them along with the corpses. Chukov had later reached the Pole but accepted that air contact had compromised his claim. In 1990 he was entirely confident of success, as were three Norwegian ski champions and four Canadians, all intending to set out from the Canadian side of the Arctic.

The Canadian team was led by Jackie McConnell. Following our Headless Valley journey in 1971 he had left the British Army and emigrated to Canada, where in 1981, he had joined our circumpolar journey for the Yukon sector. Jackie's hobby was the annual international 'Iron Man' competition and he visited us in London early in 1990 on his way to one of them. At the time the police had removed my driving licence and Jackie agreed to drive my Occidental-supplied Rover to a nearby car wash for me. Approaching Hammersmith bridge at thirty miles per hour he noticed a steel bollard set in the middle of the road to separate buses from cars. His judgement was poor and he collided with it. The impact was such that one wheel was ripped off its axle and the entire car forced out of alignment. As Jackie explained to the policeman, he lived in Moose Jaw, where there were few cars, only one set of traffic lights and no bollards. The next I heard from him was the news that he was to lead a North Pole attempt of his own in the spring.

Mike and I trained hard in the winter of 1989 and, before our departure, passed through numerous body analysis tests in the experimental chamber at the RAF Institute of Aviation Medicine in Farnborough, Hampshire. Our bodies proved to be remarkably resistant to cooling. A two-hour immersion in a cool tank designed to lower the core temperature of most men of normal build produced a report that my 'resistance was extreme with core temperature actually *rising* slightly during the course of the immersion'. The fitness report stated that I was twice as fit as a normal serviceman ten years my junior. Mike, who was eleven years younger, was stronger and fitter but much lighter than me.

We left Heathrow with Flo and Morag Howell who were to run our Siberian base. For a while we would be joined there by Paul Cleary and his film team as well as Terry Loyd from ITN who had covered many of our previous Arctic journeys. From Moscow a Soviet Air Force cargo aircraft flew us for many hours over Siberia until bad weather forced us to land at the Siberian mining town of Vorkuta. At Shredniy in the Sedov district we stayed in a scientific camp with eighty or ninety contractors. This was a highly classified part of the then USSR where only a year earlier, before Gorbachev's advances towards democracy, we would never have been allowed. The station was the Soviet equivalent of a Defence Early Warning (DEW) base in Canada.

Two heavy lorries drove us for three hours along a snow track to the remote station of Golomiany. One of the six inmates, whilst checking a generator outside, had recently been killed and partially eaten by a bear and the cook at the base showed us photographs of the poor fellow's mauled body lying in the snow outside the main hut. The camp huskies had subsequently frightened the bear away but one still had a long livid scar along her back, inflicted during her brave fight to ward off the bear. None of the five remaining staff spoke English but they explained through our interpreter that we were to be their guests that night at a dinner they wished to hold for us, for we were the very first foreigners to visit Golomiany 'since the days of the Czar'. Two days later an ex-Afghan gun-ship helicopter flew us one hundred miles to Cape Arktikiski, the most northern point of land in Novaya Zemlya.

After photographs taken with Dmitri and holding our respective national flags, we moved off into broken pack towing 300lbs each. Ahead lay a greater distance by a hundred miles than the Canadian route to the Pole and beset with far stronger sea currents. There would be a great deal more open water than we had experienced on earlier attempts but our sledges were lined with buoyant foam. Mike Stroud wrote in his diary:

> The terrain consists of broken, moving ice, a fragile skin on an ocean more than 3000 metres deep. On the seventh day my ski binding broke and I was condemned to wade through knee or thigh-high snow. We carry no spare bindings since every extra pound is at the expense of fuel or food for a journey that will entail cold and hunger.
>
> Despite my handicap we have made good progress for a week now and even when a three-day blizzard broke up the pack with winds in excess of ninety-five kilometres per hour we continued to travel, stumbling through the white-out and cursing the horizontally flung

pellets of ice that filled our hoods and stung our eyes. We knew that if we became separated we would never find each other again. The man without the tent would die. Visibility was down to a couple of metres, footsteps were covered up as soon as they were made and our shouts were immediately lost in the storm.

We have been hindered by numerous areas of open water. It is slow work to lash our sledges together since our hands are clumsy in their frozen mitts. Any time lost through water-crossing delays was made up at the end of the day but the resulting thirteen- or fourteen-hour shifts have taken their toll and we are beginning to have a serious starvation problem.

On the other side of the world the group of three Norwegian ski champions had openly declared their intention to reach the Pole first, and two separate teams of Soviet skiers were somewhere behind us, having set out, like us, from Novaya Zemlya in Siberia. From our radio base, a Soviet Army shack on the island of Shredniy, Morag and Flo managed to make voice contact via our HF set and gave us news of our competitors.

'Kagge and his Norwegians are out of the race. One of them has been airlifted to safety with a frostbitten foot. The other two are carrying on but their challenge has been compromised by air contact.'

Now we had only the Russians to worry about. Jack McConnell's Canadian team had withdrawn with frostbite.

'Chukov's men are doing well,' Morag told me through the electronic ripples of auroral interference. 'We estimate they are less than one hundred miles to the south of you.'

'What about Fyodor Konyukhov?' I asked her.

'He is also compromised,' Morag replied. 'A Soviet helicopter picked him up. He was in trouble with breaking ice in a bear-infested zone. They dropped him off further north.' Her voice faded into the electronic clutter.

I knew that Vladimir Chukov was ranked high in the lists of Soviet polar explorers. He had led two unsupported journeys to the Pole in previous years. Both times he had reached the Pole but death and injury of team members on each occasion necessitated air contact to remove the bodies. Chukov had played by the rules and was now doggedly trying again. He had learned many lessons. He knew the hazardous nature of the drifting Soviet pack ice, far looser and more volatile than the corresponding sea ice on the Canadian side of the Pole. Here, a single error could quickly lead to death, as he had found to his cost. I knew his team's progress would be slow and methodical.

After about 400 miles Mike and I abandoned our heavy carbon-fibre sledge-boats and continued with basic food, fuel and camp gear carried in rucksacks. Because we were weak and the packs weighed nigh on 100lbs each, it was all but impossible to stand up unaided after struggling into the rucksack harnesses.

On half-rations and debilitated, our chances of making the last two degrees of latitude, 120 miles, to the Pole rested on luck and avoidance of hypothermia.

The tent, forced into a sausage shape, was strapped to my rucksack. Every action was ponderous. Our fingers were blistered; raw in places beneath the plasters. My vision was impaired. For some reason, too much glare perhaps, I seemed to be going slowly blind. I could still make out enough shape and colour to navigate through the chaos of broken ice. Sometimes I skied, sometimes I strapped my skis to the pack and walked. This was less painful for my ulcerated heel but harder work in deep snow.

Mike had no option but to walk. One of his steel bindings had broken irreparably only seven days from the start. This slowed us down to the speed of a walking expedition, which in turn yielded less mileage output per ration consumed. The fact that Mike had continued this far without skis was a tribute to his remarkable tenacity.

His eyes were deep-sunk, his eyelids hugely puffed out and discoloured. A few days previously, he had come dangerously close to hypothermia. I had erected the tent and, after hot tea, he had recovered. But the signs were ominous.

Steam-banks rolled over the wasteland of ice, brown and menacing like the smoke of distant forest fires. This resulted from massive ice-fracturing the previous night. The last thing we wanted, now that we had abandoned the sledge-boats, was open water.

Within the hour narrow cracks began to criss-cross our route. The noise of booming pressure punctured by a staccato crackle, as of automatic rifle fire, sounded to the north, rendered dull and sinister by the blanketing fog. The sun briefly broke clear, giving perspective to our immediate icescape of broken floes and tilted blocks. Only a sudden contrary wind pattern saved us from bad water problems by re-closing the newly opened channels.

One day on a drifted hummock I spotted the spaced prints of an adult bear. The spoor was but recently etched in the snow and I felt that inchoate dread, the prickling of the skin at the nape of the neck, which comes with the fear of imminent danger and personal vulnerability.

I knew I must warn Mike, for polar bears will usually attack the rear member of any group and Mike was defenceless. Only a few days previously we had buried our radio and our revolver as being too heavy to carry in the rucksacks. Some eight years before, a friend and I had been attacked by a bear in the pack ice but on that occasion we were armed with a .44 Magnum pistol. Now I bitterly regretted my decision to abandon our revolver. By doing so I had put us both at risk.

I prayed that we would escape detection by the many bears that roamed the area, and tried to banish from my mind the vivid images of the photographs shown to us a month previously by the five inmates of the Siberian radar post near Shredniy.

That week, on the other side of the world, our Norwegian competitors were attacked by a large male bear which they shot close by their tent.

I tried to bury negative thoughts but the total concentration necessary for successful navigation in broken pack ice was absent that morning.

After an hour of progress over wind-scoured, multi-year floes, we climbed a twenty-foot-high wall of tumbled blocks and immediately found ourselves in an unstable area of newly fractured, young ice. Huge blocks slowly up-ended under million-ton pressure from surrounding floes, and slithered, squealing and grinding over one another. I zig-zagged wildly, unable to hold to true north, in a vain attempt to skirt the many pools and canals of newly open, steaming, black water.

Bubbling mush zones of porridge-like *shuga* increasingly blocked our passage. Frustrated by successive false trails, I decided to jump across an open canal. Mike was some 400 yards behind, following the labyrinthine course of my tracks. The temperature was −37°C and a ten-knot breeze cut knife-like through our cotton clothing whenever we halted to reconnoitre. To survive we had to keep moving. Rest stops were out of the question.

The canal looked about five feet wide at the point where its banks came closest together but nothing was quite as it seemed. The whole world of sea and ice was in motion. The far, northern, bank was coasting to the east at about one knot per hour. Or *perhaps* my own,

268

southern, bank was moving west. There was no way of telling which was reality.

Either way, the canal was slowly opening, its banks shifting apart, for this particular zone was not under pressure from surrounding floes.

I knew I must not hesitate. If these narrows widened by the time Mike arrived, he could try to find another crossing point.

I positioned my skis parallel to the canal and as close to the edge of the bank as possible. I tried to loosen the waist straps of my rucksack but my fingers were too cold to locate the toggle. Crouching to gain maximum spring, I counted to three, then jumped. The ice block under my skis slipped sideways at the crucial moment, my balance was thrown and I plunged into the canal.

Fettered by my skis and rolled face-down by my heavy rucksack, I struggled in panic, numbed by the water's temperature.

I managed to force one mitt out of the frozen leather wrist-strap of my ski-stick. Then the other. With my hands free, I scrabbled at the four-foot vertical wall of the canal. It was smooth and afforded only a meagre grip. I screamed for Mike and swallowed sea water.

I did not feel cold but was totally aware that I could not escape. My grip began to weaken and the forces of gravity were second by second more difficult to resist.

I felt a sudden blessed lessening of the deadweight forcing me under. Mike had arrived.

'Quickly,' was all I could think to shout. Already my teeth were chattering and my mouth too numb for clear speech.

Mike had removed his pack and, lying on his stomach, reached down into the canal. He managed to grasp a loose strap from my rucksack. He weighed a fifth less than I and, although physically more powerful, he was weakened by hunger. With no means of leverage and with fingers already lacerated from broken blisters, he hauled me to safety through sheer force of willpower.

Once I was clear of the water, the wind chill factor, many times colder than a deep freeze, drained my body heat away and Mike raced to unlash the tent. My hands were useless, unable to light a match let alone thread poles into the tent lining.

Mike's own fingers had lost all feeling but he managed to partially erect the tent. Within minutes my sodden clothing and boots began to freeze. I squatted inside the tent, muttering furious inanities and tearing at my clothes.

Somehow Mike lit the cooker and things began to improve. Between frequent intervals to re-warm my fingers, I squeezed my clothes dry. It would have been best to spend the rest of the day and subsequent 'night' drying out, since we carried no spare clothes. However, our fuel allowance was sufficient only for cooking purposes, not to heat the tent nor to dry clothes: an unsupported polar journey must make do without luxuries. So there was no choice but to carry on and hope that, by the end of the day, my clothes would have dried on my back.

Over the following weeks we each fell in six or seven times, sometimes because of weak canal banks but also through misjudging weak ice. Had we both fallen in at the same time the outcome would have been quick and fatal.

Around 88° North with 447 miles behind us, our strength quite suddenly disappeared as the extreme loss of body weight reached the point where we became debilitated. Cold began to pervade our bodies and sleep, always difficult on ice that shrieks and shudders, became impossible lying on thinly padded bones. In addition my eyesight became too poor to navigate, so I took to following close behind the vague outline of Mike's body, cursing each time I tripped over unseen ice blocks.

On the forty-eighth day, by which time we were within a tantalising 89 miles of the Pole, I began to feel the icy north wind blowing on to my right ear rather than my nose. After an hour of this I tapped my stick against Mike's back. He was dazed and could hardly speak. With no idea of direction and suffering from hypoglycaemia, he was in a vulnerable state.

We were ten days away from the Pole, having lost twelve or fourteen days through the contrary drift and the broken ski binding. The surface conditions in the Arctic that year were as good as in 1986, so we would have been better off on the Canadian route. But this we could not have known in advance.

We activated a miniature radio beacon as arranged with Dmitri and within twenty-four hours a Soviet gun-ship helicopter took off from the Soviet ice island 300 miles to the north-east. The biscuits and tea they gave us tasted like nectar. The next eight days we remained on their ice floe during a major break-up which split their airstrip into seven floes and their hut camp into two.

Because my feet were very swollen, Mike gave me desiccation tablets, which had the unforesesen result of shifting a kidney stone into my urinary tract. I was violently sick and contorted with stomach pains.

A week later we returned to Moscow, where the Sovet Komsomol President gave us medals and Dmitri Shparo confirmed that we had made the longest and fastest unsupported journey in the Arctic to date. The Canadian team of Jackie McConnell had retired with frostbite problems after two weeks. The Norwegian and Soviet teams both received air contact and lost members of their team *en route*, thus compromising their attempts. This the Soviets accepted with good grace. The Norwegians did not.

Our journey has remained the world record to this day. But, I had had enough. I vowed I would never again subject my mind or my body to such stresses. Future expeditions would be confined to hot deserts or tropical rain forests. Above all I would eradicate the word *unsupported* from my dictionary of future travels.

At forty-seven years of age, I was ready to focus fully on locating the lost city of Ubar which had eluded my previous searches over a twenty-two-year period.

16

The Lost City of the Sands

Others had told me of Ubar, the Atlantis of the Sands,
but none could tell me where it lay.

BERTRAM THOMAS

'You failed again then?' Dr Hammer growled when first I met him after the Siberian Arctic journey.

'Not exactly, Doctor,' I bridled. 'We broke the existing world record by over three hundred miles.'

'Well,' he said, determinedly unimpressed, 'at least you haven't failed too many times with me.'

That, I reflected, was why he had just renewed my sixth annual contract as his European representative.

At ninety-three he was undoubtedly the oldest active chairman of a great international corporation. Later that year he told me, 'You can count on my being around, Ran, for at least another eight years. My newly installed pacemaker is guaranteed that long.'

I put my back into the Doctor's various tasks, especially the raising of £1 million he had promised Prince Charles for their mutual beneficiary, the United World Colleges.

Less than a month had passed when a phone call came from Charlie Burton and Ollie Shepard. I was to meet them in the map-room of the Royal Geographical Society without delay. I arrived to find them poring over large interlocking sheets of white paper: maps of Antarctica.

A decade had passed since the three of us had completed the longest and first one-way-only crossing of the Antarctic continent. Now they were suggesting we do it again.

'This time,' Charlie said, 'on foot and without support.'

'Impossible,' I replied. 'It cannot be done.'

Whether it was Oliver or Charlie who had first spawned the idea was unclear but they were both sold on the venture despite indisputable evidence that neither man, machine nor pack animal (huskies included) could carry sufficient food and fuel to cross Antarctica from coast to coast without resupply.

'No machine devised by man,' I prodded Charlie by way of emphasis, 'is fuel-efficient enough to make such a distance. The Americans and the Soviets have both tried and failed. As for huskies,' I added, 'Steger's 1990 journey is clear evidence that dogs would be hard pushed to make even one thousand miles unassisted.'

'We are not talking about dogs,' Ollie interjected.

'I know,' I agreed, 'but, since neither dogs nor machines can make it, humans on foot are out of the question. Amundsen *proved* that dogs outperform people trying to manhaul. If you read Roland Huntford's book on Scott and Amundsen, it is quite clear that Scott's greatest error was in trying to manhaul.'

'Balls,' Charlie shouted, 'Huntford never went to Antarctica. His book is a biased load of crap and Scott was absolutely right in reckoning manpower to be *the* efficient method. Our journey will prove it.'

I looked anxiously about the map-room. Charlie's raucous tones must be audible throughout the Royal Geographical Society.

'All right. I'll check your plan over with the experts but, in the unlikely event that it does look possible, what is the form?'

Oliver had everything worked out. 'There are two options. We could start at McMurdo, since we know the ships and planes go there annually. Ideally, our route would then go straight across the Pole to the British base of Rothera on the far coast. If this proves impossible because the Brits refuse to fly us out, then we go for a return journey from McMurdo to the Pole.'

'*Very* second best, that,' Charlie thundered.

'For God's sake keep your voice down, Charlie,' I cursed him. 'We will be thrown out.'

'If *we* don't do the journey,' Ollie commented as we packed up the maps, 'somebody else will.'

He knew my Achilles tendon.

I pondered Ollie and Charlie's proposal. They were asking me to lead the venture and Ginnie to be the base leader and radio operator. Since she had become a cattle farmer, she found it increasingly difficult to leave our Exmoor home for long periods. Her Aberdeen Angus cows were expected to calve in the English winter: the only period when Antarctica can reasonably be travelled. I knew she would not agree to the proposal, on top of which I hated the thought of leaving her for yet another lonely winter on the moors.

On the other hand, I could not push from my mind the current rumours that rippled through the polar grapevine that a Norwegian team under Erling Kagge had set their sights on crossing the Antarctic continent unassisted. Back in 1990 it had been Kagge who claimed the first unsupported success to the North Pole, choosing to ignore the fact that one of his team had been airlifted out *en route*. Any form of air contact is, within the rules of unsupported polar travel, the precise parallel of drug abuse by an Olympic competitor.

In 1990 I was quoted in the press as saying that the Norwegians had compromised their attempt (as indeed had Chukov's Russians) by receiving air contact. The Russians admitted this but the Norwegians merely reiterated their own claim and castigated me as a bad sportsman.

The Russians, the British and the Canadians refused to recognise the Norwegian claim and still accept the Fiennes–Stroud 1990 journey as the existing northerly record.

I asked Ollie and Charlie to research further into the technical problems of an Antarctic crossing and agreed in principle to join them should such a venture, on close scrutiny, appear even remotely feasible.

Another journey meanwhile had come to the fore which was far more attractive to me than the prospects of another polar struggle – to search for Ubar, the Atlantis of the Sands.

Back in 1968, in Dhofar, Nashran bin Sultan, one of the Sultanate guides, had told me of this lost city. 'Some say the finest city in all Arabia was Ubar, built like Paradise with pillars fashioned from gold. Allah destroyed the place and no man has been there for a thousand years. Ubar is over there' – he pointed his stick north towards the distant Qara mountains and west towards the Yemen – 'in the Sands beyond the Wadi Mitan.'

Since the dawn of civilisation trade between the West and the mysterious East had been monopolised by seafarers, Phoenicians and Muscat Arabs, and the keystone of their commerce was incense, primarily *olibanum*, or frankincense. Historians initially believed that this scented gum originated from Somaliland and the Hadhramaut. But further research showed that, while frankincense trees were indeed abundant in both countries, the one and only source of superior quality frankincense was Dhofar. The guardians of the frankincense orchards possessed a monopoly on a commodity more valuable even than gold, which for 4000 years provoked an insatiable worldwide demand.

My early, superficial studies led me to the ready conclusion that some fabulously wealthy city was likely to have existed, because of the inescapable need for a watering place for the thousands of men and beasts involved in transporting frankincense from Dhofar to the northern markets.

Historians stress that the incense travelled from Dhofar by sea and by land. The ocean routes were at risk from storms and pirates while the desert trails involved passage through different tribal lands, with middlemen levying taxes all the way. The routes that were chronicled in greatest detail all led west from Dhofar's northern borders into Yemen, and this made me conclude that Nashran's missing incense city, Ubar, must lie on or close to that border. Somewhere there was, or once had been, a great deal more water than might be drawn from a single desert well.

The first geographers to map the Arabian Peninsula were based in Alexandria, and using information received from merchants and seafarers they produced treatises giving the positions of the main Arab cities and trade centres. By AD 200 Alexandrian professors had recorded the existence of a major market town well into the region now known as the Empty Quarter, the greatest sand desert in the world. They located this entrepôt in the lands of the Iŏbaritae, close to the Sachalitae (men of Salalah Plain), and gave it the name Omanum Emporion, meaning 'coastal market centre of Oman'. This was the first time the word Oman had appeared in writing: until then most references to the country used the Persian name Mazun.

The Qur'an (Koran) was written some four centuries later and mentioned neither Ubar nor Omanum Emporion (later Latinised into Emporium). The word of God, as passed on by the Prophet Muhammad in the Qur'an, told of desert cities whose inhabitants had behaved badly and as a result incurred the wrath of God. These doomed cities were named as Thamud, Ophir, Ad and Irem. The locations of the first three were clearly not in Oman but Irem's identity, past or present, was unknown. The Prophet, in the Qu'ran's Chapter of the Dawn, stated that Irem was destroyed in the same way as Ad. 'Irem of the columns, the like of which has not been created in the land' is the exact Quranic description.

The tenth book of Genesis gives the names of the original rulers of Arabia and states that Joktan occupied the south-western region, while his cousin Ad settled to the east between the Empty Quarter and the Indian Ocean. King Ad's son, Shedad, according to *bedu* legends, written and spoken, built Irem in a fertile area of the desert where he attempted to imitate the wealth and splendour of Paradise.

At the time of the Norman Conquest of England, the Arab historian al-Himyari wrote: 'Wabar is the name of the land which belonged to Ad in the eastern parts of Yemen and which is today an untrodden waste owing to the drying up of the desert. There are to be found in it great buildings which the wind has smothered in sand.'

When the traveller Raymond O'Shea visited T. E. Lawrence (Lawrence of Arabia) in 1934 at Clouds Hill, his Dorset retreat, E. T. Shaw, as Lawrence then called himself, said he was intensely interested in the legend of the lost city reputed to exist in the middle of the Rub al Khali. 'I am convinced that the remains of an ancient Arab civilisation are to be found in that desert,' he told O'Shea. 'I have been told by the Arabs that the ruined castles of the great King Ad, son of Kin'ad, have been seen by wandering tribes in the region of Wabar. There is always some substance in these Arab tales.'

Lawrence's desert deeds inspired many of his countrymen of later generations, two of whom, not much younger than himself, were to bring Ubar to the attention of the public in the West for the first time.

Bertram Sidney Thomas, an administrator in Palestine, was selected by the Sultan of Muscat in 1925 as his personal financial adviser. Oman was then a forbidden place for foreigners, especially Christians, and only a handful had penetrated even the edge of the great deserts of the Interior. Thomas's dream was to cross the length of the Empty Quarter from south to north and he discussed his plans in secret with the Sultan's heir, Said bin Taimur. No one else knew of his intentions when he slipped aboard a dhow that took him from Muscat to Salalah and, in the closing days of 1930, he set out with Murra and Rashidi guides into the great and waterless unknown.

The subsequent 900-mile camel journey took Thomas fifty-eight days. He received the personal congratulations of King George V, the Founder's Medal of the Royal Geographical Society and the eternal chagrin of Mr. H. St. J. B. Philby, the father of one of Britain's better-known spies. Philby senior was an adviser to His Majesty King Abdul Aziz of the Saudis and, with a secrecy equal to that of Thomas, had for a dozen years nurtured the grail of being the first non-Arab to cross the Empty Quarter.

In the debating forums of the Royal Geographical Society and the editorial pages of the *Journal of the Central Asian Society*, the two explorers exchanged terse letters on various differences of opinion. What seemed to especially niggle both men was the name used by the other for the lost city. Philby, who favoured Wabar, wrote: 'Who can have a better claim to know how the word was spelt than myself, for I have actually been there?' Thomas, who described Ubar as the 'Atlantis of the Sands', pointed out that Ubar was in south Arabia, a region never reached by Philby and one where every member of every tribe he had met used the term Ubar and had never heard of Wabar. Thomas had unearthed evidence indicating that the lost Quranic city was well into the southern reaches of the Empty Quarter.

The passage of time cannot have dulled Philby's fascination for the lost city since in London in the early 1960s, by which time his son was a KGB general in Moscow, he told the American explorer Wendell Phillips that he believed 'Wabar and Ubar both refer to the same ancient city of tradition which still remains to be discovered'.

The mystery of Ubar remains unsolved. In a completely inaccessible area where today there is little or no camel traffic, a well-marked highway centuries old, made by thousands of camel caravans, leads west for many miles from the famous spice lands of Dhofar and then, on a bearing of N75°W, mysteriously disappears without a trace of the great sands. A dozen Ubars could well be lost among these high dunes, unknown even to the present day *bedu*. I firmly believe some day some explorer will solve the mystery of Ubar, Arabia's most intriguing lost city.

My own on-off search, since 1968, for the lost frankincense city had slowly evolved into a joint venture with an old friend, Nick Clapp from Los Angeles, who had edited Dr Hammer's film of the Transglobe Expedition. In 1990 he was working full time for Hammer Productions and often contacted our London Occidental office.

Many years before he had spent three days filming the golden oryx in Oman and had fallen in love with that country. Keen to find any excuse to go back there, he happened upon tales of the lost city and decided to make a film about a search for its location. Remembering my own past Ubar expeditions, he suggested we meet to discuss pooling our resources. An agreement was soon reached that I would lead the expedition in the field, organise all liaison with His Majesty the Sultan of Oman and his ministries and obtain the necessary vehicles and equipment.

Nick's responsibilities were to include all historical research and filming matters. He had approached NASA for space photos taken by the shuttle which could 'see beneath the sand' to a depth of some two metres. Sadly our naïve hopes that these 'space images' might produce an outline of the lost city were soon dashed. The best NASA came up with was a geometrically shaped outline way out in the sand dunes of the Empty Quarter which we dubbed the *L-site* due to its silhouette.

The shuttle also spotted a series of ancient camel trails in the dunes which came from nowhere and led nowhere. These same tracks had been seen by previous desert travellers in the 1930s and their exact location recorded so, when all was said and done, NASA's useful information consisted solely of the *L-site*.

I asked David Douglas-Home, the banker son of Lord Home, if he could advise me of possible British sources of funding. Since he was a confidant of many influential Omanis and of the company directors with whom they did business, I rated his advice as the best. Nevertheless, I enjoyed as little success as had the Americans in raising UK-based funds. So I visited Muscat and called on a number of old friends. The response was cautious but never negative, which in itself was a massive improvement on London. However, since Dr Hammer was not well at the time I was able to devote much of my working hours to seeking backers in Britain as well. So when Edward Heath asked us to lunch at his Salisbury home, I approached him for help. His response was to introduce me to the paraplegic son of the Chinese President with a request for help to establish a hospital for paraplegics in Peking.

As things turned out, I raised every penny in Muscat itself.

Dr Omar Al Zawawi, who had helped sponsor the polar expeditions over a period of sixteen years, kindly made it possible for the Omani International Bank, of which he was the most influential director, to become our holding sponsor. The bank's Board agreed to co-ordinate all fund-raising activities from Muscat and to consider a cash donation.

In the summer of 1990 I spent four days visiting twenty-two Omani company executives and sixteen expatriates. The result was immediate. Gene Grogan of Occidental Oil Oman, with whom I had previously worked, agreed to give $20,000 worth of help, plus whatever field survey and camping gear we might need.

I checked out various food companies and received a generous offer from Mattrah Cold Stores of food and cooks for the expedition. BP of Oman promised us unlimited fuel anywhere in Oman and Land Rover's local distributor, Sheikh Mohamed Haider Darwish, promised me three free Rover Discovery vehicles, which are unquestionably better for long periods in soft sand than any of their competitors.

For transport of personnel and cargo, insurance and a thousand and one other necessities I made agreements with other local companies, and as for accommodation, free living in great luxury was assured by the Al Bustan Palace Hotel of Muscat and the Holiday Inn in Salalah. The former magnificent structure had just been voted the best hotel in the world by a European travel magazine, so the Ubar project was showing distinct signs of becoming an excursion rather than an expedition.

I wrote to His Majesty Sultan Qaboos to say the Ubar expedition was now financed and to ask if we could complete a reconnaissance as soon as possible. He agreed and told me to arrange it through his Minister of Palace Affairs, General Ali Majid.

The General had served in the Dhofar War and I remembered him well as an outstandingly brave officer. I visited him in Medina Qaboos and asked if the Army would help the reconnaissance with an escort, vehicles and a helicopter. After making enquiries he decided that the Royal Oman Police were better placed to help and he gave orders accordingly. I signalled Nick Clapp in Los Angeles; he was still working on the complex arrangements needed to make his documentary film of our search. I told him that everything was now in place and the reconnaissance must begin in midsummer.

The reconnaissance would hopefully enable us to visit one or two sites such as Andhur, Fasad and Hanun, all places noted by previous archaeologists, then to search other regions of Dhofar for historical clues and finally to go into the Sands by helicopter to examine the space imaged *L-site*.

The archaeologist who had volunteered to join us, Dr Juris Zarins, worked at the South-west Missouri State University and the love of his life was Arabian archaeology. Any excuse for fieldwork in Oman was manna from heaven to Juris.

In selecting an archaeologist to join a lengthy expedition it is tempting to go for the person with the most resounding reputation for previous discoveries in the relevant region or period of history. This is likely to produce a mad professor or an embittered genius, someone perhaps who creates a feisty atmosphere that is likely to affect the rest of the team.

My own reading on the subject of archaeologists, mainly written by the archaeologist Paul Bahn, had given me a jaundiced view of what to expect. Some typical observations by Bahn:

Never let the fact that nothing is really known about past events stand in your way: instead, use it to your advantage.

Eccentricity is a hallmark of the profession. So is an addiction to alcohol (in fact archaeology could be a synonym for alcoholism). You can wryly attribute this fact either to the need to drown one's sorrows in the face of unattainable solutions, or simply to acute embarrassment at practising an inherently ridiculous and often futile profession.

Field archaeologists undergo long periods of nothing much happening but there are compensations. Few other occupations enable you to go off into the wilds at regular intervals with a bunch of nubile youngsters who are eager to have fun and obtain good grades.

Juris Zarins was a pleasant surprise and, apart from a vague similarity to Indiana Jones, complete with a battered brown trilby, there was nothing traditionally professional about him. He was not stuffy, narrow-minded, humourless or susceptible to the attractions of his students.

When the chance to join the Ubar search came his way, Juris saw it as a wonderful chance to visit Oman. He knew well that no new excavation work had been permitted in Dhofar for eighteen years and that prime sites existed that were almost certainly ripe for plucking. He gave little credence to the tales of Ubar and he did not like the thought that a high degree of interference with his work was likely from Nick's film team but, for the opportunity to work in Dhofar, he was prepared to put up with a lot.

The reconnaissance journey was to take place in July 1990, at the time Saddam Hussein was about to invade Kuwait. Luckily nobody then knew of Saddam's intentions, so the Sultan's Office stamped all our visas. The team would consist of Nick and me, Juris, Ron Blom from NASA, Nick's wife Kay and George Hedges, the fund-raiser for Nick's film. Once we reached Dhofar our main guide and adviser would be Major Trevor Henry, my instructor on the SAS jungle course back in the 1970s.

The American members of the Ubar team arrived in London in mid-July and we flew into Muscat on one of the hottest days of the Omani summer.

Polar expeditions normally start in dark, freezing shacks with a handful of comrades who know each other well and understand the minutiae of the straightforward aim to get to the Pole. The Ubar reconnaissance expedition began in Muscat's plush Al Bustan Palace Hotel and involved a group who were mostly strangers to each other, none of whom knew how best to set about searching for their goal and each of whom had a different motive for being there.

Juris Zarins, the archaeologist, was not particularly interested in the concept of the lost city of Ubar, nor did he feel that we stood a cat's chance in hell of finding it – if indeed such a city ever existed. He was extremely keen to conduct archaeological work in southern Oman and if searching for Ubar provided a pretext, fair enough.

Nick Clapp, a maker of documentary films for thirty years, had known since his three-day visit to Oman in 1980 that he must find a reason to come back and make a film here. He had rifled through the history and folklore of Oman until Bertram Thomas's Ubar story had come his way, providing him with an appealing 'search story' with all the ingredients for a magnificent documentary. Whether or not the search was to strike metaphorical gold in the shape of a lost city, Nick was in Oman to make a film of that search.

Ron Blom, a geologist and interpreter of satellite images of Earth's geology, loved his work and was fascinated to think that his ultramodern techniques might be applied to search for ruins 2000 years old. He hoped to learn a great deal about the effectiveness of these techniques by matching up his satellite pictures with actual ground features such as the *L-site*. To find the city would be a nice bonus, but he would lose no sleep if we failed.

George Hedges, the Los Angeles lawyer and Nick's fund-raiser for the documentary, had no skill remotely useful to the expedition but I gathered from Nick that he had personally risked funds towards the making of the film so he deserved to be present.

Kay Clapp, Nick's wife, was a charming lady from Jackson, Texas, with long blonde hair and the key ability to look after and account for the sponsored funds I had raised in Oman. She had accompanied Nick on many film-making projects as his producer and, as a federal probation officer in Los Angeles of twenty years' standing, was unlikely to be fazed by the occasional scorpion or snake.

The fact that nobody but myself had staked his or her reputation on locating the lost city made for a loose and easy atmosphere from the start. Juris was an affable bear of a professor with a gentle sense of humour, eyes that really did twinkle behind his thick spectacles with every awful pun that he produced and an affinity with deserts that came of two decades grubbing about in them.

Trevor Henry took us under his wing as soon as we reached Salalah, a ninety-minute flight by jet to the south of Muscat. Despite the time of year the heat was bearable, and since we were based in the air-conditioned comfort of the Salalah Holiday Inn with a palm-fringed Indian Ocean beach attached, there were no complaints.

Trevor had completed land patrols to, or flights over, all the desert sites that I had queried on account of unusual features on satellite photographs or rumours of artefacts found by *bedu*. He showed us his map and told us in his concise measured way that, were there to be any surface ruins in Dhofar, they would have been seen by oil prospectors, talkative *bedu* or patrols by land or air from the Sultan's Armed Forces.

'If the city is out there at all,' he murmured, 'then, in my opinion, it has to be sub-surface.'

Together we planned a tight schedule which in eight days would take us to every worthwhile archaeological site in southern Oman. With Juris's practised eyes as our antennae, we should pick up any clues that existed by visiting every site thought to have been involved with the frankincense trade. Since Ubar's *raison d'être* could only have been the servicing of incense caravans, bound mostly for the fleshpots of the Roman Empire, such clues could lead us to Ubar through step-by-step detective work.

Before this sleuthing process began, we intended to fly by police helicopter to the northern deserts to inspect the mysterious *L-site*, our great white hope for a quick and easy Ubar discovery.

We strapped ourselves into a Bell 205 helicopter at Salalah airbase and flew north over the monsoon clouds of the Qara Hills.

An hour or so later we entered dune country, at first mere yellow pimples but then strips, and, finally, widening bands of sand that rolled from horizon to horizon and made me think of those awesome ocean rollers that power around the South Atlantic, tamed by no land mass and fuelled by the spin of the world.

The *L-site* feature that we sought was as apparent on the ground as in the picture taken from 160 miles in space. Different surface patterns and the movement of the sand had shaped a letter L between two separate dune formations. Juris quickly announced that, sadly, mankind had taken no part in forming the *L-site*. It was merely an ancient lake bed and our only excitement was his chance discovery of a nearby pre-Islamic site with artefacts testifying to ties with the Qara hills, 300 miles away. He later found ruins, of enigmatic date, 300 yards from the *L-site* and close to a sandy pass between two great dunes. Stone patterns of ancient dwellings and hearths, and even an intermittent connecting wall, became clear with prompting from the eagle-eyed Juris.

In order to refuel and save valuable flying hours, the helicopter pilot told me he would leave us with a cold-box of Cola tins and return in an hour or so, by which time our appraisal of the area should be complete.

An hour passed by and, the inspection completed, we sat or squatted on a *mesa* top, high enough to catch any breeze to alleviate the oven-like heat of midsummer. But there was no breeze, not even the slightest of zephyrs, to cool our sweat-soaked shirts. The cold-box was soon empty.

I walked around the rim of the *mesa* and, peering over the western side, spotted an aperture, more a slit in the rock than a cave. There was enough room for all of us and an aperture in the ceiling caused a slight through-draught. After an hour and a half I noticed a certain apprehension in my companions. Even Juris was not his usual talkative self. The thought was slowly dawning that, if the wheel of fortune was to cause the helicopter to crash, we could moulder here on the *mesa* until the end of time.

'Ssh!' Kay whispered. 'Listen.' She thought she had heard the distant beat of the helicopter. There is nothing easier than to hear the vibration of imagined sounds when hoping for a rescue. Many a time in deserts and polar wastes I have distinctly caught the approaching beat of an aircraft engine, expected to bring vital supplies or to remove an injured colleague. But the sound was as often as not merely my imagination.

Two hours passed by before our pilot returned. We flew to Thamrait base and then to the little-known ruins of Andhur. On the journey I reflected how, in some ways, I was now back at square one. By hoping for space-age technology to identify the actual site of Ubar, I had fallen into the trap of suggesting as much to the sponsors. I had known that the glamorous mix of satellites and buried cities would excite even the most reluctant sponsor. Now, with all our 'space cards' a busted flush, I still had to convince His Majesty and our sponsors to back the main expedition.

Over the seven days that remained of our reconnaissance we must come up with something new, some rationale to keep our search on the rails with our backers. Trevor had arranged a schedule that would cover visits to every known archaeological site that might have a bearing on the frankincense trade with relevance to Ubar.

He took us into the Wadi Naheez, the most heavily wooded valley in the Qara Hills, and picked up two Bait Qatan guides: one a fat and talkative fellow, the other a young aspiring geologist. The humidity was high and monsoon flies were about, raising red pimples that itched for days, and Nick nearly trod on a deadly carpet viper.

Centipedes, scorpions and spiders added interest to our trek, up a side valley to a wonderful cave that, in the past, I had only visited by night, for purposes of ambush. We slithered on the orange mud and avoided the dripping lianas with their colonies of stinging ants. The cave was wide and as high as a church, with a floor deep in the animal dung of centuries. Bats chirped from the dark recesses of the rock roof and Trevor led us to the mouth of an interior passage.

'Leopards live in here,' he told us, indicating the outline of feline spoor.

We searched many caves and jungle-clad ravines. In one sunny nook below the village of Shair, Trevor pointed out aloe trees – 'very good for curing wounds' – castor-oil trees – 'you know what that's good for' – and three deadly poisonous but pretty plants: euphorbia, the Sodom apple and datura. We tramped through dry bushveld that looked for all the world like Kenyan outback without the monkeys. Trevor led us to the Jebel Kasbah (or Kaysh), a lofty crag 2000 feet above the spring of Tobruk. Hidden by thorn and mimosa, a tangle of ruined, half-buried walls puzzled Juris, who had for once no ready solution to explain or date the site. A large rectangular room, well plastered and hardly damaged over the centuries, stood still in the centre of the hill-top ruins where once, perhaps, it had served as a reservoir for trapped monsoon water.

Since any occupants of this place could observe much of the Plain of Salalah, including the pre-Islamic ruins of Taqa and other coastal landing points, it was reasonable to deduce that this was a mountain garrison from which the incense trade was policed. If so, and should these ruins tie in time-wise with the pre-Islamic city of Sumhuram, then we could draw a theoretical line over the mountains towards Andhur and the only other known frankincense storage centre, Hanun. No invaders from the sea could head inland for either of these key storage sites without being spotted from this key vantage point. It was an interesting fragment of our jigsaw puzzle but not a clue to Ubar.

Forays with Trevor and other guides took us to Ayun and the ruins at Hanun and Mudayy. Juris was fascinated but found nothing that directly helped our search. For him a dozen new areas of interest were revealed every day. The country brimmed with archaeological potential and sites that were crying out to be investigated by his trowel. Such places needed no vague and endless searching: unlike Ubar, they were right here, ripe for plucking.

Poor Juris had to exercise great patience, for I had little immediate interest in anywhere without Ubar connections. Thus it was onwards to ever-new nooks and crannies that might or might not hold a key to our grail, dragging with us the drooling Juris, since none of us but he could read portents in the strange relics that we were daily shown.

When our whirlwind tour of the Plain, the mountains and the Nejd was done, we moved back to the edge of the Sands, this time without a helicopter and, in two Land Cruisers, drove west from Thamrait to my old Ubar hunting grounds of Shis'r and Fasad. Both places had undergone considerable change. Where, in 1968, there was only barren desert, now there flourished cultivated plots of palms, fruit and vegetables. Houses too had sprung up around the water sources. At Fasad there were mostly wood and tin shacks, but at Shis'r there was a modern, Arab-style housing development designed to catch the breeze and to attract the few remaining nomads in from the nearby Sands to a stable existence and planned crop rotation to feed their goats and camels.

Fasad was now the local headquarters of the civilian 'frontier patrol force', a *firqat* with a difference, made up of young Dhofaris with desert skills whose duty was to know everything that happened along the sensitive borders with Yemen and Saudi Arabia. They greeted us with warmth, curiosity and varying degrees of credulity or scepticism regarding Ubar. I spoke to their leader, a Rashidi with a cruel hawk face that transformed, when he smiled, into open friendliness. He spoke of Irem's fate as though it were an integral part of his people's history.

'Maybe Irem lies in Yemen, or Saudi or Oman. In those days there were no such borders, so, no matter. Allah was good to the people of Ad who built the city, a paradise on earth. But *they* were bad and forsook Him for other gods, so He destroyed Irem.'

The Rashidi made a pile of sand between us and then, scooping up another handful dashed it down violently on to his makeshift city.

'Like this,' he said, 'so did Allah treat the people of Ad.'

'Is Irem of the Qur'an the same place as Ubar?' I asked him.

'Maybe,' he said with a shrug. 'Who knows?'

Juris spoke the Arabic of the Saudi *bedu* and, as long as he kept to the field topics that he had for so many years discussed at desert digs, he could converse well enough with Omanis. He learnt from our hosts that the Fasad region was barren of artefacts other than Neolithic flints. The arrowhead, some 8000 years old, known to archaeology as the Fasad Point, which has one fluted side only and includes a stubby shaft extension, was found first close to the village. However, Juris was interested in pottery of a more recent age and of that there were no traces.

Later Juris struck lucky at the village of Heilat Araka, 60 miles east of Fasad, where he found fragments lying about on the gravel plain and a football-sized stone graven by the repeated friction of ropes. This was our first find of significance, but it was well to the south-east of the Sands where Ubar was meant to be.

From Fasad we returned to Shis'r. Previous visitors told of tracks running west to the Sands from Shis'r and others heading *to* Shis'r from Andhur. Its very location, so close to the edge of the Sands and astride the best aquifer in the steppe region, indicated that the ancient camel trains must have watered here *en route* for Yemen with their cargo of incense. Our satellite photographs had confirmed that these old trails were still visible in fragmented sections but so were many others elsewhere, so at the time we read nothing of import into them.

Nevertheless Shis'r was worth a visit along with all the other main watering points at key geographical locations. Especially since the ruins, where I had twice camped before Ubar searches in the 1960s, were of unknown age and might be of some interest to Juris.

Although the local *bedu* had always told me that Shis'r rubbish pile, for such was the most apt description of the ruins, was no more than a hundred years old, others had different ideas. Wendell Phillips, possibly using Bertram Thomas for source material, wrote: 'Legend attributed the construction of this stone fort to the early sixteenth-century Hadhraumi ruler Badr bin Tuwairiq.'

Juris had told me at Sumhuram that successive civilisations built on top of each other's ruins, so perhaps Tuwairiq's fort was sited on an earlier Adite fort. My erstwhile boss, Sultan Said bin Taimur, had built his own tiny fort close to the Tuwairiq ruins and obtained most of his building materials from them.

We spent three hours wandering about the heap of rubble above the thirty-foot-high cliff overhang that protected the well. Juris was delighted, for he found fragments of pottery and various ambiguous mounds, which he called tufa, evidence of former springs. He felt sure that sedentary people had used the place for longer than the 300 years theorised by the only explorers to have previously visited Shis'r. We did not entertain visions of Ubar at Shis'r or Fasad, Heilat Araka or Andhur, but at least there was potential at these places for excavation work and the finding of clues. By contrast, out in the Sands, since our space technology had unearthed no outlines of man-made dwellings, there was *no* tangible starting-point for our search.

A fortnight after we left Muscat, Saddam Hussein pushed his troops into Kuwait and Oman joined the other Gulf States in condemning this aggressive move against an Islamic country. At this point our chances of keeping to our schedule looked poor, but I was expected by the relevant Omani ministries, as well as our sponsors, to send them a concise report summarising the results of the reconnaissance and plans for the major project. I needed first and foremost to have the considered opinion of Juris.

He was nothing if not frank. 'Didn't see any real places,' he said. 'Just some pottery at Shis'r. I didn't think anything about any of the sites. Nick kept asking me and I kept saying, "I don't know." They just looked like interesting sites. I do *know* there was *nothing* in the Sands. We have done the reconnaissance and have *nothing* to show for it.'

This was all very well, but were I to admit it to His Majesty or the sponsors I feared the main expedition would not be allowed to take place.

The report which I eventually sent to the Sultan, the Omani ministries and to all our sponsors made the best of a bad job.

We stressed that there were 'previously unsupported major settlements' at three of the sites Trevor had shown us, Raysut Hemara, Kohl Sawli and Ain Humran. We elevated the bits of pottery Juris had picked up at Shis'r by calling that village 'a far more ancient and significant site than previously suspected where we will excavate the water-hole area'.

An attached report added:

'Post-Neolithic sites in the region are rare. Our focus will be on Shis'r, where early surface pick-ups suggest that some of the buried ceramics may date to the Bronze Age. It is not impossible that Shis'r may turn out to be mythical Ubar . . .'

The rationale for this last hypothesis was given as Shis'r's commanding position on ancient frankincense trails and the likelihood that the water supply had once been greater, as evidenced by the tufa mounds of defunct artesian springs. It would have been extremely useful to state that satellite imagery had indicated further evidence pointing to Shis'r. But this would have been untrue, so Juris left it at that and we all hoped the report looked strong enough to impress all that read it with our progress and our chances of eventual success.

The reconnaissance finding that we did not stress in our report was the uniform conviction that the ancient trail did not lead *to* the city of Ubar. How could it be when the Sands were so hopelessly dry and wells so scarce that even a *bedu* family, travelling between them, knew they could never count on finding water? The ancient incense caravans of many hundreds of camels and cameleers would have needed far stronger and more predictable water supplies.

Since the ancient trails definitely existed and headed along a known azimuth, why, we mused, should they not lead *from* Ubar? The lost city then must lie in the *nej'd* (where there was ample water) and not in the Sands, where every *bedu* and almost every historical reference clearly put it.

One complication to all this was that the theme of Nick's film was the search for Ubar, which, from a scenic and logical point of view, needed to start in the desert. The most appealing conclusion for such a film would obviously have been the discovery of Ubar from space. This was no longer possible but at least he could re-enact our negative journey into the Sands and record in retrospect our conclusions, namely that we must thenceforward look to the east in defiance of all folklore and all previous theories.

Since Nick had an alarming part of his personal finances tied up in the film, I was happy to go along with a scenario that appeared to lead us from the NASA images to the ancient trails but beyond that I would not co-operate, since the space help had clearly ended there. As Juris later commented about the film theme: 'Nick was in a quandary wondering where Ubar was. As far as I was concerned, at the *end* of the reconnaissance they were going to have to do some spectacular punting to find anything. And that was exactly where we stood when we came back later to Dhofar. He had really banked his hopes on that L-shaped thing and this ancient caravan road and that they could see underneath the road and all that kind of crap.'

In Juris's view, we had done the reconnaissance and had nothing to show for it. However, from Nick's point of view with regard to the documentary film, this was quite wrong, since he had been able to travel around much of Dhofar and was now in a perfect position to plan the shape of the film.

As with all media reportage, in retrospect the facts can be put over in a hundred subtle ways that do not actually constitute distortions of the truth but merely selective exaggerations. With the writing of a book such as this it is, of course, also possible to remember only certain salient points and forget or ignore others. But no author will last long if he strays from the historical truth of actual events unless he writes of a solo unwitnessed endeavour that cannot be checked. If only one companion is present, an author can be sure his exaggerations or distortions will be noised abroad to the detriment of his future reputation. By contrast, in a film the voice-over of an unseen narrator is more anonymous. Additionally, the subliminal effect of, say, the facial expressions of an expedition team on the minds of documentary viewers can lead to their assumption of mutinous feelings against an expedition leader. In reality those same grimaces may have been filmed in reaction to bad food or bad news but edited into an unconnected episode under a misleading narrative.

While it is undeniably easier to shape the viewer's perception of a film in this way, I had at that time no reason to suspect Nick of doctoring his analysis of the events. Therefore we were all in agreement to spend time, during the main expedition, re-enacting our reconnaissance into the Sands the previous summer. Since there would be a limited work period of three months, the time Juris could be spared by his university, I could foresee conflicting interests between archaeological and film-documentary requirements.

I had promoted the project to His Majesty Sultan Qaboos, the ministries and the sponsors as an archaeological search that would be recorded on film, not as the making of a beautiful documentary about Dhofar with the central theme of a search for Ubar. This was a subtle difference which it was important for all parties on our team to remember and not to abuse.

The media that summer sizzled with prophecies of chemical warfare and massive bodybag counts should anyone try to force Saddam from Kuwait. The start of our main Ubar quest was scheduled for the spring of 1991 to avoid the hot season but, with the Gulf troubles in mind, I wrote to Nick suggesting we postpone our start until the autumn.

Shortly after Dr Hammer's death I had an unpleasant, near fatal, experience at my Exmoor home that was to have serious consequences for the Ubar expedition. As a result of this event I came across a London based group who asked me to write their biography. This I eventually did and the resulting book, *The Feather Men*, became number one best-seller in the United Kingdom. It also sparked a good deal of controversy with ex-SAS members and with certain past and present expatriate members of the Sultan's Armed Forces. In particular one of the Royal Oman Police Air Wing officers felt that the book smeared the good name of his unit and of its former chief.

Not long before the expedition was due to depart I was contacted by an Omani friend, who warned me that senior elements in the ROP had suggested to the Ministry of Palace Office Affairs and the Ministry of Information that the entire Ubar project should be quashed because of the revelations made in *The Feather Men*.

I telephoned the Ministry of Information in Muscat, to whom I had sent a copy of the book some weeks before. I was told that since there was nothing in the book that was even slightly offensive to Oman there could be no reason for interfering with the expedition. My contact in the Palace Office echoed this. Nevertheless, the force upon whose help we would need to survive in Dhofar was to be the Royal Oman Police, especially their Air Wing. So I contacted the complainant, an expatriate Englishman, in the hope of making peace.

On the day we set out for the Ubar expedition I discovered that, in my rush, I had collected the wrong travel bag from our London store. Instead of tropical shirts, sun-cream and malaria tablets, I had a duffle bag with snow goggles, balaclava, mitts and the like. I decided not to mention this to the Clapps in case it alarmed them. They had never been to Dhofar and the entire responsibility for our well-being out there was in my hands. They might lose confidence in my preparations if they knew the contents of my travel bag.

For co-leaders to react happily to one another on a fraught expedition is abnormal from all I have heard of previous such arrangements, especially when the two 'chiefs' are from different cultures and share no background interests. I had never before tried sharing leadership, since I find it difficult to head in a different route to my chosen path. There were two things that I think kept Nick and me the best of friends, with never a heated word between us. First, I had undisputed command of the expedition itself in Oman and Nick had total control of the film, including my own compliance as an 'extra'. But, more importantly, neither of us was an extrovert and neither tried to score over the other. Only when the expedition was done did differences of opinion arise and these were merely a question of differing memories, as with two witnesses describing the same murder.

A young Omani, Malik al Hinai, who had masterminded our preparations from his Oman International Bank office in Muscat, came to see us off on our 600-mile overnight drive to Salalah. He handed me a portable telephone on loan.

'This will get you anywhere any time, no problem,' he said.

'Anywhere at all?' I asked.

'Absolutely. The Kremlin or Buckingham Palace . . . We can try now if you'd like.'

'Go ahead, Malik.' I gave him a London number I knew by heart as a result of work with Dr Hammer. 'That's Buckingham Palace.'

Malik laughed, clearly disbelieving me, but dialled the number. The team were grouped about and we heard the East London accent of the palace telephone operator. 'Buckingham Palace,' she grunted. Malik's mouth opened wide and he held the telephone well away as though it would bite him.

Fourteen hours later, not far from Thamrait, a police patrol car stopped us. I had no official papers but our own Special Task Force escort arrived and saw the traffic police off in seconds. The pecking order was in our favour.

Nick's camera team used one of our three Discovery vehicles so that they could film wherever we went over the next three months. I was relieved to find both men were strong characters, and not 'whingers', which I had previously found to be the case with some BBC camera teams. Kevin O'Brien the cameraman, like Nick and me, had worked for Dr Hammer for a number of years. From Los Angeles, Kevin had travelled the world in style, filming the multi-millionaire Malcolm Forbes on his motorcycle and balloon expeditions to China and elsewhere.

George Ollen, the sound man, was forty years old and unmarried. Too restless by nature to settle for a single woman or job, he had forsaken a planned career in the US Marines to become a professional nomad. One night a garage attendant shot him in the shoulder for no particular reason, which led in a roundabout way to a three-year session selling video tapes – his first profitable activity – until, in October 1991, Nick had lured him into joining our team.

In Salalah, Trevor Henry, so indispensable to our reconnaissance the previous year, warned me that as part of the ongoing removal of all expatriates from the Omani Armed Forces he was due to leave Dhofar in the near future and we could no longer count on his assistance.

He had earlier referred me to another Scotsman, named Andy Dunsire, who had lived in Dhofar for some eighteen years and knew the country almost as well as Trevor. 'Andy works for Airwork, the aircraft engineers in Thamrait. He will give you any help you need,' he assured me.

One problem I foresaw was a lack of labour to excavate any ruins that we might locate. Juris Zarins was expecting two staff and four students from his university but we might need six times that number of diggers. Andy saw no problems, especially when I mentioned that the American archaeology students were mostly nubile young blondes. 'Just clear it with our boss and I'll get you the volunteers.'

I picked up an unemployed Indian hitchhiker in the mountains. He agreed to help dig with two strong friends for a modest wage and gave me his Salalah address.

Our first task involved a thorough search of the Plain and the mountains. For this work we

Southern Oman

would be comfortably based in Salalah. To the north of the mountains, the best location from which to operate in the Sands and the central steppes was Shis'r, for there was fresh water in this *bedu* village.

I drove to a wild and remote part of the *jebel* where, after many enquiries, I found my old friend Hamed al Khalas staying with a wealthy camel-herder. The quarter century that had passed since we had worked together under Sultan Said bin Taimur had been kind to Hamed. We talked for two hours over a bowl of foaming camel's milk and I told him of our plans. He promised to guide me to any of the 'old places'. There was nowhere in Dhofar that Hamed could not find.

Nashran bin Sultan was also in good health and living in Salalah, for he had long since retired from Government Intelligence. His memories of our long patrols in the *nej'd* were undimmed but he was as adamant as ever that Ubar lay to the west of the Wadi Mitan.

All the camping and excavation materials loaned by Occidental Petroleum of Oman and an oil supplies company called Desert Line arrived in Salalah on time, so we moved to the first work site on the Plain. This was a long-abandoned well some seventy feet deep which Ptolemy had described as the Oracle of Diana. Juris wanted to excavate the shaft itself and the ruined village around the well's mouth so I borrowed a mobile crane from BP of Oman in Salalah.

Nick and I were lowered into the shaft inside the crane's bucket. The smell of rotting flesh was overpowering and emanated from the bloated bodies of dead foxes. I manoeuvred the corpses into polythene bags and swatted at the fat flies that settled on my arms. I tried to keep my thoughts off the glistening carpet of insect life that crawled, leapt and slithered in that foul-smelling hole.

Even inside the swinging iron bucket we were attended by a host of flying, biting insects, but the stench lessened once the foxes' bodies were gone. Subsequent lowerings took us back with shovels and we began the task of hoisting debris into the buckets. Each time we raised a new item, be it a tattered tent canvas or a stinking mattress, hundreds of disturbed spiders, cockroaches, scorpions and unidentifiable creatures of all imaginable shapes and sizes scuttled away.

The well shaft was some sixty feet in diameter and Juris assumed that Ptolemy, Ibn Batuta and others had noted the site as an oracle because, in ancient times, some local priest had hidden down the shaft and shouted up oracular responses to questions from paying visitors. This being so, we should find traces of a cave or crevice halfway down the shaft.

Andy Dunsire, an experienced caver, fixed two harnesses to one of the Discoveries parked above and, braced against the upper neck of the shaft, we descended twenty feet to attack a suspect protuberance with pickaxes and brushes. In a while four well-cut plastered stone slabs were clearly delineated but further work began to dislodge them, so we never discovered if they led into a horizontal passageway, long since choked with dirt, which might have hidden some trickster and acted as an echo chamber to his prophetic platitudes.

The deep stratum of modern garbage and animal bones that formed the floor of the shaft defeated our attempts to reach detritus from earlier times, so we left the Naheez valley and headed north, via Shis'r and Fasad, with eight days' supply of food, fuel and water. Andy Dunsire came as our guide but, in Fasad, I asked the Imam, a gentle Rashidi named Mohamed Mabhowt, if he would take us to two nameless spots out in the Sands, the *L-site* and the ancient camel track which we had visited on the 1990 reconnaissances by helicopter.

Ron Blom produced one of his satellite pictures, taken from 160 miles above Earth and clearly delineating each and every sand dune. Mohamed made various grunting sounds that indicated comprehension if not recognition and agreed to accompany us. One thing he could promise us: *wherever* we ended up, he would be sure to find the quickest route back out again. Just as no man could, for many centuries, travel the Sands by camel better than the Rashidis, so nowadays they were accepted as the master 4WD rally drivers of the great dunes.

This no idle boast. Mohamed drove our lead Discovery, travelling over the softest sand and mounting the most severe of slopes where none of us could follow without embarrassing results.

Somewhere well within the eastern furrows of the Uruq al Hadh, with high dunes on all sides, we camped and Ron extricated his Magellan GPS satellite navigator in order to locate our position to within 100 metres. We eagerly awaited the results of this high-tech magic, the box of tricks which rendered any city-dweller a capable navigator overnight. Ron appeared non-plussed. 'Odd,' he muttered. 'Very unusual . . . They certainly never gave any warning of this.'

Magellan had decided, for unstated reasons, to make their navigation services unavailable to ground users for twenty-four hours. So much for reliance on state-of-the-art boffinry, I mused, but said nothing, not wishing to upset Ron.

The next day we reverted to old-style position-line navigation, using the satellite pictures as though they were maps. This was a slow process involving many stops and interesting debates between the film director, the explorer, the space scientist and the Imam of Fasad, through whose familiar home terrain we were hesitantly creeping. If only we could have given him a familiar name as our desired goal and he would quickly have taken us there by the best available route. But the faded tracks of the Thomas road had no name and their grid reference could not be speedily inferred from our own, until the latter was indisputably revealed at such a time as Ron's Magellan condescended to supply the relevant data.

When sixty years ago, Philby had vainly sought Wabar in this same great desert, one of his guides had sung him the age old ballad of the lost city:

> From Qariya strike the sun upon the town
> Blame not the guide that vainly seeks it now
> Since the Destroying Power laid it low.

Andy and I, keen to savour the still beauty of the desert nights, found dune folds beyond the circle of sleepers. The night skies were wild and clean, evoking all the limitless chances of life, of a future still worthy of dreams; a fine if brief antidote to the narrowing outlook of middle age.

Sirius, the Dog Star, slid brilliantly glinting into the lacuna of pre-dawn luminosity between two crested ergs. Desert dew settled and tiny grains of sand whispered in their millions as they trickled down the face of their mother dunes. Allah was close by on such a night. It is written in the Qur'an's Chapter of the Star that:

> It is He who makes men laugh and weep, it is He who kills and makes alive . . . He is the Lord of the Dog Star, He who destroyed Ad of yore, and Thamud, and left none of them, and the people of Noah before them. Their cities, he threw them down and there covered them what did cover them.

The Dog Star, if I could only speak with him, could tell me every secret of the Sands and where to find Ubar.

At the break of day the clear and mellow voice of Mohamed, Imam of Fasad, sounded the morning incantation to God. The soul of Arabia, the thunder of the Saracens and the spirit of the desert came together in the passion of the mullah's voice. No God could ignore such a sound: '*Allahu Akbar, Allahu Akbar . . .*'

Soon after dawn, and carrying all the filming gear, we plodded to the ridge of the highest dune, filling our shoes with sand and exposing the unfit to the less unfit. The view made the effort worthwhile: mile upon mile of crests and peaks, battlements and moving shadows. To capture the colouring, wonderfully soft and diffuse, would have taxed the most subtle of artists.

The ancient camel tracks at this point were clearly shown by satellite image to disappear underneath the sand dune to our immediate east. We searched with binoculars, but not until late afternoon, when the harshness began to fade from the desert light, could we distinguish the tracks. There were two main trails, which, as they became easier to see with the naked eye, did indeed appear to vanish beneath a three-hundred foot mountain of sand. This certainly seemed to provide an argument that the track had been in use many centuries ago. Exactly how old? This is difficult to say, but camels were not used as load-carrying beasts before 2500 BC, and so, if the track *is* older, then only humans, mules and horses can have used it.

Nick directed the camera team to recapture on celluloid our reaction to the disappointment suffered on our reconnaissance here the previous year and our subsequent deduction that Ubar must lie to the east of the dunes rather than within them, as was generally believed.

Where Nick and I suffer a radical divergence of opinion is as to the nature of our reasoning at that point. He believes that the series of NASA-produced images showing a network of tracks converging on the region of Shis'r led us to the assumption that Ubar must be somewhere along an arc of tracks which included those at Shis'r and stretched all the way, albeit at sporadic intervals, to the Sands and beyond.

Juris, on the other hand, agrees that our only reason for basing ourselves at was its excellent position as a base from which to work the region to the north of the mountains. This had always been the plan and no NASA data amended it. Shis'r was one of a dozen places of potential interest both for clue searching and for film-making. Our brief 1990 visit there made Juris reflect: 'Sure, Shis'r had a bit of pottery . . . You can always find something to do archaeologically but it had nothing to do with Ubar.' Later, in 1992, he told me: 'I didn't think Shis'r was Ubar even when we started digging there.'

From the early days I knew there were three main aquifers running north into Dhofar's southern fringe of the Empty Quarter. The existing water sources at Fasad, Shis'r and Mugshin all lay at a latitude through which the Thomas road may easily have passed. The water at Fasad is very sulphurous, and at Mugshin highly salty, but Shis'r's water, that of the Wadi Ghadun aquifer, is famous for its sweetness.

Since water availability is an obvious key to the siting of cities, one did not need to be an archaeologist or a student of satellite maps to deduce that Shis'r could itself be a candidate for Ubar. Nevertheless we had all, including Juris, no idea that we might find the city at Shis'r any more than at a great number of other sites which our original space images showed as interesting blips, such as the *L-site* (the most promising), or Heilat Araka, or merely places reported by Trevor and *bedu* informants. We intended to dig and film at them all. The only reason Shis'r stood out was its suitability as a base camp. Militating against Shis'r was the fact that explorers Thomas, Thesiger, Phillips, later archaeologists and every Omani we spoke to, all wrote off the Shis'r ruins as a mere three hundred years old or less.

When first I planned which areas were most suitable for Juris to visit, the key person who judged the value of each site (whether a suspect NASA blip in the Sands, an old village in the steppes or a nest of ruins on the Plain) was Trevor Henry. But in the mountains, where our clues would mostly consist of cave drawings, and in the maze of *nej'd* wadis running north from the (where the pecked rock, graves and triliths mostly lay), our chief guide and adviser would be a remarkable Dhofari of the Shahra tribe named Ali Ahmed Ali Mahash.

Back in the 1960s Ali, like many Dhofaris, had joined the British-trained Trucial Oman Scouts. His outstanding qualities of leadership soon saw his promotion to lieutenant and he was sent to Mons Officer Cadet School in England two years after I graduated from there.

In the late 1960s we both worked at the Army School of Languages in Beaconsfield, where I was a student of Arabic and he was a teacher. He was recalled to the Gulf States as a captain and, the best young officer of his generation, was selected for a three-year posting to a British regiment. Unfortunately the Gulf intelligence services discovered that Ali was promulgating revolutionary ideas and he was jailed in Muscat for seven years.

On his release he obtained a government job in Salalah but remained restless until, in March 1988, a fellow Shahri showed Ali some cave writings in the Wadi Naheez. Ali was fascinated. He knew that the history of his country, of his people the Shahra and the lost people of Ad, was locked within a pre-Islamic language that existed only in southern Arabia and especially in Dhofar. Modern progress, especially the proliferation of 4WD jeeps all over the country, was already defacing many rock drawings on valley floors.

Ali told me: 'The Phillips expeditions of 1952 and 1953 represent the only archaeological work carried out in Dhofar and the only inscriptions so far published are written in the language of the Hadhraumi coastal settlers of AD 100. There is nothing in any local language and a remarkable dearth of information about our ancient history.'

Ali decided, without official prompting or support, to make a systematic survey of all the caves in Dhofar. Since there are many thousands of caves, often deep and inaccessible, in the *nej'd*, the mountains and along the coast, Ali's intentions were enormously ambitious. He had no formal training in data recording and could only use his spare time for the project. He took many photographs of each new discovery and attended photography courses at London's Institute of Archaeology. Over the months he drew up individual groupings of different symbols that formed the cave writing at various sites. He intended to decipher the unknown early alphabet of his ancestors. To find out how the writings and the pictures were painted, he mixed dyes from over 130 different sources, vegetable and mineral, in a backroom at his Salalah home.

Ali was enthusiastic about our work and agreed to take us to his discoveries. Whether or not the paintings or graffiti would provide us with clues, we would only know when Juris could see the sites for himself. Over a three-week period Ali took us by vehicle and on foot to remote and wonderful places all over Dhofar.

Ginnie came out to establish a proper HF communications network with radio sets based at Shis'r, Thamrait and in each of our vehicles. When the archaeologists arrived and we separated into groups, good long-distance communications would speed up the search and help in an emergency. Ali went with the two of us east to Mirbat, west to Rakhyut and just about everywhere in between. We drove the track east from Sudh to Hadbin until it tapered out on a precipitous coastal trail in the mountains west of Hasik.

Although Ali and I had been trained at the same British institutions, there was a good deal of heated discussion since we had ended up fighting on opposite sides. When, in remote villages, he introduced me as an ex-officer of Sultan Said bin Taimur, I sensed a certain coolness from time to time. Under the benevolent rule of Sultan Qaboos all the old enmities have been buried but living memories of powerful events and emotions do not disappear in Arabia any more than elsewhere.

Ali took us to the homesteads of his people, the Shahra, high on the grassland downs of Kizit, where they are cattle herders, and deep in the Wadi Darbat, where they keep thousands of camel. The caves near each settlement reflected in their paintings the business of the region. Camel drawings were omnipresent, depicting camels walking, trotting, emaciated, fat with large lumps, couched in pairs or in long caravan lines, suckling babies or being milked by herders. Pictures of camels being ridden immediately told those of us who had previously listened to Juris that the paintings must be later than 2500 BC when camels were first domesticated. We were fast becoming amateur archaeologists.

With only a few of the more inaccessible caves to explore, we thanked Ali and made our way over the mountains to Thamrait and thence to Shis'r with two lorryloads of food and equipment.

Juris's archaeological team arrived not long before Christmas, all in their early twenties and none with previous experience of Arabia. The five girls were blessed with long hair, pretty faces and well-rounded figures. I thanked God (and Juris) for an excellent selection process and felt confident there would be no problem in Andy Dunsire finding a great number of volunteer diggers from among his Airwork colleagues at Thamrait. If the attraction of the actual digging was not enough, this bunch of alluring American belles would surely do the trick. I nursed mental images of hundreds of randy diggers shovelling aside vast amounts of sand from our sites over the next three months.

I handed out *shemagh* headcloths, sand goggles, camp-beds and water bottles to everyone, including the hitchhiker and two other Indians who arrived from Salalah. Together with the anticipated influx of Thamrait expatriates, we should total up to forty diggers on a good day.

I hoped that none of our girls would get too quickly involved in emotional attractions since this might put off the majority of other diggers, who might feel their chances of romance had become too slim to warrant the boring hours of desert digging in midsummer.

Once we were established at Shis'r, two partly different programmes had to be followed. Juris and his diggers were to excavate all hopeful sites in the immediate area for a month and then move south to work for a further two months in the mountain and on the Plain, based in Salalah. Nick, Kay and the camera team, with both Andy and Ali Ahmed kindly ready to take them more or less anywhere they wished, would complete the documentary film.

The month of December rushed by with preparations and a good deal of filming work. Three days before Christmas I heard the two Omani students, who worked with us on loan from the Ministry of National Heritage and Culture, commenting on the fact that we had been in Shis'r for ten days, the teams were ready and yet all we seemed to do was to film each other. This seemed a fair summary and it would not sound good in the wrong quarters. The day before Christmas Eve, I had a quiet word with Juris and suggested he do a bit of digging *anywhere* the Ministry students could see the action. He took his group, minus Andy's amateur helpers, some two hundred yards from our camp to the rubble around the old Shis'r well. Desultory work began.

By Christmas Day Juris was looking smug. I asked him why but he was guarded.

'The dig,' he muttered. 'It's good . . . interesting.'

'Is it four hundred years old,' I pressed him, 'like they say?'

'No,' he replied, winked and returned to the room where retrieved artefacts were beginning to spread all over the improvised shelves. The team were buried in site maps, lists and hushed discussions. There was an unmistakable air of excitement.

At first Juris concentrated his small force on or close to the original rubble pile. Within a week the outline of the rock heap had taken on the clear-cut silhouette of a ruined tower connected by low battlements to a second round tower and a beautifully built horseshoe tower to its east. Pottery and flints were hourly unearthed including, to Juris's great pleasure, both Roman and Greek-style urns from the period that would have been Ubar's heyday.

'You ask me when I began to think Shis'r was Ubar,' Juris was later to stress, 'but there was *no* one single day that I said, "Oh, my God, this is Ubar or this is Omanum Emporium." Until we find an inscription we can *never* one hundred per cent say that!'

Early in January 1992 Juris found a piece of red pottery identical to the pottery style of the Jemdet Nassir period in Uruq, Mesopotamia. If carbon dating proves this to be so it will pre-date previous thinking as to the commencement of trade between Mesopotamia and south Arabia from 4000 to 5000 BC. That in turn will affect many other evolving theories about our human history.

'I am not going out on a limb,' Juris told me, 'and saying this is or isn't Ubar. I will go back to the university to check out all our findings: then I can make some statement. But I can already say this is a very important Roman site. It probably goes back at least four thousand years.'

Why, I asked him, had the middle of the walled citadel (a more appropriate word than 'city' since the whole walled area was not much bigger than a football field) collapsed? It was as though a bomb had blown out a crater, leaving only the outer walls and towers with a few rooms and hearths on the inside of the walls. How many other internal structures there might have been before the collapse may never be known.

'As with many well-built walled caravanserai,' Juris said, 'this was built around a strategically sited water-hole – and what could be more of a controlling site than this?' He paused, looking down into the sandy pit below the cliff. 'I suspect that as they used up more and more water during a dry period, the water table lowered and the immediate surrounds fell in to form a typical dolina or karst collapse. An earthquake may have even assisted by undermining the solutional cavity.'

When free time was available, I took a shovel and pickaxe to the site and attacked any area that did not require more delicate attention using trowel and handbrush. The lady diggers, however, allergic to shovels, would scream and chase me away, so I spent more time plodding about in the desert six or seven miles east of the site searching the subsidiary camps rich in axe-heads and arrowheads. Once these were located I would fetch Juris with his position-locating gear to plot each new satellite site.

In the days when the area was verdant, travellers would have camped within sight of the many-towered citadel but far enough away to settle their camels and sort out their loads. Altogether we found thirty-five such campsites to the north, west and east of the citadel and up to eight miles away from it.

The central site would have appeared majestic and without equal in the land to the *bedu* cameleers. For 560 miles of desert in any direction there was no edifice even a quarter the size of Shis'r, or Ubar as I by now described it. The walls and towers would have stood out to the weary and thirsty traveller from up to twenty miles away – to them indeed a city of the desert.

Nigel Groome, once Aden's Director of Antiquities, writes of south Arabia:

The general impression gleaned from a survey of the archaeological remains that have come down from the tenth century – and they are considerable – is that cities were built on a small scale, that buildings were simple and modestly constructed from materials locally available and that the standard of living was far from luxurious when compared to that prevailing in other parts of the ancient Near Eastern world.

Of our site Juris told me, 'So far we have walls and towers that are square and round and horseshoe-shaped. There was clearly a central tower, an inner sanctum and an outer wall which had a minimum height of between ten and fifteen feet and a consistent thickness of eighty centimetres. Some of the original rooms, complete with hearths, did not collapse into the sink-hole and these have already yielded rich finds for the key periods between the second millennium BC and around AD 300, when trading activities seem to have dropped off.'

The original building work of the Ubarites was excellent, consisting of semi-dressed stones cemented with a white plaster similar to that used in the north of the peninsula by contemporary peoples such as the Nabataeans of Petra.

Our diggers came across the only ancient chess set ever to be found in south Arabia. The six soapstone pieces, each two or three inches high and well polished by the fingers of the players, had lain buried for over a thousand years. Shutrinj, the forerunner of modern chess, was a Persian war game and the king was *shah*. The word for dead is *ma'at* and a victorious player cornering his opponent's monarch would shout '*Shah ma'at*' – not so different from 'checkmate'.

After a month the diggers were three feet down in places and pottery from Rome, Greece and Syria joined Celadon and Ming plates from China, glass bracelets of bright, clear colours from Aden and Neolithic flint weapons from 5000 BC.

Words of our discovery soon reached the Omani and Gulf press and tourists in Land Rovers began to arrive from Salalah. Was this Ubar? Was it Irem? If so, where were the golden pillars and the whole fabulous city? The fantasies of the *Arabian Nights* had a lot to answer for.

By the end of January we had found no major inscription but nine towers were unearthed, some 60 per cent of the main outer wall and over 6000 individual artefacts.

Nick's documentary film had also progressed well with the help of Ali Ahmed and Trevor.

Andy Dunsire had told me of a cave system 600 feet down at the base of a giant sink-hole called Tawi Ateer, the Well of Birds. He had promised to show me a great cavern which I hoped might contain wall writings or at least paintings, for it was known, certainly until the advent of recent rockfalls, that Dhofaris used to descend into the hole by way of vertiginous pathways. Andy drove me with a Range Rover full of his friends to the village of Tawi Ateer on the high plateau of the *jebel* and a mile to the north, and we trekked into the dry bush with rucksacks and ropes. His three friends were to camp at the end of the 600-foot deep crater to ensure that our descent ropes were not removed during the night.

Because I was inept with the special rope techniques Andy used, he took an hour to make everything ready. I felt a touch giddy, for the cry of pigeons and the starling-like Tristram's grackle echoing around the vast natural chamber kept reminding me of the long drop down to the cave system.

By the time we were ready, dusk had filled the huge, perfectly rounded cauldron and, as Andy encouraged me to let go of the safety rope by the crater lip, stars were already appearing in a sky of midnight blue. I could not see below me and my helmet torch, striking a rock, went dead. This had the advantage of making it impossible to see the hundreds of yards of thin rope dangling down into the void between my swinging feet.

After many minutes of painfully slow descent the two-inch-long alloy crocodile clasp, which slid down the rope at a great speed, suddenly came up sharp against a knot of rope coils. I winced as the rope elasticated. I imagined the feel of it breaking and the sudden rush of air. Panic was not far off. Sweat stung my eyes. Because all my body weight rested on the point where the metal teeth were jammed against the knot and since there could be no upward impetus from my dangling legs, it took me many long minutes to free the impediment without disentangling my lifeline by mistake. For a while I despaired, then a lucky tug freed the coil, and ten minutes later I arrived shaky kneed at the floor of the great shaft.

The stench of civet dung hung about in the warm air and I heard the scrabble of the striped cats in the darkness. Andy arrived after twenty minutes and I followed him via boulders and sloping ledges, past stalactites and a descending series of passages, to the edge of a scum-laden lake. The beam of his head torch disturbed a cloud of flying creepy-crawlies.

On a previous visit Andy had secreted two Land Rover inner tubes close by, and stripping down to our pants and desert boots, we slipped into the evil-smelling waters.

Andy beckoned me away from one side wall where a swarm of giant mosquito-like insects rose in anger from their nest.

'There are blind fish in the caves,' Andy pointed downwards and added, 'Keep close.' I nodded, needing no second warning.

For fifty minutes I swam on my black tube and soon gave up any attempt to memorise our tortuous route. Sometimes the ceiling on the tunnel approached within inches of the water and, copying Andy, I turned over and swam on my back. There was just enough room to breathe and then, when the gap improved slightly, to haul on a long cord attached to my tube to pull it under the obstacle.

I kept a nagging claustrophobic fear at bay through total trust in Andy's cavemanship, if that is the right term. But it came to me how easily he might suffer a heart attack, for he was well into his fifties. How then would I find my way out of these evil waterways? Certainly not by memory.

My faith in Andy collapsed and my inner fears surged when his white beard lifted from the oily surface and he spluttered, 'Which way did we enter this chamber?'

I told him and he disagreed. We bobbed under an even lower ledge with no more than three inches' clearance and I smelled putrefied flesh close at hand. An animal skull with wet, green flesh attached in floating ribbons nodded against my shoulder – some civet or goat lured to its death by thirst.

After an hour and a half Andy shook his head, dislodging all manner of flying insects. 'I can't understand it,' he grunted. 'The main passageway must be underwater. I just can't locate it.' So we gave up and, to my considerable relief, he found no difficulty in retracing his route to the entry point.

We slept on a ledge free of civet dung until dawn when, back at the base of the crater and the single length of rope, Andy attached two special grips to my foot and shoulder.

'You go first. If you get into trouble, shout, but do not look down.'

After about two hundred feet the tautly stretched rope felt as thin as string. The swish and shriek of disturbed grackles and my empty stomach combined to make the climb unenjoyable, but I managed to force from my mind the tiniest thought about the ever-increasing drop below.

When Andy joined me at the upper rim of the crater, he looked disappointed. 'Never mind,' he said, 'we'll come back when the water-level drops.'

My enthusiasm to find the cave graffiti had lessened but I took care not to show it.

Some five weeks after the first key finds at Shis'r, a police van with four armed officers arrived around midnight with a summons for me to go at once to the Palace in Muscat. The police drove me to Salalah and, by ROP flight, I reached Muscat the next morning. A Royal limousine took me to Seeb Palace, where various new ambassadors were being accredited. After an hour's wait in what must rank among the most splendid palaces in the world, I was shown in to His Majesty Sultan Qaboos' *majlis*. He was delighted with the success of the expedition and keen to ensure continued excavation at Shis'r until the ruins were fully revealed. He asked me to give him a list of actions I thought might best be taken to follow up the discovery.

'Is it definitely Ubar?' he asked me.

'I believe so, Your Majesty. It is difficult to know what else it could be.'

The warmth of his smile and the strength of his handshake reminded me of my meeting with his father twenty-four years before. I felt that the long years of hoping, the set-backs and the false trails had all been worthwhile.

I asked in my report to Sultan Qaboos that Ali Ahmed be appointed Field Director for Archaeology in Dhofar, that Juris be contracted to continue excavations and that the Shis'r site be protected against damage by visitors.

Back in Salalah I handed over all the equipment and organisational details to Juris. Apart from the archaeologists, all the team left Oman early in February. The search for Ubar was over. A few weeks later I returned to report to the Minister of Information, His Excellency Abdul Aziz bin Mohomed al Rowas, who had been appointed by the Sultan to chair a ministerial committee to oversee all aspects of archaeology in southern Oman.

To my delight, Ali Ahmed Ali Mahash had been appointed as director, with responsibility for all future work in Dhofar. I was to ensure that all artefacts were handed over to him before Juris and the team left Oman. Since I had previously signed a government document taking full responsibility for all such items, I was keen to comply. We were able to hand Ali more than 13,000 artefacts fully computerised with individual reference numbers.

There were Fasad Points, arrowheads from between the sixth and fourth millennia BC. The first buildings, in a Shis'r satellite camp, Bil Rizat, dated back to 2000 BC, and this was where Juris found the pottery shard likely to have come from Uruq.

The majority of the pottery, soapstone lamps and incense burners stem from Shis'r's trading heyday, probably between 500 and 300 BC, which was the Roman, Greek and south Arabic period. This confirms Shis'r's case for identification with Ptolemy's Omanum Emporium. The Greek word *emporion* was applied to cities on or close to the coast. This is confusing until the point of view of the *bedu*, who used the city, is considered. After travelling 560 miles south through the Sands, they would have considered Shis'r in the southern steppes more coastal than central. The informants of Ptolemy would not have seen Shis'r for themselves, but they would have relied on information that stemmed from these *bedu* traders. For hundreds of years the precise locations of important incense sources were purposely kept hidden from the Romans and the Greeks by means of secrecy and misinformation.

There was an abrupt dearth in materials between 300 BC and AD 300. This was the period when Shis'r declined and its original name is likely to have fallen into disuse. Quite when the current *bedu* name of Shis'r, or 'cleft', came into usage is not known, but by the time of the Qur'an, in the seventh century AD, the location of Ubar or Irem was no longer known.

Chinese porcelain, both Celadon and Ming, the chess set, copper needles, coins, bracelets and fine glass from Aden were plentiful and bear witness to a renewal of trade in the Arabic, early

Islamic period from AD 650 to 1200. This ties in with the Islamic network of trading horses from central Arabia to the Dhofar coast at that time.

My preconception of archaeology was born of work with ice-core drilling in polar regions. With ice, all data is stratified so that, at a certain depth, analysis will show traces in the ice of a known volcanic eruption or atomic bomb test. At Shis'r, our team located artefacts across the entire time-space of occupation from each level. Because each successive human occupation mixes up the detritus of previous inhabitants with their own rubbish, stratification does not often help with the dating process. 'So what?' said Juris. 'If you were an archaeologist of the twenty-ninth century AD and you dug up a 1990 Ford you would clearly differentiate it from a Fifties Chevvy . . . Well, pottery is just as stylised and has fashions that alter year by year. We know what period they represent, however shallow or deep we may locate them.'

Each new artefact had helped to fill in the puzzle, which Juris needed to reconstruct, that was the unknown past of Shis'r.

Between 8000 and 6000 BC the region was too arid for humans. In 5000 BC, with wetter weather, Neolithic folk from Syria and further east arrived and built hearths. Even then, Juris believed, they traded in incense and travelled the then less arid interior, now the Sands, on foot and, after 4000 BC, by donkey.

'The peoples of Ubaid, of south Iraq and Sumer,' Juris stressed, 'traded in painted ceramics by 5000 to 4000 BC. I believe incense from Dhofar was traded then too. After all, their early texts of 2500 BC already talked of incense. It is a small jump back to 4000 BC, but at that time they could not write so they left no *proof*.'

All that Juris learnt from Shis'r and its related sites about the people of Ad, the descendants of the Neolithics from the north, would help fill in our knowledge about the trading and life patterns of the age before that described to us by the classical writers of the first and second centuries AD. These men were not themselves able to penetrate Arabia. They were forced to report mere secondhand information so, although Shis'r probably did not decline until after the days of Strabo, Pliny and Ptolemy, none of them was able to go there.

By the seventh century AD, when the Qur'an and later Islamic writers described Irem, the site itself was gone, a place only of fanciful legend. The decline would partly have been due to the natural catastrophe that caused the town's collapse between AD 100 and AD 300, but Roman power faded in AD 300, Christianity spread and the demand for incense dwindled. Without the Dhofar frankincense trade, the key to Shis'r's former glories, the inhabitants of the half-ruined site returned to a *bedu* existence and for 700 years only squatters and nomads needing water came to Shis'r. After AD 1000, the time of the Ming china and the chess set, the horse trade brought back a second lesser glow to the wounded city and then, in 1970, Sultan Qaboos built homes, a mosque and a school there. Now the Bait Masan tribe, descendants in all likelihood of those early arrowhead makers and incense traders, have made it their permanent home. They too will leave their traces in the ground at Shis'r or Ubar, Atlantis of the Sands.

On 5 February 1992 an article by John Noble Wolford was splashed across the front page of the *New York Times*, giving the news of our discovery of Ubar. This article was picked up and given major coverage all across the world, for there was a shortage of hard news at the time. All major newspapers and TV networks across the USA gave the story prime rating and suggested that the project was an entirely American inspired success.

'Guided by ancient maps and sharp-eyed surveys from space,' wrote the respected Mr

Wolford, 'archaeologists and explorers have discovered a lost city deep in the sands of Arabia.'

Keen to be properly grateful to NASA who had indeed gone out of their way over a long period to try to help us, and naturally eager to tie in the romantic idea of modern technology with ancient lost cities in the documentary film of our search, Nick himself began to see things very differently to the clear events that I remember and have described in this book. I only wish satellite photography had led us to Shis'r, for it would have made a wonderful theme for this book and for the illustrated lectures which are my 'bread and butter'.

A large slice of luck, a lot of hard work and the experience-honed instincts of Juris led us to the discovery. Good vehicles, generous sponsors, the support of the Sultan and so many Omanis, a wonderful team of volunteers (including NASA personnel) and technological aids in many forms, all contributed to our success.

The Gulf media was jubilant and the Egyptian *Al Liwa Al Islami* quoted various specialists as being certain it was the same city as that mentioned in the Qur'an.

The Saudi press was clearly unhappy with any suggestion that Ubar (or Irem) was not within the Saudi borders but not all Saudis were hostile to our announcement. Professor Mohammed Bakalla of King Saud University sent me a letter:

> Your discovery is very important and I expect future work will unveil the extraordinary civilisation of Irem-al-Imad. I will not be surprised if Ad's nation cities are underneath what has been discovered by you or in the close vicinity.

The main objections voiced in the Saudi press by non-scientific sources were that our site was small, contained Islamic (not just pre-Islamic) artefacts, did not show evidence of temples and was not found fully preserved by tons of sand.

Since we had not to date unearthed an actual nameplate naming Shis'r as Ubar, Irem or Omanum Emporium, all our evidence was indeed circumstantial, but it is easy to summarise. In AD 150 Claudius Ptolemy was the only geographer to leave map co-ordinates of Arabia. In 1870 the German Sprenger analysed medieval reconstructions of Ptolemy's map and found that the principal frankincense source was close to the Plain of Salalah. Just north of the Dhofar mountains Ptolemy had placed the tribe of the Oubaritae, the men of Ubar. He gave only four other place-names in south Arabia associated with incense, which was at that time the greatest of all trading commodities and one of these was Omanum Emporion (Omani market).

A century or so before Ptolemy, an unknown Greek sea captain left behind his coastal notes. This *Periplus* survived the centuries and clearly enables Moscha to be identified as the present-day ruins of Sumhuram. It also identifies the 'Omani market-place' as a site known to seafarers of the time.

Ptolemy places this trading centre in the central steppes of Dhofar, not on the far sides of the Empty Quarter, where Jabreen and Najran are to be found.

Ptolemy, the author of the *Periplus* and other classical writers were unaware that Dhofar incense had for centuries travelled north and north-east to the coast of the Arabian Gulf. Only our 1992 discoveries in Shis'r have provided evidence of this. Five hundred years after Ptolemy, by which time our site was a long-forgotten outpost, Islamic writers were unable to provide further useful clues. They spoke of the region of Wabar as containing the lost cities that are also mentioned in the Qur'an as Irem, Ad and Thamud, but any direct link between these cities and Wabar or Ubar remains hypothetical and based merely on the Quranic fate of Ad.

The Saudi suggestion that Jabreen is Ubar is sensible from the point of view that the

The late Doctor Armand Hammer, aged ninety, and the author at a Paris function

The author tries to enunciate Russian. Mrs Raisa Gorbachev at rear. Moscow, 1989

Mrs Thatcher and the author at the Petroleum Institute's 1986 dinner

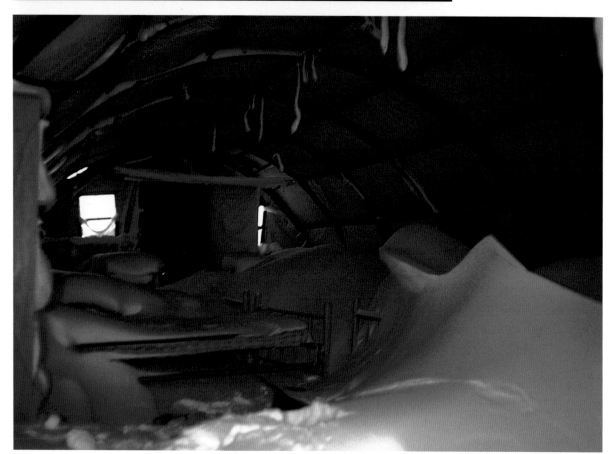

The Ward Hunt hut, long abandoned, as Ginnie found it in 1985

The Ward Hunt hut (food store), 1986

Oliver Shepard in 1986 ice-core sampling off Ward Hunt Island with the author

Flo Howell and Oliver Shepard on the edge of the Arctic Ocean at sun-up, 1986

Oliver Shepard trying to find a manhaul route through the pack-ice off Ward Hunt Island, 1986

Left: Mike Stroud

Right: Signalling the end of the 1990 North Pole unsupported attempt 89 miles from the Pole. This stands as the existing world record at the date of publishing

The author suffering another attack by Doctor Michael Stroud. Ward Hunt Hut, 1989

The author during Doctor Stroud's cold-bath immersion test at the RAF Institute of Aviation Medicine

Soviet helicopter (ex-Afghanistan). Dmitry Shparo, the USSR's top polar traveller, second from left. The start of the record-breaking journey from the Siberian coast

Oliver Shepard and Mike Stroud with the equipment needed to be manhauled for a self-sustaining fifty-day pole journey

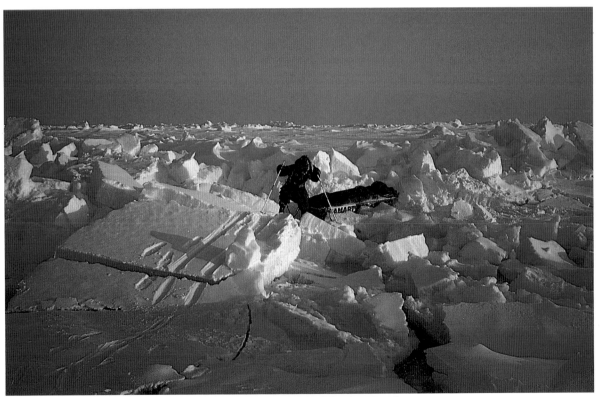

In the pressure pack: Siberian Arctic

Mike Stroud prepares to cross sea-ice a centimetre thick in the Siberian Arctic

Above left: Having no weapons, we were constantly on the alert for polar bears in the Siberian Arctic
Above right: The author's birthday in the Ward Hunt hut. Flo Howell with cake

Top right: The author with Ginnie and two of her Arctic dogs near their home in Exmoor

Bothie of Antarctica

Right: The fabulous city of Ubar as imagined by Dulac in the illustrated *Arabian Nights*; Ubar's legendary demise parallels that of Sodom

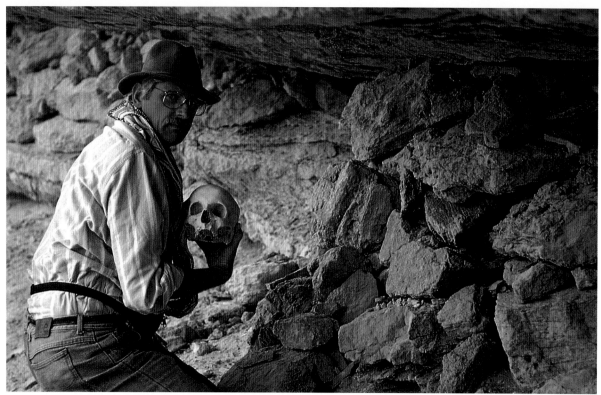
Doctor Juris Zarins with pre-Islamic skull in Dhofar's Valley of Graves, Wadi Anjodaan

In the great sand dunes of Arabia's Empty Quarter, rugged reliable vehicles like our Land Rover
Discoveries were vital

Dhofari mountain men, or *jebalis*, in a round-house, 1991

Looking south from the Dhobar hills on to the Plain of Salalah

A sandstorm threatens Thamrait

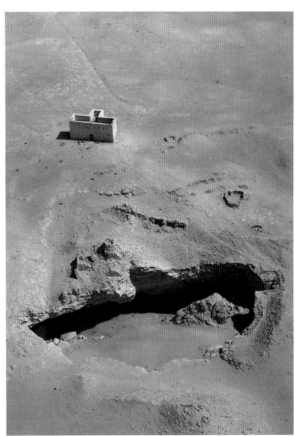

Left: Andy Dunsire and the author descend into the Oracle of Diana

Shis'r in 1959. The site is that of Ubar, Atlantis of the Sands, discovered after a twenty-four-year on-off search by the author

Lake Darbat during the Monsoon

Above: Kay Clapp by frankincense tree near Aiyun

Left: Frankincense gum recently tapped

A Dhopari *jebali* with family camels in front of the main 'living room' tent, 1968

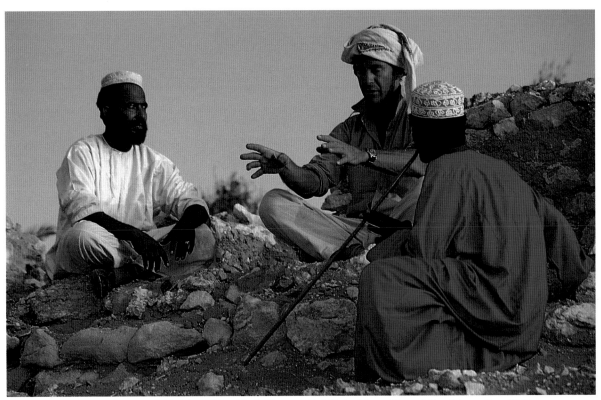

The author with Bakhait bin Abdulla and Said bin Musallim at the Ubar site, 1991

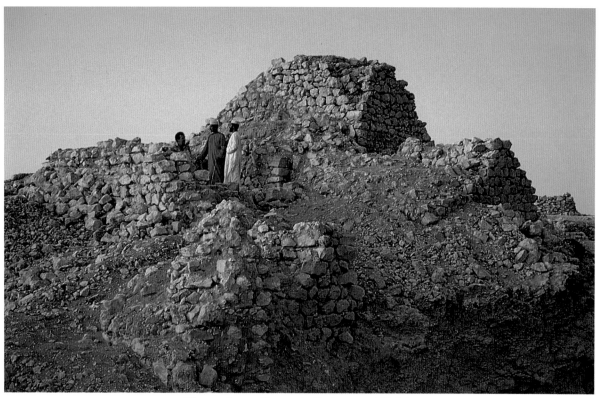

The main north-west site tower at Shis'r

The first chess set found in southern Arabia, made of soapstone and dating from around 1000 AD.
The pieces are a soldier, a king, an elephant, a bishop, a knight and a rook

discoveries there (for which Juris was also largely responsible) included Roman and Greek pottery of the correct period. But Jabreen, Juris was quick to point out, *already* had its name on the Ptolemaic map and that was Labrus. Likewise, Najran was known as Najran to Ptolemy.

Jabreen or Labrus, in Juris's opinion, was in the northern terminus of the incense route from Dhofar to Al Hasa oasis. Since it is 560 miles of desert away from the source of the incense, it would take an incense-laden camel (at the accepted daily rate of 12 miles) some seven weeks to reach it. This alone precludes Jabreen doubling as Ubar/Omanum Emporium, since Ptolemy clearly locates the latter site on the *southern* edge of the Sands, conveniently situated near Hanun, Andhur and other frankincense collection points.

Since our learned Alexandrian Greek, Ptolemy, knew of Omanum Emporium's existence in this area in AD 150, during the height of the incense trade with Rome, any site with claims to be the Emporium *must* possess signs of Roman trade. Our Shis'r has great quantities of such evidence.

Juris summed it up: 'You can go all over the Rub al Khali looking for Roman pottery and, apart from in Jabreen and Shis'r, you won't find it.

'In between these two sites there are spaced water-holes. Some, according to Philby in the 1930s, still had well-cut stone faces. But Shis'r is not just a water-hole. If it was, why all the mass of pottery? And why build a great structure like this out in the middle of nowhere only fifteen miles from the dunes? Trade is the only reason and many of our artefacts can only have come from the north. That,' Juris paused for emphasis, 'is the greatest result we have. Proof that this Ubar/ Jabreen route is the oldest of the incense routes and connected ancient Mesopotamia with Dhofar.'

'Could there not be other Ubar sites yet to be dug up?' I asked him.

'Sure there could be, but where? I have been all over Saudi and the Empty Quarter for twenty years and nobody has come up with another site, let alone one that is both where Ptolemy put it and has Roman pottery. Something as big as Shis'r shows up on air photos. Aramco and PDO oil surveyors have tracked all over the Sands for thirty years, never mind the *bedu* and the Army. Yet nobody has reported an alternative. Perhaps it is buried in sand, but sand doesn't move that fast, as you can see at Shis'r.' Juris thumped his knees. 'Shis'r is unique. There is nowhere like it in the desert for 560 miles.'

Professor Barri Jones from Manchester Univesity visited Shis'r at the request of Oman and drew up a report on behalf of UNESCO. He wrote:

> The purely archaeological discoveries that are emerging from Shis'r are of the greatest import-ance for south Arabian archaeology in their own right . . . The archaeological integrity of the site should not be allowed to be affected by possible disputes regarding its name.

The worldwide attention aroused by the expedition brought tourists and television teams aplenty to Shis'r. Sultan Qaboos knows that oil revenues will diminish and a lucrative alternative source of income could be tourism once the Omani government decides the country's infra-structure is ready to accept an invasion of package tours. At present only groups likely to behave in an 'inoffensive manner' are welcomed as tourists and these are the sort of people who are best enticed by cultural attractions. Well-organised tours of the 'frankincense trail' to Al Balid, Andhur, Hanun, Shis'r/Ubar and Sumhuram are already providing such groups with a rewarding and memorable visit. I like to think that the eventual success of my long search for Ubar has in a small way repaid the people of Oman, the country that has given me the best times of my life.

17

Mind Over Matter

Whatever you can do, or dream you can . . . begin it.

GOETHE

While I had been in Oman plans for the Antarctic expedition had been progressing smoothly, but I now learned that we might have a rival – Erling Kagge, an exceptionally fine cross-country skier. Speed and endurance would now be an even higher priority for our team and I was concerned about our collective stamina.

In mid May 1991 I went to the London Wine Trade Fair at Olympia where Oliver had organised a sales stand for his employers. By chance, Charlie Burton was in charge of security, so I was able to explain my worries to them both, and suggested that I ask Mike Stroud to join our team.

'He is like a bull terrier,' I told them, 'small in stature but incredibly powerful.'

'That's great,' Charlie remonstrated, 'but where does that leave us oldies? Surely a team moves at the pace of its slowest member?'

It was agreed that some thought would be given to the idea and, not long afterwards, Ollie called me to say they had both decided to change their role in the project. 'We would want to *enjoy* the experience,' Charlie told me later, 'and I know that, once *you* get competitive, any signs of enjoyment are tantamount to mutiny and a clear sign that we should be travelling faster.'

So they took on the role of organisers from London and I approached Mike Stroud by telephone.

Usually, the only position that I can tolerate on an expedition is that of team leader. Ollie, Charlie and Mike were totally aware of my peculiarity in this respect, but all three were strong personalities and not 'yes-men'. My policy with everyone on any journey is to follow the democratic route (*when* there is time), of talking about options rather than pronouncing dictatorial and unilateral decisions. If others, whether or not they form a majority, favour an opinion which I believe to be stupid, dangerous or unlikely to help attain the goal of the expedition, then I overrule them no matter how disaffected this may make them feel. In fact, because most fellow-polar travellers know how to progress over snow and ice, we normally all agree on the best way forward, so contretemps are quite rare.

I knew very little in depth about Mike. This may seem strange since he had, by 1990, already come on four of my Arctic expeditions and we had been through a great deal together. To take *friends* on stressful expeditions has always seemed to me to be foolish, since I can think of no easier way of marring a friendship for ever. An expedition's aim is best achieved by individuals who can look after themselves, need little or no directing or nursing and are tough in body and mind. I look for professional or dogged people and treat any friendship resulting from an expedition as an unexpected bonus.

Polar expeditions are well known for causing stress and enmity between participants and quite why Ollie, Mike and I had never come to blows, literally or even verbally, during our Arctic journeys remains a mystery to me.

'I know you like to lead from the front,' Mike said to me before he finally agreed to join on the understanding that he would conduct an extensive physiological research programme throughout the journey. This was bad news since I hate the sight of blood, especially my own, but it seemed a reasonable penalty in order to secure Mike's participation.

Chris Brasher of Reebok called with the unwelcome news that the American and European headquarters of his company were not prepared to share the sponsorship. He gave me the name of the man whose company, the Pentland Group, had sold Reebok to the Americans. The Chairman of the Pentland Group consented to see me for a breakfast meeting and a month or two later he agreed that Pentland become the overall sponsor. 'I do not think we will gain a great deal of publicity from the association' – he did not mince words – 'but my belief is that *all* companies should give at least one per cent of their annual profits to the local community. We have a number of multiple sclerosis sufferers in Finchley and your expedition will benefit them greatly, even if you only get halfway.'

This was true. Our Patron, the Prince of Wales, had asked that we should use the expedition to raise funds for a Multiple Sclerosis Research Centre in Cambridge, to which, of course, we agreed. Our sponsoring of multiple sclerosis was partly based on members of the public plegding a penny for every mile we covered. Since Antarctica is over fifty times the size of Great Britain, a lot of pennies were involved.

Because the Antarctic plateau is so high, and so cold, the period when humans can travel over it is severely limited. Since it is both hazardous and uneconomical to keep ships and aeroplanes all year round on a continent where they can only be safely used from November until March, the few countries that do operate either form of transport are careful to remove them to warmer climes outside the short southern summer.

Since Pentland's sponsorship covered only the cost of Adventure Network (the *only* air transport company flying commercially to Antarctica), delivering us to the Atlantic coast and dropping us there, I had to make other plans for escaping from the Pacific coast before the onset of winter.

Three cruise ships take tourists to McMurdo base in mid-summer each year and one of these was due to depart from Antarctica at 6.30 a.m., and not a minute later, on 16 February 1993. If we could reach the coast by then the ship's operators, Seaquest, kindly agreed to remove us at no cost and take us to Australia (providing we took passports).

The prospect of walking 1700 miles between 1 November 1992, the very earliest date Adventure Network could drop us off, and the Seaquest date of 16 February concentrated our minds on pulling at least sixteen miles a day for 108 days with loads likely to exceed 350lbs each. I knew this was a performance well in excess of any manhauling achievement in history. There was every likelihood that it was not technically feasible.

As the weeks to departure passed by, my worries about the sledge-loads increased. Certain weight totals were not available until the last month and these included the rations being specially put together by Brian Welsby, who had provided us with Arctic rations for some fifteen years.

By early October it was becoming apparent that the weight of the rations would entail sledge-loads of over 400lbs each. We were entering the realms of the theoretically impossible but it was too late to back out.

More worrying to me than the sheer weight of our sledges was the results of my personal training. In the past I had kept fit by jogging on the moors after work and, on every seventh day, spending an hour on a Nordic Track ski machine in order to put some strength into my naturally weak arms. Mike supplemented his jogging with a good deal of bicycling and we both consumed a great deal of rice and pasta in order to put on weight and increase our glycogen storage levels.

Since the Siberian journey two years before I found myself less and less motivated to train and increasingly prone to muscle damage. I *was* still training as hard as ever, but the going was tougher. Sprains took longer to disappear and past problems kept resurfacing. Two months before we were due in Antarctica my back went into spasm and jogging was out of the question.

Dr Bernard Watkin of Wimpole Street is an expert at easing back pains by deep injections of dextrose/glycerine/phenol solution into the ligaments of the lower back either side of the spine. After two sessions I felt rejuvenated, but then an attack of haemorrhoids sent me scuttling to Dr Notares, who injects the relevant parts with some form of long-lasting anaesthetic. I had first suffered from this affliction not in polar regions but on SAS training in Brunei. Then one of my ankles became swollen and awkward to run on.

Two years earlier Mike had announced that my physical fitness, measured aerobically, was far above that of most twenty-year-olds and highly unusual in a forty-seven-year-old. This time, however, my ratings had dropped considerably. Since I was training just as hard as before, I could not explain my physical deterioration but realised it did not bode well for the coming venture.

Ten days before leaving England we met in the underground London garage where I stored all my old expedition gear, some of it twenty years old. I divided all the new items sent by sponsors and gave half to Mike. This was our first chance to load the sledges with everything we would be taking. Miraculously, and by dint of a good deal of force, the loads fitted into or on to the sledges. We tried to pick up a loaded sledge between us but it was impossible. We packed everything into custom-made boxes and a KLM van took the entire cargo to Heathrow Airport.

The testing and packing of all items had taken us just one day. On previous journeys this task had taken weeks, sometimes months, to complete but Mike and I both led busy lives and seldom met up outside the confines of polar journeys.

On a gusty morning in late October Ginnie drove me to Heathrow. We said goodbye in the carpark for there would be many people in the terminal. I waved as she drove off and thanked God for her. I had told myself after many previous journeys that I would never again leave her at our bleak Exmoor home for the long and lonely winter. As she left I felt wretchedly guilty. It occurred to me that *I* had never spent a single night alone at our house on the moor.

As Mike and Morag Howell chatted *en route* to South America, I idly considered their motives. There is usually a great difference between the explanation that a person chooses to give and the truth.

Mike had spent two years of his life, seven years earlier, hoping to walk to the South Pole with Swan and Meare but, to his dismay, another man was selected, leaving him merely first reserve. Now, whether or not we managed to cross the whole continent, he knew that he stood a chance of at least making it to the Pole.

When asked for *my* motives I openly admitted that expedition leadership was my chosen way of making a living: my passport for twenty-five years has stated 'Travel Writer'. Mike found this upsetting and 'commercial'. His own rationale, on the most basic level, was more romantic. He talked of stunning landscapes and equated his adventures with a more intense version of the pleasures he found as a boy from mountaineering, hill-walking and rock-climbing.

'It sounds ridiculous on this scale,' Mike would say, 'but that simple drive is a very important reason for me. However, on top of that, the places themselves are amazing; they may be empty but they are incredibly beautiful and you feel a sort of privilege, on being on what amounts to another planet. This gives you a different and interesting perspective on your life . . .'

I am not introspective and find it awkward having to dig within myself to produce pat replies. Jean-Louis Étienne was asked why he went on polar expeditions and replied: 'Because I like it. You never ask a basketball player why he plays: it is because he enjoys it. It is like asking someone why he likes chocolate.'

The KLM Boeing stopped at Sao Paulo, Montevideo, Santiago, Puerto Montt and finally Punta Arenas in southern Chile. We were met by Annie Kershaw of Adventure Network. She was the widow of our Transglobe Expedition pilot, Giles Kershaw. Her truck took us through country-side bleak and littered with low buildings of singular ugliness though enlivened by coats of bright paint. Wild sea channels and coastlines were never far away; Cape Horn but a short flight to the south. Beyond the Cape and 1000 miles of the roughest seas on earth lies Antarctica, the reason for Adventure Network's presence in Punta.

In 1985 two Canadian mountaineers had joined with Giles to form Adventure Network (ANI) to provide a means for other climbers and adventurers to reach Antarctica by air, previously out of the question except for millionaires or government funded civil servants. Giles, sadly, was killed in an accident whilst flying a gyrocopter. Annie determined that his work with the company should not have been in vain. Her first DC6 passenger flight of the year was scheduled to depart for Antarctica two days after our arrival in Punta. My original timings, based on the need to catch the Seaquest ship out of Antarctica, *depended* on starting out on 2 November. The anticipated two-day stop-over in Punta would allow us to rest after the long flight from London and to complete last-minute checks on the sledge-loads.

The worst was soon confirmed. The weight of our sledge-loads was at least 400lbs each. I dreaded the possibility that even this ridiculous total would creep upwards. To mention 400lbs per load to anyone with the slightest knowledge of manhauling was to invite ridicule . . . so we didn't.

I went over our mathematics again and again to see how we could cross the entire continent with less weight. Every avenue I explored turned out to be a dead end.

By the time we completed our final weight checks on Annie's scales the loads had reached *450lbs* each. Fuel increments and modifications to gear were liable to add 30lbs more. In Army phraseology we were confronting a Mission Impossible. Our inner thoughts, shared only between the three of us, led Morag to write home from Chile: 'Expect me back in a fortnight.'

Due to engine problems with Annie's DC6 our take-off was delayed until 8 November. Even if there were no further problems, our chances of success had been seriously dented by the eight-day delay.

We flew south over the South Atlantic for nine hours. Nobody looked unduly joyful. Too many stories about evil Antarctic ice-landings had made the rounds. The DC6 broke through cloud cover. We banked abruptly and descended towards the ice. We glimpsed a flash of tiny figures, tents and two Twin Otters. Twice our Canadian pilot rehearsed the landing with dry runs to test the sixty-knot cross-winds. Then, with a shattering impact that could not have done any part of the DC6 much good, we struck the ice and bounced, rattling over the rippled blue surface.

I do not remember any other landing even half as impressive in thirty years of arriving at remote spots in small aircraft.

Three hours later Mo, Mike and I were flown on having trans-shipped our equipment to a small ski-plane. The engine noise prevented conversation and various fuel smells made me feel queasy. I tried to check my maps and memorise the route I had selected from the drop-off point, 78° 14' South on the edge of the floating Filchner Ice-Shelf to the actual continental coast some 200 miles to the south.

Charles Swithinbank, the British glaciologist unequalled in his knowledge of Antarctica, had warned me that *any* route could run into heavy crevasses and rough ice, but his advised route would be at least as good as any alternative. He ended his advice note: 'Either way you will have to climb to 3280 feet even to get level with the Argentinas. What a sweat it will be with gigantic loads. It makes my bones ache.'

Long before we could even gain the foothills of the great climb to the Pole, before even coming to the continental start-point of the coastline, there would be many navigational problems to face on the ice-shelf itself.

On the map in the darkened fuselage I could make out two variations to Swithinbank's suggested route. We could try forcing a route up the Support Force Glacier in a straight line from the drop-off point to the Argentinean western edge, thereby risking huge crevasse fields, or we could gain many southerly miles at no risk from crevasses by simply crossing a 3280 feet high, 170 mile long feature, Berkner Island. Kagge, I knew, favoured the latter course. For safety reasons I agreed with him, but our loads were too heavy to attempt Berkner. By ascending the glacier itself, however hazardous, we would avoid up to 3280 feet of extra climbing.

Major flow lines of glaciers and heavily crevassed zones were marked on the chart but I knew there would be many other crevasses, unmarked and therefore unavoidable, whichever route I selected.

Berkner Island divides the Filchner from the far larger Ronne Ice-Shelf to the west. The two shelves cover an area as big as France and vary in thickness from 660 feet at the seaward edge, where we were about to land, to 2000 feet at the point where it flows over the coastline 200 miles to our south.

Our Twin Otter briefly roared over the ice-front of the Weddell Sea, a vertical cliff forming the seaward face of the Filchner Ice-Shelf. After several cautious rehearsals, Warren found a relatively smooth stretch of snow at the point where Berkner Island meets both the ice-shelf and the sea. We were down at 78° 19.8' South, 43° 47' West.

Morag helped us unload and wished us well. For the next few months she would attempt to keep radio contact with us and with our UK base, which was manned by her husband Flo at their home in Aberdeen. When Flo returned from work each evening he would switch on his sets and tune in the antennae which he had erected in a seven-acre field outside the kitchen window. This, at least, was our plan.

We watched the little aircraft depart until the engine noise was a distant drone and the great silence of Antarctica closed about us.

Months of unspoken apprehension were coming to a head. The key question was whether or not *full* loads, including the 100 days' fuel taken on at Patriot Hills, could be moved by the two of us.

The main bulk was the rations. These were equally important both to our chances of success and to Mike's physiological research. Each bag was packed to provide two men with twenty-four

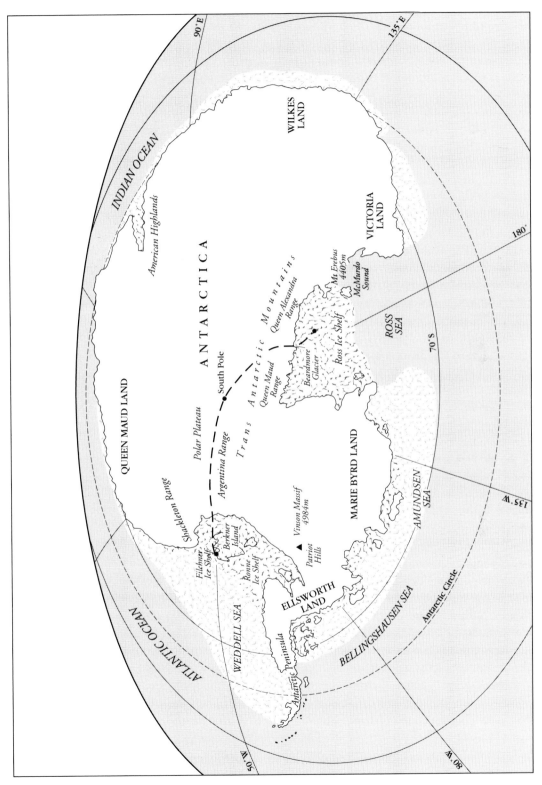

The Continent of Antarctica

hours of food at a daily intake of 5200 calories. They had evolved over a period of 16 years of polar journeys beginning with my first North Pole attempt in 1976.

I find figures both confusing and boring and hope not to clutter this book with them, but calories were critical to our survival: lack of them was to all but kill us over the months ahead. The average daily intake of both Scott's and Amundsen's teams was 4500 calories per man. This proved enough for the Norwegians who skied unencumbered and with husky power. To counter the grotesquely hard labour of the British manhaulers, the amount was insufficient and they slowly starved to death. The first man to weaken and die was the biggest and heaviest on Scott's team; the man they 'least expected to fail'.

I considered our team's vital statistics. I was eleven years older than Mike and approaching my fiftieth birthday. I was taller by five inches and heavier by three stone (42lbs). But, in terms of sheer strength, especially the vital lower limb power base, Mike was clinically tested as considerably stronger.

At home, Ginnie gives me twice her own food portions although she works harder – she on the farm and me at my desk. She also feeds her large water-dogs four times what she feeds her Jack Russell terrier although he is by far the most active of our dogs. Over the months ahead I would be consuming *exactly* the same calorific intake as Mike. I feared that, like the heavily built Evans on Scott's team, my performance would deteriorate first and more markedly than Mike's. I determined from the outset, therefore, to avoid my normal course of forging ahead at maximum output.

As each piece of equipment was loaded we ticked it off in our notebooks, alongside its weight, down to the nearest ounce. The total was 485lbs each: a figure well beyond our worst nightmares. Only by studying previous Antarctic journeys could we estimate our own chances with these dismal loads. In 1903 Scott, Shackleton and Wilson hauled loads of 175lbs each. Eight years later, on the 'worst journey in the world' Wilson, Bowers and Cherry-Garrard started out with 'enormous weights for such travelling, 253lbs a man'. Especially unnerving was the evidence of our only manhauling predecessors, Messner and Fuchs, in 1990. Reinholt Messner, revered internationally as the greatest mountaineer in history, is a man of exceptional physical stamina and an iron will. His colleague, Arved Fuchs, is Germany's top polar explorer. I had serious doubts that Mike and I could outperform such a team. Of his journey Messner wrote:

With sledge-loads of 264lbs, the longest stretch would be murderously strenuous. Perhaps even impossible . . . 264lbs is a load for a horse not a human being.

I could not ignore such warnings. Mike and I faced a journey of 1700 miles, much of it above 10,000 feet altitude with start loads of *485lbs* each. Not far short of 1000lbs between us. If we failed to manage these loads the fault would be entirely mine. I should have anticipated the unarguable force of the mathematics. As leader I could blame nobody else.

There was no excuse for delay; nothing to be gained by considering any further the unpalatable facts. Goethe wrote: 'Whatever you can do or dream you can . . . begin it. Boldness has genius, power and magic in it.' A spot of magic would be more than welcome.

We adjusted the manhaul harnesses about our stomachs and shoulders. I lent against the traces with my full 210lbs bodyweight. The near half-ton sledge paid *no* attention.

I looked back and spotted an eight-inch ice rut across the front of the runners. I tugged again with my left shoulder only, and the sledge, avoiding the rut, *moved forward*. I will never forget that instant. Never. I *could* pull the sledge. The fear that the full load would prove immovable had been growing into an ogre. That was now dispelled.

After a hundred yards I stopped. Mike was labouring hard but he too could move his load. The expedition was under way nine days behind its own very tight schedule. The thought of pulling my sledge for an entire mile, never mind to the South Pole and beyond, was appalling.

The map, or strictly speaking chart (since the sea was beneath us), showed a rash of blue lines, the crevasse symbol, running south along the foot of Berkner Island for some eighty miles.

Should we fix a safety line between us before reaching the first crevasse? I knew this was our agreed drill but the sheer weight of the sledge had already biased me against *any* action beyond the sheer task of progress. Even though we were descending a gentle incline, the sledge was totally inert. The very instant I stopped pulling, it stopped moving. There was not the least glissade. I conjured up a parallel. If I were to lash together three average-sized adults, each weighing 160lbs, dump them in a fibreglass bathtub with no legs and then drag them through sand dunes for 1700 miles, the difficulties involved would be similar.

My sledge-load soon grew to represent something animate and hostile. I knew the pattern well. First my inner anger would be directed at the weather, the equipment and the ice. Later at my companion. The same would hold good for Mike. I determined *never* to allow myself to think unnecessarily far ahead. Sufficient unto each day is the mileage thereof . . . providing daily progress tallies with the schedule.

After two hours I felt certain we had reached the ice-shelf. About a mile to our immediate north was the ice-front, a chaotic jumble of giant fragments where shelf met true sea ice. In every other direction there was nothing but mirage shimmer and the great white glare of Antarctica.

After five and a half hours it was time to halt for we had been awake for twenty-four hours since leaving Punta Arenas. For navigation purposes, we must keep to a carefully timed daily schedule. I intended to use my watch and body shadow to establish direction all the way to the Pole and that meant keeping the sun due north at local midday. There were, I reasoned, only another 1696 miles to cover and since we had rations for a hundred days, there was yet time to find a way of increasing the daily average to sixteen miles. There must be absolutely *no* rest days or we would fail.

The hard surfaces of the immediate sea front soon gave way to softer snow and I began to find the going harder. Shooting pains in my shoulder blades were the result of manhauling with our standard bandolier harnesses. To counter this, I loosened off the shoulder traces and tightened up my waistband. Within minutes both my hips and the skin at my waist began to complain. By the end of the day my midriff was raw on both sides where the waistband was pulled inwards at each forward strain.

Each and every step of progress was possible only due to a forceful tug on the 485lb load. The pressure points involved, apart from our shoulders and waists, were chiefly our feet, boots and skis.

Our course had settled down and ran about a mile out to the east of, and parallel with, Berkner Island. Remembering my promise to Mike, I alternated the navigation with him at hourly intervals. I found this increasingly annoying since I had spent well over twenty years leading expeditions from the front and mistrusted anyone else's navigating abilities.

I had to force my irritation down each time my hour ended and I halted to let Mike take over. This inner struggle was a great help in the ongoing problem of trying to face the slow passage of time. Time was our enemy. Every minute was long and tedious. At all costs, we had to avoid pondering the ever-increasing bodily pains, which would lead to self-pity, and at this early stage God alone knew what that would result in. But, instead of antipathy for Mike (since he happened to be the only other human available at whom to aim my feelings), I was able to indulge in apprehension and fill my mind with thoughts about crevasses, how best to avoid them, what to do if and when either or both of us fell into them, what it would feel like to plunge unroped into the maw of a 200 foot deep ice-hole, how to retrieve Mike from even a small fifty-foot fissure? All these and many other allied thoughts helped the long hours and the slow miles to pass by without our dwelling on the sheer size of the task and the knowledge that an increasing amount of discomfort was likely to accrue as our bodies slowly broke down.

I remembered a journalist, as we left England, telling me: 'Of course it isn't the same nowadays as it was eighty years ago. Now you have all the trappings of the technical age. The sense of adventure and the dangers are gone.' I tried to think what technical items I carried on my sledge which might stop me descending into a crevasse or help me out once I was down one.

We were on a flat stretch, with not the least sign of an undulation, when I found myself suddenly shooting downwards and flung both arms out, ski sticks flailing. My descent stopped short at my armpits. I felt my legs involuntarily treading air, swimming on the void. Gingerly I tried to turn my neck to look backwards at the sledge. My greatest fear at that moment was that it too would break through the thin trapdoor and I would cartwheel downwards to snap my spine or crack open my skull on some sharp icy ledge down below.

Crevasses are today, just as in the time of Scott and Mawson, the chief threat to Antarctic travellers, and the danger has not lessened one iota over the intervening years. This does not stop ignorant media reporters (who have never travelled through crevasse fields), nor old buffs (who have, but regard their own heyday in the 1930s, 1940s or 1950s as being the end of the heroic era of no gadgetry), from denouncing polar travellers of today as cossetted joyriders who have but to press a red knob to receive instant rescue from all predicaments.

Up to my armpits in deep soft snow, with my lower torso dangling over nothingness, I only wished that the 'red knob' fallacy had some basis in reality. Too much movement on trying to extricate my body could in an instant collapse the whole snow bridge. My attempt to look back at my sledge failed, for the hood of my parka and my cotton balaclava prevented sufficient lateral movement of my neck. Furthermore I had breathed into the balaclava as I fell, which had the immediate effect of misting up my goggles. The mist had quickly frozen across the inside of the lens. To all intents and purposes I was blind since I had no hand free to tear off the goggles.

The alloy trace leading back from my harness to the sledge had snapped in half close behind me – which, in a perverse way, helped me by allowing sufficient movement to wriggle up, inch by inch, until my hips were out of the hole. The rest was easy.

Sweating with relief, I crawled to one side of the crater and hauled the sledge well away from its vicinity before I again dared to stand up, make a botch-up repair to the trace and carry on.

Many of the crevasses were over a hundred feet wide with sagging bridges. The weakest point was not, as might be expected, in the centre but along the fault-line, where the bridge was joined to the crevasse wall's lip. In the most dangerous cases the whole bridge had already descended a few feet down into the maw before catching on some unseen temporary 'stopper'. New snow had then partially filled the resulting gap.

Hauling the sledges *down* on to such teetering bridges presented no great physical task since gravity was on our side. If the bridge held, under our initial weight, we pulled onwards over the centre span. At this point the going became singularly off-putting because, in order to manhaul our monster loads *up* the far side of the disintegrating bridge, maximum downwards pressure with skis and sticks must be applied at its weakest point. There were moments of sickening apprehension as our straining ski sticks plunged through the crust, or part of a sledge lurched backwards, its prow or stern having broken through.

I never grew inured to the crevasse hazard and continued to sweat and silently curse as each new death trap loomed ahead or to my immediate flank.

Suddenly, I looked up. Mike must have shouted. Then, there followed an immediate sound of rushing air and snow thunder from the bridge beneath him, as it collapsed. I was about 500 yards away and could now see nothing but his head, a dark blob against the snow, apparently quite bodiless, and then the alloy manhaul poles and the sledge itself.

A crevasse of only six feet in width but with sheer, clean sides had opened up beneath both Mike and his sledge. Mike's hips were athwart the far lip and his arms reaching out for a grip. But his alloy traces prevented him from moving in any direction because the sledge was poised for half its length over the chasm. If Mike moved at all, he was liable to precipitate disaster.

I tore myself clear of my harness and grabbed the back of Mike's sledge. My first priority was to stop the sledge moving even fractionally forwards. Once it began to slide into the hole I would not be able to stop it and Mike would certainly be jerked off his precarious perch by its downward-plunging bulk.

Although my instinct was to pull the sledge towards me and away from the crevasse, common sense luckily prevailed as I remembered a similar situation in the Arctic with Mike poised over a narrow water canal.

'I'll try to push, Mike,' I shouted, 'and you try to crawl as far forwards as your traces allow. Hopefully you will be on firm ground before the sledge drops.'

Once Mike was clear, after an inch-by-inch process that must have been most incredibly frightening for him, he unclipped his harness. Now, if the sledge did go down, it would not drag him too. We each took up a firm position on either side of the crevasse and together applied sudden force to his sledge. I pushed and he pulled. The resulting forward momentum narrowly defeated gravity as, his face red with the strain, Mike flung himself backwards and dragged the 485lb deadweight over the far lip of the fissure.

For three days foul weather closed in on the ice-shelf. Exposed skin was frost-nipped. Crotch-rot developed on the inside of our thighs and I suffered a resurgence of haemorrhoids despite the deep injections in London. My back and shoulders continued to complain through the long hours.

Harnesses, skis and skins needed frequent repairs but the repair materials were not limitless. Like everything else they had been cut down to the bare minimum.

On Friday 13 November, I began to aim west of south but a rash of great holes kept us out on the shelf.

Mike: 'The crevasses seem to be everywhere' . . . 'Today I fell through. It was a vertical-sided chasm. My ski was pressed against one side. My arm and shoulder on the other. I could see no bottom at all, just blue-grey going to black.'

From time to time we were sufficiently scared by near escapes into fixing safety ropes to our waists but this was a last resort since the rear person is forever treading on the rope, which jerks the navigator off-balance and provides yet another general embuggeration factor at a time when toleration levels are low.

My crotch-rot reached the stage where both scrotum and inner thighs were raw and uncomfortable despite the daily application of Canesten powder. My cotton boxer shorts (which I wore under a pair of thin wick-away long johns and some Army baggy cotton trousers) were continually rucking up and exacerbating the raw patches.

I buried the pants, my only pair, and the crotch-rot did in due course begin to get better. But the remaining two protective layers of underclothing were not enough even at sea level and, with the sharp winds off Berkner, my private parts were nipped and swelled up. When I mentioned this to Mike, it turned out that he was having the same problem only worse, with a blistered end. He was circumcised and therefore, in effect, had one less layer of insulation. I made a note of this factor in terms of selecting future candidates for polar expeditions.

Fifteen miles above us, as was first discovered by the British Antarctic Survey nine years before, a hole in the ozone layer opened up at this time of the year (at its worst in November) and allowed dangerous levels of ultraviolet rays to descend unfiltered to Antarctica and southerly lands like Australasia and Patagonia. Since we were travelling directly under the ozone hole's epicentre at the worst time of the year, it made sense to cover our skin. But we needed to breathe without fogging our goggles, so the sun shone day after day on our lips and noses. Perhaps Mike protected himself the better with sun-cream or merely manhauled in a more hunched position, shading his face. Whatever the reason my lips deteriorated rapidly from burns and my nose swelled into a bulbous blister. When we scooped our evening meal from the communal cook-pot, my spoon would invariably contain dribbles of the blood which welled out of the deep cracks in my blistered lips.

The scabs always grew together overnight and, when I woke, the act of tearing my lips apart (in order to speak and drink) invariably opened up all the raw places. Breakfast consisted of porridge oats in a gravy of blood. Mike gave me three different lip balms but none of them seemed to help the deep ultraviolet burns.

Our minds churned over against the inescapable fact that our loads were too heavy and we were progressing too slowly. Despite no rest days, no halts for bad weather and a mere ten minutes' rest daily for Thermos stops, our eight or nine hours per day were still averaging under ten miles. We *had to* cut the loads.

'Mike, I'm chucking my duvet. I have hardly worn it all week. We work so hard we will keep warm even when winter comes.'

He nodded. We both knew it was a big decision. The weather was now warm – in polar, not European, terms – and we were still close to sea-level with some effect from the comparative warmth of the Southern Ocean. Maybe we would have second thoughts later on. But there would be no later if we could not get a move on *now*. Next morning we buried the two down-filled jackets along with the empty ration packs. From now on our only clothing would be the light, mainly cotton garments that were just enough to protect us in the current coastal conditions. In retrospect I sorely regret the decision but it is easy to be wise with hindsight.

At the end of the first week we entered a zone of great instability. A thunderous roar sounded through my facemask. I glanced right and saw that Mike was not in trouble. I must have imagined the noise. But a minute later my heart missed a beat as the rumble of some great unseen disturbance took several seconds to die away.

I listened intently. Within the space of two minutes I found myself flinching to the thunder of three further explosions. I felt the deep vibrations as though the source of each sound was right beneath my feet. I wanted to warn Mike but he would never hear me and anyway there was, as far as I could see, no specific danger to avoid. I suspected avalanches somewhere in the vicinity, because of the noise, yet I could see no features liable to avalanche. It was much like hearing sonic booms with no evidence of aircraft. Mike must have heard or sensed something for I saw that he had now also halted and packed away his sail. I moved across and was close behind him when a cloud of snow dust rose immediately to his front and, simultaneously, the thunderclap of another 'avalanche' reverberated through the ice-shelf. The real source of the phenomenon was now frighteningly clear. This whole region of the ice-shelf had entered a hyperactive phase causing hitherto 'safe' snow bridges to collapse into the great crevasses that laced the entire feature. It was by terrible bad luck that we were in such a place at such a time.

No amount of experience or ice-lore could keep us out of trouble. The gaping hole some ten paces ahead of Mike was 45 feet wide by 120 feet in length and lay directly across his intended path. In another minute he and his sledge would have disappeared along with several tons of plunging snow bridge.

All around us renewed mumbles announced further cratering. The sensation was memorably frightening. We must escape at once to a safer area. But where *was* safer? Only the looming bulk of Berkner Island offered certain stability. We roped up with nervous fingers, fearing that at any moment the snow beneath us would open up and drop us hundreds of feet.

The surface rumbled and reverberated again and again. Puffs of snow dust rose into the air. The feeling was similar to closing on enemy troops when under mortar fire. As each new crump exploded at random, the fear increased that the next would have your name on it.

The nylon rope between us was sixty feet in length. We moved as fast as the sledges and the wings of fear allowed. Time stood still.

I came to an abrupt halt as a wave of cold air rushed past, accompanied by the loudest and closest of the explosions. I ducked, for the all-engulfing sound seemed to pass both overhead *and* underfoot.

Immediately *between* Mike and me an immense crater appeared. One moment the ice-shelf ahead was solid and white. The next a maw like the mouth of the Underworld, steaming gently with snow vapour, lay across our ski track and wide enough to swallow a double-decker bus. The roaring echoes of imploding snow cascading into the bowels of the ice-shelf returned in successive waves, like shore-ripples from an undersea volcano.

Although a cold wind scoured the ice-sheet, I sweated with fear. The next hour was a nightmare of apprehension; *nowhere* was safe. Only pure luck enabled us to escape from this volatile zone.

Later that night we came at last to the ice-foot of Berkner Island and camped, with a luxurious feeling of safety, on the narrow causeway which, wrongly or rightly, we felt to be clear of crevassing.

On the ninth day the ice-shelf beside the island showed signs of climbing towards the interior. There were no spot heights on my local chart and my small-scale map of Antarctica showed only that we were about to enter the largest crevasse field on the Filchner Ice-Shelf, a disturbed area of some fifty square miles which appeared to collide, on its western boundary, with the very edge of Berkner Island.

Mike agreed that we *seemed* to be climbing but maintained that the undulating series of rising steppes, which I could see through the wafting mists, was in reality only an illusion caused by the heavy loads and mirage effects.

Fortunately the deep drifts of the ice-shelf did not extend to the island's wind-scoured flanks so the going was easier than at any time since the firm coastal strip. Temperatures of around

−15°C were not low enough to coarsen the surface and Mike, when navigating, set a pace that seemed to me as the day went by increasingly and unnecessarily fast.

I resolved to make no comment and at first found no difficulty in keeping hard on his heels. My shoulder blades and lower back screamed at me but the old competitive urge came back. Why let this guy steam ahead? For almost twenty years now I have pulled sledges, in all conditions, faster than any colleague of any age, and for the past six years I have out-pulled Mike, day after day, in even the worst of Arctic conditions.

I talked persuasively to myself in this vein but all the time Mike's small but powerful legs pulled on piston-like and I began to realise it was self-defeating for me to keep up such a pace. Quite why I should be experiencing this problem for the first time was unclear. Perhaps I was having an off-day. Mike was as strong a man as any I had travelled with. In particular his lower limbs were unusually powerful. In leg-strength tests monitored by Research Establishment scientists, two months before, Mike had proved far superior in general aerobic fitness and in leg power. Only two years previously, just prior to our Siberian journey, the reverse had been true. Despite training more consistently and for longer hours during the interim years I had for some reason achieved far lower results in 1992. Two years before, the scientists had described my physiological measurements as those of 'a top-flight athlete'. At thirty-nine Mike was in his prime. In Siberia, when he was thirty-six and I was forty-seven, I had no difficulty keeping well ahead as in previous years. So, at that stage, his eleven-year advantage made no difference. Something must have happened since. I began to suspect the inescapable effects of the ageing process. Just as my eyes first turned short-sighted at forty-seven, I believe that, at the same age, my body began to deteriorate markedly. I could no longer happily run a daily marathon (which is what we were now doing in terms of energy expenditure), week after week, without rest and with ever-dwindling calorific replacement.

Morbid pondering of these hard facts during the endless hours of struggle over the ice-shelf led me to accept two principles. Firstly, I had made a serious mistake in attempting a journey of such physical hardship at my age. Secondly, since there was no point in 'crying over spilled milk' I must make every effort from now on to conserve my energy by adapting a 'polar plod', which would use up minimal energy and preserve what body strength I had for the many hundreds of hours and miles which lay ahead. At first I resolved to say nothing of this to Mike in the hope that he would realise his own need for long-term conservation. And the less said between individuals under extreme stress the better. Especially when the matter is likely to prove contentious.

By the evening Mike's energetic pace was naturally taking its toll. He wrote: 'Each day is a battle not to make some excuse to stop early.' My own diary notes were not effusive: 'Bad visibility all day but a faint outline of crevasse shadows halfway up the island's flanks gives us enough direction. Agony from shoulder blades and hips. Bottom lip now like raw blubber. Crotch bad and lower back twinges. M. cooked excellent spaghetti. His willy is frostbitten and blistered.'

Mike told me whilst lancing my foot: 'To be attempting this journey while you're approaching fifty is quite extraordinary.' This served to make me think my body might be on the verge of breaking up, of suddenly yielding to reality. I remembered the words of Dr Phillip Law, head of Australia's Antarctic Services, when selecting men for Antarctica: 'Our standards of fitness are very high. It is unusual for a man past forty years to possess the necessary physical drive and energy we require.'

Like Shackleton I seemed to be growing utterly preoccupied by the ageing process. I attempted to shake off the obsession but this was no place to break free of the nightmares loose in your skull. All I could see was the greatest void on Earth. Be it grey with fog, or blinding from the glare, it yielded nothing at all upon which to fix my gaze and concentrate, nothing to take my mind off the festering broth of my thoughts. The slightest niggle soon achieved obsession rating and bodily sores screamed their presence through every long and toilsome day. I swore silently when Mike changed gear and I was forced by pride to abandon the rhythm of my polar plod. Self-pity is not an attractive trait and I do not remember indulging in it on previous occasions. At this stage I said nothing to Mike, but there were many hundreds of miles ahead of us and the worst of it by far was yet to come, including the 11,000-foot climb described by Charles Swithinbank as bone-crushing toil.

The first clouds began to gather between us as we crept across the ice-shelf before we even reached the Atlantic coast of Antarctica.

Our cooker caught fire one night. Without warning vapour began to escape through the seals and caught fire. Flames ran over the tent floor and under our sleeping bags. Flashbacks of previous Arctic tent fires when Geoff Newman and I had narrowly escaped immolation sent me instantly to the door-zipper, diving out into the snow and screaming at Mike to throw the lethal cooker outside. He did so and quickly smothered the flames with one of our jackets.

Dr Phillip Law, describing his life's work in Antarctica and relationships in polar bases, wrote: 'Personal habits of others can be intolerable, even the way someone eats, talks or laughs. The weaknesses or mistakes of others also become unbearable and the unfortunate individual is blamed and hated for them.' Mike and I were well aware of this and tried to watch ourselves for annoying traits. If either of us started to develop such a wart, the other quickly pointed it out. We did not allow resentment to fester if we could help it. I used my penknife scissors to cut off my eyebrows, moustache and beard soon after we left Berkner Island. This was anti-social. Mike, who was cooking, found bits of hair in the stew and the porridge. After one oblique comment from Mike, I took the hint and conducted future barber operations into a bag on my lap.

As the days struggled by and the stress mounted, we faced increasing tensions between us. We could not ease the pain, the fear, above all the sheer burden of the sledge-loads, by kicking our sledges. We took it out on each other, at first silently, as had been our wont in the Arctic, but then with controlled outbursts 'in public'.

The first open forum was calm enough and consisted of a fairly even discussion about relative pace. We both acknowledged that the pace difference was small, at most three minutes in the hour, so our ability to attain the daily ten-mile yardstick was not affected. None the less it did adversely affect the morale of the man with the slower pace on any given day whilst boosting the morale of the other. We agreed that the obvious answer was to balance the weight of our sledge-loads accordingly.

After only five miles of progress on the seventeenth day Mike's foot blisters became painful and he told me he thought it would be sensible to stop. I said nothing in the interests of diplomacy and we camped four hours early; to my mind a dangerous precedent.

The very fact there were to be no 'days off' on our schedule and no shortening of hours of travel, was a further mental burden that turned the screws on our fragile relationship. If two saintly monks were to manhaul heavy loads, whilst increasingly deprived of food and subjected to mounting discomforts, *they* might maintain at least an outward show of mutual tolerance. If so, they would be the exception to the rule.

Although Mike and I had travelled so many polar miles together in harmony over the past six years, I had never forgotten my ancient prejudices based on the adage 'small Yorkshire spectacles'. In a nutshell I had spent many years on many expeditions following the general rule that a great deal of trouble can be avoided by *never* selecting Yorkshiremen for my teams, because they are dour and nurse grievances, small men because they need to work hard to make themselves seen and heard, and bespectacled men because, when their spectacles break, they may become pains in the neck.

Mike was not a spectacled Yorkshireman but he was undeniably short. I had read Meare's book about that journey and would never have even contemplated Mike for one of my journeys had I not met him *prior* to reading the book.

An American naval psychologist based at McMurdo had been asked to assess the characters of the expedition team including Mike. Her report, as published in the appendix to *Footsteps of Scott*, ran:

All five individuals did not function well as a group. Michael Stroud had extremes in his character greater than most of the expedition members. He sees himself as expedient, dominant, forthright and undisciplined. Secondly, and almost equally, he sees himself as enthuiastic, tender-minded, imaginative and experimenting.

Individuals like Mike see themselves as assertive to aggressive, authoritative, competitive and stubborn. People like him disregard rules and feel few obligations. They do not feel group pressure to conform.

In a group his type may slow up group performance and upset group morale by undue fussiness. Being inner-directed and self-motivated, while also imaginatively creative, this sometimes can lead to unrealistic situations accompanied by expressive outburst.

The Antarctic coast passed under our feet sometime during the twentieth morning. At first any uphill gradient was imperceptible but, by the afternoon, each and every heave on the traces required concentrated mental and physical effort.

For quite a while I was fascinated by a shape floating on the glare-blurred horizon to our front, as of something different, and visible a good half-hour before we came upon it. '*Sastrugi*,' Mike breathed, for our change-over coincided with our arrival beside the two-foot-high six-foot-long wall of ice. There was no obvious reason for its presence but memories came rushing back of the great *sastrugi* fields I had crossed with Charlie and Oliver in 1980. God forbid that Mike and I should meet such obstacles. I sent up a silent but fervent prayer. There was no way we could shift our current loads through even ten miles of giant *sastrugi*. In 1980 we crossed some sixty miles of unexplored snowfields on the high plateau where prevailing winds had cut the ice-sheet into a ploughed field. Each furrow was of ice averaging three feet in height, like athletes' hurdles, but set only five feet apart. In many places we had progressed only by cutting a path with tree axes. You do not force a way through these ridges, for the wind has cut them from snow into smooth and slippery ebony, as hard as concrete.

Our first lone *sastruga* was joined by other solitary outrunners until a great rash of iron-hard furrows lay directly across our route. My determination to conserve energy could cope with the competitive urge to race Mike (if shackled tortoises can race), but crumbled before my instinctive reaction to *attack* ice obstacles. I knew of no other way to advance when the ice gets nasty. You must attack it head-on and with every ounce of gristle at your disposal. There can

312

be *no* holding back. Tightening my harness and stick-straps, I focused on each successive wall of ice and threw energy conservation to the winds.

My various blisters and chaffing sores were not helped by this onslaught but there was now an identifiable enemy, not just the endless flat glare of the ice-shelf where the persistent struggle was all in the mind. Now there was no difficulty following Mike. Indeed, I found it necessary to take pauses every few minutes as he slipped and fell. His legs were stronger but mine were longer. To a great extent this advantage was cut down by the skis – extensions to our legs – which were approximately the same length. When I navigated, Mike could not keep up. I would pull for fifteen or twenty minutes, then wait, so that we were never out of sight.

In addition to the *sastrugi*, we experienced our first major slope. I began to appreciate Swithinbank's 'bone-crunching toil'. The work was breathtaking. Even the briefest of halts, with sledge pointing downhill or astride a *sastruga*, was a bad mistake for, once the load began to slide backwards, skis followed suit and then an undignified tangle of falling body, flailing sticks and more bruises on the sharp-edged ridges.

Towards the end of the day, after eleven hours of uphill hauling, we came to an especially rugged zone of serrated ice and Mike lagged well behind, despite my many pauses for him to catch up. At the end of the final hour I had the tent up in time for his arrival and knew at once that he was livid. Now that we were openly expressing our concerns Mike let rip. I had surged ahead despite the evil terrain and, worse, I had gone *straight* at the *sastrugi* instead of taking a sensible, though less direct, route between the worst ice walls. For some reason the often hostile feelings that I nursed towards Mike, whilst on the move, almost invariably evaporated once we were back in the tent. This appeared to apply also to Mike – which saved the journey for both of us from becoming a non-stop nightmare.

In early December the gradient began to increase in severity. There were times when our skis slipped backwards at every step and the only way upwards was to tack at 45° to the slope, adding a deal of extra distance to the whole. On the interminable, grinding ascents there was little to be done but grit your teeth together and force any images of *future* or distance *ahead* out of your thoughts.

When periods of no wind coincided with a cloudless sky, the sun beat down 'through the ozone hole' and we grew so hot that we stripped to our vests. Sweat dribbled into our eyes. Our unwashed hair and bodies itched and emitted a powerful stench. The sweat-salt stung my crotch sores and the renewed assault from ultraviolet burns further damaged my lips, from which blood and pus leaked into the chin cover of my face-mask.

The joys of sun and warmth quickly ceded to a twenty-five-knot easterly wind. Mike had circulation troubles in one hand and, due to severe *sastrugi* patches, found it hard work to keep up.

After twenty-five days we both looked and felt worn out. Overall, if we could somehow keep going, there was still a slim chance of success. We might even reach the Seaquest ship by its departure date given a long list of favourable ifs and buts. Mike was stricken by stomach trouble in the night. 'Rough,' he wrote. 'Got diarrhoea three times overnight. With one disaster I missed the empty ration bag and got shit on my sleeping bag cover. I then spilled a load of water from the cook pot as I tried to clear up – Thank God Ran was asleep.'

I did notice an unusual aroma the next morning but we set out on time and I was surprised and dismayed when, after only forty minutes, Mike halted and told me he felt weak as a kitten and must stop. I tried to appear sympathetic and to cover my impatience as I unpacked the tent.

After hot tea and Lomotil tablets Mike slept for four hours and I buried my frustration by forming the plot for a novel to be written on our return.

Mike woke and we drank more tea. I refrained from pressurising him and was delighted when he said he would try to go on. There was still time to get in five hours of hauling, but at seven in the evening he again halted and told me he felt drained of energy. I seethed inwardly. How dare Mike comment earlier on my polar plod when, by *twice* cutting full days short due to mere blisters and diarrhoea, he had wasted the equivalent of many weeks of polar plods. Whatever our pace, and no matter whether he or I was on any given day slower than the other, we had invariably managed to complete our vital ten-mile minimum. Only when his problems had caused early halts had we dropped miles which would be hard ever to regain.

Mike further riled me with the sudden news that his watch had stopped with a dead battery. He acknowledged that, two months before we left London, I had asked if he would send me his watch for a free check-up at Rolex. He had been too busy to post it off. We depended for our navigation, on sunny days, entirely on our watches. To keep fastening or unfastening my watch *every* hour, when we changed over to navigate, was unthinkable. It seems simple enough on the face of it but, with two pairs of mitts and cold fingers, it would be asking for frostbite and we both knew this. Without our being able to look at a watch the time *within* each hour could seem endless. I knew that Mike, a zealous time-keeper like most doctors, was especially keen on regulating the moments for change-overs to suit our ever-changing state of energy level. There was only one answer. I gave Mike my watch.

'When *my* hour ends,' I suggested 'just shout at me to stop. It should act as a brake to stop me getting too far ahead in *sastrugi* zones since I will not want to be out of hearing distance.' From then on I was to be watch-less all day and every day of the journey.

Before I had made up my mind to deliver some peroration after our meal, Mike announced that his abscess was so swollen that he had decided to operate. I watched with intense admiration as he gave himself two deep injections of Xylocaine anaesthetic and then plunged a scalpel blade deep into the swelling with diagonally crossed incisions. Pus poured out of the wounds and the swelling visibly decreased. Mike then bandaged up his heel and packed away his medical kit. I am not sure whether or not he felt faint but I certainly did. I said nothing about the early halt or the stricken Rolex.

Most of the plasters over our blisters and crotch-rot were not changed daily. They became semi-permanent fixtures because plasters, like everything else, were in short supply. This state of affairs sometimes caused sores to deteriorate and after thirty days my right foot began to hurt when travelling. I removed the bandage one evening and noticed that a two-inch area was soggy and swollen. Mike incised the area with a half-inch slit and relieved the pain immediately. I rubbed haemorrhoid cream, of which Mike had a plentiful supply, into the foot slit (and also on to my raw lips) before re-plastering the foot. By now there were nine separate bandaged areas on my feet. Mike had applied Granuflex pressure-sore pads to his blisters and swore by the results which seemed to have miraculously cured some of his worst sores. I tried one but found it too bulky for my relatively tight fitting plastic boots.

Over the next three days we climbed to 5000 feet above sea level with constant Force Eight winds in our faces.

For two days my stomach felt loose but the cold wind strengthened my resolution not to take my pants down *en route*. Our long practised custom, diarrhoea excepted, was to defecate just before striking camp, using the lee of the tent, or a sledge, as an imperfect windbreak. When

Ascent from Atlantic Ocean to Antarctic Plateau

outside conditions were especially foul (or when my haemorrhoids were playing up) we would use an empty ration bag strategically positioned inside the tent. This was, of course, a smelly affair and kept to a minimum.

In the tent my face-mask was firmly embedded in my beard and, despite trying to remove it with care, a chunk of skin and beard came away, attached to the chin pad, leaving a raw and bleeding patch the size of a silver dollar. This was annoying since I had tried hard to avoid just such a recurrence of chin troubles. In a few days my chin became swollen. I tried to avoid the balaclava tearing off bits each evening by cutting away the beard hairs with my penknife scissors, but the damaged area grew more poisoned and Mike gave me antibiotics from his dwindling supply.

Arriving some distance ahead of Mike one evening I began to erect the tent by fixing a safety line to my sledge before trying to slot the ten-foot-long alloy poles into the sleeving. The fourth and last pole was almost positioned when an especially violent blast tore the tent from my mitts and buckled one of the poles. Since I only carried a single eighteen-inch spare pole section for the entire journey I left the bent pole in place and prayed we would be spared a 'big katabatic' in the days ahead.

I thought of Ginnie back on Exmoor. She had lit a church candle and intended to keep it burning day and night until I returned. It was four feet long but so many hundreds of miles stretched ahead of us I could not help but think the candle would run out long before I came home.

One morning I noticed a small black item behind Mike's sledge. It turned out to be a spare battery – Mike looked grim, as well he might, for he had packed the battery deep inside his load and there was no way it could have escaped but through a hole in the hull. Earlier Mike had crashed down into a crevasse and his sledge had followed him into the maw. A chance snow ledge had saved Mike from certain death and his sledge had appeared but slightly damaged. We rolled the sledge on to one side and then the other, revealing a ragged split across its entire width. The sledge was now sundered and held together only by the two narrow longitudinal runners. Many of the half-inch screws which held the runners to the base of the hull were loose but, fortunately, responded to tightening by the screwdriver on Mike's knife.

We erected the tent as a new gale blew up and, having unloaded all contents, pulled the front end of the stricken sledge inside. Away from the wind, we were now able to detach the custom-made alloy strong points from the front end of the sledge which was now both smaller and more damaged than the rear section.

Mike restacked his more solid gear, mainly the food and fuel, into what was now the front end, about two-thirds of the sledge, and stowed only bulky light equipment, such as his sleeping bag, in the broken rear section.

We then retreated to the tent shivering, to stir up our circulation with soup from the Thermos. This we discovered, through its unusual taste, had fermented due to the difficulty of cleaning it out on a daily basis. Our recurring diarrhoea troubles might be partially caused by well-brewed Thermos bacteria.

'The whole sledge could fall apart any day,' Mike ruminated.

'You could always tow half of it,' I added unhelpfully. 'Moby MacLean once designed an edible sledge, made from toughened pemmican, which he aimed to consume from back to front.'

'And what happened?'

'It never got off the drawing board. Polar buffs whom he approached cut the idea to ribbons.'

'Exactly,' said Mike, wholly unimpressed at the idea of towing half a sledge anywhere.

I carried Mike's bed mat for him but everything else fitted well enough and the undamaged runners seemed unaffected.

'Oh well.' I picked up my mitts from the tent floor. 'If we are to catch up the remaining four hours, we had better be going.'

'Is it worth it?' Mike commented. 'Just for four hours! Now we've camped we might as well stay put.'

Rather hurriedly I assured him that there was every point and, without stopping to argue the issue, pushed out of the door flap.

Allowing for slight improvement to our current rate of progress the sledge-loads slowly lessened, but taking no account of altitude or bodily deterioration, I estimated that we were now halfway to the Pole time-wise. Thirty-four days behind us and thirty-four to go.

The following day brought our first true white-out along with uneven *sastrugi* and heavy crust snowdrifts, through which the sledges ploughed only with the most determined haulage.

For twenty years, largely in the Arctic, I had navigated in the worst of glare-ice, month after month, without eye protection. But in Siberia this stupidity, born of the frustration of misted goggles, had caught up with me and the best London ophthalmic surgeon had warned me I would risk blindness if I ever again subjected my retinas to further overdoses of blue and ultraviolet light. Frightened, I no longer gave in to the temptation to tear off misted goggles but I fully sympathised when Mike did so.

Under true white-out conditions it is quite possible for people to walk off cliffs and for aircraft to 'land' by mistake. Some individuals are physically sickened by white-out travel and, that morning, Mike complained of feeling 'disturbed and totally disorientated', when he removed his jacket hood to prevent his goggles misting. As a result he kept his hood up, his goggles became unwearable and, in an especially bad *sastrugi* field, he removed them for a period of two hours.

Towards noon the clouds shifted and a slight horizon was visible. This enabled us to hold our bearing by simply crossing successive *sastrugi* trenches at an angle of 70°.

When we camped, after a memorably nasty ten hours lurching over unseen obstacles, crossing ski-tips and crashing into invisible trenches, I found both my cheeks burning and inflamed by UV rays. A mole on one cheek was especially tender. I had exposed my cheeks to help demist my goggles but it had been a mistake. The cheeks were later to blister because the burn conditions had been so bad. Mike's eyes, even though he wore goggles for all but two hours throughout the day, were also damaged. Soon after we camped he developed snow blindness symptoms. Only the mildest of attacks, but enough to have him lying back in considerable pain. We carried a bottle of amethocaine eye drops and these provided Mike with exquisite relief for about an hour, after which he would wake in renewed pain and apply further drops.

Since our overall speed and rate of progress for the first forty days were slightly better than for any previous Antarctic manhauling journey on record, our pace should not theoretically have caused dissension. But we were both under increasing strain and our bodies, under the stress of slow starvation combined with enormous energy expenditure, were altering chemically.

Subsequent analysis of our blood samples was to show that our whole enzyme system, everything that controlled our absorption of fat, was changing and we were getting levels of gut hormones twice as high as were previously known to science. We were adapting to our high-fat rations in a way hitherto unrecognised. Furthermore, we were losing muscle and weight from our hearts as well as our body mass.

During this period of the steep climb to the Pole and beyond we were losing muscle fast. Mike later said, after our results were analysed, 'Ran was at times using nearly 10,000 calories a day. This is more than has been documented *ever* for any length of time.'

By the fifth week Mike's surges were telling on him. Entries in his diary at this time included, 'I felt a bit hypoglycaemic in the last hour,' and 'I feel totally bushed in the last hour, sick and lightheaded.' One evening he wrote: 'Felt terrible. Thought I had reactive hypoglycaemia.' He told me that he could 'feel the weight falling off'.

At the beginning of a day of hauling through the clinging wet cement of snow-crud, it was truly difficult to master your thoughts and banish the insistent desire to halt because this whole huge task was simply *too hard*.

I often wished to scream my feelings to the sky. Cherry-Garrard wrote: 'Sometimes it was difficult not to *howl*. I *did* want to howl many times every hour but I invented a formula instead which I repeated to myself constantly. Especially, I remember, it came in useful at the end of the march with my feet frostbitten, my heart beating slowly, my vitality at its lowest ebb and my body solid with cold. Then I would repeat: "Stick it. Stick it. Stick it. Stick it."'

Some aspects of Mike's behaviour, or some chance phrase, would lodge itself in my mind unbidden and the more I chewed the cud the more it would rile me. This I found an especially useful thought-tactic, for *where there is anger there is no room to brood*.

By Christmas Eve we had staggered to 6000 feet above sea level. That afternoon, for the first time, a southerly wind allowed us to sail through mists and weirdly convoluted banks of *sastrugi*. We both fell heavily many times but, by some miracle, escaped injury. The wind appeared to pick up again on the morning of Christmas Day, but in a short while veered well to the west and we quickly packed the sails.

By noon my stomach, loose all morning, was in sharp revolt. I felt weak and sick and was forced to squat, bare bottomed, beside my sledge in a bitter south-west wind. The terrain was as foul as ever with wet-cement, or drag-anchor crud, clinging all day to the sledge runners.

Christmas lunch was a bitterly cold affair sitting side-by-side and hunched against the wind to crunch two squares of chocolate and gulp down a pint of tepid glutinous soup.

Our mitts had to come off in repeated combined attacks to unscrew the frozen lid of the vacuum flask. We eventually battered it off against the hull of my sledge but by then we both had cold hands which took an hour of hard hauling to recover.

Whenever I felt my core temperature drop, the alarm bells rang and I would pull harder. At such times Mike would drop behind until, recovered from 'the shivers' and remembering my polar plod policy, I would slow down again. One side of me would fiercely condemn such wimpish behaviour . . . Why limp along when capable of greater speed? But a more cautious voice would prevail: 'There are over a thousand miles to go . . . You are too old, sick, tired and hungry. Keep plodding. Never stop, but never race. Forget the urge to compete with him. Don't pander to pride. Think long-term. If he wishes to squander his energy reserves, let him go ahead.'

Mike's diary:

The willy-warmer extra padding that I sewed in my underwear last night gives little benefit and the end of my penis was markedly swollen . . . we are exhausted . . .

Day Fifty: Desperately hard day. Ran finding it very hard to cope with going slower than I although, in reality, it is not that much slower and both of us are now feeling as though we are running on empty. I think that our steadily pushing up the hours to approaching ten haul-hours is getting too much and we need a break . . . I think I can say that today was the first time that my legs were tired even when I left the tent in the morning.

Day Fifty-One: A terrible day of crushing morale, physical decrepitude and difficult terrain. Last night I weighed us. Ran has lost forty pounds and me thirty pounds. Twenty per cent of our body weight.'

When Mike broke the news of this further weight deterioration, I made up my mind to counter future enfeeblement by drastic changes. In only fifty days of eating *exactly* the same food as Mike I had lost 25 per cent more weight than he had. I refused to ask for extra food to cope with my greater bulk so I asked him to begin using more rations off his sledge over the next few days. This should, I hoped, even out our rate of bodily weakening.

Whenever I kept well ahead of Mike, he would remind me that I was heavier and longer of leg. He maintained that both these physical attributes were an advantage. Yet, in scientific papers that he had previously written, he held the opposite view as regards heavy, bulky manhaulers. Of the death of Scott's heaviest team member, Evans, Mike wrote: 'Sheer starvation with consequent emaciation might have been the more significant factor [of their death]. For example, Evans was the biggest man in Scott's team and could have lost over thirty pounds by the time he reached the Pole, let alone what he lost on the return journey . . . Of course the other men would also have suffered from only slightly less devastating weight losses.' Mike's study of the three men on the Meare/Swan 1986 South Pole Expedition led him to realise that the heaviest member of that team lost far more weight than the lightest *despite* eating more. This he now chose to ignore.

Because of my recent bouts of diarrhoea I was again suffering on the march from haemorrhoids. The only benefit of this was a tendency to forget the pain of my feet due to the new aggravation.

Mike produced two small bottles from his science pack and we each drank the contents, which consisted of very expensive water. He explained the purpose. 'This stuff is deuterium and is made up of heavy hydrogen and O_{18}. Like atomic *heavy water*, but non-radioactive. Each bottleful costs hundreds of pounds, so don't spill any.'

'So what good does heavy water do us?'

'None at all. It just gets mixed up with all the other water in our bodies which we will slowly rid ourselves of and I will slowly collect. The O_{18} will come out partially in the form of carbon dioxide. We will burn everything up sooner or later but the O_{18} disappears first. I can use the differing disappearance rates revealed by analysis of our urine samples to measure our daily energy expenditure.'

I never ceased to admire Mike's dedication to his research work. However sick he happened to be feeling at the time, he would never skimp the tiniest detail of his science schedule.

On our fifty-third day Mike slowed right down, so that even my polar plod overhauled him. He wrote: 'A desperate day for me. The pulling seemed so hard that I very nearly gave in to the wish to have a rest day . . . I diagnosed a state of near-terminal, physical decline.'

The next day, after two hours of steep, yard-by-yard progress, Mike was forced by another diarrhoea attack to stop and drop his trousers 'by the roadside'. A few minutes later he told me he could not continue. He must rest. I was furious. We erected the tent and made tea. After Mike had rested for an hour or two I told him we must get going. He was angry and said I was boorish and graceless; in short a prick of the first order.

Mike's diary: 'I began to feel ill early and got diarrhoea after two and a half hours. Ran was unsympathetic, angry and a right sod.'

I told him that the mounting number of delays caused by his halts were costing us vital time. The few minutes of difference between our relative speeds were of no consequence since our time-keeping methods simply prolonged our marching hours to cover any such difference. This was not true of his stops. I stressed, in my anger, that if he could not take it, I would go on without him and that we must be hard not soft in our approach to every side of our schedule, or we would never reach the Pole never mind the Beardmore Glacier.

This outburst futher soured poor Mike and certainly did not increase his readiness to break camp. I settled back to accept the inevitable and to wait for his recovery. After a couple of hours and more hot tea, we set out again, but, after a further three hours, his track began to curve from side to side and then he collapsed in the snow and lay still. I drew up beside him and waited. He recovered in a few moments and stood up. I took over the navigation but, fifteen minutes later, he suffered further stomach upsets and told me he must stop. In the tent I apologised for my previous anger and by the time the evening meal was over the atmosphere was clear of tension.

We had reached 8500 feet above sea-level and I was feeling increasingly tight-chested. I eased off my shoulder straps as much as possible but *any* constriction of the lungs led to heavy breathing and the noise in my ears of blood rushing to my head. It became difficult to eat a chocolate square on the move because any interruption to the breath-taking process had me gasping for air. Even to bend over to tighten a ski-binding made me breathless and weak.

Although we did not then know it, and Mike continued to assure me that altitude would not affect us, I learned later that the relatively low air pressure near to the Poles markedly increases the effect of altitude on humans. Eight thousand five hundred feet here gave the same conditions as 11,500 feet on, say, Mount Everest. At 11,500 feet the thinness of the air and the consequent lack of oxygen causes many people to suffer from altitude sickness; shortness of breath, dizziness, even nausea and confusion. One of Scott's men collapsed from altitude sickness at 9000 feet, and Amundsen, although ten dogs hauled his sledge, found 'it was hard to work and breathing was an effort'.

I saw huge hill features up ahead but thanked God when, hours later, they turned out to be part mirage, part cloud formations.

On our sixtieth day Mike had a very bad time and told me he must be wrong about the effects of altitude. He was worried within himself about his ability to continue fending off negative thoughts. 'If things go on like this beyond the Pole, I can see myself wanting out. I simply don't have the same resolute resolve as you do.' He wrote: 'Last night I did express to Ran my fears of not being able to hack it if things go badly. Needless to say I got a sort of "we will be tough" type talk rather than true understanding. He gets *his* strength from *"God and family and the whole clan here inside me"*. All very useful but I know it won't help me if I can see the whole chance of success slipping away and us just slogging on.'

That night I gave Mike two chocolate squares and he seemed to appreciate the gesture. I am not good at being sympathetic. I knew that Mike was agnostic and did not expect him to gain any mental help in that direction. I had hoped, however, that he might be able to invoke his family and the knowledge that they were all 'gunning for him' but he seemed to scoff at this as too contrived a mental aid.

My practice was to 'hype up' my mind during the first hour of every day, when the pain from my feet was at its worst, by simply remembering that I was not alone in facing the dreaded hours ahead. I pictured my grandfather who had trapped in northern Canada and fought for his country all over the world. I thought of my father and uncle who were killed in the two World Wars. I pictured my wife, my mother and my sisters and I knew that all of them were right behind me helping to suppress the ever-lurking urge to put a stop to the pain and the cold.

The last 200 miles before the Pole involved us in climbing above 10,000 feet. The altitude effects added to our debilitation and the heavy loads were beginning to change us in many subtle ways. Mike said later: 'I had all day these endless thoughts about how to give up, on what excuse. I was on the point of calling Ran and I was going to say: "This is it." On the day before we got to the Pole, when it was within sight, I was going to give up – but because I *wanted* to give up not because I couldn't take it.'

That was on our sixty-seventh day. The wind chill factor was −84°C with thick fog. In such conditions it is all too easy to make some small effort that can quickly lead to serious trouble.

Over the weeks of gradually dropping temperatures we had each modified our clothes with needle, Dentafloss and patches cut from such items as the tent bag. Mike was still unhappy with his trousers. I have always held it as vital that I can undo my trouser zip when wearing mitts and accordingly fix a long loop of plastic wire to the zip-toggle. Mike had a complete pee-flap which required ungloved hands to manoeuvre.

I was unable to adjust my face-mask that morning to protect my nose without causing fogged-up goggles. Frequent attempts to scratch all the resulting grime off the lens had failed and, short of pitching the tent, it was dangerous to halt for more than three or four minutes in such conditions to make radical face-mask alterations. I therefore asked Mike to navigate in my place since he could still see reasonably well. This was the only stint that Mike navigated 'my hours' during the entire journey and the timing could not have been better for it certainly saved his life.

During the second hour of the morning Mike stopped to have one of many wayside pees and fumbled the job of fastening his trousers. His hands, colder than usual, would not fit back into his oiled wool Dachstein mitts. I stood waiting behind him, cursing silently as my swollen foot seemed to vibrate with shafts of pain. Less than fifteen miles away, in the frozen swirling mists, the South Pole waited.

Mike turned round, a cumbersome business wearing skis and in harness, but he needed to face away from the bitter south-easterly wind.

I knew he was in trouble when I heard him moaning, then sobbing with pain and fear. I knew what he was experiencing, the anguish that comes with allowing your fingers or toes to go that touch too far down the road to frostbite and permanent loss.

Mike had been trying to force hands with no feeling into mitts that were slightly too tight. Because both hands were now senseless lumps of bloodless meat he could no longer do anything with them. In his moment of blind panic he forgot the most obvious answer.

Normally we do not spring to each other's aid. There is an unspoken pride in being self-sufficient and it can be irritating fending off attempts at nursemaiding. If and when one of us is quite obviously about to drown (in the Arctic), or fall further into a crevasse (in Antarctica), then the other does what is necessary, but day-to-day hazards are coped with individually.

When I saw that Mike was on the point of losing his fingers for good I wrenched off my fogged-up goggles, removed my clumsy Canadian Army mitts and tried to force Mike's frozen hands into his Dachsteins. My own fingers cooled in seconds to the point that they were of no help to Mike so I thrust them back into mitts and screamed at Mike to shove his hands into his crotch. Even this was difficult for him but desperation gave him added strength and, still whimpering through gritted teeth, he managed to force the hands which he could not feel down between his sledge-jacket and his trousers to the only warm place (other than *my* crotch) within fifteen miles. Forcing his thighs together Mike gradually squeezed blood back into his hands and eventually down to his fingertips but not before five of his fingers were badly nipped. This was to lead to further troubles at a later date but at least the current danger was averted.

By the time we were ready to move on, both of us were extremely cold, our body core temperatures lower than at any time in the journey so far. Knowing that Mike was more prone to hypothermia, I lent him my outer mitts and took his own Gortex outers which, normally excellent, were less than adequate in such conditions. The delay had rendered my own hands unworkable in terms of trying to de-fog my goggles and the only feature I could see in the near white-out was Mike's indistinct silhouette eight yards ahead of me. His tracks were invisible.

After an interminable time, during which I bitterly regretted the fact that I had not brought a second watch with me, I came to an abrupt halt as my ski-tips struck the rear of Mike's sledge. Normally when he halted to announce that ninety minutes were up and it was my turn to navigate, he would shout the word 'Time' loud enough for me to hear above the screech of my ski-sticks. There had been no shout and, as I came alongside to detach the compass from Mike's chest harness, I noticed something unaccountably different about his behaviour. My standard practice, having clipped the compass to my own chest-strap, was to move a few yards ahead of him and check the correct bearing before setting off for my next ninety-minute session. It was not my habit *ever* to look back, except in a zone of crevasses or other hazards, and if, on this occasion, I had followed my normal procedure, Mike would certainly have died. As it was some aspect of Mike's stance, perhaps just a total lack of movement, alerted my subconscious and, removing my near useless goggles, I peered at his face.

I could not focus for a while as the cold wind whipped at my tear ducts and Mike's face gave me no clues through his goggles and balaclava. Ice spikes poked horizontally from his chin as from a grotesque clown's mask. 'Are you OK, Mike?' I screamed at him, and struck him on the shoulder. There was no response at all and his head seemed to loll.

I remembered seeing him once before in this state, somewhere in the Siberian Arctic, and realised he was about to succumb to hypothermia. Because my fingers were numb and a steady Force Seven wind made things awkward, I spent several minutes unpacking and erecting the tent. When the inner tent was up I shouted to Mike to go inside and start the cooker whilst I fixed up the fly sheet.

A couple of minutes later I found that Mike was still kneeling in the snow and staring vacantly into space. I hustled him through the door-flap and, unpacking his sledge, threw his mat and bag inside. Once the cooker was going, Mike began to remove his clothes as though in a trance. He said nothing but accepted a mug of tepid soup from the Thermos. He slept for an hour and when he awoke spent some time staring at the tent ceiling. His memory, which had entirely gone as far as the last few hours were concerned, gradually returned. I made him two cups of tea and he ate two of his chocolate bars.

My mind was in turmoil. I had little doubt but that he was pushing himself far too hard. Time and again I had tried to make him see the sense of the polar plod policy but he suspected my motives, believing I was merely protecting my own interests, and could not bring himself to manhaul at less than his maximum capacity.

The next day the wind dropped, the mists cleared and we carried on. Towards the evening I screamed at Mike, 'Look ahead. Over there. There's a *thing*.' For the first time in over 700 miles a man-made object was visible in the snow. We had a two-part wager between us. Whoever spotted the first sign of the Pole would get a free hamburger snack and, for sighting the Pole itself, a free 'slap-up' lunch.

The *thing* turned out to be a half-buried meteorological balloon and its presence was a definite boost to morale.

At 7 p.m., glancing ahead as I topped a slow rise, I thought I saw movement. Removing my goggles and squinting to focus, I could just make out a series of dark, blurred objects: five or six black marbles dancing on the shimmer of the southern horizon.

I turned back and shouted to Mike. It was a rare moment of sheer elation. The journey was far from over but we had dragged to the Pole *just* enough stores to allow us to cross the continent and survive. If our luck held.

The American Pole station, known as Amundsen-Scott Base, was ten miles from the point where we first glimpsed its buildings. A series of rising steppes kept hiding the site but, after seven hours' hauling on 16 January, we topped the final rise and came to the first of many isolated science domes at 17.00 hours Greenwich Mean Time on the eighty-first anniversary day of Scott's sad arrival there.

All the isolation of the past months fell away. The polar site had vastly altered even in the twelve short years since my last visit. Strangely shaped installations on jack-up steel legs reared monstrously in every direction from the main central feature, the black-roofed dome, in which over-wintering scientists live and work.

Constructed over an area of two square miles, the site no longer resembled the moonscape of my memory with its small huddle of Earth Stations. We were now confronted by a film set vista as of a long-deserted industrial estate, littered with oil drums, pipes, construction materials and many thousands of large wooden crates.

Time-wise, Mike and I arrived at the Pole well before the station's working day began, but a huddle of nine figures in full polar clothing stood waiting beneath the colourful array of national flags at the world's most southerly point.

Mike's face was a picture of conflicting emotions. He leant forward briefly on his ski stick and there were tears in his eyes. He was clearly elated. I felt pleasure for him, knowing that he had tried for so long and so hard to reach this place. Back in 1985, when Roger Mear turned him down and chose Gareth Wood in his place, Mike had admitted, 'Not going to the Pole is hurting, hurting like hell.'

Unbidden thoughts of the food available inside the dome canteen tripped about my taste buds as we forced ourselves north from the station. In all, we had paused at the Pole for eighty minutes.

A mile beyond the Pole we entered a region of snowquakes. Without warning I heard a crashing roar and felt an instant of extreme panic as the solid snow surface under my feet dropped away.

When snow builds up into a patch of wind crust several inches thick, whether as big as a sports arena, or merely room-sized, the pressure of even a dog's foot can be enough to trigger a sudden collapse of the whole suspended mass. Never more than a few inches, but enough to petrify the ignorant passer-by and to spark off thunderous sound waves for several seconds.

By the time we made camp in thick mist we had hauled over ten miles despite the delay at the Pole. I cut my last Mars Bar in half and we silently savoured the exquisite taste for a minute of luxury by way of self-congratulation for reaching the Pole.

I was worried by our body weight figures. I had weighed in that afternoon at eleven and a half stones (161lbs) and Mike at nine and a half stones (133lbs). We had each lost some 25 per cent of our body weight, in my case 49lbs, and Mike now forecast that I would probably lose a further 21lbs over the next thirty days.

Neither of us could afford this sort of weight loss since the colder temperatures now setting in with the imminent onslaught of winter would cut right into our body cores. Normally our body fat would have provided natural thermic protection but we were already devoid of fat and, especially in Mike's case, vulnerable to hypothermia.

Unless he settled down to a sensible polar plod I could see Mike running himself into the ground. He refused to accept this and, since *he* was the doctor, I stood little chance of persuading him. Since his erroneous diagnosis of the effects of altitude on our performance, I no longer considered his cold weather theories as omnipotent.

I told him that since I was losing more weight than he was, but naturally did not expect to eat more than my half-rations share, the only sensible course I could suggest was that we use up more of the rations I was carrying so that I lightened up by 25lbs before he did. This should continue until he moved at the same slow plod as I did, even on flat surfaces and in easier temperatures.

Mike naturally revolted against such a suggestion. Why, he queried, should he carry more than someone who had talked of going on without him and muttered, 'We must be tougher,' when he, Mike, had wished to pause through sickness?

All our previous sufferings were as nothing compared with the days which followed the Pole. Much of this was my fault for underestimating the extreme cold at 11,000 feet above sea level and the effect it would have on our battered bodies. I should have obtained and packed *more* protective clothing and I should not have suggested abandoning our down jackets and outer sleeping bags. We were now suffering for these mistakes, and the immediate future looked grim.

Only now, beyond the Pole, were we discovering the true meaning of *cold*. Our conditions in terms of body deterioration, slow starvation, inadequate clothing, wind chill temperature, altitude and even the day of the year, exactly matched those of Scott and his four companions as they came away from the Pole. Dr Wilson, Scott's friend, wrote: 'Thin air, low pressure and oxygen deficiency reach a point, at about 10,000 feet, above which even well-fed, fit humans will be affected by altitude "sickness". It is best not to exert yourself but, if you must, you will find every movement is an effort. The pulse rate races away and to breathe is to gasp as your lungs and heart fight to pump oxygen around the body.' Additionally, because both our vacuum flasks were broken, we were drinking too little liquid to replace the enormous amounts we lost daily through hard work at altitude and in great cold.

I could sense that Mike was in a bad way despite his continued 'power surges'. I knew that even now he would never recognise that his pace was his own worst enemy. He looked to be near the end of his tether and I feared that any further attempts by me to 'bully' him into copying my polar plod, any further 'gracelessness' should he again need to camp early, might prove to be the final straw. I resolved, from now on, to compromise with him over matters of pace whenever necessary.

That afternoon, on a high place that could have been the summit of Mount Everest without the view for all its wind-blasted, frozen hostility, Mike stopped at the end of our fifth hour. We slumped, breathless and weak, on to a sledge and feebly tried to crack the ice jamming the top of our Thermos. Gulping at tepid soup, we agreed that something would have to change.

When Mike tried to get off the sledge, his legs crumpled and he fell backwards. On his third attempt he stood up swaying. We both laughed or at least emitted sounds which I took to be laughs. I was surprised at such signs of muscle deterioration in Mike who has amazingly powerful lower limb muscles in terms of sheer effective pulling power.

That night we reached an agreement that Mike would slow himself down by taking rations for the next three days off my sledge, and that we would eat the last of the six cannibalised rations over the next ten days whilst still under maximum altitude stress. If we could only survive as far as the Beardmore Glacier and start to lose height, *then* we could compensate by cutting to half-rations.

Mike unpacked a sterilised scalpel and lanced my infected foot in several places, releasing quanties of surface poison. That side of my foot was now death-white, spongey and hyper-sensitive.

Even inside our tent, with the cooker rehydrating the spaghetti, it was intensely cold. I forced myself to take down my trousers in order to apply haemorrhoid cream to various places, including the raw regions of my crotch, scabbed lips, nose and chin.

'I don't believe it,' Mike exclaimed staring at my legs. 'You can't pull anything with *those*. They're Belsen-like.'

The following day was purgatory. Mike wrote:

Cold is an understatement . . . it became very unpleasant indeed and I nearly blew it by delaying putting on my outer jacket in the morning. I suffered both general cold and severely cold hands as a result.

A desperately cold day, perhaps −40°C with a stiff wind that kept us deeply chilled despite wearing all our clothing and going as best we could. My hands were very bad and, after each pee, they took thirty minutes to recover. Even then they would still be weak which led to further problems at the next pee – a vicious circle. My morale was not too bad: just a brief spell of 'Let's get out now with an illness/injury' phase and, the rest of the day, just quiet recognition that after seventy-four days of this it's not much fun. Still, Ran has calculated that, at this pace and with no help from the wind, we should make the glacier top in seventeen days. Surely I can last that long . . . Ran and I have such a profoundly different approach to planning and coping. He finds it necessary to be as pessimistic as possible and then work up from that point while I do the opposite. It is strange to have him trying to help me mentally (for he is being as attentive as he can in this regard) by putting a *black* picture of success. All I want is a *white* picture of what could be, to keep me going – although I do accept that knowing even the black one will give us something is worthwhile.

My own diary was beginning to lapse into a mere record of impressions. 'New kind of chisel-hard hoar-frost surface in sudden patches. It is now horribly body-cold. I feel as though naked. When waiting for Mike, I have to clasp my arms around my torso and jump and sing or swear. We have run out of glue for our skins. Every six days now the average temperature drops two degrees.'

Sometimes I stopped to gasp for air and was forced to loosen my chest harness. This I hated for the waist strap immediately began to chafe my hip-sores along the edges of the plasters which I had placed over the original raw areas. My stomach churned all day and bouts of dizziness came and went. Two explosive attacks of diarrhoea involved taking my trousers down and squatting clear of my skis. This reopened my haemorrhoids which in turn made leg movement a misery. I dislike people who whinge when they are uncomfortable, and now I started disliking myself, for my thoughts dwelt increasingly on my various sources of bodily discomfort. Since the wind chill factor was around −85°C I pulled my trousers back with alacrity and without careful attention to detail. This soiled my trousers and mitts but the excrement quickly froze solid and was then easily knocked off.

Mike came alongside and said, 'We can stop if you want.' My churlish response, which I regretted as soon as it was said, was, 'I don't stop for diarrhoea.'

I spent the next hour ruminating on how extremely unpleasant I must be as a travelling companion and ended up quite thankful that Mike was not carrying the revolver which in the Arctic was usually his responsibility. On earlier journeys he had admitted nursing thoughts of using it when I left him way behind and his morale had dropped to rock bottom.

On the seventy-fifth day I woke from a night of throbbing foot pain with an almost phobic dread of my rigid ski-boots. If some modern-day Gestapo had threatened me with the torture of squeezing my feet into those boots, I would have told all and sold my soul to avoid the experience. As it was, there was no such option. The porridge gruel and coffee were ruined by having to count down the minutes to execution, the moment when I must gingerly draw my socks over the mess of my feet. As the textile hairs brushed against the damaged areas, I would grind my teeth together. Then came the unyielding pressure of the boots themselves and the beginning of the twelve-hour ordeal during which I would have only one thing in mind: the moment of release from the boots.

Painkillers tended to make me drowsy – not a good state to be in when working in cold places, so I had fought against taking them for the past two months. Mike now gave me two to take at breakfast along with antibiotics to stave off gangrene. At the time I was on Erythromycin and the mixed effect of the pills was a general feeling of gut sickness.

Mike tried hard to stop the poison spreading in my foot but, as he explained, the safest treatment in addition to antibiotics was immediate prevention of any further trauma to the damaged areas. His diary commented:

> This morning Ran actually said, 'I feel like chucking it all in,' when talking of his foot. Although he never would, I welcome such signs of weakness which are so familiar to me, although he has my every sympathy, since I find it hard enough and I am essentially pain-free.

The following day Mike diagnosed possible 'deep-seated infection in the foot bone' and put me on Metronidazole and Flucloxicillin. Unfortunately we were running short of these antibiotics which seemed most effective. The cold in the afternoon and evening was so penetrating it had the excellent effect of taking my mind off my feet. Mike said I had hauled 'incredibly fast', which naturally made me feel both guilty and hypocritical.

In the night I woke to stabbing pains from one frostbitten toe. Mike was asleep so I tried to emulate his scalpel incisions with my penknife. That seemed the best way of relieving the pressure. A good deal of pus and tea-like liquid escaped but the pains continued, so I swallowed two painkillers and eventually slept. I woke a few minutes later, or so it seemed, with a head full of rats. Mike checked the infected foot after porridge and squeezed it successfully.

I realised now how lucky I had been for fifty years of experiencing comparatively little pain. Broken bones and teeth, torn-off digits, frostbite and chronic kidney stones had seemed unpleasant at the time. But now I knew *real* pain and I feared lest it overwhelm me, to my everlasting shame. I tried to think up ways of attacking it mentally on the basis that whenever there were lethal crevasses about, or when navigational worries were preoccupying my brain, the constant pain receded. The pain behaved like a circular railway track with a steam train chugging relentlessly around it . . . when it went through the tunnels it was still there but less noticeable. So I tried to invent tunnels, by day and by night, to programme my mind with vivid thoughts of past happenings. When this failed, especially after I slipped or caught my boot and triggered raw shrieks from one or other foot, I tried to imagine the pain as a living *thing*. Sometimes as a red-hot poker or an electric drill. At those times I would try to imagine I was part of the poker or the drill and I was working to stoke a fire or drill a gatepost. This would lead me to think of a myriad other 'jobs' that my pain could attack. I never won the fight with these tactics, but nor did I lose it.

Our current sorry state had largely been caused by the long weeks of calorie deficiency. As Mike put it, 'Our calorie *deficit* has been the equivalent of the total *input* of a normal person. It is exactly as though a normal person had eaten nothing, I repeat nothing, all this time. After several weeks they would get weak and desperately hungry. In fact they would starve. We *are* slowly starving.'

This, of course, was a godsend for Mike's research work. After sixty days of watching Mike divide our daily ration in two and hand me one vitamin tablet, four small-size milk chocolate bars, eight sheets of loo paper (inedible) and one crunchy flapjack, I began to nurse horrible suspicions that he was handing me the smaller of the flapjacks every day. This irked me as I grew more ravenous until, on the sixty-first day, I suggested that we take turns to choose the daily flapjacks. Mike agreed readily enough.

By Day Eighty, to my eternal disgrace, I found myself suspecting a less than mathematically precise division of the contents of the porridge pot each morning. When I could no longer bear the sight of Mike licking even the most innocently 'empty' cook's porridge spoon, I suggested that we take turns at scraping out any porridge remains. Mike again responded with good grace and I felt renewed shame at my greed.

On January 30 we recorded our first barometric descent of a few hundred feet, but this welcome news was balanced by a potentially disastrous event.

At noon Mike caught me up after a twenty-minute delay to announce that both his ski-sticks had somehow fallen off his sledge. He had already scanned his back-track but could see nothing. We could have wasted the rest of the day searching to no avail so I gave Mike one of my sticks and suggested we try to progress with one each.

Even on flat stretches we found it exceptionally difficult to progress with only half our previous thrusting power.

I could not help considering the irony that, all this time, we had thought life as about as bad as could possibly be and yet we had the luxury of *two* sticks. If only we had known how lucky we then were.

Working at only half-thrust, I began to freeze and was forced to step up the pace. Mike lagged far behind and, every time I stopped to await him, I became colder, until my body shook as though with the ague. I would have given anything for more clothes or even some newspaper, or straw, to stuff under my jacket and trousers. I considered cutting up the remaining polythene ration bags and stitching them to the inside of my jacket.

Our hauling was now ridiculously slow and especially painful for whichever foot corresponded with the stick-wielding arm. I moved slowly but, none the less, Mike dropped far behind and, waiting, I became so cold that my feet went numb. In something of a panic I could think of no answer but to stop early, which was taboo, or to encourage Mike's pace by giving him my remaining stick. This he accepted gratefully and he resumed a much steadier pace.

For thirty minutes we advanced through less than ideal wind chill conditions but Mike's speed gradually decreased to a crawl and his head began to loll with exhaustion. I spoke to him and his response was blurred. I grew frightened. He was clearly heading for hypothermia again. Some twenty-five minutes before stop time, I erected the tent and made hot tea which tasted exceptionally good.

Our bodily condition was becoming highly suspect. I was not in the business of leading suicide expeditions. We were approaching the edge of our ability to cope safely with very extreme conditions and this was, we both knew, because we were starving.

Mike wrote about the loss of his sticks:

We were both very cold today and I have further frostbitten my fingers. Three p.m. saw us hauling initially with one stick each. But then with me on two sticks and Ran with none (how he goes with none amazes me). Later, on opening up my sledge, I found devastation. The aerial of the Sarsat beacon was smashed despite being wrapped in my sleeping bag. The lid of our remaining Thermos is chipped and frozen soup is all over my bag. I was horrified and so, no doubt, was Ran although he has taken it remarkably philosophically despite real concern about the Sarsat. Much to my guilt, Ran says he can walk without sticks so my great concern there is much lessened (I am useless without arm power). My shoulder is painful but manageable.

The next day Mike began to work out a satisfactory way of forcing his sledge to move with just one stick and we carried on at a goodish rate in a lop-sided manner. Although the sun was visible for much of the day I constantly checked the compass for I knew we would need great accuracy to enter the Mill Glacier, the start of the long and lethal descent from the plateau down to the Pacific coast, by a relatively crevasse-free route. The slightest deviation could lead us into vast fissure fields, as bad as any in the world.

I was uncertain at what distance we would first glimpse the peaks of the Trans-Antarctic Mountains. Maybe twenty miles away or maybe only ten. On my map there were many small peaks with no names which dotted the region to our immediate south.

At last, at 11 a.m., I spotted a definite black peak directly ahead. We both shouted our delight and relief. An end at least to the many hundreds of miles of whiteness where evidence of progress could be measured only at the end of the day.

On seeing the mountain, I determined to take over all navigation down the glacier. I had no personal reason to trust or mistrust Mike's navigating abilities since, on all our previous journeys, I had been sole navigator apart from six days when I was partially blind. Until now, all our Antarctic navigation had consisted of following a simple compass bearing or keeping to a

Crevasse practice in London, 1992

Above: The author at the hand-over of 13,000 artefacts to Ali Ahmed Ali Mahash

Charlie Burton: Organiser and Originator of the 1992/93 Antarctic Crossing

Above: Dr Michael Stroud, the author's companion on five major polar expeditions

Above right: Laurence (Flo) Howell

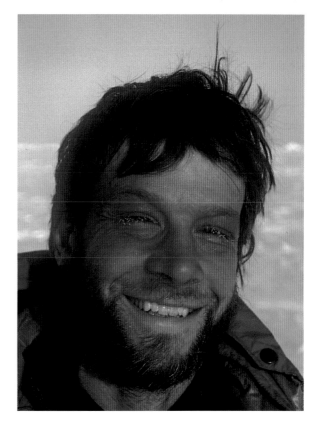

Right: Oliver Shepard: Organiser and Originator, with Charlie Burton, of the 1992/93 Antarctic Crossing

Left: Morag (Mo) Howell. She and Laurence (Flo) Howell are probably the most efficient and experienced polar communicators in the world. Mo was the Antarctic Base Leader and Flo manned the UK radio base during the 1992/93 crossing

Flight to the start of the Crossing Journey, November 1993

Above: The author and Doctor Stroud set out. Mike's sledge (at rear) was split in two within the week. Note crevasse shining on the skyline ahead

Right: The author manhauling beside the Berkour Island on a rare clear day

Below: Two fleas at the edge of a vast ice sheet

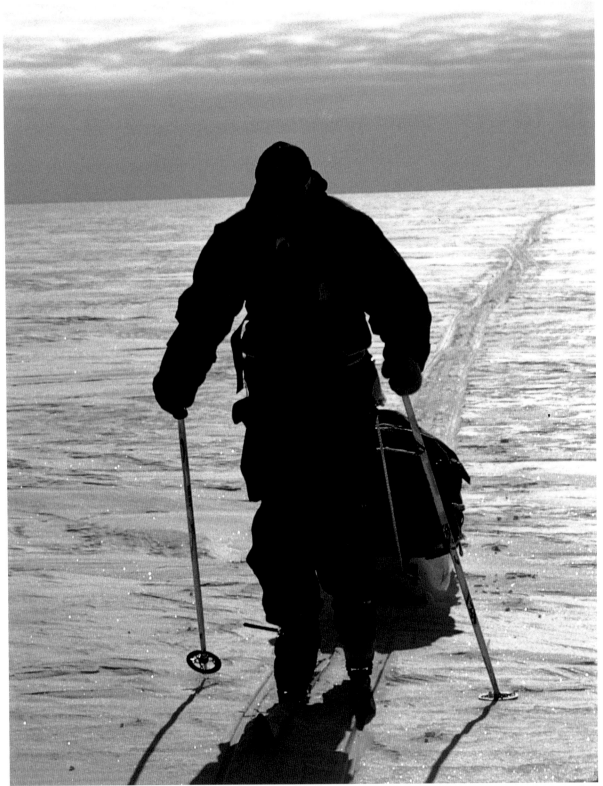

The time is local noon and the author is treading on his shadow as a means of navigating due south

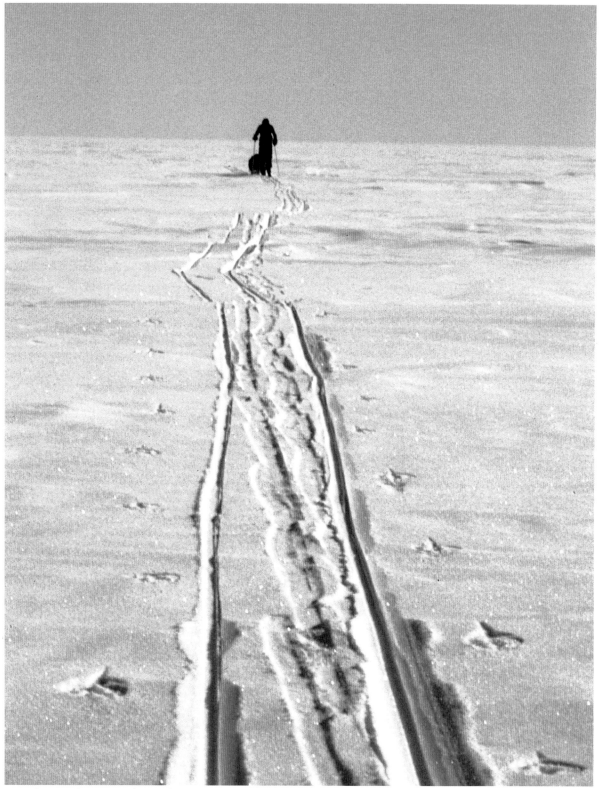

The gap between the author and Doctor Michael Stroud . . . the cause of much friction on every Antarctic manhaul expedition

The author feeling cold and exhausted in Antarctica

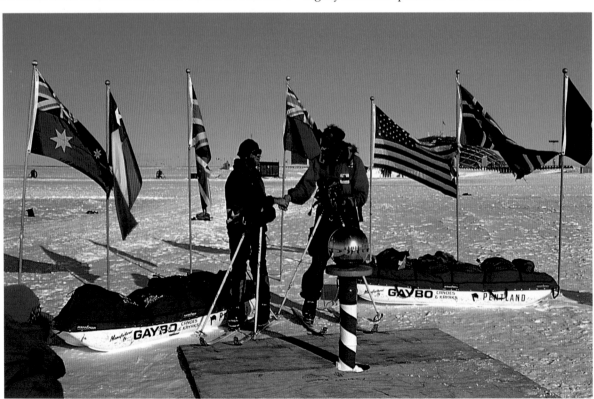

Eighty minutes' pause at the South Pole

This photograph of the author's chin was taken in 1990 in the Siberian Arctic. Exactly the same wound re-opened on this expedition

The author's left foot with frost damage soon after the South Pole was reached

One of the author's Transglobe team (Beverly Hoover) with toe-end frost damage; fairly common on manhaul journeys in extreme temperatures. Thankfully this problem wasn't encountered this time around

Above: Doctor Michael Stroud inspects a frost-damaged finger

Left: A collapsed and partially snowed-in crevasse on the Beardmore Glacier

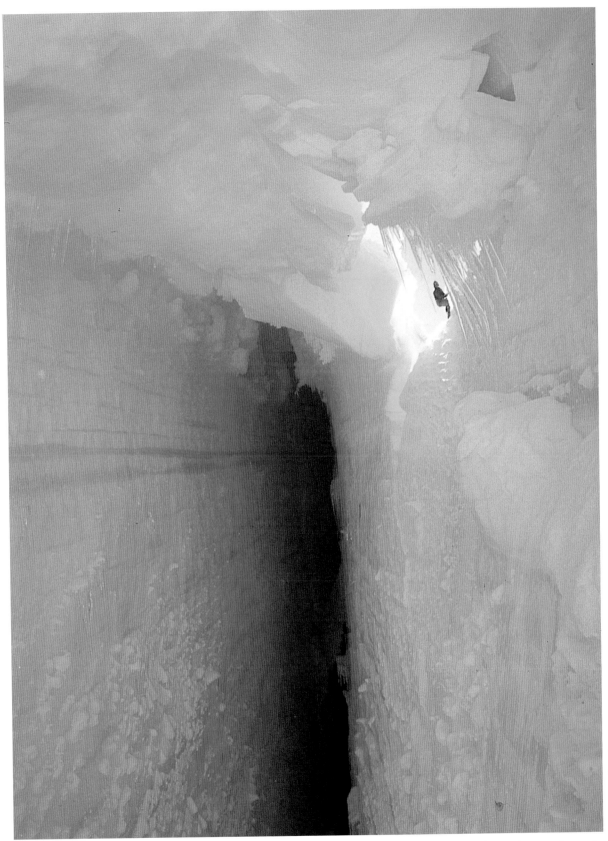

Crevasses often look harmless enough from a bird's eye view but a single step on a weak trap-door of snow can quickly lead to a long drop. This crevasse, with one climber just visible at its upper lip, was photographed by a British Antarctic Survey member some way down its interior

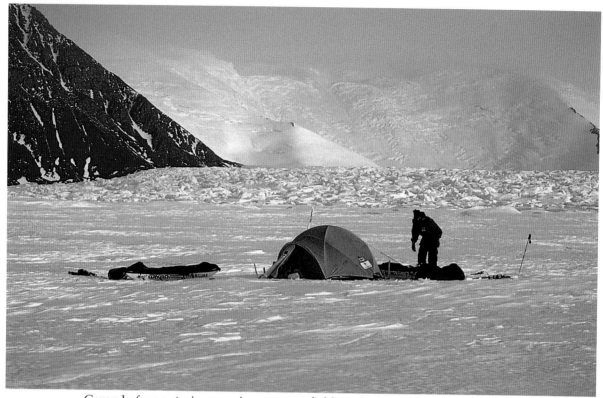

Camp before entering a major crevasse field on the Beardmore Glacier, 1993

Left: The author makes a ski stick from a spare ski during the descent of the Mill Glacier

Right: Chess on the cook-box with urine-sample vials

Above: Among the pressure waves and 180 foot deep fissures of the Wedge crevasse field

Right: The original cuddly penguin

Left: Baby seal (child of E.T.)

Below: A penguin rookery on the Atlantic coast of Antarctica

Right: On two of the polar journeys, the author lost up to eighty pounds through insufficient calorie intake and substantial exertion in a hostile environment

Below: Deep muscle biopsy without anaesthetics at the end of the Antarctic Crossing

The author, at fifteen stone, one week before leaving London for Antarctica (October 1992)

The author a week after returning to London from Antarctica (February 1993)

course dictated by the position of shadows, *sastrugi* or wind direction. From now on success would depend entirely upon selecting the correct tortuous pathway between the myriad man-killer crevasse fields of the second largest glacier on Earth.

I had total confidence in my navigating abilities and no confidence in anybody else's. I remembered a telling incident during a journey made by Mike, Roger Meare and a friend to re-enact Cherry-Garrard's 'worst journey in the world'. The leader was Meare but he had allowed too much democracy to creep into the process of navigating. He was soon to regret this because continued contradictory suggestions from Mike undermined his own vital self-confidence. He wrote:

> We were heading due east when Mike began to urge a more southerly course. In situations such as these decisions have to be made based on something more than correct evaluation of known facts. Much is conjecture . . . Mike was angry with me for, once again, he felt that his ideas had been treated with contempt. He had suggested, when the uncertainty of our position began to be felt, that we were heading in the wrong direction and it might be safer to turn east . . . It is impossible to be guided by reason in all one's decisions, and yet, because I had lost faith in Mike's judgement, I am forced to treat all my decisions as infallible.

Meare added: 'Indecision caused us to continue blindly on in what had become a howling gale.'

I wanted no such pressures on my instinctive navigation processes on this next, most hazardous and final stage of the continental crossing. On the other hand I did not wish to antagonise Mike, as Roger Meare apparently had, where I could avoid doing so. I could see I would have to be as tactful as was possible once we reached the mountains and I made my intentions clear.

I was alarmed that about to enter 200 miles of notorious icefall and great stretches of slippery blue-ice, we had no crampons between us and only two ski-sticks, both of which had recently lost their baskets and their pointed ends. That night, probably some ten miles still from the first rock features but already flanked by fearsome crevasse fields, I began to manufacture crampons to fit our four ski-boots. Using knotted lengths of our safety rope, our last repair wire and the pin-nose pliers, I put together some rough and ready crampons just before we reached the first blue-ice.

We were both a touch subdued. Grateful to be escaping, as we believed, from the unbearable cold of the high plateau, but apprehensive of the 9000-foot labyrinth below. This massive bastion, which effectively dams a mile-deep ocean of ice, is 2000 miles long and 200 miles wide. When the moving sea of inland ice, descending from the polar plateau, laps against the upper flanks of the range, even 6000-foot-high peaks seem vulnerable to the surging forces of ice which have drowned two-thirds of their rock mass. The scale of rock and ice is massive, the pent-up power of nature threatening, the jumble of gigantic tributary glaciers, contorted ice-falls and deep hidden valleys more grandiose than anywhere on earth.

Many thousands of great glaciers have forced a path through this range, tearing away mountainsides and burying anything and everything in their wake. Of all these glaciers the Beardmore is king, the second biggest glacier in the world and twice the size of Alaska's Malaspina which was the record-holder until Shackleton discovered and named the Beardmore in 1908.

Ice plays games in Antarctica where God has franchised all power to its whim. Ice is solid only to the eye, for its sinuous eddies are endlessly renewed, constantly revitalised. Mankind is trivial and of no concern to the ice. Unstoppable and unpredictable, sheering and truncating every solid thing that stands in its way, ice lays a thousand traps and snares for those who trespass in her southern playpen.

Mike and I needed to make *no* mistakes from now on. We were committed to the 9000-foot descent as in a rubber boat at the moment of yielding to the first pull of a great rapid. Around us the polar ice plunged silently over the rim of the Trans-Antarctic Range, to our immediate west sucked down into the Beardmore Valley and, dead ahead, into the maelstrom of the Mill Glacier's upper icefalls. We trod at our peril through God's most menacing minefield, a place shot through with fissured snares and hidden plunges.

My own intention was to use Charles Swithinbank's overall advice but to react flexibly to each new set of obstacles. Reinhold Messner had tried to follow Charles's suggested route but, despite his unparalleled experience in glacier icefalls, had soon become lost in a maze of huge interlocked crevasses.

For two hours we skidded and slid down the ice-clad slopes of Mount Ward until, a mile to the north of its peak, I came to an unbroken west–east wall of boulders deposited by centuries of glacial flow and forming a barrier between the Ward Ridge and the Davis Peaks, three miles to the north-west.

We spent less than an hour manhandling the sledges up and over this moraine. I watched the runners of Mike's sledge curve snake-like over rocks and ice ridges and marvelled at the workmanship of the designer of the sledge, which had now come over a thousand miles with its two broken segments attached only by two thin runners and a handful of screws.

I noticed that Mike was wearing his rope crampons and working well with them. I envied him his ability, even with blistered fingers, to handle ropes and lines. Even at home in summer I am cack-handed with knots; 'rope dyslexia' I call it. Either I donned my crampons in the tent first thing or it was best to forget them . . . The circulation in my hands is bad and always has been, so fixing rope crampons *al fresco* was not on my menu.

Once over the moraine I took a bearing to the left of the most northerly peak of Ward Ridge and we ascended a gentle snow slope for two hours right up to the rim of a fissure-field that fell away steeply to our front. I pitched the tent some twenty yards from the dip of the first crevasse.

After a memorably unpleasant night Mike and I followed an unnamed tributary that descended steeply into the crevasse-streaked maw of the Mill Glacier. The horizons which now opened to us in slow motion were awesome, a sprawling mass of rock and ice locked in suspended motion. These were the headwaters of a *moving* ice-river. Constrictions caused by 15,000-foot-high mountains had formed, and were even now renewing savage whirlpools and mighty maelstroms of cascading pressure-ice. Huge open chasms leered from distant foothills and standing ice-waves reared up at the base of black truncated cliffs.

I found this canvas full of power and wonder and thanked God for this moment of being alive. Nothing else lived here nor ever had since the dinosaurs of Gondwanaland. No birds nor beasts nor the least bacteria survived. Only the deep roar of massive avalanche, the shriek and grind of splitting rock, the groan of shifting ice, and the music, soft or fierce, of the winds from a thousand valleys, moved to and fro across the eternal silence.

Like Shackleton and Scott we were but temporal and irrelevant shadows against such a backdrop, our personal pains, hopes and grudges as petty as an eddy in the breeze.

I scanned the skies north and saw no clouds. So long as I could *see*, I could find the best route. I felt a God-given confidence and, for the first time on this journey, the warm pleasure of

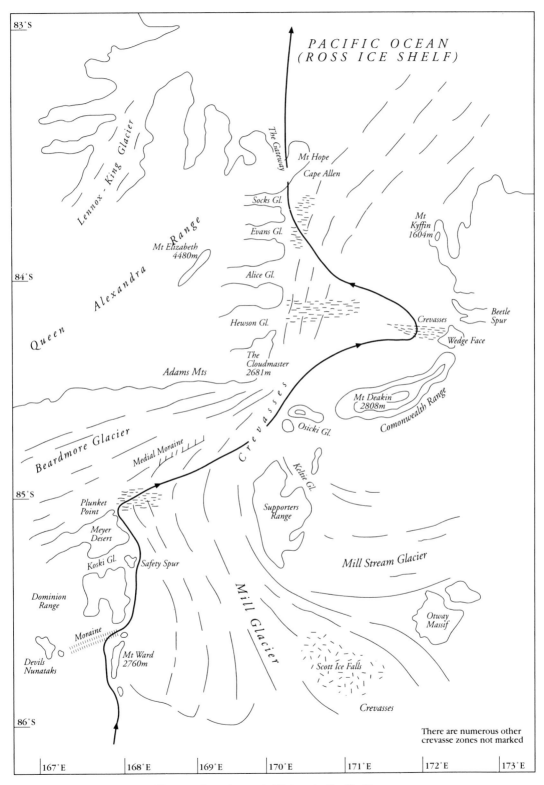

Descent from Antarctic Plateau to Pacific Ocean

331

challenge. I knew the rules. Never waste a minute. Pause for nothing. Here there could be no place for my polar plod. So long as the weather held we must go like the wind, for every hidden hole, every snow-covered snare, would double in danger once white-out closed down on the glaciers.

This was the region of the monster holes described by Cherry-Garrard as 'vast crevasses into which we could have dropped the *Terra Nova* with ease'. We crossed many great fissures by way of their sagging lids, our hearts beating fast, especially on these trapdoors where the danger of bridge-collapse was greatest. Our loads were still in excess of 200lbs and, at the end of the Antarctic summer, the bridges were at their most fragile, mere crumbling gangplanks spanning unseen voids. As we joined the mainstream of the Mill the great width of the ice-valley narrowed to only eleven miles between its cliff banks; this constriction had created wide regions of chaos to be avoided. The passageways between the disturbances were themselves far from idyllic. After five hours we reached descending blue-ice races where skis were useless. Without them, I once again faced the need for crampons, but cold fingers kept me from trying to fit them to my boots. Countless crevasses with narrow lips threaded the blue-ice.

The wind gathered strength through the afternoon. At forty knots the wind chill was probably in the −80°s. I could only keep my balance with one stick and bare boots by maintaining a lop-sided trot, concentrating, with each step, on avoiding the crust-snow traps every few feet between the blue-ice pans. There were many steep descents where our sledges took control and knocked us over and dragged us, teeth clenched, over fragile bridges. My feet and Mike's ankle complained bitterly.

Increasingly I found myself waiting for ten or fifteen minutes, with Mike a distant black spot, often blurred or wiped out by blown snow crystals. I do not remember *ever* feeling so deeply chilled. I stamped and slapped myself and swore viciously at Mike. To my left a second katabatic slammed down the face of the Vandament Glacier. I counted to a thousand again and again, all the while, jogging and slapping. I racked my mind for some ingenious way of keeping warm. As the travel hours passed by at a tortuously slow pace, I told Mike, when he finlly joined me beneath the great red cliff of Safety Spur, that I would not wait again as I was dangerously core-cold. I would *try* to find a place to camp off the blue-ice and out of the vicious wind. Mike nodded his agreement.

The wind roared against the cliffs in Force Eight strength and, donning my skis, I found it possible to body-sail over lakes of wind-scoured blue-ice. The wind struck my back with enough power to move me, sledge and all, with the blessed bonus of less boot action needed and a corresponding reduction in foot pain. My arms became numb with cold since they were no longer pumping with the rhythm of the ski-stick.

Antarctica is by far the coldest place on earth with still air temperatures of −88°C. In such temperatures mercury turns to solid metal, tin falls apart into granules, the flame of a candle becomes hooded by a wax helmet and a carelessly dropped steel bar is liable to shatter like broken glass.

I have met people who have been in Canada or Minnesota and laugh: 'Oh, I was working at −60°C last year. It was easy.' As like as not these polar veterans experienced their 'cold' wearing adequate clothing, with full stomachs, healthy and about to return to a nice warm bed.

For humans in Antarctica the danger is chiefly the wind. Each knot of wind has the effect on human skin of a drop of one degree in temperature. We, like Scott, found ourselves starving, freezing and in danger of falling into crevasses without hope of rescue. As I waited for Mike on a scoured ice sheet and the wind knifed through me, I found my body chattering beyond control with violent shivering seizures. The ever-nagging pain from my feet disappeared, at least from my awareness, with this utterly new experience which had not even accompanied previous Arctic soakings and the subsequent waiting, sodden, with clothes turning solid. At least my *core* resistance had on those occasions been in fighting form. We were now experiencing the coldest 'flesh' temperatures of the expedition. In the 48 hours we had dropped some 4000 feet in height but we were still at 6000 feet above sea level. This was the worst of conditions, for we battled now against altitude cold *and* katabatics fed by gravity from slopes above. As the elevation drops and air 'warms', gusting katabatics are wont to grow stronger. They have been known to reach 200 miles an hour. Tents are ripped into shreds by katabatic gusts, and I knew we must find a camp spot somehow protected from the full blast that polished this blue-ice canyon.

Rounding a bend in the cliff-walk I spotted, through the blowing snow, a sudden steep descent of several hundred feet. This was the confluence of the Koski Glacier with the Mill and liable to present too many dangers to attempt at the end of the day in such wind conditions.

I retraced my northward trail and headed straight for the rockface in the hope of finding some nook of protection for the night. Small rocks began to litter the ice floor and these increased in size until we were clambering between boulders, manoeuvring the sledges with care for they tended to jam.

Battered by katabatic blasts, but afforded some shelter by the boulders, we made camp working carefully together to avoid the tent being torn from our grasp as, with our near lifeless fingers, we tried to push the rods into the billowing cotton dome. With considerable relief we crawled into the tent. This was the first of our nights on half-rations. For some reason I remember it as the only night when I smelled a powerful aroma of stale body odour in the tent. Whether the stench was mine or Mike's I am unsure. We never washed in three months.

Mike's hands had gradually deteriorated since his mitt problems just before the Pole and now looked quite impressive, for three of the main finger blisters had burst, the dead skin falling away to reveal raw stumps like red sausages. He continued to handle our evening cooking and turned down my offer to help (my fingers were in good shape). What pained him most, it seemed, was the removal of his mitts for their wool sometimes stuck to the raw finger flesh.

Freezing winds blew all day but the steep descent past Koski Glacier proved no problem due to a patchwork of *névé* blotches which descended haphazardly to gentler slopes and which gave enough grip to prevent a headlong glissade.

With exceedingly painful feet from hours of trotting on ribbed blue-ice and falling into crust-covered holes, we came by noon to Plunket Point where the Mill joins the Beardmore and another breathtaking vista opens ahead. Here the Beardmore is more than thirty miles in width and pours down its valley in a cataract of spectacular chaos, a devil's cauldron with crevasses large enough to devour St Paul's Cathedral if Scott's men are to be believed.

The only other person to have *tried* to follow my intended route was Reinhold Messner who is unequalled in strength, skill and experience when it comes to dangerous ice work.

Within a few hours of leaving Plunket Point, Meissner and his colleague Fuchs began to lose the way. Messner wrote: 'The hardest and most dangerous day so far. For the most part we move between and over gigantic crevasses. We have to overcome an ice fall which looks like the upper part of the Khumbu Glacier on Mount Everest.'

Mike began to lag again and the colder I felt, the faster I needed to travel. I again gave him my remaining ski-stick but soon regretted this because we entered a region of successive pressure waves where progress became a near-impossibility with no sticks and no crampons.

Scott, in similar conditions, wrote: 'Blue ice showed on the crests of the waves; soft snow lay in the hollows. We had to cross the waves in places thirty feet from crest to hollow and we did it by sitting on the sledge and letting her go: then following a fearfully tough drag to the next summit.' Like Scott I lay on my sledge and rushed down the ice waves. The trouble was that, unlike Scott, I had no spiked boots nor pointed ski sticks with which to drag my sledge *up* the bare slopes and resorted to tearing at the tiniest ledges with my boot edges and mitts to gain some leverage. Often my sledge slid sideways and pulled me back down into the troughs. My knees were bruised and my language was bad but, at least for a while, I kept from freezing.

Mike wrote: 'Whole day on bare ice. Fell innumerable times. Couldn't keep up with cold Ran who finally gave me the second ski-stick. I *still* couldn't keep up but, although *he* thought we were going "unbelievably slowly" our distance belies this and in fact he was near trotting at times. High katabatic winds continue.'

When we had hauled for eleven hours I looked for snow on which to camp and eventually found a scrap of crusted *névé* no bigger than the area of the tent floor. We anchored the tent to the sledges since the metal pegs would not drive into the ice. Throughout the night the winds roared down the narrow furrow, where we slept between two curving waves. All around, as far as the eye could see, were pressure mounds and cracks. This was a bad place and worse lay ahead for the Keltie Glacier debouched into the Beardmore thirteen miles ahead of the tent. Knowing there were badly fractured ice-fields in every possible direction, I considered our safety rope, but I was cold and tired and said nothing. My hips were sore from falls and from the old harness wounds so I pulled from the shoulders only. Suddenly, a third of the way across the mouth of the Keltie Glacier, the many hundreds of lightly bridged crevasses that we had been crossing for two or three hours began to converge and to increase in size. To our left, and for at least twenty miles over a 180° front, there stretched a sea of havoc which I preferred not to contemplate.

The crevasses were for a while interrupted with a field of sharp *sastrugi*. Unable to cross these with my skis on I made the fatal error of unclipping and strapping them to my sledge. Mike was some 400 yards away and himself involved in tricky negotiations of crevasse bridges which I might well have weakened prior to his reaching them.

The very first crevasse bridge I attempted to cross without skis was a minor affair, no more than four feet wide and similar to hundreds we had safely traversed. My boot broke through close to its far wall and I dropped straight down as through a trap door. Because my harness waistband was unfastened the sledge ropes did not restrain me as they should have done, and my abrupt plunge into the dark shaft was halted only by the thin webbing strap of my ski-stick looped over my right wrist.

I dangled for a moment more surprised than frightened. The fear came as soon as I realised that only my ski-stick had saved me from certain death. The stick had wedged itself at an angle between one wall of the crevasse and a knob of crusty snow on the other. Any movement that dislodged the stick was liable to send me downwards for the unfastened harness was loosely draped about my neck.

The *feel* of the void below my feet brought instant panic and, throwing caution to the wind, I lunged upwards with my free hand and grasped the handle of the stick above my captive mitt. With my foot scrabbling against each smooth ice wall, I fought to loosen the wrist strap but my mitt was caught so I tore my bare hand free. With my arm strength quickly sapping, I lifted my body high enough to reach the crevasse lip with my mitted hand and then heaved my chest over to safety. For a minute I lay shaking with relief until, with horror, I realised that my stick and the mitt in its wrist loop were loose down the hole. There was no spare mitt. Fearing lest I knock the stick, I inched to one side until I could squint downwards. My breath rushed out in a sigh of relief as I spotted the ski-stick now loosely lodged some four feet down the hole. Using my boots as grabs, I thankfully retrieved both the stick and the vital mitt.

Mike arrived and his eyebrows rose as he saw where I had been. We agreed to fix up a safety rope between is since the region was clearly lethal.

With extreme care we edged our way through a formidable crevasse field. Whenever I moved too fast, Mike shouted so that he could keep our rope manoeuvrable but taut between us. My route was tortuous and very unsafe. We both broke through on many occasions and the rope often enough spanned two separate gaping holes at different points along the zig-zag trail between us. Had there been *any* way of avoiding such a nightmare route, we would have taken it.

By good fortune we had found the very narrowest point of the upheavals where the Keltie meets the Mill, and, some two hours after entering the disturbances, the crevasses began to separate into individual features which could be more easily circumnavigated. As we reached the first unbroken flow band, deep soft snow layers covered every trap and we breathed again.

The next day, once the heights of Mount Deakin were behind my right shoulder, I set 210° on the compass and headed out towards the central fields of the Beardmore. We camped at the mouth of the central crevasse field, relieved to be free of the stomach-gripping dread that is never far away when one is tip-toeing over such masked holes of death.

Next day, we passed between the snow-capped leviathans of the Commonwealth Range and the giddy walls of the Queen Alexandra massif. The 8000-foot-high ramparts of the Cloudmaker were, usually, clear of mist, and for three blessed hours I felt merely chilled instead of unutterably cold. To our immediate west lay an area through which some of Scott's men 'tumbled into the horrible pressure about the Cloudmaker'.

Some three miles south of Mount Patrick, in the teeth of a bitter Force Eight windstorm, I took a bearing some 20° west of Wedge Face buttress. At first the wind-blown ice-fields ahead, dark and forbidding in the shadow of Wedge Face, were simple enough. At this point of Reinhold Messner's descent he wrote: 'We go two miles to get one mile north. From above we have no view of the route. We try to reach the middle of the Beardmore by crossing side-streams. We go three hours with crampons on bare ice and come to a widely shattered ice-fall marked on no map. We get stuck. We go back. In part the crevasses are so big one could put a church inside.' I knew we should soon be stopping, having travelled for over nine hours, but fear of imminent bad weather forced me to continue in the desire to camp where I could see beyond the Wedge Face to the fjord mouth below.

The wind was spinning spray from distant peaks and lifting snow. The sun played about with the mountain shadows and I gasped as I saw, or thought I saw, the ravaged face of the land ahead. For a moment I considered turning back and starting a wide ten-mile loop, perhaps more, to circumvent the pock-marked ice cauldron to our front. Tiredness or idleness overcame common sense and, with Mike twenty minutes or more behind and my body shaking with cold, I hunched my shoulders and promised myself we would rope up if things became really bad. Too late, apprehensions turned to the realisation that I had made a mistake.

Mike said of the place that we now entered: 'The crevasses were huge and the combination of icy surfaces, slopes and changes of direction totally knackered me.'

Such turbulent confusion is difficult to convey. To plot any route through its midst or indeed to fix upon any less convulsed region as a goal of safety was impossible. In such conditions you can turn back or rush on. I looked back at Mike who seemed to be progressing well, and, strapping my skis to the sledge, slid twenty feet down a narrow ramp between two ninety-foot-deep sink-holes. They might have been deeper.

My hands were numb, incapable of donning my rope crampons. I hoped that Mike would be able to affix his own. Towering walls of grey ice loomed above and around me. For some while I could not work out my intended direction for my tracks were invisible and high ridges encompassed me on every side.

Of these conditions Cherry-Garrard wrote: 'I cannot describe the maze we got into and the hair breadth escapes we have had to pass through today. Fathomless pits fell away on each side too numerous to think of. Often and often we saw openings where it was possible to drop in the biggest ship afloat and lose her.' So it was with Mike and me on our eighty-eighth day but, unlike Cherry-Garrard, we had no crampons nor pointed sticks to help grip the ice as we crept along slanting, slippery crater rims and knife-end ridges between deep, dark craters.

Mike was especially at risk since, although I had lost more weight than he, he was still the lighter of the two and so more prone to succumb to the nerve-racking behaviour of our sledges. At moments when, with dizzy drops on both sides and virtually no traction, we traversed slanting gangplanks, our sledges would sometimes slip sickeningly sideways, and their weight, heavier than our own bodyweight, would try to tear us from our precarious foothold.

In one way I was thankful that Mike was far behind and could not hear my gasps of terror as I fought to keep my balance and struggled, veins bulging, to fight the pull of my sledge down to some waiting maw. But then I feared that, where hard ice hid my tracks, Mike might take a wrong turning through the maze. Then we would be in serious trouble. I began to beckon him on. My chief dread was being caught in this awful place in a white-out. The whole breadth of this Wedge Face crevasse-field stretched over many miles and, after an hour within the maze of its fractures, I climbed an ice hillock which at last gave me a glimpse of the far side. For another mile, if we could only continue to avoid cul-de-sacs, there was a steeply descending shoulder to the north-west, riven with fissures but leading to gentler slopes and, eventually, the edge of the troubled zone. During the last hour I often found it necessary to descend slopes which I knew we would not be able to renegotiate should my route lead to a dead end. That this never happened was due to exceptionally good fortune, for a more corkscrew, zig-zag rabbit warren of a journey would be hard to devise. Mike kept lagging way behind and, partly to keep warm, partly to speed him up, I gesticulated with both arms. I suspect this had little effect but to annoy him.

When at last we emerged from that perilous place, we had travelled non-stop for twelve hours and I pitched the tent on a patch of snow crust amidst a spider's web of narrow ice crevasses.

Next day the glacier and the weather both relented.

A wondrous fairyland floated, inch by inch, past our goggles. Progress was not apparent for the panorama was simply too huge. The 13,000-foot-high snow queen, Mount Elizabeth, reigned with majestic serenity to the west, wreathed in ever-changing veils of cloud whilst, to the north-east, the soaring red cliffs of Mount Kyffin marked the very edge of the Antarctic Continent. Mike recorded: 'Only two days from crossing the continent, an amazing thought.'

At this point we had travelled hundreds of miles further than any of our unsupported predecessors, including Scott's men. But we were sorely debilitated. Mike was hovering, as is evidenced by his own diary, on the edge of a dangerous hypoglycaemic state. We had both lost nigh on one-third of our body weight and were already in a state of extreme vulnerability to the cold. Nothing, I felt, could now stop us reaching the very edge of the continent, but beyond that point our chances of reaching the Seaquest ship were, to put it mildly, remote. I decided to think no further than the coastline some forty miles ahead.

We camped some distance short of Mount Kyffin and, on our ninetieth day, heavy cloud banks warned of possible weather change. I feared the onset of the white-out conditions and storms for which the snout area of the Trans-Antarctic glaciers are well known. Our immediate vicinity was one where good visibility was vital. Wild described it as 'an awful place exactly like a rough sea in appearance but in every hollow there was a crevasse. The strain on one's nerves was greater than on the muscles.'

Once we had rounded the Granite Pillars, so named by Shackleton, we passed through a number of small crevasse fields in misty conditions. I tried to steer east of these obstacles without much success but all minor troubles were forgotten as we entered the pass which separated the island of Mount Hope on our right from the mainland's foothills to the west. This three-mile passageway, the Gateway, involves a steep climb to the summit of a giant snowdrift several hundred feet high.

With many halts for Mike, anxious when he failed to appear over the summit of the Gateway's col lest he had gone down a crevasse, I at length reached a steep slope some 500 feet above the edge of the Ross Ice-Shelf and pitched the tent in a rising wind.

Mike's diary: 'I felt pretty rough for the first half of the day despite eating all my chocolate early on. We had our soup stop half an hour early because I had big cramps and felt rough – and that is after only six days on half-rations. But, if not elated now, after a very long twelve-hour day, I certainly recognise that we have achieved something very special.'

We took stock of our rations and fuel. Ten days. The blizzard season was imminent during which a single storm can prevent all travel, on foot or by air, for two or even three weeks without a break.

I took two painkillers from our dwindling supply and tried to sleep. However uncertain the future, we were within half a mile of walking over the highest, coldest, most inhospitable continent on Earth from Atlantic to Pacific.

This was our last and ninetieth camp on the Antarctic continent. Should we try to continue on over the shelf? How much further did we stand a chance of surviving? Since all our main aims were now achieved, the only practical rationale for continuing must be to reach the ship before its departure in eight days' time. Three hundred and sixty miles in eight days meant 45 miles daily, probably impossible.

I said nothing to Mike since I was increasingly aware of his mental struggles. Half the time he spent in black moods looking as though he wished to accept the continental edge as our final target but then, mercurial as ever, his mood would change and he would swing the other way. His thoughts and his motives were complex and contradictory. It seemed to me that he feared that I would secretly seek to blame him for any decision to abort, *whenever* such a decision might occur.

This placed him in the highly awkward position of needing to continually demonstrate his strength and not give in to a deteriorated state which, in other circumstances, he would quickly have identified as potentially lethal. I felt he needed *somebody else* to make the decision to abort and, further, to do so for reasons unconnected to his own vulnerable state. Should anything happen to Mike at this stage I would, as leader, be held responsible. The question would then be asked: Why had I risked further travel after it was blatantly pointless from most aspects?

I did a good deal of tossing and turning and eventually concluded that, even if I *should* be calling for evacuation right now, we would still need to traverse the turbulent ice to our immediate front in order to find a safe place for the ANI ski-plane to land. Nine days of food remained. Without wind help and on half-rations it might be possible to reach the science base at the far edge of the ice-shelf but *not* in time to catch the ship. Such a journey lacked the clearly delineated goals which had driven me and probably Mike as far as the edge of the continent.

After a bad start caused by a cooker fire, we set out in a semi-white-out, not ideal conditions to thread our way through the complex labyrinth of fissures around the glacial shear-zone. I used the compass and chart with great care but Mike twice spotted deep crevasses narrowly avoided. We zig-zagged through the gloom along three distinct bearings, switching from one to the other at set times. After three hours the worst of the ridges and rifts fell away until, some five miles out from the Gateway, we came to a deep trench that stretched away to west and east as far as the eye could see.

After four hours of concentrated travel we cleared the last obstacle. From now on the ice-shelf should be free of obstacles and as flat as the Filchner.

With the going flat and easy, I reverted thankfully to the polar plod for the first time in almost two weeks and noticed with relief that Mike also seemed to be 'plodding'. This was a pleasant surprise for any flat going normally saw him hauling as hard as he could. But now he slowed down until, some five hours into the day, he came to a complete halt with his head drooping forwards.

Recognising the signs of imminent hypothermia I grew fearful and erected the tent immediately, for there was no wind. Mike's lisping attempts to talk were inaudible. He sat listlessly on his sledge and I asked him in a loud voice to collect snow for tea. He hit the plastic shovel against one of his fingers and whimpered with pain. As I waited for the tea to boil, the foolishness of continuing to travel in so vulnerable a state and for so fragile a purpose was rammed home by Mike's collapse after only five hours of travel in comparatively friendly conditions. I determined to take the sensible decision as soon as I could without upsetting Mike's sensitivities. Many a time after past expeditions he had told me how much he had regretted my decisions to abort. Mike had always worried lest it should be thought that I had based my thinking on *his* state of health. I knew that now, more than ever before, any decision to abort, however sensible and responsible, would be anathema to him.

Yet, I had grown daily more worried that I would be powerless to help should his obvious susceptibility to hypoglycaemia take him 'over the edge'. I remembered five or six occasions when I had guided Mike into the tent just in time. A person with hypothermia can die quickly even during a weekend hike in wet weather. For someone semi-starved and debilitated, the dangers are great.

I was in a no-win situation. Either I told Mike we *must* abort before he died – in which case he would never forgive me for terminating due to his fallibility, for making him look weak – or I kept going with the ever-present danger that, the next time he fell hypothermic, I might be navigating and fail to notice his absence until too late.

I wondered to myself which his wife and children would prefer, a bold Mike who had never 'given in' until it was too late, or a live one who had swallowed his pride and known when enough was enough. That night, even as Mike wrote in his diary, 'Ran is considerably supportive,' his worry that he must not be the one to 'yield' made him add: 'But nice for him.'

Since I did not know what Mike was writing in his diary until after the end of the expedition, I could not at the time be sure how weak he was feeling. If I had known then what he wrote that night, I believe I would have overruled his request for 'one more chance' and taken the responsible course to abort no matter how much he would undoubtedly have damned me thereafter.

He wrote:

A very black day. Debilitation seems to be knocking me down and there's nothing I can do about it. I only lasted five hours before I went gaga in my head and had severe cramps in both legs. I was cold but I don't know how much was hypothermia and how much hypoglycaemia. The cramps are probably a lack of some food for the muscles. It's just like Siberia. Anyway, tent up, tea and chocolate and I was much better.

Since then there has been the talking. Ran sees me as chronically deteriorated with no hope of recovery and he's almost certainly right. He would therefore think it best to radio for the aircraft now.

I, however, have great difficulties in being 'the cause for failure' although I do feel what we have already done is beyond expectations. I, therefore, have determined to try again tomorrow although I already know that, if it gets too tough, I have a 'let-out' that he will accept and so I am concerned about the psychological aspects of forcing myself on. Anyway we shall see . . . I dread turning round and counselling the end (although I would also love it!).

My diary:

Mike says my sledge is now eight pounds heavier than his. It makes no difference to the drag of the thing. He feels it is *very* cold. I agree. But we both know it's really our dwindling lack of resistance. I fear for him if we continue. When he 'goes', it's with little or no warning and I will be blamed, perhaps rightly, by his family if he 'goes' once too often. He accepts that my 'conserve energy' policy has now paid off for me. He is always exhausted but he *cannot* see that it is largely due to his totally unnecessary pushing himself on the flat stretches.

Starving and inadequately clothed, we are feeling the cold horribly. We must push ourselves when the cold *forces* us to, but otherwise we should keep to the most non-taxing form of progress possible to conserve every calorie.

In his phobic desire to outdistance me, even by a few hundred yards, he has convinced himself that any complaint from me is selfishly motivated and not for his own good. We human beings are pretty weird when you think about it.

On the ninety-second day, clear of the crevasses, we hauled for ten and a half hours on flat soft snow. The wind, so vital to our chances of catching the ship, stayed away and far from making the necessary forty-five miles per day we just managed thirteen.

Mike wrote: 'Three months today with no re-supply! Quite a feat by any standards.'

On 12 February, our ninety-fifth day of travel, the last US aeroplane left Antarctica to escape the imminent winter blizzards. In five days' time, at 7 a.m., precisely, our ship would steam out of the Ross Sea. We were still 289 nautical miles from Ross Island. The time for procrastination was over. Now we would need to achieve fifty-eight miles each day for the next five days to catch the ship. We were struggling to manage even twelve miles daily; there was no point in continuing up a cul-de-sac.

At 1 p.m., I made up my mind to delay no longer and turned to tell Mike we must erect the tent to discuss calling it a day. I dithered and explained my halt as merely to suggest curtailing the travel days from now on to combat the alarmingly decreased resistance to the cold that we both acknowledged. I immediately cursed myself for giving in to procrastination and, two hours later, I finally crunched the bullet. We put up the tent having hauled some forty-one miles since crossing the Pacific coastline.

Within fifteen minutes, we had agreed that the realistic course was to call a halt. Our key hope was that the ANI ski-plane reached us before a long period of bad weather arrived on the ice-shelf. Our satellite transmitter was irreparable so I laid HF antenna wires on the ice and made contact with ANI. I was fortunate since, given bad solar conditions, several days might have passed without communications.

Mike told me he had found himself falling asleep that morning simply standing beside his sledge and, despite feeling so cold, it was 'like having no clothes at all'. In his diary he wrote: 'Every day begins, continues and ends in pain.' He was delighted and relieved that *he* had not made the decision to stop even though he agreed with it. 'The decision,' he wrote, 'is only hours old and already I feel regrets. I hope I can live happily with this achievement. It's too late to change now. At least Ran precipitated it . . . I want to get out very quickly to family . . . When the wind blew it was as if we were naked . . . However hard we worked the cold gnawed at the bone, and hands and feet cried out for release.'

The weather held and the Twin Otter ski-plane which had dropped us off three months before on the Atlantic coast now picked us up from the ice forty miles 'out to sea' on the Pacific ice. Only when back in the diesel-fumed warmth of 'civilisation', the little aircraft's narrow fuselage, did our bodies begin to show the full state of their debilitation. Within hours our legs became horribly swollen as with dropsy, we felt sick, giddy and disorientated and concentrated effort was required even to rise from the lying position. Neither of us could focus our vision.

Most fatal climbing accidents happen during the descent of the mountain. Our highest mountain peak had been the moment of crossing the continent. Our resolve had long been focused on the Gateway. Once we reached the ice-shelf, I should have delayed no longer but, then and there, called a halt to our undertaking and remembered Shackleton . . .

Within an ace of reaching the South Pole but aware each further mile would overstretch his eventual chances of survival, Shackleton had not wavered but turned around to head back for the Ross Sea. Whether or not his team were grateful to him, he saved their lives. When his wife asked him how he had found the strength of mind to turn back (an act described by Roland Huntford as 'one of the bravest acts of polar exploration') Shackleton had replied, 'I thought you would rather have a live donkey than a dead lion.'

Whether or not London Insurers would pay for the ANI costs of retrieving us would depend on their definition of our state of health when found. Mike's medical summary included, along with details of various wounds, a description of my feet as 'toes infected and ulcerated due to frostbite with large areas of devitalised tissue' and 'eroding ulcer on right foot, present for seventy days but increasing in severity since supplies of appropriate antibiotics finished'.

He described his own debilitation: 'Rapidly increasing vulnerability to cold demonstrated by an episode of hypothermia two days prior to pick up. Additionally, episodes of mild hypoglycaemia, due to starvation and high levels of exercise, are increasing in frequency and severity and posing the probability of a very dangerous situation.'

We will never know how much further we could have continued because there are too many ifs and buts. If, like Scott, we had no option but to battle on, it is my opinion that we would have died short of Ross Island.

Scott's modern detractors make much of his 'narrow-minded stupidity' in championing manhaul travel over the use of dog teams. Amundsen's colleague Hanssen is often quoted as concluding: 'What shall one say of Scott and his companions who were their own sledge dogs? . . . I don't think anyone will ever copy him.'

All attempts for a century, whether by Norwegians, Soviets or Americans, to cross the continent unaided and using snow-machines, or dog teams, had failed miserably. In hauling our own loads across this area, greater in mass by far than the United States, we have shown that manpower can indeed be superior to dog-power and, in doing so, have partly exonerated Scott's much-abused theories on the matter.

The 1993 *Guinness Book of Records* now states: 'The longest totally self-supporting polar sledge journey ever made and the first totally unsupported crossing of the Antarctic landmass were achieved by R. Fiennes and M. Stroud. They covered a distance of 2170 km (1350 miles).'

Back in Punta Arenas a week later, I joined Mike and Morag buying Chilean trinkets for our families. I reflected that it would be difficult to find two better people, one a doctor, the other an engineer. Both are very 'normal'. Cherry-Garrard wrote of Scott's team: 'If you are a brave man you will do nothing: if you are fearful you may do much, for none but cowards have need to prove their bravery. Some will tell you that you are mad, and nearly all will say, "What is the use?" For we are a nation of shopkeepers. And so you will sledge nearly alone, but those with whom you sledge will not be shopkeepers.'

What are we then, those of us who like to dangle in the void and test the cutting edge of our ability? Are we eccentric? I think not, for I am always put off by individuals showing signs of abnormality. Nine out of ten of all those I have selected, for twenty-five years of expeditions, have been conventional people with everyday jobs and families. I seldom look for people with particular skills. The ideal criteria are level-headedness, patience and, above all, good nature towards fellow human beings. Under stress these characteristics will be sorely tested whether the strain comes during a polar expedition, a marriage undergoing a difficult period or a business challenge.

As far as determination is concerned, any human being, however meek and unambitious they may think themselves, can develop and nurture a single-minded desire to fulfil a particular goal. Mike and I *had* been determined but we had also been lucky. The frozen continent that we crossed is, after all, ruled by the untamed might of Nature. A single storm could have wiped us out, but Antarctica suffered our passing as a giant that allows a fly to crawl across his face.

When we returned home from Antarctica in 1993, Morag, Laurence, Mike and I were invited to 10 Downing Street to chat with the Prime Minister who congratulated us, as did our Patron, the Prince of Wales, at Kensington Palace. Mike and I were awarded OBEs and I was sent some 4000 letters by members of the public. One of these enclosed a news cutting which read:

It is one of the symptoms of this age of nerves and hysteria that we magnify everything, that our boasts are frantic and our scares pitiable, that we call a man who plays well at football a hero and that all successes are triumphs. Just now, when we are feeling a little downhearted at seeing our supremacy in sport and in more serious matters slipping away from us, it is a moral tonic to find that in exploration we are still the kings of the world.

This was a cutting from the *Sketch* newspaper following Shackleton's return from Antarctica in June 1909.

Plus ça change . . .

There were also the usual carping columnists in 1993: Anne Robinson in the *Mirror* – 'That tiresome and unnecessary trek across Antarctica nearly cost them their lives'; and Margaret Maxwell of the *Independent* on 'how pointless it all was'. Few people bother to counter-attack columnists unless they feel very strongly. Several letters bounced back this time, including from the leader of the first ascent of Mount Everest:

> In these depressing times, I derived some comfort from the rejoinders to Margaret Maxwell's denigration of the trans-polar journey. It ill becomes Ms Maxwell to question the motives underlying this astonishing feat of human endurance and courage which was also concerned for people who suffer from a particularly sad and intractable illness. Surely at a time when, as never before, we need to develop these qualities in the young generation, this story should be accepted at its face value, as a shining example to Britain's youth.

Various letters flurried between the polar pundits as to precisely what had been the previous record. Dr Geoffrey Hattersley-Smith, a great polar traveller of the 1950s, wrote: 'Shackleton's party, without support, covered a distance of 1215 statute miles. They picked up depots laid by themselves on the outward leg of the same march. It is this record that they have broken. All honour belongs to both Sir Ernest's and Sir Ranulph's parties, men of different eras whose achievements approached the limits of endurance. Comparisons are superfluous if not impossible to make.'

When Messner returned to Europe from his supported crossing of Antarctica he received heavy criticism. This he summarised as coming from

> citizens who were indirectly angry with themselves when they saw one person living out his dreams to the ultimate. But I understood better the criticism of my neighbours who considered my activities irresponsible. That somebody should think it right to evade his middle-class responsibilities was an affront to their morality. That I, despite my family commitments, for months escaped from day-to-day pressures, in order to follow my private ambitions, was for them not justifiable.

When Reinhold Messner, the world's greatest mountaineer, and Arved Fuchs, Germany's top polar traveller, completed their journey they were reasonbly friendly, but things changed once they returned to the civilised world and the temptations of the media. Messner wrote:

> With a single news article, and through no fault of ours, a quarrel broke out which would for ever affect relations between us. Once he had let himself appear the quiet hero of this quarrel provoked by others, Arved suppressed the facts more and more. It pleased him to play the role of the oppressed . . . I had made the speed and track in order to save the expedition. Now, suddenly, all that had been Arved's tactics.
>
> Was I supposed to be the 'fall guy' twice? First used, then slandered? Was Fuchs so sly? The quarrel with him made me ill and sleepless. I was hurt and as after a broken love affair. The breach of trust gave me so much pain at first that I needed a long time to recover.
>
> This argument was not the first with my touring partners. Time and again I had been publicly slandered by 'comrades', always *after* the relevant expedition, always only *after* a great

success. Thus one or other managed to come out from under 'my shadow' on the title page of magazines or daily papers.

The *Stern* utilised the 'media lust' of some of my 'quiet, oppressed' climbing partners shamelessly, in order to concoct a story out of falsehoods, half-truths and distortions, which I was able to expose as deliberate character assassinations. Nevertheless some of it stuck with the readers, above all because Fuchs knew how to disguise the facts.

For eighteen years of polar expeditions mostly with Charlie Burton and Oliver Shepard, we had survived exactly the same post-expedition strains that Messner listed. Both Ollie and Charlie were loyal and honourable men. They had their grudges, as I did, but they kept them to themselves and we have remained the most solid of friends as a result and despite constant rumours to the contrary.

After their 1985 South Pole journey, Meare and Swan erected a screen over the intense antagonisms between themselves. 'It was part of the rules,' Meare wrote, 'that an outward pretence of cohesion be maintained.' In their joint book they were open and honest about one another's failings and their relationship did not degenerate into a mud-slinging match that would ruin whatever mutual feelings of respect had withstood the journey itself. Sensible partners in marriage or business do likewise.

The Director of the Scott Polar Research Institute, Dr John Heap, told me that he considered that Mike and I were 'a marriage made in heaven, with your initiative and drive and Mike's scientific ability'. After our return, Mike's sister, Debbie, told a reporter: 'When I heard that Mike nearly died through hypothermia, I didn't know whether to run up to Ran and hug him for saving my brother or whether to shout at him for putting him in that danger in the first place.' Mike told the press that we had got on 'extraordinarily well' together and, when asked if he would consider another expedition with me, replied: 'I can think of nobody I would rather do these things with.' My own responses had been on similar lines when asked about Mike and Morag.

Five peaceful months after our return from Antarctica, a tabloid reporter produced a full-page article which claimed to be based on Mike's writings, which began: 'The smiles and mutual backslapping that marked the return of Fiennes and Stroud from their record-breaking Antarctic expedition was a sham and their ninety-five-day trek was peppered with bitter arguments.'

Mike phoned me the very evening that the article appeared, apologised profusely and explained that he was furious with the newspaper which had completely misquoted him. So no harm was done between us. He wrote back to the newspaper to say:

> I have been bitterly hurt by the allegations that the smiles and handshakes on our return were a sham. It is not true – worse, it is unadulterated rubbish. I feel so bad about what was printed, I had to apologise. Despite difficulties and immense hardships, we came back smiling and acting like friends, because that is what we are. There were some arguments on the expedition – but that is hardly surprising when you have just one man's company for so long. They were not frequent, they were not bitter and they did not spoil our relationship. We have since hinted at another expedition together, and personally, I hope we are able to do so.

On return from Antarctica I began work to form an agency to export UK-made goods to the Far East in partnership with one of Ginnie's brothers. This is based from an office built on top of our generator shed at home on Exmoor.

Ginnie's Aberdeen Angus herd slowly expanded in the early 1990s. She is out in all weathers looking after her beloved cows each of which has a name (not a good sign, to my mind, in terms of future beef sales). Ginnie also breeds wildfowl and looks after our Arctic dogs, the descendants of Blackdog of Tuktoyuktuk who, like Bothie, died peacefully of old age after many adventures and much disgraceful behaviour.

Fifty seems to me to be a good age to switch from physically demanding projects to a more sedentary, if not sedate, existence but I remember thinking along similar lines when I was forty and that came to nothing.

Only last week Charlie Burton called with ambitious polar plans for 1995 and he is a difficult person to say no to.

APPENDIX 1
The Fiennes Family

I believe we are each very much congenital victims or beneficiaries. Of course there are twists of fate whereby the occasional housepainter's bastard becomes a Führer or a grocer's daughter an Iron Lady, but in the main we run life's course the way we do because of our hereditary make-up. We are each the sum total of a chain of ghostly sires, generation upon generation of evolving characters, of actions good or evil, the vibrations of which pass silently on, foetus to foetus, until there is you and there is me.

On the pages that follow is a family tree of my ancestors. They have owned land in southern England since the days of an Ingelram Fiennes who lived around AD 1100. His family became anglicised and have lived here continuously since 1260. Earlier they were based in the village of Fiennes, which lies between Calais and Boulogne in France.

There are, of course, many members of the family, dead and still alive, not included on this simplified family tree.

KING CHARLES the GREAT
AD 800
(EMPEROR CHARLEMAGNE)

His daughter, BERTHE

The Dukes of PONTHIEU

EUSTACHE FIENNES
Fought for the Normans at Battle of Hastings, 1066, but other Fiennes family members fought on the English side. Eustache was given English land by William the Conqueror. His brother-in-law founded Beaulieu Abbey.

INGELRAM FIENNES
married SYBIL de TINGRIES, heiress to the Dukes of Ponthieu. Through Sybil's dowry, the Fiennes family inherited English manors at Martock, Wendover and Carshalton, all of which they lost in the Hundred Years' War. Ingelram was killed at the Battle of Acre in 1189, as was his cousin Tougebrand Fiennes, close companion to King Richard Coeur de Lion. Another cousin killed in the Crusades, John Fiennes, donated his heart to the citizens of London along with a burial plot, still known as Finsbury Square.

ENGUERRAND FIENNES
Married the daughter of King Alexander of Scotland. Enguerrand, Lord of the Fiennes clan in Artois, was responsible for the Wars of the Roses since his direct descendants included the main protagonists, Edward IV, Richard III, Henry IV and Henry V, Henry Stafford, Duke of Buckingham.

ENGUERRAND FIENNES
Married Isobel, daughter of King Edward III.

WILLIAM DE SAYE I
(died 1144)
Moved from Saye, Normandy, to England. Fought with the Earl of Essex against King Stephen. Killed at Burwell.

WILLIAM DE SAYE II
(died 1177)
Captured seven knights single-handed at the Battle of Saintes. At the Battle of Lewes, he fought with King Henry III against the barons.

His brother,
GEOFFREY DE SAYE I
(died 1214)
Helped ransom King Richard I from the Germans. He was one of the twenty-five barons to sign Magna Carta.

GEOFFREY DE SAYE III
(died 1321)
Fought for King Edward II vs. the Scots and the Earl of Lancaster. In 1318 he was jailed for consorting with the outlaw Robert Coleman.

GEOFFREY DE SAYE IV
(died 1359)
Fought at Crecy, 1346. In 1339 as Admiral of the Fleet, he captured the French fleet at the battle of Sluys.

JEHAN FIENNES
Fought against King Edward III's English. Jehan was one of the five famous 'Burghers of Calais' who offered their lives in exchange for a promise not to massacre the citizens.

His son, an MP, married **MAUDE MONCEUX**. Fiennes family inherit Herstmonceux.

JOAN SAYE married WILLIAM FIENNES

ROGER FIENNES
A constable of the Tower of London. He married the heiress of the Dacre family, so this branch became the Lord Dacres of Herstmonceux.

THOMAS FIENNES, LORD DACRE
Imprisoned for collusion with thieves.

THOMAS FIENNES, LORD DACRE
Courtier of King Henry VIII. On jury of Anne Boleyn's trial. Bore canopy at Jane Seymour's funeral. Hanged at Tyburn for poaching neighbour's deer.

JAMES FIENNES, 1st LORD SAYE AND SELE
Because the male descendants of the Sayes died out, their grandson James inherited. He was born in 1395 at the dawn of the Civil War. Created a baron in 1447, he chose the title Saye and Sele after a Benedictine Priory which he owned. He became Lord High Treasurer but, in 1459, things went sour. For years, with his son-in-law the Sheriff of Kent, he had practised large-scale extortion in Sussex and Kent, to the fury of the locals, including various Fiennes cousins. Now, an angry mob of southern gentry and clerics, including several Fiennes cousins, went to London and demanded retribution from King Henry VI. Their leader, Jack Cade, lived at Herstmonceux and may even have been a member of the Fiennes family, since Cade is known to have been an alias. Cade had James Fiennes beheaded in 1450.

WILLIAM FIENNES, 2nd LORD SAYE AND SELE
Married the heiress of William of Wykeham and inherited Broughton Castle near Banbury. As a soldier in France he was twice taken prisoner and ransoms forced him to sell the Knole estates in Kent. During the Wars of the Roses he fought for Earl Warwick, the King Maker, at the Battle of Northampton, where King Henry VI was deposed. At the Battle of Towton in 1471 he fought for the Yorkists while his cousin, Ranulph Fiennes, a Lord Dacre, was killed fighting for the Lancastrians at the Battle of Barnet.

GREGORY FIENNES, LORD DACRE
Queen Elizabeth I restored the Dacres' lands confiscated after his father's disgrace.

(This branch of the family died out.)

NATHANIEL FIENNES
Roundhead Colonel.

CELIA FIENNES
Famous traveller who rode around England on horseback annotating everything she saw. A nursery rhyme about her survives to this day: 'Ride a cockhorse to Banbury Cross to see a Fiennes (fine) lady upon a white horse . . .'

WILLIAM FIENNES, 8th LORD SAYE AND SELE
Founded a settlement along the Connecticut River which he called Saybrook. With Hampden and Pym he plotted against King Charles I, although he was not in favour of regicide. When war broke out in 1641, William and his four sons raised a cavalry regiment. Prince Rupert's Royalists routed the Fiennes troops at Edgehill and King Charles's troops captured Broughton Castle. William became known as 'Old Subtlety', for he managed to retain the trust of both sides throughout the Civil War. After the restoration, Charles II elevated William to Lord Privy Seal.

JAMES FIENNES, 9th LORD SAYE AND SELE
Hero of Baroness Orczy's novel The Honourable Jim.

Daughter ELIZABETH FIENNES married COLONEL TWISLETON

Daughter CECIL TWISLETON, BARONESS SAYE AND SELE eloped, aged fifteen, with her cousin GEORGE TWISLETON

GEORGE FIENNES TWISLETON, 11th BARON SAYE AND SELE
Fought with Duke of Marlborough. Adjutant-General during Quebec Campaign.

JOHN FIENNES, 12th BARON SAYE AND SELE
Constable of Dover Castle.

GREGORY TWISLETON FIENNES, 14th BARON SAYE AND SELE
Lived to be the 'Oldest Whig in the House of Lords'.

WILLIAM FIENNES, 15th BARON SAYE AND SELE
Friend of the Prince Regent. He once left a note to his valet: 'Put 6 bottles of port by my bedside and call me the day after tomorrow.'

FREDERICK FIENNES, 16th BARON SAYE AND SELE
Archdeacon of Hereford. His mother's second cousin was Jane Austen. By Royal Licence, this Baron restored the old family name to make him Twisleton-Wykeham-Fiennes.

JOHN TWISLETON-WYKEHAM-FIENNES, 17th LORD SAYE AND SELE
His horse Placida won the Oaks.

GEOFFREY TWISLETON-WYKEHAM-FIENNES, 18th LORD SAYE AND SELE

IVO TWISLETON-WYKEHAM-FIENNES, 20th LORD SAYE AND SELE

EUSTACE TWISLETON-WYKEHAM-FIENNES
After three years as a fur-trapper and later as a Canadian Mountie, he travelled widely in Africa and fought in the Boer War. Became Private Secretary to Winston Churchill and served in Gallipoli during the First World War. Was later created Baronet of Banbury. Governor of the Seychelles and, later, the Leeward Islands.

LT COL. SIR RANULPH TWISLETON-WYKEHAM-FIENNES, BARONET
Commanded Royal Scots Greys 1942–3. Died of wounds in Italy 1943.

THE AUTHOR married Virginia Pepper 1970.

NATHANIEL FIENNES, 21st LORD SAYE AND SELE
Current incumbent of Broughton Castle, open to the public.

OLIVER TWISLETON-WYKEHAM-FIENNES
Dean of Lincoln.

APPENDIX 2
List of Expedition Members
(excluding the author)

Norway 1961: Simon Gault, Maggie Rayner

Pyrenees 1962: Hamish Macrae, Maggie Rayner, Patrick Offord

Norway 1967: Peter Loyd, Simon Gault, Nick Holder, Don Hughes, Martin Grant-Peterkin, Vanda Allfrey

Nile 1969: Peter Loyd, Nick Holder, Charles Westmorland, Mike Broome, Anthony Brockhouse UK: Ginnie Pepper

Norway 1970: Roger Chapman, Patrick Brook, Geoff Holder, Peter Booth, Brendan O'Brien, Bob Powell, Henrik Forss, David Murray-Wells, Vanda Allfrey, Rosemary Alhusen, Jane Moncreiff, Johnnie Muir, Gillie Kennard   UK: George Greenfield

Canada 1971: Jack McConnell, Joe Skibinski, Stanley Cribbett, Ginnie Fiennes, Sarah Salt, Bryn Campbell, Ben Usher, Richard Robinson, Paul Berriff, Wally Wallace   UK: Mike Gannon, Spencer Eade

Greenland – North Pole 1976–1978: Oliver Shepard, Charlie Burton, Ginnie Fiennes, Geoff Newman, Mary Gibbs   UK: Mike Wingate Gray, Andrew Croft, Peter Booth

Transglobe Expedition 1979–1982: Oliver Shepard, Charlie Burton, Ginnie Fiennes, Simon Grimes, Anton Bowring, Les Davis, Ken Cameron, Cyrus Balapoira, Howard Willson, Mark Williams, Dave Hicks, Dave Peck, Jill McNicol, Ed Pike, Paul Anderson, Terry Kenchington, Martin Weymouth, Annie Weymouth, Jim Young, Geoff Lee, Nigel Cox, Paul Clark, Admiral Otto Steiner, Mick Hart, Commander Ramsey, Nick Wade, Anthony Birkbeck, Giles Kershaw, Gerry Nicholson, Karl Z'berg, Chris McQuaid, Lesley Rickett, Laurence Howell, Edwyn Martin, John Parsloe, Peter Polley and others.   UK: Anthony Preston, David Mason, Janet Cox, Sue Klugman, Roger Tench, Joan Cox, Margaret Davidson, Colin Eales, Elizabeth Martin and others. Sir Edmund Irving, Sir Vivian Fuchs, Mike Wingate Gray, Andrew Croft, George Greenfield, Sir Alexander Durie, Peter Martin, Simon Gault, Tommy Macpherson, Peter Windeler, Peter Bowring, Lord Hayter, Dominic Harrod, George Capon, Anthony Macaulay, Tom Woodfield, Sir Campbell Adamson, Jim Peevey, Eddie Hawkins, Eddie Carey, Peter Cook, Trevor Davies, Bill Hibbert, Gordon Swain, Captain Tom Pitt, Alan Tritton, Jack Willies, Graham Standing, Muriel Dunton, Edward Doherty, Bob Hampton, Arthur Hogan-Fleming, Dorothy Royle, Annie Seymour, Kevin and Sally Travers-Healy, Jan Fraser, Gay Preston, Jane Morgan

North Pole 1986–1988: Oliver Shepard, Mike Stroud, Laurence Howell, Paul Cleary, Beverly Johnson   UK: Ginnie Fiennes, Alex Blake-Milton, Andrew Croft, George Greenfield, Perry Mason

Index